SOCIALIST LAW IN SOCIALIST EAST ASIA

Since China's reform and opening up started in 1978 and Vietnam's *Doi moi* reforms were initiated in 1986, these two East Asian economies have adopted capitalistic models of development while retaining and reforming their socialist legal systems along the way. Tracking the trajectory of socialist laws and their legacy, this book offers a unique comparison of laws and institutional designs in China and Vietnam. Leading scholars from China, Vietnam, Australia and the United States analyse the history, development and impact of socialist law reforms in these two continuing socialist states. Readers are offered a varied insight into the complex quality and unique features of socialist law and why it should be taken seriously. This is a fresh theoretical approach to, and internal critique of, socialist laws which demonstrates how socialist law in China and Vietnam may shape the future of global legal development among developing countries.

FU HUALING is Professor of Law and Associate Dean at the University of Hong Kong.

JOHN GILLESPIE is Professor of Law in the Monash Business School at Monash University, Australia.

PIP NICHOLSON is Professor of Law and Dean at Melbourne Law School, Australia.

WILLIAM PARTLETT is Associate Professor at Melbourne Law School, Australia.

SOCIALIST LAW IN SOCIALIST EAST ASIA

Edited by

FU HUALING

The University of Hong Kong

JOHN GILLESPIE

Monash University

PIP NICHOLSON

The University of Melbourne

WILLIAM PARTLETT

The University of Melbourne

CAMBRIDGE
UNIVERSITY PRESS

CAMBRIDGE
UNIVERSITY PRESS

University Printing House, Cambridge CB2 8BS, United Kingdom

One Liberty Plaza, 20th Floor, New York, NY 10006, USA

477 Williamstown Road, Port Melbourne, VIC 3207, Australia

314–321, 3rd Floor, Plot 3, Splendor Forum, Jasola District Centre, New Delhi – 110025, India

79 Anson Road, #06–04/06, Singapore 079906

Cambridge University Press is part of the University of Cambridge.

It furthers the University's mission by disseminating knowledge in the pursuit of education, learning, and research at the highest international levels of excellence.

www.cambridge.org
Information on this title: www.cambridge.org/9781108424813
DOI: 10.1017/9781108347822

© Cambridge University Press 2018

First published 2018

Printed and bound in Great Britain by Clays Ltd, Elcograf S.p.A.

A catalogue record for this publication is available from the British Library.

ISBN 978-1-108-42481-3 Hardback

Cambridge University Press has no responsibility for the persistence or accuracy of URLs for external or third-party internet websites referred to in this publication and does not guarantee that any content on such websites is, or will remain, accurate or appropriate.

CONTENTS

CONTRIBUTORS

SARAH BIDDULPH is Australian Research Council Future Fellow (2014–2018) and Professor of Law at Melbourne Law School, Melbourne, Victoria. Sarah's research focuses on the Chinese legal system with a particular emphasis on legal policy, lawmaking and enforcement as they affect the administration of justice in China. Her particular areas of research are contemporary Chinese administrative law, criminal procedure, labour, comparative law and the law regulating social and economic rights.

Her recent publications include: *The Stability Imperative: Human Rights and Law in China* (2015); *Law and Fair Work in China: Making and Enforcing Labour Standards in the PRC*, co-authored with Sean Cooney and Ying Zhu (2013); *Justice: The China Experience* (Cambridge University Press, 2017); *Legal Reforms and the Deprivation of Liberty in China* (2016); and *The Politics of Law and Stability in China*, co-edited with Susan Trevaskes, Elisa Nesossi and Flora Sapio (2014).

JASON BUHI teaches at the Peking University School of Transnational Law in Shenzhen, Guangdong, China, where he focuses on constitutional law and comparative political developments. He holds a JD from the Pennsylvania State University and a PhD in Constitutional Law from the University of Hong Kong. His dissertation represents the first comprehensive treatise on Macau's constitutional development in the English language, and he has authored several articles on developments in Hong Kong and greater China. Dr Buhi is a member of the Maryland, Washington, DC and US Supreme Court bar associations. He was first introduced to China as a Rotary International Ambassadorial Scholar from the United States to Hong Kong and Macau (2007–2008).

LEI CHEN is Associate Professor and Associate Dean at the City University of Hong Kong Law School in Hong Kong. His research areas are property theory, contract law, comparative law and Chinese legal history.

He has been an associate member of the International Academy of Comparative Law since 2010 and a Fellow of the European Law Institute since 2013. He is also a Council Member of the Chinese Civil Law Association and a Fellow of International Academy of the Belt and Road. He is a fellow of Hong Kong Institute of Arbitrators and on the panel of arbitrators in HKIAC, KLRCA, CIETAC, SCIA and BAC.

MICHAEL W. DOWDLE is Associate Professor at the National University of Singapore (NUS) Faculty of Law. Prior to joining NUS, he held positions at New York University, Columbia Law School, the Australian National University, and the Chair in Globalization and Governance at Sciences Po in Paris. His research interests are in comparative public law – in particular, public law and Asian constitutionalism – and in 'regulatory geography'. Ongoing projects include a monograph on regulatory geography with Chantal Mak, and a textbook to be entitled *Transnational Law: Texts and Materials* with Chantal Mak and Mariana Prado.

CYNTHIA ESTLUND is the Catherine A. Rein Professor at the New York University School of Law in New York City, and a leading scholar of labour and employment law. Her writings explore workplace regulation and governance; freedom of expression and procedural fairness at work; diversity, integration and affirmative action; and many aspects of collective labour law, both in the United States and in comparative perspective. Her most recent book, *A New Deal for China's Workers?* (2017), offers a comparative perspective on reform and its limits in the wake of rising labour unrest in China. Estlund received her BA from Lawrence University and her JD from Yale Law School. She clerked for Judge Patricia M. Wald on the US Court of Appeals for the DC Circuit, and then practiced law for several years before entering law teaching, first at the University of Texas School of Law and then at Columbia Law School before moving to New York University in 2006.

JOHN GILLESPIE is a professor in law and Director of the Asia Pacific Business Regulation Group at Monash Business School, Monash University in Melbourne, Australia. He is the author and editor of eight books on Asian law; his most recent with Hualing Fu is *Resolving Land Disputes in East Asia: Exploring the Limits of Law* (Cambridge University Press, 2014). His research focuses on law and development in Asia with a particular interest in land reform, environmental conflict and dispute resolution.

DO HAI HA is a lecturer at the Faculty of Law and International Relations at the University of Economics and Finance in Ho Chi Minh City, Vietnam, with more than thirteen years working for different law schools in Vietnam. Ha holds an LLB degree from Hanoi University of Law, and LLM and PhD degrees from University of Melbourne. He has spent several years advising on corporate, commercial, investment and labour law matters and has also served as an independent expert in multiple labour law reform projects sponsored by the International Labour Organization (ILO) and other foreign donors in Vietnam. His research interests include comparative and international labour law, and legal reform and transplantation in transitional socialist states (with a focus on Vietnam). Ha has many single/co-authored pieces in these fields which will be soon published in edited collections.

AARON HALEGUA is a practicing lawyer, consultant and a research fellow at New York University Law School's US–Asia Law Institute and its Center for Labor and Employment Law in New York City. He is an expert on labour and employment law, legal aid, dispute resolution and corporate social responsibility in the United States, China and internationally. Halegua is the author of the report *Who Will Represent China's Workers? Lawyers, Legal Aid, and the Enforcement of Labor Rights* (2016) and numerous other book chapters, law review articles and op-eds. He has consulted on labour rights issues for numerous entities, including Apple, the International Labour Organization and the Ford Foundation. Halegua holds a JD from Harvard Law School and an AB from Brown University. After law school, he was a Skadden Fellow at The Legal Aid Society in New York City and served as a law clerk in the federal court for the Southern District of New York.

FU HUALING is Professor of Law and Associate Dean at the University of Hong Kong in Hong Kong. His research interests include constitutional law and human rights, with a special focus on legal institutions and criminal justice in China. He teaches courses on Corruption, Human Rights in China and Legal Relations between Hong Kong and Mainland China.

TOAN LE is a lecturer in the Department of Business Law and Taxation at the Monash Business School in Melbourne, Australia. His research interests include comparative land and constitutional law in transitional market economies and interpreting the continuing impact of socialist ideals and ideologies in Vietnam and China. He has published widely on these issues in international journals and edited publications.

PIP NICHOLSON is Dean and Professor of Law at Melbourne Law School in Carlton, Australia. With degrees in Arts, Law and Public Policy from the University of Melbourne and the Australian National University, Pip's research focus is law and development and the Vietnamese courts, constitutions, legal profession and criminal justice. Pip also works comparatively on legal sector reform in socialist East Asia.

WENDY NG is a lecturer at Melbourne Law School in Carlton, Australia. Wendy researches on competition law, focusing on China, international and comparative law and political economy issues. Her upcoming book, *The Political Economy of Competition Law in China*, will be published by Cambridge University Press. Prior to joining Melbourne Law School, Wendy worked as a lawyer at leading commercial law firms in Melbourne and New York and as a lecturer at the University of Adelaide. She has also worked with the Australian Competition and Consumer Commission to deliver competition law and policy capacity building workshops in South East Asia. She is an editor of the China Competition Bulletin and on the editorial board of the China Antitrust Law Journal.

PHAM DUY NGHIA graduated at Leipzig University in Leipzig, Germany. At Fulbright University in Vietnam, he teaches Law and Public Policy, Public Governance, Business Law, Commercial Transactions, Contract Law and Dispute Settlement.

As arbitrator at VIAC, Nghia has served in several tribunals hearing transnational business disputes, including commercial disputes, investment, construction, insurance, corporate disputes, mergers and acquisitions and intellectual property disputes.

Besides teaching, research and practicing law, Nghia is a frequent commentator in leading newspaper and media in Vietnam. The areas concerned include protection of basic citizen's right, voice and accountability in public governance, regulatory quality, rule of law and access to justice.

WILLIAM PARTLETT is Associate Professor at Melbourne Law School in Carlton, Australia. Before coming to Melbourne, Dr Partlett was an assistant professor at the Faculty of Law of Chinese University Hong

Kong, a postdoctoral research fellow and lecturer at Columbia University Law School, and a fellow at the Brookings Institution. Dr Partlett holds a JD from Stanford Law School as well as a DPhil in Soviet History and MPhil in Russian and East European Studies from the University of Oxford (where he was a Clarendon Scholar). He also holds an honours bachelor's degree in International Affairs and Public Policy from Princeton University and speaks Russian.

Dr Partlett's research broadly focuses on the role of institutions in comparative public law. His work is currently focused on two projects. First, his research explores the institutional dimensions of constitution making. Second, his research draws on his background in Soviet history to explore the distinctive institutional legacies of the socialist system of law in the former Soviet Union and Asia.

PHAM LAN PHUONG is a PhD candidate at Melbourne Law School in Carlton, Australia. Her research interests include Vietnamese and comparative criminal law and human rights issues.

She holds a Master of Law Degree from Melbourne Law School and a Bachelor of Law Degree from Vietnam National University in Hanoi. Prior to her PhD candidature, she was a lecturer at the Professional Training School for Procurators in Ho Chi Minh City, where she specialised in international cooperation issues. Phuong was also a lecturer at the Royal Melbourne Institute of Technology (RMIT University) in Vietnam.

BUI NGOC SON is Senior Research Fellow in the Centre for Asian Legal Studies of the Faculty of Law at the National University of Singapore. He holds a PhD in law at the University of Hong Kong. His research focuses on comparative constitutional law and theory, and comparative law from an interdisciplinary perspective. He has written on socialist law, Confucian law, Confucian constitutionalism, popular constitutionalism, constitutional mobilisation, constitution making, globalisation of constitutional identity, the global diffusion of constitutional rights and constitutional review. His work includes the book *Confucian Constitutionalism in East Asia* (2016), and journal articles published in the *American Journal of Comparative Law*, the *Law & Social Inquiry*, the *Illinois Law Review*, the *Fordham International Law Journal*, the *Washington University Global Studies Law Review* and the *Washington International Law Journal*.

GLENN TIFFERT is a historian of twentieth-century China, and a visiting fellow at the Hoover Institution in Stanford, California. His research centres on China in the nationalist and early PRC periods, using a combination of traditional and computational methods. He has published on the construction of the modern Chinese court system and judiciary, the 1954 PRC Constitution, and on the spectre of censorship in the digital age. His present book project re-theorises the 1949 revolution and the position of the PRC in Chinese history via a deep empirical dive into the origins of the PRC judicial system.

PART I

Socialism and Legality

PART I

Socialism and Equality

1

Socialist Law in Socialist East Asia

FU HUALING, JOHN GILLESPIE, PIP NICHOLSON AND WILLIAM PARTLETT

More than fifty years ago, socialist states in Asia turned to the Soviet Bloc for inspiration in developing their political and legal systems. They enacted constitutions and laws, and established institutions that, with varying degrees of faithfulness, replicated Soviet regulatory models. The collapse of socialism in the Soviet Bloc was accompanied by the literal collapse of structures and bodies previously considered indestructible, such as the Berlin Wall and statues venerating socialist heroes. Mirroring this decline, much subsequent analysis about socialist Asia promptly devalued and dismissed socialist institutions, legal theories and forms of knowledge – presupposing a linear transition from socialism to liberal legalism. Far from linear, legal reform in this region has been variegated and complex – raising the question of whether socialist laws and institutions were more resilient and adaptable than previously thought.

This book argues that the scholarly focus on the emergence of liberal legalism has marginalised the ongoing normative and structural legacy of Asian socialism found in various guises in contemporary Vietnam and China. The assumption of the inevitable export of Western capitalism, together with versions of liberalism and its institutional manifestations, is, we suggest, flawed, or at least misconceived, in socialist Asia. The chapters suggest that, at least in part, a failure to recognise the normative and structural legacy of Marxist–Leninist approaches to socialism constrains our capacity to interpret the contemporary Vietnamese and Chinese reforms. Further, and significantly, a failure to recognise the socialist legacy risks overlooking a key reason for ongoing local support for strong/authoritarian states in socialist Asia, which seek to promote 'development' while also resisting its destabilising effects. As will become evident, the impacts of contemporary socialism vary across countries, jurisdictions and institutions.

We commence this Chapter with a brief review of the history of socialism, including recalling socialist debates before the advent of the Russian Revolution. Subsequently, we briefly trace the 'import' of Soviet

3

socialism into both the People's Republic of China and the Socialist Republic of Vietnam. We turn then to the 'puzzle' of socialism's resonance and relevance today, outlining the debates about its resilience and adaptation in socialist Asia.

1.1   A Brief History of Socialism Pre-Russian Revolution

Socialist ideas predate the Russian Revolution and the subsequent export of Marxist–Leninism around the world. In its narrowest sense, socialism is a theory of society where the means and benefits of production are collectively owned and enjoyed by labour. This definition reflects the political economy of the nineteenth century, where the means of production was almost exclusively factories and land. Owning the means of production enabled the reorganisation of the political economy to advance the interests of the labouring classes. With the emergence of post-industrialisation in the late twentieth century, what constitutes the means of production has become an increasingly open-ended question. Whether the core values underlying socialism – equality, community and fairness – require the socialisation of the means of production is unclear. However, as the discussion about the historical development of socialist ideas makes clear, for socialism to realise its objectives it is necessary to retain some type of central coordination over the political economy.

Socialist ideas arose from the interpretation of the French Revolution by French and German intellectuals. The French philosopher and businessman Henri de Saint-Simon is credited with distinguishing between the industrial and idling classes, and developing a notion of class that continues to animate social critiques.[1]

Taking the analysis further, Lorenz von Stein developed a 'sociological interpretation of the proletariat as the labour force in modern society and as a class-conscious unit struggling for power in pursuit of their interests'.[2] He was influenced by Hegel's historical idealism, and viewed the

---

[1] Albert S. Lindemann, *A History of Modern Europe: From 1815 to the Present* (Oxford: Wiley-Blackwell, 2013), p. 67; Kaethe Mengelberg, 'Introduction', in Lorenz von Stein, *The History of the Social Movement in France, 1789–1850* (ed. and trans. Kaethe Mengelberg, New York, NY: Bedminster Press, 1964), pp. 1, 27 [translation of: *Geschichte der sozialen Bewegung in Frankreich von 1789 bis auf unsere Tage* (first published 1850)]; Werner Sombart, *Socialism and the Social Movement* (M Epstein, translated from 6th German edition, London: J.M. Dent; New York, NY: J.P. Dutton & Co, 1909), p. 2.

[2] Mengelberg, 'Introduction', pp. 1, 27; Friedrich Muckle, *H. de Saint-Simon* (Jena: Fischer, 1908), p. 329.

French Revolution as the perfect example of a mass of people energised by the notions of liberty and equality, and cognisant of the unequal nature of their participation in the economic system. The principles of equality underlying socialism arose in France because the proletariat toiled ceaselessly for the capitalists – the owners of the means of production – who deprived them of the surplus value of their labour. Stein preferred political reform to revolution as a means of allowing the proletariat to acquire property through labour.[3]

Drawing on the utopian ideas of French philosopher Charles Fourier,[4] Robert Owen argued that human distress was caused by the competition of human labour with machinery. Like other utopian socialists, Owen proposed that the poor should form communities that allowed members to achieve a state of human flourishing by participating in varied and fulfilling occupations.[5] Although experiments during the nineteenth century with 'utopian' socialist communities failed, they provided inspiration for later communist projects.

Marx and Engels were attracted to the 'utopian project', but disagreed with 'utopian' socialists that mere exhortation and good example would convince the bourgeoisie to relinquish power.[6] Marx and Engels regarded revolution as a necessary process for socialising the means of production. Their 1848 publication of the *Manifesto of the Communist Party* provided a clarion call for the proletariat to arise and overthrow the capitalists that controlled the means of production.[7] Marxist ideology consisted of four interrelated elements: (1) that society was divided into classes, including the proletariat and bourgeoisie; (2) that those classes had general interests; (3) that those interests were implacably opposed; and

---

[3] Lorenz von Stein, *The History of the Social Movement in France, 1789–1850* (ed. and trans. Kaethe Mengelberg, New York, NY: Bedminster Press, 1964), pp. 73–75 [translation of: *Geschichte der sozialen Bewegung in Frankreich von 1789 bis auf unsere Tage* (first published 1850)].

[4] Jonathan Beecher, *Charles Fourier: The Visionary and His World* (Berkeley, CA: University of California, 1986), p. 355. See also Lindemann, *A History of Modern Europe.*

[5] Letter from Robert Owen to the Committee of the Association for the Relief of the Manufacturing and Labouring Poor, 12 March 1817, in Robert Owen, *The Life of Robert Owen Written by Himself* (1857–1867), vol. 2 (Fairfield, NJ: A.M. Kelley, 1977).

[6] See especially K. Marx, F. Engels, S. Moore and D. McLellan, *Manifesto of the Communist Party* (Oxford: Oxford University Press, 1992), ch. 3.

[7] Famous last line of the *Manifesto of the Communist Party*. See *Marx and Engels Selected Works*, vol. 1 (Moscow: Progress Publishers, 1969), pp. 98–137.

(4) that class struggle was the only way to eliminate dependence of labour on capital.[8]

It is possible to extract from this body of socialist literature a cluster of characteristics that describe socialism. A socialist-inclined position tends to favour centrally organised political economy decision making that redistributes production according to notions of equality. It also favours the aims and values of community or society, over those of the individual. Marx, for example, privileged commitments to universal social and moral perspectives over individual perspectives.[9] Finally, socialism tends to favour cooperation above hierarchy and competition. For Michael Newman, socialism is 'based on the values of solidarity and cooperation ... it promotes a relatively optimistic view of human beings and their ability to cooperate with one another'.[10] Socialism places a premium on working together for the service of the state and furthering communal reciprocity. This spirit of (idealised) cooperation, or state mandated collectivisation, contrasts with the pursuit of material self-interest underlying capitalism, a point that Dowdle will elaborate further in Chapter 2.

1.2   Socialism and Legal Development

Socialist legal theory is relatively underdeveloped when contrasted with theories of socialist political economy. Questions about the particular legal and institutional arrangements required of a socialist state – to grant supervisory jurisdiction to a procuracy or not, for instance; a topic discussed by Partlett in Chapter 3 – were peripheral to the socialist theories of the nineteenth century. As Schleiermacher noted, '[l]aw is the expression of existing conditions'.[11] It is reflective of the distribution of power among the classes in society. In a similar fashion, Stein stated '[a] valid legal system contains two elements: it is the pronounced will of the state, and it is a result of circumstances'.[12] The key circumstance of socialism – the socialisation of the means of production – had not taken

---

[8] Sombart, *Socialism and the Social Movement.*

[9] Will Kymlicka, *Contemporary Political Philosophy: An Introduction* (New York, NY: Oxford University Press, 2002, 2nd edn.).

[10] Michael Newman, *Socialism: A Very Short Introduction* (New York, NY: Oxford University Press, 2005), p. 3.

[11] Quoted in Sombart, *Socialism and the Social Movement*, p. 48.

[12] Von Stein, *The History of the Social Movement in France, 1789–1850.*

place, and without this social change, socialist doctrine had not formulated legal institutional arrangements.

Marx's theory of historical materialism[13] was much clearer than previous socialist writings in linking the rate and direction of social progress to the development of the means of production and exchange.[14] Although his writings draw on this theory to provide a practical approach to questions of law, he did not develop a detailed and systematic theorisation of law.[15] Marx's main contribution to our understanding of law resides in his analysis of the social relations that underlie, but are often obscured by, formal legal categories, such as private property and state property. The core insight is that legal rights are not natural attributes of individuals or the product of state power, but rather a set of social relationships that emerge in particular historical circumstances. For example, Marx concluded that despite the appearance of voluntariness, the commodity economy establishes abstract rules that governed trade and labour contracts. Workers in commodity economies are forced to price their labour at market rates, rather than according to the value of the products or services they produce.

When socialism finally triumphed in 1917 in the former imperial Russian Empire, a fierce struggle emerged between a decentralised, 'utopian' version of socialist law and a more centralised, 'statist' approach grounded in the imperial Russian tradition. Evgeni Pashukanis was the leading utopian, applying Marx's critique of political economy to jurisprudence.[16] Pashukanis concluded that legal thinking, which arose in bourgeois societies, was inextricably linked to its origins and would wither away in socialist political economies. Andrei Vyshinsky was the leading statist, arguing that the use of formalist and centralising imperial

---

[13] Best elucidated in the preface to Karl Marx, *A Contribution to the Critique of Political Progress* (Moscow: Progress Publishers, 1977).

[14] John Spargo and George Louis Arner, *Elements of Socialism* (New York, NY: Macmillan, 1912), p. 77.

[15] Hugh Collins, *Marxism and Law* (Oxford: Oxford University Press, 1984), p. 9; Robert Fine, 'Marxism and the Social Theory of Law', in Reza Banakar and Max Travers (eds.), *Law and Social Theory* (Oxford: Hart, 2013) pp. 95–109.

[16] As Harold Berman writes: E. B. Pashukanis was, until 1936, the Director of the Institute of Soviet Construction and Law, attached to the Communist Academy. After this post he was a member of the USSR Academy of Social Sciences. See Harold J. Berman, *Justice in the USSR* (Cambridge, MA: Harvard University Press, 1963), pp. 31, 389–390. Extracts of Pashukanis' writing are located in V. I. Lenin et al., H. W. Babb (trans.), 1951, cited in John N. Hazard, *Communists and Their Law* (Chicago, IL: University of Chicago Press, 1969), p. 18.

Russian legal institutions was necessary to overcoming the exploiting class and attaining a socialist state. Relying on the ideas of Lenin and Marx, this approach placed a highly centralised bureaucratic state – rather than the individual or community organisations – at the centre of a transition to socialism. In short, a powerful and centralised socialist state itself was a normative good for progress to socialism; something that could smash the class enemy, allow the Soviet Union to catch up with the West, and manage economic inequality or destructive competition. This Marxist–Leninist and statist conception of socialist law as a centralised and coordinated legal system was transferred to China and Vietnam during the 1950s and has shown considerable resilience since then.

1.3   Borrowing from the Soviet Union: China

China's embracing of the Soviet-style socialist system was a significant departure in terms of the trajectory of its legal history, but the shift was partial.[17] Chinese legality and legal practices after 1949, in substantive terms, were more profoundly shaped by the unique sequence of revolutionary experience prior to 1954 when the first Constitution was promulgated under a strong Soviet influence. The Land Reform Law and the Marriage Law, both enacted one year after the establishment of the People's Republic of China, were the defining characteristics of an indigenous revolution in legal innovation. The Land Reform Law, as brutal as it was in its enforcement, gave land title to individual farmers, fulfilling an essential revolutionary understanding to give land to its tillers.[18] The Marriage Law had a powerful emancipatory impact in freeing women from traditional bondage. The formation of a joint government in 1949 composed of multiple parties to represent the interests of all classes allowed the Communist Party to exercise leadership with meaningful participation from other political forces supportive of the Communist Revolution.[19]

---

[17] Albert Chen, *An Introduction to the Legal System of the People's Republic of China* (Hong Kong: LexisNexis Butterworths, 2011, 4th edn.).

[18] William Hinton, *Fanshen: A Documentary of Revolution in a Chinese Village* (Berkeley, CA: University of California Press, 1977); and Edwin E. Moise, *Land Reform in China and Northern Vietnam: Consolidating the Revolution at the Village Level* (Chapel Hill, NC: University of North Carolina Press, 1983).

[19] Xiaoping Cong, *Marriage, Law and Gender in Revolutionary China, 1940–1960* (Cambridge: Cambridge University Press, 2016); and Neil J. Diamant, *Revolutionizing the*

The making of the 1954 Constitution brought the full impact of the Soviet constitution to bear, formally incorporating China into the Bolshevik orbit, even if it would never be a satellite of the USSR. With Stalin's personal intervention modelled on the Soviet 1936 Constitution, the Chinese Communist Party (the CCP) followed the footsteps of 'Soviet Old Brothers', as they were colloquially referred to, in creating a constitutional order based on congressional supremacy and democratic centralism.[20] The new Constitution ended the multi-party joint government that had been practiced since 1949, clipping the wings of the non-CCP political forces into a consultative body and entrenching the CCP's monopoly on political power. The 1954 Constitution also laid a foundation for the abolition of private ownership in production and central economic planning, and formally nullified the promises that the CCP had made to the ethnic minorities that the new China would be built upon a federal structure that would maximise ethnic autonomy.

The Constitution also created a legal system modelled on other Soviet examples, in which the court is directly accountable to the congress at the corresponding level and the procuracy has a general supervisory power to ensure faithful implementation of state law. From legal theories (e.g. the jurisprudence of state and law and the four elements of crime), legislative drafts (e.g. for criminal law and in the general principles of civil law), institutional designs (e.g. the creation of a super procuracy) and legal practices (e.g. formalised popular participation), China witnessed a revolutionary change in its political and legal systems.[21]

The legal revolution was both deep and comprehensive. In 1949, the CCP declared the abolition of all laws that were enacted by the regime it overthrew and applied revolutionary norms in their places. The 1954 Constitution created a wide range of new legal institutions guided by new ideologies aimed at achieving new missions. In the meantime, the CCP initiated a systematic rectification campaign to remove legal professionals, judges and lawyers who worked for the previous regime from the newly created institutions. The transformation was thoroughgoing and total; historical continuity was intentionally rendered impossible.[22]

Family: Politics, Love, and Divorce in Urban and Urban China, 1949–1962 (Berkeley, CA: University of California Press, 2000).

[20] Han Dayuan (ed.), *1954 Nian Xianfa yu Zhingguo Xianzheng* [*The 1954 Constitution and Chinese Constitutionalism*] (Wuhan: Wuhan University Press, 2004, 2nd edn.).

[21] Chen, *An Introduction to the Legal System of the People's Republic of China*.

[22] Ji Pomin, 'Liufa Quanshu Feichu Qianhou' ['Before and after the Abolition of the Six Laws'], available at www.iolaw.org.cn/shownews.asp?id=7314, accessed 12 January 2018.

The creation of a socialist legality in a revolutionary society was an uncertain endeavour, and in terms of the rules of the game the legal system experienced dramatic fluctuations. Conflict in a revolutionary society is reflected by a duality whereby law withers away and at the same time a socialist legality is created that cannot be abolished automatically. While the need for social and economic progress requires the laws of bureaucratic command and hierarchical organisation, the ideological mission to create a socialist, egalitarian and self-regulating society required political mobilisation to achieve substantive justice. Roberto Unger well captures the revolutionary tension embedded in socialist legality. For him, socialism fluctuates between the law 'of self-education' in a 'self-regulating community' and the law of 'government control' though 'industrial organisation and political centralisation'.[23]

Similarly, Brady and others have interpreted the legal history of communist China as reflecting the 'two-line struggles as ideology and history', in which an antagonism between the 'ethic of social revolution' and the 'ethic of bureaucratic centralisation' unfolded.[24] Indeed, for Brady and many others, the fluctuation between 'continuous revolution and legal order' is a 'unifying theme' in the legal history of the socialist China in which the pragmatists wanted stability and discipline while the 'idealists' sought social change and continuous revolution.[25]

Central to this dichotomy is the periodisation of legal development in communist China. Accordingly, the legal history of communist China since 1949 is roughly periodised into several phases, with each model of law dominating each successive phase. During the periods of 'formal', 'bureaucratic' and 'juridical' law, such as between 1953 and 1956 and between 1962 and 1965, there was a drive towards formalism, all in relative terms of course, with legal procedures specified, institutions established and legal professionals playing a leading role. On the contrary, during the periods of 'societal' and 'informal' law, such as between 1957 and 1961 and between 1966 and 1976, formal rules and legal institutions were displaced by mass mobilisation and

---

[23] Roberto Unger, *Law in Modern Society* (New York, NY: Free Press, 1976).

[24] James Brady, *Justice and Politics in People's China: Legal Order or Continuing Revolution?* (London: Academic Press, 1982).

[25] Leng Shao-chuan and Hungdah Chiu, *Criminal Justice in Post-Mao China: Analysis and Documents* (Albany, NY: State University New York Press, 1985).

popular participation, with procedures simplified, courts closed and judges and lawyers alike sent down to the labour camps.[26]

Socialist legality did not have a stronghold in the political system as it had in the USSR. The CCP learned from the Soviets how to construct a one-party state, albeit one that differed from the Soviet template. The CCP had much less faith in the imported legal institutions and tended to rely more on its own institutions to exercise control over important areas such as anti-corruption and censorship, whereas the Bolsheviks tended to rule indirectly through legal institutions – for example, in deploying the procuracy as an anti-corruption agency. CCP leaders, and Mao in particular, were more dedicated to the pursuit of a continuous revolution in the cultural and other spheres, and demonstrated a marked tendency to sabotage their own legal institutions and procedures through the mass-line populism.[27] The CCP, in comparison with its Soviet counterpart, was insistent on the continuation of a class struggle without an enemy class, and had been openly critical of what it perceived as class reconciliation advocated by the Bolsheviks; and as a result it was more willing to treat law as a dictatorial tool against its enemies, real or imagined. Three years after the creation of a constitutional order and a functioning legal system in 1954, the CCP initiated a series of violent campaigns to undo the brave new socialist legality. Those were the years of legal nihilism, when revolutionary lawlessness was openly advocated.[28]

Mao's anti-bureaucratic inclination was a decisive factor in perpetuating Chinese informalism. The Maoists argued that law was socialist when it was sensitive to social needs and when legal actors were responsive to the interests of the masses. What was wrong with legal institutions was their inherent bureaucratic tendency, by which they meant when legal actors were divorced from social practices and made judgements only according to technical rules. To overcome the problem was not so much to dismantle the legal system, but to break bureaucratic isolationism and to purge elite arrogance. This is typified by the Maoist popular saying: 'Cadres must not be judged solely on whether they have obeyed the laws and the formal obligations of the position, but also on their performance against the mass line.'[29]

---

[26] James R. Townsend, *Politics in China* (Boston, MA: Little, Brown and Company, 1980); Victor Li, 'The Role of Law in Communist China' (1970) 44 *The China Quarterly* 66.

[27] Michael Dutton, *Policing Chinese Politics: A History* (Durham, NC: Duke University Press, 2005).

[28] Brady, *Justice and Politics in People's China*.

[29] Ibid.

In the Maoist view, just as schooling is mistaken as education and medication as health care, law became the embodiment of justice. The bureaucratic, rule-based form of justice was defined as little more than the activities of judges in their chambers. Ultimately, the integrity of the legal system is maintained only at the cost of substantive justice. In that sense, the Maoist position was not so much strictly against legality but simply insisted on the law's responsiveness to social needs.[30]

Law, not unlike other fields, is a mechanism for achieving substantive justice. A socialist law must in its rules and operation be consistent with this ultimate goal. In that sense, the Maoist legality resembled the 'result-oriented' responsive law that Nonet and Philip have popularised.[31] Rules are to be followed rigidly and uncritically, but interpreted and adjusted so as to reflect social pressures and meet social needs. Bureaucratic legality naturally becomes self-serving and parasitical unless opened up to social supervision. After all, a revolutionary state should wield its power in a way that minimises the degree of stability and institutionalisation and maximises flexibility and innovation. Without the socialisation of justice, the legal system would be self-serving and alienated from the society.[32]

It is in that political and legal context that the post-Mao legal reform and the open-door policy began in China in the late 1970s. There was significant continuity in following the legacy of socialist legality as defined in 1954: laws were passed that were first drafted in the 1950s; legal actors who were trained in the 1950s and 1960s were called back to work in newly restored legal institutions. The 1982 Constitution, which establishes a reform-oriented political order, is based on its 1954 predecessor. In the end, it is the restoration of a legal order under the same authoritarian one-party state. The aim was to institutionalise and professionalise the legal system to create a degree of certainty and order in politics, as well as in the economy and social life.[33]

As such, this marked a significant departure from the Russian-dominated legality of the 1950s. The production relationship that was essential for the

---

[30] Ibid.

[31] Philippe Nonet and Philip Selznick, *Law and Society in Transition* (New York, NY: Harper & Row, 1987).

[32] Brady, *Justice and Politics in People's China*; Leng Shao-chuan, 'The Rule of Law in the People's Republic of China as Reflected in Mao Tse-Tung's Influence' (1977) 68(3) *Journal of Criminal law and Criminology* 356–372.

[33] Randall Peerenboom, *China's Long March toward Rule of Law* (New York, NY: Cambridge University Press, 2002); Chen, *An Introduction to the Legal System of the People's Republic of China*.

understanding of socialist law was changing, and Chinese law now operates according to a different economic framework. China started to decisively move away from public ownership and state planning of the economy by de-collectivising farmland, privatising small-to-medium-sized state-owned enterprises, and securitising state assets. China no longer claimed to have reached full-blown socialism, and humbly conceded that it was still at a preliminary stage of socialism struggling for a low level of economic prosperity for its people. To develop a market-oriented economy, China looked to the West, the United States in particular, for legal inspiration and assistance. This trend has continued to the present day.

While the Russian impact on Chinese law remains, it is now largely limited to the constitutional structure and a function of the repressive state apparatuses. That impact is likely to remain as long as China's one-party state, that Stalin helped to build, survives current economic and social transitions.[34] With recent constitutional amendments allowing the president more than two terms in office, the stage seems set for the party to further consolidate power in the future.

1.4 Borrowing from the Soviet Union: Vietnam

Like China, Vietnam looked to the Soviet Union for ideas regarding the construction of a socialist state.[35] Also like China, the commitment to a socialist state did not immediately follow the Declaration of Independence in 1945. As has often been stated, Vietnam's first independence Constitution of 1946 reflected a range of influences, including that of the United States and France.[36] It made clear commitments to freedom and democracy, and did not position Vietnam explicitly as a part of the community of socialist nations.

By the mid-1950s, Vietnam potentially had the benefit of two socialist models: the USSR, particularly Russia, and the PRC. And both nations

---

[34] See Chapter 6 in this volume.

[35] Pip Nicholson, *Borrowing Court Systems* (Leiden: Martinus Njihoff Publishers, 2007), pp. 3–5, 173–191; V. Kolesnikov, 'The Supreme People's Court – Highest Judicial Organ in the Democratic Republic of Vietnam', *Byulletan Verkhognogo SSSR*, No. 3, Moscow, 1961, JPRS.

[36] David Marr, 'Ho Chi Minh's Independence Declaration', in K.W. Taylor and John K. Whitmore (eds.), *Essays into Vietnamese Pasts* (Ithaca, NY: Studies on Southeast Asia, Cornell University, 1995), pp. 221–231; Pip Nicholson, 'Vietnamese Legal Institutions in Comparative Perspective: Contemporary Constitutions and Courts Considered', in Kanishka Jayasuriya (ed.), *Law, Capitalism and Power in Asia: The Rule of Law and Legal Institutions* (London: Routledge, 1999), pp. 257–282.

were advising Vietnam, whose leading Party was divided about to which state their loyalty should be accorded. Gradually, Russia became the dominant influence over socialist state building in Vietnam.[37]

The Soviet hold as a reform model can be attributed to several factors. First, Vietnam has long had to resist Chinese expansionism and control. Vietnam was not independent of China until 939 AD and remained a tributary state for centuries.[38] Vietnamese leaders have consistently harboured fears that China nurtures expansionist policies. This doubt, while ever-present, was arguably at an all-time low while China embarked on Mao's continuous revolution (see above). Nevertheless, fear of Chinese intervention moderated any *a priori* hold the Chinese had on Vietnamese policy development through either proximity or alleged shared cultural values. Secondly, the Chinese leadership contributed heavily to the land reform campaigns in socialist Vietnam between 1953 and 1956.[39] Chinese cadres coached Vietnamese officials in bloody trials held by 'special courts' to oust landholders from their lands and prosecute them for political offences.[40] The Vietnamese abandoned the land reform campaign given the popular backlash, which cast doubt on the Chinese 'way forward'.[41] Thirdly, as China descended into lawlessness, Vietnam constructed a nascent legality during a protracted war, supported by Russian foreign aid.[42] At the same time, Chinese aid was decreasing. With the Sino-Soviet split in the early 1960s, Vietnam elected to side with the USSR, producing recourse to Soviet aid. Russian aid took many forms, including offering legal codes for transplantation, legal training and tested legal institutions – particularly the procuracy, as set out in Chapter 9.

---

[37] Nicholson, *Borrowing Court Systems*, pp. 173–191.

[38] Keith Taylor, *The History of the Vietnamese* (New York, NY: Cambridge University Press, 2013), pp. 183–192.

[39] Nicholson, *Borrowing Court Systems*, pp. 68–70.

[40] Nicholson, *Borrowing Court Systems*, pp. 68–70. See also J. Price Gittenger, 'Communist Land Policy in North Vietnam' (1957) 28(2) *Far Eastern Survey* 113–126 and Wilfred Burchett, *North of the 17th Parallel* (Hanoi: Foreign Languages Publishing House, 1955), pp. 168–169.

[41] Nicholson, *Borrowing Court Systems*, p. 69.

[42] Robert F. Turner, *Vietnamese Communism: Its Origins and Development* (Stanford, CA: Hoover Institution Press, Stanford University, 1975), pp. 131–146 and Georges Boudarel, 'Influences and Idiosyncrasies in the Line and Practice of the Vietnam Communist Party', in William S. Turley (ed.), *Vietnamese Communism in Comparative Perspective* (Boulder, CO: Westview Press, 1980), p. 145.

In effect, as the most developed socialist state, Soviet laws and legal institutions were preferred by Vietnamese leaders as a model to 'strengthen the role of law'.[43] The 1959 Constitution announced Vietnam's 'sympathy and support' from the world's socialist states.[44] Vietnamese writers during the 1960s described socialist legality as a tool of proletarian dictatorship (*chuyên chính vô sản*) to defeat enemies, protect the revolution and collective democratic rights, and to organise and manage a command economy.[45]

Drawing on Marxist–Leninist theory, writers argued that worker-controlled societies require legal systems that reflect proletarian aspirations.[46] They explained the relationship between law and class with the familiar assertion that law reflects the 'will of the ruling class' (*ý chí của giai cấp thống trị*). As the executive committee of the ruling class, the Communist Party of Vietnam assumed the exclusive right to determine the content of law. In order to lead society, the Party used law as a 'management tool' (*công cụ quản lý*) to adjust or balance (*điều chỉnh*) social relationships – a practice that sanctioned the substitution of party policy for law.

Not only was socialist doctrine appropriated by Vietnam, but new institutions also were established that were to have a lasting legacy. First and foremost among these was the establishment of the Indochinese Communist Party (the precursor to the CPV) in 1930. Once officially established as the leader of newly emerging independent Vietnam, the Party consolidated its hold on power through the construction of statist institutions reflecting their Soviet Stalinist roots. The procuracy was an import from Russia. The introduction of the mass line in the work of

---

[43] See Nguyễn Duy Trinh, 'Phát Triển Chế Độ Dân Chủ Nhân Dân và Bảo Đảm Quyền Tự Do Dân Chủ Của Nhân Dân' ['Developing the People's Democratic Regime and Ensuring People's Liberties and Democratic Rights'] (1956) 3 *Học Tập* 26–32.

[44] Preamble, DRVN Constitution 1959. See also Art. 9 where Vietnam is characterised as 'marching toward socialism'. See also Vu Dinh Hoe, 'Les Quatres Constitutions du Vietnam' (1995) 2 *Vietnamese Law Journal* 2; William J. Duiker 'Socialist Republic of Vietnam: The Constitutional System of the Socialist Republic of Vietnam', in Lawrence W. Beer (ed.), *Constitutional Systems in Late Twentieth Century Asia* (Seattle, WA: University of Washington Press, 1992), pp. 331–62. Smith et al., *Area Handbook for North Vietnam* (Washington, DC: The American University, 1966), pp. 165–80; Bernard B Fall, 'Constitution-Writing in a Communist State: The New Constitution of North Viet-nam' (1960) 6 *Howard Law Journal* 157.

[45] Đinh Gia Trinh, 'Mấy Ý Kiến Đóng Góp Về Vấn Đề Bảo Vệ Pháp Chế' ['Some Comments on the Protection of Legality'] (1961) 3 *Tập San Tư Pháp* 20–32.

[46] Writing in the Vietnamese Court Review (*Tap San Tu Phap*) several Soviet law professors set out the basic principles of Soviet law (Lets Noi 1961: 36–41).

courts, determining cases on the basis of morality and staffed by a panel including two lay judges and cadres rather than lawyers, for example, were also Soviet borrowings. These institutions did not operate as replicas of Soviet institutions, but Russia was the source of the institutional settings established by the nascent CPV between the 1950s and 1970s.[47]

With the unification of Vietnam in 1976, the 1980 Constitution is best understood as the 'unification constitution'; heralding socialist Vietnam and the export of its institutions south to the former Republic of Vietnam.[48] The 1980 Constitution also explicitly incorporated for the first time Soviet political-legal ideology such as pháp chế xã hội chủ nghĩa (socialist legality), tập trung dân chủ (democratic centralism) and làm chủ tập the (collective mastery).[49] It also established the CPV as the 'only' force leading the state.[50]

1.5   *Doi Moi* and the Turn to Law in Vietnam

Following widespread economic collapse in the early 1980s and unprecedented division within the Party, the Party leadership searched for new ways of shoring up and projecting its authority into society.[51] A resolution issued by the Fifth Party Congress in 1982 complained that:

> Many officials, including leaders of state agencies, are unaware that socialist law is the institutionalisation of the Party's political line, and is a means of implementing Party leadership, they do not respect the law, and even violate the law, leading to a political influence that adversely affects the people.[52]

Little concrete action was taken, however, until Truong Chinh declared at the Sixth Party Congress in 1986 that law needed to replace party

---

[47] Nicholson, *Borrowing Court Systems*, pp. 173–230.
[48] See Editorial, 'The Strength of the Socialist Legal System', *Nhan Dan*, 1 April 1977, trans. 6 FBIS East Asian Daily Report (67), 7 April 1977, K7. See also Preamble & Art. 2, SRVN Constitution 1980.
[49] Preamble & Art 2, SRVN Constitution 1980.
[50] Art. 2, SRVN Constitution 1980.
[51] Thai Quang Truong, 'The Fifth Party Congress of the Vietnamese Communist Party' (1982) 4(2) *Contemporary Southeast Asia* 236–245.
[52] CHỦ TỊCH HỘI ĐỒNG BỘ TRƯỞNG [Resolution Council of Ministers], VỀ VIỆC ĐẨY MẠNH CÔNG TÁC TUYÊN TRUYỀN, GIÁO DỤC PHÁP LUẬT 315-CT 1981 [Promoting Propaganda Work on Legal Education], available at http://thuvienphapluat.vn/van-ban/Giao-duc/Chi-thi-315-CT-day-manh-tuyen-truyen-giao-duc-phap-luat-44011.aspx.

morality as the chief instrument of governance.[53] In its place he argued for the promotion of 'socialist law' to regulate new forms of economic activities and instil a sense of order into society. Law, he argued, would cultivate vigilant citizens and corrall potential social conflicts into channels controlled by the party-state. To further this policy, he urged the party-state to inculcate legal consciousness – a social awareness about law – among citizens, and also encourage legal compliance in all social spheres. In signalling this shift, Vietnam embarked on socialist construction according to law, which was confirmed with the passage of Vietnam's fourth Constitution in 1992.[54]

The turn to law was supported by a comprehensive program designed to train legally qualified cadres. Universities teaching law grew in number and expertise,[55] albeit reflecting evolving curricula.[56] Media outlets were required to promote legal consciousness, while Party members were expected to set an example by 'living and working according to the law'.[57] Legal journals critically explored how the Party could adapt socialist law to unleash creativity and stimulate the economy. Some writers argued that markets were the site of knowledge creation and law needed to promote the exchange of ideas.[58] This involved reshaping the legal framework to encompass the different types of ownership generated by economic markets.[59] Others emphasised the transitional nature of law

---

[53] John Gillespie, 'Changing Concepts of Socialist Law in Vietnam,' in *Asian Socialism & Legal Change: The Dynamics of Vietnamese and Chinese Reform* (Canberra: Australian National University Press, 2005), pp. 45–75.

[54] Art. 4, SRVN Constitution 1992.

[55] From ten law schools in the mid-1980s Vietnam today has in excess of forty law teaching programs. Do Hai Ha and Pip Nicholson 'Lawyers and Lawyering in Socialist Vietnam: Cadres to a "Managed" Profession', in Richard Abel, Hilary Sommerland, Ulrike Schultz and Ole Hammersley (eds.), *Comparative Sociology of Legal Professions* [forthcoming: copy on file with authors].

[56] Bui Bich Thi Lien, 'Legal Education in Transitional Vietnam', in John Gillespie and Pip Nicholson (eds.), *Asian Socialism and Legal Change: The Dynamics of Vietnamese and Chinese Reform* (Canberra: ANU E Press, 2005), pp. 135–158.

[57] Chủ tịch hội đồng bộ trưởng, {Council of Ministers} Về việc đẩy mạnh công tác tuyên truyền, giáo dục pháp luật 315/CT 1988 [On Accelerating the Propagation of Legal Education], Sở khoa học và công nghệ Đồng Nai [Department of Science and Technology, Đồng Nai], available at https://motcua.dost-dongnai.gov.vn/Pages/LegalDocumentFullText.aspx?DocID=16949.

[58] Phạm Ngọc Quang, 'Để bảo đảm quyền con người – cần đổi mới nhận thức về nhân tố con người trong chủ nghĩa xã hội' ['Change our Conception of Human Agency in Socialism to Ensure Human Rights'] (1989) 10 *Nhà Nước Pháp Luật* 20–28.

[59] Nguyễn Niên, 'Mấy suy nghĩ về đổi mới tư duy pháp lý' ['Some Ideas on Renovating Legal Thinking'] (1987) 3 *NNPL* 44.

and the need for a flexible legal system capable of resolving contradictions generated by the introduction of market forces.[60] The writers agreed, however, that during the early stage of *Doi moi* reforms, the law should continue to suppress enemies of socialism.

Over the intervening three decades, laws and regulation have changed significantly from this transitional period. As the chapters in this volume demonstrate, in some areas socialist law has taken on new meanings, while in other areas it has remained more faithful to its Soviet roots and the Marxist–Leninist belief that a powerful and centralised socialist state is a normative good.

The chapters in the book reveal that the socialist legal past is not dead; it regularly re-emerges to frame present experience, while acquiring new meanings in everyday political, economic and social struggles. For example, socialist legal practices and concepts (such as democratic centralism) are themselves part of a normative tradition that rejects key assumptions underlying Western rule of law, such as the necessity of an independent judiciary.

1.6   The Puzzle: Legal Resilience after the Fall of Socialist Economics

The chapters in this book address one of the most important puzzles at the intersection of law and governance in socialist Asia: the resilience of socialist legal forms after the collapse of socialist economics. Since the 1980s, many have sought to introduce Western economic ideas and associated regulatory institutions across Asia, including in socialist Asia. Along with this, scholars have viewed Asia through the lens of Western laws. Both these attempts at legal engineering and the Western view have not necessarily been successful. In fact, they have missed the critical fact that socialist Asia has been able to integrate institutions of legal liberalism, while retaining a normative commitment to the statist underpinnings of a Marxist–Leninist understanding of socialist law. This explains why, despite China's apparent adoption of the institutions of capitalism (such as joint stock companies and corporations, competition law and policy), certain institutions have also proved hard to instil in the booming Chinese economy. Fundamental reforms, whether targeting the development of global capitalism or judicial independence, have proven elusive in China and Vietnam.

---

[60] Lê Minh Thông, 'Mấy vấn đề lý luận chung về pháp luật trong thời kỳ quá độ ở Việt Nam' ['Some Issues with the General Theory of Law in the Transitional Period in Vietnam'] (1988) 3 *NNPL* 41.

Many commentaries about legal reform in socialist Asia equate the failure to adopt liberal legalism to the role of local culture or 'Asian values' in the region,[61] conceptual reinterpretation,[62] path dependency,[63] 'palace wars'[64] or selective adaptation.[65] These approaches have been variously used to explain the take-up, rejection of and/or adaptation of liberal legal transplants. Scholars note the following as fundamental to the transplant debate: political will;[66] receptivity to change in laws, institutions and norms;[67] and technical and cognitive capacity.[68] Some scholars have focused on the 'modernisation' that results from transplants of Western-based laws and institutions into transforming East Asia, while others have argued that local understandings of law and legal institutions have been marginalised at the expense of supply-sided conceptions of reform and change,[69] also seen as limiting local sovereignty over the shape and scope of reforms.[70] The principal argument of this book is that the socialist legacy is fundamental to understanding law and legal institutions in Vietnam and China.

---

[61] See, e.g., Amartya Sen, *Human Rights and Asian Values*, available at www.nyu.edu/classes/gmoran/SEN.pdf.

[62] John Gillespie 'Developing a Discursive Analysis of Legal Transfers into Developing East Asia' (2008) 41(2) *New York University Journal of International Law and Politics* 101–161.

[63] Douglass C. North, *Institutions, Institutional Change and Economic Performance* (Cambridge: Cambridge University Press, 1990).

[64] Yves Dezalay and Bryant G. Garth, *The Internationalization of Palace Wars: Lawyers, Economists, and the Contest to Transform Latin American States* (Chicago, IL: University of Chicago Press, 2002).

[65] Pitman Potter, 'Legal Reform in China: Institutions, Culture and Selective Adaptation' (2004) 29 *Law and Social Inquiry* 465–493.

[66] Kahn-Freund, Otto, 'On Uses and Misuses of Comparative Law' (1974) 37 *The Modern Law Review* 1–27 and Daniel Berkowitz, Katharina Pistor and Jean-Francois Richard, 'Economic Development, Legality and the Transplant Effect' (2003) 47 *European Economic Review* 165–195.

[67] John Gillespie, 'Localizing Global Competition Law in Vietnam: A Bottom-Up Perspective' (2015) 64(4) *International and Comparative Law Quarterly* 935–963.

[68] John Gillespie and Pip Nicholson 'Taking the Interpretation of Legal Transfers Seriously: The Challenge for Law and Development', in J. Gillespie and P. Nicholson (eds.), *Law and Development and the Global Discourses of Legal Transfers* (Cambridge: Cambridge University Press, Cambridge, 2012), pp. 1–26.

[69] Ibid.

[70] Pip Nicholson and Sally Low, 'Local Accounts of Rule of Law Aid: Implications for Donors' (2013) 5 *Hague Journal on the Rule of Law* 1–43.

1.7   Legacy, Adaptation and Resilience

This book shifts the analytical focus away from liberal legalism. It treats socialist thought and institutions as subjects worthy of study in their own right. A key argument repeated throughout this book is that differences between socialist law and liberal legalism are often exaggerated. Rather than constituting an alien 'other', socialist institutions and forms of knowledge offer an alternative vision for modernity with advantages as well as drawbacks. It is the exploration of this alternative vision, rather than an explanation of why socialism turns local regulators away from liberal legalism, that animates this book.

In short, this book offers a different approach. It draws on history and context – and specific case studies – to examine the development of a Marxist–Leninist approach to socialist law and how China and Vietnam's commitment to this form of 'socialist' law has changed over time. In particular, it will examine how a 'socialist' legal system carries particular institutions and conceptual approaches that are compatible with economic capitalism, but that fundamentally reject key legal institutions and concepts of Western-style legal liberalism, including the political neutrality of state organs, judicial independence or autonomy of the civil society as some of the examples.

Put another way, the book inverts the analytical optic for socialist transforming East Asia: the study is not of how new forms of regulation are accommodated in transforming East Asia, but what conceptions of law, normativity and legal practice remain socialist and steadfast in contemporary socialist East Asia. Thus, rather than assuming a progressive movement towards Western liberal legal reform (enabled by transplantation), this inquiry asks: What is the continuing normative traction of the Soviet socialist and/or locally Asian socialist legal legacy? It explores the resonance and tenacity of these socialist projects – as well as their ongoing reinterpretation – in China and Vietnam. It explores how deeply rooted historical approaches to law have been justified as socialist and therefore themselves remain persistent, even as conventional socialist practice fades away.

This book argues that this Soviet and/or Asian socialist legacy has a profound ongoing influence on contemporary legal development. We contend that there are important continuities that bring together the Soviet socialist legal system with that of China and Vietnam and their socialist laws (public law, in particular), and that these help us more broadly understand the conception of today's socialist legal project.

Putting to one side the debate about what makes a socialist legal system socialist, we argue that most countries with socialist legal systems have, and continue to, prioritise state interests over the individual. The state – both centralised and effective – has a profound normative importance in the form of socialist law that we are tracing. The socialist focus on the importance of the state in development has drawn on deeply rooted conceptions of the need for the state to guide economic growth and ensure state security. This point is made clearly in Chapter 3, which deals with the Soviet experience and highlights how the founders of the socialist law system – the Soviet Union – interpreted socialism in a statist way. This statist orientation feeds the ongoing influence of Marxist–Leninist organisational structures, such as democratic centralism and the *nomenkultura* system, in contemporary Chinese and Vietnamese legal systems.

Scholars, we argue, have largely ignored the ramifications of this continued commitment to socialist law and legal institutions. Socialist law remains an important category of law in East Asia, even with the collapse of the communist bloc and the end of the Cold War. To take just one example, article 5 of the Chinese Constitution describes the importance of upholding China's '*socialist* legal system', and all the ongoing legal reform emphasises that it is underpinned by socialist values and serves a socialist agenda. Furthermore, article 2 of the Vietnamese Constitution describes Vietnam as a '*socialist* rule of law state'. However, a majority of foreign scholars have largely assumed these commitments to socialist law to be purely semantic and have instead sought signs of a (linear) transition to Western-style legal systems.

The reluctance to seriously engage with the socialist aspects of Chinese and Vietnamese law is problematic. By ignoring the socialist aspects of these legal systems, and the normative justifications for them, scholars have neglected the distinctive institutions and approaches embedded within the Chinese and Vietnamese legal systems. For instance, Party leadership in both China and Vietnam have made use of a public prosecutor's office that exercises both prosecutorial and supervisory powers. This supervisory role is a reflection of how the institutional organisation of the socialist legal system is in tension with Western conceptions of separated powers. While this trend continues in Vietnam, China is in the process of creating a Supervision Commission, which will incorporate a significant part of the procuracy and other organs, to exercise the supervisory power centrally and comprehensively.

1.8   Project Scope

The book comprises three parts. Part I explores the question of what makes socialist law socialist. Professor Michael Dowdle argues that there is very little that is intrinsically socialist about socialist legal systems. More particularly, Dowdle argues that there are much greater political-legal commonalities between Asia and the West than the current discourse on socialism allows. He asserts that this is the result of the conflation of socialism with communism, anti-capitalism, state capitalism, Leninism and 'socialism with Chinese characteristics'. Dowdle suggests disaggregating this confusion and demonstrates that the nature of socialist law depends on its context. For example, in the Soviet Union and contemporary Asia, socialist law has adopted a statist guise that is very different from the one that it has assumed in Western European socialist thinking.

Part II explores the basis of the socialist legal system in the Soviet system (Chapter 3) and its legacies in China (Chapter 4) and Vietnam (Chapter 5). More particularly, Chapter 3 asks what imperial Russian institutions and mentalities were critical in the construction of the socialist legal system. This Chapter adopts a social and conceptual historical approach to understanding how socialist law evolved in Soviet society, concluding that it reflected formalist and statist lines. This reinvention of institutions placed many of the institutions and approaches to law taken by Imperial Russia at the centre of a powerful state, which allowed a transition to socialism. The subsequent chapters in this section reflect on how China and Vietnam adapted this Soviet ideological and structural legacy for themselves.

Parts III–VII (Chapters 6–15) offer empirical analyses of the socialist legacy in China and Vietnam. They examine how socialist law is conceived, practised and understood across both countries. The contributors analyse the resilience of socialist precepts and practices, along with studies of Chinese and Vietnamese adaptations of these tenets. The focus is on constitutions; the tension between the Soviet-inspired notion of democratic centralism and conceptions of justice; labour-based disputes; regulatory approaches to the (socialist) economy; and land laws.

In each case, the contributors explore whether there is an identifiable transition 'out of' socialism or whether the study reveals transforming socialism. If the latter, the question is asked: What remains resilient of the socialist roots – whether Soviet, Chinese or Vietnamese?

What Is *Not* 'Socialist' about Socialist Law

MICHAEL W. DOWDLE

2.1 Synopsis

Because understandings of what constitutes 'socialism' are so contested, in this Chapter I try more limitedly to explore what socialism – and hence what might be 'socialist' about socialist law – is not. This is an important question because there is good reason to try to preserve the idea of socialism, even in its vagaries; and understanding what socialism is not allows us, at the minimum, to prevent visiting semantic harm on that concept. Included among the things I identify that socialism is not are nationalism, Leninism, communitarianism, state capitalism and 'socialism with Chinese characteristics'. I conclude by arguing how the search for what is 'socialist' in socialist law is a very difficult operation; one that must be done with great care if we are to preserve socialism as a worthy human endeavour.

2.2 Why the Meaning of Socialism Is Important

Socialism is a powerful word. Few other words have generated such social upheaval and division over the past 200 years. On the west side of the North Atlantic, they fear the very word itself.[1] Elsewhere, it is worn as a badge of honour, even by those who would appear quite apathetic to its real concerns.[2] Correspondingly, socialism is also a very vague word. People bend and twist it to use its power to address their particular causes.

Socialism is a word worth preserving. Of course, there is nothing wrong with a word changing its meanings – it happens all the time. But at least in the context of the word 'socialism', I think there is a

---

[1] See Eric Foner, 'Why Is There No Socialism in the United States?' (1984) 17 *History Workshop Journal* 57–80.

[2] See, e.g., C. V. Devan Nair (ed.), *Socialism That Works ... the Singapore Way* (Singapore: Federal Publications, 1976).

two-fold utility in boundary keeping. First, the term socialism carries a certain moral weight. To apply it to a particular phenomenon lends that moral weight to the phenomenon. Misapplication serves to valorise something in a way that it does not deserve and/or serves to diminish the strength of the moral truth the word seeks to capture. Relatedly, the word 'socialism' uniquely captures a valuable insight – that capitalism has its problems, and that there just might be something we can do about it. Our ability to conceptualise, express and explore this insight is threatened when the meaning(s) of the word 'socialism' comes to be attached too strongly to other kinds of conceptualisations.

2.2.1   A Brief History

I will not attempt to offer a definition of socialism. Words need their leeway if they are to be used to teach about our world.[3] Nevertheless, in order to preserve the value of the word, we have to understand what it was that the word was working to provoke (if for no other reason than to know if the word still deserves its relevance). For that, it would help to explore its history.

In English, the modern usage of the word 'socialist' first appears in the early nineteenth century, although the idea that it sought to capture dates back to the French Revolution. In the latter part of the eighteenth century, Western European society – France and England in particular, and later Germany – began experiencing a profound shift in the way that the production of material goods was organised, and how industrial production fit within the larger systemic structure of the European world economy. Today, we refer to this shift as the Industrial Revolution (or more precisely, the first Industrial Revolution).

Early industrialisation drastically changed the nature of production and work in Western European society in a couple of ways. First, it made production the principal source of wealth generation (previously, it had been commerce) and through that, the principal constructor of European socio-economic ordering.[4] Second, it centralised the activities of production – labour – by removing these activities from individual homes and locating them, and the workers who performed them, in factories.

---

[3] George Lakoff and Mark Johnson, *Metaphors We Live By* (Chicago, IL: University of Chicago Press, 2003).

[4] Fernand Braudel, *Civilization and Capitalism, 15th–18th Century, vol. 3: The Perspective of the World* (trans. Siân Reynolds) (Berkeley, CA: University of California Press, 1992).

The wealth that is generated by production is called surplus value. Industrialisation greatly increased the surplus value that could be generated from productive labour. In the free-market economies of the early industrial era, the allocation of surplus value was made by those who organised production. And they would invariably allocate it to themselves. Surplus value could be increased by reducing labour costs. So those who organised production – let's call them 'capitalists' – had strong incentives to pay workers as little as possible, in order to maximise the surplus value that would go to capitalists.[5]

The factory system exacerbated the capitalists' ability to suppress the amount workers received for their work. Centralisation of production allowed for more intrusive monitoring of workers' activities, increasing the amount of labour a worker performed (by increasing hours and restricting breaks).[6] It tied the worker to a particular firm and a particular place, thus preventing them from pursuing a higher income elsewhere.[7] As a result, capitalists became increasingly wealthy, as workers became increasingly impoverished.

But the factory system also made the asymmetries between capitalist income and worker income more visible. And herein, it is asserted, lie the roots of socialism. The germinal intellectual figures associated with the birth of socialism were all motivated by the sense that there was something deeply immoral about an industrial system in which those many who actually laboured to create goods had to live in abject poverty, while those few who organised their labour were able to live in increasing opulence.[8]

We see this in the famous distinction that Henri de Saint-Simon (1760–1825) – often referred to as the founder of French socialism – drew between what he called the 'working class' and the 'idling class', and in his call for the creation of a new kind of industrial society that would be led by the former rather than the latter.[9] This was the concern that led Charles

---

[5] Karl Marx, *Theories of Surplus Value: Books I, II, and III* (New York: Prometheus Books, 2000).

[6] E. P. Thompson, 'Time, Work-Discipline, and Industrial Capitalism,' (1967) 38 *Past & Present* 81–83, 85–86.

[7] Sidney Pollard, 'Factory Discipline in the Industrial Revolution,' (1963) 16 *The Economic History Review* 254–271.

[8] Sheldon Richman, 'Libertarian Left,' *The American Conservative*, March 2011, p. 30.

[9] Henri de Saint Simon, *Henri de Saint Simon, 1760–1825: Selected Writings on Science, Industry and Social Organization* (ed. and trans. Keith Taylor, New York, NY: Holmes and Meier Publishers, Inc., 1975), pp. 158–161.

Fourier (1772–1837) to advocate that workers should be paid according to their actual contributions to production via communal distribution of profits;[10] and that Pierre-Joseph Proudhon (1809–1865) sought to capture in his famous assertion that 'property is theft'.[11] Concern for the plight of the working poor also motivated Robert Owen (1771–1858) to establish his famous New Lanark Mill as a symbol of the possibilities of utopian socialism (also called 'Owenism'), and thus popularise the idea of socialism in England.[12] And of course, this was also the problem to which Karl Marx devoted much of his life, developing the key theoretical vocabulary that we associate with socialism, such as 'exploitation', labour theory of value, capital accumulation, means of production, and surplus value.[13]

However, just as there was general agreement about the problem, there was much disagreement about its exact causes and what should be done about it. Some saw labour exploitation (the capitalists' appropriation of all the surplus value generated by labour) as a product of new-found systems of state organisation, and so advocated living in small, intimate communities that operated outside of the state's reach.[14] Others, such as Mikhail Bakunin, argued for the elimination of the state entirely.[15] Some saw the state as a solution, advocating for the development of more scientific state administration of industrial production and allocation of the wealth and livelihood opportunities it created.[16] Others argued for much more confrontational political action.[17]

---

[10] Jonathan Beecher and Richard Bienvenu (eds.), *The Utopian Vision of Charles Fourier: Selected Texts on Work, Love, and Passionate Attraction* (Boston, MA: Beacon Press, 1971).

[11] Pierre-Joseph Proudhon, 'Letter to Villiaume (24 January 1856),' reprinted in *Property Is Theft!: a Pierre-Joseph Proudhon Anthology* (trans. Paul Sharkey, Oakland, CA: AK Press, 2011), p. 603.

[12] Robert Owen, 'Report to the Committee of the Association for the Relief of the Manufacturing and Labouring Poor,' 12 March 1817, reprinted at http://la.utexas.edu/users/hcleaver/368/368owenrptcom.html.

[13] Marx, *Theories of Surplus Value*.

[14] Jonathan Beecher, *Charles Fourier: The Visionary and His World* (Berkeley, CA: University of California, 1986), p. 355.

[15] George Woodcock, *Anarchism* (Harmondsworth: Penguin Books, 1962), p. 158.

[16] See, e.g., 'The Gotha Program (1875)' in J. H. Robinson (ed.), *Readings in European History*, vol. 2 (Boston, MA: Ginn, 1906), pp. 617–619, available at *Hanover Historical Texts Project*, https://history.hanover.edu/texts/gotha.html.

[17] Henry Tudor and J. M. Tudor (eds.), *Marxism and Social Democracy: The Revisionist Debate 1896–1898* (Cambridge: Cambridge University Press, 1988), p. 3.

2.2.2   Identifying Core Concerns

Given this history, I think we can identify a number of core concerns that recommend socialism as an important moral critique of capitalism (even if it remains very unclear how we should respond to this critique).

- Socialism Carries a Particular Moral Weight
  As discussed, socialism emerged out of a concern for a particular kind of injustice, that which attends to labour exploitation. For this reason, appeals to socialism, if they are to carry the valourising impact that brought the idea of socialism to our attention in the first place, must ultimately be moral appeals. They cannot be grounded simply in their subject's contribution to our material or pragmatic comfort.
- Socialism Focuses on the Moral Implications of Material Inequality, and Not Simply on Inequality of Opportunity
  From its inception, socialism has been motivated by the material inequalities that are generated by one person's ability to usurp the surplus value generated by another's labour. This would suggest a concern for material inequality (that is, substantive inequality) rather than simply a concern for inequalities of opportunity. This distinguishes it from liberalism, which tends to be concerned with the latter over the former.[18] This is not to argue that socialism is necessarily anti-liberal, or that liberalism is necessarily anti-socialist. There is no reason why one cannot place moral value in both procedural and substantive equality. Socialism does not even necessarily deny that that the moral value of procedural equality might sometimes have to condition our moral pursuit of material equality. It is just that socialism focuses its particular moral attentions on problems of material inequality.
- Socialism Is a Cosmopolitan Phenomenon
  Because socialism conveys a particular moral view of the world, its application is not conditioned by political borders. Morality knows no geography (even if the sociology of morality is geographically contingent). This is not to say that the particular duties that socialism promotes cannot have geographical constraints. There may be very good reason why the polity of a socialist state might choose to limit the reach of its socialist policies (including its socialist legalities) to its own

[18] See, e.g., John Rawls, *A Theory of Justice*, rev. edn. (Cambridge, MA: Belknap Press, 1999), p. 118.

domestic terrain.[19] But the moral insights that socialism seeks to capture cannot but be universal.

Of course, to say that socialism is a cosmopolitan phenomenon is not to say that every place is equally deserving of its particular concerns. Marx, for example, did not believe that the goals of socialism were relevant to pre-industrial economies, since he thought that industrialisation was a necessary precondition for socialism. The point here is simply that socialism does not regard its concerns as being limited to a particular kind of culture (such as Western culture). For example, the pre-industrial societies of East Asia might not have been well suited to socialism. But assuming they were, then the socialist goals to which they aspired were and are ultimately a cosmopolitan project and not an East Asian project.

2.3   What Socialism Is Not

The discussion so far allows us to see how many legal practices that are commonly equated with 'socialist law' or 'socialist legality' are not *necessarily* socialist in nature. This is not to suggest that these practices are always illegitimate or morally suspect – indeed, many of these practices are often used to promote socialism. But they can also be used for other purposes; even to promote conditions that are inapposite to socialism. The point is that the mere deployment of these practices does not establish a country as a socialist state or polity; their deployment alone does not necessarily merit the moral valourisation that the term 'socialism' is meant to bestow.

2.3.1   Socialism Is Not a Proper Noun

Many states label themselves 'socialist' in either their official name (for example, 'The *Socialist* Republic of Vietnam') or in their constitution (for example, '[t]he People's Republic of China is a *socialist* state under the people's democratic dictatorship' [PRC Const., art. 1, emphasis added]). Oftentimes, self-labelled 'socialist' states will label some of their legal practices as being therefore distinctly 'socialist' as well. Alternatively, some will presume that if a particular state calls itself socialist, this is

---

[19] Compare with Thomas Nagel, 'The Problem of Global Justice' (2005) 33 *Philosophy & Public Affairs* 113–147.

enough to establish that some distinctive legal practice found in that state is therefore socialist as well.

Obviously, such presumptions are fallacious – one cannot claim socialist legitimacy simply by saying that one is a socialist.[20] It is the values of socialism that identify socialism, not the mere presence of some noun or adjective. Whether or not a particular country or legal practice is 'socialist' is determined by evidence that the country or the practice is actually working to prioritise material equality and non-exploitation over other values. And this involves an inquiry into more than just the name of the country or practice. If a country wishes to enjoy the legitimacy benefits that socialism bestows, it has to actually promote socialist equalities and freedom. It can't simply *call* itself 'socialist'.

2.3.2 Socialism Is Not 'Socialism with "X" Characteristics'; It Is Not a Form of Nationalism

'A White Horse is not a Horse'.[21] A variant of the socialism as a proper noun fallacy is the labelling of some particular practice as being one of 'socialism with "x" characteristics'. The most famous example of this is the People's Republic of China's invention of a 'socialism with Chinese characteristics'.[22] But China is not unique in this – during the 1970s, well before Deng came up with his famous characterisation, Singapore, upon being evicted from the Socialist International for its suppression of labour activism, briefly advanced the claim that it was in fact a socialist country, but that it had simply been practising socialism 'the Singapore way'.[23]

In evaluating this fallacy, we should distinguish between two different kinds of claims. Every country, indeed every socialist, has their own

---

[20] David Hackett Fischer, *Historians' Fallacies: Toward a Logic of Historical Thought* (New York, NY: Harper & Row, 1970).

[21] Gongsun Longzi, 'The White Horse Dialogue' (ca. circa 300 BCE), reprinted in Bryan W. Van Norden, 'Gongsun Longzi: "On the White Horse",' in Philip J. Ivanhoe and Bryan W. Van Norden (eds.), *Readings in Classical Chinese Philosophy* (Indianapolis, IN: Hackett Publishing, 2005, 2nd edn.), p. 364.

[22] Deng Xiaoping, 'Building a Socialism with a Specifically Chinese Character' (30 June 1984) in *Selected Works of Deng Xiaoping. Vol III, 1982–1992* (Beijing: Foreign Language Press, 1994), p. 73.

[23] Nair, *Socialism That Works.*

distinct vision of how the values of socialism would be best realised.[24] And it is undoubtedly the case that what works to promote socialism in one locale may not work to promote socialism somewhere else. But we need to distinguish the question of how socialism is best realised from the question of what socialism refers to. China may be realising socialism in its own way, but that does not make the socialism it is realising a different kind of thing. Again, the question as to whether something is really socialist (or even socialism with 'x' characteristics) depends on *what* is being realised (that is, socialism), not on *how* it is being realised. To the extent that the 'socialism with Chinese characteristics' is working to promote material equality and non-exploitation among the working classes, then it is just socialism pure and simple. But to the extent that it is being used to place other values (such as nationalism or the development of state power) above these socialist concerns, then it is not really 'socialist' at all, in the sense of being deserving of the moral valourisation that the term is being used to convey. (Note that this is true even if it were the case that these other values also represent a particular kind of moral good.)

Of course, it is possible for a country to use nationalism or development of state power as a tool for promoting socialism.[25] But that does not alter the nature of that socialism itself. Again, as with the self-labelling of socialism, whether or not a particular practice is actually socialist depends on what the practice is being used for, not on who is doing the using.[26]

2.3.3   Socialism Is Different from Communitarianism

Socialism is also frequently associated with communitarianism. For our purposes, communitarianism refers to a moral prioritisation of the community over the individual. It represents a moral demand that the individual subordinate his or her own interests to the corporate interests of the community taken as a whole. The conflation of socialism with communitarianism probably derives in considerable part from the fact that many early socialists, particularly the utopian socialists like Robert

---

[24] Chris M. Hann (ed.), *Socialism: Ideals, Ideologies, and Local Practice* (London: Routledge, 2003).

[25] Tudor and Tudor, *Marxism and Social Democracy*, p. 3.

[26] Jamie Peck and Jun Zhang, 'A Variety of Capitalism ... with Chinese Characteristics?' (2013) 13(3) *Journal of Economic Geography* 357–396.

Owen and Charles Fourier, were communitarians. Many socialist thinkers also often contrasted the distinctly cooperative and social character of socialism against the competitive and socially alienating character of capitalism.

Even if it were the case that all socialism is innately communitarian, it is certainly not the case that all communitarianism is innately socialist. Communitarianism can obviously be used in service of values that are clearly not socialist. Indeed, as well analysed by Antonio Gramsci, appeals to communitarianism are frequently deployed in order to support the very kinds of material inequalities and class exploitation that socialism seeks to overcome. According to Gramsci, one of the principal ways in which a ruling class maintains its domination over the working classes is by encouraging the working classes to accept their exploitation in the name of larger communal values such as cooperation, integration and identity – a practice he famously termed 'hegemony'.[27]

2.3.4   Socialism Is Not State Capitalism

Socialism is also commonly conflated with state capitalism. State capitalism is a practice in which the state assumes the role of the capitalist in the structuring of the industrial order.[28] The theory is that since the state is a public entity rather than a private entity, it will be more sensitive to issues of exploitation and material inequality, and thus will be naturally inclined to pursue socialist goals. State capitalism is a prominent feature of many of the countries iconically identified with 'socialism' in the United States – such as the Soviet Union, the People's Republic of China, and the Socialist Republic of Vietnam.

State capitalism can of course be a means of promoting socialism. Indeed, state capitalism was originally conceptualised as a way of allowing pre-industrial countries to attain socialism without having to first transit through the exploitative stage of private capitalism (see discussion of Leninism in Section 2.3.5).

But states have their own corporate interests, and these interests can often be promoted by processes of capital accumulation (for example, national reserves). This, in turn, can give the state the same incentive to

---

[27] Douglas Litowitz, 'Gramsci, Hegemony, and the Law,' (2000) 2 *BYU Law Review* 515–551.

[28] Raymond Williams, *Keywords: A Vocabulary of Culture and Society*, rev. edn. (New York, NY: Oxford University Press, 1985), p. 52.

exploit labour for its benefit as private capitalists have to exploit labour for their benefit. Indeed, many so-called 'socialist' states have expressly engaged in such exploitation to promote corporate-state interests such as national strength. A good example of this is the People's Republic of China during the Great Leap Forward. Here, China heavily exploited the labour of its rural population, forcing them to live in conditions of subsistence (or less), to generate enough surplus value to construct a higher-end manufacturing sector to enhance the Chinese state's global geo-political interests.[29]

Even if this were the right decision for China to make at the time (for example, in terms of China's future ability to protect its population from external domination), it was not at all consistent with the moral vision of socialism. As discussed previously, a moral wrong is a moral wrong. If exploitation is a moral wrong, it is just as much a wrong when practised for the benefit of 'the state' as when practised for the benefit of private capitalists. Indeed, many non-socialist societies (such as the United States during the late nineteenth century) embrace capitalist exploitation precisely because they see it as contributing to their national power in the same way that self-designated 'socialist' countries justify state exploitation as contributing to state power.

2.3.5 Socialism Is Not Leninism

Many self-proclaimed 'socialist' states are also Leninist, and this sometimes causes socialism to be conflated with Leninism. Leninism is probably best seen as being the political side of state capitalism. As discussed, socialism emerged out of a moral revulsion to the exploitations of industralisation. In 1850, Karl Marx, in his germinal theorisation of socialism, famously argued that exploitative industrial capitalism was a necessary stage on the historical path to socialism.[30] Such an argument posed a problem for those seeking to establish socialism in pre-industrial societies, like Vladimir Lenin was trying to do in Russia.

---

[29] Jonathan Spence, *The Search for Modern China* (New York, NY: W.W. Norton, 1991), pp. 574–583.
[30] Karl Marx and Friedrich Engels, *The Communist Manifesto* (trans. Samuel Moore, New York, NY: Penguin, 2002), ch. 3.

Lenin's response was to claim that pre-industrial societies could bypass the exploitative state of capitalism by having the state assume the role of the private capitalist class (aka state capitalism).[31] This still posed a problem, though. In contrast to labourers in industrial societies, labourers in pre-industrial societies would have not yet developed class consciousness.[32] They therefore could not be expected to pursue socialism on their own, in the way they could be expected to do in the more industrialised countries of Western Europe. Instead, they would have to be organised and led by an enlightened political elite, a 'natural socialist aristocracy' as it were.

Like political socialism in Western Europe, this socialist aristocracy would take the form of a political party. But in contrast to the socialist political parties of Europe, the pre-industrial socialist party would have to be paternalistic and dictatorial (often referred to as a 'revolutionary vanguard party') rather than democratic,[33] since pre-industrial workers could not be expected to appreciate on their own the short-term sacrifices that would be needed to bring about the ultimate goal of socialism. Hence was born the political ideal of Leninism.[34] Like Russia, Asian societies (excluding Japan) were not yet industrialised at the time they first encountered the political ideal of socialism. For this reason, they found the Leninist vanguard party path to socialism appealing.[35]

But paternalistic and dictatorial parties may call themselves 'socialist' without necessarily being socialist in fact. Many self-proclaimed socialist Leninist party-states have ended up being as exploitative of industrial labour as any capitalist state (often confusing socialism with nationalism in the process).[36] Again, important social good might be served by such exploitation, but that does not justify aligning that particular exploitation with the values of socialism.

---

[31] Nikolai Bukharin, *Imperialism and World Economy* (London: Merlin, 1972), p. 158.

[32] Vladimir Ilich Lenin, *Two Tactics of Social Democracy in the Democratic Revolution* (Miami: Hard Press Publishing, 2012).

[33] James Ryan, *Lenin's Terror: The Ideological Origins of Early Soviet State Violence* (London: Routledge, 2012), p. 19.

[34] See generally Neil Harding, *Leninism* (Durham, NC: Duke University Press, 1996).

[35] Zhu Suli, '"Judicial Politics" as State-Building,' in Stéphanie Balme and Michael W. Dowdle (eds.), *Building Constitutionalism in China* (New York, NY: Palgrave MacMillan, 2009), pp. 23–36.

[36] Peck and Zhuang, 'A Variety of Capitalism ... with Chinese Characteristics?', pp. 357–396.

2.4 Conclusion

Socialism is a concern worth preserving. The evolution of global capitalism into neo-liberalism makes socialism's moral reminders more important today than they have been in the last seventy years. But the idea of socialism also seems particularly subject to abuse, and too easy to corrupt and pervert. Reminding ourselves that capitalism has its dangers requires us to be alert to the abuses of socialist appeal, in law as in everything else.

PART II

Socialism and Legacies

The Historical Roots of Socialist Law

WILLIAM PARTLETT

3.1 Introduction

This Chapter will explore the importance of history to socialist law. It will describe how the ultimately triumphant Leninist version of socialism valuing state centralisation drew heavily on a historically rooted imperial Russian practice of 'supervisory legality' that competed with and undermined binding judicial control of legality. This supervisory tradition – justified as a way of ensuring a centralised vertical of power for Party policy, as well as a method for efficiently entertaining and monitoring complaints from individual petitioners – enforced legality through a bureaucratic process of checking and rechecking administrative and judicial decision-making. This supervisory practice was transplanted to other socialist countries and remains influential to this day because of a continued value for centralised state power in the countries of the former socialist bloc. Current efforts at understanding legal systems and judicial reform in these countries requires understanding both the practices and institutions of this tradition of supervisory legality, as well as its internal justifications.

> The Russian czars did a great deal that was bad. They robbed and enslaved the people. But they did one thing that was good. They amassed an enormous state, all the way to Kamchatka ... We have united the state in such a way that if any part were isolated from the common socialist state, it would not only inflict harm on the latter but would be unable to exist independently and would inevitably fall under foreign subjugation.
>
> Joseph Stalin[1]

Associate Professor, Melbourne Law School. I would like to thank Melbourne University for a generous grant that supported this research.

[1] Joseph Stalin, 1937. Quoted from Ivo Banac (ed.), *The Diary of Georgi Dimitrov 1933–1949* (New Haven, CT: Yale University Press, 2003), p. 65.

In 1936, the Soviet Union adopted a constitution that would define the socialist legal model.[2] The key legal institutions mirrored those of Western European civil law systems: the Constitution described a Public Prosecutor's Office (hereafter, procuracy) alongside a Supreme Court. However, the Constitution also afforded both of these institutions broad powers of 'supervision' (*nadzor*). As this model spread to other newly socialist countries, scholars in the socialist bloc described these 'supervisory' powers over administrative and judicial decision-making as a socialist improvement on 'bourgeois' separation of powers principles.[3] Western scholars followed suit, tying supervision to socialist political and economic ideology.[4] Despite the end of the Cold War and the rise of capitalism, however, 'supervision' still remains important in constitutional text and practice across many of the former socialist bloc countries.[5]

---

[2] John Hazard, 'Soviet Model for Marxian Socialist Constitutions' (1975) 60 *Cornell Law Review* 985–1004 (discussing whether the 1936 Constitution has become a 'model to which Marxist-oriented statesmen must adhere on pain of loss of membership in the socialist commonwealth'.).

[3] George Ginsburgs, 'The Soviet Procuracy and Forty Years of Socialist Legality' (1959) 18 *American Slavic and East European Review* 34, 34 (describing the how Soviet jurists saw supervision 'as a vast improvement over Western practice'.). More recent scholars still assume that these types of legal powers were socialist in nature. Rafal Manko, 'Is the Socialist Legal Tradition "Dead and Buried"? The Continuity of Certain Elements of Socialist Legal Culture in Polish Civil Procedure', in Thomas Wilhelmsson, Elina Paunio, Annika Pohjolainen and Helsingin Yliopisto (eds.), in *Private Law and the Many Cultures of Europe* (Alphen aan den Rijn: Kluwer Law International, 2007), pp. 94–98 (discussing legacies of supervisory powers in Polish civil procedure as socialist in nature).

[4] Leon Boim, 'Party-State Control in the Soviet Union', in Leon Boim, Glenn Morgan and Aleksander Rudzinski (eds.), *Legal Controls in the Soviet Union* (Leyden: A. W. Sijthoff, 1966), p. 11 (explaining this form of supervisory control as necessary given 'the nationalisation of the means of production and the planned economy of the communist state'.). Others saw supervision as a feature of an 'absolutist' government which does not 'utilise the constitutional machinery of the West for challenging the legality of administrative enactments'. Glenn Morgan, 'The "Protest" of the Soviet Procuracy – A Means of Challenging Subordinate Legislation' (1960) 9 *American Journal of Comparative Law* 499, 507. Hiroshi Oda, 'The Procuracy and the Regular Courts as Enforcers of the Constitutional Rule of Law: The Experience of East Asian States' (1986–1987) 61 *Tulane Law Review* 1339–1363.

[5] William Partlett and Eric C. Ip, 'Is Socialist Law Really Dead?' (2016) 48 *New York University Journal of International Law and Politics* 463 (describing how key institutions from the Russian tradition continue to shape institutional discourse in China). Russia's post-communist constitution from 1993 placed the Procuracy and the Courts in a chapter entitled 'Judicial Power'. See also the European Court of Human Rights' criticism of supervision in the Russian court system.

A historical perspective helps us better understand the persistence of this critical aspect of socialist law.[6] History demonstrates that supervision in the 1936 Soviet Constitution was not an innovation tied to socialist ideology. Instead, supervision was a socialist rebranding of a deep-rooted imperial Russian practice for the political review of the legality of administrative and judicial decision-making.[7] During the imperial Russian period, this practice had been justified on two grounds. First, and most importantly, supervision was seen as an effective method for modernising the Russian Empire, by centralising and unifying legal decisions. Second, it was justified as a statist tool for entertaining (and monitoring) the large number of informal petitions and complaints from individuals.[8] Stalin's statist version of socialism drew heavily on these justifications and supervisory practices. And these justifications remain present in the state capitalist systems today in many former socialist bloc countries.

This story of continuity begins with the 1917 Russian revolution. In the years after the Russian Revolution, one of the most pressing challenges for the builders of socialist law was the form of the socialist legal system.[9] A critical question emerged: What role would the state and imperial-era legal concepts and institutions (such as supervision) play in socialist law? Would these concepts continue or disappear?

The 'utopians', drawing on an experimental and decentralised conception of socialism (closer to socialism's Western European roots), argued that socialist ideology should lead to a complete abandonment of imperial Russian approaches to law in favour of a less formal and more decentralised form of technical-administrative rules.[10] Perhaps the clearest example of this school of thought was Evgeny Pashukanis, who

---

[6] Martin Krygier, 'Law as Tradition' (1986) 5 *Law and Philosophy* 237, 244.

[7] David Christian, 'The Supervisory Function in Russian and Soviet History' (1982) 41 *Slavic Review* 73. In fact, the Soviet conception of supervision drew in part on a tradition of supervision that pre-dated the 1864 reforms.

[8] Elise Wirtschafter, 'Legal Identity and the Possession of Serfs in Imperial Russia' (1998) 70(3) *Journal of Modern History* 561–587 (discussing the role of the Senate and the procuracy in responding to petitions from individual serfs in eighteenth and nineteenth century imperial Russia).

[9] Zigurds Zile, *Ideas and Forces in Soviet Legal Theory: Statutes, Decisions and Other Materials on the Development and Processes of Soviet Law* (Madison, WI: College Printing & Publishing Inc, 1970), p. 50. ('Prior to the revolution, no one had thought of drawing up (whether in detail or in a general form) the legal relations to be established and adjusted during the transition from the proletarian revolution to the consolidation of socialism and communism ... At present, therefore, research in this area is like plowing virgin soil.').

[10] See, e.g., Csaba Toth, 'Most Wild and Visionary': Social Change and the Legacy of Robert Owen' (1996) 7(1) *Utopian Studies* 108–112.

argued that a socialist legal system would look very different from imperial Russian law because the legal 'form' of the bourgeois state was linked to commodity exchange.[11]

The 'statists', by contrast, interpreted socialism through the imperial Russian tradition, and argued that socialist ideology required a centralised state that could ensure Russia's 'transition' from capitalism to communism. One of the critical aspects of this statist program was the continuance of imperial-era practices of supervision.[12] This form of supervisory legality – now labelled as socialist – would have the same effect as its imperial Russian predecessor: centralise the state by ensuring 'that local organs of authority decide such matters in conformity with law'.[13] This position was best represented in the writing of Andrei Vyshinsky, himself the head of a key supervisory institution – the procuracy.

The statists were ultimately successful. Their success was constitutionalised in the 1936 Soviet Constitution.[14] This constitutional order featured a vertically controlled procuracy that combined the power to initiate and supervise criminal prosecutions with vast powers of 'general supervision' over administrative law (*vyschii nadzor*).[15] It also included a supreme court that had wide powers to 'supervise the judicial activities of lower courts' and develop the law that went well beyond the appellate powers of Western supreme courts.[16] The statist supervision in the 1936 Soviet Constitution was then exported to newly socialist East Asia in the post–World War II period. In this process of transplantation, the formal supervisory institutions themselves were superimposed on East Asian traditions of political review of legality.[17]

---

[11] Evgeny Pashukanis, 'The General Theory of Law and Marxism', in *Russian Legal Theory* (New York, NY: New York University Press, 1996)

[12] Christian, 'The Supervisory Function in Russian and Soviet History', 73.

[13] Andrey Y. Vyshinsky, *The Law of the Soviet State* (New York, NY: Macmillan, 1948), p. 526.

[14] Glenn Morgan, *Soviet Administrative Legality: The Role of the Attorney General's Office* (Stanford, CA: Stanford University Press, 1962), p. 21 ('reached back into the past and revived the supervisory functions of the Procuracy in an effort to promote observance of legality in its sprawling bureaucracy and to ensure the conformity of local enactments with central decrees.').

[15] Article 113, Constitution of the Soviet Union 1936, available (in Russian) at www .hist.msu.ru/ER/Etext/cnst1936.htm#9.

[16] Article 104, Constitution of the Soviet Union 1936.

[17] Though one differing in important ways from that of the Russian. Charles O. Hucker, 'The Traditional Chinese Censorate and the New Peking Regime' (1951) 45 *American*

Today, supervision remains a powerful practice across the former socialist bloc, despite the collapse of the Soviet Union and the rise of capitalism in East Asia. Underpinning this persistence is a continued desire for centralisation and state coordination – now in the context of state capitalism. In fact, these practices are now justified as mechanisms for overcoming problems of state weakness and coping with the challenges of transitioning to a 'socialist market economy'.[18] They have also been justified as a less formalistic way for the people to petition for remedies to violations of their rights. These normative justifications complicate attempts to move towards the judicial control of legality and, in turn, rule of law.[19]

This Chapter will develop this argument in seven sections. Section 3.2 will explore why scholars of socialist law have ignored history and what insights history can bring to our understanding of this legal system. Section 3.3 will describe one of the key foundations of socialist law: the imperial Russian tradition of supervision. Section 3.4 will describe the two competing approaches to socialist law in 1920s and 1930s Soviet Russia. Section 3.5 will describe how these different approaches competed for dominance in the first two decades of the Soviet period. Section 3.6 will explain how the 1936 Soviet Constitution represented the final triumph of the statist approach to socialist law. Section 3.7 will describe how this statist approach remains influential in the former Soviet republics. Section 3.8 will turn to its adaptation and continuing influence in socialist East Asia.

3.2   Socialist Law and History

During the Cold War, legal scholars understood 'socialist law' to be one of the major legal families alongside the common law and civil law

---

Political Science Review 1041, 1041 ('the Censorate provided a service in Chinese government that has no institutionalised counterpart in any modern western nation.')

[18] Partlett and Ip, 'Is Socialist Law Really Dead?', 463, 485.

[19] Independent and binding judicial review of legality is at the core of all definitions of rule of law. Lord Bingham, for instance, explains that the 'core' of the principle of rule of law is that all persons and authorities shall be bound by 'laws that are publicly and prospectively promulgated and publicly administered in the courts'. Lord Bingham, 'The Rule of Law' (2007) 66(1) Cambridge Law Journal 67, 69. Joseph Raz also includes in his thinner version of rule of law the importance of guaranteeing the 'independence of the judiciary'. Joseph Raz, The Authority of Law: Essay on Law and Morality, (Oxford: Oxford University Press, 2009), p. 216.

systems. In comparison with common law and socialist law, however, socialist law was viewed as a 'young' legal tradition with very little basis in Russian history.[20] Rene David, for instance, commented on the 'weakness of the legal tradition and the idea of law in Russia'.[21] Stripped of any national roots, the history of socialist law was assumed to be the Western European civil law tradition.[22] This perception has weakened our understanding of the unique debates and approaches to law in countries that were or still identify as socialist, and the role of ideology in shaping these distinctive approaches to law.

3.2.1   An Ahistorical Approach to Socialist Law

This ahistorical approach to socialist law in the West was driven by two main motivations. First, during the Cold War, many scholars were driven by a 'know-thy-enemy' motivation to understand the legal systems in the socialist bloc.[23] Underpinned by government funding, this justification became particularly strong during the détente years in the 1970s.[24] Ironically, this approach drew in part on the work of socialist legal scholars based in the Soviet Union. These scholars – constrained by ideology – argued that socialist law had no historical roots in imperial Russia and was instead a simple product of political ideology, and therefore 'administered in the interest of the defense and education of the proletariat as the only class which can give the Union, and the world, a classless society'.[25] To accord with the dominant ideology of the time, socialist law was portrayed as a new legal system that completely broke with the Tsarist past.

---

[20] John Merryman and David S. Clark, *Comparative Law: Western European and Latin American Legal Systems: Cases and Materials* (Charlottesville, VA: The Michie Company, 1978), p. 4.

[21] Rene David and John C. Brierley, *Major Legal Systems in the World: An Introduction to the Comparative Study of Law* (London: Stevens and Sons, 1968), p. 11.

[22] John Quigley, 'Socialist Law and the Civil Law Tradition' (1989) 37 *American Journal of Comparative Law* 781–783.

[23] Leonard Shapiro, 'The Importance of Law in the Study of Politics and History', in Leonard Shapiro, Ellen Dahrendorf and Harry Willetts (eds.), *Russian Studies* (New York: Penguin Books, 1988) (discussing law as simply a mechanism of repression).

[24] William Partlett, 'Reclassifying Russian Law: Mechanisms, Outcomes and Solutions for an Overly Politicised Field' (2008) 2 *Columbia Journal of East European Law* 1, 37–42.

[25] John Hazard, 'Soviet Law: An Introduction' (1936) 36 *Columbia Law Review* 1236, 1249.

Much of the English-language research drew on this approach, focusing on the role of ideology in the construction of socialist law.[26] John Hazard – who trained under these socialist theorists in the early 1930s, while on exchange in Soviet Russia – expressed an ideological understanding of the socialist legal system when he commented that the 'first mark of distinction' of the socialist legal system was 'an economic factor ... evidenced by the degree of involvement of all elements of society and of its institutions in the operation of a fully state-owned and planned economy'.[27] If scholars saw a historical basis for Russian law, they pointed to its basis in the Western European civil law tradition. John Merryman thus commented that socialist law imposed 'certain principles of socialist ideology on existing civil law systems and on the civil law tradition'.[28]

In the late 1980s, scholars began to argue that socialist ideology had done little to distinguish the socialist legal systems from these Western European, civil law roots. For instance, John Quigley argued that socialist legal systems were firmly part of the civil law tradition.[29] As the distinctiveness of socialist law was criticised, the study of socialist law ended with the collapse of the Soviet Union. Funding and research on the law in many post-socialist countries began to disappear. Socialist law was thought to have disappeared from comparative law casebooks and was declared 'dead and buried'.[30] Freed of Marxist ideology, researchers now argued that these socialist law countries were transitioning back to their historical roots in Western European civil law systems.[31] For instance, a recent book on the Russian legal system states that 'Russian law is gradually returning to the civil law family from which it came'.[32]

---

[26] Marxist theory held that the means of production (what theorists know as 'the base') ultimately determined the nature of the law and legal institutions (known as 'the superstructure'). Thus, to build communism required creating an economic system with public ownership over the means of production.

[27] John Hazard, *Communists and Their Law: A Search for the Common Core of the Legal Systems of the Marxian Socialist States* (Chicago, IL: University of Chicago Press, 1969), p. 523.

[28] Merryman, *Comparative Law*, p. 4.

[29] Quigley, 'Socialist Law and the Civil Law Tradition', 781.

[30] Hein Kötz, 'Preface to the Third Edition', in Konrad Zweigert and Hein Kötz (eds.), *Introduction to Comparative Law* (Oxford: Clarendon Press, 1998).

[31] Ugo Mattei, 'Codifying Property Law in the Process of Transition: Some Suggestions from Comparative Law and Economics' (1995) 19 *Hastings International and Comparative Law Quarterly* 117, 122.

[32] Peter Maggs, Olga Schwartz and William Burnham (eds.), *Law and Legal System of the Russian Federation* (New York, NY: Juris Publishing, 2015), p. 7.

Second, socialist law has been of interest to Western legal theorists seeking to explore socialist alternatives to present-day legal approaches.[33] These researchers saw opportunities to 'learn-from-thy-enemy'.[34] Although diminished today, scholars have continued to explore the possibilities and dimensions of socialist law as part of critical projects.[35] If these scholars take any interest in history at all, it is simply to suggest how the Soviet Union ultimately abandoned the correct socialist approach to law.[36] Thus, most of the work focuses heavily on thinkers like Evgeny Pashukanis, who were closer to Western concepts of socialism, but (as we will see) ultimately had very little influence on the historical *practices* of socialist law.

3.2.2   Historicising Socialist Law

There were a few exceptions to this ahistorical approach to socialist law. Writing in 1950, Harold Berman identified the deeper historical roots of the socialist legal system in the USSR.[37] Describing how law is 'built up slowly over centuries' and is therefore 'impervious to social upheavals',[38] Berman explained that 'the Soviets again and again were forced to yield to history'.[39] In particular, Berman pointed to the persistence of critical Russian institutions in the socialist legal system, including the procuracy. Other scholars made similar claims. For instance, Gordon Smith's work has also traced the continuities between socialist law and the Russian legal tradition.[40]

This Chapter will expand on this work by exploring the interaction between socialist ideology and historically rooted forms of law. Underpinning this approach is the idea that law is more than just a product of

---

[33] See, e.g., Michael Head, *Evgeny Pashukanis: A Critical Reappraisal* (Abingdon: Routledge-Cavendish, 2007).

[34] See, e.g., Michael Mandel, 'Marxism and the Rule of Law' (1986) 35 *UNB Law Journal* 7–34. Alice Erh-Soon Tay and Eugene Kamenka, 'Marxism, Socialism and the Theory of Law' (1985) 23 *Columbia Journal of Transnational Law* 217–249; John Quigley, *Soviet Legal Innovation and the Law of the Western World* (Cambridge: Cambridge University Press, 2007).

[35] See, e.g., China Mieville, *Between Equal Rights: A Marxist Approach to International Law* (Leiden: Brill, 2004).

[36] See, e.g., Head, *Evgeny Pashukanis*, n. 34.

[37] Harold Berman, *Justice in the USSR: An Interpretation of Soviet Law* (Cambridge, MA: Harvard University Press, 1978, 5th edn.), 5–7.

[38] Ibid., 5.

[39] Ibid., 269.

[40] Gordon Smith, 'The Impact of Socialism on Soviet Legal Institutions and Procedures' (1984–1985) 23 *Columbia Journal of Transnational Law* 315, 324 ('Soviet legal institutions bear a marked resemblance to those of the tsarist regime they replaced.').

shifting ideological commitments.[41] Law necessarily contains a set of historically rooted normative debates and practices.[42] These historically rooted practices are not static or, therefore, ultimately self-replicating; on the contrary, historical practices of law are inconsistent, dynamic and 'speak[] with many voices'.[43] The history of law matters because it presents the individuals within a tradition the 'substance, models, exemplars and a language in which to speak within and about law'.[44] These practices and models are in turn only relevant to present law when they present 'solutions to present problems'.[45] Ideology then helps to explain what aspects of the tradition are emphasised. In this case, the founders of the socialist legal system operated within the imperial Russian legal tradition. The ultimately triumphant statist interpretation of socialism led them to revive a weakening, but still existing, tradition of supervision.

3.3   Supervision in Imperial Russia

Supervision has been at the centre of the imperial Russian legal system since the early eighteenth century. In general, this tradition involved a set of non-judicial and centrally coordinated practices and institutions that checked and rechecked both administrative and judicial decisions for 'conformity to the law and the commands of their superiors'.[46] This approach rejected Western normative arguments about the necessity of independent judicial supervision over the execution of the law,[47] and instead represented the top-down political control of legality.[48] In the late

---

[41] Eugene Huskey, 'A Framework for the Analysis of Soviet Law' (1991) 50(1) *Russian Review* 53, 54.

[42] H. Patrick Glenn, *Legal Traditions of the World* (Oxford: Oxford University Press, 2014) (discussing the importance of the concept of traditions in understanding legal development).

[43] Krygier, 'Law as Tradition', 242.

[44] Ibid., 244.

[45] Ibid., 248.

[46] Christian, 'The Supervisory Function in Russian and Soviet History', 73.

[47] Jack Rakove, 'The Original Justifications for Judicial Independence' (2006) 95 *Georgetown Law Journal* 1061 (tracing the idea of control over legality to an independent judicial branch to Montesquieu); Henry Monaghan, '"Marbury" and the Administrative State' (1983) 83 *Columbia Law Review* 1 (discussing the roots of judicial review of administrative action in the United States); Felix Frankfurter, 'Task of Administrative Law' (1927) 75 *University of Pennsylvania Law Review* 613, 615 (describing the task of administrative law to be one studying 'the field of control exercised by courts over such agencies'.).

[48] Christian, 'The Supervisory Function in Russian and Soviet History', 81 (describing how a 'division of powers never made sense' in Imperial Russia). Charles O. Hucker, 'Governmental Organisation of the Ming Dynasty' (1958) 21 *Harvard Journal of Asiatic Studies* 1, 55 (no 'special autonomous status to the judiciary' in the Chinese system).

Tsarist period, this tradition was weakening as imperial Russia moved towards the Western European civil law approach of independent, judicial determinations of legality.

The normative basis for the supervisory tradition has largely eluded characterisation because of its rejection of 'European political theory'[49] such as the separation of powers. Supervisory legality, however, did have deep roots of justification. First, it was seen as a way of responding to the ineffectiveness and weakness of the Russian state. After travelling through Europe, Peter the Great proclaimed the need for a centralised bureaucratic apparatus to ensure the 'co-ordination, unity and supervision of the subordinate organs' to compete with Europe.[50] Supervision – with its ability to relay political orders from the centre – was viewed as a way to ensure that the state could collect taxes and raise a military.[51] Furthermore, as the bureaucracy grew in size, supervision emerged as a way of coping with the growing amount of contradictory and self-interested administrative and sub-legal acts that were issued with little reference to law.[52] Second, it was seen as a method for allowing citizens a less onerous and procedural method for challenging illegal decisions, and a way for the state to monitor these complaints.[53] Petitioning had a long history in Russian imperial governance that predated Petrine Russia.[54] As time went on, this tradition provided individual petitioners with the ability to challenge the growing number of contradictory sub-legal normative acts in imperial Russia.[55] These two justifications have remained at the centre of justifications of supervisory legality to this day.[56]

---

[49] Christian, 'The Supervisory Function in Russian and Soviet History', 73.

[50] Dominic Lieven (ed.), *The Cambridge History of Russia*, Volume 2: Imperial Russia, 1689–1917 (Cambridge: Cambridge University Press, 2006), p. 435.

[51] Zhand Shakibi, 'Central Government', in D. Lieven (ed.), *The Cambridge History of Russia*, Volume 2: Imperial Russia, 1689–1917 (Cambridge: Cambridge University Press, 2006), p. 430.

[52] Karl V. Ryavec, *Russian Bureaucracy: Power and Pathology* (Lanham: Rowman & Littlefield, 2005), pp. 64–65 (discussion of the 'essentially unfettered' local administrative agencies).

[53] Wirtschafter, 'Legal Identity and the Possession of Serfs in Imperial Russia', 561 (discussing the role of the Senate and the procuracy in responding to petitions from individual serfs in eighteenth and nineteenth century imperial Russia).

[54] Valery Kivelson, *Autocracy in the Provinces: The Muscovite Gentry and the Political Culture in the Seventeeth Century* (Stanford, CA: Stanford University Press, 1996).

[55] Ryavec, *Russian Bureaucracy*, 95 (estimating that in the late Soviet period there were ten thousand sublegal acts in force).

[56] Sergei Kazantsev, 'The Judicial Reform of 1864 and the Procuracy', in Peter H. Solomon (ed.), *Reforming Justice in Russia, 1864–1996: Power, Culture, and the Limits of Legal Order* (Armonk, NY: M.E. Sharpe, 1997), p. 47 (describing how the procuracy began to develop a number of administrative and quasi-ministerial functions which ultimately

Peter the Great placed two institutions at the centre of this tradition of supervisory legality.[57] The first institution in this supervisory tradition was the Senate. Created in 1711, this institution was charged with 'administering the empire', and rapidly developed into a body that formulated law and exercised 'coordination and supervision' over the implementation the empire's laws.[58] It therefore helped to pass laws while overseeing a vast array of undermanned and poorly staffed courts.[59] The second key institution was the procuracy.[60] This centrally accountable institution developed into a hierarchical organisation at the centre of the imperial legal system.[61] It exercised wide power, not only to initiate criminal prosecutions but also to carry out 'general supervision' over judicial and administrative decision-making.[62] These powers of 'general supervision' included quasi-ministerial and adjudicatory functions.[63] Two are most important. First, the procuracy could demand a formal review of acts or decisions by an agency or a court through a 'protest', a document containing a detailed legal analysis that looked very similar to the reasoning in a court opinion.[64] Second, the procurator could provide a 'proposal' (*predstavlenie*), which contained more positive demands about 'what must be done'.[65] Although these actions were not technically binding, they were almost always complied with because of the centralised bureaucratic power exerted by the procuracy.[66]

Alexander II's great reforms of 1864 weakened this supervisory system in order to strengthen judicial control over legality.[67] These reforms stripped the procuracy of its powers of general supervision over

---

meant that the procuracy represented 'such a mosaic of borrowings as to produce an original Russian picture'.).

[57] Shakibi, 'Central Government', p. 435.

[58] Ibid.

[59] Natasha Assa, 'How Arbitrary Was Tsarist Administrative Justice? The Case of the Zemstvos Petitions to the Imperial Ruling Senate, 1866–1916' (2003) 24 *Law and History Review* 1, 40.

[60] Gordon Smith, *The Soviet Procuracy and the Supervision of Administration* (Alphen aan den Rijn: Sijthoff & Noordhoff, 1978), p. 4.

[61] Ibid., p. 14.

[62] Christian, 'The Supervisory Function in Russian and Soviet History', 76.

[63] Kazantsev, 'The Judicial Reform of 1864 and the Procuracy', 47.

[64] Morgan, *Soviet Administrative Legality*, p. 13.

[65] Ibid.

[66] Gordon Smith, *Reforming the Russian Legal System* (Cambridge: Cambridge University Press, 1996), p. 107 (describing how over 95 per cent of procuratorial protests were complied with).

[67] Berman, *Justice in the USSR*, p. 241.

administrative acts.[68] In the final decades of imperial Russia, the Senate grew in power as the upper house of the legislature, as well as a body for reviewing individual cases and issuing guiding explanations on broad points of law (after abstract study of court practice) that could ensure central control over the development of law.[69] This was not a complete reform, however; the procuracy retained its powers to supervise and protest judicial decisions.[70]

3.4 Socialist Law and the Transition to Communism

This tradition of supervision – and its roots in a normative desire to overcome state weakness – would play a critical role in the formulation of a socialist legal system in the early Soviet Union. Soviet reformers broadly agreed that a transitional period was needed to achieve communism. Two competing visions for law emerged during this transitional period. One school of thought – which I call the utopians – saw this transition happening without many of the pre-existing forms of law from the imperial period. Unleashed by the sense of possibility in the wake of the collapse of the Tsarist state, this approach envisioned this transitional period as beginning a move towards an entirely new approach to law.

The other school of thought – which I call the statists – saw the need for a strong state in the 'transition' from capitalism to socialism. They therefore vigorously argued for a return to a strongly supervisory approach to legality. I do not want to overstate the nature of this split – throughout the early Soviet period, many individuals found themselves making statements that drew on ideas from both sides. Despite these shortcomings, however, this dichotomy is a useful way of understanding a critical early debate about the nature of 'socialist law'.

3.4.1 *Utopianism and Anti-Formalism*

The utopians grounded their approach to socialist law on the view that imperial Russian legal practices and institutions should play little role in the transition to communism. In this way, the utopians drew on a

---

[68] Jorg Baberowsky, 'Law, the Judicial System and the Legal Profession', in D. Lieven (ed.), *The Cambridge History of Russia*, Volume 2: Imperial Russia, 1689–1917 (Cambridge: Cambridge University Press, 2006), p. 346.

[69] Alexander Vereshchagin, *Judicial Law-Making in Post-Soviet Russia* (Abingdon: Routledge-Cavendish, 2007), p. 97.

[70] Morgan, *Soviet Administrative Legality*, p. 17.

decentralised and more experimental conception of socialism that was closer to Western socialism. This fact is at least partly reflected in the greater Western interest in the work of Russian legal thinkers such as Evgeny Pashukanis.

In his seminal book, *The General Theory of Law and Marxism*, Evgeny Pashukanis explained that law was ultimately grounded in capitalist commodity exchange.[71] In his conception, law ultimately draws on the market bond between individual enterprises (either capitalist or petty commodity production) and groups of enterprises (either capitalist or socialist). In so doing, law becomes a tool of class dominance. Pashukanis therefore criticised conceptions such as the rule of law as a 'mask' that obscures the repressive aspects of bourgeois law.[72] As soon as the bourgeoisie is threatened as a class, this mask slips and it reveals the 'essence' of the law as the 'organised force of one class against another'.[73]

Pashukanis then described how socialist economic relations would spawn a fundamentally new approach to law, in which key legal concepts like crime and punishment would wither away.[74] This approach towards law was underpinned by the idea that a new system of regulation would emerge spontaneously in the Soviet Union, in response to the replacement of market relations by a socialised economy.[75] The 'narrow horizons' of Tsarist legal forms were a conceptual, and therefore a practical, absurdity in this kind of socialist economic system.[76] Pashukanis argued that, in the place of bourgeois forms will rise 'a technical-expediency relationship with one another', which will destroy any bourgeois conception of 'legal personality'.[77] In particular, this would include regulation through the administrative-technical rules of the plan.[78] This type of regulation would cease to look like law; instead, administrative-technical modes of governance would emerge in its place.[79]

---

[71] Head, *Evgeny Pashukanis*, p. 191.

[72] Evgeny B. Pashukanis, 'The General Theory of Law and Marxism' in William Butler (ed.), *Russian Legal Theory* (New York, NY: New York University Press, 1996), p. 290.

[73] Ibid.

[74] Ibid., p. 277.

[75] Ibid., pp. 277–278.

[76] Quoted from Berman, *Justice in the USSR*, p. 314.

[77] Pashukanis, 'The General Theory of Law and Marxism', p. 279.

[78] Piers Beirne and Robert Sharlet, 'Toward a General Theory of Law and Marxism: E. B. Pashukanis', in Piers Beirne (ed.), *Revolution in Law: Contributions to the Development of Soviet Legal Theory, 1917–1938* (Armonk, NY: M.E. Sharpe, 1990), p. 25.

[79] Pashukanis wrote that '[t]he withering away of certain categories of bourgeois law in no way implies their replacement by new categories of proletarian law.' Rett R. Ludwikowski,

3.4.1.1   Anti-Formalism

In part because it constituted a rejection of the imperial Russian legal tradition, the precise form of this regulatory form of law was never fully developed in practice. Suggesting that even the utopians could not be completely free of the grip of past Tsarist practices and approaches, the most concrete example that existed of this new form of law could be found in the proposals for a new criminal code. Underlying these pro-posals was a strong belief that criminal law should adopt flexible, anti-formalist approaches that would allow 'a politically inspired judiciary the tools to control and, when necessary, reverse the formality of the statute'.[80]

This anti-formalist approach emerged clearly in drafts of a new criminal code. As committed Marxists, the utopians understood crime to be something that was ultimately conditioned by the environment. More flexibility would allow judges to take environmental factors into account. For instance, Pashukanis had argued that a socialist approach to criminal law should not involve a judge in determining guilt or innocence, but instead in considering 'how to change the conditions of life of a given person – in order to influence him in the sense of correction'.[81]

Those views were part of the work by Nikolai Krylenko on a new criminal code. Krylenko was in many ways a classic utopian – he had no legal training at all; after studying for a history and philology degree, he had spent most of his life as a professional revolutionary and then a political operative.[82] In the new criminal code, Krylenko proposed to completely eliminate the 'specific' part of the prior criminal code that catalogued crimes, and instead include the 'general' part. This would leave the general part of the criminal code as the main section, and would allow judges considerable flexibility to apply the 'penalty' deemed neces-sary to deter future violence and therefore assure the protection of

---

'Socialist Legal Theory in the Post-Pashukanis Era' (1987) 10 *Boston College International and Comparative Law Review* 323, 326.

[80] Gianmaria Ajani, 'Formalism and Anti-Formalism Under Socialist Law: The Case of General Clauses within the Codification of Civil Law' (2002) 2(2) *Global Jurist Advances*.

[81] Quoted from Head, *Evgeny Pashukanis*, p. 185.

[82] Donald Barry, 'Nikolai Vasil'evich Krylenko: A Reevaluation', in Piers Beirne (ed.), *Revolution in Law: Contributions to the Development of Soviet Legal Theory, 1917–1938* (Armonk, NY: M.E. Sharpe, 1990), p. 157. His undergraduate degree was in philology, p. 159.

society.[83] Underlying this idea was the deeper conception that crime was often a product of individual circumstances, and that fixed penalties for certain crimes were inherently unfair.[84]

3.4.2 Statism and Centralised Supervision

In contrast to the anti-formalism of the utopians, statists grounded their view of the socialist legal system on the needs of centralising the Soviet state.[85] This viewpoint was grounded on a statist interpretation of social-ist ideology in Lenin's *The State and Revolution*, which argued that a centralised version of the bourgeois imperial Russian state was an important tool for the proletariat in vanquishing the 'capitalists' in the transitional period of socialism.[86] In particular, Lenin argued that the transitional period to communism requires 'not only bourgeois law, but even the bourgeois state, without the bourgeoisie!'[87] Stalin also drew on this statist conception of socialism in later proclaiming the 'Marxist formula' to be the 'highest possible development of the power of the state'.[88] This justification reflected a much broader – and Petrine – normative justification for law: a need for a strong state to compete with Europe.

The leading figure in this statist approach was Andrei Vyshinsky. As head of the procuracy himself, he criticised the utopians' anti-formalist approach to law. Vyshinsky explained that legal discipline was necessary to allow the state to play a role in strengthening the state for the top-down Party construction of socialism.[89] This approach, he argued, rejected bourgeois conceptions of judicial independence. Instead, a dic-tatorship of the proletariat was the only way to truly guarantee 'civil rights' to the proletariat.[90]

---

[83] Hazard, Reforming Soviet Criminal Law (1939) 29 *American Institute of Criminal Law and Criminology* 157, 164–165.

[84] Eugene Huskey, 'Vyshinsky, Krylenko, and Soviet Penal Politics in the 1930s', in Piers Beirne (ed.), *Revolution in Law: Contributions to the Development of Soviet Legal Theory, 1917–1938* (Armonk, NY: M.E. Sharpe, 1990), p. 181.

[85] For a comprehensive critique of the statist approach to law, see Ludwikowski, 'Socialist Legal Theory in the Post-Pashukanis Era', p. 323.

[86] Vladimir I. Lenin, *The State and Revolution*, (trans. Robert Service), (London: Penguin Books Limited, 1992), p. 87.

[87] Ibid., p. 89.

[88] Quoted from Hazard, 'Soviet Law', 1266.

[89] *Socialist Legality*, 1934, at http://istmat.info/files/uploads/26308/no_1.pdf.

[90] Vyshinsky, *Law and the Soviet State*, p. 538.

3.4.2.1 Supervision

In order to craft the state into a powerful tool of socialist 'transition', the statists drew on pre-1864 aspects of the imperial Russian tradition of supervision.[91] These long moribund, but highly centralising, elements were seen as carrying out the 'socialist' need for intensified state unity, coordination and centralisation. This unified and powerful state, they argued, would in turn achieve a key requirement of socialist ideology: to carry out the central directives of the Party and ensure the transition to communism. Supervisory institutions therefore once again found themselves at the centre of a new push for state modernisation – but this time in the language of socialism, rather than imperial advancement.

To achieve this goal, the statists drew on the same two key institutions that Peter the Great had established in the eighteenth century to build the Russian state. The statists first repackaged the procuracy in the language of socialism, describing it as the critical institution in ensuring 'socialist legality'.[92] In 1934, under the tutelage of the Procuracy, the statists started a monthly journal called 'Socialist Legality', which would serve as a key platform for justifying the procuracy.[93] In this journal and elsewhere, they argued that the procuracy should be given the powers of 'general supervision' that it had lost during the reforms of 1864. Furthermore, the statists argued that a powerful supreme court should also be placed at the top of the Soviet Union's system of courts. They argued that the broad powers of legal supervision and control lodged in the Tsarist Senate should instead be placed in the Soviet Supreme Court.

3.5 Historical Development: 1917–1936

These competing approaches to socialist legal construction waxed and waned in the first two decades of Soviet power. Both sides sought to justify their approaches in both the needs of the day, as well as the language of Marxism–Leninism. In the end, the statist approach triumphed, as it was ultimately better suited to the practical needs of the Soviet state to strengthen top-down legality. As a result, the key supervisory institutions

---

[91] Ekaterina Trendafilova-Batcharova, 'The New Legal Status of the Bulgarian Prosecutor's Office' (1997) 4(1) *Annual Survey of International and Comparative Law* 132, 139–142.

[92] Eugene Huskey, 'Vyshinskii, Krylenko, and the Shaping of the Soviet Legal Order' (1987) 46 *Slavic Review* 414.

[93] Ibid., 418. (The journal was originally named 'For Socialist Legality' (Za Sotsialisticheskuiu Zakonnost') and renamed 'Socialist Legality' (Sotsialisticheskaya Zakonnost').

of the Tsarist period – the procuracy and a highly centralised court system – became key institutions in the socialist legal model.

3.5.1 Early Period: War Communism and the Civil War (1917–1921)

The early Bolshevik approach to law was highly anti-formalist and utopian.[94] Captured by the possibility of revolution, many Bolshevik leaders openly discussed ways of completely refashioning the entire legal system by 'smash[ing] the old bureaucratic apparatus', and, therefore, the Tsarist legal system.[95] For instance, Anatolii Lunacharsky, the Commissar of Education, described how the revolution would create a new form of law involving a 'popular mass trial over the hated system of privilege'.[96] Lunacharsky went on to describe how, in a socialist legal system, law would be based on what he termed 'intuitive law', which would be grounded on 'direct, revolutionary legal creativity'.[97]

These utopian visions of socialism were paired with key practical challenges of eliminating the Tsarist legal elite. The first piece of legislation pushed through by the Bolsheviks abolished the centralised hierarchy of tsarist courts under the Senate and replaced them with a far more decentralised system of local people's courts and revolutionary tribunals.[98] New judges, who often had no legal training, were encouraged to proceed by their 'revolutionary consciousness' in applying the law.[99] Next, in 1918, another key law abolished the procuracy.[100]

Both pragmatism and principle lay behind these legislative moves. First, these moves reflected the experimentalism and anti-formalism unleashed by the revolution. Many justified the flexibility of the more decentralised and organic approaches as allowing people to resolve disputes without the 'elaborately organised tribunals' and 'a labyrinth of rules of procedure and evidence' that existed in bourgeois legal systems.[101] For instance, in criminal law, judges could now take into

---

[94] Beirne and Sharlet, 'Toward a General Theory of Law and Marxism', p. 24.
[95] Quoted from Ginsburgs, 'The Soviet Procuracy and Forty Years of Socialist Legality', 35.
[96] Quoted from Head, Evgeny Pashukanis, at p. 115.
[97] Ibid., p. 117.
[98] Ibid., p. 97.
[99] Ibid., p. 93.
[100] Pamela A. Jordan, Defending Rights in Russia: Lawyers, the State, and Legal Reform in the Post-Soviet Era (Vancouver: University of British Columbia Press, 2006), p. 33.
[101] John Hazard, Settling Disputes in Soviet Society: The Formative Years of Legal Institutions (New York, NY: Columbia University Press, 1960), p. vi.

consideration the circumstances of the crime, as well as the personal insecurity and class antagonisms of capitalism in determining a penalty. Second, there was a more pragmatic need to eliminate the old Tsarist elite that existed within many of these institutions. As Lenin said:

> Comrade workers! Remember that you yourselves now administer the state. No one will help you if you yourselves do not unite and fail to take all the affairs of the state into your own hands. Your soviets are henceforth the organs of state power, plenipotentiary organs of decision-making.[102]

3.5.2 New Economic Policy Period (1921–1928)

With the end of the civil war, the leaders of the Soviet state realised the need to re-establish stability and order. World War I and the Civil War had immense economic, social and human costs. Amidst the chaos of war-torn Soviet Union, contradictory laws and administrative orders had proliferated. In order to rebuild the state, the Bolsheviks now turned to Tsarist-era legal institutions and concepts to create the New Economic Policy (NEP) period. Although justified in the language of Marxism, these institutions had key practical goals.

The Bolsheviks first moved to re-establish the procuracy after its short period of dissolution. Lenin himself intervened decisively in this debate. In a now famous letter, he criticised the anti-formalist, utopian approach as 'pandering to the ancient Russian view and semi-savage habit of mind, which wishes to preserve Kaluga law as distinct from Kazan law'.[103] The procuracy, he argued, was critical in overcoming the 'ocean of illegality and local influence' in the Soviet Union and securing state unity and coordination.[104] This supervisory institution – organised in a system of vertical accountability – could solve these problems and ensure compliance with law.[105]

Second, a clear judicial hierarchy was reintroduced during the NEP period in the 1922 Judiciary Act.[106] This 'uniform' organisation of judicial power was justified on similar grounds as necessary for 'safeguarding the state' and 'the rights of toilers'.[107] This law gave the provincial court

---

[102] Zile, *Ideas and Forces in Soviet Legal Theory*, p. 12.
[103] Vladimir I. Lenin, *Dual Subordination and Legality*, at www.marxists.org/archive/lenin/works/1920/may/20.htm.
[104] Ibid.
[105] Ibid.
[106] W. J. Wagner, 'The Russian Judiciary Act of 1922 and Some Comments on the Administration of Justice in the Soviet Union' (1966) 41 *Indiana Law Journal* 420–453.
[107] Ibid., 442.

supervisory power over 'all courts in the territory of the province or oblast'.[108] Another 1922 statute on the procuracy returned powers of 'general supervision' to the newly reinstituted Procuracy.[109]

Despite the return of these statist institutions, NEP also witnessed utopian thinking. In fact, the NEP period saw the publication of a key book of the utopian movement. In 1924, Evgeny Pashukanis produced his famous treatise *The General Theory of Law and Marxism*. This book argued that law was a 'bourgeois category' that regulated relationships between isolated individuals.[110] Bourgeois law would not be replaced by 'new categories of proletarian law'.[111] Instead, bourgeois conceptions of law would fade away as economic concepts of value and capital disappeared.

3.5.3 The Great Break (1929–1932)

In 1928, a more revolutionary and anti-formalist conception of socialism arose once more. Key elements of the utopian approach again became highly influential. Consequently, decentralised and discretionary forms of administration were considered as replacements for formal law and the restored Tsarist institutions of the late Tsarist period.[112] The legal codes restored in the 1920s were attacked and some called for 'the thicket of bourgeois laws [to] be cleared out'.[113]

Pashukanis grew in influence, arguing that criminal law was a product of commodity exchange. Under this theory, as commodity exchange disappeared so should criminal law. In 1930, he worked to introduce the changes that would bring the 'decay' of criminal law as the natural progression of a society that was achieving socialism.[114] During this time, Pashukanis' influence was very high. John Hazard – who studied under Pashukanis at the time – described his influence as 'so marked' that 'the course in civil law in the law school [was] abolished, and to replace them (sic) there appeared a course called economic-administrative law,

---

[108] Ibid.
[109] Ibid., 432.
[110] Quoted from Ludwikowski, 'Socialist Legal Theory in the Post-Pashukanis Era', 327.
[111] Ibid., 326.
[112] Huskey, 'Vyshinskii, Krylenko, and the Shaping of the Soviet Legal Order', 174.
[113] Beirne and Sharlet, 'Toward a General Theory of Law and Marxism', 33.
[114] John Hazard, 'Reforming Soviet Criminal Law' (1938) 29 *Journal of Criminal Law and Criminology* 157, 160.

concerning itself with regulation of the relations between state enterprises'.[115]

Furthermore, adversarial elements in criminal law largely disappeared during this period. Defence attorneys appeared in only a small minority of trials, and even then judges had the right to dispense with 'debate between the sides'.[116] Work begun on a new criminal code under the tutelage of Krylenko.

3.5.4 High Stalinism (1933–1940)

With the end of the collectivisation drive and the introduction of Stalin's concept of 'Socialism in One Country', these utopian elements receded. As before, statists argued that the anti-formalist and decentralising aspects of the utopian approach were poorly suited to contemporary needs. In particular, these approaches threatened to undermine the ability of the state to function as a centralised tool for socialist transition. Supporters of 'socialism in one country' wanted the Soviet Union to catch up with the West. This rapid development required an efficient system of legal supervision over compliance with central Party policy.

In a presentation at the Communist Academy, Vyshinsky viewed increased formalisation as critical to solving these problems. He declared that 'the Party now demands of us the strengthening of the legal form, the court and the procedural norm'.[117] Vyshinsky argued that '[h]istory demonstrates that under socialism ... law is raised to the highest level of development'.[118] Others criticised the utopian Krylenko for attempting to 'undermine' the authority of Soviet law and courts that are necessary in strengthening socialist legality.[119] Statists pointed to the poor education level of many members of the legal community. For instance, in 1935, 85 per cent of people's court judges had no more than a primary school education.[120]

---

[115] Quoted from Bill Bowring, *Law, Rights and Ideology in Russia: Landmarks in the Destiny of a Great Power* (Abingdon: Routledge, 2013), p. 54.

[116] Huskey, 'Vyshinsky, Krylenko, and Soviet Penal Politics in the 1930s', 180.

[117] Quoted from Robert Sharlet and Piers Beirne, 'In Search of Vyshinsky: The Paradox of Law and Terror', in Piers Beirne (ed.), *Revolution in Law*, p. 151.

[118] Quoted from Head, *Evgeny Pashukanis*, p. 108.

[119] Hazard, 'Reforming Soviet Criminal Law', 157.

[120] Huskey, 'Vyshinsky, Krylenko, and Soviet Penal Politics in the 1930s', 184.

Vyshinsky therefore emphasised the importance of strengthening the Tsarist-era institutions that had been restored during the NEP period.[121] In particular, Vyshinsky saw Tsarist-era supervision as a powerful way of ensuring the more rigid adherence of administrative acts to socialist legality.[122] Drawing on the arguments advanced by Lenin when he reintroduced the procuracy in 1922, he argued that an increased role for the procuracy in general supervision would help in the fight against localism and protect socialist property.[123] A 1933 law on the 'position' of the procuracy described its non-prosecutorial roles as those of general supervision over administrative acts and judicial practice, as well as safeguarding socialist property.[124] A 1934 Handbook tasked the local procurator with 'struggl[ing] against all defects and distortions in the policy adopted toward criminal justice adopted by the people's courts'.[125] Furthermore, the Supreme Court recognised in a resolution that its work should be directed towards fulfilling 'the directive institutions of the party and the government in the province of revolutionary legality'.[126]

Vyshinsky's vision soon became the official line as Stalin criticised the 'leftist prattle' of those advocating a less formalist approach to legality.[127] Stalin described how, during a period of capitalist encirclement, 'the land of the victorious revolution should not weaken, but in every way strengthen its state'.[128] In this situation, Stalin argued, 'we need stability of laws now more than ever'.[129] The idea of 'socialist legality' enforced clearly by supervisory institutions like the procuracy and the Supreme Court would better allow the state to serve its role – in the words of Stalin – as the 'transmission belt' for the decisions of the Party (the 'motor').[130]

---

[121] Ibid., p. 175.

[122] Quoted from Morgan, *Soviet Administrative Legality*, p. 29.

[123] Huskey, 'Vyshinsky, Krylenko, and Soviet Penal Politics in the 1930s', p. 186.

[124] Polozhenie o prokurature Soyuza SSR, Zakon, www.law.vl.ru/history/showhist.php?his_range=0&his_id=13.

[125] Eugene Huskey, *Executive Power and Soviet Politics: The Rise and Decline of the Soviet State* (Armonk, NY: M.E. Sharpe, 1992), note 5, p. 239.

[126] Vladimir Gsovski, *The Soviet Concept of Law and State* (Georgetown: Georgetown University, 1935), note 66, p. 18.

[127] Sharlet and Beirne, 'In Search of Vyshinsky', in Piers Beirne (ed.), *Revolution in Law*, p. 151.

[128] Quoted from Christine Sypnowich, *The Concept of Socialist Law*, (Oxford: Clarendon Press, 1990), p. 20.

[129] Quoted from Head, *Evgeny Pashukanis*, p. 108.

[130] Boim, 'Party-State Control in the Soviet Union', p. 14.

3.6   A Socialist Version of Supervision?

The success of the statists under Vyshinsky led to the insertion of close
prototypes of the Petrine supervisory institutions in Chapter IX of the
1936 Constitution.[131] This placement itself carried significant symbolic
power. The 1936 Constitution proclaimed the end of a period of experimentation with different approaches to socialism. Stalin described this
Constitution as representing the attainment of socialism through the
'struggles' of the working people and a blueprint for a transitional state
that would then attain 'a higher phase of communism'.[132]

Supervision was justified in two official ways. First, it was described as
an effective way for the Party to ensure a unified state apparatus, which
could then enable the 'transition' from capitalism to socialism.[133] Second,
it was described as an efficient method for the state to solve problems
raised by citizens in petitions against the actions and regulations of local
officials. For instance, many Soviet scholars justified the procuracy's
broad powers of supervision as an improvement on the 'weak position'
of the ombudsmen in Western legal systems.[134] A key monthly journal
called *Socialist Legality* began publication in 1934 and stressed the
importance of supervision to ensuring socialist legality.[135]

3.6.1   The Procuracy

The procuracy occupied a prominent role in the 1936 Constitution.
Article 113 entrenched 'supreme supervisory power' over the execution
of laws in this institution. This provision signalled a formal return to the
pre-1864 powers of the procuracy. Reflecting Lenin's arguments about
the need for overcoming local control, the procuracy exercised this power
as part of a strict vertical of power, with all appointments coming from
the Procurator of the USSR.[136] This strict hierarchy was guaranteed by a

---

[131] 1936 Constitution of the USSR, at www.departments.bucknell.edu/russian/const/
36cons03.html#chap09.
[132] Joseph V. Stalin, On the Draft Constitution of the U.S.S.R: Report Delivered at the
Extraordinary Eighth Congress of Soviets of the USSR, 25 November 1936, at
www.marxists.org/reference/archive/stalin/works/1936/11/25.htm.
[133] Vyshinsky, *Law and the Soviet State*, p. 40.
[134] Leon Boim, '"Ombudsmanship" in the Soviet Union' (1974) 22 *American Journal of
Comparative Law* 509, 513.
[135] Huskey, 'Vyshinskii, Krylenko, and the Shaping of the Soviet Legal Order', 414.
[136] Article 113, 1836 Constitution of the Soviet Union.

provision stating that the organs of the procurator 'function independently of any local organs whatsoever'.[137]

The Soviet Procuracy developed into a legal institution that existed at the centre of the legal system. In the criminal law process, for instance, the procuracy had broad powers, not to just prosecute crimes but to oversee and control criminal investigation.[138] It also exercised wide powers to supervise courts, having the authority, for instance, to reopen final cases (through a protest). Finally, and perhaps most importantly, it also possessed wide power to supervise the 'compliance' of administrative law with higher law through the issuance of a 'protest' against a specific administrative law (general supervision) or a proposal.[139] The procuracy also had wide powers to issue 'proposals' (*predstavleniia*) that allowed it be involved in the positive drafting of administrative acts. This practice meant that courts played only a minor role in the consideration of the legality of administrative decrees.[140]

Finally, as designed, the procuracy developed into an institution that carried out the political commands of the central Party apparatus. Soviet Procurators were ranked hierarchically into eleven, military-type classifications.[141] Each was accountable to the procurator at the next highest level.[142] Its effectiveness relied on hierarchy – its non-binding protests and proposals gained compliance because of the ever-present threat of sending a supervisory request to a superior. As a result, although procuratorial protests were not binding, they almost always were accepted by the issuing agency or court.[143] Thus, this supervisory power has largely been seen as a 'watchdog' for the central authorities, and not one that oversees the central authorities themselves.[144] The 1955 law on the

---

[137] Article 117, 1936 Soviet Constitution.

[138] Harold Berman, *Soviet Criminal Law and Procedure: The RSFSR Codes* (Cambridge, MA: Harvard University Press, 1966), pp. 104–105.

[139] There was some debate over where this protest should be made. Some laws suggested it should be protested in a higher agency. Practice, however, suggested that protests were lodged in the agency or department issuing the decree. Morgan, 'The "Protest" of the Soviet Procuracy', 505.

[140] Morgan, 'The "Protest" of the Soviet Procuracy, 500.

[141] Gordon Smith, The Soviet Procuracy and the Supervision of Administration (1978), 14.

[142] Ibid., 15.

[143] Leon Boim and Glenn Morgan, *The Soviet Procuracy Protests: 1937–1973: A Collection of Translations*, Law in Eastern Europe Series, No. 21, (Alphen aan den Rijn: Sijthoff & Noordhoff, 1978).

[144] Quoted from Berman, *Soviet Criminal Law and Procedure*, p. 100.

procuracy suggested precisely this, specifically directing the General Procuror to guard against any 'local differences' or 'influences'.[145]

3.6.2   The Court System

A powerful supreme court was also a critical aspect of the 1936 Soviet socialist legal model. The Constitution granted the Supreme Court power over 'the supervision of the judicial activities of all the judicial organs of the USSR and of the Union Republics'.[146] This system therefore entrenched the highly centralised and bureaucratic nature of the courts. All lower courts were institutionally subordinated to a powerful supreme court with vast power to control the work of lower courts and 'articulate judicial policy'.[147]

The Supreme Court itself possessed a number of 'supervisory' powers that went far beyond the appellate supervisory jurisdiction of high courts in the West. These powers were drawn in part from the practices of supervision over law developed by the imperial Russian Senate. First, when the entire Supreme Court sat together – in what was called a Plenum – it exercised a number of broad supervisory powers over lower courts. This practice included the issuing of 'guiding explanations' for lower courts grounded in an abstract analysis of judicial practice.[148] These directives were obligatory for lower court judges and reflected the Senate's prior role of clarifying the vast array of conflicting Soviet laws and directives and ensuring centralisation. Second, the Supreme Court also retained power to reopen cases that had become final. Individuals could protest a final decision and have it reconsidered by a small panel of Supreme Court judges, called a 'presidium'.[149] The presidium had the power to reopen cases 'that have entered into force' in order to safeguard 'the unity of judicial practice or legality'.[150] Finally, the Chairman of the Supreme Court also possessed wide power over the judges in

---

[145] Ibid., pp. 100–101.

[146] Article 104, 1936 Soviet Constitution.

[147] Peter Solomon, 'The U.S.S.R. Supreme Court: History, Role, and Future Prospects' (1990) 38 *American Journal of Comparative Law* 127.

[148] Ibid., 131. This Senate developed the power to issue instructions to guide court practice. Vereshchagin, *Judicial Law-Making in Post-Soviet*, p. 97.

[149] Kirill Koroteev and Sergei Golubok, 'Judgment of the Russian Constitutional Court on Supervisory Review in Civil Proceedings: Denial of Justice, Denial of Europe' (2007) 7 *Human Rights Law Review* 619–620.

[150] Article 7, Section 1, Law on The Supreme Court. Also Article 391.1, Russian Code of Civil Procedure.

his or her court, ultimately controlling important benefits like salaries and housing.

3.7 The Legacy of Supervision in the Former Soviet Union

With the collapse of communism in Eastern Europe and the former Soviet republics, comparative law scholars described the socialist legal system as 'dead and buried'.[151] Comparative law casebooks simply omitted the category altogether, leaving what one scholar has described as a 'black hole'.[152] Underlying this 'death' was the logic that when market-based capitalism replaced state-centred Marxist economics, the legal systems in the former Soviet Union would automatically begin 'transitioning' back towards the capitalist civil law system. In one of the major casebooks, John Merryman argued that 'socialist law was little more than a superstructure of socialist concepts imposed on a civil law foundation' and 'with the end of the Soviet empire the superstructure is being rapidly dismantled, and nations once considered "lost" to the Western European civil law are returning to it'.[153]

Many reformers shared these aspirations. They hoped to end supervisory legality and replace it with judicial control over legality. In Estonia, Latvia and Lithuania, reformers successfully ended the practice of supervision. This success was itself a product of history – these Baltic countries always saw their inclusion in the Soviet Union as illegitimate, so their post-Soviet reforms reflected a strong desire to move away from Russian and Soviet legacy and to return to their Western European roots.[154] Furthermore, even when these countries were part of the Russian empire, they occupied an autonomous status, and viewed themselves as apart from Russian imperial development and its normative debates.[155]

In the other Soviet republics, however, supervision has continued to exert a powerful influence alongside judicial control of legality in most of the former Soviet republics. Legal actors and politicians have continued

---

[151] Zweigert and Kötz, *Introduction to Comparative Law*.

[152] Zdeněk Kühn, *The Judiciary in Central and Eastern Europe: Mechanical Jurisprudence in Transformation?* (Leiden: Martinus Nijhoff Publishers, 2011), p. 293.

[153] John Merryman, David S. Clark and John O. Haley, *The Civil Law Tradition: Europe, Latin America, and East Asia* (Charlottesville, VA: The Michie Company, 1994).

[154] William Partlett, 'Restoration Constitution-Making' (2015) 9(4) *ICL Journal: Vienna Journal on International Constitutional Law* 514, 516–518.

[155] Thomas Lane, Artis Pabriks, Aldis Purs and David J. Smith, *The Baltic States: Estonia, Latvia and Lithuania* (London: Routledge, 2002), pp. 1–32.

to argue for its importance in solving problems.[156] First, they have argued that supervision is necessary to ensure state unity amidst the centrifugal forces unleashed by a transition to capitalism.[157] Second, supervision is justified as an important method for protecting individuals from bureaucratic lawlessness.[158] Underlying both of these justifications is a belief that supervision is needed to respond to the unique challenges of post-Soviet governance.

3.7.1   Prosecutorial Supervision

In the 1990s, reformers attempted to weaken the procuracy in order to reassert the power of the courts over the control of legality.[159] Yet, despite the reforms, the vast powers of the procuracy have proved remarkably persistent outside of the Baltic countries. At the formal level, constitutional text in many post-Soviet republics remains largely unchanged. For instance, many post-Soviet constitutions continue to place the procuracy in a section entitled 'Judicial Power'. Furthermore, many still explicitly afford the procurator powers of general supervision. Article 125 of the Belarus Constitution, for example, states that the procurator 'shall be entrusted to supervise the strict and unified implementation of the laws'. Furthermore, all five of the Central Asian republics have also preserved the tradition of supervision.

   Even countries that did not grant general supervision to the procuracy in the constitution have afforded these powers through legislation.[160] In Russia, for instance, reformers successfully blocked the constitutionalisation of supervisory power in the procuracy. However, Russian legislation affords the procuracy powers of general supervision through legislation.

---

[156] The monthly journal *Legality* (*Zakonnost'*) – which changed its name from *Socialist Legality* (*Sotsialisticheskaya Zakonnost'*) – has emerged as one of the key publications for these justifications.

[157] See, e.g., A. Alexseev, 'General Supervision: Problems and Perspectives' (1998) 2 *Zakonnost* 8. Iu. Paraskun, 'Net Demokratii bez zakonnosti' ['There is no democracy without legality'] (1993) *Zakonnost*, M. Shalumov, *Prokuratura v pravavoi sisteme gosudarstva* [*The Procuracy in a Law-Based State*] (Moscow, 1993).

[158] Ibid.

[159] Brian Taylor, 'From Police State to Police State? Legacies and Law Enforcement in Russia', in Mark Beissinger and Stephen Kotkin (eds.), *Historical Legacies of Communism in Russia and Eastern Europe* (New York, NY: Cambridge University Press, 2014), p. 136.

[160] William Partlett, 'Post-Soviet Constitution-Making', in David Landau and Hanna Lerner (eds.), *Handbook on Comparative Constitution-Making* (Cheltenham: Elgar, 2017).

In fact, Russian procurators continue to have the power to issue protests and proposals, and are statutorily required to consider and formally respond to requests from citizens.[161] These protests have a similar format and reasoning to judicial decisions.

The justifications for these continuing supervisory powers have shifted from enforcing socialist legality to protecting the interests of the state in fighting terrorism, ensuring territorial integrity and combatting legal nihilism (particularly in administrative regulations).[162] Russia is again illustrative. In the mid 1990s, the procuracy successfully argued that its powers of supervision were critical to managing the 'upheavals' in the country, such as 'skyrocketing crime'.[163] In the early years of President Vladimir Putin's presidency, the procuracy used its supervisory powers to 'scrutinise the legality' of acts of regional and local authorities.[164] The procuracy ended up playing a critical role in that process, issuing thousands of protests against regional laws that brought laws in line with federal legislation.[165]

Despite claims of convergence, supervision remains a point of difference with Western European civil law systems. For instance, the Venice Commission has said that the procuracy 'exercises too many functions which actually and potentially cuts across the sphere of other State institutions' and 'raises serious concerns of compatibility with

---

[161] See in general the law on the procuracy: Articles 23 and 24, Law on the Procuracy, at www.consultant.ru/document/cons_doc_LAW_262/. S. Bratanovskii and A. Uryvaev, *Prokuratura Rossisskoi Federatsii v mekhanisme zashchity konstitutsionnykh prav i svobod cheloveka I grazhdanina* [*The Procuracy of the Russian Federation in a Mechanism of Protection of Constitutional Rights and Freedoms of the Individual and Citizen*] (Moscow, 2012), pp. 99–100.

[162] Article 4, Section 1, Belarus Law on the Procuracy: states the 'goals' of the procuracy are to protect the 'verticality of law, legality, and legal order, as well as the interests of people, organisations, and the state'.) Article 1(2), Law on the Procuracy of the Russian Federation: similarly states the procuracy's purpose is to protect the 'verticality of law, unity, and strengthening of legality' as well as the interests of both citizens and the state. See also Stephen Thaman, 'Reform of the Procuracy and Bar in Russia' (1996) 3(1) *Parker School Journal of East European Law* 1, 15.

[163] Taylor, 'From Police State to Police State? Legacies and Law Enforcement in Russia', 136.

[164] Gordon B. Smith, 'The Procuracy, Putin, and the Rule of Law in Russia', in Ferdinand J. M. Feldbrugge (ed.), *Russia, Europe and the Rule of Law* (Leiden: Martinus Nijhoff, 2007), pp. 9, 11.

[165] Gordon Smith, 'The Procuracy: Constitutional Questions Deferred', in Gordon Smith and Robert Sharlet (eds.), *Russia and Its Constitution: Promise and Political Reality* (Leiden: Martinus Nijhoff Publishers, 2008), p. 113.

democratic principles and the rule of law'.[166] But these powers have proven resilient. In fact, legal actors have justified supervision as important to solving legal problems unique to the region. These justifications are frequently found in the monthly legal publication *Zakonnost'*, which explores different ways in which supervision can be used.[167]

These practices have proven highly resilient in countries seeking to break with the Russian tradition. In Ukraine, for instance, legal reforms have failed to alter key aspects of supervisory power.[168] The procuracy has the power to interpret customary international law and is present during the formulation of guiding explanations of the law by the Plenum of the Supreme Court.[169] The law also affords the procurator the power to issue decrees requiring administrative agencies to alter their activities, procedures or substantive rules and powers of review over legislative acts.[170]

3.7.2   Judicial Supervision

With the fall of communism, a great deal of judicial reform was also carried out in the former Soviet world. For instance, reformers introduced jury trials and adversarial procedure. The supervisory powers lodged in the supreme courts, however, have persisted. Supreme courts across the region exercise broad pseudo-legislative and administrative powers when sitting in a plenary session. These sessions – which include participation and submissions by non-judicial officials, including the general procurator and the minister of justice – carry out a number of duties for overseeing the administration of court practice.[171] Most notably, they provide 'judicial supervision' and 'provide instructions (*raziasnenie*) on the issues of court proceedings',[172] based on the general study of a number of cases and these instructions are binding on all lower

---

[166] European Commission for Democracy Through Law, Opinion on the Federal Law on the Prokuratura (Prosecutor's Office) of the Russian Federation, Opinion No. 340–2005, CDL-AD(2005)014, at http://www.venice.coe.int/webforms/documents/default.aspx?pdffile=CDL-AD(2005)014-e

[167] Zakonnost [Legality] is available online (in Russian) at http://pressa-lex.ru/.

[168] William Partlett, Agendas of Constitutional Decentralisation in Ukraine, Constitution-Net, 23 July 2015, at http://www.constitutionnet.org/news/agendas-constitutional-decentralization-ukraine.

[169] 'Recent Developments' (1993) 34 *Harvard International Law Journal* 563, 616.

[170] Ibid., 618.

[171] Article 5, The Law on the Supreme Court.

[172] Article 126, 1993 Russian Constitution.

courts. Finally, a smaller body of the Supreme Court – the presidium – retains broad power to reopen cases.

The persistence of judicial supervision has also caused significant friction with the European Court of Human Rights (ECHR).[173] This court has held that judicial supervision violates the principle of legal certainty in article 6 of the European Convention for the Protection of Human Rights.[174] After finding the power problematic for Ukraine and Romania, the ECHR turned to Russia.[175] In a 2003 case, the Court stated that 'no party is entitled to seek a review of a final and binding judgment merely for the purpose of obtaining a rehearing and a fresh determination of the case'. The Court went on to argue that the rights of a litigant would be 'illusory' if a final and binding decision could be 'quashed by a higher court on an application made by a state official'.[176]

Laws describing these powers of judicial supervision point to the need for supervision in order to ensure 'legality' and the 'unity of the legal system'.[177] Furthermore, the Russian Constitutional Court has argued that judicial supervision is a critical part of the Russian constitutional system. In a 5 February 2007 judgment, the constitutional court held that supervision was based on the 'objective realities' of Russia.[178] Later, in a public statement, the Chairman of the Constitutional Court explained that the ECHR did not understand the importance of this kind of supervision to the Russian legal system. Judicial supervision, he argued, must remain a critical aspect of the Russian legal system in order to correct 'judicial mistakes'. He cautioned that 'numerous problems' had

---

[173] Koroteev and Golubok, 'Judgment of the Russian Constitutional Court on Supervisory Review in Civil Proceedings', 620–622.

[174] Case 48553/99, *Sovtransavto Holding v. Ukraine*, [2002] ECHR 621; [25 July 2002].

> judicial systems characterised by the objection (protest) procedure and, therefore, by the risk of final judgments being set aside repeatedly, as occurred in the instant case, are, as such, incompatible with the principle of legal certainty that is one of the fundamental aspects of the rule of law for the purposes of Article 6(1) of the Convention.

[175] William Pomeranz, 'Supervisory Review and the Finality of Judgments under Russian Law' (2009) 34(1) *Review of Central and East European Law* 15, 19.

[176] Application No. 5284/99, *Ryabykh v. Russia*, [2003] ECHR 396; [24 July 2003].

[177] Article 7, Law on the Supreme Court.

[178] Koroteev and Golubok, 'Judgment of the Russian Constitutional Court on Supervisory Review in Civil Proceedings', 619, 626. This has a parallel in the way that the court relied on the 'developing socio-historical context'.

arisen in other countries that had abandoned judicial supervision as a practice.[179]

3.8   Supervision in East Asia

The supervisory legality embedded in Chapter IX of the 1936 Soviet Constitution has exerted significant influence on formal constitutional design in socialist East Asia. At a textual level, all constitutions afford powers of supervision. The extent of this supervisory power and its manifestations, however, has developed in a very different way. Much of this will be described in the following Chapters in this book. This final part will therefore only sketch the bare outlines of an East Asian socialist supervision system that is grounded on local history and developing interpretations of socialist history.

3.8.1   Textual Similarities

The process of constitutional transplantation from Soviet Union to socialist Asia was not consistent over time. In the People's Republic of China (PRC), for instance, the 1954 Constitution adopted a version of supervisory legality but then abandoned it after the Cultural Revolution. The PRC then reintroduced supervisory legality – in much the same form – in the 1982 Constitution.[180] Vietnam, by contrast, instituted this model in 1959, and has retained it to varying degrees throughout the rest of the socialist period.[181]

Today, most of the major socialist constitutions in socialist East Asia formally follow the 1936 Soviet constitutional model. First, they place the courts and the procuracy in the same section of the constitution, and afford these institutions supervisory power. They also place supervision at the centre of their constitutional orders. In China, for instance, article 129 states that the procuracy is a 'State organ[] for legal supervision'.[182] It describes how the Supreme People's Court 'supervises the administration of justice by the people's courts at various local levels and by the special

---

[179]   Ekaterina Butorina, Vremiya Novostei, Viperson, at http://viperson.ru/articles/valeriy-zorkin-v-nashey-strane-nadzor-neobhodim-ks-zaschitil-rossiyskoe-sudoproisvodstvo-ot-evropeyskoy-kritiki

[180]   Partlett and Ip, 'Is Socialist Law Really Dead?', 485.

[181]   George Ginsburgs, 'The Genesis of the People's Procuracy in the Democratic Republic of Vietnam' (1979) 5 *Review of Socialist Law* 179.

[182]   Article 130.

people's courts'.[183] In Vietnam, the Constitution gives the procuracy the power to 'supervise judicial activities'. The Constitution also describes how the Court 'supervises and directs the judicial work of other courts', as well as ensuring 'the uniform application of law in trials'.[184] Thus, these supreme courts remain powerful bodies that exert significant power over lower courts through a number of different mechanisms.

3.8.2 Selective Adaptation

This formal reception has led to some key similarities. Most notably, many courts in socialist East Asia exercise similar powers of supervision to those found in the former Soviet Union. For instance, the Chinese Law on Courts grants the Supreme People's Court the power to promulgate 'explanations on questions concerning specific applications of laws and decrees in judicial procedure'.[185] These judicial explanations are legally binding rulings, which are not case judgments but are instead abstract decrees and replies.[186] With regard to the procuracy, practice varies. In China, for instance, the procuracy serves a similar statist goal, taking cases involving 'acts to dismember the state', or other cases 'impeding the unified enforcement of State policies, laws, decrees and administrative orders'. Second, much like its Soviet counterpart, it exercises wide powers to oversee judicial practice (article 5(4)) and protest individual cases (article 18). For instance, procurators have the power to protest against a legally effective judgment, even if it involves a 'mediation agreement harmful to state interests or social public interests'.[187] Finally, the procuracy also plays an important role in the long tradition of citizen petitions (*xinfang*).[188] The Chinese central government has recently encouraged this practice, issuing regulations to formalise this process. The stated goal of these regulations is to 'maintain[] connections between

---

[183] Article 127.

[184] Article 104, Section 2.

[185] Shao-Chuan Leng and Hungdah Chiu, *Criminal Justice in Post-Mao China: Analysis and Documents* (Albany, NY: State University of New York Press, 1985), p. 63.

[186] Supreme People's Court of the People's Republic of China [Sup. People's Ct.] June 6, 1997, Several Regulations for Judicial Interpretation, Judicial Distribution [1997] No. 15 (repealed); Supreme People's Court, March 9, 2007, Regulations on the Work of Judicial Interpretations, Judicial Distribution [2007] No. 12.

[187] Yuwen Li, *The Judicial System and Reform in Post-Mao China: Stumbling towards Justice* (London: Routledge, 2017).

[188] Carl Minzner, 'Xinfang: An Alternative to Formal Legal Chinese Institutions' (2006) 42(1) *Stanford Journal of International Law* 103–179.

the government and the masses'.[189] The procuracy has also played an important role in this continuing tradition. In a four-year period, Guandong procuracy received 13,444 petitions for protest and filed official protests in about 5 per cent of these cases.[190]

These formal similarities, however, mask critical differences in operation. Again, historical context helps to ensure how these formal transplants are selectively adapted to each country.[191] A particularly difficult institution to transplant was the procuracy and its vast powers of general supervision over administrative law making. For instance, in China, in the early days of the procuracy, there was confusion about how general supervision should operate.[192] The Procurator General is reported to have said, 'What to do and how to do it?'[193] Other countries without similar traditions of procuratorial control also had trouble in implementing this institution. For instance, in Poland, the procuracy – used to focusing on criminal prosecutions – lacked the resources and trained staff to successfully carry out general supervision.[194] In 1956, Polish lawmakers introduced changes to a comprehensive code of administrative procedure that increased the legal powers of courts in administrative law.[195]

Despite the failure to fully implement the supervisory powers of the procuracy, the supervisory tradition of the political review of legality remains important in China today. General supervision in the PRC is exercised by other institutions – for example, the standing committees of the National People's Congress, at different levels themselves, possess wide-ranging powers of supervision.[196]

---

[189] Cited from ibid., 120.

[190] Randall Peerenboom, 'The Dynamics and Politics of Legal Reform in China', in Tim Lindsey, *Law Reform in Developing and Transitional States* (London: Routledge, 2012), p. 222.

[191] Alan Watson, 'Aspects of the Reception of Law' (1996) 44 *American Journal of Comparative Law* 335–351 (discussing how the 'reception' of law is one of the most important sources of legal change).

[192] Oda, 'The Procuracy and the Regular Courts as Enforcers of the Constitutional Rule of Law', 1342.

[193] Ibid., 1343.

[194] Klaus-Jurgen Kuss, 'Judicial Review of Administrative Acts in East European Countries', in George Ginsburgs, Gianmaria Ajani, Gerard Pieter van der Berg and William B. Simons (eds.), *Soviet Administrative Law: Theory and Policy*, Law in Eastern Europe Series, No. 40 (Dordrecht: M. Nijhoff Publishers, 1989), p. 474.

[195] Ibid., p. 475.

[196] Chapter IV, Law of the People's Republic of China on Supervision by the Standing Committees of the People's Congresses at All Levels, at www.npc.gov.cn/englishnpc/

Furthermore, the Ministry of Supervision (MOS), as well as the Central Discipline Inspection Commission (CDIC) and their subordinate bodies also have supervisory power.[197] These bodies also rely on the frequent practice of petitioning. For instance, during one period, petitions were responsible for the disciplining of about 80 per cent of cadres for illicit conduct.[198]

Other Chapters in this volume describe the adaptation of supervision in socialist East Asia. For instance, Chapter 9 describes the operation of the procuracy and its relevance to Vietnam's legal system. They describe how Ho Chi Minh established the procuracy 'to ensure that the law was observed strictly and uniformly, and people's democratic legality was maintained'.[199] Since the 2001 reforms, the procuracy has shifted its rationale closer to that of the post-Soviet countries, supervising court practice and compliance with human rights. This change was introduced in part to ensure better control over legality during large-scale market reforms.[200] Despite this difference, however, a key similarity emerges in socialist East Asia: despite judicial reform, socialist law continues to employ the top-down political control of legality. This centralised supervision is in turn a critical tool in East Asian consolidation of state capitalism.

3.9 Conclusion

This Chapter demonstrates the importance of history in understanding how legal systems respond to political ideologies like socialism. In

---

Law/2008-01/02/content_1388018.htm. (Key provisions demonstrate that standing committees are charged with ensuring that key laws are enforced correctly.). China has also introduced supervisory legality into its governance of Hong Kong. The key institution of supervision over the interpretation of the Hong Kong Basic Law is the National People's Council Standing Committee (NPCSC). Furthermore, Beijing has also established a Basic Law Committee that would assist the NPCSC in its interpretation of the Basic Law. Eric Ip, 'Prototype Constitutional Supervision in China: The Lessons of the Hong Kong Basic Law Committee' (2015) 10(2) Asian Journal of Comparative Law 323–342.

[197] Yasheng Huang, 'Administrative Monitoring in China' (1995) 143 The China Quarterly 828.

[198] Ibid., 835.

[199] Article 2, Law on the Organisation of the People's Procuracy (LOOPP), 1960.

[200] Brian Quinn, 'Vietnam's Continuing Legal Reform: Gaining Control Over the Courts' (2003) 4 Asian-Pacific Law & Policy Journal 431.

particular, it reminds us that to understand a legal system requires more than just understanding how those within a new dominant political ideology describe their system. Instead, it requires understanding how this political ideology interacts with a historically situated set of often contradictory practices and concepts in the pre-existing legal system.[201] This suggests that no matter how revolutionary the language of political change, the practice of legal systems changes much more slowly and involves far more continuity.

Understanding socialist law in this way yields three important conclusions. First, it demonstrates how the Leninist, statist version of socialist supervision reinvigorated supervisory practices that ultimately frustrated the judicial monopoly over the review of legality and challenged Western conceptions of judicial power. For instance, supervision invested the review of administrative legality in procuracies or other non-judicial bodies. It also gave a small group of court leadership (in the presidium) the authority to reopen final Supreme Court judgments. In this way, socialist law helped to re-energise politicised methods of ensuring legality.

Second, this historical perspective helps deepen our understanding of the internal debates and practices of supervision. Seen this way, supervision is best understood as the bureaucratised and political control of legality that exists alongside, and in some tension with, independent and binding judicial enforcement of legality. Evolving out of needs to discipline the vast bureaucratic apparatus of the imperial state and respond to a tradition of individual petitions, supervision was justified as a more flexible and effective approach to legality in comparison with judicial proceedings. Although it has varying institutional manifestations, supervision remains an important lever for ensuring state control over the potentially centrifugal forces of capitalism and persistent administrative illegality in the former Soviet bloc.

Finally, these justifications allow us to better understand the persistence of non-judicial supervision across the former socialist bloc countries today. These statist justifications and practices remain persuasive in many parts of the former socialist world, and therefore represent a

---

[201] For a reflection of this approach to understanding law, see Patrick S. Atiyah and Robert S. Summers, *Form and Substance in Anglo-American Law: A Comparative Study of Legal Reasoning, Legal Theory, and Legal Institutions* (Oxford: Clarendon Press, 1987).

significant divergence from the trend towards judicial resolution of legal disputes in the rest of the civil law world. The persuasive power of these justifications is not inevitable; in fact, there have been moves in some former socialist bloc countries to strengthen judicial power.[202] But, as long as a normative value for strengthening centralised state power remains robust, supervisory legality is likely to continue.

---

[202] William Partlett, 'The Elite Threat to Constitutional Transitions' (2016) 56(2) *Virginia Journal of International Law* 407–457.

4

Socialist Rule of Law with Chinese Characteristics

A New Genealogy

GLENN TIFFERT

In October 2014, the Fourth Plenum of the 18th Central Committee of the Chinese Communist Party (CCP) adopted a widely hailed *Decision Concerning Some Major Questions in Comprehensively Advancing Governing the Country According to Law*.[1] This decision offers one of the most authoritative public statements of legal policy and goals ever issued by the CCP's top leadership. Analysts accordingly devoured the text for clues to new priorities and initiatives, and for shifts in the tone and overall agenda of legal reform in the People's Republic of China (PRC).[2]

With most eyes trained on the future, the ways in which the decision uses the past to serve its purposes have remained largely unexamined. This diminishes our insight into PRC legal reform because how we understand its trajectory depends in large measure on how we characterise its starting points. To the extent that we rely unduly on local information and cognitive maps supplied by the CCP, we are prone to reproduce their priorities and biases, and may miss material features they overlook or obscure. This is particularly the case when we reflect on what is socialist about socialist law in the contemporary PRC. In recent years, and most notably since the 2014 plenum decision, the CCP has promoted a doctrine dubbed 'Socialist Rule of Law with Chinese

---

[1] 'Decision of the Central Committee of the Chinese Communist Party Concerning Certain Major Questions in Comprehensively Advancing Ruling the Country According to Law', *People's Daily*, 29 October 2014.

[2] Randall Peerenboom, 'Fly High the Banner of Socialist Rule of Law with Chinese Characteristics! What Does the 4th Plenum Decision Mean for Legal Reforms in China?' (2015) 7(1) *Hague Journal on the Rule of Law* 49–84; Albert H. Y. Chen, 'China's Long March towards Rule of Law or China's Turn against Law?' (2016) 4(1) *The Chinese Journal of Comparative Law* 1–35; Eva Pils, 'China, the Rule of Law, and the Question of Obedience: A Comment on Professor Peerenboom' (2015) 7(1) *Hague Journal on the Rule of Law* 83–90.

Characteristics' with increasing vigor, and it has substantiated the legitimacy of that doctrine by adducing a supporting pedigree that reaches back to Mao, Lenin and, ultimately, Marx.

This follows an established practice in the PRC of forcing modern Chinese history through the filters of CCP ideology, which reduces it to scarcely more than a branch of Party history. It buries or excises discordant and incompatible elements to yield a tidy, teleological narrative that preempts or forecloses alternatives, and depicts the CCP as perennially farsighted and steadfast. Furthermore, on this basis, the Party promotes itself as the indispensable representative of popular will, and the guarantor of discipline and progress across both state and society. Such narratives propagate in the PRC by dint of official sponsorship, persistent repetition and tight Party control over information. With few alternative sources to work from, foreign observers frequently pick up and disseminate traces of these anointed narratives abroad, with the result that Party orthodoxy has, to a surprising degree, colonised scholarship outside of China, as well.

This paper takes a different approach. By delving into suppressed chapters of the CCP's Mao-era engagements with the rule of law, it challenges the genealogy through which the Party today authenticates a dubiously socialist and proprietary variant of that concept and arrives at an ideologically provocative conclusion about the provenance of 'Socialist Rule of Law with Chinese Characteristics' that remaps how we understand the arc of the revolution, the legacies of socialism and the context for legal reform.

Official speeches, policy documents and the secondary academic literature are common sources of insight into how the rule of law is theorised in the PRC, but perhaps the most authoritative statement on the subject is a widely overlooked textbook published by the CCP's apex Political-Legal Committee in 2009.[3] Intended as a study guide for Party members, cadres and university faculty and students, the volume covers the basic principles and objectives of socialist rule of law, and illustrates how the CCP has shrewdly asserted ownership over the concept and revamped it from the ground up, conferring upon it the distinctive socialist and Chinese characteristics that now define its official interpretation in the PRC.

---

[3] Central Committee of the Chinese Communist Party, *Textbook on the Concept of Socialist Rule of Law* (Beijing: China Chang'an Press, 2009).

Of particular interest, the textbook catalogues the orthodox sources of authority from which socialist rule of law derives. Exemplifying what Horwitz called 'roaming through history looking for friends', it assembles a star-studded pedigree, beginning with Marx, Engels, Lenin, Mao and Dong Biwu, and then concludes with the prime movers behind current 'Socialist Rule of Law with Chinese Characteristics' thought, namely Deng Xiaoping, Jiang Zemin and Hu Jintao.[4] If the textbook is updated, then Xi Jinping and his call to 'comprehensively govern the nation according to law', will no doubt round out the list. Interestingly, it also credits imperial China and the capitalist nations of the West as offering lessons that China can study critically, admissions that would have been counterrevolutionary in the Mao era. Hence, there are sections with titles such as 'Lenin's thought on the rule of law', 'Conscientiously implement the requirements of the *Three Supremes* in every aspect of socialist rule of law' and the 'Ideology of Using *Li* (rites) and *Fa* (law) together'.

To put it plainly, this volume commits audacious feats of legerdemain. First, the Party invokes 'Chinese characteristics' to surgically excise the rule of law's imported, liberal associations, but not its Marxist–Leninist ones, which are instead Sinicised by the likes of Mao and Deng. In an age when 'Western values' are again under assault in China, why socialism is intrinsically amenable to this localisation but liberalism is not remains an open question. Secondly, 'Chinese characteristics' also offer a vehicle for relaxing the Party's original verdict on the imperial period, once held as a reactionary and feudal encumbrance to be overcome, but now described as 'China's excellent traditional culture' and a source of inspiration for rule of law's necessary complement, traditionalistic 'rule of virtue (*dezhi*)'.[5] Thirdly, the volume 'waves the red flag to oppose the red flag'; that is to say that it wraps the concept of the rule of law in the banner of socialism to release it from its Mao-era ignominy. Needless to say, this is not Mao's socialism, but the contrasting socialism of today's 'socialist market economy', which, owing to its early stage development, in turn authorises a muscular statism and a commensurate, supporting legal system. Taken together, these gambits amount to a quiet but fundamental reversal of former revolutionary verities. While the nature of 'Chinese

---

[4] Morton J. Horwitz, 'Republican Origins of Constitutionalism', in Paul Finkelman and Stephan E. Gottlieb (eds.), *Toward a Usable Past: The Use of History in Law* (Athens, GA: University of Georgia Press, 2009), pp. 148–149.

[5] 'Communique of the Fourth Plenum of the Eighteenth Central Committee of the Chinese Communist Party', *People's Daily*, 24 October 2014.

characteristics' and socialism may have shifted dramatically, the labels and rhetorical strategies connected to them remain deceptively static.

Of course times change, and with them ideas, and the issue is therefore not the current contradictions with the Party's past positions, but rather the contortions the Party goes through to mask those inconsistencies in order to maintain the façade of ideological constancy. Perhaps nowhere is this more evident than in the official pedigree constructed for socialist rule of law. The attentive observer will notice, for instance, that among the expansive range of influences acknowledged in the 2009 textbook on the subject, the Republican period (1911–1949) is conspicuously absent. The relevant history blithely skips from imperial China to the CCP's revolutionary base areas and the PRC. The most that leading statements will generally say about the Republican period is that: 'After the Opium War broke in 1840 ... people with lofty ideals tried to transplant to China modes of the rule of law from modern Western countries, but failed for various historical reasons.'[6]

It bears asking: Why should the CCP continue to single out the Republican period for such casual disregard when the taboos against other eras have noticeably relaxed? The answer is: Because the Party's genealogy of socialist rule of law is a fragile construct that would suffer the challenge. Asserting Republican failure and summarily casting that period to the margins of history maintains the fiction that the 1949 revolution was a purifying break with the past, preserves the concept of the rule of law in the current PRC against an inference of prior contamination from the West, validates the folly of transplanting foreign paradigms to present-day China, and therefore awards the CCP a monopoly of credit for the rule of law's subsequent success. As with many other subjects, the CCP brooks no competitors; Party history must always be in command.[7]

A problem arises, however, when Party history collides against the empirical record. Particularly during the late Republican period, the rule of law was a topic of fierce public debate, very often pitting the Nationalist government against jurists and political progressives who found its

---

[6] State Council, 'China's Efforts and Achievements in Promoting the Rule of Law' (2008) 7(2) *Chinese Journal of International Law* 515.

[7] State Council, 'China's Efforts and Achievements in Promoting the Rule of Law', in Central Committee of the Chinese Communist Party, *Textbook on the Concept of Socialist Rule of Law*. 'Decision of the Central Committee of the Chinese Communist Party Concerning Certain Major Questions in Comprehensively Advancing Ruling the Country According to Law'.

implementation of the concept to be gravely lacking. Much more than 'lofty ideals' were at stake; critics chafed at the creeping authoritarianism, corruption and politicisation of the legal system under the Nationalist regime, especially the elevation of Kuomintang party ideology as a guiding framework for adjudication, the extra-judicial interference of Kuomintang party members in the handling of concrete cases and the partification (*sifa danghua*) of judicial recruitment, training and evaluation.[8]

The Nationalist government and Kuomintang party routinely defended their approaches to the rule of law by referencing China's 'national conditions', shorthand for its cultural, economic, geographic, political, social and technological idiosyncracies. They notoriously maintained, for example, that these conditions did not initially suit constitutional government, and that the nation therefore required a preparatory period of political tutelage, which dragged on to 1947. Accordingly, in the same year, in a section devoted to Kuomintang 'Party Principles' (*dangyi*), the national judicial exam tested the ideological fitness of candidates for state judicial office and the bar by asking: 'Why was it necessary to undergo a period of political tutelage before it was possible to reach the period of constitutional government?'[9] In May 1948, as the civil war raged, the Nationalist government and Kuomintang party again cited exigent conditions, this time to suspend key provisions of the new constitution and declare martial law, a 'temporary' situation that lasted in Taiwan until 1991.

Constitutional government did not usurp the Kuomintang's primacy over the law. In fact, Nationalist and Kuomintang officials insisted that the rule of law was a pluralistic concept, which they could reformulate on their own terms. Accordingly, they proclaimed a localised variant, dubbed 'Three People's Principles Rule of Law' (*sanmin zhuyi fazhi*), grounded in Kuomintang ideology, and the morality and discipline of traditional 'rule by rites' (*lizhi*). In 1940, Ju Zheng, President of the Nationalist Judicial Yuan, argued:

---

[8] Zaiquan Li, *Rule of Law and Party Rule: The Kuomintang Regime's Judicial Partification (1923–1948)* (Beijing: Social Science Academic Press, 2012); Xiutao Han, *Judicial Independence and Modern China* (Beijing: Tsinghua University Press, 2003); Jinfan Zhang, 'Overview of a Century of Legal Science and Rule of Law in China' (2005) 5 *China Legal Science* 185–192.

[9] '1947 Judicial Examination Questions' (1947) 3(7) *Revue Juridique et Économique de L'Université L'Aurore*.

> The rule of law must suit the age ... Currently, there are many forms of
> rule of law being implemented by various nations. There is capitalist
> nation rule of law, socialist nation rule of law and fascist nation rule of
> law. However, we need none of those. The rule of law that we need is one
> that harmoniously joins with the spirit of the Three People's Principles,
> that has the elements of the Three People's Principles within the rule of
> law's spirit.[10]

The parallels with the CCP's efforts to establish a distinctive brand of
'Socialist Rule of Law with Chinese Characteristics' are obvious, and
extend further. Recall that the Kuomintang and CCP were once partners.
Each styled itself a Leninist party at the vanguard of history, and both
favoured highly statist, centrally planned models of economic development and social organisation. Still, in contrast to the CCP, the Kuomintang abjured communism and class struggle.[11] Thus, while the Three
People's Principles Rule of Law explicitly subordinated the liberty of the
individual to that of the greater nation, 'the people were not divided into
classes and had equal rights'.[12] Ironically, this is effectively the CCP's
position today, and contrasts strikingly against the policies it pursued
during the Mao era.

Furthermore, the two parties often spoke of law in remarkably similar
terms. If Zhang Zhiben, secretary-general of the Nationalist Judicial
Yuan, invoked the Three People's Principles to assert that 'the administration of justice is an important branch of politics', then the president of
the CCP's Shaanganning Border Region High Court, Lei Jingtian, could
concur with a Marxist argument that 'law and politics have an intimate
connection. Law is a branch of politics, and serves politics'.[13] Both parties
also welcomed the creative destruction revolution dialectically wrought
on law and society. The CCP demonstrated this by abrogating the
Nationalist legal system in 1949, but the Kuomintang position on this
subject was equally forthright. In 1929, Hu Hanmin, president of the
Nationalist Legislative Yuan, declared:

---

[10] Zheng Ju, 'Prospects for the Rule of Law in China' (1940) 37(13) *Eastern Miscellany* 11.
[11] William Kirby, 'The Nationalist Regime and the Chinese Party-State, 1928–1958', in
Merle Goldman and Andrew Gordon (eds.), *Historical Perspectives on Contemporary East
Asia* (Cambridge, MA: Harvard University Press, 2000).
[12] Ju, 'Prospects for the Rule of Law in China', 11.
[13] Zhiben Zhang, 'Knowledge Judicial Officers Should Have in Wartime' (1938) 7 *Decretal
Weekly* 8. Jingtian Lei, 'Lei Jingtian's Report to the Shaanganning Border Region Judicial
Work Conference (1941)' (2004) 5 *Analects of Legal History* 379.

> Revolution is an undertaking in which destruction and construction advance in tandem. Destruction is the beginning of construction. Construction is the culmination of destruction ... on the one hand we must abolish all unsuitable laws from the old era, while on the other hand formulating laws that suit the new era ... we must now in a China with a rotting old society and old order create a new nation and new society.[14]

Likewise, almost two decades later, in an article defending the Kuomintang's tarnished position on the rule of law, Zhang Zhiben argued that the concept went hand in hand with revolution:

> Revolution must have order, but it must destroy the old order and create a new one. Not only must revolution not repudiate the rule of law, on the contrary it needs the rule of law, only then can it guarantee success. The constitutions of various countries around the world are all products of revolution. You could say that the goal of revolution is to destroy the old law, and follow with new law.[15]

These manifold correspondences caution us against taking at face value the CCP's self-representations of what is intrinsically socialist or proprietary about its current approach to the rule of law, particularly because what it today calls socialism departs extravagantly from the policies of that name promoted by the founding generation of revolutionaries it traces its origins to. Furthermore, if in China the Nationalist regime pioneered the Leninist party-state, the planned economy, a doctrine of close party leadership over the legal system, a dialectical understanding of law and revolution, and a localised variant of the rule of law putatively defined by party ideology and China's national conditions, then the official CCP genealogy of 'Socialist Rule of Law with Chinese Characteristics' seems mortally deficient, and the Party's dismissal of the Republican period looks calculated and disingenuous.

One explanation for these correspondences is parallel evolution from a common Soviet root, since both political parties studied Soviet models. Such evolution indeed transpired, but even so, the above examples underscore the importance of not conflating Soviet influence with socialism. To

---

[14] Hanmin Hu, 'The Legislative Essentials and Legislative Program of the Three People's Principles', in Party History Committee of the Central Committee of the Chinese Kuomintang (ed.), *Collected Works of Hu Hanmin: Revolutionary Theory and Revolutionary Work* (Pt. 2) (Taipei: Party History Committee of the Central Committee of the Chinese Kuomintang, 1978), pp. 774, 778.

[15] Zhiben Zhang, 'The Rule of Law Spirit of the Chinese Kuomintang' (1946) 2 *Three People's Principles Semi-Monthly* 3.

appreciate that point, consider that Nationalist judges and procurators studied the methods of the Soviet secret police (NKVD), in part to suppress Chinese communists more efficiently, frequently charging and convicting them with the crime of counter-revolution. Moreover, parallel evolution is only a fraction of the story behind socialist rule of law. CCP historiography has buried a still more subversive mode of development.

In the early 1940s, many left-leaning intellectuals disillusioned with the Nationalist government were drawn to the CCP's Shaanganning Border Region headquarters at Yan'an. Among them was a small group of law students and legal professionals, who the Party quickly elevated to leading positions in the Border Region's rudimentary legal system. Committed to adapting elements of the Nationalist legal system to the CCP's emerging policy of New Democracy, in 1941 they organised a New Law Society that proposed a New Democratic Rule of Law Campaign (*xin minzhu zhuyi de fazhi yundong*). They advocated a burst of codification, higher professional standards and greater procedural regularity in adjudication, and hoped to make the legal system more responsive and accessible to the public. As their manifesto declared: 'Having a fine legal system that the people cannot use is for that fineness to be in vain and for the rule of law to remain an open question.'[16]

The prime mover behind the New Law Society was Li Mu'an. Li was one of China's earliest modern law graduates, and during the early Republican period he served as a procurator and organiser of the professional bar in Beijing. From June 1942 to December 1943, Li served as acting president of the Border Region High Court, a lionised institution in the pedigree of the PRC legal system. True to the goals of the New Law Society, Li's 1942 work report announced the court's intention to 'eliminate the vestiges of guerilla-ism, establish revolutionary procedures, and cultivate the habits of the rule of law'.[17] More remarkably still, to ground adjudication in solid legal foundations, Li encouraged judicial cadres to cite Nationalist codes as complements to Border Region legislation, and their decisions reflect this practice.[18]

---

[16] Xinyi Hou, 'The Chinese School of Legal Science: Causes, Methods, and Results – A Study of the Yan'an New Law Society' (2006) 11 *Tribune of Political Science and Law: Journal of the Chinese University of Politics and Law* 13.

[17] Xinyi Hou, *From Justice for the People to People's Justice: Research Into the Popularization of the Judicial System in the Shaanganning Border Region* (Beijing: Chinese University of Politics and Law Press, 2007), p. 133.

[18] Yongheng Hu, *Sources of Civil Law in the Shaanganning Border Region* (Beijing: Social Science Academic Press, 2012), pp. 27, 30–31.

By the end of 1943, Li's ambition to ameliorate the Border Region judicial system was foundering on inadequate institutional and human capital, and on the ideological radicalisation accompanying Mao's rise to hegemony. The chairman of the Border Region government, Lin Boqu, later denounced 'the tendency towards judicial Kuomintang-ification (mainly in the leading organs)', and labelled Li's stewardship of the legal system as 'thoroughly Kuomintang'.[19] Lei Jingtian, Li's predecessor at the court, said: 'In his work at the Border Region High Court, Li Mu'an implemented the New Law Society's program, and made Border Region judicial work completely Kuomintang.'[20] Lei then took the motif of Chinese characteristics one step further by arguing that Li and his associates 'deny the special circumstances of the Border Region's historical environment, and regard the Border Region in the same way as the territory under Nationalist rule, and therefore emphasise that capitalist law is completely applicable to the Border Region'.[21] Xie Juezai summed up the verdict against them: 'The New Law Society was an out-and-out Old Law Society. The old law, this we do not need.'[22]

Xie's clever rectification of names was typical of the discursive strategies the CCP employed to isolate and stamp out heterodoxy, and it prefigured the fate of the rule of law in the early PRC, not least of all because it added a new weapon to the Party's arsenal, the epithet of the 'old law standpoint' (jiufa guandian), which stood for the reactionary technocratic, procedural and positivist commitments associated with Republican legal reform. By definition, old law had no place in New China, and neither did its proponents. Thus, as a consequence of the 1943 rectification movement, Li was forced from office, and a savage wave of purges washed over the judicial system, claiming 17 of the High Court's 36 cadres, including judges and tribunal presidents. Afterwards, the CCP covered up this initial, ill-fated experiment with the rule of law,

---

[19] Boqu Lin, 'The Experience of the 3–3 System in the Shaanganning Border Region and Deviations That Should Be Corrected', in Shaanxi Provincial Archives and Shaanxi Provincial Social Sciences Institute (eds.), Selected Shaanganning Border Region Government Documents, vol. 8 (Beijing: Archives Press, 1988), p. 115. Shirong Wang et al., Cornerstone of New China's Judicial System: The Shaanganning Border Region High Court (1937–1949) (Beijing: Commercial Press, 2011), p. 104.

[20] Hu, Sources of Civil Law in the Shaanganning Border Region, pp. 27, 30–31.

[21] Yongheng Hu, 'Study of the Cessation of Citation to the Six Codes in the Shaanganning Border Region: The Influence of the Rectification and Cadre Investigation Campaigns on the Administration of Justice in the Border Region' (2010) 4 Anti-Japanese War Studies 93.

[22] Juezai Xie, Diary of Xie Juezai (Beijing: People's Press, 1984), p. 557.

but could not escape repeating it because the commitments underlying it endured among segments of the Party. Thus, for the remainder of the Mao era, the CCP would alternately promote codification, higher judicial standards and legal institutionalisation only to turn abruptly against those initiatives, and persecute their representatives for allegedly harbouring the old law standpoint.

At the time, it was not enough for the CCP leadership to discredit the New Democratic Rule of Law, they also had to provide a compelling alternative around which to mobilise the legal system, and within a week of Li's resignation from the court, the Party leadership found one: the Ma Xiwu style of adjudication. Celebrated as a crystallisation of the 'Yan'an Way', the Ma Xiwu style is legendary in the PRC because it endowed the CCP with a revolutionary legal heritage the Party could call its own.[23] Briefly, the Ma Xiwu style stressed the primacy of the mass line over positive law, and the common wisdom of rural judicial cadres, who typically had little to no formal education. It required judicial cadres to adopt flexible and simplified procedures, and to venture forth from the courtroom to investigate personally the circumstances behind the cases before them. They were supposed to seek the opinions of the masses so that they might better understand pertinent facts and the potential ramifications of their rulings, grasp the conjunctions between law and local society, spread the teachings of Party policy, and deliver more timely and responsive justice. While, strictly speaking, the Ma Xiwu style referred to trial work, its populist spirit applied equally well to mediation, and the CCP has therefore tended to promote the two together ever since.

The fact that the CCP's iconic paradigm of revolutionary judicial practice grew out of the backlash to the Party's initial foray into the rule of law hangs like a cloud over current CCP efforts to claim a rule of law tradition endogenous to the Party. Moreover, time and again the CCP promoted the Ma Xiwu style as an antidote to the legal formalism and professionalisation associated with the rule of law. The two opposing paradigms of justice have long co-existed in an unstable balance, each rising or falling in inverse relation to the other as political winds shifted.[24]

---

[23] Xipo Zhang, *The Ma Xiwu Style of Adjudication* (Beijing: Law Press, 1983); 'The Ma Xiwu Style of Adjudication', in Yanping Wu and Genju Liu (eds.), *Collected Reference Materials on the Law of Criminal Procedure*, Vol. 1 (Beijing: Peking University Press, 2005), pp. 159–161. Carl Minzner, 'China's Turn against Law' (2011) 59(4) *American Journal of Comparative Law* 935–984.

[24] Minzner, 'China's Turn against Law'.

The CCP's second major experiment with the rule of law began in May 1948. Tasked with establishing a North China People's Government (NCPG) in preparation for assuming national power, Liu Shaoqi, secretary of the Party's North China Bureau, invited Xie Juezai and Chen Jinkun to lead the NCPG's prospective judicial department and people's court. Xie was a Party elder who had played a major role in appointing and then dismissing Li Mu'an five years earlier in Yan'an, and was the principal drafter of the 1946 Constitutional Principles of the Shaanganning Border Region. Chen was a renowned law professor who had briefly led the Nationalist Ministry of Justice's Civil Division. Liu privately told them: 'The North China region for the most part already has no enemy [presence], [we] may set about establishing proper rule of law (*jianli zhenggui fazhi*) ... first revise the old criminal and civil laws a bit, revising as you implement, something is better than nothing.'[25]

These instructions are historiographically explosive for two principal reasons. First, they revived the discredited language of the rule of law in Party circles for the first time since 1943, when senior cadres had attacked the concept as a reactionary fraud. Crucially, this comeback was initiated at the highest levels of the Party leadership. That steered CCP legal discourse back towards the mainstream of Republican legal reform for a time, and it became possible once again for cadres to invoke the rule of law as integral to the Party, though usually prefaced by words such as 'socialist', 'people's' or 'revolutionary' as a prophylactic against fatal associations with the 'old law' and the Kuomintang. Even NCPG regulations and decisions began incorporating references to the rule of law.[26]

Importantly, it was also in this context that Dong Biwu first suggested 'handling matters according to law' (*yifa banshi*), the seed from which the post-Mao revival of the rule of law in China would eventually sprout. Dong articulated an ambitious agenda for state building that briefly carried over into the early PRC under the rubric of 'democratic regime

---

[25] Chongwen Liu and Shaochou Chen (eds.), *Chronicle of Liu Shaoqi (1898–1969)* (Beijing: Central Party Literature Press, 1996), p. 148.

[26] 'General Order of the North China People's Government on Regularizing Prison Ration Quotas, Abolishing Litigation Fees, and Regional Villages Introducing a System for Filing Lawsuits', in Yanping Wu and Genju Liu (eds.), *Collected Reference Materials on the Law of Criminal Procedure*, vol. 1 (Beijing: Peking University Press, 2005), p. 617; 'General Order of the North China People's Government: Regulations on Handling Suspects Who Flee Various Counties for Beiping, Tianjin, and Other Large Cities', in Wu and Liu (eds.), *Collected Reference Materials on the Law of Criminal Procedure*, p. 639.

construction' (*minzhu jianzheng*).[27] This agenda attacked localism, promoted codification, institution building and tighter discipline, and impressed upon cadres the habits of strictly abiding by policies, instructions and procedures. For example, in October 1948, Dong said:

> Creating a new regime naturally requires establishing new laws, regulations and systems. We have smashed the old, we must definitely establish the new. Otherwise it would be anarchism. If we do not have laws, regulations and systems, how (can we) maintain the new order? Consequently, after establishing the new, we demand that matters be handled according to laws, regulations and systems. These kinds of new laws, regulations and systems everyone must formulate on the basis of the wills and interests of the proletarian class and the vast laboring masses. I (once) wrote a sentence, 'Bad law is better than no law,' which means that although for the time being our law cannot be perfect, it is generally still better than no law at all.[28]

At the time, the CCP had just emerged from devastating intra-Party violence appurtenant to land reform, and the revival of the rule of law was in part a response to this trauma. But a much larger game was also afoot. China was buzzing with discussions about the rule of law, stirred by the entry into force of a new constitution in 1947, which ended nineteen years of one-party political tutelage by the Kuomintang, and famously shifted the doctrinal basis of Nationalist governance from 'ruling the country using the Party' to 'ruling the country using law'.[29] Whether Liu took his cues from these discussions or from the commitments to the rule of law expressed years earlier by Li Mu'an and the New Law Society (and the answer was probably both), all evidence points to a common Nationalist root. There simply were no other rule of law traditions at hand in China for him to draw upon, and the Soviet Union did not use that particular vocabulary.

Nationalist models seem particularly likely because of the second astonishing aspect of Liu's instructions. In 1943, the judicial conference that denounced Li Mu'an singled out his advocacy of citing Nationalist

---

[27] Biwu Dong, 'The Principal Form of Current Democratic Regime Construction', in *Collected Works of Dong Biwu on Politics and Law* (Beijing: Law Press, 1986), pp. 106–115.

[28] Biwu Dong, 'On the Question of a New Democratic Regime' in *Collected Works of Dong Biwu on Politics and Law*, p. 41.

[29] Haopei Li, 'The Question of Implementing the Rule of Law' (1947) 2(12) *The Observer* 3–6; Guansheng Xie, 'The Mental Construction of the Rule of Law' (1948) 52 *Thought and Times* 4–5.

law in Border Region adjudication. The conference summary denounced this practice, saying: 'Law is a class product; we cannot cherish any fantasies or thoughts of retaining the sham [Nationalist] Six Codes, we must thoroughly smash [them].'[30] Nevertheless, in 1948, Liu Shaoqi overturned that judgement by instructing his senior judicial cadres to implement Nationalist codes as a step towards establishing the rule of law.

Two months later, in response to that call, Chen Jinkun, president of the North China People's Court, presented a draft civil procedure code consisting of 375 articles based explicitly on revisions to the corresponding Nationalist law.[31] In an accompanying explanatory note, he wrote:

> In this transitional period – the period of replacing old with new law, and drafting laws, we should revise the old law. We cannot obliterate it out of existence. We consult the old law to create the new law so that the transitional period can be properly managed. This is not at all inheriting the old legal system or neglecting the revolutionary standpoint.[32]

Up until December 1948, about six weeks before Beijing fell to the People's Liberation Army (PLA), Chen implored Party leaders to maintain this course. But the rapid collapse of Nationalist armies in Manchuria and North China during the intervening months hardened attitudes towards the Nationalist legal system, and the CCP began to prepare its imminent abrogation.

In theory, abrogation severed the PRC legal system from the legacies of the Nationalist past. But in reality, the legal organs of the new regime, especially in the cities, could not escape the shadow of Republican legal reform. As of late 1951 and early 1952, legacy judicial personnel (*jiu sifa renyuan*), the CCP's term for non-Party judicial cadres trained under the old regime, made up 56 per cent of adjudication personnel on the courts of

---

[30] Hu, 'Study of the Cessation of Citation to the Six Codes in the Shaanganning Border Region', 97.

[31] Jinkun Chen, 'Draft Civil Procedure Law of the Republic of China (1948)' in Civil Procedure Group of the Chinese Academy of Social Sciences Institute of Law and the Civil Procedure Group of the Beijing Institute of Politics and Law Procedural Law Teaching and Research Group (eds.), *Reference Materials on Civil Procedure Law*, vol. 2 (Pt. 1) (Beijing: Law Press, 1981), pp. 119–193.

[32] Jinkun Chen, 'Guiding Principles for the Draft Civil Procedure Law of the Republic of China (1948)', in Civil Procedure Group of the Chinese Academy of Social Sciences Institute of Law and the Civil Procedure Group of the Beijing Institute of Politics and Law Procedural Law Teaching and Research Group (eds.), *Reference Materials on Civil Procedure Law*, pp. 114–115.

Beijing, Guangzhou, Shanghai and Wuhan. Contrary to received wisdom, many of them were not Nationalist holdovers at all, but had been freshly hired since 1949.[33] They, along with elements inside of the Party who subscribed to the rule of law, carried the concept across the 1949 divide and sought to keep it alive by adapting it to Party ideology.

Thus, on the first anniversary of the PRC's founding, Dong Biwu listed among the central government's most important political and legal tasks 'building a people's judicial system and constructing the rule of law'.[34] The following month, Tao Xijin spoke to former Nationalist personnel about building a 'revolutionary people's rule of law'.[35] In 1951, Xu Deheng, Vice Chairman of the PRC Legal Affairs Commission, introduced the Provisional Statute on the Organisation of 'the People's" = the Provisional Statute on the Organisation of the People's Courts by noting that it would help the courts to 'raise the people's capacity for rule of law' and 'publicise the state's rule of law spirit'.[36] Similarly, in 1956, Li Qi, Peng Zhen's political secretary, called for overcoming China's traditionally weak respect for the rule of law by improving China's legal system and establishing 'the spirit of strict rule of law'. Li explained that this required strengthening legislative work, the judicial system, academic legal science and using education to inculcate law-abiding behaviour, areas highlighted in the 2014 plenum decision, as well.[37]

As this suggests, when senior cadres espoused the rule of law in the opening years of the PRC, it was most often in the context of state-building, administrative discipline, codification, legal construction and institutionalisation, and this usage flowed directly out of the initiatives launched in 1948 by the NCPG and their connections to Nationalist

---

[33] 'Report to the Central Committee and the North China Bureau by the Beijing Municipal Committee of the Chinese Communist Party on Early Conditions in the Judicial Reform Campaign, and Future Work Plans' in Beijing Municipal Archive and Beijing Municipal Chinese Communist Party Committee Party History Office (ed.), *1952: Selected Major Documents from Beijing* (Beijing: China Archives Press, 2002); Jieying Dong, *Chinese Legal Education 1949–1957* (Jilin: Jilin People's Press, 2008), pp. 87–88.

[34] Dong Biwu, 'Several Major Tasks in Politics and Law by the Central People's Government Over the Past Year', *People's Daily*, 1 October 1950.

[35] Xijin Tao, 'Certain Questions in Strengthening People's Judicial Work' in Xijin Tao (ed.), *The Construction of New China's Legal System* (Tianjin: Nankai University Press, 1988), p. 3.

[36] Xu Deheng, 'Explanation of the "Provisional Statute on the Organization of the People's Courts of the PRC"', *People's Daily*, 5 September 1951.

[37] Qi Li, 'The Struggle to Perfect Our Country's People's Democratic Legal System', *People's Daily*, 6 November 1956.

practice. However, like the New Law Society's abortive reforms years earlier, this agenda ultimately fell prey to radicalised politics, too.

The 1952 Judicial Reform Campaign is notorious for its public vilification and purges of legacy judicial personnel, but the Party hid from view the scale and intensity of the attacks it directed against its own veteran cadres. The old law standpoint was again at the centre of the storm. Members of the CCP leadership internally denounced Dong Biwu's project of 'democratic regime construction' as a 'capitalist slogan', on the grounds that the power of regime construction was not within the purview of state organs at all, but rather of the Party. Dong was forced to retreat and deliver a self-criticism.[38] In Beijing, the city government lambasted the veteran cadre leadership of its own municipal court and forced senior cadres to submit to fierce struggle sessions.

> In employing veteran cadres, the court leadership also stressed having a foundation in the old law as a standard ... veteran cadres occupy all of the important positions, but these cadres for the most part have some foundation in the old law, and some still have a pronounced old law standpoint ... not a few of the cadres who have studied and applied the old law believe that law transcends class and can only manifest its impartiality if it separates from politics ... Also, some believe that the new law is born of the old, which can be used critically, and some do not study policies and decrees because they believe that since there are no provisions [of law in them], there is no law to adjudicate (*wufa kesi*).[39]

This episode left deep fissures and bitter enmities within the legal system, which would erupt into conflict again before the decade was over. Technocratic legal modernisers within the CCP coped by seeking shelter under Soviet models, which for a time seemed to offer an ideologically unimpeachable way for them to advance their objectives, without triggering the toxic associations of the old law standpoint. Accordingly, high-level endorsements of the rule of law tapered off significantly from 1953 onwards, and cadres tended to describe their projects in the language of Soviet socialist legality (*shehui zhuyi fazhi*) instead.

In some areas, the uptake of Soviet models was deceptively rapid and far-reaching. This was most pronounced in textual representations of the

---

[38] Qi Sun, 'Interview with Mr. Wang Huai'an' (2003) 2 *Global Law Review* 176.

[39] 'Report to the Central Committee and the North China Bureau By the Beijing Municipal Committee of the Chinese Communist Party on First Phase of the Judicial Reform Campaign and Preliminary Summary', *1952: Selected Major Documents from Beijing*, p. 532.

law, such as teaching materials, legal doctrine and legal drafting. By contrast, legal practice changed much more slowly, and assimilated Soviet models to a lesser degree. Indeed, many aspects of Soviet legal practice that were initially embraced in the PRC with great fanfare fizzled, including enterprise-level comrade courts, special rail and water transport courts, the people's assessors system and the reconstituted bar. When Sino-Soviet relations began to sour towards the end of the 1950s, Soviet models were criticised as quickly and energetically as they had earlier been praised, and the safe harbour they offered legal modernisers in the PRC closed. During the years that followed, the trajectories of the two legal systems diverged dramatically, a testament to how little their underlying dynamics overlapped.

Following well-established patterns, the CCP's authoritative textbook on socialist rule of law regards the Soviet legacy ambivalently. On the one hand, it celebrates the trailblazing role Lenin and Stalin played in developing the theory and practice of socialist rule of law, and the 'early', foundational influence this had on the CCP. On the other hand, it sidesteps later developments, especially the PRC's embrace and abandonment of Soviet-style socialist legality during the 1950s, and the mutual polemics following the Sino-Soviet split. The Soviet Union re-enters the narrative only in the late 1980s, when its communist party errantly abandoned Marxism as a guiding ideology, and was 'drawn into the political model of certain Western capitalist states'. The textbook admonishes that this 'historical tragedy ... furnishes a useful lesson'.[40]

To be sure, the primacy of Party leadership and Party ideology were as fundamental to the CCP's version of the rule of law as they had been to the Kuomintang's. This much had not changed, though the specifics of the ideologies surely had. Steeped in Leninism, both the CCP and Kuomintang insisted that the bedrock principle of Party leadership distinguished their own respective variants of the rule of law from 'American-style' or capitalist rule of law, and they each charged their critics with fundamentally misunderstanding that the latter forms were inappropriate and misguided in a Chinese context.[41] Whereas Ju Zheng

---

[40] Central Committee of the Chinese Communist Party, *Textbook on the Concept of Socialist Rule of Law.*

[41] Liang Shi, 'All Judicial Cadres United Around the Party, Thoroughly Defeat the Rightists' Savage Attack: Speech by Shi Liang', *People's Daily*, 13 July 1957; Zheng Ju, 'Why Must We Reconstruct China's Judicial System? (September, 1946)', in Zhongxin Fan, Chenjin You and Xianzhai Gong (eds.), *Why Must We Reconstruct China's Judicial System?*

had propounded the singularity of the Three People's Principles Rule of Law, in 1957, Tao Xijin argued: 'The rule of law that we need is proletarian socialist rule of law, and the dictatorship of the proletariat is the highest law. Anything that departs from the dictatorship of the proletariat basically cannot be called rule of law at all.'[42] Again, while contemporary Soviet theorists pioneered such contempt for bourgeois rule of law (*pravovoe gosudarstvo*), they did not articulate an explicit, socialist variant of the concept so brazenly.[43] The PRC was still exorcising its Republican demons.

Arguments over judicial independence highlighted the contested boundaries of Party leadership of the legal system. Critics of the Nationalist and PRC governments spoke freely of judicial independence (*sifa duli*), and attacked both regimes for trampling on the principle. While such criticisms carried moral and political weight, as legal arguments they were flawed because both governments tended to speak instead of the more limited remit of *adjudicatory* independence (*shenpan duli*), which is the term used in every Chinese constitution since 1914. Adjudicatory independence referred only to the narrow, technical act of applying law to facts in judicial decision making, and not to the surrounding frames of public policy and judicial administration. It provided the justification for the Kuomintang program of judicial partification, and fulfills a similar function for the CCP, with one major difference. For the CCP, adjudicatory independence applied only to courts as institutions and not, as in Nationalist China, to individual judges. Thus, individual CCP judges remained liable to internal supervision, correction and command from judicial superiors while deciding cases. Considering the immature state of the legal system and the low level of training and basic education CCP judicial cadres had, this made a certain amount of sense, and indeed the 1914 draft Republican constitution endorsed the same accommodation.

The problem was that Nationalist standards nevertheless coloured how some CCP judges understood the balance between adjudicatory independence and Party leadership. It could not have been otherwise,

---

Selected Works by Ju Zheng on Law and Politics (Beijing: China University of Politics and Law Press, 2009).

[42] Xijin Tao, 'The Struggle in the Legal Community', *People's Daily*, 13 September 1957.

[43] Eugene Huskey, 'From Legal Nihilism to Pravovoe Gosudarstvo: Soviet Legal Development, 1917–1990', in Donald D. Barry (ed.), *Toward the 'Rule of Law' in Russia? Political and Legal Reform in the Transition Period* (Armonk, NY: M.E. Sharpe, 1992).

considering that article 1 of the 1939 Organisation Statute of the Shaan-ganning Border Region High Court – which, for the first time in CCP history, codified the ideas that the 'court exercises its judicial official powers independently' and 'tribunal presidents and judges carry out their adjudicatory powers independently' – proclaimed 'this statute was drafted on the basis of the Law on Court Organisation promulgated by the national government'.[44] Histories of the PRC legal system typically omit this inconvenient parentage and instead misattribute the roots of adjudicatory independence in the PRC to the Soviet Union.

Among judges who took statutory law seriously and hoped that the CCP might set a higher standard than the Kuomintang, the results were predictable. In a veiled reference to Li Mu'an's tenure on the Shaangan-ning High Court, Xie Juezai wrote in 1944: 'We had this sort of thing happen: certain judicial personnel who were Party members refused to obey Party leadership, and did not implement Party instructions. They used judicial independence as their excuse, and were at odds with leading administrative cadres. But this has nothing to do with judicial independence.'[45]

Despite concerted efforts to stamp out such impertinence, the ten-dency among many judicial cadres to read the law through the lens of Republican controversies survived into the PRC. In 1955, Minister of Justice, Shi Liang, reported to Zhou Enlai that judicial cadres, pulled by the old law standpoint, were veering alarmingly off message in their interpretations of the new PRC Constitution and Law on the Organisa-tion of the People's Courts:

> Their understanding is confused to the point of committing errors. Some do not understand that the legal system and laws of our country and those of capitalist countries have fundamental differences. They are not clear that our past criticism of the hypocrisy of capitalist 'equality before the law' and 'judicial independence' was necessary, still is and will be in the future. They mix those up with 'the law is applied equally to all' and 'the people's courts adjudicate independently, subject only to the law' and other principles that we put forward today, and that gives rise to doubts.[46]

---

[44] 'Statute on the Organization of the Shaanganning Border Region High Court', in Wu and Liu (eds.), *Collected Reference Materials on the Law of Criminal Procedure*, p. 98.

[45] Xie, *Diary of Xie Juezai*, p. 755.

[46] 'Report on Conditions and Issues at the Symposium on the Study and Implementation of the Statute on the Organization of the People's Courts (May 18, 1955)' in *Notices Related to Staffing Work from the State Council Editorial Board, Finance Department, Judicial*

Likewise, in 1956, the president of Beijing's Intermediate People's Court, a veteran cadre with nearly a decade of experience in CCP legal organs, boldly pushed back at extra-judicial Party interference in adjudication. He noted that district courts in the city were deadlocked with the extra-judicial joint Party groups recently established above them over the disposition of live cases. Reflect for a moment on what this meant – the courts were refusing to budge, despite higher Party authorities ordering them to handle specific cases differently.

The intermediate court tried to finesse the issue, but ultimately insisted that the Law on the Organisation of the People's Courts gave the judiciary precedence. If a district joint Party group did not like the result, then it could follow the law, and prevail upon the district procuratorate to lodge an official protest, effectively an appeal. Either way, a court – not an extra-judicial Party group – would have the final say.

> Currently, there are resolutions by the district court adjudication committees that are not in accord with the opinions of district joint Party groups, and the deadlocks are unresolved. In order to prevent these kinds of problems from recurring, we propose that district court adjudication committees not exceed five members, with CCP members in the majority. After vetting from the district committee, they [should be] appointed by the district people's committee. Before a president of a district court sends major cases to [the court's] adjudication committee for discussion, the president should first get a decision from the joint Party group, then send the case to the adjudication committee for discussion and adoption [of the joint Party group decision]. If the opinions of the adjudication committee and the joint Party group differ, then the case should still be decided on the basis of the stipulations of the Law on the Organisation of the People's Courts, and the sentence should be pronounced according to the resolution of the adjudication committee. In addition, it can be resolved according to trial supervision procedure if the procuratorate protests the original decision, or the higher-level court [independently] reviews it, etc.[47]

Such assertiveness ran against the grain of Party ideology and was punished. Two years later, this episode featured prominently in the litany of offences cited when the court's president was declared a rightist. 'He

---

Bureau, and Municipal People's Committee (Beijing Municipal Archive Folio 123–001–00499).

[47] 'Report By the Beijing High and Intermediate People's Courts on Trial Work Conditions (Draft) (1955)' in Collected Reports to the Municipal Committee by Various Work Units of the United Front and Political-Legal System (Beijing Municipal Archive Folio 001–006–01248), p. 12.

completely opposed Party leadership over the courts', and he was not alone.[48] By 1958, a page one editorial in People's Judicature, the internal journal of the Supreme People's Court, laid to rest the debate over which flavour of the rule of law was orthodox by repudiating the concept all together: 'Our law conforms to our country's characteristics, national customs and concrete conditions ... Rightists wanted to use "adjudicatory independence" to oppose the leadership of the Party over judicial work ... Is this rule of law or rule of man? We have rule of man. What is called the rule of man is relying on Party leadership, relying on the masses, giving free rein to the dynamism of human subjectivity.'[49]

That set the dominant tone for the next twenty years, and favourable invocations of the rule of law would not return publicly to CCP discourse until its champions were rehabilitated after Mao died. Indeed, two months before the landmark Third Plenum of the Eleventh Party Congress in 1978, Chen Shouyi, the CCP's leading authority on legal education and a graduate of one of Republican China's most prestigious law schools, made a splash at the first academic law conference held since the Cultural Revolution by provocatively putting the rule of law back on the table. Almost overnight, a vigorous discussion sprang up about the competing ideas of rule of law, rule by man and rule by the Party, with Mao and the trial of the Gang of Four very much the elephants in the room.

An article by Li Buyun, entitled 'Insist on All Citizens Being Equal Before the Law', was one of the earliest such efforts.[50] For authority, it began with quotes from the 1954 Law on the Organisation of the People's Courts, then still in effect, and was written from the perspective that various principles enshrined in that law had yet to be realised because radical ideological positions had derailed them, the implication being that the moment was now ripe to make up for lost time. This observation alone exposes the orthodox genealogy's account of socialist rule of law's Mao-era roots as hollow. Moreover, the following year, Li struck again with a draft article originally entitled 'On Ruling the Country Using Law' (*lun yifa zhiguo*). Awkwardly, this was the same formulation adopted by

---

[48] 'The Rightist Faces of He Zhanjun and He Shenggao Have Been Thoroughly Exposed: Absolutely Never Let Rightist Elements Seize the Leadership of Judicial Organs', *Beijing Daily*, 10 March 1958.

[49] 'Bring the Spirit of on-the-spot Meetings to Practical Work' (1958) 19 *People's Judicature* 4.

[50] Buyun Li, 'Insist That Citizens Are All Equal Before the Law', *People's Daily*, 6 December 1978.

the Nationalist government in 1947 and had never been part of main-stream PRC legal discourse before. Out of caution, Li's article was given a new title upon publication: 'We Must Implement Socialist Rule of Law'.[51]

The new title sprang from an authoritative Party document on 'social-ist rule of law' Li had helped draft at the behest of Hu Yaobang after the 1978 plenum.[52] Known popularly as 'Document 64', this document was pivotal to the post-Mao reconstitution of the legal system. For the first time, the CCP Central Committee formally endorsed 'implementing socialist rule of law as an important standard' and, while some of the text's promise remains unrealised today, it fundamentally changed the climate for legal reform in China by giving ideas regarded as apostasies for much of the Mao era the imprimatur of orthodoxy.[53]

> Party committees and judicial organs each have their own special respon-sibilities. One cannot substitute for the other, and they must not be mixed up. Consequently, the Centre decides to eliminate the system of Party committees approving the adjudication of cases ... Relevant work units and individuals must resolutely implement judgements and decisions issued by judicial organs according to the law, and if they do not agree, they should file an appeal according to judicial procedure, which the relevant judicial organ has the responsibility to accept ... The Party leads judicial work mainly through programmatic and policy leadership. Party committees at various levels must resolutely change the past [practice] of substituting the Party for the government, or of words for law.[54]

Let us step back for a moment to review the dizzying fluctuations the CCP has elided in its schematic pedigree for 'Socialist Rule of Law with Chinese Characteristics'. The concept of the rule of law first achieved currency in Party circles in 1941. At the time, CCP critics rightly connected this to Nationalist influence. The brutal campaign that followed in 1943 to eradicate Nationalist legal ideas and practices from the base areas by labelling them the 'old law standpoint' set a powerful precedent. Nevertheless, every time the Party subsequently reached for

---

[51] Buyun Li, Deyang Wang and Chunlong Chen, 'We Must Implement Socialist Rule of Law', *Guangming Daily*, 2 December 1979.

[52] Buyun Li and Qing Li, 'From "Legal System" to "Rule of Law": 20 Years Changed One Character' (1999) 7 *Legal Science* 3.

[53] Min Cui, 'Document 64: Are Officials or the Law More Important?' (2009) 12 *Annals of the Yellow Emperor*.

[54] 'Instruction of the Central Committee of the Chinese Communist Party on Resolutely Guaranteeing the Conscientious Implementation of the Criminal Law and Criminal Procedure Law (1979)' in Wu and Liu (eds.), *Collected Reference Materials on the Law of Criminal Procedure*, p. 955.

that precedent, it underscored how thoroughly it had assimilated the offending ideas and practices, and how resilient they were. Multiple bouts of self-harm to expunge this unwelcome part of its identity, or at least suppress it, ensued. Unsure of how to deal with that miscegenation, Party historiography has either ignored it or twisted in stupendous knots to avoid it.

For instance, in 1948, Liu Shaoqi reconsecrated the 'rule of law' in the NCPG and proposed in the same breath to adopt revised editions of Nationalist codes. In concert with that, Dong Biwu introduced the supporting ideas of 'handling matters according to law' (*yifa banshi*) and building a state apparatus distinct from the Party.[55] Not coincidentally, this happened just after the Nationalist government shifted the basis of its authority from 'ruling the country using the Party' (*yidang zhiguo*) to 'ruling the country using law' (*yifa zhiguo*), a transition the CCP would echo fifty years later.

The NCPG's rule of law and 'handling matters according to law' evolved into formulations like 'people's revolutionary rule of law' in the early 1950s, and then, in the mid-1950s, reasserted themselves through socialist legality.[56] This came with a palette of strong claims about buffering the state from the Party, and about the importance of codified law and adjudicatory independence. The Anti-Rightist Campaign and the Cultural Revolution drove this discourse underground, but did not extinguish it and, in 1978, it suddenly roared back to life, full of pent-up energy. The following year, the Central Committee formally recognised 'socialist rule of law' in Document 64 and revived the call for recasting the party–state relationship in the legal system.

Then, a step backward into socialist legality occurred in the 1980s, after the Gang of Four trial, followed by a leap forward into socialist rule of law again during the mid-1990s. In 1993, a complementary jump

---

[55] Songfeng Wang, 'The Lessons and Significance of Administering According to Law Thought in the North China People's Government Period', in Jianxin Ren (ed.), *Harbinger of Administering According to Law: Commemorating Study of the Laws and Decrees of the North China People's Government* (Beijing: China Law Society Dong Biwu Legal Thought Study Society, 2011), p. 111; Ji Guo, 'Study the Administrative Experience of the North China People's Government, Advance the Construction of a Service Government: Speech to the 60th Anniversary Symposium Commemorating the Establishment of the North China People's Government', in Jianxin Ren (ed.), *Harbinger of Administering According to Law*, p. 10.

[56] 'Strengthen and Consolidate the People's Revolutionary Rule of Law', *People's Daily*, 5 September 1951.

occurred when the Central Committee widened debate about the rule of law and marketisation by publicly endorsing the iconic NCPG slogan 'handling matters according to law' (*yifa banshi*) for the first time. Through this, it introduced the related concept of 'administering according to law' (*yifa xingzheng*), which in short order became 'ruling the country according to law' (*yifa zhiguo*), a slogan the Party hastened to distinguish from the similar sounding 'ruling the country using law', once favoured by the Nationalists and reintroduced by Li Buyun three decades later.[57] Notably, Guo Daohui observed at the time that the meaning of 'administering according to law' and 'ruling the country according to law' was for all intents and purposes identical.[58] But the change in wording suited the circumstances and was part of a larger plan; in 1999, 'socialist rule of law' and 'ruling the country according to law' entered the PRC constitution together, each for the first time.

Such discursive acrobatics are necessary in the arcane, ritualised world of Party doctrine. They provide a mechanism for adaptation within the ostensibly timeless frame of CCP orthodoxy, where the nuances of every slogan are scrutinised carefully. By reaching into the past for serviceable precedents with revolutionary pedigrees, they confer legitimacy on present goals, burnish the gilt of CCP exceptionalism and inoculate the legal system against competing, foreign sources of authority. Of course, the irony is that there is not much here that is peculiarly socialist. With every passing year, the attempts by the Party to insist otherwise grow more laboured, and perhaps more suggestive of its own insecurities on this point.

Today the CCP's talents for reinvention are being put to new purposes. For decades, the Party tried hard to bury its early assignations with the rule of law because its uncompromising revolutionary line on the abrogation of the Nationalist legal system left no room for 'capitalist' legal constructs. Now that the CCP has embraced the market and wears the rule of law like a badge, controlling the narrative is of equal concern, but in a different way.

When it comes to the professionalised judiciary, academic legal education and a host of affiliated concepts such as adjudicatory independence,

---

[57] 'Decision of the Central Committee of the Chinese Communist Party on Certain Questions in Establishing a Socialist Market Economy System', *People's Daily*, 17 November 1993.

[58] 'Summary of the Academic Symposium on Ruling the Country According to Law and Constructing a Socialist Rule of Law Country' (1996) 18(3) *Chinese Journal of Law* 7.

equality before the law and the presumption of innocence, the road unavoidably leads back to Republican sources. As we have seen, the official 2009 textbook on socialist rule of law deals with this awkward history by ignoring it, as does a more recent supporting line of scholarship. What is more, they construct an alternative backstory that turns the past on its head by suggesting that the Party championed those institutions and ideas, when it more often attacked and strained to eradicate them.[59]

Just the same, positions that were heterodox in the 1950s, and progressive in the 1980s now sustain an originalist brief for conservatism. They demonstrate how far the CCP has come, but also reveal the limits of how much further it is willing to go. Grafted on to a market economy, the only discernible traces of 'socialism' in the CCP's version of the rule of law are forceful statism and a declarative identification with the popular will, made manifest through its rightful representative, the vanguard party.[60] This is, more properly, twentieth-century authoritarianism of a very pedestrian sort. Insofar as the CCP is proclaiming a vision of legal modernity that celebrates exceptionalism, promotes neo-traditionalism, demands social and administrative discipline, and upholds the supremacy of one-party rule, it is not breaking new ground, but recapitulating a defensive crouch pioneered in China three generations ago by the Kuomintang. From the Party's perspective, it is apparently far better to sidestep that history than to acknowledge how the argument has come full circle, and to invite unwelcome comparisons.

Only time will tell if the Party's reconstruction of the past will buoy the legal system and help to ameliorate some of the congenital defects that

---

[59] Runshi Yang, 'From Handling Matters According to Law to Ruling the Country According to Law: Comment on the Theoretical Contribution of Dong Biwu to the Construction of the Socialist Legal System', in Mingshan Zhu and Wangzhong Sun (eds.), *Collected Research into the Legal Thought of Dong Biwu: Commemorating the 115th Anniversary of Comrade Dong Biwu's Birth* (Beijing: People's Courts Press, 2001); Central Committee of the Chinese Communist Party, *Textbook on the Concept of Socialist Rule of Law*; Chunyan Zhao, *The Initial Dream: Discourse and Practice in the Legal System During the Early Period of New China's Construction* (Beijing: Law Press, 2012). Long Li, *Outline of the Theoretical System of Socialist Rule of Law with Chinese Characteristics* (Wuhan: Wuhan University Press, 2012).

[60] 'Decision of the Central Committee of the Chinese Communist Party Concerning Certain Major Questions in Comprehensively Advancing Ruling the Country According to Law'; 'Explanation of the "Decision of the Central Committee of the Chinese Communist Party Concerning Certain Major Questions in Comprehensively Advancing Ruling the Country According to Law"', *People's Daily*, 29 October 2014; Xiaodong Ding, 'Law According to the Chinese Communist Party: Constitutionalism and Socialist Rule of Law' (2017) 43(3) *Modern China*.

have weighed heavily on reformers for decades. Based on experience and the recent tightening of archival access on relevant documents, the prospects are not encouraging. If the CCP succeeds in exercising a proprietary claim over the rule of law and converts yet another rich aspect of China's legal heritage into a neatly sculpted, fenced off topiary in the garden of Party history, then it will have lamentably robbed the concept of much of its dynamism, and starved PRC legal reform of its fullest potential.

5

The Soviet Legacy and Its Impact on Contemporary Vietnam

PHAM DUY NGHIA AND DO HAI HA

5.1 Introduction

Decades after the collapse of the Soviet Union and the Eastern bloc, Vietnam remains one of a few countries that portrays itself as a socialist state. Nevertheless, the country has also undergone enormous transformations since the Communist Party of Vietnam (CPV or Party) launched its economic program – *Đổi mới* – in 1986. Walking along the lively streets in Hanoi or Ho Chi Minh City, formerly Saigon, it is easy to observe that the capitalist market is present at every corner of life in Vietnam. Not much nostalgia for the Soviet era is left. Vietnam is now said to develop a market-oriented economy which has increasingly integrated into the global market.

However, the Soviet-style economic, political and legal systems that once existed in Vietnam have not entirely disappeared. The CPV now labels its new economic model as a 'socialist-oriented' economy. The international media regularly characterises Vietnam as a Marxist–Leninist state with one-party rule and limited spaces for secondary associations and dissident behaviour. Rejecting the Western rule-of-law concept, the CPV is developing a 'socialist law-based state'.[1]

This Chapter seeks to understand to what extent the Soviet legacy has endured, and how fundamental socialist ideals and Marxist–Leninist principles continue to transform and influence contemporary Vietnam. Drawing on desk research, the Chapter argues that socialist and Marxist–Leninist conceptions play an important role in the economic, political and legal systems of contemporary Vietnam. However, while these conceptions endure, the fundamental socialist ideals underpinning Marxism–Leninism have gradually lost their influence.

The authors would like to express sincere thanks for the insightful comments made by Professors John Gillespie and Pip Nicholson on early versions of this Chapter.
[1] See Art. 2.1, Constitution 2013.

The next section of this Chapter chronicles the importation of Soviet economic, political and legal models into Vietnam during the high socialist era. The third section highlights economic changes since 1986 and the persistent, but eroding, impact of socialist and Marxist–Leninist economic thinking. Section four reviews political developments after *Đổi mới*, showing that Leninist political principles continue to dominate the Vietnamese polity. The fifth section reviews the transformation of the legal system since economic reforms have been introduced and the imprint of the Soviet legacy on this process. The last section concludes with general reflections on the endurance, transformation and influence of the Soviet legacy in transitional Vietnam.

5.2   Pre-*Đổi mới* Socialist Vietnam and the Importation of Soviet-Style Economic, Political and Legal Models

The Democratic Republic of Vietnam (DRVN) declared independence in 1945. Yet the French attempt to re-assert its colonial regime resulted in a war between France and the *Việt Minh*, a Vietnamese communist-led nationalist movement. This war, known as the First Indochina War, lasted until the conclusion of the 1954 Geneva Peace Accords, according to which national elections would be held within two years to determine the future of Vietnam. However, such elections did not take place, leading to the split of the country into two states at war with each other (the Second Indochina or Vietnam War) for two decades. North of the seventeenth parallel was the DRVN or North Vietnam, a communist state receiving support from the Soviet Union, China and other communist countries. South of the line was the Republic of Vietnam ('RVN') or South Vietnam, a capitalist state backed by the United States and the Western alliance. This protracted war ended in 1975 with the collapse of the Southern regime. A year later, the country was formally reunited as the Socialist Republic of Vietnam.[2]

Along with its growing ties with communist states, the DRVN gradually developed Soviet-style economic, political and legal systems – namely, a centrally planned economy, a Leninist political system and a socialist legal system.[3] This process can be traced back to at least the early 1950s, when

---

[2]   See Melanie Beresford, *Vietnam: Politics, Economics, and Society* (London: Pinter Publishers, 1988), pp. 17–52 for a brief history of Vietnam from the 1945 declaration of independence to the 1975 national reunification.

[3]   Carlyle A. Thayer, 'Mono-Organisational Socialism and the State', in Benedict J. Tria Kerkvliet and Doug J. Porter (eds.), *Vietnam's Rural Transformation* (Boulder, CO: Westview Press; Institute of Southeast Asian Studies, 1995), pp. 39, 44–46; Melanie Beresford, 'Vietnam: The Transition from Central Planning', in Garry Rodan, Kevin

the CPV began to receive extensive support from the People's Republic of China and, to a lesser degree, the Soviet Union in the form of military aid, policy advice and technical expertise.[4] The importation of Soviet-style models accelerated in 1958 (as the DRVN officially commenced to construct socialism in northern Vietnam)[5] and these models were extended to southern Vietnam after the 1975 national reunification.

5.2.1   Developing a Centrally Planned Economy

Inspired by the Chinese and, to a lesser extent, Soviet examples, the DRVN undertook an agrarian reform in 1953–1956 to redistribute land from landlords and rich peasants to poor and middle-class peasants, followed in 1958 by a large-scale collectivisation of agriculture.[6] In 1960, the CPV announced the first five-year plan to pursue 'socialist industrialisation' (following the nationalisation of industrial factories in 1958–1960).[7] By the mid-1960s, North Vietnam was basically a Soviet-style economy, based chiefly on public ownership of the means of production and a comprehensive command system whereby the state extensively regulated economic activities.[8] Once the country was reunified, the CPV employed rapid and radical measures to export this economic model south.[9]

Like other Marxist–Leninist parties, the CPV declared that public ownership and central planning were necessary to eliminate the economic foundation of the old (in the case of Vietnam, half-colonial/half-feudal) society, and to construct a new economy which would be more efficient, free from exploitation and mastered by the working class.[10]

Hewison and Richard Robison (eds.), *The Political Economy of South-East Asia: Markets, Power and Contestation* (Oxford: Oxford University Press, 3rd edn., 2006), pp. 197, 199–200; Pip Nicholson, 'Renovating Courts: The Role of Courts in Contemporary Vietnam', in Jiunn-Rong Yeh and Wen-Chen Chang (eds.), *Asian Courts in Context* (Cambridge: Cambridge University Press, 2014), pp. 528, 529–530.

[4] See, e.g., William J. Duiker, *Ho Chi Minh* (Crows Nest: Allen & Unwin, 2000), pp. 425–440; Vu Tuong, 'Workers and the Socialist State: North Vietnam's State – Labour Relations, 1945–1970' (2005) 38 *Communist and Post-Communist Studies* 329, 334.

[5] See DRVN National Assembly, *Nghị quyết về nhiệm vụ kế hoạch 3 năm và kế hoạch phát triển kinh tế năm 1958* [Resolution on the Tasks of the Three-Year Plan and the Plan for Economic Development in 1958] (29 April 1958).

[6] Beresford, 'Vietnam', pp. 199–200.

[7] Ibid., p. 200.

[8] Ibid.

[9] Ibid., pp. 151–152; Charles Harvie and Tran Van Hoa, *Vietnam's Reforms and Economic Growth* (Hampshire: MacMillan Press Ltd, 1997), pp. 34–39.

[10] CPV, *Nhiệm vụ và phương hướng của Kế hoạch 5 năm lần thứ nhất phát triển kinh tế quốc dân (1961–1965)* [Tasks and Orientations of the First Five-Year Plan for the

The adoption of the Soviet economic model did not merely reflect the socialist criticism of capitalism, the socialist ideal of public ownership and a Marxist–Leninist emphasis on economic central planning. To a degree, it was also to secure Chinese and Soviet aid, which was vital to the success of the DRVN in the First and Second Indochina Wars.[11] Further, it was believed that some economic measures, like land reforms, would help the Party to win popular support for its military efforts.[12]

Despite resembling a planned economy, the Vietnamese socialist economy, however, differed from its European counterparts in two respects. It had a more decentralised state sector which allowed a high degree of practical autonomy within local economic units.[13] In addition, it had a larger informal, private sector, a consequence of 'fence breaking' (*phá rào*) practices – namely, spontaneous unplanned activities from below and unorthodox experiments by local authorities.[14]

5.2.2   Installing a Leninist Political System

The construction of a Leninist political system, characterised by the monopolistic and authoritarian rule of the Communist Party, took place in North Vietnam no later than the 1950s.[15] This system was imposed

Development of the National Economy (1961–1965)] (7 September 1960) particularly pt I.2; CPV, *Nghị quyết của Hội nghị Trung ương lần thứ 16 (mở rộng) về vấn đề hợp tác hoá nông nghiệp [Resolution of the 16th (Expanded) Plenum of the Central Committee on Agricultural Collectivisation]* (April 1959) particularly pt. III.1. See also John Murphy, *Socialism and Communism* (Chicago, IL: Britannica Educational Publishing, 2015), pp. 17–18, 26 for general account of ideological ideas behind socialist economics.

[11] See Duiker, *Ho Chi Minh*, p. 440; Võ Nguyên Giáp, *Chiến đấu Trong Vòng vây [Fighting Within an Encirclement]* (Hanoi: Nhà xuất bản Quân đội nhân dân [People's Army Publishing House], 1995), p. 412.

[12] See CPV, *Cương lĩnh về vấn đề ruộng đất [Political Program for the Issue of Agricultural Land]* (November 1953) noting that land reforms were to mobilise peasants to participate in the Anti-French Resistance War.

[13] Börje Ljunggren, 'Market Economies under Communist Regimes: Reform in Vietnam, Laos and Cambodia', in Börje Ljunggren (ed.), *The Challenge of Reform in Indochina* (Cambridge, MA: Harvard Institute for International Development, Harvard University, 1993), pp. 39, 58; Pietro P. Masina, *Vietnam's Development Strategies* (London: Routledge, 2006), p. 52.

[14] Dang Phong, 'Stages on the Road to Renovation of the Vietnamese Economy: An Historical Perspective', in Melanie Beresford and Angie Ngoc Tran (eds.), *Reaching for the Dream: Challenges of Sustainable Development in Vietnam* (Copenhagen: NIAS, 2004), pp. 19, 40–42; Adam Fforde and Stefan de Vylder, *From Plan to Market: The Economic Transition in Vietnam* (Boulder, CO: Westview Press, 1996), pp. 60–69.

[15] Duiker, *Ho Chi Minh*, p. 429; Thayer, 'Mono-Organisational Socialism and the State', pp. 44–46.

throughout the country after 1975,[16] and has remained very much in place until today. Like several other communist parties, the CPV justified its Soviet-inspired political system based on two ideological propositions.[17] One is that socialism can be achieved only through the establishment of 'dictatorship of the proletariat' (*chuyên chính vô sản*).[18] The other proposition is that the working class does not exercise its dictatorship directly, but through the leadership of a 'vanguard party' (*đảng tiên phong*) – namely, the communist party.[19]

As a Leninist party, the CPV has operated on the principle of 'democratic centralism' (*tập trung dân chủ*),[20] which contains two essential aspects. The democratic aspect encourages wide circulation and discussion of pluralist and conflicting views in decision-making.[21] Meanwhile, the centralist aspect requires all party members to unquestionably comply with decisions that have been made by majority vote.[22] Though permitting pluralism, the actual priority of this principle is centralism, as demonstrated in the following Party rule:

> All party resolutions must be observed unconditionally. Party members must follow party organizations; the minority must yield to the majority; lower organizations must obey upper organizations; [and] party organizations throughout the country must submit to the National Representative Congress and the Central Executive Committee.[23]

As in other Leninist political systems,[24] the CPV maintained absolute control over the political system by setting policy orientation and directing the operation of all members of this system, including representative

---

[16] See generally Beresford, *Vietnam*, pp. 79–126.

[17] See Janos Kornai, *The Socialist System: The Political Economy of Communism* (Oxford: Oxford University Press, 1992), pp. 49–61 for a general account of political ideology and its relation to power structures in communist states.

[18] Lê Duẩn, 'Tăng cường Pháp chế Xã hội Chủ nghĩa, Bảo đảm Quyền Làm Chủ Tập thể Của Nhân dân: Bài Nói Tại Hội nghị Toàn Ngành Kiểm sát Ngày 22 Tháng 3 Năm 1967' [*Enhancing Socialist Legality, Guaranteeing the People's Mastery: Speech Delivered at the Procuracies' Conference on 22 March 1967*] in Lê Duẩn (ed.), *Cách mạng Xã hội Chủ nghĩa Tại Việt Nam. Tập I* [*Socialist Revolution in Vietnam. Vol I*] (Hanoi: Nhà Xuất bản Sự thật [Truth Publishing House], 1980), pp. 594, 596–599.

[19] Ibid., pp. 620–624.

[20] See, e.g., Art. 10, CPV Statute 1960. See also Kornai, *The Socialist System*, pp. 34–35 for a general account of democratic centralism.

[21] See, e.g., Art. 10, CPV Statute 1960.

[22] Ibid.

[23] Ibid., Art 10.6. See also Kornai, *The Socialist System*, pp. 17, 35 for a similar situation in other communist states.

[24] See Kornai, *The Socialist System*, pp. 33–48 for a general account of Leninist political systems.

bodies, administrative agencies, judicial institutions, military forces and mass organisations.[25] To give effect to its policy choices and directive instructions, the Party relied on its control over the appointment of leadership positions in other political institutions, and the penetration of the party apparatus into every functional branch, territorial level and organisational unit of the state and mass organisations.[26]

The CPV did not recognise pluralism in political life. Party ideology and policy were essentially non-contestable, and political opposition was by and large unacceptable.[27] Nor were there free elections,[28] given their potential to challenge Party supremacy. The space for secondary associations was limited, and was occupied by state-sponsored organisations, such as sectoral mass organisations (e.g. those for workers, peasants, women and youth) and special interest/professional groups (e.g. those for lawyers, researchers and writers).[29] These organisations played a dual function in state-society relations: mobilising the masses to carry out Party policy, on the one hand; and communicating their voices to the Party, on the other hand.[30] Yet, since these organisations were subordinate to the Party, the mobilisation function often prevailed.[31]

As in other communist states, the CPV also tightly controlled the media through state ownership, censorship and control over media personnel, including leadership staff, and through the monitoring by party cells and members within media organisations.[32] As such, the media was essentially

---

[25] Thayer, 'Mono-Organisational Socialism and the State', p. 44.

[26] Ibid., p. 45.

[27] Carlyle A. Thayer, 'Political Reform in Vietnam: Đổi Mới and the Emergence of Civil Society', in Robert F. Miller (ed.), *The Developments of Civil Society in Communist Systems* (Crows Nest: Allen & Unwin, 1992), pp. 110, 111; Jonathan London, 'Vietnam and the Making of Market-Leninism' (2009) 22(3) *The Pacific Review* 375, 379.

[28] Gareth Porter, *Vietnam: The Politics of Bureaucratic Socialism* (Ithaca, NY: Cornell University Press, 1993), pp. 153–156.

[29] Thayer, 'Political Reform in Vietnam', p. 111.

[30] Edwin Shanks et al., 'Understanding Pro-Poor Political Change: The Policy Process – Vietnam' (Report, Overseas Development Institute, April 2004), pp. 36–37.

[31] Tran Thi Thu Trang, 'Local Politics and Democracy in Muong Ethnic Community', in Benedict J. Tria Kerkvliet and David G. Marr (eds.), *Beyond Hanoi: Local Government in Vietnam* (Copenhagen: NIAS Press; Institute of Southeast Asian Studies, 2004), pp. 137, 146. For a general situation in communist states, see Vu Tuong, 'Workers under Communism: Romance and Reality', in Stephen A. Smith (ed.), *The Oxford Handbook of the History of Communism* (Oxford: Oxford University Press, 2014), pp. 471, 479–480.

[32] London, 'Vietnam and the Making of Market-Leninism', 379; Benedict J. Tria Kerkvliet, 'Authorities and the People: An Analysis of State-Society Relations in Vietnam', in Hy V. Luong (ed.), *Postwar Vietnam: Dynamics of a Transforming Society* (Singapore: Institute of Southeast Asian Studies; Lanham, Md: Rowman & Littlefield, 2003), pp. 27, 37–40.

a vehicle for mass propaganda and mobilisation which, together with the repression of dissident behaviour, constituted the major means for the Party to secure popular support and loyalty.[33]

Notwithstanding Leninist influence, the political system of pre-*Đổi mới* socialist Vietnam allowed more pluralism within the party-state and greater spaces for state-society interaction than its counterparts in China and the Eastern bloc.[34] Arguably, this indicates the inability of the CPV and its central leadership to exert total control over economic, political and social relations. Yet, the higher degree of pluralism and liberalisation in the Vietnamese polity also reflected a more decentralised and polycentric power structure and the CPV's greater responsiveness to pressure from below.[35] This, in turn, had roots in Vietnam's political and cultural traditions, as well as the wartime conditions which required the Party to secure popular support and promote political participation.[36]

5.2.3   Constructing a Socialist Legal System

Soviet jurisprudence gained influence in the DRVN from the early 1950s.[37] However, the extensive borrowing of Soviet-style legal principles and institutions merely took place in North Vietnam from the late 1950s, marked by the adoption of a Soviet-style constitution in 1959 and the introduction of Soviet-style people's courts and procuracies in 1960.[38] This socialist legal system was exported to southern Vietnam after 1975.[39]

---

[33] London, 'Vietnam and the Making of Market-Leninism', 380; Kerkvliet and Marr, *Beyond Hanoi*, pp. 37–40.

[34] Chris Dixon, 'State, Party and Political Change in Vietnam', in Duncan McCargo (ed.), *Rethinking Vietnam* (London: RoutledgeCurzon, 2004), pp. 15, 16–18. See also Chapter 6 this volume.

[35] Ibid., pp. 17–18.

[36] Ibid., p. 17.

[37] See Hồ Chí Minh, 'Trích Bài Nói Của Chủ tịch Hồ Chí Minh Tại Hội nghị Học tập Của Cán bộ Ngành Tư pháp 1950' ['Excerpt of the Speech of President Hồ Chí Minh at the Study Workshop of Judicial Cadres 1950'] in Viện Khoa học Pháp lý [Institute of Legal Science], *Xây dựng Hệ thống Pháp luật và Nền Tư pháp Nhân dân Dưới Sự Lãnh đạo Của Đảng* [*Constructing the Legal System and Judicial System of the People under Party Leadership*] (Hanoi: Nhà Xuất bản Tư pháp [Judicial Publishing House], 2005), p. 18.

[38] Penelope (Pip) Nicholson, *Borrowing Court Systems: The Experience of Socialist Vietnam* (Leiden: Martinus Nijhoff, 2007), p. 1; John Gillespie, 'Concepts of Law in Vietnam: Transforming Statist Socialism', in Randall Peerenboom (ed.), *Asian Discourses of Rule of Law: Theories and Implementation of Rule of Law in Twelve Asian Countries, France and the US* (London: RoutledgeCurzon, 2004), pp. 142, 146.

[39] Nicholson, 'Renovating Courts', pp. 529–530.

As in other communist states, the Vietnamese legal system before Đổi mới was built on the Soviet doctrine of 'socialist legality' (*pháp chế xã hội chủ nghĩa*), which was officially introduced at the 1960 Party Congress.[40] On its face, 'socialist legality' is not so different from 'rule of law', requiring that state bodies, economic and social organisations, public officials and citizens strictly abide by the law.[41] The Soviet doctrine, however, differs from its Western counterpart in that it rests on a class-based, positivist conception of law inspired by Marxism–Leninism. In this conception, law is a system of rules which is promulgated by the state and guaranteed by its coercive measures.[42] Further, law is considered a mere reflection of the 'will of the ruling class' (*ý chí của giai cấp thống trị*) and their control over the means of production.[43] Hence, socialist law serves the interests of the proletariat and their dictatorship.[44]

The Marxist–Leninist conception of law has several implications. It denies the existence of natural law.[45] In addition, it prioritises collective

[40] CPV, *Nghị quyết Của Đại hội Đại biểu Toàn quốc Lần Thứ III Về Nhiệm vụ và Đường lối Của Đảng Trong Giai đoạn Mới* [*Resolution of the Third National Party Congress on the Tasks and Lines of the Party in a New Period*] (10 September 1960), pt. IV.6.

[41] Hoàng Quốc Việt, 'Xây dựng Pháp chế Xã hội Chủ nghĩa và Giáo dục Mọi Người Tôn trọng Pháp luật' ['Developing Socialist Legality and Educating People to Respect the Law'] (1963) (9) *Tạp chí Cộng sản* [*Communist Review*] reproduced in Viện Khoa học Pháp lý [Institute of Legal Science], *Xây dựng Hệ thống Pháp luật và Nền Tư pháp Nhân dân Dưới Sự Lãnh đạo Của Đảng* [*Constructing the Legal System and Judicial System of the People under Party Leadership*] (Hanoi: Nhà Xuất bản Tư pháp [Judicial Publishing House], 2005) pp. 67, 71; Gordon B. Smith, 'Development of Socialist Legality', in F.J.M. Feldbrugge and William B. Simon (eds.), *Perspectives on Soviet Law for the 1980s* (The Hague: Martinus Nijhoff, 1982), pp. 77, 80–91.

[42] Lê Minh Tâm, 'Bản chất, Đặc trưng, Vai trò, Các Kiểu Và Hình thức Pháp luật' ['Nature, Characteristics, Role, Types and Forms of Law'] in Lê Minh Tâm (ed.), *Giáo trình Lý luận Nhà nước Và Pháp luật* [*Textbook on Theory of State and Law*] (Hanoi: Nhà Xuất bản Công an Nhân dân [People's Police Publishing House], 2003), pp. 61, 64; Smith, 'Development of Socialist Legality', p. 77.

[43] Gillespie, 'Concepts of Law in Vietnam', p. 146; Lê Minh Tâm, 'Bản chất, Đặc trưng, Vai trò, Các Kiểu Và Hình thức Pháp luật' ['Nature, Characteristics, Role, Types and Forms of Law'], pp. 61–65.

[44] Hoàng Quốc Việt, 'Xây dựng Pháp chế Xã hội Chủ nghĩa và Giáo dục Mọi Người Tôn trọng Pháp luật' ['Developing Socialist Legality and Educating People to Respect the Law'], pp. 67–71; Lê Duẩn, 'Tăng cường Pháp chế Xã hội Chủ nghĩa, Bảo đảm Quyền Làm Chủ Tập thể Của Nhân dân: Bài Nói Tại Hội nghị Toàn Ngành Kiểm sát Ngày 22 Tháng 3 Năm 1967' ['Enhancing Socialist Legality, Guaranteeing the People's Mastery: Speech Delivered at the Procuracies' Conference on 22 March 1967'], p. 634.

[45] Gillespie, 'Concepts of Law in Vietnam', p. 146; Lê Minh Tâm, 'Bản chất, Đặc trưng, Vai trò, Các Kiểu Và Hình thức Pháp luật' ['Nature, Characteristics, Role, Types and Forms of Law'], p. 61.

interests over individual rights.[46] Marxist–Leninist jurisprudence does not position law higher than the state; rather, it requires that law derive from and be enforced by the state.[47] Significantly, as party leadership is deemed essential for proletariat dictatorship, socialist law becomes a political instrument of the communist party.[48] Put differently, socialist law is not regarded as a means to protect citizens' rights, but as a tool of party leadership and state governance.[49] As a corollary, law is generally subordinate to and replaceable by party policy and administrative commands, a common practice in pre-*Đổi mới* Vietnam.[50] Similarly, legal institutions, including the courts, are never meant to be independent, but a political vehicle in the hands of the party-state.[51]

Though substantially replicating a Soviet-style legal system, the Vietnamese legal system in the high socialist era remained unique. Compared with its Eastern European counterparts, the CPV placed a stronger emphasis on leadership through revolutionary morality (*đạo đức cách mạng*).[52] The Vietnamese legal practice was also inspired by the Maoist theory of the 'mass line' (*đường lối quần chúng*), which emphasised the importance of popular participation and support and, therefore,

---

[46] V. Gsovski, 'The Soviet Concept of Law' (1938) 7 *Fordham Law Review* 12–3.

[47] Gillespie, 'Concepts of Law in Vietnam', p. 146; Lê Minh Tâm, 'Bản chất, Đặc trưng, Vai trò, Các Kiểu Và Hình thức Pháp luật' ['Nature, Characteristics, Role, Types and Forms of Law'], pp. 68–69.

[48] Hoàng Quốc Việt, 'Tăng cường Pháp chế Trong Sự Hoạt động Kinh tế Của Các Cơ quan, Xí nghiệp Nhà nước' ['Promoting Legality in Economic Activities of State Bodies [and] Enterprises'] (1962) (6) *Tạp chí Cộng sản* [Communist Review] reproduced in Viện Khoa học Pháp lý [Institute of Legal Science], *Xây dựng Hệ thống Pháp luật và Nền Tư pháp Nhân dân Dưới Sự Lãnh đạo Của Đảng* [*Constructing the Legal System and Judicial System of the People under Party Leadership*] (Hanoi: Nhà Xuất bản Tư pháp [Judicial Publishing House], 2005), pp. 55, 61–62; Lê Duẩn, 'Tăng cường Pháp chế Xã hội Chủ nghĩa, Bảo đảm Quyền Làm Chủ Tập thể Của Nhân dân: Bài Nói Tại Hội nghị Toàn Ngành Kiểm sát Ngày 22 Tháng 3 Năm 1967' ['Enhancing Socialist Legality, Guaranteeing the People's Mastery: Speech Delivered at the Procuracies' Conference on 22 March 1967'], p. 637.

[49] Gillespie, 'Concepts of Law in Vietnam', p. 146.

[50] Ibid., p. 147; Nguyen Nhu Phat, 'The Role of Law During the Formation of a Market-Driven Mechanism in Vietnam', in John Gillespie (ed.), *Commercial Legal Development in Vietnam: Vietnamese and Foreign Commentaries* (Singapore; Hong Kong: Butterworth Asia, 1997), pp. 397, 400–402.

[51] Nicholson, *Borrowing Court Systems*, pp. 196–197; Porter, *Vietnam*, pp. 14–15.

[52] Nguyễn Khắc Viện, *Tradition and Revolution in Vietnam* (Berkeley, CA: Indochina Resource Centre, 1975), p. 50. See also Gillespie, 'Concepts of Law in Vietnam', pp. 145–146; Margaret Kohn and Keally McBride, *Political Theories of Decolonisation: Postcolonialism and the Problem of Foundations* (Oxford: Oxford University Press, 2011), pp. 61–68; Shaun Kingsley Malarney, 'Culture, Virtue, and Political Transformation in Contemporary Northern Viet Nam' (1997) 56(4) *The Journal of Asian Studies* 899, 907–909.

promoted the use of motivating the masses ('mass mobilisation') (*dân vận*) to assist with bureaucratic and legal work.[53] As a result, Vietnamese party-state officials were encouraged to adopt a flexible and outcome-oriented rather than a principle-based approach to legal problems.[54] This not only weakened the role of law and legal institutions, but also encouraged flexible interpretation and application of or even departure from legal rules in view of moral precepts or political expediency.[55] As a result, Vietnam's pre–*Đổi mới* socialist legal system was considerably less developed than the legal systems in the Eastern bloc.[56]

In summary, the Vietnamese economic, political and legal systems in the high socialist era substantially replicated Soviet-style models, which were built on both fundamental socialist ideals and Marxist–Leninist principles. Nonetheless, considerable divergence existed between the Vietnamese system and its Soviet parent, which appeared to stem from local conditions, culture and traditions as well as the Chinese influence.

5.3   From Socialist Planned to Socialist-Oriented Market Economy: *Đổi mới* and Influence of Socialist and Marxist–Leninist Economic Thinking

5.3.1   A Snapshot of Đổi mới

The CPV initiated an ambitious program for socialist construction soon after the 1975 reunification.[57] However, the socialist economy quickly

---

[53] John Gillespie, 'Changing Concepts of Socialist Law in Vietnam', in John Gillespie and Pip Nicholson (eds.), *Asian Socialism & Legal Change: The Dynamics of Vietnamese and Chinese Reform* (Canberra: Australian National University E Press: Asia Pacific Press, 2005), pp. 45, 49; Hoàng Quốc Việt, 'Về Sự Lãnh đạo Của Đảng Đối với Viện Kiểm sát Nhân dân' ['Party Leadership over the People's Procuracies'] (Speech delivered at Hội nghị Tổng hợp Ngành Kiểm sát [Procuracies' Conference], Hà Nội, October 1966) reproduced in Viện Kiểm sát Nhân dân Tỉnh Đăk Lăk [The People's Procuracy of Dak Lak], 20 May 2015, available at http://vksdaklak.gov.vn/index.php?option=com_content&task=view&id=4296&Itemid=306

[54] For further elaboration, see Do Hai Ha, *The Dynamics of Legal Transplantation: Regulating Industrial Conflicts in Post-Đổi mới Vietnam* (PhD Thesis, University of Melbourne, 2016), pp. 69–72.

[55] See Nicholson, 'Renovating Courts', p. 529.

[56] See John Gillespie, 'Understanding Legality in Vietnam', in Stephanie Balme and Mark Sidel (eds.), *Vietnam's New Order: International Perspectives on the State and Reform in Vietnam* (New York, NY: Palgrave Macmillan, 2007), pp. 137, 145; Nicholson, *Borrowing Court Systems*, pp. 224–227.

[57] CPV, *Báo cáo chính trị của Ban chấp hành Trung ương Đảng tại Đại hội đại biểu toàn quốc lần thứ IV* [Political Report of the Central Executive Committee at the 4th National Party Congress] (14 December 1976).

suffered from stagnation and decline.[58] The late 1970s saw a grave economic crisis, characterised by widespread shortages of food, crucial shortfalls in material supplies and severe reduction in industrial output.[59] These economic difficulties triggered 'fence breaking' activities.[60] Production units and local authorities increasingly employed flexible solutions that tested the boundaries or even explicitly violated central regulations (such as selling industrial products to the market or applying contract systems in agriculture).[61] The prevalence of spontaneous change and the gravity of the economic crisis resulted in increasing policy debates within the party-state, leading to partial decentralisation reforms in agriculture and industrial enterprises between 1979 and 1981.[62] These reforms, followed by recentralisation attempts in 1982–1985, were inadequate to save the economy.[63] By the mid-1980s, Vietnam's economy nearly collapsed, facing acute economic problems such as hyperinflation, food shortages and structural imbalances.[64] This generated widespread civil disobedience and unrest,[65] threatening the legitimacy and survival of the regime. Against this background, the 1986 Party Congress launched a bold program of economic reforms: Đổi mới.

Under the slogan of Đổi mới, the CPV implemented a series of fundamental market-oriented reforms, including decollectivising agriculture, liberalising prices and trade, restructuring state enterprises and promoting a private economy.[66] Incremental reforms were also made in respect of external economic policy, such as extending foreign

---

[58] Harvie and Tran, *Vietnam's Reforms and Economic Growth*, p. 39; Brian Van Arkadie and Raymond Mallon, *Viet Nam – A Transition Tiger?* (Canberra: ANU Press, Asia Pacific Press, 2004), p. 47.

[59] Beresford, *Vietnam*, p. 154; Harvie and Tran, *Vietnam's Reforms and Economic Growth*, p. 39.

[60] Fforde and De Vylder, *From Plan to Market*, p. 130.

[61] Ibid., pp. 130–131; Dang Phong, 'Stages on the Road to Renovation of the Vietnamese Economy', pp. 31–35.

[62] Fforde and De Vylder, *From Plan to Market*, pp. 131–132; Harvie and Tran, *Vietnam's Reforms and Economic Growth*, pp. 41–46.

[63] Fforde and De Vylder, *From Plan to Market*, pp. 131–143; Harvie and Tran, *Vietnam's Reforms and Economic Growth*, pp. 41–48.

[64] Fforde and De Vylder, *From Plan to Market*, pp. 142–143; Harvie and Tran, *Vietnam's Reforms and Economic Growth*, p. 48.

[65] For various illustrations see Tuổi trẻ [The Youth], Đêm trước Đổi mới [The Night before Đổi mới] (Ho Chi Minh City: Nhà Xuất bản Trẻ [Youth Publishing House], 2006), compiling fifteen articles originally published in Tuổi trẻ Newspaper between 2005–2006.

[66] Harvie and Tran, *Vietnam's Reforms and Economic Growth*, pp. 49–60; Van Arkadie and Mallon, *Viet Nam – A Transition Tiger?*, pp. 68–75.

economic relations beyond the socialist bloc, easing foreign trade limitations, endorsing a more export-oriented strategy and encouraging foreign investment.[67] Consequently, Vietnam gradually shifted from a closed, planned economy towards a more open, market-oriented economy.

Unlike market transitions in post-communist Eastern Europe, Đổi mới was not a sudden reform, but a gradual process.[68] It also differed from the Chinese economic reform in that it was more spontaneous and bottom-up.[69] It was the economic crisis from the late 1970s that triggered 'fence-breaking' activities, forcing the top party leadership to accept incremental reforms.[70] At first, these reforms were merely intended to save the planned economy rather than to promote a new (market-oriented) economic model.[71] Yet, through this incremental process, the planned economy was gradually dismantled and transformed into some form of market economy. Initially labelled as a 'multi-sectoral commodity economy' (kinh tế hàng hoá nhiều thành phần), it was renamed 'socialist-oriented market economy' (kinh tế thị trường định hướng xã hội chủ nghĩa) in the 2001 Party Congress.[72]

5.3.2   The Persistence of Socialist and Marxist–Leninist Influences

While endorsing a more market-oriented economy, Đổi mới has never meant abandonment of orthodox socialism and Marxism–Leninism. As demonstrated below, socialist and Marxist–Leninist thinking has had a strong impact on economic policy and practice throughout the post-Đổi mới era.

To begin with, the CPV relied on Marxist–Leninist conceptions to justify its departure from the Soviet economic model. In particular, the

---

[67] Pietro P. Masina, *Vietnam's Development Strategies* (London: Routledge, 2006) p. 100–112; Vu Tuan Anh, 'Economic Policy Reforms: An Introductory Overview', in Irene Nørlund, Carolyn Gates and Vu Cao Dam (eds.), *Vietnam in a Changing World* (Florence: Taylor and Francis, 1995), pp. 25–26.

[68] Masina, *Vietnam's Development Strategies*, pp. 71–72.

[69] Đặng Phong, 'Phá rào' Trong Kinh tế Vào Đêm trước Đổi mới ['Fence Breaking' in the Economic Sphere on the Eve of Đổi mới] (Hanoi: Nhà Xuất bản Tri thức [Knowledge Publishing House], 2009), p. 487.

[70] Ibid., pp. 491–493.

[71] See CPV, *Báo cáo chính trị của Ban chấp hành Trung ương Đảng tại Đại hội đại biểu toàn quốc lần thứ VI* [Political Report of the Central Executive Committee at the 6th National Party Congress] (15 December 1986) ('Political Report 1986').

[72] Pham Duy Nghia, 'From Marx to Market: The Debates on the Economic System in Vietnam's Revised Constitution' (2016) 11(2) *Asian Journal of Comparative Law* 263, 268.

Party argued that the continuing existence of non-socialist economic sectors is unavoidable during the transition to socialism.[73] This argument rests on the proposition of Marxist–Leninist historical materialism that the relations of production must be compatible with the nature and developmental level of production forces.[74] Based on this proposition, the Party reasoned that because its production forces remained under-developed, Vietnam could not immediately eliminate the private economy.[75] Further, Lenin's New Economic Policy (NEP) endorses a mixed economy during the transitional era.[76] This indicates that the CPV did not intend to abandon, but only reinterpret, orthodox Marxist–Leninist conceptions.

Significantly, socialist and Marxist–Leninist ideas continue to shape post-*Đổi mới* economic policy and practice. This is evident in the endorsement of three essential principles in the CPV's vision and implementation of the 'socialist-oriented market economy'. The first is 'party leadership' (*sự lãnh đạo của đảng*).[77] This principle upholds the leadership role of the CPV in setting economic policy and its supreme supervision over economic activities and institutions,[78] substantially replicating the Leninist notion of a vanguard party.

The second principle is 'state economic management' (*quản lý nhà nước về kinh tế*).[79] This principle urges the government to extensively intervene in economic affairs to ensure socio-economic and political

---

[73] CPV, *Political Report 1986*, pts. I and II.

[74] Ibid.

[75] Ibid.

[76] Ibid., pt. II.

[77] See, e.g., CPV, *Báo cáo chính trị của Ban chấp hành Trung ương Đảng tại Đại hội đại biểu toàn quốc lần thứ XII* [Political Report of the Central Executive Committee at the 12th National Party Congress] (January 2016) ('Political Report 2016'), pt. IV.2; CPV, *Nghị quyết 21-NQ/TW Về Tiếp tục Hoàn thiện Thể chế Kinh tế Thị trường Định hướng Xã hội Chủ nghĩa* [Resolution 21-NQ/TW on Developing Socialist-Oriented Market Economy Institutions] (30 January 2008) pts. I.2, II.5.

[78] See generally, Nguyễn Minh Tuấn, 'Tiếp tục Đổi mới Nội dung, Phương thức Lãnh đạo Kinh tế Của Đảng' ['Continuing the Reform of the Substance [and] Methods of the Party's Economic Leadership'] (2014) *Tạp chí Cộng sản Điện tử* [*Communist Review Online*], available at www.tapchicongsan.org.vn/Home/xay-dung-dang/2014/27193/Tiep-tuc-doi-moi-noi-dung-phuong-thuc-lanh-dao-kinh-te.aspx.

[79] For the recognition of this principle in Party documents since 1986, see Nguyễn Thanh Tuấn, 'Kinh tế Thị trường Định hướng Xã hội Chủ nghĩa Qua Các Văn kiện Của Đảng Trong Thời kỳ Đổi mới' ['Socialist-Oriented Market Economy in Party Documents of the *Đổi mới* Era'] (2016) *Tạp chí Cộng sản Điện tử* [*Communist Review Online*], available at www.tapchicongsan.org.vn/Home/xay-dung-dang/2016/37544/Kinh-te-thi-truong-dinh-huong-xa-hoi-chu-nghia-qua-cac.aspx.

objectives.[80] For this purpose, the government has been encouraged to utilise various means, including – among other things – large-scale public investments; tight control of the banking and finance system; price controls on several commodities; state enterprises; and strict licensing regulations.[81]

The third essential principle endorsed by the CPV is the 'leading role' (*vai trò chủ đạo*) of the socialist – cooperative and state – economic sectors.[82] It has urged the government to provide the socialist sectors, especially state-owned enterprises (SOEs), with substantial preferential treatment regarding market entrance, access to capital and resources and governmental subsidies, to name a few.[83] Accordingly, it has substantially impeded the growth of the private sector, especially in the early stage of *Đổi mới*.[84]

The emphasis on state economic management and state sector domination reveal that the socialist ideal of public ownership and social control of the means of production and the Marxist–Leninist emphasis on state-directed resource allocation continue to significantly influence party-state economic thinking.[85] Yet, while invoked to explain the new economic model, these socialist and Marxist–Leninist principles have been conflated with other economic (developmental/protectionist) perspectives. For instance, the principle of state economic management has been substantiated by the experience of other Asian economies, where the state played a proactive role in coordinating economic activities.[86] Likewise, the CPV justifies the promotion of giant state economic groups

---

[80] Le Thanh Vinh, *Competition Law Transfers in Vietnam from an Interpretive Perspective* (PhD Thesis, Monash University, 2011), pp. 127–128.

[81] See, e.g., Song Hà, 'Nhà nước "Can thiệp Trực tiếp Quá Lớn" Vào Nền Kinh tế' ['"Excessive Direct Intervention" in the Economy by the State'], *VnEconomy* (online), 3 March 2014, available at http://vneconomy.vn/thoi-su/nha-nuoc-can-thiep-truc-tiep-qua-lon-vao-kinh-te-20140303022341964.htm (summarising the Ministry of Planning and Investment's report on the five years' implementation of Party Resolution 21-NQ/TW on socialist-oriented market economy institutions).

[82] See, e.g., CPV, *Báo cáo chính trị của Ban chấp hành Trung ương Đảng tại Đại hội đại biểu toàn quốc lần thứ IX* [*Political Report of the Central Executive Committee at the 9th National Party Congress*] (April 2001) ('Political Report 2001') pt. IV.2; CPV, *Political Report 2016*, pt. IV.2.

[83] Vu-Thanh Tu-Anh, 'The Political Economy of Industrial Development in Vietnam' (Working Paper 2014/158, World Institute for Development Economics Research, United Nations University, December 2014), pp. 2–3.

[84] Ibid.

[85] See particularly CPV, *Political Report 2001*, pt. III.

[86] Le Thanh Vinh, *Competition Law Transfers in Vietnam from an Interpretive Perspective*, p. 131.

on the basis that this would enhance the competitiveness of the Vietnamese economy.[87]

Moreover, the CPV appears to have been inspired more by the Marxist–Leninist emphasis on party leadership and state control than core socialist ideals like material equality and social cooperation. While emphasising the importance of state ownership and management, Party documents have seldom paid substantive attention to other socialist ideals, such as the democratic control of economic resources and redistribution of wealth and income in a socialist-oriented market economy.[88] Put differently, the main concern has been the control of the party-state over economic resources, rather than the use of these resources to achieve socialist objectives.

Finally, the endorsement of state economic management and state sector domination is not merely ideologically oriented. It is also utilised by interest groups within the party-state to protect their economic and political interests and privileges.[89] These groups are diverse, loosely divided along institutional, regional and sectoral lines, and increasingly connected with private business interests.[90] As a result, the endorsement of socialist-inspired economic principles reflects not only socialist commitments, but also crony business interests.[91]

5.3.3   The Erosion of Socialist and Marxist–Leninist Influences

Although socialist and Marxist–Leninist economic thinking has remained significant throughout the post-*Đổi mới* era, it appears to have declined in influence over time as the emergent criticism of state economic management within the party-state exemplifies. Under pressure from international donors, (domestic/foreign) business communities and liberal-oriented scholars, certain party-state officials – including those at the top leadership level – have supported a shift from an interventionist to a facilitative approach to business regulation.[92] This has facilitated some moderate reforms, such as the relaxation of business licensing requirements.[93]

---

[87] Ibid., pp. 162–163.
[88] See, e.g., CPV, *Political Report 2001*, pt. IV.2; CPV, *Political Report 2016*, pt. IV.2.
[89] Pham Duy Nghia, 'From Marx to Market', 279.
[90] Ibid., 278–279; Dixon, 'State, Party and Political Change in Vietnam', p. 19.
[91] Pham Duy Nghia, 'From Marx to Market', 279.
[92] Le Thanh Vinh, *Competition Law Transfers in Vietnam from an Interpretive Perspective*, p. 132.
[93] Ibid., p. 137.

The public ownership ideal and the leading role of the state sector have also been challenged. Relying on empirical data, reform-minded officials have maintained that despite receiving special privileges, the performance of SOEs and their contribution to the economy are significantly lower than private enterprises.[94] Pointing to scandals in state enterprises and land management, they have further argued that public ownership, SOEs and their privileges opened spaces for corruption and mismanagement.[95]

The notions of public ownership and state sector domination have also been contested in theoretical terms. Citing the Marxist–Leninist maxim that 'theory must be proved by practice', reform-minded officials have contended that these notions are not supported by the experience of Vietnam (before and after Đổi mới) and other socialist states.[96] Some have also stressed that classical socialist theorists like Marx did not envisage a complete picture of socialism, but only offered certain suggestions and predictions.[97] In addition, reform-minded officials have argued that the state and private sectors should be treated equally,[98] echoing neoliberal economic thinking.

Liberal-oriented party-state officials have failed to press for the abandonment of the leading role of the state economic sector. Nevertheless, their attempts have gradually reshaped the Party's view about both the state and private sectors. In particular, the CPV has redefined the leading role of the state economic sector to accommodate criticism.

At first, it was defined as SOEs occupying a significant share of the economy.[99] Subsequently, state sector domination has been reinterpreted

---

[94] Ibid., p. 152.

[95] See, e.g., Toan Le, 'Interpreting the Constitutional Debate Over Land Ownership in the Socialist Republic of Vietnam (2012–2013)' (2016) 11(2) *Asian Journal of Comparative Law* 287, 297–299; Thu Hằng, 'Hãy Để Kinh tế Nhà nước Cạnh tranh Bình đẳng' ['Let the State Sector Compete [with Other Sectors] in a Fair Manner'], *Pháp luật Thành phố Hồ Chí Minh* [HCMC Law] reproduced in *Dân trí* (online), 31 August 2010, available at http://dantri.com.vn/kinh-doanh/hay-de-kinh-te-nha-nuoc-canh-tranh-binh-dang-419136.htm; V. V. Thành, 'Xác định Rõ Vai trò Kinh tế Nhà nước' ['Clarifying the Role of the State Sector'], *Tuổi trẻ* [*The Youth*] (online), 8 October 2010, available at http://tuoitre.vn/tin/kinh-te/20101008/xac-dinh-ro-vai-tro-kinh-te-nha-nuoc/404516.html.

[96] See Le Thanh Vinh, *Competition Law Transfers in Vietnam from an Interpretive Perspective*, p. 152; Toan Le, 'Interpreting the Constitutional Debate Over Land Ownership in the Socialist Republic of Vietnam (2012–2013)', 294–295.

[97] Le Thanh Vinh, *Competition Law Transfers in Vietnam from an Interpretive Perspective*, p. 152.

[98] See Huy Đức, *Bên Thắng Cuộc: II. Quyền Bính* [*The Winning Side: II. The Power*] (Los Angeles, CA: OsinBook, 2012), ch. XXI.

[99] Ibid.; Le Thanh Vinh, *Competition Law Transfers in Vietnam from an Interpretive Perspective*, pp. 145–146.

as the SOEs' capacity to intervene, control and regulate the economy, particularly in key econmic fields and domains.[100] This changed definition has paved the way for a slow process of SOE reform and equitisation since the late 1990s.[101]

The policy regarding the private sector has also significantly changed. Substantially restricted in the early phase of Đổi mới, private enterprises were subsequently permitted to 'develop to unlimited scope and locations in those industries not prohibited by law' and, more recently, accepted as 'an important component of the economy'.[102] More recently, the private sector has been recognized as 'an important driving force of the economy'.[103] This transformation has resulted in the easing of legal restrictions on private business and a more equal, if still discriminatory, treatment between private and state enterprises.[104] In addition, private capitalists have been allowed to join the Party on a pilot basis since 2011,[105] undermining the orthodox Marxist–Leninist conceptions of the exploitative nature of capitalists and of workers as the leading class in the socialist revolution.

In a noteworthy move, the 2011 Party Congress declined to recognise the 'public ownership of the main means of production' as a characteristic of the socialist society that the Party aims to develop.[106] Instead, this Congress chose to state in the Party's political manifesto that the socialist society would have 'modern production relations that suit the development level of production forces'.[107] Though reflective of the eroding

---

[100] Huy Đức, Bên Thắng Cuộc: II. Quyền Bính [The Winning Side: II. The Power], ch. XXI; Le Thanh Vinh, Competition Law Transfers in Vietnam from an Interpretive Perspective, pp. 146–148.

[101] Huy Đức, Bên Thắng Cuộc: II. Quyền Bính [The Winning Side: II. The Power], ch. XXI.

[102] See CPV, Political Report 1986; CPV, Báo cáo chính trị của Ban chấp hành Trung ương Đảng tại Đại hội đại biểu toàn quốc lần thứ VII [Political Report of the Central Executive Committee at the 7th National Party Congress] (June 1991); CPV, Political Report 2001.

[103] CPV, Political Report 2016, pt. IV.2.

[104] Huy Đức, Bên Thắng Cuộc: II. Quyền Bính [The Winning Side: II. The Power], ch. XXI; Le Thanh Vinh, Competition Law Transfers in Vietnam from an Interpretive Perspective, pp. 136–142.

[105] CPV, Báo cáo chính trị của Ban chấp hành Trung ương Đảng tại Đại hội đại biểu toàn quốc lần thứ XI [Political Report of the Central Executive Committee at the 11th National Party Congress] (January 2011).

[106] Le, 'Interpreting the Constitutional Debate Over Land Ownership in the Socialist Republic of Vietnam (2012–2013)', 295.

[107] See CPV, Cương lĩnh Xây dựng Đất nước Trong Thời kỳ Quá độ Lên Chủ nghĩa Xã hội (Bổ sung, Phát triển năm 2011) [Political Program for National Construction in the Transitional Period to Socialism (Revised in 2011)] ('Political Program 2011') (19 January 2011).

belief of party-state officials in the public ownership ideal, the vague term 'modern production relations' is insufficient to create a breakthough development. Despite calls for reforms, the party-state chose not to recognise private forms of land ownership in the 2013 constitutional reforms.[108]

In short, socialist and Marxist–Leninist ideas continue to play an important role in post-*Đổi mới* economic thinking and practice. However, these ideas have been conflated with and, to a degree, eroded by new ideals of economic developmentalism, protectionism and neoliberalism. Particularly, the continued reliance on socialist and Marxist–Leninist conceptions does not only reflect the enduring commitment to socialist objectives, it has also become a strategic means for various interest groups within the party-state to defend their own power and economic privileges.

5.4   Post-*Đổi mới* Political Transformation and the Continual Dominance of Leninist Political Principles

5.4.1   Political Changes after Đổi mới

While undertaking bold economic reforms, the CPV has strategically sought to maintain political stability.[109] Notwithstanding this, remarkable developments have occurred indicating the decentralisation of political power and the liberalisation of state–society relations.

5.4.1.1   The Decentralisation of Political Power

The post-*Đổi mới* era has witnessed several changes towards a more polycentric power structure. First, there was a relative withdrawal of Party organisations from state governance, which enabled state bodies to have more autonomy in performing their functions.[110] A major

---

[108] Le, 'Interpreting the Constitutional Debate Over Land Ownership in the Socialist Republic of Vietnam (2012–2013)', 296–306.

[109] CPV, *Báo cáo chính trị của Ban chấp hành Trung ương Đảng tại Đại hội đại biểu toàn quốc lần thứ VIII* [Political Report of the Central Executive Committee at the 8th National Party Congress] (June 1996) pt. IV.2.

[110] Dang Phong and Melanie Beresford, *Authority Relations and Economic Decision-Making in Vietnam: An Historical Perspective* (Copenhagen: NIAS, 1998), p. 85; Jonathan D. London, 'Politics in Contemporary Vietnam', in Jonathan D. London (ed.), *Politics in Contemporary Vietnam: Party, State, and Authority Relations* (Basingstoke: Palgrave Macmillan, 2014), pp. 1, 7.

contributor to this development is the expanding market economy, which makes it impossible for the Party to intervene in every respect of economic management and, concurrently, requires the use of state laws rather than party directions in economic governance.[111] In addition, the Party has gradually recognised that its frequent intervention causes delays and diminishes state efficiency.[112]

Another transformation of the Vietnamese polity after Đổi mới is the growing role of the National Assembly (NA). Unlike in the preceding period, this institution has become increasingly active and influential in reviewing government plans and budgets, promulgating statutes and supervising other arms of state power.[113] This can be attributed to the Party's decreasing intervention in state governance.[114] The change can also be explained in view of the newly introduced doctrine of 'socialist law-based state' (nhà nước pháp quyền xã hội chủ nghĩa).[115] By promoting the use of law as a major means for state governance and the 'distribution' (phân công) and 'control' (kiểm soát) of power between state bodies, this doctrine requires that the NA's lawmaking and supervisory functions be enhanced.[116]

Thirdly, the administrative apparatus has drastically increased its work load, size and power.[117] The relative withdrawal of party organisations from state affairs arguably has contributed to this transformation. The development of the economy, especially where state economic intervention remains prevalent, has also fostered the growth of the administration.

The fourth change is the rising position of local authorities in the national polity. This can be seen in the increasing numbers of local representatives in the Central Executive Committee – one of the most

---

[111] John Gillespie, Transplanting Commercial Law Reform: Developing a 'Rule of Law' in Vietnam (Aldershot: Ashgate Publishing Company, 2006), p. 115; Nguyen Nhu Phat, 'The Role of Law During the Formation of a Market-Driven Mechanism in Vietnam', pp. 397–440.

[112] Porter, Vietnam, p. 85.

[113] See Edmund J. Malesky, 'Understanding the Confidence Vote in Vietnamese National Assembly: An Update on "Adverse Effects of Sunshine"', in London, Politics in Contemporary Vietnam, pp. 84, 86–87; Van Arkadie and Mallon, Viet Nam – A Transition Tiger?, p. 60.

[114] Dang and Beresford, Authority Relations and Economic Decision-Making in Vietnam, p. 85; Thayer, 'Political Reform in Vietnam', p. 120.

[115] See CPV, Political Program 2011, pt. IV.2.

[116] Ibid.

[117] Dang and Beresford, Authority Relations and Economic Decision-Making in Vietnam, p. 95; Thaveeporn Vasavakul, 'Vietnam: Doi Moi Difficulties', in John Funston (ed.), Government and Politics in Southeast Asia (Singapore: Institute of Southeast Asian Studies, 2001), pp. 372, 385.

powerful organs of the CPV – and the growth of local autonomy in managing investment projects, state enterprises, land and other natural resources.[118] Particularly, fiscal reforms have permitted local authorities to generate and retain surplus funds.[119] These and other changes have promoted the position of provincial authorities, especially rich cities and provinces, and permitted them to have a weighty voice in policy making and significant discretion in implementing central policies, including departing from those policies and experimenting with their own.[120]

Lastly, there is growing tension between different political factions within the party-state.[121] As many commentators observed, the division between such factions is relatively complicated, loosely tied to various factors, including ideological and policy perspectives, economic and political interests, institutional, regional or sectoral divisions, as well as leadership personalities.[122]

5.4.1.2   The Liberalisation of State-Society Relations

Although Vietnam is still an authoritarian state, there has been a gradual liberalisation of state–society relations after Đổi mới. As lawmaking consultation has become a more regular and institutionalised practice with discernible impact, law production is now more democratic and publicly accessible.[123] In addition, while mass organisations remain an extended

---

[118] Dixon, 'State, Party and Political Change in Vietnam', pp. 18–19; Thayer, 'Mono-Organisational Socialism and the State', pp. 60–61; Vu-Thanh Tu-Anh, 'The Political Economy of Industrial Development in Vietnam', pp. 16–17.

[119] Dixon, 'State, Party and Political Change in Vietnam', p. 18.

[120] See, e.g., Thomas Jandl, *Vietnam in the Global Economy: The Dynamics of Integration, Decentralisation, and Contested Politics* (Lanham: Lexington Books, 2013), pp. 225–238; Edmund J. Malesky, 'Push, Pull, and Reinforcing: The Channels of FDI Influence on Provincial Governance in Vietnam', in Kerkvliet and Marr (eds.), *Beyond Hanoi*, pp. 285, 289–290.

[121] See, e.g., Martin Gainsborough, 'From Patronage to "Outcomes": Vietnam's Communist Party Congresses Reconsidered' (2007) 2(1) *Journal of Vietnamese Studies* 3, 16–17; David Koh, 'The Politics of a Divided Party and Parkinson's State in Vietnam' (2001) 23(3) *Contemporary Southeast Asia* 533, 537–538; Vasavakul, 'Vietnam: Doi Moi Difficulties', pp. 400–402; Alexander L. Vuving, 'Vietnam: A Tale of Four Players' (2010) *Southeast Asian Affairs* 367, 367–368.

[122] Gainsborough, 'From Patronage to "Outcomes"', 537–538; Koh, 'The Politics of a Divided Party and Parkinson's State in Vietnam', 537–538; Vasavakul, 'Vietnam: Doi Moi Difficulties', pp. 400–402; Vuving, 'Vietnam: A Tale of Four Players', 367–368.

[123] Matthieu Salomon, 'Power and Representation at the Vietnamese National Assembly: The Scope and Limits of Political Doi Moi', in Balme and Sidel, *Vietnam's New Order*, pp. 198, 204–205; John Gillespie, 'Localizing Global Rules: Public Participation in Lawmaking in Vietnam' (2008) 33(3) *Law & Social Inquiry* 673, 687–688.

arm of the CPV, they have managed to improve their representative function.[124] The Vietnam General Confederation of Labour (VGCL) is a noteworthy example. The VGCL has been relatively vocal in defending the interests of workers in labour law reforms.[125] Further, under the pressure of transforming industrial relations, it has undertaken many reforms, such as provision of legal aid to workers and promotion of collective bargaining, with a view to better protecting the interests of workers.[126]

Moreover, the post-Đổi mới era has witnessed a boom of new social organisations which are affiliated to the party-state to varying degrees.[127] Several of these organisations have become increasingly vocal and effective in communicating the views of their members and the public to the authorities.[128] The activism and rising voice of the business community illustrates this. Since its restructuring in the 1990s, the Vietnam Chamber of Industry and Commerce (VCCI) has become an important voice in shaping economic laws and policies and their implementation.[129] Domestic and foreign entrepreneurs have also succeeded in utilising other business organisations, business-government fora and personalised networks to exert influence on the authorities.[130]

---

[124] Benedict J. Tria Kerkvliet, 'An Approach for Analyzing State-Society Relations in Vietnam' (2001) (2) *Journal of Social Issues in Southeast Asia* 238, 247; Benedict J. Tria Kerkvliet, 'Introduction', in Benedict J. Tria Kerkvliet, Russell H.K. Heng and David W.H. Koh (eds.), *Getting Organized in Vietnam: Moving in and around the Socialist State* (Singapore: Institute of Southeast Asian Studies, 2003, Vietnam Update Series), pp. 1, 9–10.

[125] See Do Hai Ha, *The Dynamics of Legal Transplantation*, chs. 6 and 9; Jonathan R. Stromseth, *Reform and Response in Vietnam: State-Society Relations and the Changing Political Economy* (PhD Thesis, Columbia University, 1998), pp. 176–226.

[126] Do Hai Ha, *The Dynamics of Legal Transplantation*, pp. 176, 299–301.

[127] Thaveeporn Vasavakul, 'From Fence-Breaking to Networking: Interests, Popular Organisations and Policy Influences in Post-Socialist Vietnam', in Kerkvliet, Heng and Koh, *Getting Organized in Vietnam*, pp. 26–28; William Taylor et al., 'Civil Society in Vietnam: A Comparative Study of Civil Society Organizations in Hanoi and Ho Chi Minh City' (Report, Asia Foundation, October 2012), pp. 6–7. Taylor et al. note that there were nearly 15,000 organisations of this kind across the country in 2010.

[128] Vasavakul, 'From Fence-Breaking to Networking', pp. 34–53; Jorg Wischermann, 'Governance and Civil Society Action in Vietnam: Changing the Rules from within – Potentials and Limits' (2011) (3) *Asian Politics & Policy* 383, 395–405.

[129] See John Gillespie and Bui Thi Bich Lien, 'Unacknowledged Legislators: Business Participation in Lawmaking in Vietnam', in John Gillespie and Randall Peerenboom (eds.), *Regulation in Asia: Pushing Back on Globalisation* (London: Routledge, 2009), pp. 163, 176–177; Jonathan R. Stromseth, 'Business Associations and Policy-Making in Vietnam', in Kerkvliet, Heng and Koh, *Getting Organized in Vietnam*, pp. 62, 88–92.

[130] See, e.g., Gillespie and Bui, 'Unacknowledged Legislators', p. 163; Malesky, 'Push, Pull, and Reinforcing'; Nguyen Hung Quang, 'Legal Diffusion and the Role of Non-State

Several factors have contributed to the rising entrepreneurial influence. The growing importance of the private sector, the pro-investment policy of the party-state and its transforming attitude towards private business have increased the position of entrepreneurs in national politics. Another contributing factor is the increasing interconnection between vested interests within the party-state and emergent business interests.[131] Structural changes like the institutionalisation of consultation about lawmaking, the introduction of business-government fora, the renovation of state-sponsored business associations like the VCCI and the emergence of new business associations, have also helped entrepreneurs to communicate more effectively with the party-state.[132]

Despite the continual existence of political control, liberalisation has also taken place with respect to state-sponsored media. Commercialisation and a slightly more relaxed censorship have created spaces and incentives for state-supervised newspapers to go beyond the role of being a mere mouthpiece of the party-state.[133] Quite often, they are an active platform for state–society communicative exchanges, or even engage in mass action that pushes the authorities to respond to social needs.[134] Even when

Actors in Shaping the Regulatory Environment in Vietnam', in John Gillespie and Albert H. Y. Chen (eds.), *Legal Reforms in China and Vietnam: A Comparison of Asian Communist Regimes* (New York, NY: Routledge, 2010), p. 350; Nguyen Phuong Tu, 'Rethinking State-Society Relations in Vietnam: The Case of Business Associations in Ho Chi Minh City' (2014) 38 *Asian Studies Review* 87.

[131] See Dixon, 'State, Party and Political Change in Vietnam', p. 19; Nguyen Phuong Tu, 'Business Associations and the Politics of Contained Participation in Vietnam' (2014) 49 *Australian Journal of Political Science* 334, 347.

[132] See Gillespie and Bui, 'Unacknowledged Legislators', pp. 174–178; Stromseth, 'Business Associations and Policy-Making in Vietnam', pp. 64–77.

[133] Geoffrey Cain, 'Kill One to Warn One Hundred: The Politics of Press Censorship in Vietnam' (2014) 19(1) *International Journal of Press/Politics* 85, 102; Cari An Coe, 'Minding the Metaphor: Vietnamese State-Run Press Coverage of Social Movements Abroad' (2014) 9(1) *Journal of Vietnamese Studies* 1, 4; Russell Hiang-Khng Heng, 'Media Negotiating the State: In the Name of the Law in Anticipation' (2001) 16(2) *Journal of Social Issues in Southeast Asia* 213, 227.

[134] See, e.g., Cain, 'Kill One to Warn One Hundred'; Catherine McKinley, 'Can a State-Owned Media Effectively Monitor Corruption? A Study of Vietnam's Printed Press' (2008) 2(1) *Asian Journal of Public Affairs* 12; Nguyen Vu Hoang, 'Constructing Civil Society on a Demolition Site in Hanoi', in Hue-Tam Ho Tai and Mark Sidel (eds.), *State, Society and the Market in Contemporary Vietnam: Property, Power and Values* (Hoboken, NJ: Taylor and Francis, 2012) p. 193; Angie Ngoc Tran, 'The Third Sleeve: Emerging Labor Newspapers and the Response of the Labor Unions and the State to Workers' Resistance in Vietnam' (2007a) 32(3) *Labor Studies Journal* 257; Andrew Wells-Dang, 'Political Space in Vietnam: A View from the 'Rice-Roots' (2010) 23(1) *Pacific Review* 93.

state-controlled newspapers act as the political leadership's instrument, their role has become more dynamic and complicated because the party-state (of which state-controlled newspapers are a constituent) has become more diverse. Active journalists have often attempted to exploit spaces created by unclear or conflicting party directions.[135]

Finally, the Party, albeit inconsistently, has become more tolerant of criticism and associational activities outside the official framework, including large public protests or even criticism by dissidents.[136] Additionally, it has to a considerable extent attempted to accommodate public concerns, criticisms and demands beyond authorised channels, particularly from workers and peasants (the supposed political foundation of the regime).[137] Unlike its Chinese counterpart, the CPV has not censored social media too strictly.[138] This has enabled social media to become a powerful channel to express public views and concerns, as well as an effective means for social activism, including social campaigns on various economic, political and social issues.[139]

5.4.2   The Party's Loyalty to Leninist Political Principles and the Limits of Post-Đổi mới Political Changes

Despite some degrees of political decentralisation and liberalisation, the CPV has continuously maintained a Leninist political system.[140] Party leadership – or in other words, the 'vanguard role' of the CPV – remains strongly upheld in Party documents and the Constitution.[141] Similarly,

---

[135] Cain, 'Kill One to Warn One Hundred', 102–103; Coe, 'Minding the Metaphor', 4–5; Heng, 'Media Negotiating the State: In the Name of the Law in Anticipation', 226–231.

[136] See, e.g., Benedict J. Tria Kerkvliet, 'Governance, Development, and the Responsive-Repressive State in Vietnam' (2010) 37(1) *Forum for Development Studies* 33, 36–46; Benedict J. Kerkvliet, 'Government Repression and Toleration of Dissidents in Contemporary Vietnam' in London (ed.), *Politics in Contemporary Vietnam*, 100; Wells-Dang, 'Political Space in Vietnam'.

[137] Kerkvliet, 'An Approach for Analyzing State-Society Relations in Vietnam', 247–250; Kerkvliet, 'Governance, Development, and the Responsive-Repressive State in Vietnam', 36–46; Carlyle A. Thayer, 'Political Legitimacy of Vietnam's One Party-State: Challenges and Responses' (2009) 28(4) *Journal of Current Southeast Asian Affairs* 47, 63–64; Carlyle A. Thayer, 'Political Legitimacy in Vietnam: Challenge and Response' (2010) 38(3) *Politics & Policy* 423, 439–441.

[138] See Bui Hai Thiem, 'The Influence of Social Media in Vietnam's Elite Politics' (2016) 35(2) *Journal of Current Southeast Asian Affairs* 89, 104–106.

[139] Ibid., 92–103.

[140] London, 'Vietnam and the Making of Market-Leninism', 379.

[141] CPV, *Political Program 2011*, pt. IV.4; Art. 4.1, Constitution 2013.

'democratic centralism' is still the main organising principle of the Party.[142] In upholding these principles, the CPV has, however, re-configured itself as the vanguard of not only the working class, but also the entire people,[143] thereby softening the Marxist notion of class struggle. In a similar vein, while the CPV still posits workers as the leading and vanguard class in socialist construction, it now avoids using the orthodox Marxist–Leninist term 'dictatorship of the proletariat'.[144]

Given the Party's adherence to Leninist political principles, the impact of post-Đổi mới political transformation is modest. While reducing its intervention in state affairs, the CPV still firmly controls state agencies by appointing their leaders and through permeation of Party organisa-tions.[145] The past five years have also seen an attempt to re-assert party control over the state by, for example, re-establishing functional party bodies like Commissions of Economic Affairs (Ban Kinh tế) and Com-missions of Internal Affairs (Ban Nội chính).[146]

More particularly, the CPV has tightened its control over the armed forces through special measures. For example, it has strengthened direct control over party organisations within the People's Army and the People's Police.[147] The General Secretary (Tổng Bí thư) of the Party is the Head of the Army's Party Committee (Quân uỷ Trung ương) by charter,[148] and has recently participated in the Police's Party Committee (Đảng uỷ Công an Trung ương) as a standing member.[149] Indeed, the Party has strongly rebuffed the call for the 'de-politicisation' (phi chính trị hoá) of the armed forces, including in the 2013 constitutional reform.[150]

[142] CPV, Political Program 2011, pt. IV.4.

[143] Ibid.

[144] Ibid., particularly pt. III.2.

[145] London, Politics in Contemporary Vietnam, p. 7.

[146] See Ngọc Hà, Thanh Xuân and Văn Công, 'Việt Nam Hoàn thiện Cơ chế Kiểm soát Quyền lực' ['Vietnam Has Perfected the Mechanism for Power Control'], VTV News (online), 13 February 2016, available at http://vtv.vn/chinh-tri/viet-nam-hoan-thien-co-che-kiem-soat-quyen-luc-20160213183907453.htm.

[147] Art. 25.1, CPV Statute 2011.

[148] Ibid., Art 26.1.

[149] Anh Hiếu, 'Tổng Bí thư Lần đầu Tham gia Đảng uỷ Công an Trung ương' ['General Secretary Has Participated in the Police's Party Committee for the First Time'], Công an Nhân dân [People's Police] (online), 21 September 2016, available at http://cand.com.vn/Su-kien-Binh-luan-thoi-su/Tong-Bi-thu-lan-dau-tham-gia-Dang-uy-Cong-an-Trung-uong-409050/.

[150] Nguyễn Mạnh Hưởng, '"Phi Chính trị hoá" Lực lượng Vũ trang: Một Thủ đoạn Trong Chiến lược "Diễn biến Hoà bình"' ['"De-politicising" the Armed Forces: A Ruse of the "Peaceful Evolution" Strategy], Tạp chí Cộng sản Điện tử [Communist Review Online], 4 May 2013, available at www.tapchicongsan.org.vn/Home/Nghiencuu-Traodoi/2013/21305/Phi-chinh-tri-hoa-luc-luong-vu-trang-mot-thu-doan-trong.aspx.

Party paramountcy has also impeded the acceptance of the doctrine of separation of powers – though the CPV has realised that state power must be distributed and controlled by and between different state bodies.[151] In addition, it has restricted more substantive changes within the NA. As in the past, the NA is elected through a process that is carefully orchestrated by the CPV and is overwhelmingly dominated by Party members.[152] Accordingly, it remains subject to political boundaries set by the Party and its directives.[153] This and many other problems, such as its part-time operation, high proportion of part-time delegates (with limited expertise, budgets and resources) and membership that overlaps with other arms of state power, have substantially constrained the NA's role and its discharge of law-making and supervisory functions.[154]

Despite the growing pluralism within the party-state, the CPV has strongly affirmed 'democratic centralism', considering criticism of this principle as an indicator of 'self-transformation' (*tự diễn biến*) and 'self-degradation' (*tự suy thoái*) among its members.[155] This has by and large prevented democratic reforms within the CPV and the whole political system. For example, Party members are prohibited from nominating themselves or accepting nominations to state positions without Party approval, including in national elections.[156] The Party also tightly controls the selection of candidates for the Central Executive Committee and, therefore, substantially disregards the right to nomination and self-nomination of Party members in the Party Congress.[157]

---

[151] CPV, *Nghị quyết số 04-NQ/TW Về Tăng cường Xây dựng, Chỉnh đốn Đảng* [*Resolution 04-NQ/TW Regarding Reinforcing the Construction and Reorganization of the Party*] ('Resolution 04/2016'), 30 October 2016, pt II.3; Bùi Văn Học, 'Tam quyền Phân lập Không Phù hợp Với Thể chế Chính trị Ở Nước ta' ['Separation of Powers Does Not Suit Our Political Regime'], *Công an Nhân dân* [People's Police] (online), 10 September 2013, available at http://cand.com.vn/Su-kien-Binh-luan-thoi-su/Tam-quyen-phan-lap-khong-phu-hop-voi-the-che-chinh-tri-o-nuoc-ta-237626/.

[152] London, 'Politics in Contemporary Vietnam', pp. 9–10.

[153] Malesky, 'Understanding the Confidence Vote in Vietnamese National Assembly', p. 87; Salomon, 'Power and Representation at the Vietnamese National Assembly', p. 210.

[154] Edmund Malesky and Paul Schuler, 'Paint-by-Numbers Democracy: The Stakes, Structure, and Results of the 2007 Vietnamese National Assembly Election' (2009) 4(1) *Journal of Vietnamese Studies* 1, 7–9; Van Arkadie and Mallon, *Viet Nam – A Transition Tiger?*, p. 60.

[155] CPV, *Resolution 04/2016*, pt. II.3.

[156] See Regulation No. 47-QD/TW of the Central Executive Committee dated 1 November 2011 on Acts Not Permitted to Commit by Party Members [I.7].

[157] See VV Thành, 'Không Được Giới thiệu Sẽ Không Ứng cử Và Nhận Đề cử, Nhưng ...' ['Those Not Selected [by the Central Committee] Will Not Self-Nominate or Accept

The space for political participation and civil society, albeit increased, remains limited. This is not only because the CPV still controls national elections tightly. Consultation for lawmaking has become more regular, but its effectiveness has been substantially restricted by state control over the scope, focus and participants in lawmaking discussions and weak political accountability.[158] Additionally, mass organisations continue to adhere to the CPV closely and, serve the interests of the party-state more than their members.[159] Meanwhile, newly emerged organisations are hampered by state control, the legal environment, and a lack of resources, organisational capacity, and political connection.[160]

The state-sponsored media also remains tightly controlled by the party-state through various means including state funding, control of leadership personnel in media agencies, regular meetings with party-state authorities, and punishment of journalists and agencies who break censorship rules.[161] Although social media is not entirely banned, the authorities have applied different measures to monitor this emerging space, including establishing firewalls against independent or dissenting websites, using 'rumourmongers' (dư luận viên) to manipulate public opinion and repressing dissident bloggers.[162] While the Party has become more tolerant of secondary associational activities and dissident behaviour, repression against vocal, complaining and self-organised citizens remains intense and regular, especially when they threaten political stability and Party paramountcy.[163]

In conclusion, Leninist political principles (particularly, party leadership and democratic centralism) remain the backbone of the post-Đổi

Nomination, but . . .'], Tuổi trẻ [The Youth] (online), 20 January 2016, available at http://tuoitre.vn/uy-vien-khong-duoc-gioi-thieu-se-khong-ung-cu-va-nhan-de-cu-nhung-1041931.htm.

[158] See Gillespie and Bui, 'Unacknowledged Legislators', pp. 173–178; Salomon, 'Power and Representation at the Vietnamese National Assembly', pp. 213–215.

[159] See, e.g., Do Hai Ha, The Dynamics of Legal Transplantation, pp. 275, 329; Tran Thi Thu Trang, 'Local Politics and Democracy in Muong Ethnic Community', p. 146.

[160] See, e.g., Nguyen Phuong Quynh Trang and Jonathan R Stromseth, 'Business Associations in Vietnam: Status, Roles and Performance' (Report 13, The Asia Foundation, August 2002), pp. 38–43; Taylor et al., 'Civil Society in Vietnam', pp. 28–30.

[161] See Cain, 'Kill One to Warn One Hundred'; Pham Doan Trang, 'Media Censorship in Vietnam', Asia Sentinel (online), 24 July 2014, available at www.asiasentinel.com/society/media-censorship-vietnam/.

[162] Bui Hai Thiem, 'The Influence of Social Media in Vietnam's Elite Politics'; Pham Doan Trang, 'Media Censorship in Vietnam'.

[163] Kerkvliet, 'Governance, Development, and the Responsive-Repressive State in Vietnam', 46–51.

mới political system. Nonetheless, the CPV has somewhat adapted these principles by redefining itself as the leader of both the working class and society as a whole and by reducing direct referral to proletariat dictatorship. Additionally, the devolution of political power and some liberalisation of state-society relations indicate that the Party has reformed its methods of leadership over the political system and the society since *Đổi mới*. This has permitted a more democratic space for political activities, both within and outside the party-state system. And as Fu and Buhi demonstrate in Chapter 6, this space is considerably greater than the space for political democracy in China.

As shown previously, the transition to a more open and market-oriented economy has played a critical role in enabling moderate developments in post-*Đổi mới* politics. The market transition has resulted in increasingly diversified interests and perspectives within the party-state. In addition, it has transformed the range of actors involved in political life and their relative influence. The growing power of local authorities, the weightier position of the business community and the emergent influence of foreign and international donors exemplify this. These changes have promoted a more pluralistic political system and society.

Finally, economic reforms have created many challenges for the party-state, such as in relation to dealing with new economic relations, identifying and handling social demands in an increasingly vibrant, diverse and uncontrollable society and managing an increasingly commercialised media, the Internet and social media. These challenges have forced the party-state to review and renovate its traditional methods of party leadership and state governance, paving the way for political developments.

5.5   From Socialist Legality to Socialist Law-Based State: Legal Developments after *Đổi Mới* and the Imprint of the Soviet Legacy

5.5.1   The Socialist Law-Based State and Post-*Đổi Mới* Legal Developments

Vietnamese law has developed significantly since the initiation of *Đổi mới*. At the doctrinal level, this development is marked by the introduction of a new political-legal doctrine, namely, 'law-based state' (*nhà nước pháp quyền*) since the late 1980s.[164] The concept was officially endorsed

---

[164] See Đỗ Mười, 'Bài Phát biểu Tại Hội nghị Tư pháp Năm 1989' [Speech delivered at 1989 Judicial Conference] reproduced in Dương Thanh Mai et al., *Xây dựng Hệ thống*

by the CPV in 1994 and has become a constitutional doctrine since 2001, after being renamed 'socialist law-based state' (*nhà nước pháp quyền xã hội chủ nghĩa*).[165] It has roots in the Russian/German-originated doctrine of *pravovoe gosudarstvo*, which was reintroduced to Soviet jurisprudence in the *perestroika* era.[166]

The doctrine of 'socialist law-based state' differs from the pre-existing doctrine of 'socialist legality' in three important points. First, it adopts a softer version of the class rhetoric, as evident in Article 2 of the 1992 Constitution:

> The State of the Socialist Republic of Vietnam is a state of the people, by the people, for the people. All state power belongs to the people whose foundation is the alliance of the working class with the peasantry and the intelligentsia.[167]

Thus, the 1992 Constitution (as well as its 2001 and 2013 successors)[168] diverge markedly from the 1980 Constitution – the charter of the high socialist era – in that it portrays the socialist state primarily as 'a state of the people' rather than 'a state of proletariat dictatorship'.[169] Further, it has expanded the political foundation of the regime to include intellectuals. In a similar vein, Vietnamese jurists now contend that in addition to its 'class-based nature' (*bản chất giai cấp*), law reflects 'social values' (*giá trị xã hội*) and 'national identity' (*bản sắc dân tộc*).[170]

Pháp luật Và Nền Tư pháp Nhân dân Dưới Dự Lãnh đạo Của Đảng [Building the Legal System and People's Judicial System under Party Leadership] (Hanoi: Nhà Xuất bản Tư pháp [Judicial Publishing House], 2005), pp. 148, 154.

[165] CPV, *Báo cáo Chính trị Tại Hội nghị Đại biểu Toàn quốc Giữa Nhiệm kỳ Khoá VII* [Political Report to the Mid-Tenure National Representative Party Conference of the Seventh Tenure] ('Political Report 1994'), January 1994, pt One I(2); Art. 2, Constitution 1992 (revised in 2001).

[166] Gillespie, 'Concepts of Law in Vietnam: Transforming Statist Socialism', p. 147. For a historical development of *pravovoe gosudarstvo*, see H. Oda, 'The Emergence of Pravovoe Gosudarstvo (*Rechtsstaat*) in Russia' (1999) 25(3) *Review of Central and East European Law* 373.

[167] Art. 2, Constitution 1992.

[168] Art. 2, Constitution 1992 (revised in 2001); Art. 2.2, Constitution 2013.

[169] Cf Art. 2, Constitution 1980.

[170] Đào Trí Úc, Đinh Ngọc Vượng and Nguyễn Như Phát, 'Khái niệm Và Những Mối Liên hệ Của Pháp luật', in Đào Trí Úc (ed.), *Những Vấn đề Lý luận Cơ bản Về Nhà nước Và Pháp luật* [Fundamental Theoretical Issues of State and Law] (Hanoi: Nhà Xuất bản Chính trị Quốc gia [National Political Publishing House], 1994), pp. 120, 122–125; Nguyễn Minh Đoan, *Giáo trình Lý luận về Nhà nước Và Pháp luật* [Textbook on Theory of State and Law] (Hanoi: Nhà Xuất bản Chính trị Quốc gia [National Political Publishing House], 2010), pp. 75–77.

Secondly, 'socialist law-based state' posits law as the principal means to regulate the economy and society.[171] This represents a remarkable departure from the pre–*Đổi mới* regulatory practice, which relied extensively on Party policy, administrative commands and moral principles rather than law.

Finally, the new doctrine declares the 'supreme role of law in society'.[172] This declaration does not only require that all state bodies, social organisations, business entities and individuals abide by law, as purported by 'socialist legality'.[173] To a degree, it also indicates the party-state's greater commitment to be bound by law.[174] This is evident in Article 4.3 of the 2013 Constitution which provides that: 'All Party organizations and members operate within the framework of the Constitution and the law.'[175] In addition, the Party has officially affirmed that whereas 'citizens can do everything not expressly prohibited by law', 'state agencies [and] officials can do nothing other than what is permitted by law'.[176]

The introduction of the 'socialist law-based state' has opened spaces for remarkable changes in the Vietnamese legal system. The promotion of a law-based approach to state governance has led to the enactment of numerous statutes in the past three decades. Additionally, the weakening class-based conception of state and law paves the way for the adoption of market-based laws and legal borrowings from capitalist states, which were once considered an instrument of bourgeois dictatorship. Meanwhile, the idea of the supremacy of law creates the possibility of limiting the power of party-state agencies[177] and, therefore, fosters public law reforms.

---

[171] CPV, *Nghị quyết Số 08-NQ-HNTW Hội nghị Lần Thứ Tám Của Ban Chấp hành Trung ương Đảng Khoá VII Về Tiếp tục Xây dựng Và Hoàn thiện Nhà nước Cộng hoà XHCN Việt Nam, Trọng tâm Là Cải cách Một Bước Nền Hành chính [Resolution No. 08-NQ/HNTW on Continuing to Construct and Perfect the Vietnamese Socialist State, with a Focus on Reforming the Administrative System]* ('Resolution 08/1995'), 23 January 1995, pt. 1.

[172] Nguyễn Minh Đoan, *Giáo trình Lý luận về Nhà nước Và Pháp luật* [Textbook on Theory of State and Law], pp. 261–263.

[173] Ibid., pp. 263–265.

[174] Nicholson, *Borrowing Court Systems*, p. 244.

[175] Art. 4.3, Constitution 2013. See also Art. 4, Constitution 1992; Art. 4, Constitution 1992 (revised in 2001). Cf Art. 4, Constitution 1980.

[176] CPV, *Nghị quyết Số 48-NQ/TW Của Bộ Chính trị Về Chiến lược Xây dựng Và Hoàn thiện Hệ thống Pháp luật Việt Nam Đến Năm 2010, Định hướng Đến Năm 2020* [Resolution No. 48-NQ/TW of the Politburo on Strategy for Development and Improvement of the Vietnamese Legal System up to 2010 and Vision up to 2020] ('Resolution 48/ 2005'), 24 May 2005, pts II.1.4, II.3.

[177] Gillespie, 'Concepts of Law in Vietnam: Transforming Statist Socialism', p. 143; Nicholson, *Borrowing Court Systems*, p. 244.

Business law has undergone the most outstanding development, with the emergence/re-emergence of property law, contract law, corporate law, competition law, consumer protection law and labour law – to a name a few.[178] As demonstrated in several studies, these laws are constructed extensively on legal ideas and principles transplanted from capitalist market economies.[179] Extensive reforms have also been made in respect of public law, including constitutional law, administrative law, civil proceedings, criminal law and procedure.[180] Nonetheless, legal transformation in this sphere appears to be less radical, with considerably less impact from capitalist states.[181]

Moreover, the CPV has initiated a broad program of 'judicial reform' (*cải cách tư pháp*), which aims to promote judicial independence, professionalise the courts and enhance their accountability.[182] Under this reform program, the function of the People's Procuracies has been narrowed.[183] These institutions are now no longer responsible for supervising legal compliance in general, but only legal compliance in judicial activities.[184] This indicates the decline of Marxist–Leninist jurisprudence, which has traditionally seen People's Procuracies as the main means to ensure socialist legality.[185] Aside from these changes, there has been a revival in legal education and the profession after decades of disruption.[186]

---

[178] See, e.g., Civil Code 2015; Law on Intellectual Property 2005 (as revised in 2009); Law on Enterprises 2014; Law on Competition 2004; Law on Protection of Consumers' Rights 2010; Labour Code 2012.

[179] See, e.g., Do Hai Ha, *The Dynamics of Legal Transplantation*; Gillespie, *Transplanting Commercial Law Reform*; Le Thanh Vinh, *Competition Law Transfers in Vietnam from an Interpretive Perspective*; Nguyen Van Cuong, *The Drafting of Vietnam's Consumer Protection Law: An Analysis from Legal Transplantation Theories* (PhD Thesis, University of Victoria, 2011).

[180] See, e.g., Constitution 2013; Civil Procedure Code 2015; Law on Access to Information 2016; Penal Code 2015 (as revised in 2017); Criminal Procedure Code 2015.

[181] See, e.g., Mark Sidel, *Law and Society in Vietnam* (Cambridge: Cambridge University Press, 2008); Balme and Sidel, *Vietnam's New Order*, pt. II; Matthieu Salomon and Vu Doan Ket, 'Achievements and Challenges in Developing a Law-Based State in Contemporary Vietnam', in John Gillespie and Albert H.Y. Chen (eds.), *Legal Reforms in China and Vietnam*, p. 134.

[182] Brian J. M. Quinn, 'Vietnam's Continuing Legal Reform: Gaining Control Over the Courts' (2003) 4 *University of Hawaii Asian-Pacific Law & Policy Journal* 431, 449–457; Penelope (Pip) Nicholson, 'Vietnamese Courts: Contemporary Interactions between Party-State and Law', in Balme and Sidel, *Vietnam's New Order*, pp. 178, 181–182.

[183] Quinn, 'Vietnam's Continuing Legal Reform', 460–464.

[184] Ibid.

[185] See George Ginsburgs, 'Genesis of the People's Procuracy in the Democratic Republic of Vietnam' (1979) 5 *Review of Socialist Law* 187.

[186] Pip Nicholson and Do Hai Ha, *Lawyers and Lawyering in Socialist Vietnam: Cadres to a 'Managed' Profession* (manuscript in preparation, 2017).

5.5.2   The Imprint of the Soviet Legacy on Contemporary Vietnamese Law

While experiencing enormous changes after *Đổi mới*, Vietnamese law remains substantially shaped by the economic, political and legal legacies of the high socialist era. Socialist legality continues to exist in policy documents, statutory laws, legal scholarship and regulatory practice.[187] Importantly, several aspects of this doctrine and its application have been assimilated into the newly introduced doctrine. The class-based conception of law retains a place in the 'socialist law-based state'.[188] Despite the call for rule by law, Party policy theoretically and practically continues to be a primary regulator directing the interpretation and application of law.[189] Further, even if the bureaucracy has relied more on law to regulate the economy and society, its discretionary power remains significant because the implementation of law normally requires administrative guidance.[190]

Party paramountcy – rather than the supremacy of law – remains the dominant political-legal principle. Party documents have consistently underlined that Party leadership is a core feature of the 'socialist law-based state'.[191] Still, law is considered a means to realise Party policy.[192] Where divergence between law and policy exists, state officials – who are usually simultaneously Party members – tend to follow the latter.[193]

It is noteworthy that while promoting a socialist law-based state, the CPV continues to view revolutionary morality and mass mobilisation as major instruments for Party leadership and state governance.[194] Invoking

---

[187] Socialist legality was not removed from the Vietnamese constitution until the 2013 reform. Even so, it has remained existent in newly adopted statutes. See, e.g., Law on Organization of People's Courts 2014; Law on Organization of People's Procuracies 2014. See also Nguyễn Minh Đoan, *Giáo trình Lý luận về Nhà nước Và Pháp luật* [*Textbook on Theory of State and Law*].

[188] See, e.g., CPV, *Political Program 2011*; Nguyễn Minh Đoan, *Giáo trình Lý luận về Nhà nước Và Pháp luật* [*Textbook on Theory of State and Law*], pp. 75–77.

[189] See Lê Minh Tâm, 'Bản chất, Đặc trưng, Vai trò, Các Kiểu Và Hình thức Pháp luật' [*Nature, Characteristics, Role, Types and Forms of Law*], p. 334; Nicholson, 'Renovating Courts', p. 557.

[190] Van Arkadie and Mallon, *Viet Nam – A Transition Tiger?*, p. 60.

[191] See, e.g., CPV, *Resolution 08/1995*; CPV, *Resolution 48/2005*.

[192] Nguyễn Minh Đoan, *Giáo trình Lý luận về Nhà nước Và Pháp luật* [*Textbook on Theory of State and Law*], pp. 298–301.

[193] Nicholson, 'Renovating Courts', p. 545.

[194] See, e.g., CPV, *Nghị quyết Số 04-NQ/TW Hội nghị Lần Thứ Ba Của Ban Chấp hành Trung ương Đảng Khoá X Về "Tăng cường Sự Lãnh đạo Của Đảng Đối với Công tác Phòng, Chống Tham nhũng, Lãng phí"* [Resolution No. 04-NQ/TW on "Enhancing Party Leadership over the Prevention of [and] Combat against Corruption [and]

'Hồ Chí Minh Thought', Party scholars regularly propose that 'legalism' (*pháp trị*) be combined with 'virtue-rule' (*đức trị*).[195] The CPV and its leaders consistently note that while governing society by law, the socialist law-based state still gives weight to 'education [and] promotion of socialist morality'.[196] Likewise, mass propaganda and mobilisation continue to be considered an important means for Party leadership, state governance and law enforcement.[197] As Nguyễn Phú Trọng, now General Secretary of the Party, put it: the law-based state has to 'combine the power of law with the power of the masses'.[198]

Soviet-inspired economic, political and legal concepts have also significantly shaped legal change and transplantation. For instance, the socialist ideal of public ownership has discouraged the recognition of private forms of land ownership.[199] The idea of state sector domination postponed efforts to unify the legal frameworks for private and state

Dissipation"], 21 August 2006; CPV, *Nghị quyết Số 25-NQ/TW Ngày 3/6/2013 Hội nghị Lần Thứ Bảy Của Ban Chấp hành Trung ương Đảng Khóa XI Về Tăng cường Và Đổi mới Sự Lãnh đạo Của Đảng Đối với Công tác Dân vận Trong Tình hình Mới* [Resolution No. 25-NQ/TW on Enhancing and Renovating Party Leadership over Mobilisation Work in the New Situation] ('Resolution 25/2013'), 3 June 2013.

[195] Bùi Thị Ngọc Mai, 'Một Số Vấn đề Của Tư tưởng Hồ Chí Minh Về Pháp luật' ['Some Issues of Hồ Chí Minh Thought on Law'] (2009) (7) *Tạp chí Tổ chức Nhà nước* [Journal of State Organisation] 15; Thái Vĩnh Thắng, 'Tìm hiểu Tư tưởng Triết học Pháp quyền Của Chủ tịch Hồ Chí Minh' ['Understanding President Hồ Chí Minh's Philosophical Thought on Rule of Law'] (2011) (1–2) *Tạp chí Nghiên cứu lập pháp* [*Journal of Legislative Research*] 24.

[196] CPV, *Resolution 08/1995*, pt. 1. See also Nguyễn Phú Trọng, *Phát huy Dân chủ, Tiếp tục Xây dựng Nhà nước Pháp quyền Xã hội Chủ nghĩa Của Nhân dân, Do Nhân dân Vì Nhân dân* [*Promoting Democracy [and] Continuing to Construct the Socialist Law-Based State of the People, by the People, for the People*] (Hanoi: Nhà Xuất bản Chính trị Quốc gia – Sự thật [National Politics – Truth Publishing House], 2011), pp. 87–88; Tô Huy Rứa, 'Quan điểm Của Hồ Chí Minh Về Xây dựng Nhà nước Pháp quyền Xã hội Chủ nghĩa Của Nhân dân, Do Nhân dân Và Vì Nhân dân' ['Hồ Chí Minh's View on the Socialist Law-Based State of the People, by the People and for the People'] (2005) (22) *Tạp chí Cộng sản* [*Communist Review*] 23, 25–27.

[197] CPV, *Resolution 48/2005*, pt. II.1.1; CPV, *Nghị quyết Số 49-NQ/TW Của Bộ Chính trị Ngày 02/6/2005 Về Chiến lược Cải cách Tư pháp Đến Năm 2020* [Resolution No. 49-NQ/TW on Strategy for Judicial Reform up to 2020], 2 June 2005, pt. II.2.5; CPV, *Resolution 25/2013*, pts. II–III.

[198] Nguyễn Phú Trọng, *Phát huy Dân chủ, Tiếp tục Xây dựng Nhà nước Pháp quyền Xã hội Chủ nghĩa Của Nhân dân, Do Nhân dân Vì Nhân dân* [*Promoting Democracy [and] Continuing to Construct the Socialist Law-Based State of the People, by the People, for the People*], p. 87.

[199] Le, 'Interpreting the Constitutional Debate Over Land Ownership in the Socialist Republic of Vietnam (2012–2013)', 304–305.

enterprises until 2005.[200] The notion of state sector domination has also distorted the implementation of the bankruptcy law – as the government has often intervened to save insolvent SOEs.[201] In another example, the doctrine of socialist legality has been invoked to defend the continued existence of procuracies and prevent the transformation of these state bodies in the form of prosecution bodies only.[202] Meanwhile, the socialist critique of capitalism and the Marxist–Leninist class-based conception of state and law have contributed to legal recognition of the right to strike and the frequent tolerance of strike action.[203]

There are various other examples of socialist and Marxist–Leninist influences. And although we do not have space to cover all of them, the importance of the Leninist principle of party leadership is worth mentioning. As shown earlier, this principle has prevented radical political and, therefore, constitutional reforms, including democratic elections, the separation of powers and the removal of the armed forces from Party influence. Further, it has substantially restricted the impact of court reform on judicial independence.

Despite the call to strengthen judicial independence in Party documents, the CPV has never meant to exclude the courts from its leadership.[204] Rather, it aims to protect the courts against the interference of other party-state actors, which can be, at times, difficult to distinguish from the Party leadership.[205] Several factors severely circumscribe judges from acting independently, including political credentials for appointment, short tenure, guidance from upper courts, influence of senior judges, monitoring by party cells, and extremely low payment.[206] Party supremacy has also deterred bold reforms in legal education due to

[200] Le Thanh Vinh, *Competition Law Transfers in Vietnam from an Interpretive Perspective*, pp. 133–134.

[201] Nguyên Hà, 'Kiến nghị Xoá bỏ Ưu đãi Cho Doanh nghiệp Nhà nước' ['Proposal for Elimination of Privileges for SOEs'] *VnEconomy* (online), 27 October 2011, available at http://vneconomy.vn/thoi-su/kien-nghi-xoa-bo-moi-uu-dai-cho-doanh-nghiep-nha-nuoc-20111027121553344.htm.

[202] Bui Ngoc Son, 'Constitutional Developments in Vietnam in the First Decade of the Twenty-First Century', in Albert H.Y. Chen (ed.), *Constitutionalism in Asia in the Early Twenty-First Century* (Cambridge: Cambridge University Press, 2014), pp. 194, 213.

[203] Do Hai Ha, *The Dynamics of Legal Transplantation*, pp. 354–355.

[204] Nicholson, 'Vietnamese Courts', pp. 181–182; Gillespie, 'Concepts of Law in Vietnam: Transforming Statist Socialism', p. 162.

[205] Nicholson, 'Vietnamese Courts', pp. 181–182; Gillespie, 'Concepts of Law in Vietnam: Transforming Statist Socialism', pp. 163–164.

[206] Nicholson, 'Renovating Courts', pp. 542–548.

concerns about departing from the Party line.[207] Additionally, it has nurtured Party control over the legal profession and, thus, the development of lawyers and their role in the contemporary society.[208] In effect, the upholding of Party leadership has severely limited post-Đổi mới legal development.

In summary, the emergence of the doctrine of the 'socialist law-based state' has laid down doctrinal ingredients for important changes in the Vietnamese legal system, including an increasing role for the law, the explosion of legislation, market-oriented law reforms and extensive borrowing from capitalist states. However, the new legal doctrine has also embraced important aspects of the Soviet-imported doctrine of 'socialist legality' and its application in the pre-Đổi mới era. Further, economic, political and legal notions inherited from the Soviet Union continue to significantly impact on the Vietnamese legal system.

5.6 Concluding Remarks: Eroding Socialist Ideals vs. Persistent Marxist–Leninist Principles

The Soviet Union collapsed, but its economic, political and legal models and their underpinning ideas have persisted. This Chapter has demonstrated that the Soviet legacy continues to play an important role in contemporary Vietnam, despite enormous changes taking place in this country after Đổi mới. It shows that the socialist ideal of public ownership and social control of production means and the Marxist–Leninist emphasis on state control over economic resources substantially influence economic policy, practice and regulation. Significantly, Leninist political principles – Party leadership and democratic centralism – remain to dominate party-state thinking and, thus, critically shape post–Đổi mới economic, political and legal systems. The Soviet legal legacy – especially the doctrine of 'socialist legality' – is also relevant, continuously determining the shape of the transforming legal system.

Further, while still relevant, socialist and Marxist–Leninist economic, political and legal notions have changed considerably. The conflation of Soviet economic thinking with Asian-style developmental or protectionist perspectives, the re-configuration of the communist party as the vanguard of the entire society, the innovation of new methods of party leadership and the assimilation of 'socialist legality' into the doctrine of a

---

[207] Nicholson and Do, *Lawyers and Lawyering in Socialist Vietnam*.
[208] Ibid.

'socialist law-based state' exemplify this. In addition, continuing pre–*Đổi mới* practice, the application of Soviet-imported conceptions has substantially reflected the local context. Political decentralisation and liberalisation and the ongoing emphasis on rule by virtue and mass mobilisation are prominent examples. Moreover, socialist-inspired economic principles, such as state economic management and state sector domination, have been strategically deployed by party-state interest groups to protect crony capitalist interests rather than achieve socialist objectives.

Importantly, the Chapter has illustrated the eroding impact of the Soviet legacy. This is especially evident in the case of fundamental socialist ideals like material equality and social cooperation. Some Marxist–Leninist economic, political and legal conceptions, such as state economic management, proletariat dictatorship and socialist legality, have also declined somewhat in influence. Overall, the Marxist–Leninist legacy, especially the principles of party leadership and democratic centralism, have nonetheless strongly persisted. In short, whereas Marxist–Leninist economic, political and legal principles remain very strong and influential, the core socialist ideals underpinning Marxism–Leninism have become increasingly irrelevant.

PART III

Constitutions

6

Diverging Trends in the Socialist Constitutionalism of the People's Republic of China and the Socialist Republic of Vietnam

FU HUALING AND JASON BUHI

6.1 Introduction

The People's Republic of China and the Socialist Republic of Vietnam are probably the best reference points for each other in comparative studies of socialist constitutionalism, not just for their extensive similarities, but also their growing differences. For at least a decade, and especially since 2011,[1] the two East Asian party-states have been pursuing increasingly distinct paths towards the future. Although history records that Vietnam has taken important governance cues from China for centuries,[2] a discernable pattern exists whereby some of Vietnam's more independent moves occur during periods of tension with its neighbour to the north.[3] We seem to be

Fu Hualing, Professor of Law, University of Hong Kong Faculty of Law; Jason Buhi, Visiting Assistant Professor, Peking University School of Transnational Law (Shenzhen). The authors would like to thank John Gillespie, Keith Hand, Andrew Harding, Pip Nicholson and Wang Chenguang for their comments on the earlier versions of this paper.

[1] We assert that China has been growing more insular since the 18th Party Congress in 2012, while Vietnam has been trending more open since its 11th Party Congress in 2011.

[2] China dominated Vietnam for much of the period from 112 BC to 939 AD, and the Chinese influence continues with varying intensity to the present era. For example, the nineteenth-century Nguyen Dynasty's Gia Long Code was heavily based on the Qing Code. During the 1940s, Chinese advisers shaped the stance of the Communist Party of Indochina. For a compilation of various historical notes, see John Gillespie and Albert Chen, *Legal Reforms in China and Vietnam: A Comparison of Asian Communist Regimes* (New York, NY: Routledge Press, 2010), pp. 3–6; also Joern Dosch and Alexander L. Vuving, *The Impact of China on Governance Structures in Vietnam* (Bonn: German Development Institute, 2008).

[3] Vietnam, like China, attempted a near-wholesale importation of the Soviet political-legal system but remained closer to Moscow upon the Sino-Soviet split in 1968. Relations deteriorated as the countries fought a border war in 1979. Deference reappeared in the mid-1980s as Vietnam's *doi moi* reforms aligned Vietnam with China's reform policies, but the Vietnamese counterbalanced that with more internationalist initiatives after 1989,

at such a geopolitically inspired crossroads right now, as China pursues aggressive territorial claims in waters off the Vietnam coast.[4]

Despite their significant differences in size, population and economic scale, the two systems invite comparison because they share common cultural (Confucian)[5] and political (Soviet)[6] origins. Both state apparatuses are subordinate to the leadership of a communist party whose supremacy is entrenched in the national constitution. Both claim to be committed to building a socialist rule of law that offers protection of human rights, although the substance differs greatly from Western expectations.[7] Both have been experiencing rapid socioeconomic transformations after liberalising policies under the banner of developing a socialist market economy.[8]

---

as many major laws were borrowed from or inspired by multilateral institutions in the 1990s. Gillespie and Chen, *Legal Reforms in China and Vietnam*, pp. 7–8.

[4] Whereas the Preamble of the Vietnamese Constitution of 1992 twice thanked 'the precious assistance of friends across the world, *especially of the socialist and neighboring countries*' (emphasis added) in achieving revolutionary victories, the 'especially' clause was dropped from the new Constitution of 2013. Similar language was removed from the new Article 12 (previously Article 14) describing the substantive bases of Vietnam's foreign policy. Indeed, the HYSY 981 oil-rig incident invited speculation that Vietnam will revisit its 'Three Nos' defence policy (i.e., having no formal military alliances, not allowing any foreign military bases on Vietnamese territory, and not relying on other countries in combat operations). See Ankit Panda, 'After HYSY-981: A U.S.-Vietnam Alliance?', *The Diplomat*, 22 July 2014, available at http://thediplomat.com/2014/07/after-hysy-981-a-u-s-vietnam-alliance.

[5] Bui Ngoc Son, 'The Confucian Foundations of Ho Chi Minh's Vision of Government' (2013) 46(1) *Journal of Oriental Studies* 35–59.

[6] The Preamble of the 1982 Constitution explicitly entrenches the leadership of the CCP and, according to Article 1, China remains a socialist country practicing 'democratic dictatorship' based on the alliance of workers and peasants. The Preamble of the 2013 Vietnamese Constitution notes the leadership of the VCP, while Article 4 declares that the VCP, 'acting upon the Marxist-Leninist doctrine and Ho Chi Minh's thought, is the leading force of the State and society'. Constitution of the Socialist Republic of Vietnam (as amended in 2013), unofficial translation available at www.constitutionnet.org/vl/item/constitution-socialist-republic-vietnam-amended-2013.

[7] See, e.g., Albert H. Y. Chen, 'Conclusion: Comparative Reflections on Human Rights in Asia', in Randall Peerenboom et al. (eds.), *Human Rights in Asia* (London: Routledge, 2006); Sonya Sceats and Shaun Breslin, 'China's Indirect Impact on the International Human Rights System', in *China and the International Human Rights System* (London: Chatham House, 2012), pp. 41–45; 'Human Rights Watch World Report: Vietnam 2013', Human Rights Watch, available at https://www.hrw.org/world-report/2013/country-chapters/vietnam.

[8] Both are middle income countries, although China is at the higher-middle end of the per capita income scale (USD 7,589) while Vietnam is at the lower-middle end (USD 2,052). In terms of GDP per capita (nominal), China ranked 78/184 in 2014 with USD 7,589 per capita; and Vietnam's was USD 2,052, ranked 132/184. To put this in perspective,

Noting these similarities, several comparative studies have been undertaken in recent years,[9] but the field lies outside the mainstream of international constitutional discourse and is therefore still open to development. Conventional liberal criticism of constitutional law in Leninist states centres around its lack of constitutionalism – that is, the text does not outline and establish a system that functions to constrain the real political power of (or behind) the state, especially through an independent judiciary.[10] Thus described, the constitution's only operative provisions are the decrees justifying the exercise of absolute political power by the ruling party; all other provisions – especially those involving individual liberties – are merely irrelevant 'window dressing'.[11] If true, the Chinese and Vietnamese constitutions are ineffective and inconsequential. Yet these critiques cannot explain why such meaningless constitutional provisions are robustly debated and frequently resorted to, with varying degrees of effectiveness, by aggrieved parties, both through the courts and on the streets, as discussed below.

Many argue that socialist constitutions are, at least, aspirational,[12] and history demonstrates that once inspired there is little the people of China

Vietnam in 2014 was where China was in 2006. IMF ranking available at www.indexmundi.com/facts/indicators/NY.GDP.PCAP.CD/compare?country=cn#coun try=cn:vnm.

Meanwhile, the United Nations Development Program's (UNDP) Human Development Index (HDI) provides another apt comparison. In 2013, China was ranked as a high development country with a HDI score of .719, while Vietnam was a middle development country with a score of .638. Once again, Vietnam in 2013 was about where China was in 2004–2005 in terms of HDI. UNDP HDI Index available at http://hdr.undp.org/en/con tent/human-development-index-hdi.

[9] See, e.g., Gillespie and Chen, *Legal Reforms in China and Vietnam*; John Gillespie and Pip Nicholson, *Asian Socialism and Legal Change: The Dynamics of Vietnamese and Chinese Reform* (Canberra: Asia Pacific Press, 2005); Teresa Wright, *Accepting Authoritarianism: State-Society Relations in China's Reform Era* (Stanford, CA: Stanford University Press, 2010), pp 162–179. Bui Ngoc Son, 'The Discourse of Constitutional Review in Vietnam' (2014) 9 *Journal of Comparative Law* 175–205; Mark Sidel, *Law and Society in Vietnam: The Transition from Socialism in Comparative Perspective* (Cambridge: Cambridge University Press, 2008); Dosch and Vuving, *The Impact of China on Governance Structures in Vietnam*.

[10] Albert H. Y. Chen, 'The Achievement of Constitutionalism in Asia: Moving Beyond 'Constitutions without Constitutionalism'', in Albert H. Y. Chen (ed.), *Constitutionalism in Asia in the Early Twenty-First Century* (Cambridge: Cambridge University Press, 2014).

[11] Tony Saich, *Governance and Politics of China* (Basingstoke: Palgrave Macmillian, 2010, 3rd edn.), p. 148.

[12] This characterisation has been around for many years. See, e.g., William B. Simons (ed.), *The Constitutions of the Communist World* (Germantown, MD: Sijthoff and Noordhoff,

or Vietnam cannot achieve. The party-states, having codified normative rights, face credibility crises if they violate the peoples' expectations by ignoring those undertakings for too long. Indeed, constitutional inter-pretation, enforcement and/or reform sometimes legitimately occur through alternative processes known as either 'political constitutional-ism' (wherein political mechanisms such as legislative processes assume and manage constitutional enforcement),[13] or 'popular' or 'civic' consti-tutionalism (wherein citizens spontaneously assert ownership over con-stitutional interpretation and compel a dialogue and a settlement with the state on matters relating to constitutional rights).[14] While the former can be used to capture popular demands within the authoritarian system, the latter may be more worrisome to authoritarian rulers, as the spon-taneous demand for constitutional rights is 'gain[ing] new cohesion and momentum',[15] demonstrating a nascent constitutional awareness among

1980), p. xv ('The constitutions of the communist world have always been used for internal as well as external consumption – to proclaim what has been achieved and to lay down the program of what is still to be accomplished.'); He Weifang, Stephanie Balme and Michael Dowdle, among others, point out that a significant part of the 1982 Chinese Constitution declares goals to be achieved in the future, including a system of democratic political representation, as well as a wide range of political, social and economic rights. Balme and Dowdle refer to China's constitutionalism as 'development potential, not developmental accomplishment', Stephanie Balme et al., 'Introduction: Exploring for Constitutionalism in 21st Century China', in Stephanie Balme and Michael Dowdle (eds.), *Building Constitu-tionalism in China* (New York, NY: Palgrave Macmillan, 2010), p. 10.

[13] See Chen Duanhong, 'The People Must Be Present' ['Ren Min Bi Dei Chu Chang'], in *Constituent Power and Fundamental Law [Zhi Xian Quan Yu Gen Ben Fa]* (Beijing: China Legal Publishing House), pp. 46–110; Jiang Shigong, 'Written and Unwritten Constitution: A New Approach to the Study of Constitutional Government in China' (2010) 36(1) *Modern China* 12–46.

[14] Bruce Ackerman, *We the People: Foundations* (Cambridge, MA: Harvard University Press, 1993); John E. Finn, 'The Civic Constitution: Some Preliminaries', in Sotirios A. Barber and Robert P. George (eds.), *Constitutional Politics: Essays on Constitution Making, Maintenance, and Change* (Princeton, NJ: Princeton University Press, 2001), p. 44; Larry Kramer, *The People Themselves: Popular Constitutionalism and Judicial Review* (Oxford: Oxford Univer-sity Press, 2004); Richard Bellamy, *Political Constitutionalism: A Republican Defense of the Constitutionality of Democracy* (Cambridge: Cambridge University Press, 2007); Bui Ngoc Son and Pip Nicholson, 'Activism and Popular Constitutionalism in Contemporary Viet-nam' (2016) *Law & Social Inquiry Law*; and Mark Tushnet, 'Popular Constitutionalism as Political Law' (2006) 81 *Chicago-Kent Law Review* 991; Zhang Qianfan, 'A Constitution without Constitutionalism? The Paths of Constitutional Development in China' (2010) 8(4) *International Journal of Constitutional Law* 950.

[15] Keith Hand, 'Resolving Constitutional Disputes in Contemporary China' (2011) 7 *East Asia Law Review* 51, 65–66.

the public outside of the party-states' master plan.[16] Inspired citizens are increasingly usurping judicial roles by interpreting and implementing constitutional rights through online mobilisations, peaceful vigils, religious ceremonies, labour strikes and street actions.[17] Such resilient demands have made constitutional supremacy a subject of lively debate,[18] with the positive potential of generating more healthy dialogue between party-state and society. Indeed, a diverse range of legal and accommodative approaches are now being deployed.[19] As such, if constitutional studies concern the distribution and exercise of political power, then research on the Chinese and Vietnamese constitutions must venture into a 'results-oriented pragmatic approach'.[20] The failure to explore such avenues is fatal to an academic understanding of different national governance schemes, comparative scholarship generally and, specifically, to the aspirations of citizens and reformers in socialist states who seek to develop ties to mainstream constitutional discourse.

This Chapter provides an overview to a comparative study of Sino–Vietnamese comparative constitutionalism by exploring the bases of three core substantive pillars of socialist constitutionalism: insistence on Party leadership, reliance on socialist rule of law and adaptation to populism. After considering several examples of how constitutional rules

[16] See Stephanie Balme, 'China's Constitutional Research and Teaching: A State of the Art', in Balme and Dowdle, *Building Constitutionalism in China*, p. 107; Keith Hand, 'Citizens Engage the Constitution: The Sun Zhigang Incident and Constitutional Review Proposals in the People's Republic of China' in Balme and Dowdle, *Building Constitutionalism in China*, p. 221. See also Stephanie Balme, 'The Judicialisation of Politics and the Politicisation of the Judicary (1978–2005)' (2005) 5 *Global Jurist Frontiers* 1; Randall Peerenboom, 'Law and Development of Constitutional Democracy: Problem or Paradigm?' (2005) 19 *Columbia Journal of Asian Law* 185, 204.

[17] Hand, 'Resolving Constitutional Disputes in Contemporary China' 51, 92, also citing Carl Minzner, 'Xinfang: Alternative to Formal Chinese Legal Institutions' (2006) 42 *Stanford Journal of International Law* 103, 143–145.

[18] Of course, both China and Vietnam make the controversial assertion that their national constitutions are the supreme law of the land (Art. 5, 1982 Chinese Constitution; Arts. 4,8,9, 2013 Vietnamese Constitution), but the lack of rigorous judicial enforcement does not necessarily mean the constitution is an empty letter.

[19] Judicial enforcement is obviously preferable as it is more transparent, structured and formal; political and popular constitutionalism are both characterised by opacity and informal trade-offs, while popular constitutionalism can be informal or occasionally chaotic. See, e.g., Keith Hand, 'Constitutionalising Wukan: The Value of the Constitution outside the Courtroom' (February 2012) 12(3) *China Brief*; Minzner, 'Xinfang', 143–145.

[20] Randall Peerenboom, *The Social Foundations of China's Living Constitution* (2010), available at SSRN: https://ssrn.com/abstract=1542463 or http://dx.doi.org/10.2139/ssrn.1542463, 41.

are currently operating through political and popular constitutionalism in all three areas, we conclude that Vietnam is presently moving in a direction that offers more prospects for convergence with international norms,[21] as the current Vietnamese party-state is relatively less politically monolithic, more open to the influence of international laws and more tolerant of civil society than its Chinese counterpart. That being the case, we predict that, for the foreseeable future, Vietnam will likely continue to depart from the increasingly insular Chinese model of constitutional development.

6.2   Leadership of the Communist Parties

At a foundational level, there have been few structural changes to the authoritarian Chinese and Vietnamese party-state constitutional orders, in spite of the pervasive social and economic reforms of the last three decades. With the exception of the first Vietnamese Constitution of 1946,[22] all of China and Vietnam's post-revolution constitutions (each of which has had five) have enshrined Leninist political supervision. Party leadership is a prime directive consistently entrenched in both the Chinese and Vietnamese national constitutions, clearly declared in their respective Preambles and core text. The respective Chinese Communist Party (CCP) and the Vietnamese Communist Party (VCP) monopolise political and military power,[23] institutionalise democratic centralism and prohibit threatening discourse.

Though Party leadership cannot be changed through any legal means, the organisation of that power is significantly different in China and Vietnam. While decisive and effective implementation characterises both countries, the Vietnamese party-state is presently more open to

---

[21] Some institutional limits on this flirtation are evaluated by Thiem Bui, 'Liberal Constitutionalism and the Socialist State in an Era of Globalisation: An Inquiry into Vietnam's Constitutional Discourse and Power Structures' (2013) 5 *The Global Studies Journal* 2.

[22] Perhaps this is because that 1946 Constitution represented a synthesis of Western and Ho Chi Minh Thought, calling for a tripartite separation of powers and guaranteeing fundamental rights. David G. Marr, 'Ho Chi Minh's Independence Declaration', in K. W. Taylor and John K. Whitmore (eds.), *Essays into Vietnamese Pasts* (Ithaca, NY: Cornell University Press, 1995), pp. 221–231.

[23] Article 4 of the Vietnam Constitution (2013) makes the party the vanguard and representative not only of the Vietnamese working class, but of the whole Vietnamese people and nation, further narrowing the legal space to exercise the right to pluralistic and freely contested elections. Article 65 follows the government lead in enshrining a new legal requirement for Vietnam's armed forces to be absolutely loyal to the Communist Party.

constructive debate within the Party forum, as evinced by having more diffuse executive authorities and a more competitive selection process for membership in its Central Committee.

Indeed, both nations feature a party-state that operates on the basis of democratic centralism. This ensures a decisive decision-making process, thus establishing 'effective' states in which policy making and implementation is swift, owing in part to a denial of separation of powers and a lack of mechanisms through which formal checks and balances can be exercised.[24] While these structural deficiencies perpetuate other systemic problems, they need not undercut raw 'government effectiveness', which – as defined by international institutions – simply measures whether a regime can implement meaningful change.[25] Fukuyama forcefully argues that state effectiveness is a necessary condition for successful constitutional and legal reform, as strong leaders in the Confucian tradition are well positioned for nation-building, demonstrated by the cases of South Korea, Japan, Taiwan and Singapore.[26] Once there is the political will to promote reform, effective states have strong institutions to rely upon and competent bureaucrats to implement programs with a high degree of efficiency.[27] Accepting that both states have high implementation capacity,[28] it becomes a question of political values and will.

---

[24] As the 2014 Decision Concerning Some Major Questions in Comprehensively Promoting the Rule of Law [Zhonggong zhongyang guanyu quanmian tuijin yifa zhiguo ruogan zhongda wenti de jueding] explains, China will not admit any separation of powers and will not tolerate any institution to have a veto on the Party's decisions. English translation and Chinese original available at https://chinacopyrightandmedia.wordpress.com/2014/10/28/ccp-central-committee-decision-concerning-some-major-questions-in-comprehensively-moving-governing-the-country-according-to-the-law-forward/.

[25] The World Bank provides this definition: 'Government effectiveness captures perceptions of the quality of public services, the quality of the civil service and the degree of its independence from political pressures, the quality of policy formulation and implementation, and the credibility of the government's commitment to such policies.' Available at https://info.worldbank.org/governance/wgi/pdf/ge.pdf.

[26] Francis Fukuyama, *Political Order and Political Decay: From the Industrial Revolution to the Globalisation of Democracy* (London: Profile Books, 2014).

[27] 'Regardless of the degree of government intervention, the fast-growing economies of East Asia share a common feature: they all possess competent, high-capacity state.' Ibid., p. 335.

[28] For instance, the World Bank's Worldwide Governance Indicators (WGI) index measures governance ability via six indicators: voice and accountability; political stability and absence of violence; government effectiveness; regulatory quality; rule of law; and control of corruption. China and Vietnam performed the best in government effectiveness among the six indicators in the 2014 survey. Importantly, China outperformed its 'East Asian and Pacific' neighbours in 'government effectiveness' while lagging behind in the

It is perhaps on those bases that several meaningful and consequential differences between the political designs of the two party-states is emerging. Since the Tiananmen crackdown in 1989, the CCP has demonstrated a much higher concentration of political power in the hands of a smaller number of men, while the VCP has demonstrated signs of political diffusion, splitting into contesting blocs. As a result, the nascent checks and balances within the Vietnamese system are more apparent. Former Chinese President Hu Jintao found the trend so disturbing that he felt compelled to issue an internal Party document:

> criticis[ing] the Vietnamese authorities for moving 'too quickly toward inner-party democracy', even warning that a destabilising Mikhail Gorbachev-like figure could come to power. The CCP also banned public discussion of Vietnam's reforms, deploying party intellectuals to argue publicly against such a political development in China.[29]

This fear likely emanates from the fact that developments in Vietnam indicate the emergence of more political constitutionalism, as there is more intra-party democracy in the VCP than the CCP.

At the level of elite politics, the commanding heights of Vietnam's party-state feature a broader policy-making coalition involving more diverse stakeholders in the decision-making process.[30] This is true in both the executive and legislative arenas. Speaking of the executives first, China has endowed its supreme leader with a 'trinity' of positions that unify command of the party-state: President of the State, General Secretary of the CCP and Commander-in-Chief of the Armed Forces. That makes the officeholder, now Xi Jinping, incredibly powerful. Meanwhile,

---

other five indicators. Vietnam closely tracked the regional averages. As a lower–middle income country, Vietnam clearly outperformed other similarly situated countries in terms of both 'political stability' and 'government effectiveness'. These assets generate confidence and legitimacy in the durability of the system and hope for its capacity to improve. World Bank Worldwide Governance Indicators, Government Effectiveness, available at http://info.worldbank.org/governance/wgi/index.aspx#doc.

[29] Regina Abrami, Edmund Malesky and Yu Zheng, 'Vietnam through Chinese Eyes: Divergent Accountability in Single-Party Regimes', citing Gu Sanyue, 'Yuenan chule ge Deng Xiaoping' ['There Is a Deng Xiaoping in Vietnam'], Blog China, December 2006, (on file with authors) Martin K. Dimitrov, 'Understanding Communist Collapse and Resilience', in Martin K. Dimitrov (ed.), *Why Communism Did Not Collapse: Understanding Authoritarian Regime Resilience in Asia and Europe* (Cambridge: Cambridge University Press, 2013), p. 238.

[30] Edmund Malesky, Regina Abrami and Yu Zheng, 'Institutions and Inequality in Single-Party Regimes: A Comparative Analysis of Vietnam and China' (2011) 43(4) *Comparative Politics* 409.

in Vietnam, the posts are separate: the Prime Minister, the President and the General Secretary of the VCP are separate positions held by separate persons.[31] Although political power was consolidated by a more conservative faction at the 12th National Congress of the VCP in 2016, political observers indicate that those three individuals can and have represented different political factions within the VCP, perhaps reflecting a grand bargain.[32]

Power is also more diffuse throughout the legislative organs of the Vietnamese party-state. For example, the ultimate political power in China rests in the CCP Politburo (twenty-five members before October 2018) and especially its Standing Committee (currently seven members, down from nine in 2013), with the Central Committee (205 full members and 171 alternate members) playing only a ceremonial role.[33] Adding the 2,987 representatives of the National People's Congress, that is a total of roughly 3,395 representatives for 1.3 billion people, each representing 435,000 souls. In Vietnam, the 150-strong VCP Central Committee has been grappling for power with the smaller Standing Committee (fifteen members), while the state's National Assembly contains 498 members. That amounts to roughly 660 people presiding over 90 million souls, or one representative for every 136,000 people.

The VCP's broader Central Committee has been a relevant decision maker since the demise of General Secretary Le Duan in 1986, with some claiming that it is superior to a Standing Committee that has been reduced to 'a glorified secretariat'.[34] Indeed, that Central Committee has grabbed attention for an ability, though rarely manifested, to reject recommendations on significant political decisions from the Politburo.[35] The Central Committee's apparent power was demonstrated in October 2012, when it reversed a Politburo decision initiated by General Secretary Nguyễn Phú Trọng to discipline Prime Minister Nguyễn Tấn Dũng for economic mismanagement and nepotism.[36] It next rejected Trọng's recommendation of two persons to the Politburo in May 2013, opting

---

[31] At present, the President of Vietnam is Truong Tan Sang; the Secretary-General is Nguyen Phu Trong; and the Prime Minister is Nguyen Tan Dung.

[32] http://thediplomat.com/2015/07/vietnam-after-2016-who-will-lead/.

[33] The Name List of the 18th Communist Party of China Central Committee [Zhongguo gongchandang di shibajie zhongyang weiyuanhui mingdan] , available at http://news.ifeng.com/mainland/special/zhonggong18da/detail_2012_11/14/19165234_0.shtml.

[34] Malesky, Abrami and Zheng, 'Institutions and Inequality', 13.

[35] Ibid.

[36] Available at http://thediplomat.com/2015/07/vietnam-after-2016-who-will-lead/.

for its own favoured candidates.[37] Another unprecedented vote of no confidence for twenty top party officials was overcome by Prime Minister Dũng's faction in the Central Committee in January 2015.[38] Meanwhile, across the divide, senior members of the National Assembly have boldly criticised the Prime Minister,[39] while another proposed that Vietnam should adopt a bicameral legislature, with the National Assembly serving as the lower house and the VCP's Central Committee as the senate.[40] While corruption, patronage and factional politics are common issues facing both the CCP and VCP, power is much more centralised in the CCP, where political competition is much less visible.

While what we know of these events clearly suggests significant internal power struggles, this broader coalition enables wider political participation and more fierce competition for power in Vietnam than in China. There is, for example, no formal, competitive procedure for joining Politburo or the Standing Committee in China, and the rejection rate of nominees to the ceremonial Central Committee is only between 4 to 8 per cent. However, in Vietnam, the gap between nominated candidates and elected members in the Central Committee is 23 per cent for full members and 54 per cent for alternate members.[41] A larger circle of decision makers composed of more representative competing factions can produce different political consequences and so, in Vietnam, the political process appears relatively more open, more representative of diverse interests and potentially more accountable to the larger society.

Vietnam's broader political participation and fiercer political competition make the VCP more accountable, both horizontally and vertically, than the CCP.[42] Political pluralism at the elite level has had a cascade effect in making the atmosphere surrounding legal processes more transparent. There has been more competition between the Party and the state, and disagreements among different state organisations can be openly manifested. In one famous case, the Vietnamese police promulgated a 'one person, one motorcycle' policy, and following that policy, the

---

[37] Le Hong Hiep, 'Power Shifts in Vietnam's Political System', East Asia Forum, 5 March 2015, available at www.eastasiaforum.org/2015/03/05/power-shifts-in-vietnams-political-system/.

[38] Votes in June 2013, November 2014, and January 2015, respectively. See www.bloomberg.com/news/articles/2014-11-15/vietnam-confidence-vote-reveals-jockeying-among-political-elite.

[39] Available at www.bbc.com/news/world-asia-20322830.

[40] Le Hong Hiep, 'Power Shifts in Vietnam's Political System'.

[41] Malesky, Abrami and Zheng, 'Institutions and Inequality', 17.

[42] Martin K. Dimitrov, 'Understanding Communist Collapse and Resilience', p. 32.

Hanoi government suspended registration of motorcycles in some of the city's districts.[43] The restriction inspired deep hostility and resistance among Vietnam's motorcycle users, leading to fierce social mobilisation and public debate over constitutional property rights. The Hanoi government and the police held their ground, but the Ministry of Justice and National Assembly eventually threatened legal challenges, forcing them to back off.[44]

In contrast, CCP elites are more monopolistic and retain more extensive and institutionalised control over state apparatuses, even overriding state organs in making and implementing decisions. The CCP is deeply embedded in government departments, and exercises routine political control of state institutions and public authorities.[45] It relies on informal institutions under the control of the Party, known as 'small leading groups', which cut across any perceived boundary between Party and state.[46] These CCP cells play a key role in decision making within Chinese state organs, and are increasingly asserting political control in private sector law firms, accounting firms and non-governmental organisations (NGOs).[47]

There also appears to be a stronger political will for, and deeper commitment to, structural reform in Vietnam. After fierce debate, the Vietnamese chose to ratify a new constitution in 2013, rather than amend the old. During the debates, the National Assembly took a strong position in supporting a proposed Constitutional Council.[48] Prior to the abrupt final decision against its adoption, elements of Vietnamese society undertook a rich discussion of constitutional review that advanced the concept of building such an independent constitutional adjudication forum quite

---

[43] Bui Ngoc Son, 'Constitutional Developments in Vietnam in the First Decade of the 21st Century', in Albert H. Y. Chen, *Constitutionalism in Asia in the Early Twenty-First Century* (Cambridge: Cambridge University Press, 2014), pp. 206–207.

[44] Interestingly, when the Guangdong police banned the use of motorcycles in the city, the police only faced a legal challenge by the motorcycle manufacturers. Jim Yardley, 'In City Ban, A Sign of Wealth and Its Discontents', *New York Times Asia Journal*, 15 January 2007, available at http://www.nytimes.com/2007/01/15/world/asia/15china.html?_r=0.

[45] Ibid. at Abrami, Malesky and Zheng, 'Vietnam through Chinese Eyes', pp. 259–61.

[46] Ibid.

[47] Ibid. Also Sarah Biddulph, *The Stability Imperative Human Rights and Law in China* (Vancouver: UBC Press, 2015).

[48] Le Nhung, 'Will Vietnam Have Constitutional Council or Constitutional Court?', Vietnam-NetBridge, 21 February 2013, available at http://english.vietnamnet.vn/fms/government/66904/vietnam-will-have-constitutional-council-or-constitutional-court-.html; http://vietnamnews.vn/politics-laws/240346/na-deputies-discuss-constitutional-council.html

far.[49] To date, the only known comparable example in China was for a retired Chief Justice to call for the creation of a similar institution at a quasi-official function.[50] The CCP largely associates such suggestions as heresies associated with colour revolutions, to be perpetrated by Western powers and their domestic agents.[51] Indeed, whereas Vietnam appears to be liberalising its perspective on consultation, input and debate since 2013, China has opted to go in the opposite direction, rendering the terms 'constitutionalism', 'civil society' and 'judicial independence' (among others) taboo in academic discourse.[52]

Intriguingly, the Vietnamese are currently debating procedural rules both for holding public demonstrations and voting in referendums. The former is meant to actualise a limited and issue-specific freedom to assemble granted in article 25 and has been boosted by recent nationalist sentiment against China.[53] Of more structural interest, article 29 grants the right to vote in a referendum to any person over eighteen years old in

---

[49] Ibid., 'NA deputies' two-day discussion on draft amendments to the Constitution, which was broadcast live on national radio and TV, drew great attention from voters around the country.' For a discussion of the drafting process, see Bui Hai Thiem, 'Pluralism Unleashed: The Politics of Reforming the Vietnamese Constitution' (2014) 9(4) *Journal of Vietnamese Studies* 19–22; Pip Nicholson, 'Vietnamese Constitutionalism: The Reform Possibilities' (2016) 11 *Asian Journal of Comparative Law* 199–207.

[50] Beijing Youth Newspaper, 'Former Chief Justice of the Supreme People's Court Suggesting the Establishment of a Constitutional Court', available at www.chinalawinfo.com/news/NewsFullText.aspx?NewsId=70635&NewsType=0.

[51] According to Hand, one of the main reasons not to introduce a constitutional committee within China's NPC to police the legislative order is the concern that creating such a constitutional committee will further generate citizen activism and offer a forum for politically sensitive questions. Keith Hand, 'An Assessment of Socialist Constitutional Supervision Models and Prospects for a Constitutional Supervision Committee in China: The Constitution as Commander?', in John Garrick and Yan Chang Bennett (eds.), *China's Socialist Rule of Law Reforms Under Xi Jinping* (London: Routledge, 2016); See also Rogier Creemers, 'China's Constitutionalism Debate: Content, Context and Implications' (July 2015) 74 *The China Journal* 91–109.

[52] The Party issued a document which lists seven topics which are off limit in public discussion, commonly referred to as seven prohibitions. It is telling that the Party classified the said document as a state secret and sentenced Ms Gao Yu, a seventy-year veteran journalist, to seven years' imprisonment for leaking the document. *See* 22 April 2013, 'Report Concerning the Present Situation in the Ideological Area'; Stanley Lubman, 'Document No. 9: The Party Attacks Western Democratic Ideals,' *Wall Street Journal* China Real Time Report, 27 August 2013.

[53] Dang Ngoc Tung, president of the Vietnam General Confederation of Labor, and Tran Thi Quoc Khanh, a Hanoi deputy, also said they agreed with the suggestion that the Bill on Demonstrations be effective in 2016. 'In the context that China has committed wrongdoings that violated our country's sovereignty, many people want to express their patriotism and aspirations,' Tung said. Tuoi Tre News, 28 May 2015, 'Vietnam lawmakers want

any referendum declared by the National Assembly (article 70) and organised by the Standing Committee of the National Assembly (article 74). Although there have not been any referendums to date, the matter was warmly debated at a series of three conferences in 2015, including by legal academics and members of the Ho Chi Minh City Bar Association.[54] Though unlikely to be implemented in the near future, such a move would be a remarkable leap in socialist constitutional development. In terms of Vietnamese constitutional text, it would help promote 'the People's mastery' (article 2) and assist the VCP in developing 'close ties with the People', 'submitting to People's supervision', and assure that the VCP is 'accountable to the People in its decisions' (article 4[2]).

In any event, it is probable that the Central Committee will continue to aggregate power after the upcoming 12th National Congress in 2016 if Dũng ascends to Party Chairman and the Central Committee can defend and maintain its ability to conduct confidence votes on top party officials. In concert, these developments indicate that the VCP appears to be relatively more open-minded and pluralistic in its exercise of political power within its authoritarian context, rendering its current state of reform progress more 'politically consequential' than that of China.[55]

6.3   Commitment to Socialist Rule of Law

Both China and Vietnam advocate the development of a so-called socialist rule of law. Since shedding their totalitarian approach decades ago, both parties have been more reluctant to exercise naked political power. They instead resort to legal institutions to manage and coordinate massive socioeconomic transitions and maintain credibility. Legal reform in authoritarian states is a contradictory process, however, because it can generate tremendous societal demand for individual rights and

---

Law on Demonstrations to be Passed Next Year,' available at http://tuoitrenews.vn/society/28354/lawmakers-want-law-on-demonstrations-to-be-passed-next-year.

[54] Domestic commentators were quite clear in arguing that a referendum must be binding, because to make it advisory would change the definition of the word referendum to equate it with 'consultation'. The majority of their efforts in drafting a recommendation paper to the government focused on narrowing substantive matters capable of submission to referendum. Foreign speakers from Sweden, Canada, and the United States presented alternative views, and the chairman announced that twenty sample referendum laws from other jurisdictions had been officially translated for sending to the government.

[55] Bui Ngoc Son, 'The Discourse of Constitutional Review in Vietnam' (2014) 9(2) *Journal of Comparative Law* 175–205.

government accountability. Thus, while the party-states employ law to achieve certain objectives, they attempt to limit legal reform so as to prevent any political spillover. Vietnam's experiment has been proceeding in a more internationalist fashion, however, as it has been more welcoming of foreign normative influences, especially in the field of human rights.

What comprises socialist rule of law is the subject of much debate. What classifies the Chinese and Vietnamese orders as 'socialist', perhaps more than anything else, is their self-identification; what separates them most obviously from European models is their Leninist political structure. Leninism includes a doctrine positing that vanguard communist parties do not have an interest independent of that of the 'People', as they completely discern and represent their common interest. As Nathan put it, the Party asserts that it and the people 'have a fundamental harmony of interests' which makes democracy and accountability redundant and potentially harmful.[56] A fundamental change occurred upon the collapse of this doctrine in China and Vietnam during the period of economic reform, which was accompanied by the surfacing of diverse, pluralistic social interests. Having recognised the perennial existence of social conflict, the parties must design rules and institutions to manage and preserve harmony. Both the CCP and the VCP have managed developments in response to complex socioeconomic circumstances and, as a result, there have been visible expansions or contractions of constitutional 'space'.

The main thread of constitutional change has been an emphasis on the rule of law and individual rights in promoting social and economic development. In China, significant constitutional amendments include the recognition of the privately-owned economy in 1988, the promotion of rule of law and construction of a socialist state of rule of law in 1999, and the duty of state to respect human rights in 2004.[57] The CCP Central Committee's Fourth Plenum in 2014 recommitted China to further development of a socialist rule of law system.[58] The new Vietnamese Constitution of 2013 contains significantly more phrasing of substantive

---

[56] Andrew Nathan, *Chinese Democracy* (Berkeley, CA: University of California Press, 1986), p. 228.

[57] 1982 Chinese Constitution, amendments of 1988 (first), 1999 (third), 2004 (fourth).

[58] Communique of the 4th Plenary Session of the 18th Central Committee of CCP (23 Oct. 2014), available at www.china.org.cn/china/fourth_plenary_session/2014-12/02/content_34208801.htm.

rights than before. Meanwhile, legal reform in both countries has included an explosion of legislation, the professionalisation and institutionalisation of legal institutions, a growing number of legal professionals to channel disputes from society to state institutions and, above all, an effort to inculcate a new popular legal culture.[59]

Rule of law, in order to be credible in the eyes of the public, must be able to regularise, normalise and discipline the exercise of power. The CCP and VCP have thus established self-limiting and self-correcting mechanisms, such as the strengthening of intra-Party anti-corruption enforcement,[60] although the Chinese efforts have been much stronger in this regard. The Chinese central inspection system was strengthened in 1990 and codified in the CCP Constitution at the 17th Party Congress in 2007, with a series of new measures being unveiled since, especially after a renewed anti-corruption drive began with the ascendancy of Xi Jinping in 2012.[61] Meanwhile, the Vietnamese issued a resolution on 'urgent issues in Party building' at its fourth plenum of the 11th Party Conference in 2011, but elaboration has been relatively lacking, and a comprehensive 'Law on the Party' proposal put forward by the Fatherland Front was rejected in 2013.[62] The new 2013 Constitution did add two important stipulations to the old article 4, however, declaring the accountability of the VCP to the people in its decision-making capacity,

---

[59] See Fu Hualing, 'Access to Justice in China: Potentials, Limits and Alternatives', in Gillespie and Chen, *Legal Reforms in China and Vietnam*, pp. 163–187; Brian J. M. Quinn, 'Vietnam's Continuing Legal Reform: Gaining Control Over the Courts' (2003) 4(2) *Asian Pacific Law & Policy Journal* 431, 449–457.

[60] Earlier, the fourth plenum of the 11th Communist Party Central Committee issued a resolution on '*urgent issues in Party building*'. These measures aimed to create a sort of checks and balances mechanism within the CPV with the goal of resolving the challenges the party faces. (http://thediplomat.com/2015/02/2015-challenges-for-the-communist-party-of-vietnam/).

[61] Given that the commanding heights of Chinese elite politics are now more monolithic than in Vietnam where power is more diffuse among factions, this perhaps indicates that such 'anti-corruption' measures can be hijacked and conflated with more political purposes.

[62] Hoàng Thái, a former standing member of the VFF Central Committee, made a very sharp comment in 2013: 'There are laws all on the State, the NA, the VFF, but no law on the party. There must be a law on the party to ensure openness and transparency as well as to avoid arbitrariness' in 'Góp ý sửa Hiến pháp: Phải có luật về sự lãnh đạo của Đảng' ['Contribution to the Constitutional Amendments: There Must be a Law on the Party's Leadership'], *VnEconomy*, February 2013, cited in Bui Hai Thiem, 'Pluralism Unleashed: The Politics of Reforming the Vietnamese Constitution' (2014) 9(4) *Journal of Vietnamese Studies* 16.

as well as the subjugation of VCP members to the Constitution and the law.[63] Incentives for such self-regulation exist despite the lack of an institutionalised system of checks and balances. Indeed, both countries appear to have reached a stage where their party-states must figure out how to commit themselves to the rule of law systems they themselves created. This is not because of a serious and credible commitment to the rule of law on the part of the party-state, but due to internal corruption scandals and a demand emanating from civil society to hold the party-state accountable to its own rhetoric.

The development of socialist rule of law in China and Vietnam differs from the liberal conception of rule of law in at least three other major respects: the prevalence of a statist stance in imposing legal norms and creating institutions, selective rights extension and thin (versus thick) legal protections. In developing socialist rule of law, China and Vietnam demonstrate unique characteristics that are strongly associated with their national cultures and ideological debates.[64] Yet, by placing both countries in the larger historical and comparative context, Peerenboom argues that they have been following a fairly typical East Asian Model (EAM) of development despite their professed allegiance to communism.[65] Thus, there are a number of similarities between the two countries in key areas of law reform and legal development.

First, owing to their statist stances in imposing legal norms and creating institutions, both states prioritise the 'supply side' of the rule of law and rights protection while managing a gradual shift to the demand side.[66] The supply side includes establishing both constitutional

---

[63] Bui Hai Thiem, 'Pluralism Unleashed', 13–19.

[64] Gillespie and Chen, *Legal Reforms in China and Vietnam*; and Sidel, *Law and Society in Vietnam*.

[65] That model begins with a state-led economic reform, followed by the development of commercial rule of law to facilitate a market economy. In the initial stage, the state promotes civil law rights (i.e., freedom of contract) and socio-economic rights (i.e., consumer and labour rights), while limiting collective rights and political rights. As the economy grows, the state invests more in institutions, improves education and professional training (including for legal professionals), and diverts resources to human development. From that stage onward – the argument goes – the state is on the defensive and starts to guard its power and privilege, refusing to make further concessions unless absolutely necessary, although there is persistent demand for rule of law, accountability, and an expansion of rights. Randall Peerenboom, 'Rule of law, democracy and the sequencing debate: lessons from China and Vietnam', in Gillespie and Chen, *Legal Reforms in China and Vietnam*, p.29.

[66] Fu Hualing, 'Challenging Authoritarianism through Law: Potentials and Limits' (2011) 6(1) *National Taiwan University Law Review* 331, 345–346.

and legal rules, and institutions (that is, courts) to apply them.[67] The demand side includes rights awareness on the part of the citizens, as well as the cooperation of lawyers and social organisations in channelling disputes into legal institutions that facilitate rights protection.[68] It is to be expected at the beginning of a rule-of-law-building process that rule making, as a top-down process, has priority. After all, rules must be in existence before they can be enforced. Once promulgated, the issue becomes whether those rules are actually enforced or remain mere 'window-dressing'.[69] Therefore, the second stage of reform regards institutional capacity building.

Both China and Vietnam have an adequate supply of baseline rules and institutions, but there seems to be insufficient channelling into dispute resolution forums.[70] This weak channelling function appears to be a critical bottleneck in both efforts towards law reform, as it has been in other developing countries.[71] As Epp argues, what distinguishes a weak legal system from a strong one is not rules or institutions, but what he refers to as the 'support structure', which includes the legal profession, legal aid, access to justice, NGOs and other intermediaries that perform a channelling function.[72] Both China and Vietnam are developing legal aid services, improving access to courts and other dispute resolution mechanisms, and otherwise strengthening the demand side of the rule of law. But, they are also deeply concerned about the political risk of increasing legal consciousness among the citizenry and at the same time placing the supply side of the legal system, the judiciary in particular, under the Party's firm control.[73]

Second, both party-states are selective in terms of which rights they liberalise. Within limited political contexts, both demonstrate that it is

---

[67] Ibid.

[68] Ibid.

[69] Tom Ginsburg and Alberto Simpser describe 'window dressing', in Tom Ginsburg and Alberto Simpser (eds.), *Constitutions in Authoritarian Regimes* (Cambridge: Cambridge University Press, 2014), pp. 7–8.

[70] Scholars have observed that the problem is not with having laws to follow, but rather people disregarding the law. See James D. Seymore, 'Human Rights and the Law in the PRC', in Victor C. Falkenheim (ed.), *Chinese Politics from Mao to Deng* (New York, NY: Paragon House, 1989), pp. 271–299, 272.

[71] Fu Hualing, 'Access to Justice and Constitutionalism in China', in Balme and Dowdle, *Building Constitutionalism in China*.

[72] Charles Epp, *The Rights Revolution: Lawyers, Activists and Supreme Courts in Comparative Perspective* (Chicago, IL: Chicago University Press, 1998), pp. 6–21.

[73] Mark Sidel, *Law and Society in Vietnam*, p. 60; see also Nicholson and Pham in this volume and Fu Hualing, 'Building Judicial Integrity in China' (2016) 39(1) *Hastings International and Comparative Law Review* 167–181.

possible for authoritarian states to respect some degree of personal free-dom, individual rights and rule of law. Indeed, the CCP has proven itself adaptable and resilient in the eyes of the general public because of the promulgation and enforcement of a bundle of legal rights.[74] Meanwhile, the ratification of a new, more approachable 2013 Constitution signals that Vietnam has the will and capacity to pursue more progressive changes. But, like other transitional states, both China and Vietnam prioritise rule of law and the protection of rights in selective policy areas depending on perceived necessity and feasibility. There is greater rule of law in matters of commerce than in media, religion, criminal law and other politically sensitive areas.[75] It is therefore not surprising that Vietnamese constitu-tionalism was most forcefully asserted in the aforementioned motorcycle case,[76] while the Chinese Supreme People's Court chose to test the feasi-bility of constitutional review in a case regarding educational rights.[77]

In contrast, there are areas, such as anti-corruption and media gov-ernance, where formal law remains largely silent.[78] A dualism exists wherein professional justice serves the vast majority of ordinary cases, while politicised justice caters to a range of exceptional cases.[79] That

[74] See David Shambaugh, *China's Communist Party: Atrophy and Adaptation* (Washington, DC: Woodrow Wilson Center Press, 2008).

[75] During the 1990s, Vietnamese lawmakers borrowed or drew inspiration from laws multilateral international institutions such as the World Bank, including in drafting the 1993 Law on Business Bankruptcy, 1995 Civil Code, 1997 Commercial Law, and the 1999 Enterprise Law. Gillespie and Chen, *Legal Reforms in China and Vietnam*, 8.

[76] Bui Ngoc Son, 'Constitutional Developments in Vietnam in the First Decade of the 21st Century', in Albert H. Y. Chen, *Constitutionalism in Asia in the Early Twenty-First Century* (Cambridge: Cambridge University Press, 2014), pp. 206–07.

[77] In *Qi Yuling v. Chen et al.* (2001), China's Supreme People's Court (SPC) recognized a PRC citizen's constitutional right to education under Article 46 of the Chinese Consti-tution of 1982. After much controversy, the SPC unceremoniously abolished the case without explanation in December 2008. SPC Vice-President Judge Huang Songyou was also detained for corruption by the CCP. Robert K. Morris, 'China's Marbury: Qi Yuling v. Chen Xiaoqi – The Once and Future Trial of Both Education and Constitutionalisation' (2012) 2 *Tsinghua China Law Review* 273–316.

[78] Fu Hualing, 'Wielding the Sword: President Xi's New Anti-corruption Campaign', in Susan Rose-Ackerman and Paul Lagunes (eds.), *Greed, Corruption, and the Modern State: Essays in Political Economy* (Cheltenham: Edward Elgar Publisher, 2015), pp. 134–157.

[79] Such as the high-profile trials of Bo Xilai, Zhou Yongkang and others in the current Xi Jinping anti-corruption campaign in China. Meanwhile, Vietnamese Prime Minister Nguyen Tan Dung also declared anti-corruption a priority, establishing a new anti-corruption agency to be headed by the Deputy Prime Minister. A major corruption scandal within the Ministry of Transport in 2006 led to high-level resignations and arrests, including the Vice Minister of Transport.

dualism causes a dilemma for the judiciary when facing cases of different political natures. For example, Chinese judges are beholden to political instructions in exceptional cases, but perhaps too independent in other ordinary cases.[80] Both China and Vietnam have been regularising and professionalising their court procedures,[81] but such measures encounter insurmountable difficulties inherent to the political system.[82] Dissident trials, which have become a regular practice in both countries, illustrate the pain of authoritarian states struggling with rule of law.

Third, in both countries, the present state of reform promotes a thin/formal version of the rule of law, without dealing with the hard questions posed by a thick/substantive rule of law. The thin version focuses on the internal qualities of law, such as the requirements that law must be public and accessible, generally applicable and largely consistent.[83] It also focuses on the institutional dimension of enforcement, and requires valid rules for law making, fair application, effective enforcement and general acceptance of rules.[84] Critics who challenge the existence of a thin rule of law point out that it does not provide a normative foundation, and is not supported by the sort of rights-based system commonly observed in a liberal democracy.[85] Indeed, legal reform in this context is largely illiberal in the sense that the legal system under construction is not rights-based. Instead, reform efforts have been concentrated on developing a system that better ensures certainty, clarity and, to some extent, procedural fairness. Such law reform is thus aimed at improving government effectiveness and enhancing state capacity.

Despite these underlying similarities, China and Vietnam differ in interesting ways on their official commitment to, and societal demand

---

[80] Fu Hualing, 'Putting China's Judiciary into Perspective: Is It Independent, Competent and Fair?', in Erik Jensen and Tom Heller (eds.), *Beyond Common Knowledge: Empirical Approaches to the Rule of Law* (Stanford, CA: Stanford University Press: 2003), pp. 193–219.

[81] See Gillespie and Chen, *Legal Reforms in China and Vietnam*.

[82] 'Vietnam's 2005 Anti-Corruption Law requires government officials to declare their assets and sets strict penalties for those caught engaging in corrupt practices. Implementation and enforcement, however, continues to remain problematic. Vietnam also signed the United Nation Convention on Anti-Corruption in July 2009.' U.S. Department of State, '2013 Investment Climate Statement – Vietnam', February 2013, available at www.state.gov/e/eb/rls/othr/ics/2013/204760.htm.

[83] Randall Peerenboom, *China's Long March toward Rule of Law* (Cambridge: Cambridge University Press, 2005), pp. 3–7.

[84] Ibid.

[85] Brian Tamanaha, 'A Concise Guide to the Rule of Law', St. Johns University School of Law, Legal Studies Research Paper Series, Paper #07–0082, September 2007, pp. 16–20.

for, the rule of law. Rhetoric that praises the rule of law and the supremacy of the constitution is more often relied upon in China by emerging political leaders when facing challenges from more established authorities. Once those leaders consolidate their power, however, rule of law and constitutionalism typically become less relevant.[86] Due to the broader participation of, and fiercer competition among, different factions, Vietnam may depend more upon the rule of law as a fundamental code of the political game. This – and the apparent rise of a pro-reform faction – may help to explain why the Vietnamese Constitution evinces deeper normative commitments than its Chinese counterpart.

Though abuses persist, Vietnamese leaders have been more receptive to incorporating international best practices, especially in the field of human rights. Human rights received constitutional recognition in the Vietnamese Constitution of 1992, twelve years before it was added via amendment to the Chinese Constitution in 2004.[87] Prior to that, Vietnam ratified the International Covenant on Civil and Political Rights (ICCPR) in 1982.[88] Article 70(14) of the 2013 Constitution mentions a general commitment to international human rights treaties and fundamental citizens' rights,[89] while article 31 showcases a commitment to human rights norms vis-à-vis the practice of criminal justice at a level of detail matched by few national constitutions.[90] The partial entrenchment of the ICCPR has the potential to open the door for further reform. While the Basic Laws of Hong Kong and Macau incorporate the ICCPR,[91] it remains wishful thinking on behalf of Chinese constitutional scholars to entrench such core rights in the national Constitution. China signed the ICCPR sixteen years after Vietnam and has yet to ratify it.[92]

---

[86] Fu Hualing, 'Challenging Authoritarianism through Law'.

[87] Art. 50, Vietnamese Constitution 1992 read '[i]n the Socialist Republic of Vietnam, human rights in all respects, political, civic, economic, cultural and social are respected, find their expression in the rights of citizens and are provided for by the Constitution and the law'.

[88] United Nations Office of High Commissioner for Human Rights, Status of Ratification [ICCPR], available at http://indicators.ohchr.org/.

[89] Art. 70(14), Vietnamese Constitution 2013.

[90] Art. 31(1–5), Vietnamese Constitution 2013 include: presumption of innocence (1), timely access to trial (2), prohibition of double-jeopardy (3), access to attorneys (4), and right to punitive damages for unlawful prosecution (5).

[91] Article 39 of the Basic Law of the Hong Kong Special Administrative Region; Article 40 of the Basic Law of the Macau Special Administrative Region.

[92] United Nations Office of High Commissioner for Human Rights, Status of Ratification [ICCPR], available at http://indicators.ohchr.org/.

This may have practical effect. Vietnam appears relatively more committed to reforming the use of the death penalty. It abolished execution by firing squad in favour of legal injection more decisively than China.[93] Extraordinarily, in 2007 Vietnam abstained from the UN resolution calling for a global moratorium on execution with the ultimate goal of abolishing the death penalty, effectively making Vietnam the only Asian retentionist country that did not object to the resolution.[94]

6.4 Responsiveness to Civil Society and Public Demands

Party-states must be responsive to popular will to ensure regime survival and political stability. While the promotion of rule of law generates further demand for rights in both countries, their limited legal systems are hard pressed to meet the challenges brought by massive socioeconomic transition due to a lack of capacity and credibility. The party-states must directly face those challenges and may at times choose to supplement or subvert the legal systems they have created. Chinese and Vietnamese constitutional practice therefore necessitates a responsive and proactive state, based on political expedience rather than established legal rules, in managing and coordinating popular demand for rights and interests. The Vietnamese party-state appears to be situated in a 'better' (that is, less defensive) posture than its Chinese counterpart, as the Vietnamese order is more tolerant of input from a more autonomous civil society. Indeed, some Vietnamese politicians have called for an even more resilient civil society.[95] Nonetheless, both systems often fail to meet such demands, resulting in extrajudicial action by the people themselves.

---

[93] An Dien, 'Vietnam Switched from Firing Squad to Lethal Injection in 2011', *Thanh Nien News*, available at www.thanhniennews.com/politics/is-vietnam-ready-to-abolish-death-penalty-37916.html.

[94] David T. Johnson and Michelle Miao, 'Chinese Capital Punishment in Comparative Perspective', in Bin Liang and Hong Lu (eds.), *The Death Penalty in China: Policy, Practice, and Reform* (New York, NY: Columbia University Press, 2015).

[95] http://vneconomy.vn/thoi-su/da-den-luc-thua-nhan-xa-hoi-dan-su-20140429110559789.htm (this article cites the statement of Mr Truong Dinh Tuyen, former Minister of Industry and Trade, at the 2014 Spring Economic Forum, a regular event of the Vietnamese National Assembly, that Vietnam should accept civil society to address shortcomings of a market economy and the bureaucratic government.); www.thesaigontimes.vn/115717/Dai-bieu-Quoc-hoi-Dung-ao-tuong-ve-16-chu-vang.html (this article reports that Mr Ha Sy Dong, a delegate of the National Assembly, called in a plenary session that civil society be promoted. Interestingly, this call was made in the context of the China-Vietnam conflict in the Southeast China Sea.)

Constitutionally, the people are the master of the state in China, and they are the protector of the Constitution in Vietnam.[96] Thus, a feasible theory of socialist constitutionalism demands that law reflect and reinforce popular will in both countries. Both the CCP and VCP have proven responsive (sometimes over-responsive) to popular demand, yet the Vietnamese party-state is presently far more respectful of voices from civil society than its Chinese counterpart. That Vietnam would possess a more structured and vibrant public sphere is consistent with Vietnam's higher degree of political pluralism and deeper commitment to international norms. It boasts a healthier interface between the party-state and civil society, as evinced by: a more activist labour sector; a more vibrant religious community; and a more independent lawyers' bar association. In comparison, the Chinese party-state has been more decisive and harsher in cracking down on civil organisations and silencing dissenting voices.

6.4.1   Labour

Labour unions in both countries are dominated by their respective communist parties and serve a 'transmission belt' of intelligence.[97] Faithful to their ideological roots, both constitutions devote special attention to protect the rights of the toiling people. For example, Chinese workers enjoy constitutional rights to work and rest.[98] In that sense, the Chinese Constitution is nominal, but its constitutional provisions are not fully implemented, due to the lack of resources and issues of implementation. The Vietnamese Constitution, meanwhile, grants constitutional status to a trade union intended to protect workers' rights.[99] In practice, Vietnam's labour relations regime

---

[96] Article 2(2), Vietnamese Constitution 2013 reads: 'The people are the masters of the Socialist Republic of Vietnam; all state powers belong to the people whose foundation is the alliance between the working class, the peasantry and the intelligentsia.' Preamble, paragraph 2, Chinese Constitution 1982, reads 'the Chinese people took state power into their own hands and became masters of the country'. The phrase is repeated in Article 42.

[97] Erwin Schweisshelm, 'Trade Unions in Transition – Changing Industrial Relations in Vietnam', Friedrich Ebert Stiftung, Vietnam Office Briefing Paper, September 2014, available at www.fes.de/gewerkschaften/common/pdf/2014_09Vietnamese_TU_in_Transition.pdf, p. 1.

[98] Arts. 42 and 43, Chinese Constitution 1982.

[99] Art. 10, Vietnamese Constitution 2013 reads: 'The Trade Union is the socio-political organisation of the working class and labourers, established on a voluntary basis that represents the workers, looks after and protects the legitimate and legal rights and interests of the workers; participates in state administration and socio-economic management; participates in the control, inspection, and supervision of the activity of State bodies, organisations, units and enterprises with respects to the matters concerning the rights and duties of the workers; propagandises, mobilises learning, development of

more closely tracks the International Labour Organisation (ILO) standards. For example, Vietnamese labour law includes a National Wage Council that is modelled on a South Korean example, with technical assistance from the ILO. Composed of members from the government, unions and business associations, this tripartite body has been effective in advising decision makers on minimum wages.[100] Vietnam is thus ahead of China in legalising industrial action. These developments may come in handy as both countries experience interest-based industrial action and mass strikes, which are likely to increase in size and frequency.[101]

Vietnamese labour law has long authorised strikes under certain circumstances (although these conditions are hard to fulfil),[102] while unions and professional organisations, in spite of their dependence on the VCP, can be relatively more spontaneous and representative than their Chinese counterparts in representing workers' interests against both the state and employers.[103] For example, a significant difference between the two countries is that an enterprise's union chair is paid for by unions at the next level up in Vietnam, while their Chinese counterpart is paid for by the very enterprise the union chair serves.[104] This openness reflects the historical fact that Vietnamese unions, Vietnam General Confederation of Labour (VGCL), are more politically powerful in dealing with employers and structurally more independent from the VCP than their

---

abilities and professional skills, conformity of law, and construction and defence of the Fatherland among the workers.'

[100] Vietnamese Prime Minister Nguyen Tan Dung approved Decree 49/2013/ND-CP, which commissioned the establishment of a National Wage Council to oversee national wage levels throughout the country. Vietnam Briefing, 'National Wage Council Established in Vietnam, Minimum Wage Rises', 16 July 2013, available at www.vietnam-briefing.com/news/national-wage-council-established-in-vietnam-minimum-wage-rises.html/#sthash.n13yVLtv.dpuf.

[101] China Labour Bulletin, 'Worker Activism Is Now the New Normal as Strikes and Protests Erupt Across China', 7 April 2015, available at www.clb.org.hk/en/content/worker-activism-now-new-normal-strikes-and-protests-erupt-across-china; Vu Trong Khanh, 'Vietnamese Workers Strike Over End of Option on Retirement Money', *Wall Street Journal Asia*, 1 April 2015, available at www.wsj.com/articles/vietnamese-workers-strike-over-end-of-option-on-retirement-money-1427889688.

[102] Trinh K. Y. Khanh, 'The Right to Strike in Vietnam's Private Sector' (2015) 2 *Asian Journal of Law and Society* 115–135.

[103] Anita Chan and Irene Norlund, 'Vietnamese and Chinese Labour Regimes: On the Road to Divergence', *China Journal*, July 1998, pp. 192–93, available at www.researchgate.net/profile/Anita_Chan5/publication/260388138_Vietnamese_and_Chinese_Labour_Regimes_On_The_Road_to_Divergence/links/53fd46f00cf2364ccc08a891.pdf.

[104] Ibid., p. 173.

Chinese counterpart, the All-China Federation of Trade Unions (ACFTU).[105]

The relative strength of Vietnamese workers is also reflected in the fact that, despite the large number of illegal wildcat strikes in Vietnam, few organisers have been prosecuted (although harassment does occur beyond view).[106] While there is a legal procedure for the government to petition courts to declare a strike illegal, the government has never utilised it. Instead, the dismissal of a striker often leads to renewed strikes, forcing management to reinstate the dismissed workers.[107] As Clarke points out, official tolerance of such strikes provides the most powerful incentive for Vietnamese workers to achieve what they want through extralegal means.[108] In Khanh's view, an over-responsive state 'has given rise to a negative precedent, making workers believe compliance with the official mechanism for collective labour dispute resolution is unnecessary'.[109]

6.4.2   Religion

The relative open space for religion also reflects a more resilient and rigorous demand for religious freedom in Vietnamese society. Unlike the CCP, the VCP does not prohibit its members from exploring religious beliefs, as long as the religion is properly recognised by the state.[110] Unlike the CCP, it has not created a parallel Catholic Church that is independent of Rome; it does not force its Catholics to renounce allegiance to the Vatican; and it does not ordain bishops who are not endorsed by the Vatican, although it does occasionally veto the Vatican's

---

[105] A significant difference between the two countries is that an enterprise union chair is paid for by unions at the next higher level and the Chinese counterpart is paid for the enterprise the Chair serves. Ibid., p. 185.

[106] Ibid. For further deliberations see Chapter 11 in this volume.

[107] Simon Clarke, 'The Changing Character of Strikes in Vietnam' (2006) 18(3) *Post-Communist Economies* 346, 355.

[108] Ibid., 345–361.

[109] Khanh, 'The Right to Strike in Vietnam's Private Sector', 127.

[110] Art. 24, Vietnamese Constitution 2013; Eleanor Albert, 'Religion in China', Council on Foreign Relations, 10 June 2015, available at https://www.cfr.org/backgrounder/religion-china. For a comprehensive review of religious policy in Vietnam, see John Gillespie, 'Human Rights as a Larger Loyalty: The Evolution of Religious Freedom in Vietnam' (2014) 27 *Harvard Human Rights Journal* 107–149; and Thomas J. Reese and Mary Ann Gledon, 'How Vietnam Respects and Protects Religious Freedom Has Implications beyond Its Own Borders', (2016) *America: The Jesuit Review*, www.americamagazine.org/issue/report-vietnam.

recommended candidates.[111] Where restriction and repression undoubtedly continue in Vietnam, the CCP has been far less tolerant of independent religious activities.

With the general improvement of relations between Vietnam and the Vatican, Vietnamese religious groups maintain stronger ties with foreign countries. While both party-states impose strong bureaucratic control over religious organisations, Vietnamese believers are allowed to openly practise their faith with greater confidence: they can be registered as independent religious organisations with the government and thereby authorised to operate legitimately in public, in parallel with directly state-controlled religious organisations. In China, no independent religious groups can legally exist outside of direct state control. They are either incorporated into the state-controlled institutions or they operate as house-churches in the long shadow of the state, suffering routine harassment and crackdown.[112]

The VCP started to loosen its grip over religious organisations and practices in 1990, and one key development was to accept and tolerate Party members from religious communities.[113] The removal of a religious ban on Party members was a recognition and reflection of the importance of religion in the Vietnamese society, and contributed to the creation of a more vibrant religious community that cuts across party-state and societal boundaries.[114] The participation of VCP members in religious activities legitimises religion in general, opens a space for interaction between the state and the religious sector, and makes police harassment of the faithful less likely. The ability of VCP members to practise religion may help to explain why Vietnamese believers practise largely in the open, while their Chinese counterparts do so 'underground'.

---

[111] Kevin Boyle and Juliet Sheen (eds.), *Freedom of Religion and Belief: A World Report* (London: Routledge, 1997), p. 256; Andrew Batson, 'China Set to Name Catholic Bishop without Consent', *Wall Street Journal*, 29 November 2006, available at www.wsj.com/news/articles/SB116475889349535058.

[112] Vietnam to date has not suppressed any cult groups as China has done against Falun Gong and Vietnamese middle-class churchgoers have not suffered nearly as much as members of the Shouwang church in Beijing. David C. Schak, 'Protestantism in China: A Dilemma for the Party-State' (2011) 2 *Journal of Current Chinese Affairs* 71–106.

[113] Gillespie, 'Human Rights as a Larger Loyalty', 124; and Reese and Gledon, 'How Vietnam Respects and Protects Religious Freedom Has Implications beyond Its Own Borders'.

[114] The idea was mooted by some religious scholars in China but was never taken seriously by the CCP.

6.4.3   The Legal Profession

Legal professionals in both countries actively hold the party-state accountable to its rule of law rhetoric, despite tight government control over lawyers, law firms and bar associations.[115] Lawyers in both nations are endeavouring to achieve a degree of autonomy from government control but are met with a swift and harsh response, with leading lawyers selectively prosecuted for sedition, subversion or other offences.[116] Yet ad hoc evidence indicates that while Chinese rights lawyers are at least as zealous as their Vietnamese counterparts, their representative professional organisations are more timid.[117]

While the size of the legal profession is much smaller in Vietnam than in China,[118] the phenomena of 'die-hard lawyers' vigorously challenging the prosecution's cases (on largely procedural matters) began in Vietnam at least as early as 2003,[119] several years before China. Meanwhile, the CCP is more aggressive at penetrating and controlling organised challenges from the legal profession, while the VCP appears relatively more tolerant of their institutional autonomy. Vietnam's National Bar Association has little control over regional and local bar associations, as the latter openly challenge the former's lack of autonomy from the government.[120] The Ho Chi Minh City Bar Association, in particular, is much more active than its Chinese counterparts in seeking autonomy from regulators, and is more responsive to the interests of its members when in conflict with the

---

[115] John Gillespie, 'The Juridification of Cause Advocacy in Socialist Asia: Vietnam as a Case Study' (2014) 31 *Wisconsin International Law Journal* 672–701.

[116] See, e.g., 'Vietnam Lawyer Charged with Subversion', *BBC*, 24 December 2009, available at http://news.bbc.co.uk/2/hi/asia-pacific/8429351.stm; 'China Dissident Lawyer Gao Zhisheng "Destroyed by Jail"', *BBC*, 14 August 2014, available at www.bbc.com/news/world-asia-china-28793055.

[117] Recently, however, having witnessed the increasing level of prosecution and harassment of human rights lawyers in China, some lawyers have petitioned the NPC to have the All China Lawyers' Association abolished for failing to speak on behalf of its members. 'Chinese Lawyers Call for the Abolition of Their Professional Body', Asian Pacific Star, vol. 417, 8 October 2015, available at www.asiapacificstar.com/index.php/sid/237422049.

[118] Nguyen Hung Quang and Kerstin Steiner, 'Ideology and Professionalism: The Resurgence of the Vietnamese Bar', in Gillespie and Nicholson, *Asian Socialism and Legal Change*, p. 191.

[119] For a discussion of the aggressive defense against the prosecution of the Godfather of Saigon, see Ibid. and Sidel, *Law and Society in Vietnam*, pp. 166–194.

[120] Bui Thi Bich Lien, 'Legal Education and the Legal Profession in Contemporary Vietnam: Tradition and Modification', in Gillespie and Chen, *Legal Reforms in China and Vietnam*, p. 299.

government.[121] Of course, it is hard to predict whether stronger challenges from better organised lawyers' organisations will lead to deeper political reform and a more credible commitment to the rule of law.

Both party-states engage in the arrest and harassment of individual defence lawyers who take on politically sensitive cases. Le Cong Dinh, a Western-trained lawyer who won a major World Trade Organisation (WTO) case for Vietnam, was imprisoned from 2009 to 2013 and then disbarred for defending dissidents and bloggers.[122] In 2011, Cu Huy Ha Vu was sentenced to seven years in prison for filing lawsuits against the prime minister and defending clients that included a Roman Catholic parish.[123] But the scale and severity of repression against human rights lawyers in China has been far worse, as amply demonstrated by the 2015 crackdown that resulted in the criminal conviction and administrative punishment of dozens of lawyers.[124]

The question thus remains: Will a party-state rely on the formal legal system to resolve disputes according to proper procedures, or will it resort to repression or other unprincipled informal mechanisms based on political expedience? As numerous studies have shown, dispute resolution that bypasses the legal system eventually exacerbates social conflict and becomes a destabilising factor unto itself.[125] There is an emerging consensus among political elites that dispute resolution that is based on the rule of law and predictable legal principles is the most cost-effective way to resolve the vast majority of cases.[126]

---

[121] Jerome Cohen, 'Introduction to Part V', in Gillespie and Chen, *Legal Reforms in China and Vietnam*, p. 271.

[122] Sherif Mansour, Maria Snegovaya, Zachary Abuza, 'Stifling the Public Sphere: Media and Civil Society in Egypt, Russia, and Vietnam', Report by the International Forum for Democratic Studies, National Endowment for Democracy, 15 October 2015, available at www.ned.org/stifling-the-public-sphere-media-and-civil-society-in-egypt-russia-and-vietnam/.

[123] Ibid.

[124] Fu Hualing, 'The July 9th (709) Crackdown on Human Rights Lawyers: Legal Advocacy in an Authoritarian State' (forthcoming 2018) *Journal of Contemporary China*; Alex W. Palmer, ''Flee at Once': China's Besieged Human Rights Lawyers', *New York Times*, 25 July 2017, available at www.nytimes.com/2017/07/25/magazine/the-lonely-crusade-of-chinas-human-rights-lawyers.html.

[125] Liangjiang Li, Mingxing Liu and Kevin J O'Brien, 'Petitioning Beijing: The High Tide of 2003–2006' (2010) 210 *China Quarterly* 313–34; Carl F. Minzner, 'Xinfang'; Yanhua Deng and Kevin. J. O'Brien 'Relational Repression in China: Using Social Ties to Demobilise Protesters' (2013) 214 *China Quarterly* 533–552.

[126] Randall Peerenboom, 'The Future of Legal Reforms in China: A Critical Appraisal of the Decision on Comprehensively Deepening Reform', available at http://papers.ssrn.com/sol3/papers.cfm?abstract_id=2379161.

When discourse signals a constitutional commitment on the part of the party-state, citizens in both nations have responded by seizing that discourse. Constitutional rhetoric gives space for articulation and action by civil society, and has inspired people to fight for their rights, even in authoritarian states. The gap between a high normative standard of constitutional rights and low levels of practical enforcement sharpens the contrast between entitlement and reality, creating further incentives and opportunities for mobilisation. It is commonly agreed that rights awareness has been rising steadily, with political and legal consequences in both countries,[127] and aware citizens are demanding to exercise those rights through available institutions. If those institutions fail to deliver, people will create or resort to non-institutional means for remedies. Ultimately, the authoritarian party-state's flirtation with rule of law is a double-edged sword that has been wielded with great caution, mindful of law's inherent threat to authoritarian rule.

6.5   Conclusion

Constitutional rights are on the agenda in both China and Vietnam, as grassroots constitutional demands unfold on a daily basis. While judicial development is severely constrained, citizens actively interpret and implement constitutional rights in forums across both countries, including in the streets, factories, churches and classrooms. This Chapter conceptualised the similarities and differences between three substantive foundations of constitutional practices in both states – the leadership of the communist party, faith in developing a socialist rule of law and the requisite state responsiveness to popular will.

Regime survival is the ultimate goal for any single party that desires to perpetuate its command of power. The party-state model is adapting to new circumstances and continues to evolve incrementally to develop and defend its credibility and legitimacy. One core strategy is reliance upon legal rules to discipline the state and impose order on society. While the party-state purposely maintains a weak legal system to satisfy its own political agenda,

---

[127] See, e.g., Michael Dowdle, 'Introduction to Part II', in Gillespie and Chen, *Legal Reforms in China and Vietnam*, p. 106; Zheng Ge, 'Toward Regulatory Neutrality in a Party-state? A Review of Administrative Law Reforms in China', in Gillespie and Chen, *Legal Reforms in China and Vietnam*, p. 119; Dang Xuan Hop, 'Vietnam: The Past 25 Years, the Present and the Future', in E. Ann Black and Gary F. Bell (eds.), *Law and Legal Institutions of Asia: Traditions, Adaptations and Innovations* (Cambridge: Cambridge University Press, 2011), p. 210.

a weak system cannot contain the socio-economic problems it is designed to resolve. The resort to extrajudicial forums undermines the state's legal system while delegating some degree of constitutional enforcement to the people.

Both constitutional orders are presently locked in a cycle of mobilisation and counter-mobilisation, in which societal forces demand change that the party-state considers, manages and, occasionally, concedes. This requires the Party to constantly balance its position against popular action that pushes for a redistribution of interests or incremental change while the legal system attempts to impose a degree of regularity. Where civil society is consulted, rather than resisted, the process is more likely to run smoothly. The Sino–Vietnamese comparison indicates that the limits of the Chinese experiment with constitutionally-based legal reform over the past several decades seem to have hardened, at least for the time being. While China and Vietnam may share common constraints, the scope for reform appears greater in Vietnam, whose system currently has the advantage of being more receptive to new ideas, both internal and external in origin. Thus, the 'socialism with Vietnamese characteristics' outlined herein may allow the Vietnamese party-state to rejuvenate itself while overcoming some of the institutional barriers that have stalled reform in China.

7

Constitutional Dualism

Socialism and Constitutionalism in Contemporary Vietnam

BUI NGOC SON

7.1 Introduction

In early 2013, when the Socialist Republic of Vietnam released the draft Constitution to the public for comment, people called for, among other things, a change to the nation's name by eliminating the term 'socialist'. They proposed alternative names such as Democratic Republic of Vietnam, Republic of Vietnam and People's Democratic Republic of Vietnam.[1] The new Constitution approved by the National Assembly of Vietnam on 28 November 2013 rejects the call to change the nation's name, and other substantive reforms. It retains fundamental socialist constitutional principles and the overall Leninist constitutional structure. However, it also introduces some concepts and principles that are unconventional to the socialist constitutional tradition and that resonate with the normative requirements of constitutionalism. The Constitution has still functioned as an instrument to describe the party-state's socialist principles and goals in constitutional terms, but at the same time it has begun to perform prescriptive function. This Chapter examines these two competing functions of the Constitution in socialist Vietnam, with a particular focus on the 2013 Constitution.[2]

Senior Research Fellow, Centre for Asian Legal Studies, Faculty of Law, National University of Singapore; PhD (The University of Hong Kong).

[1] The Editing Board of the Vietnam Constitutional Amendment Committee, *BÁO CÁO Tổng hợp ý kiến nhân dân về Dự thảo sửa đổi Hiến pháp năm 1992 (từ ngày 02/01/2013 đến ngày 30/4/2013)* [*Synthesised Report on People's Opinion on the Draft Amendments to the 1992 Constitution (from February 01, 2013 to April 30, 2013)*], available at: http://duthaoonline.quochoi.vn/DuThao/Lists/DT_DUTHAO_NGHIQUYET/View_Detail.aspx?ItemID=32&TabIndex=2&TaiLieuID=1066.

[2] In this Chapter, when the term constitution is capitalised, it refers to a specific constitution. When the term is not capitalised, it refers more generally to a fundamental document of a country.

International scholars, namely John Gillespie,[3] Pip Nicholson[4] and Mark Sidel,[5] have provided useful explorations of Vietnamese constitutional law, although they have not yet accounted for the 2013 Constitution. Recently, the *Asian Journal of Comparative Law* published a special issue on Vietnamese and comparative constitutional law, focusing on the constitutional debates leading to the birth of the 2013 Constitution.[6] The featured scholars helpfully demonstrated how fundamental socialist constitutional principles were subject to social contestations, contributing to the understanding of the dynamics of constitutional law within the socialist regime. They did not, however, consider the function of the new Constitution.

In this Chapter, I will focus on the function of the Constitution in Vietnam. I propose the concept of 'functionalist constitutional dualism', which denotes two competing functions of a constitution in response to competing concerns. Within that conceptual framework, I argue that, in response to competing demands of state and social actors, the Constitution in Vietnam now has dual functions – its traditional, hegemonic

---

[3] John Gillespie, 'Evolving Concepts of Human Rights in Vietnam', in Randall Peerenboom, Carole J. Petersen and Albert H. Y. Chen (eds.), *Human Rights in Asia: A Comparative Legal Study of Twelve Asian Jurisdictions, France and the USA* (Abingdon Oxon: Routledge, 2006), p. 452; John Gillespie, 'Changing Concepts of Socialist Law in Vietnam', in John Gillespie and Pip Nicholson (eds.), *Asian Socialism and Legal Change: The Dynamics of Vietnamese and Chinese Reform* (Canberra: ANU E Press and Asia Pacific Press, 2005), p. 45; John Gillespie, 'Concept of Law in Vietnam: Transforming Statist Socialism', in Randall Peerenboom (ed.), *Asian Discourses of Rule of Law: Theories and Implementation of Rule of Law in Twelve Asian Countries, France and the U.S.* (London: Routledge Taylor & Francis Group, 2004), p. 146.

[4] Penelope (Pip) Nicholson, *Borrowing Court Systems: The Experience of Socialist Vietnam* (Leiden: Martinus Nijhoff Publishers, 2007); Pip Nicholson, 'Renovating Courts: The Role of Courts in Contemporary Vietnam,' in Jiunn-rong Yeh and Wen-Chen Chang (eds.), *Asian Courts in Context* (Cambridge: Cambridge University Press, 2015), p. 528. See also Pip Nicholson, 'Vietnamese Courts: Contemporary Interactions between Party-State and Law', in Stéphanie Balme and Mark Sidel (eds.), *Vietnam's New Order: International Perspectives on the State and Reform in Vietnam* (New York: Palgrave Macmillan, 2007); Pip Nicholson, 'The Vietnamese Courts and Corruption', in Tim Lindsey and Howard Dick (eds.), *Corruption in Asia: Rethinking the Good Governance Paradigm* (Annandale: Federation Press, 2002), p. 201.

[5] Mark Sidel, *The Constitution of Vietnam* (Oxford: Hart Publishing, 2009); Mark Sidel, 'Analytical Models for Understanding Constitutions and Constitutional Dialogues in Socialist Transitional States: Re-Interpreting Constitutional Dialogues in Vietnam' (2002) 6 *Singapore Journal of International and Comparative Law* 42–89. See also Mark Sidel, *Law and Society in Vietnam* (Cambridge: Cambridge University Press, 2008).

[6] 'Special Issue on Vietnamese and Comparative Constitutional Law' (2016) 11(2) *Asian Journal of Comparative Law*.

socialist function and a new, nascent constitutionalist function. On the one hand, in response to the concern of the socialist elite, the constitution has predominantly remained the instrument for the party-state to describe the socialist principles, structure and goals in constitutional language. On the other hand, in response to the concerns of society, it has incrementally assumed constitutionalist function: it establishes normative constraints upon constitutional politics.

First, I will describe the background on how socialism informed constitutional history in Vietnam. Next, I critically review several relevant theories and consider how functionalist constitutional dualism may be a useful concept. I then examine the two functions of the constitution in Vietnam, before concluding with some discussions and reflections.

7.2   Historical Background

7.2.1   The 1946 Constitution

In the early twentieth century, when Vietnam was under French colonialism as a part of Indochina, there were different constitutional movements that struggled for a constitutional government and national independence.[7] During this period, the influence of Western constitutionalism on Vietnamese constitutional intellectual life was more prominent than constitutional socialism. The influence of Soviet constitutional concepts and principles was limited to the communists and was adapted to the local context. For example, Xô viết Nghệ- Tĩnh (Nghệ-Tĩnh Soviets) (1930–1931)[8] compelled the communists to change the previous Soviet model of a 'workers', peasants' and 'soldiers' government' to a people's government so as to rally all stratum and revolutionary groups.

Notably, the presence of Soviet constitutional concepts on the constitutional discourse of Ho Chi Minh, the father of the Communist Party of Vietnam, was far from dominant. During the prerevolutionary time and the early years after the August Revolution of 1945, his political discourse presented a mixture of Western liberal constitutionalism and socialism. Ho Chi Minh's revolutionary ideology is shaped by the socialist/communist ideas of violent revolution, the leadership of the communist party

---

[7] See generally Phan Đăng Thanh, *Tư tưởng Lập hiến Việt Nam nửa đầu Thế kỷ 20 [Vietnamese Constitutional Thoughts in the First Half of the Twentieth Century]* (Hanoi: Judicial Publishing House, 2006).

[8] Martin Bernal, 'The Nghe-Tinh Soviet Movement 1930–1931' (1981) 92(1) *Past and Present* 148–168.

and the international connection of communist forces. However, his discourse on constitutional government for an independent Vietnam was informed by Western constitutionalist concepts, such as a written constitution as a document to limit despotic power and to protect democratic rights, and a democratic government operating within the framework of a 'democratic constitution'.[9]

Reflecting the discordant constitutional movements, the 1946 Constitution of the Democratic Republic of Vietnam (DRV), though created after the triumph of a communist revolution, was not a socialist document. It adopted fundamental concepts of Western liberal constitutionalism that drew mainly on French and American constitutional experiences, such as popular sovereignty, popular constitution-making power, political pluralism, fundamental liberal rights and a Montesquieuian tripartite government with an independent judiciary.[10] However, this does not mean that there is no socialist influence on the 1946 Constitution. In this regard, it is necessary to consider the debate between David Marr and Alec Holcombe about the Soviet influence on the 1946 charter.

In his seminal book *Vietnam: State, War, and Revolution (1945-1946)*, Marr argues that the 1946 Constitution was influenced by the French Third Republic.[11] He said: 'Almost surely the 1946 drafting committee canvassed the French constitution that had been defeated by popular referendum on 5 May, and managed to peruse the text of the constitution that was eventually ratified on 27 October.'[12] Marr, however, also carefully noted that: 'There were a few borrowings from the Soviet constitutional model in the DRV text, notably people's councils and administrative committees meant both to serve their constituency and to obey directives from above.'[13]

In an extensive review essay, Holcombe criticises Marr for 'not exploring the clear Soviet inspiration for the DRV's 1946 Constitution'.[14]

---

[9] Bui Ngoc Son, 'Anticolonial Constitutionalism: The Case of Ho Chi Minh' (forthcoming, 2018) 19 *Japanese Journal of Political Science* (on file with author).

[10] For more details, Bui Ngoc Son, 'Restoration Constitutionalism and Socialist Asia' (2015) 37(1) *Loyola of Los Angeles International and Comparative Law Review* 67-116.

[11] David G. Marr, *Vietnam: State, War, and Revolution (1945-1946)* (Berkeley, CA: University of California Press, 2013), p. 106.

[12] Ibid.

[13] Ibid.

[14] Alec Holcombe, 'The Role of the Communist Party in the Vietnamese Revolution A Review of David Marr's *Vietnam: State, War, and Revolution (1945-1946)*' (2016) 11(3-4) *Journal of Vietnamese Studies* 298, 333.

He draws on Bernard Fall's argument that the DRV borrowed the concept of the Presidium of the Supreme Soviet from the 1936 Soviet Constitution.[15] Holcombe asserts that the DRV's National Assembly Standing Committee was 'a small-scale replica of the Soviet Union's Presidium of the Supreme Soviet. In a nutshell, both institutions were small committees derived from much larger "elected" bodies (the USSR's Supreme Soviet and the DRV's National Assembly)'.[16] To further this argument, he compares the similarities between article 49 of the Presidium of the Supreme Soviet in the 1936 Soviet Constitution and article 15 of the Standing Committee in the original draft of the first constitution released by the DRV in November 1945, which was produced by a seven-person drafting committee established by the provisional government.[17] The Standing Committee and the Presidium are seen to have five similar powers, namely: convening the sessions of the parliament, interpreting the law, dissolving the parliament, annulling executive legal instruments inconsistent with the law and proclaiming a state of war.[18] Holcombe eventually concludes: 'Reading through the two versions, we can see that the original drafters of the DRV 1946 Constitution must have had a copy of the 1936 Stalin Constitution in hand as they framed Vietnam's political system.'[19]

When the 1946 Constitution makers prepared the nation's first constitution, they might actually have had copies of the constitutions of different countries at hand, including the USSR's. However, I argue that the influence of Western liberal constitutionalism in the 1946 Constitution is dominant, while there are only vestiges of Soviet constitutional socialism in the document. I have discussed the former in length elsewhere,[20] and for the purposes of this Chapter, I will focus more on the latter. The 1946 Constitution makers had more incentive to adopt Western, rather than Soviet, constitutional values so as to socialise the new-born DRV into the civilised world and gain more international acceptance, especially from Western powers like the United States and France.[21] However, Marr correctly points out a few influences of the Soviet constitutional model in the 1946 charter, evidenced by the

---

[15] Bernard Fall, *The Viet-Minh Regime: Government and Administration in the Democratic Republic of Vietnam* (Ithaca, NY: Department of Far Eastern Studies, Cornell University, 1954), p. 14.

[16] Holcombe, 'The Role of the Communist Party', 334.

[17] Ibid., 334–335.

[18] Ibid.

[19] Ibid., 335.

[20] Son, 'Restoration Constitutionalism'.

[21] This is connected to the historical fact that 'no foreign government recognised the DRV's existence.' Marr, *Vietnam: State, War, and Revolution*, p. 1.

design of the local government to include the people's councils and administrative committees, somewhat mirroring the Soviet system.

In the design of central institutions, the 1946 Constitution makers were less influenced by the Soviet constitutional model – specifically, the DRV's Standing Committee is not a copy of the USSR's Presidium of the Supreme Soviet. Methodologically, it is problematic to rely on the original draft Constitution to argue for the influence of the socialist institution of the Presidium on the DRV's Standing Committee. Holcombe is aware of the fact that the National Assembly created its own eleven-person constitutional drafting committee,[22] the membership of which was totally different from the government's membership. In addition, the constitutional draft was released for public discussion and was debated among the National Assembly – a pluralist institution that included both communist and non-communist members – before its approval on 9 November 1946.[23] The deliberative process might result in the change to the original draft, and hence it is far from true that 'compared to the original 1945 draft, the later version approved by the National Assembly a year later shows minimal substantive change'.[24] One example of the substantive change is that in the final Constitution, the Standing Committee only had the power to convene the sessions of the People's Parliament.[25] They did not have four other substantive powers – to interpret the law, dissolve the parliament, annul executive legal instruments inconsistent with the law and proclaim a state of war – which existed in the government's original draft and in the Soviet Constitution. Most importantly, the Standing Committee is, by nature, different from the Presidium of the Supreme Soviet – the former is essentially the permanent body of the parliament while the latter is essentially the collective head of state. The 1946 Constitution provided for an individual presidency separate from the Standing Committee, according to which the head of state was concurrently the head of the government, which resonates with the American presidency.

7.2.2 The 1959 and 1980 Constitutions

After the Geneva Conference divided Vietnam into two separate zones – the North and the South – the communist leadership in North Vietnam enacted the new 1959 Constitution as a charter to implement socialism in that part

---

[22] Holcombe, 'The Role of the Communist Party', 333.
[23] For more details see Marr, *Vietnam: State, War, and Revolution*, pp. 99–106.
[24] Holcombe, 'The Role of the Communist Party', 333.
[25] Article 36, 1946 Constitution.

of the country, modelling the Soviet constitutional system. Bernard Fall provides a useful description of the socialist features of this Constitution.[26] He argues that this document 'deals in extreme detail with economic theories and makes abundant use of stereotyped communist phrases and ideas'.[27] To illustrate, its preamble 'contains all the communist cliches of the past decade, from the "planned development of agriculture" to the "wholehearted solidarity" with the other nations of the Soviet orbit'.[28] On institutional structure, the National Assembly was introduced to replace the former People's Parliament, now defined as '"the highest organ of state authority", a turn of phrase that can be found in all constitutions of the Soviet bloc'.[29] Its standing committee's new powers 'are strictly parallel to those of the USSR's Presidium of the Supreme Soviet'.[30] Socialist influences can also be found in the constitutional provisions on the 'state control organs', people's courts, the Leninist people's procuracies, local government, the rights and duties of citizens, and 'new economic policy'.[31]

After the Vietnam War, the new Constitution of the Socialist Republic of Vietnam (SRV) was promulgated as the charter for enforcing socialism across Vietnam. The 1980 Constitution strictly adhered to the 1977 Constitution of the USSR, evident by the confirmations of the principle of dictatorship of the proletariat, the exclusive leadership of the Communist Party, the centrally planned economy, citizens' duties and statist rights, and the Leninist constitutional structure consisting of the supreme National Assembly, the collective presidency called the Council of State, the subordinate government called the Council of Ministers, the procuracies and the courts.[32]

During the periods when the 1959 and 1980 Constitutions were implemented, Vietnamese constitutional vison was dominated by Marxist–Leninist political and legal ideology. This is understandable in circumstances where political leaders were gravitating towards the Soviet model and in an intellectual environment where most constitutional scholars were educated in the Soviet Union. The 1959 and 1980 Constitutions were established with

---

[26] Bernard B. Fall, 'Constitution-Writing in a Communist State: The New Constitution of North Vietnam' (1960) 6 *Howard Law Journal* 157.

[27] Ibid., 159.

[28] Ibid.

[29] Ibid., 163.

[30] Ibid.

[31] Ibid., 164–167.

[32] On the 1980 Constitution, see William J. Duiker, 'The Constitutional System of the Socialist Republic of Vietnam', in Lawrence W. Beer (ed.), *Constitutional Systems in Late Twentieth Century Asia* (Seattle, WA: University of Washington Press, 1992).

the hegemony of communist ideology, and this stymied the dynamics of constitutional discourse. As Professor Mark Sidel points out, from 1959 to 1980, in Vietnam, 'there were only occasionally alternative voices heard in the north on issues of constitutionalism'.[33] Statements of political elite and 'scientific work' on the 1956 and 1980 Constitutions were dominated by the dogmas emulated from 'historical materialism', 'scientific communism' and Soviet constitutional tradition, including: the class nature of state and law, the dichotomy of capitalism and socialism, the dictatorship of the proletariat, the leadership of the communist party, democratic centralism, the concentration of power and socialist legality.[34] 'Constitutional law' was even conceived as a 'bourgeois' product and was not taught at law schools. The alternative course called 'Law on the State of Vietnam' was taught in a highly ideological manner.

The mechanism of diffusion of socialist constitutional ideas in the 1959 and 1980 Constitutions is a coercive one. It was not undertaken in the forthright manner of 'imposed constitution' as in the case of Japan's post-war Constitution, but in the subtle gesture of a reward to the Soviet Union for its material and military assistance to Vietnam in its struggle against foreign invaders.[35]

7.2.3 The 1992 Constitution and Its 2001 Amendments

The situation began to change in 1986, when the Communist Party of Vietnam initiated an important economic reform program known as Đổi mới (Renovation), which was meant to transform the centrally planned economy into a socialist-oriented market economy. The renovation policies stimulated active debate on 'democratisation' and 'legalisation'.[36] To meet the new demands of this renovation, the new Constitution of the SRV was adopted in April 1992. The 1992 Constitution continued to

---

[33] Sidel, *The Constitution of Vietnam*, p. 62.

[34] See, e.g., Institute of Legal Studies (ed.), *Hiến pháp nước Cộng Hòa Xã Hội Chủ Nghĩa Việt Nam* [*The Constitution of the Socialist Republic of Vietnam*] (Hanoi: Legal Publishing House, 1980); Vietnam Lawyers Association (ed.), *Nhà nước và pháp luật* [*State and Law*], Volume 1- *Những vấn đề cơ bản về hiến pháp Việt-Nam (31-12-1959)* [*Fundamental Issues on the Vietnam Constitution (31 December 1959)*] (Hanoi: Labor Publishing House, 1971).

[35] For more details, Bui Ngoc Son, 'The Global Origins of Vietnam's Constitutions: Text in Context' (2017) 2017(2) *University of Illinois Law Review* 553.

[36] See generally Zachary Abuza, *Renovating Politics in Contemporary Vietnam* (Boulder, Co.: Lynne Rienner Publishers, 2001), pp. 75-130.

follow the socialist constitutional tradition, but in a more moderate manner. Notably, it introduced competing visions, which promote economic liberalisation.[37] It recognised the role of private economic sectors, indicative of a shift from Soviet to capitalist values.[38] The Constitution also included provisions that facilitated global political and economic integration and, at the same time, released the restrictions on the commitment to exclusive diplomatic relationships with socialist nations, established by the preceding Constitution.[39]

New constitutional provisions facilitating economic reform were adopted, together with a revised institutional setting. Notably, the 1992 Constitution removed any forms of dictatorship whether proletariat or 'democratic'. The Leninist constitutional structure was continued but was modified to make power less concentrated: the government was vested with more independent administrative authority, no longer merely the subordinate body of the National Assembly; the prime minister had more individual authority and responsibility; and the individual presidency was established. So, the diffusion of socialist constitutional ideas now operated as more of a learning process rather than being forced to borrow from the outside world.[40]

The 1992 Constitution also featured for the first time the idea of 'human rights'.[41] The constitutional amendments in 2001 introduced more new ideas and principles that were unconventional to the Soviet constitutional tradition, such as the socialist rule of law state, distribution of power and the institution of vote of confidence. Notably, one amendment truncated the procuracies' 'general supervision' function, challenging the rationale of this imported Leninist institution.[42]

A new constitution was enacted in late 2013, replacing the 1992 Constitution. The 2013 Constitution continues the socialist constitutional legacy,

---

[37] On the 1992 Constitution, Ngô Bá Thành, 'The 1992 Constitution and the Rule of Law', in Carlyle A. Thayer and David G. Marr (eds.), *Vietnam and the Rule of Law* (Canberra: Department of Political and Social Change, Research School of Pacific Studies, The Australian National University, 1993), pp. 81–115.

[38] Article 15.

[39] Article 14.

[40] Bui Ngoc Son, 'The Global Origins of Vietnam's Constitutions', 554.

[41] Article 50, 1992 Constitution.

[42] Bui Ngoc Son, 'Constitutional Developments in Vietnam in the First Decade of the Twenty First Century', in Albert Chen (ed.), *Constitutionalism in Asia in the Twenty First Century* (Cambridge: Cambridge University Press, 2014), p. 201. See also Chapter 3 in this publication detailing the imperial roots of the procuracy in Russia.

but also incorporates new constitutional ideas. This is because it has dual functions: the traditional socialist function and the new constitutional function. Before exploring this functional complexity in detail, relevant constitutional theories should be considered.

7.3 Theoretical Considerations

7.3.1 Authoritarian Constitutionalism

Constitutional theories tend to be dichotomic – for example, centralised and decentralised judicial review; federalist and unitary state; presidential and parliamentary system; 'global north' and 'global south'; particularism and universalism.[43] One such dichotomy is authoritarianism and constitutionalism, which has its root in McIlwain's negative definition of constitutionalism as a legally limited government, 'the antithesis of arbitrary rule'.[44] In its modern form, constitutionalism is comprised of fundamental elements such as a normative constitution, popular sovereignty, the separation of power and other forms of checks and balances, and the protection of fundamental rights.[45]

Socialist/communist regimes are normally identified as examples of authoritarian regimes.[46] Socialist/communist constitutions are normally considered irrelevant to constitutionalism. To illustrate, Walker describes Europe's former communist constitutions as anti-constitutionalist documents – they fail to constitute the polity objectively because they put power fully and formlessly at the disposal of its wielders.[47] Louis Henkin holds a similar view, stating that Europe's communist constitutions are merely descriptive rather than normative to the government, as these documents simply 'describe the kind of government and the institutions of government that have already been established and indicate plans and make promises for the future' rather than 'ordain what must be, establishing a blueprint for how government is to be organised and what the

---

[43] See generally Ran Hirschl, *Comparative Matters: The Renaissance of Comparative Constitutional Law* (Oxford: Oxford University Press, 2014).

[44] Charles Howard McIlwain, *Constitutionalism, Ancient and Modern* (Clark, NJ: The Lawbook Exchange, Ltd., 2005), p. 24.

[45] See generally Dieter Grimm, *Constitutionalism: Past, Present, and Future* (Oxford: Oxford University Press, 2016).

[46] Tom Ginsburg and Alberto Simpser (eds.), *Constitutions in Authoritarian Regimes* (New York, NY: Cambridge University Press, 2014).

[47] Graham Walker, 'The Constitutional Good: Constitutionalism's Equivocal Moral Imperative' (1993) 26(1) *Polity* 94.

governors must do if government and governors are to have constitutional legitimacy'.[48] This theory remains the powerful lens through
which scholars can understand communist constitutions that have
remained after the collapse of the Soviet Bloc, like those of China and
Vietnam.[49]

The dichotomy between authoritarianism and constitutionalism, and
the consequent theory of 'constitution without constitutionalism', may
not fully capture the complexity of the constitutional life in general and
of complex functions of the socialist constitutions in particular. Constitutionalism is an ideal. No country can claim that it has fully realised
constitutionalist ideals. Therefore, in theory, there may be some authoritarian aspects in even a well-established constitutionalist regime,[50] and
conversely, an authoritarian constitution may perform constitutionalist
function to some extent.

In contrast to the dichotomy between authoritarianism and constitutionalism, Mark Tushnet has recently called for 'pluralizing the category
of constitutionalism' and proposed the concept of 'authoritarian constitutionalism'.[51] Accordingly, a regime can be controlled by a dominant
party that can make public policies without a legal basis for challenging
its choices, which makes the regime authoritarian. However, the same
regime does not depress political opponents arbitrarily, 'allows reasonably open discussion and criticism of its policies', 'operates reasonably
free and fair elections', 'is sensitive to public opinion and alters its
policies', and ensures reasonable independence of courts and their capacity to 'enforce basic rule-of-law requirements',[52] which makes the
regime constitutionalist.

Tushnet's study suggests that there is not a clear separation between
authoritarianism and constitutionalism, and that constitutionalist
elements can also exist under an authoritarian regime. However,
Tushnet has not yet accounted for the potential of the constitutionalist

---

[48] Louis Henkin, 'Elements of Constitutionalism' (1998) 60 *Review of The International
Commission of Jurists* 10.

[49] Qianfan Zhang, 'A Constitution without Constitutionalism? The Paths of Constitutional
Development in China' (2010) 8(4) *International Journal of Constitutional Law* 950–877;
Duiker, *The Constitutional System of the Socialist Republic of Vietnam*, p. 331.

[50] See, e.g., Robert Diab, 'The Embrace of Authoritarian Legality', in Robert Diab, *The
Harbinger Theory: How the Post-9/11 Emergency Became Permanent and the Case for
Reform* (New York, NY: Oxford University Press, 2015), pp. 23–98.

[51] Mark Tushnet, 'Authoritarian Constitutionalism' (2015) 100 *Cornell Law Review* 395.

[52] Ibid., 449–450.

function of a constitution in an authoritarian regime. For example, while using Singapore as a case study, he focuses more on the country's electoral system and personal freedoms than the function of its constitution.

7.3.2 Negative Constitutional Theories

There is a body of recent scholarship that focuses on the way constitutionalism is constitutionally undermined by authoritarianism, which can be called 'negative constitutional theories'.

That idea resonates in recent negative constitutional theories. For example, William Partlett's theory of 'the elite threat to constitutional transitions' argues that constitution making in post-communist Europe and Asia provided the platform for self-interested elites to incorporate constitutional rules that fortify their power and undermine individual rights.[53] Similarly, David Landau's theory of 'abusive constitutionalism' suggests that would-be autocrats can constitutionally use the process of constitutional amendment and constitutional replacement to undermine democracy, evidenced by the experience in Hungary, Egypt and Venezuela.[54] In the same vein, Ozan O. Varol's theory of 'stealth authoritarianism' argues that post–Cold War authoritarians 'learned to perpetuate their power through the same legal mechanisms that exist in democratic regimes'.[55]

Negative constitutional theories also resonate in some accounts of socialist constitutions. In a recent study, Thomas E. Kellogg argues that China's Constitution functions as a 'false blueprint', in the sense that the communist party in China 'seeks to use the Constitution to legitimize its rule by maintaining the political fiction that China is transitioning to constitutional governance'.[56] Similarly, Brad Adams of Human Rights Watch criticises Vietnam's 2013 Constitution as it 'leaves the door wide

---

[53] William Partlett, 'The Elite Threat to Constitutional Transitions' (2016) 56(2) *Virginia Journal of International Law* 407.

[54] David Landau, 'Abusive Constitutionalism' (2013) 47 *UC Davis Law Review* 189.

[55] Ozan O Varol, 'Stealth Authoritarianism' (2015) 100 *Iowa Law Review* 1673.

[56] Thomas E. Kellogg, 'Arguing Chinese Constitutionalism: The 2013 Constitutional Debate and the "Urgency" of Political Reform' (2016) 11(3) *University of Pennsylvania Asian Law Review* 351.

open to the continued use of harsh laws and politically controlled courts to target activists and critics'.[57]

While negative constitutional theories help disclose the downside of authoritarian constitutional practices, they may not fully appreciate the potential positive sides. A more balanced approach is necessary, which would consider both the negative (instrumentalist) and positive (constitutionalist) functions of authoritarian constitutions.[58] At least in the case of Vietnam, the Constitution is not merely an instrument for political control. It can also control politics to a certain extent.

Moreover, negative constitutional theories have a normative impulse. In these theories, liberal constitutionalism is implicitly or explicitly the desirable outcome that authoritarians fail to achieve. Liberal constitutionalism, which is defined by the central concern of the limitation of the state power to protect individual rights, is just one among many forms of constitutionalism. Tushnet has pointed out 'varieties of constitutionalism', which include liberal constitutionalism, social-democratic constitutionalism and non-liberal constitutionalism (such as authoritarian constitutionalism and Islamic constitutionalism).[59] Other alternatives to liberal constitutionalism that have been discussed by different scholars include Confucian constitutionalism, societal constitutionalism, statist constitutionalism, communitarian constitutionalism and universalist constitutionalism.[60] In short, negative constitutional theories fail to appreciate the plurality of constitutionalism, both as a practice and a normative ideal.

---

[57] Human Rights Watch, 'Vietnam: Amended Constitution a Missed Opportunity on Rights', available at https://www.hrw.org/news/2013/12/02/vietnam-amended-constitution-missed-opportunity-rights.

[58] This classification of negative and positive is different from the classification of negative and positive constitutionalism with the former underlining the disabling function of the constitution, and the latter, enabling one. See generally, Stephen Holmes, *Passions and Constraint: On the Theory of Liberal Democracy* (Chicago, IL: University of Chicago Press, 1995); Sotirios A. Barber, *Welfare and the Constitution* (Princeton, NJ: Princeton University Press, 2003).

[59] Mark Tushnet, 'Varieties of Constitutionalism' (2016) 14(1) *International Journal of Constitutional Law* 1–4.

[60] Jiang Qing, *A Confucian Constitutional Order: How China's Ancient Past Can Shape Its Political Future* (eds. Daniel A. Bell and Ruiping Fan; trans. Edmund Ryden) (Princeton, NJ: Princeton University Press, 2013); David Sciulli, *Theory of Societal Constitutionalism: Foundations of a Non-Marxist Critical Theory* (Cambridge: Cambridge University Press, 1992); David S. Law, 'Constitutional Archetypes' (2016) 95 *Texas Law Review* 153; Sanford Levinson, 'On Searching for Archetypes in Constitutional Preambles' (2016) 95 *Texas Law Review* 63.

7.3.3 Socialist Constitutionalism

In contrast to negative constitutional theories, the theories of 'socialist constitutionalism' indicate optimism about the possibility of constitutionalism under socialism, with particular reference to the case of China.

Chinese scholars have developed normative theories of socialist constitutionalism 'focusing on the value of popular sovereignty and civil society', which challenges 'the hegemonic constitutional status of the CCP [Chinese Communist Party]'.[61] Chinese theories of socialist constitutionalism adopt a bottom-up approach. Baogang He summarises four 'basic principles' of this normative model, namely: the supremacy of the constitution over the communist party; citizen welfare; common prosperity; and the extension of the 'reform and opening up' initiative to the political field.[62]

In contrast, Cuban-American legal scholar Larry Catá Backer adopts a top-down approach, proposing the normative socialist constitutional theory known as 'state-party constitutionalism'. This is a model of a 'constitutionalist' system led by the communist party and with a focus on such things as the party's institutionalisation and its internal disciplines.[63] According to Baogang He, 'many Chinese scholars immediately rejected Backer's model of party-state constitutionalism because they thought it augments the power of the CCP without taking into account the complexity of the relationship between the party and the state – a

---

[61] Baogang He, 'Socialist Constitutionalism in Contemporary China', in Michael W. Dowdle and Michael A. Wilkinson (eds.), *Constitutionalism Beyond Liberalism* (Cambridge: Cambridge University Press, 2017), pp. 176–177. See also Feng Lin, 'Idealism and Realism in in Chinese Constitutional Theory and Practice', in Maurice Adams, Anne Meuwese and Ernst Hirsch Ballin (eds.), *Constitutionalism and the Rule of Law: Bridging Idealism and Realism* (Cambridge: Cambridge University Press, 2017), p. 294.

[62] He, 'Socialist Constitutionalism in Contemporary China', p. 182.

[63] Larry Catá Backer, 'Crafting a Theory of Socialist Democracy for China in the 21st Century: Considering Hu Angang's Theory of Collective Presidency in the Context of the Emerging Chinese Constitutional State' (2014) 16(1) *Asian-Pacific Law and Policy Journal* 29; Larry Catá Backer, 'Towards a Robust Theory of the Chinese Constitutional State: Between Formalism and Legitimacy in Jiang Shigong's Constitutionalism' (2014) 40(2) *Modern China* 168; Larry Catá Backer, 'Party, People, Government, and State: On Constitutional Values and the Legitimacy of the Chinese State-Party Rule of Law System' (2012) 30(1) *Boston University International Law Journal* 331; Larry Catá Backer, 'A Constitutional Court for China Within the Chinese Communist Party?: Scientific Development and a Reconsideration of the Institutional Role of the CCP' (2010) 43(3) *Suffolk Law Review* 593.

complexity that in their minds imposed foundational limits to the unity of a party-led constitutional system'.[64]

The useful implication of the theories of socialist constitutionalism is the potential for constitutionalism even under socialism, which is consistent with the trend to pluralise the concept of constitutionalism and avoid the simple dichotomy between constitutionalism and authoritarianism. However, the theories of socialist constitutionalism are polar opposites of negative constitutional theories. These theories seem too optimistic and underestimate the constitutional realities in socialist regimes, although they do not completely ignore the realties. Again, a more balanced approach is necessary to understand both the negative and positive sides of socialist constitutions. In addition, although the theories of socialist constitutionalism are informed by the realities to some extent, their primary concern is normative. Therefore, they are a less helpful tool for understanding the actual functions of the socialist constitutions. This requires an alternative descriptive concept.

7.3.4   Functionalist Constitutional Dualism

Functionalist constitutional dualism may be a concept suited to understand empirically the function of the socialist constitutions in the contemporary world. A substantive development of the theory of functionalist constitutional dualism is beyond this single Chapter. Instead, its core idea can be exposed: functionalist constitutional dualism is a concept denoting two competing functions of a constitution as a response to competing concerns.

This concept is connected to dualist thinking in political science and constitutional theory. In political science, dualism refers to 'the two practical problems of institutional design and personal conduct require, at the fundamental level, two different kinds of practical principle'.[65] John Rawls is the most influential dualist thinker, whose theory of 'justice as fairness' incorporates competing principles applied to political institutions and individuals.[66] This normative dualism focuses on political principles. Although this is instructive to dualist thinking, it is more concerned with normative institutional design than understanding institutional functions.

---

[64] He, 'Socialist Constitutionalism', p. 188.

[65] Liam Murphy, 'Institutions and the Demands of Justice' (1999) 27(4) *Philosophy & Public Affairs* 254.

[66] Colin Farrelly, 'Dualism, Incentives and the Demands of Rawlsian Justice' (2005) 38(3) *Canadian Journal of Political Science / Revue Canadienne de Science Politique* 675.

In constitutional theory, Bruce Ackerman is famous for this theory of 'dualist constitution', or 'dualist democracy'.[67] Unlike normative dualism, Ackerman's theory is directed towards positively understanding constitutional law and politics in the United States. He argues that 'a dualist constitution seeks to distinguish between two different kinds of decision that may be made in a democracy. The first is a decision by the American People; the second, by their government.'[68] Ackerman's theory suggests the possibility of dualist constitutional thinking in an empirical way. However, his theory focuses on dualist constitutional decision making rather than constitutional function.

I propose a functionalist approach to constitutional dualism. Functionalist constitutional dualism is directed, not to the normative constitutional principles and constitution making, but to the competing functions of a constitution. Functionalist constitutional dualism holds that a constitution can potentially have two competing functions. This does not mean that a constitution has only two functions. A constitution may have multiple functions, but a dualist account is conceptually directed to its two competing functions. This conceptual model is descriptive rather than normative; it tries to describe the real complexity of the functions of constitution due to the fact that the constitution needs to respond to competing concerns of different actors in a polity. Functionalist constitutional dualism does not pursue any constitutional ideals; nor is it grounded on any normative constitutional impulse.

Functionalist constitutional dualism has distinctive traits, though it also resonates with other constitutional theories. To begin with, it shares with authoritarian constitutionalism the ideas that pluralisation of the concept of constitutionalism is necessary, that a clear dichotomy between constitutionalism and authoritarianism must be abandoned, and that constitutionalism is potentially possible under authoritarian regimes. However, functionalist constitutional dualism accounts for the constitutionalist function of authoritarian constitutions, which is the missing point in the institutions-based theories of authoritarian constitutionalism.

Functionalist constitutional dualism agrees with negative constitutional theories on the negative function of the constitutions – specifically, socialist

---

[67] 'Constitutional Dualism', *Encyclopedia of the American Constitution*, available at: www.encyclopedia.com/politics/encyclopedias-almanacs-transcripts-and-maps/constitutional-dualism.

[68] Bruce Ackerman, 'Constitutional Law/Constitutional Politics' (1989) 99(3) *Yale Law Journal* 461.

constitutions have an instrumentalist function defined by the nature of the socialist regime it serves. A dualist account would not ignore the potential positive of constitutions generally and socialist constitutions in particular. Moreover, functionalist constitutional dualism does not rest on ideals of liberal constitutionalism. It adopts a generic sense of constitutionalism as legal restraints on state power, without attaching to the particular liberal ideational foundations of constitutional restraints (such as to protect liberal rights) and the particular liberal institutional mechanisms of constitutional restraints (such as free elections, separation of powers and judicial review). Functionalist constitutional dualism, therefore, operates with the pluralist view of constitutionalism; it is open to different possibilities of constitutionalist practices.

With particular reference to socialist constitutions, functionalist constitutional dualism accepts that some practices of constitutionalism are possible under socialist regimes, but it does not pursue a normative model of 'socialist constitutionalism'. First, this is because some incipient constitutionalist ideas and practices under the socialist regimes are not necessarily associated with socialist ideas, goals and institutions. For example, a socialist constitution can adopt the global constitutional principle of proportionality, which is alien to the socialist regime. Second, the socialist party-state may tolerate some competing constitutionalist ideas and practices while retaining the hegemony of socialist ideas and practice, but to create a 'model' of constitutionalism as a prevailing spirit within a socialist regime is an extremely difficult, if not impossible, task. At its essence, constitutionalism requires constraints on different types of domination: ideational/ideological, personal, political and institutional. It is unlikely that this essential spirit of constitutionalism can prevail in the socialist polity in which the communist party and the socialist ideology play dominant roles. If the communist party and the socialist ideology do not dominate, and constitutionalism becomes the prevailing spirit, then the polity will be something other than socialist.

7.4   Analytical Exploration

Within that conceptual base, I argue that the socialist constitution in today's Vietnam performs two competing functions: it operates as a controlled instrument of the party-state, but it also establishes normative prescriptions that constrain the party-state. The first function is hegemonic and presents the socialist features; the second function is peripheral and presents a nascent constitutionalist practice.

In fact, the dual functions of the socialist constitution in Vietnam began to manifest in 2001 when the regime amended the 1992 Constitution. In his extensive investigation of the constitution amendment process, Sidel argued that the constitution in Vietnam is transformed from a text for control and motivation to a platform for dialogue and debate.[69]

> In the new analytical framework of constitutional dialogue that emerges from the recent Vietnamese experience, the Party coordinates and ultimately controls, but through a spectrum of direction and coordination that ranges from high levels of control, to substantial direction, to strong pressure, to relatively open debate – and always maintaining a role in post-debate, postadoption implementation processes. In this framework a substantially broadened array of debate takes place, while the results of the process remain under coordinated direction and, if necessary, firm control.[70]

The instrumental nature of the constitution remained, but new constitutionalist functions began to emerge. However, the dual functions of the 2013 constitution become more remarkable, as explored in the next section.

7.4.1 Hegemonic Constitutional Socialism

I use the phrase 'hegemonic constitutional socialism' to denote the idea that the constitution predominantly functions as an instrument serving the socialist regime. This function is descriptive, as opposed to prescriptive, because the socialist constitution describes the confirmed principles, policies and the existing socialist status quo. In addition, this function is hegemonic, in the sense that it prevails over the competing function. The constitution in Vietnam performs this instrumental function well, as I will illustrate using the 2013 Constitution.

To begin with, the 2013 Constitution describes the Principles and policies that had been already confirmed by the communist party. The new preamble to the Constitution explicitly states that the Constitution is enacted to 'institutionalise the Political Creed of building the nation during the transitional period to socialism'.[71] The party's Political Creed was revised in 2011 to provide guidance for comprehensive 'renovation' of both the

---

[69] Sidel, 'Analytical Models', 82.
[70] Ibid., 86.
[71] Preamble, The Constitution of the Socialist Republic of Vietnam (2013).

economic system and the political system.[72] The 2013 Constitution makers justified the enactment of the constitution on the basis that it was necessary to make the constitutional framework consistent with the Political Creed and other party documents.[73] During the constitution-making process, the Party also met to discuss and 'conclude' on several important questions, including constitutional questions. The Constitution makers acknowledged that the Party's political documents and 'conclusions' were a 'guiding opinion' in constitution making,[74] and that constitution making must be 'under the leadership of the Party'.[75] On that basis, the Constitution makers sought to reaffirm the 'socialist rule of law state', the leadership of the Communist Party over the state and society, the overall institutional structure confirmed in the previous 1992 Constitution, the unity of power and the socialist-oriented market economy.[76] The new 2013 Constitution effectively reaffirmed these socialist features, which reflect the Soviet constitutional legacy:

- *The aspirations and goals to create the socialist paradise*: '[...] a prosperous people and a strong, democratic, equitable and civilised country, in which all people enjoy an abundant, free and happy life and are given conditions for their comprehensive development.' (article 3)
- *Socialist legality*: 'The State of the Socialist Republic of Vietnam is a socialist rule of law state of the People, by the People and for the People.' (article 2)
- *Collective mastery*: 'The Socialist Republic of Vietnam is the country where the People are the masters; all the state power belongs to the People and is based on the alliance of the working class, the peasantry and the intelligentsia.' (article 2)
- *The unity of power*: 'The state power is unified.' (article 2)

---

[72] Đảng Cộng sản Việt Nam [Communist Party of Vietnam], 'Cương lĩnh xây dựng đất nước trong thời kỳ quá độ lên chủ nghĩa xã hội (Bổ sung, Phát triển năm 2011)' ['Political Creed of Building the Nation during the Transitional Period to Socialism (Amended and Developed in 2011)'], section II.

[73] Ủy ban dự thảo sửa đổi Hiến pháp năm 1992 [The Committee for Drafting Amendments to the 1992 Constitution], 'Tờ Trình Về Dự thảo sửa đổi Hiến pháp năm 1992,' Số: 194/TTr-UBDTSĐHP, ngày 19 tháng 10 năm 2012 ['Statement on the Draft Amendments to the 1992 Constitution'] No. 194/TTr-UBDTSĐHP, dated 19 October 2012], p. 1.

[74] Ibid., p. 2.

[75] Ibid., p. 3.

[76] Ibid., pp. 3–4.

- *The Communist Party*: The leadership of the Party over the state and the society and "Marxist–Leninist doctrine and Ho Chi Minh Thought" as its ideology. (article 4)
- *Democratic centralism*: 'The State shall [. . .] implement the principle of democratic centralism.' (article 8)
- *Statist rights*: '(1) Citizens' rights are inseparable from citizens' obligations. (2) Everyone is obliged to respect others' rights. (3) Citizens shall perform their obligations toward the State and society.(4) The exercise of human rights and citizens' rights may not infringe upon national interests and others' rights and legitimate interests.' (article 15)
- *The military*: 'The people's armed forces shall show absolute loyalty to the Fatherland, the People, the Party and the State.' (article 56)
- *The judiciary*: The constitutional requirement of the People's Courts and the People's Procuracies to safeguard the socialist regime, among other things. (articles 102 and 107)
- *The constitutional economy*: 'The Vietnamese economy is a socialist-oriented market economy with varied forms of ownership and economic sectors; the state economy plays the leading role.' (article 15); 'the state ownership of all lands.' (article 54)
- *Social policies*: 'The State and society shall make investments to further the protection of and care for the People's health, implement the universal health insurance, and adopt policies to prioritise health care for ethnic minority people and people living in mountainous areas, on islands, and in areas that have extremely difficult socio-economic conditions' (article 58); 'The State shall create equal opportunities for citizens to enjoy social welfare, develop the social security system, and adopt policies to support elderly people, people with disabilities, poor people, and other disadvantaged people' (article 59); 'The State and society shall create an environment for building prosperous, progressive and happy Vietnamese families, and developing Vietnamese people with good health, cultural qualities, patriotism, a spirit of solidarity, a sense of mastery and civic responsibility.' (article 60)

Thus, like previous socialist constitutions, Vietnam's 2013 Constitution functions as an instrument for the party-state to describe their goals, principles and policies in constitutional terms. The Constitution repeats nearly the exact same the language as previously adopted in the Party's political documents (such as 'socialist rule of law state', 'unity of power' and 'socialist-oriented market economy').

The Constitution also describes the existing socialist institutional settings. Made under the Party's leadership, the new Constitution successfully reaffirms the Leninist constitutional structure of the previous 1992 Constitution, featuring the leadership of the communist party as the embodiment of the socialist principle of constitutional vanguardism, the formalist supremacy of the National Assembly and subordinate executive and judicial bodies as an expression of the socialist principle of 'democratic centralism', and the centralised relationship between central and local governments as a reminder of the Soviet system.[77] The Leninist constitutional system had been already established as such, and the new Constitution simply describes this system.

Following the Party's direction, the Constitution makers effectively rejected the popular calls for non-socialist institutional changes intended to establish normative constraints on party-state power, such as an institution of constitutional review, a human rights committee or an anticorruption committee. The new Constitution also rejects several proposals intended to constrain state control over social-economic resources, such as the calls for multi-ownership of land and removing the constitutional mandate of the 'leading role' of the state-economic sectors.[78] The fact that the Constitution fails to establish structural constraints on political power indicates that it ultimately functions as an instrument for political control. The socialist elite uses the Constitution to describe their policies, principles and institutions, and would not allow any institutions that might substantively challenge their power and their socialist endeavours.

Constitutional propaganda is another aspect indicating the instrumental function of Vietnam's Constitution. After its enactment, the regime employed propaganda mechanisms to spread positivity about the Constitution. It focused on describing the Constitution as the expression of the popular will and the base 'for Vietnam to enter a new period of comprehensive renovation in economy, politics, national construction and defense, multifaceted development and proactive international integration'.[79]

---

[77] For these common features of socialist constitutions, see generally Chris Osakwe, 'The Common Law of Constitutions of the Communist-Party States' (1997) 3 *Review of Socialist Law* 155.

[78] See Le Toan, 'Interpreting the Constitutional Debate over Land Ownership in the Socialist Republic of Vietnam' (2016) 11 *Asian Journal of Comparative Law* 287; Pham Duy Nghia, 'From Marx to Market: The Debates on the Economic System in Vietnam's Revised Constitution' (2016) 11 *Asian Journal of Comparative Law* 263.

[79] Nguyen Sinh Hung, 'The Revised Constitution Is the Firm Legal and Political Guarantee for the Entire Party, People and Army to Join Force in the March toward the New Period',

Most members of the Constitutional Amendment Committee wrote papers praising the new Constitution.[80] Popular media disseminated similar sentiments written by different constitutional propagandists. Constitutional law scholars and others have produced several volumes of 'scientific comments' that describe and praise the contents of the Constitution.[81] In popular outlets and academic law journals, writings calling constitutional reforms pave way for propagandist constitutional writings.[82] The Ministry of Justice even held a national competition to encourage engagement with the new Constitution – it posed basic questions on topics such as the number of constitutions in Vietnam, the date the new constitution came into effect and the new constitutional provisions on state institutions.[83] So, the party-state used propaganda to talk up the Constitution and its contents, while controlling and even excluding critical comments about it in official media and other official fora. Those who were critical of the Constitution were forced to comment via unofficial platforms – for example, mathematician Hoàng Xuân Phú used his blog to publish a paper condemning the new Constitution as a 'Hiến pháp vi hiến' (unconstitutional constitution), in the sense that it includes provisions that negate each other.[84]

Constitutional propaganda illustrates the instrumental function of the socialist Constitution in Vietnam. The Constitution operates as the

Communist Review, 8 May 2014, available at http://english.tapchicongsan.org.vn/Home/Politics/2014/799/The-revised-Constitution-is-the-firm-legal-and-political-guarantee-for-the.aspx

[80] These writings were published in the Tạp chí Nghiên cứu Lập pháp (Journal of Legislative Studies) in 2014.

[81] See, e.g., Đào Trí Úc and Vũ Công Giao (eds.), Bình Luận Khoa Học Hiến pháp Nước Cộng hòa Xã hội chủ nghĩa Việt Nam năm 2013 [Scientific Comments on the Constitution of The Socialist Republic of Vietnam of 2013] (Hanoi: Labor and Society Publishing House, 2014); Hoàng Thế Liên (eds.), Hiến pháp Năm 2013: Những Điểm mới mang tính Đột phá [The 2013 Constitution: The Breakthrough New Points] (Hanoi: Judicial Publishing House, 2015).

[82] For example, many such articles have been published in the Tạp chí Nhà nước và Pháp luật (Journal of State and Law) and the Tạp chí Nghiên cứu Lập pháp (Journal of Legislative Studies) in post-2013.

[83] For more information see the website of the Ministry of Justice, at http://moj.gov.vn/qt/cacchuyenmuc/ctv/Pages/cuoc-thi.aspx.

[84] Hoàng Xuân Phú, 'Hiến pháp vi hiến' ['The Unconstitutional Constitution'], http://hpsc.iwr.uni-heidelberg.de/hxphu/index.php?page=readwriting&w=HienPhapViHien-20140904. The phenomenon 'unconstitutional constitution' in recent comparative constitutional scholarship has a different meaning: it is a constitutional amendment that is unconstitutional because it violates fundamental principles of the current constitution. See, e.g., Gary Jeffrey Jacobsohn, 'An Unconstitutional Constitution? A Comparative Perspective' (2006) 4(3) International Journal of Constitutional Law 460.

platform for the party-state to propagandise ideas, principles and policies that legitimise the existing socialist regime. These include ideas about the legitimacy of the Constitution itself: constitutional propagandists assert that the constitution expresses the popular will and the consensus between the Party and the people.[85]

7.4.2   Nascent Constitutionalism

On the other hand, Vietnam's Constitution has a nascent constitutional-ist function. It operates as the base for the development of a dialogue about constitutionalism. Elsewhere, I have argued that while the Consti-tution confirms fundamental socialist constitutional principles, it also adapts these principles (due to the impact of globalisation), which creates the condition of 'disharmony' that is necessary for continuing consti-tutional dialogue in Vietnam.[86] These adaptions reflect certain ideals of constitutionalism, including:

- *Constituent power*: The preamble recoginzes The Vietnam people' as the author to make the constitution, while the body of constitutiion vests the constitution-making power to the ordinary legislature (pre-amble and article 70), and constitutional referendum depends on the decision of the legislature. (article 120)
- *Accountability*: The Communist Party leads the state and society, but under the Constitution and the law it is accountable to the public and subject to popular supervision. (article 4)
- *Limited power*: The state powers are united but distributed and con-trolled. (article 2)
- *Universal human rights*: 'Human rights and citizens' rights in the political, civil, economic, cultural and social fields shall be recognised, respected, protected and guaranteed in accordance with the Consti-tution and law.' (article 14)
- *The market*: State economic sectors play the leading role, but 'all economic sectors are important components of the national economy. Entities in different economic sectors are equal before law and shall cooperate and compete with one another in accordance with law'. (article 51) The state may recover the rights to use land, but 'Land

---

[85] Nguyen Sinh Hung, 'The Revised Constitution'.

[86] Bui Ngoc Son, 'Globalization of Constitutional Identity' (2017) 26(3) *Washington Inter-national Law Journal*.

recovery must be public and transparent, and compensation must be paid in accordance with the law'. (article 54)

- *Justice*: Courts must project human rights and justice, but they must also protect the socialist regime. (article 102)
- *Political decentralisation*: While local governments are under the control and supervision of the central government, they 'may, as necessary, be assigned certain tasks of state agencies at higher levels, along with the necessary means to ensure the performance of those tasks'. (article 112) 'The People's Council shall decide on local issues as prescribed by a law; and supervise the observance of the Constitution and law in its locality and the implementation of its own resolutions.' (article 113)

The Constitution includes ambiguous language, which creates scope for dialogue to determine the meaning of the provisions. For example, the Constitution retains the principle of unity of power but adapts and legitimises it by committing to mutual control among the three state branches.[87] This echoes the Western idea of checks and balances. But, the Constitution has yet to provide detailed mechanisms for controlling state power. This provides space for active dialogue in academic fora and the popular media (such as *Thanh Niên, Tuổi trẻ, Vietnamnet, Vnexpress* and *Dân trí*) about controlling public power,[88] which resonates with the essential spirit of constitutionalism. Whether this dialogue results in institutional checks among the state actors remains to be seen. At this level at least, the Constitution operates as the platform not only to disseminate socialist ideas and principles, but also to discuss ideas and principles associated with constitutionalism.

In addition, the Constitution functions as the base for the development of what can be called 'universalist constitutionalism' in Vietnam. Universalist constitutionalism resonates with David Law's identification of the 'universalist constitutional archetype', which 'generates legitimacy by holding the state to norms and principles of a universal character that

---

[87] Article 2, The Constitution of the Socialist Republic of Vietnam (2013).

[88] See, e.g., Vũ Ngọc Hoàng, 'Kiểm soát quyền lực: 'Có những người bán rẻ Tổ quốc vì quyền lợi cá nhân'' ['Controlling the Power: There Are People Selling the Fatherland at a Cheap Price for Personal Interests''], *Vietnamnet* [22 September 2016], available at http://vietnamnet.vn/vn/tuanvietnam/tieudiem/kiem-soat-quyen-luc-co-nhung-nguoi-ban-re-to-quoc-vi-quyen-luc-329103.html; Cấn Cường - Tuấn Hợp - Hải Sâm, 'Phải kiểm soát được mặt trái của tập trung quyền lực' ['The Negative Side of Centralised Power Must Be Controlled'], Dân trí [16 May, 2016], available at http://dantri.com.vn/chinh-tri/phai-kiem-soat-duoc-mat-trai-cua-tap-trung-quyen-luc-2016051607171729.htm;

stand over and above the state'.[89] But the model of universalist constitutionalism emphasises the constitutionalist nature of the international/ universalist norms, which are mostly incorporated into international or transnational treaties, and are the source of domestic constitutional legitimacy. This constitutionalist nature is defined by the fact that these norms establish prescriptions on the behaviours of domestic state actors – to prevent them from the arbitrary use of power and to have them work for the public good.

The 2013 Constitution has some traits of 'universalist constitutionalism'. Although it is predominantly descriptive, it has begun to establish some normative prescriptions upon state power. For example, the Constitution newly requires that human rights can only be restricted for common good by legislative statutes. This provision has two important implications for constitutionalism. First, human rights can only be limited for common good, such as public order and national security, resonating the universal principle of proportionality.[90] That means the law cannot arbitrarily limit human rights. Second, human rights can only be restricted by the legislature. This is intended to restrict the discretion of administrative bodies.[91] Moreover, the Constitution introduces more human rights that are consistent with international human rights treaties, which may limit state power. These new rights include: the right to life, the right to not be expelled from home territory, the right to private family life, the right to a presumption of innocence, the right to appeal to a higher court, the right to favourable working conditions, the prohibition of child labour and the right to a healthy environment.[92] So, the Constitution operates as a domestic framework to incorporate and implement international constitutionalist norms.

More importantly, 'universalist constitutionalism' has begun to be realised. There is empirical evidence that the legislature (the National Assembly) is now, to some extent, constrained by constitutional rights provisions. A legislator told me that the National Assembly is now strongly influenced by the constitutional requirement that legislation must respect and protect

---

[89] Law, 'Constitutional Archetypes', 174.

[90] Alec Stone Sweet and J. Mathews, 'Proportionality Balancing and Global Constitutionalism' (2008) 47 *Columbia Journal of Transnational Law* 74 ('Proportionality-based rights adjudication now constitutes one of the defining features of global constitutionalism.').

[91] For the list of discretions by administrative bodies, see H. L. A, Hart, 'Discretion' (2013) 127 *Harvard Law Review* 655.

[92] For more details, see Bui Ngoc Son, 'The Global Origins of Vietnam's Constitutions', 542–543.

human rights, and that human rights must be limited only for public good.[93] As a consequence, National Assembly deputies now invoke the Constitution in their legislative debates, especially its rights provisions.[94] For example, in May 2015, the draft revision of the Civil Code provides that Vietnamese names must not exceed twenty-five characters. Some legislators and lawyers have argued that this restriction of personal rights is unconstitutional. They cite article 14 of the 2013 Constitution, which stipulates that rights can only be restricted for public interests, and argue that name length is a personal issue.[95] This restriction was therefore removed in the new Civil Code of 2015. This shows that the Constitution can be prescriptive in relation to the state's actions, albeit in limited contexts.

In reality, many legislative statutes have been revised or newly enacted to comply with the new constitutional rights provisions.[96] For example, reflecting the Constitution's newly adopted right to life, the 2015 Penal Code removes the application of the death penalty from seven crimes, namely: surrendering to the enemy, opposing order, destroying important national security works, robbery, drug possession, drug appropriation, and the production and trade of fake food.[97] The (currently suspended) 2015 Criminal Procedure Code recognises the right to silence, which echoes the constitutional recognition of the presumption of innocence (article 58). Moreover, new laws, such as the Law on

---

[93] Interview with an Assembly deputy in Hanoi on 12 January 2017.

[94] Ibid.

[95] See L. Thanh, 'Quy định đặt họ tên không được quá 25 chữ cái, có vi hiến?' ['Is the Provision That Names must not exceed 25 Characters Unconstitutional?'], Báo Pháp Luật Thành phố Hồ Chí Minh, 12 May 2015, available at http://phapluattp.vn/phap-luat/quy-dinh-dat-ho-ten-khong-duoc-qua-25-chu-cai-co-vi-hien-553222.html; Minh Hòa, 'Đề xuất đặt tên không quá 25 Chữ cái: Vi hiến và Trái luật?' ['The Proposal That Names must not Exceed 25 Characters: Unconstitutional and Illegal?'] VOV, 16 May 2015, available at http://vov.vn/phap-luat/de-xuat-dat-ten-khong-qua-25-chu-cai-vi-hien-va-trai-luat-401206.vov.

[96] Trần Ngọc Đường, 'Báo cáo đánh giá việc thể chế hóa quyền con người, quyền công dân trong các Bộ Luật, đạo Luật đã ban hành theo tinh thần và nội dung mới của Hiến pháp năm 2013' ['Report: Evaluating the Institutionalization of Human rights and Citizen Rights in Codes and Statutes enacted According to the New Spirit and Contents of the 2013 Constitution']. (Date is not provided). (On file with author). I thank Dr Vu Cong Giao for sharing this report.

[97] Vũ Hân, 'Bỏ hình phạt tử hình với 7 tội danh' ['Abolishing Death Penalty to Seven Crimes'], Báo Công an nhân dân điện tử, 27 November 2015, http://cand.com.vn/Van-de-hom-nay-thoi-su/Nguoi-tren-75-tuoi-duoc-mien-tu-hinh-374274/.

Referendum and the Access to Information Law, have been enacted to implement relevant constitutional rights.[98]

Furthermore, legislative statutes also established restrictions on the administrative bodies, preventing them from violating constitutional rights. Trần Ngọc Đường, who worked in the National Assembly for many years as a senior officer and scholar, reports that administrative regulations are now not allowed to 'arbitrarily cut off and invalidate' constitutional rights as the legislative statues create prohibitions on that.[99] For example, the 2016 Law on Children lists prohibitions on violating children rights,[100] such as blocking children from practising their rights and disclosing their personal information (article 6). These legislative prohibitions prescribe the behaviour of social actors *and* state actors, especially those in administrative authority.

Universalist constitutionalism is lively to some extent in Vietnam because its citizens are now more likely to call upon their constitutional rights. For example, Công Phượng, a famous footballer in Vietnam, was rumoured to have fabricated his age in order to play in a younger league, which prompted an investigation by Vietnam Television (VTV), the national television broadcaster. On 16 November 2014, VTV's Chuyển Động twenty-four-hour broadcast program published documents about Công Phượng, which they used to dispute his 1995 birth certificate and claim he was really born in 1993. In response, Vietnamese lawyers publicly argued that VTV's action violated article 23 of the 2013 Constitution, which provides that 'everyone is entitled to the inviolability of personal privacy, personal secrecy and familial secrecy'.[101] On 30 December 2014, VTV 'was fined VND15 million (US$701) and ordered to issue a public correction' by the Ministry of Information and Communications – not for violating a constitutional right but for 'broadcasting wrongful information' about Phượng's age.[102] While these consequences

---

[98] Trần Ngọc Đường, in 'Báo cáo đánh giá việc thể chế hóa quyền con người, quyền công dân trong các Bộ Luật, đạo Luật đã ban hành theo tinh thần và nội dung mới của Hiến pháp năm 2013.

[99] Ibid., 7.

[100] Ibid., 8–9.

[101] Vũ Hương and Trà My, 'Công Phượng có Bị xâm Phạm quyền Riêng tư? [Is Công Phượng's Right to Personal Privacy Violated'], Báo Tuổi trẻ, 20 November 2014, available at http://tuoitre.vn/tin/chinh-tri-xa-hoi/tieu-diem/20141120/cong-phuong-co-bi-xam-pham-quyen-rieng-tu/673848.html.

[102] Khánh Uyên, 'Vietnam Television Fined for Slandering Young Football Striker,' Thanh Nien News, 31 December 2014, available at www.thanhniennews.com/sports/vietnam-television-fined-for-slandering-young-football-striker-37116.html.

were not framed in terms of a constitutional violation, the case illustrates that lawyers publicly articulated arguments based on the Constitution's provision on the right to privacy.

7.5 Conclusion

The dual functions of the Constitution in Vietnam are generated by the competing concerns of the state actors and the social actors. On the one hand, the socialist leadership needs to maintain the existing (socialist) status quo to both protect their power and interests and to pursue the socialist goals. The Constitution is instrumental in expressing these socialist goals, principles and policies in and describing the existing structure in constitutional terms. This echoes what Tom Ginsburg and Alberto Simpser call the 'billboard' role of constitutions, which 'is common to both dictatorships and democracies'.[103] 'As authoritative statements of policy, constitutions can also play a role in signaling the intention of leaders within the regime to those outside it.'[104] In this way, Vietnamese leaders seek to use the Constitution to signal to the international and domestic audience the regime's authoritative and definitive commitment to socialist goals, principles and policies.

On the other hand, the Constitution must also be able to respond to the concerns of society. During the last few decades, Vietnamese society has changed significantly due to factors such as economic liberalisation, international integration, the development of the civil society and urbanisation. Vietnamese citizens (particularly those of the middle class) are now aware of the relevance of the Constitution, especially its rights provisions. They mobilised for the incorporation of international human rights into the Constitution and the realisation of these rights in practice.[105] This mobilisation was particularly vehement during the 2013 Constitution-making process, evidenced by the work of the group of seventy-two scholars, law graduates, the 'free citizens' group, the Cùng Viết Hiến pháp (Let's Draw up the Constitution) group (an online forum providing constitutional analysis), the Vietnamese Catholic bishops, and civil society groups and

---

[103] Tom Ginsburg and Alberto Simpser, 'Introduction: Constitutions in Authoritarian Regimes,' in Ginsburg and Simpser, *Constitutions in Authoritarian Regimes*, p. 6.
[104] Ibid.
[105] On social mobilisation for international human rights, see generally Beth A. Simmons, *Mobilizing for Human Rights: International Law in Domestic Politics* (Cambridge: Cambridge University Press, 2009).

organisations.[106] Consequently, the Constitution has had to respond to these social demands, leading to its constitutionalist function or its establishment of norms prescriptive to the state's behaviour. Therefore, the Constitution can serve as the framework for society to debate constitutionalist values and to demand the practice of constitutionalist norms.

This constitutionalist function of the Constitution can be tolerated within the socialist regime without rejecting its instrumentalist function and destroying the regime. This is because the constitutionalist function does not prevail over the instrumentalist function. As the socialist elite can powerfully control the regime, the instrumentalist function remains dominant. The constitutionalist demands of society are accommodated, but only insofar as the regime endures. Consequently, the Constitution provides space for discourse on constitutionalist institutions, but they cannot be systematically established in a way that challenges the existing socialist regime. For example, the debate on controlled power can lead to some checks from the National Assembly over the government, but a comprehensive system of separation of power and checks and balances could not be established within the socialist institutional settings. There is potential for the constitutionalist function to develop, but it's not guaranteed.

Moreover, in response to social concerns, the Constitution can operate as the site to incorporate and implement universalist rights. This is tolerated because the demands for rights, unlike the demands for structural change, do not fundamentally challenge the existing socialist regime. Further, the demands for personal or socio-economic rights are better tolerated than the demands for civil-political rights, which are more challenging to those in power. This can be seen in the delay in the enactment of the law on associations, although the freedom of association is constitutionally recognised.

The functions of socialist constitutions today are complex. Neither a pessimistic nor optimistic view fully captures this complexity. This Chapter argues that recognising functionalist constitutional dualism reveals the tensions and possibilities for constitutional reform in socialist states, while quarantining the assumption of liberal constitutional reform. While this view is exemplified by the case of Vietnam, it may have implications for constitutions in other socialist regimes and similar institutional settings.

---

[106] I have examined this in detail in Bui Ngoc Son, 'Constitutional Mobilization'(forthcoming 2018) 17(1) *Washington University Global Studies Law Review*. See also Bui Ngoc Son and Pip Nicholson, 'Activism and Popular Constitutionalism in Contemporary Vietnam' (2017) 42(3) *Law & Social Inquiry* 677.

PART IV

Justice and Democratic Centralism

Democratic Centralism and Administration in China

SARAH BIDDULPH

8.1 Introduction

The decision issued by the fourth plenary session of the 18th Central Committee of the Chinese Communist Party (CCP, or Party) in 2014 on *Some Major Questions in Comprehensively Promoting Governing the Country According to Law* (the 'Fourth Plenum Decision') reiterated the Party's determination to build a 'socialist rule of law system with Chinese characteristics'.[1] What does this proclamation of the 'socialist' nature of China's version of rule of law mean, if anything? Development of a notion of socialist rule of law in China has included many apparently competing and often mutually inconsistent narratives and trends. In searching for indicia of socialism in China's legal system, it is necessary at the outset to acknowledge that what we identify as socialist may be overlaid with other important influences, including at least China's long history of centralised, bureaucratic governance, Maoist forms of 'adaptive' governance[2] and Western ideological, legal and institutional imports outside of Marxism–Leninism. In fact, what the Chinese party-state labels 'socialist' has already departed from the original ideals of European

This research was supported by a grant from the Australian Research Council [FT130100412].

[1] English translation available at https://chinacopyrightandmedia.wordpress.com/2014/10/28/ccp-central-committee-decision-concerning-some-major-questions-in-comprehensively-moving-governing-the-country-according-to-the-law-forward/.

[2] That is, the capacity to respond in diverse ways to 'shocks and disturbances' in a way that furthers the resilience of the system. See discussion in Sebastian Heilmann and Elizabeth Perry (eds.), *Mao's Invisible Hand: The Political Foundations of Adaptive Governance in China* (Cambridge, MA: Harvard University Press, 2011).

socialists.[3] This Chapter does not engage in a critique of whether Chinese versions of socialism are really 'socialist'. Instead it examines the influence on China's legal system of democratic centralism, often attributed to Lenin, but more significantly for this book project firmly embraced by the party-state as a core element of 'Chinese socialism'.

Having asserted the centrality to governance of 'socialist rule of law with Chinese characteristics', it is timely to consider its distinctive characteristics and how these might assist us to better understand the trajectory of Chinese legal reforms. Two preliminary issues of context help explain the importance of understanding the basic parameters of China's legal system reforms. The first is the framework for analysis of Chinese legal development: can it usefully be seen as a form of either transition or incomplete transition? The second is the potential international impact of the Chinese model of rule of law (if one exists).

With respect to the first issue, many analyses of the development of the rule of law in China imagine that, as China's economy develops, we will gradually see development and broadening of law as a mode of governance and the strengthening of legal institutions. It is a vision that has China 'marching toward the rule of law'.[4] Will economic and legal reforms result in some form of convergence with a procedural or 'thin' version of the rule of law, if not a liberal democratic-inspired normative version of rule of law? Increasingly, this possibility seems unlikely. Many now argue that the legal system we see operating in China cannot be explained away as one of 'incomplete transition'. Landry, Tong and Shen note that key features of the Leninist party-state remain – one of which is political control over legal institutions.[5] They argue that we can't characterise unexpected features of the legal system as 'transitional because we see it as a temporary out of equilibrium phenomenon'.[6] These comments invite us to question

---

[3] The newest rendition of socialist ideology, 'Xi Jinping thought for a new era of socialism with Chinese characteristics' was included in the Party Charter at the 19th Party Congress on 24th October 2017, Yan Xiaofeng 25 October 2017 'Xi Jinping Thought for a New Era of Socialism with Chinese Characteristics' has been written into the Party Charter: raising the flag of a 'New Era' of thought' *people.com* http://cpc.people.com.cn/19th/n1/2017/1025/c414538-29608349.html

(颜晓峰 25 October 2017 '习近平新时代中国特色社会主义思想"写入党章：立起了"新时代"思想旗帜'people.com http://cpc.people.com.cn/19th/n1/2017/1025/c414538-29608349.html)

[4] Randall Peerenboom, *China's Long March toward Rule of Law* (Cambridge: Cambridge University Press, 2002).

[5] Pierre Landry, Yanqi Tong and Mingming Shen, 'Introduction: Markets, Courts and Leninism' (2009) 9(1) *The China Review*.

[6] Ibid., 2.

whether what might appear to be an anomaly in China's legal development is in fact an anomaly, or if it is actually indicative of a more stable, permanent feature of the legal system – though one that we had not expected to see. To be clear, I am not making an argument that the Chinese system is unique in this. The varieties of capitalism literature point out the diversity of legal systems, and the ways the overall structure of the legal system impacts on the nature of legal reform and legal responses to crises.[7] And China is not the only authoritarian state that is developing a version of rule of law that suits and supports authoritarian modes of governance. China is one example among a number of authoritarian states establishing a legal edifice for governance that might also produce something unexpected.

With respect to the second issue, the Fourth Plenum Decision and what it says about rule of law in China also needs to be read in the context of a broader question about the significance of China's push back against so-called 'Western' ideas, including liberal democratic visions of the rule of law and the relationship between citizen and state that that vision instantiates. There is increasing worry that rising (socialist or post-socialist) authoritarian powers, with China as one of those at the forefront, are acting to entrench counter-norms to liberal democracy, rule of law and the universal values they represent. At the international level, this can be seen in areas such as 'privileging state security, civilizational diversity (non-interference in domestic affairs) and traditional values'.[8] At the domestic level, these include prioritisation of the interests of the party-state and social order at the expense of individual rights.[9] Party leadership has explicitly rejected a number of core elements of a liberal democratic notion of rule of law – separation of powers, independence of the judiciary and constitutionalism among the most obvious.[10] So,

---

[7] Curtis Milhaupt and Katarina Pistor, *Law and Capitalism: What Corporate Crises Reveal About Legal Systems and Economic Development around the World* (Chicago, IL: Chicago University Press, 2008).

[8] Alexander Cooley, 'Authoritarianism Goes Global: Countering Democratic Norms' (2015) 26(3) *Journal of Democracy*.

[9] Sarah Biddulph, *The Stability Imperative: Human Rights and Law in China* (Vancouver: UBC Press, 2015).

[10] One instance is the 'Seven Don't Mentions' set out in the Communique on the Current State of the Ideological Sphere issued by the General Office of the Central Party Committee in May 2013 prohibiting discussion of: universal values, press freedom, civil society, civic rights, historical mistakes of the Communist Party, elite cronyism and judicial independence. Anne Henochowicz, https://chinadigitaltimes.net/2015/04/words-of-the-week-seven-dont-mentions/, *China Digital Times*, 23 April 2015, available at www.chinadigitaltimes/2015/04/words-of-the-week-seven-don't-mentions/. Another is

behind our inquiry into socialist characteristics of China's version of the rule of law lurks a question of whether these developments present a challenge or establish a counter-norm to the liberal democratic notion of rule of law? This Chapter raises, but leaves open, this broader question.

In interrogating the socialist nature of Chinese rule of law, this Chapter focuses on a core ideological and institutional principle of party and state: democratic centralism. It also notes that a dominant form of legality is the political-administrative orientation of governance. It explores the nature and extent of the role that these elements of ideology and form continue to play in structuring the legal system and influencing modes of governance more broadly.

Nicholson and Pham's Chapter in this volume (Chapter 9) examines the impact of democratic centralism on the institutional organisation of courts and the procuratorate in Vietnam. Rather than adopt a similar institutional focus for analysis, or address the question as one of ideology, this Chapter seeks to explore the practical impact of democratic centralist arrangements of power and policy making on governance – the *ways* in which power is exercised. It does not make a general claim about governance as a whole but seeks to identify how the organisational aspects of democratic centralism are at play in shaping certain areas of administration. It uses as its example campaign-style enforcement (*yundongshi zhili*) – specifically, the ongoing campaigns to redress the systemic problem of wage arrears.

The main argument of this Chapter is that there is a ready resort to the campaign form as a way to redress perceived crises arising from failures in decentralised forms of regulation and enforcement. It asserts that campaign-style enforcement depends heavily on the organisational principles of democratic centralism, with an emphasis on centralisation of analysis and strategy, target setting and reporting back. Campaigns also reflect what Tay and Kamenka have labelled the 'bureaucratic-administrative' character of governance, and have a strong centrally planned flavour.[11] Campaign-style enforcement punctuates regular decentralised enforcement and is so commonly used that I argue it could be seen as a regular feature of governance, rather than an exception to ordinary day-to-day administration.

---

the speech given by the Chief Justice of the Supreme People's Court Zhou Qiang in January 2017 in which he warned against falling into the Western ideological traps of constitutional democracy, separation of powers and judicial independence. https://www .nytimes.com/2017/01/18/world/asia/china-chief-justice-courts-zhou-qiang.html.

[11] Alice Tay and Eugene Kamenka, 'Marxism, Socialism and the Theory of Law' (1984–1985) 23 *Columbia Journal of Transnational Law* 217.

After giving a brief account of the concepts of democratic centralism as it relates to governance in contemporary China, I will develop my argument through a detailed discussion of law enforcement campaigns. Throughout, I raise questions about the organisation and form of campaigns, which rely on central organisation and control, mobilisation and propaganda. All in turn, I argue, reflect the basic principles of democratic centralism. In particular, I will focus on campaigns to address non-payment of wages – the 2004–2007 Wages Campaign and the annual wages campaigns conducted since.[12]

8.2 Democratic Centralism

8.2.1 Historical Evolution

While the focus of the discussion in this Chapter is on the CCP, it is relevant to note that the embrace of Leninist principles of party organisation was not unique to the Communists. From the early 1920s, both the Nationalist and the Communist Parties adopted democratic centralism as their fundamental organisational principle, and as the ideological basis of governance. For both, the Leninist notion of strong centralised governance exercised by a political elite was key.[13]

The CCP embraced democratic centralism in its 1928 and 1945 Constitutions.[14] Identification of democratic centralism as the fundamental principle of both Party organisation and the system of government in China is affirmed in 1940 in Mao Zedong's essay, *On New Democracy*,[15] and reiterated in 1945 in his report *On Coalition Government*.[16] In his essay *On New Democracy*, Mao drew a distinction between the 'state system' (*guoti*) and the system of government (*zhengti*). The state system was defined as the 'dictatorship of all the revolutionary classes'; defining

---

[12] My discussion of the wages campaign draws on the account of the campaign set out in Sarah Biddulph, Sean Cooney and Ying Zhu, 'Rule of Law with Chinese Characteristics: The Role of Campaigns in Law-Making' (2012) 34(4) *Law & Policy*. In discussing this campaign, I am primarily interested in the *form* of the campaign – as a mode of governance and what it might reveal about the socialist characteristics of the Chinese version of the rule of law. In our article we focused instead on questions about the impact of the campaign on law reform and the iterative cycle of law making, interpretation and implementation.

[13] With respect to the Guomindang (or Kuomintang KMT) see discussion in Yangsun Chou and Andrew Nathan, 'Democratizing Tradition in Taiwan' (1987) 27(3) *Asian Survey* 27.

[14] See discussion in Douglas Howland, 'Popular Sovereignty and Democratic Centralism in the People's Republic of China' (2012) 30(1) *Social Text*.

[15] At www.marxists.org/reference/archive/mao/selected-works/volume-2/mswv2_26.htm.

[16] At www.marxists.org/reference/archive/mao/selected-works/volume-3/mswv3_25.htm.

the status of social classes within the state. The system of government is the way power is organised and exercised – democratic centralism.

In a speech made on 1 February 1942, Mao Zedong criticised sectarian tendencies within the Party, saying:

> They do not understand the Party's system of democratic centralism; they do not realise that the Communist Party not only needs democracy but needs centralisation even more. They forget the system of democratic centralism in which the minority is subordinate to the majority, the lower level to the higher level, the part to the whole and the entire membership to the Central Committee.[17]

The Party's ideological platform (as a vanguard party) is that it represents the overall interests of the people and society. Democratic centralism is seen as the way in which integration between Party leadership, the position of the people as 'masters of the country' and (since the beginning of the reform era in 1978) the rule of law can be achieved. A core aspect of democratic centralism 'is that objective, scientific judgements can be made by Party leaders based on evidence gathered through the democratic process', but also that the political leadership is not bound to follow popular inputs.[18] In theory, there should be a correct balance between democracy and centralism. This theory holds that democracy cannot exist without centralism, and that democracy without centralism will lead to chaos.

Mao Zedong emphasised the mass line (*qunzong lüxian*) as complementary to democratic centralism, as an aspect of democracy. It was a way of ensuring the Party's close links and responsiveness to the concerns of the people. It operated by incorporating popular views in decision-making processes and then propagating these ideas and decisions back to the people. However, this process was not designed merely to act as a reflection of the popular will. It was intended to be a mechanism by which the Party guided the consciousness of the people so that they embraced these policies and decisions 'as their own'[19] (even if the policies did not ultimately reflect popular inputs), and as a way to mobilise them to action.[20] Throughout the history of the People's Republic

---

[17] Mao Zedong 'Rectify the Party's Style of Work', in *Selected Works of Mao Tse-tung* (Peking: Foreign Languages Press, 1967), vol. III, pp. 35–51.

[18] Stephen Angle, 'Decent Democratic Centralism' (2005) 33 *Political Theory* 518, 527.

[19] Mao Zedong, 'Some Questions Concerning Methods of Leadership', speech given on 1 June 1943, reproduced in Mao Zedong, *Selected Works of Mao Tse-tung*, p. 119, excepted in Roderick McFarquhar and John K. Fairbank (eds.), *Cambridge History of China*, vol. 15, Part 2 (Cambridge: Cambridge University Press, 1991). p. 3.

[20] Ibid., pp. 3–6.

of China (PRC), the balance between centralism and democracy has changed, often at the expense of democracy. The form that democracy has taken has also changed alongside the shifting politics of the time.

In terms of the relationship between the people and the Party centre, Mao's view was that participation should be allowed, though managed and controlled by the centre. In his 1956 speech 'On the Ten Major Relationships', Mao applied a similar principle to the relationship between the centre and localities, under which localities were to be consulted, allowed a degree of autonomy and permitted to take some initiatives, although this was tightly controlled by the centre and for the purpose of building a 'powerful socialist country'.[21] McFarquhar and Fairbank point out, however, that Mao did not place great weight on giving democracy an institutional form, a tendency that escalated as Mao became increasingly radical from the late 1950s.[22] The mass line increasingly became a mode of mass mobilisation and a way of waging continuous revolution. Howland argues that mass mobilisation, with the most extreme example being the Great Leap Forward, served to strengthen central control by the Party and diverted attention away from the needs and ideas of people at the grassroots.[23]

8.2.2   Ideology in the Reform Era (after 1978)

After the end of the Cultural Revolution, Deng Xiaoping reaffirmed the centrality of democratic centralism as the fundamental organisational principle and ideological basis of governance of both Party and state. In December 1978, he famously argued that the problem of governance had not been excessive .democracy, but centralism at the expense of democracy.

> One important condition for getting people to emancipate their minds and use their heads is genuine practice of the proletarian system of democratic centralism. We need unified and centralised leadership, but centralism can be correct only when there is a full measure of democracy. At present, we must lay particular stress on democracy, because for quite a

---

[21] Ibid., p. 9. The full text of the speech is available at www.marxists.org/reference/archive/mao/selected-works/volume-5/mswv5_51.htm.

[22] Ibid., p. 15.

[23] Howland, 'Popular Sovereignty and Democratic Centralism in the People's Republic of China', 7.

long time democratic centralism was not genuinely practised: centralism
was divorced from democracy and there was too little democracy.[24]

Democracy may be strengthened, he argued, by hearing the voice of
the people. However, this formulation did not represent a fundamental
departure from the pre-reform constraints that the people's participation
was to be channelled into an 'orderly' form by Party and state organisations. One of the ways in which principles of democracy were to be
institutionalised was through strengthening the system of people's congresses and instituting local elections.[25] Mass organisations such as the
trade unions (as part of the transmission belt) were also to play a key role
in transmitting popular views to the central authorities and participating
in policy formation and legislative drafting. Trade unions then had the
task of propagating Party policies and decisions back to the workers and
ensuring compliance with centrally issued policy and law. These basic
structures allow for orderly (and so, managed and constrained) public
participation in the administration of state and social affairs in accordance with the law. But at the same time, they continue to require submission of the minority to majority, the unconditional obligation of lower
agencies to carry out decisions of higher-level organs and the personal
responsibility of all Party members to implement Party decisions.[26] Deng
Xiaoping also articulated the principles that '[U]nder this system, personal interests must be subordinated to collective ones, the interests of
the part to those of the whole, and immediate to long-term interests'.[27]

The mass line as a method of leadership that places particular emphasis upon creating and maintaining a close relationship between Party and
government officials and the masses has again become prominent under
Xi Jinping since 2012. It involves mobilising and shaping popular opinion and being seen to respond to it. The mass line has been redeployed
as a way of both being seen to engage with the people and as a way of
disciplining Party and state officials. A recent example is in June 2013,

---

[24] Xiaoping Deng, 'Emancipate the Mind, Seek Truth from Facts and Unite as One in
   Looking to the Future', in Lenin Bureau for the Compilation and Translation of Works
   of Marx, Engels and Stalin under the Central Committee of the Communist Party of
   China (ed.), Selected Works of Deng Xiaoping (1975–1982) (Beijing: Foreign Languages
   Press, 1978).
[25] Howland, 'Popular Sovereignty and Democratic Centralism in the People's Republic of
   China', 8–9.
[26] Angle, 'Decent Democratic Centralism', 27.
[27] Deng, 'Emancipate the Mind, Seek Truth from Facts and Unite as One in Looking to the
   Future', p. 151.

when Xi Jinping launched a mass line campaign stating that official work should focus on the needs and interests of the ordinary people and cracking down on what he labelled four types of official decadence: formalism, bureaucratism, hedonism and extravagance.[28]

A vision of democratic centralism is also reflected in the Fourth Plenum Decision, which represents the latest authoritative statement about the Party's view of the nature, objectives and priorities of rule of law in China. It asserts the 'organic unity' of the interests of the Party and the people, with rule of law as a means to achieve both Party leadership and people's democracy.[29] Rule of law, according to the Fourth Plenum Decision, not only affirms Party leadership over socialist rule of law, but also equates socialist rule of law with Party leadership: 'Party leadership and socialist rule of law are identical, socialist rule of law must persist in Party leadership, Party leadership must rely on socialist rule of law.'[30] Law is also seen as a way to institutionalise and legalise democracy. The Fourth Plenum Decision asserts:

> We must persist in the fact that rule of law construction is for the people, relies on the people, benefits the people and protects the people, guarantees the people's basic rights and interests into a starting point and stopover point, guarantees that the people enjoy broad rights and freedoms according to the law, bearing the duties they should, safeguards social fairness and justice, and stimulates common prosperity.

The Fourth Plenum Decision asserts that the rule of law is a way to guarantee the 'people's democracy'. Rule of law and the Constitution do not, Ding argues, stand outside of and above the Party or the people, as a liberal interpretation of rule of law would insist. Instead, he argues that law should be understood as reflecting the people's will; where the Party leads and represents the people in authoring the law and where both the Party and the people are also the guarantors of enforcement and respect for law. Rather than being governed by law, according to Ding, rule of law should be seen as a form of self-governance.[31] Viewed in this way,

---

[28] 'About CPC's Mass Line Campaign', *China Daily*, 19 July 2013, available at www.china daily.com.cn/china/2013massline/2013-07/19/content_16800244.htm.

[29] Xiaodong Ding, 'Law According to the Chinese Communist Party: Constitutionalism and Socialist Rule of Law' (2017) 43(3) *Modern China* 322.

[30] *Some Major Questions on Comprehensively Promoting Governing the Country According to Law* (Fourth Plenum Decision).

[31] Ding, 'Law According to the Chinese Communist Party: Constitutionalism and Socialist Rule of Law', 324, 331–332.

ongoing legal popularisation campaigns[32] (or legal propaganda) that seek to increase legal consciousness and law-abiding behaviour do not aim to strengthen individual rights consciousness, which can be used against the party-state. Instead, they aim to increase responsibility to the law, encourage popular engagement with Party programs and strengthen Party legitimacy as both leading and reflecting the popular will through law.[33] Law is thus one of the institutional mechanisms that gives specific form to the relationship between the Party and the people, imagined under a model of democratic centralism.

8.2.3 Institutional Form

The principle of democratic centralism as both ideology and institutional form is also articulated in both the Party Charter and state Constitution. The state Constitution at article 3 provides that: 'The state organs of the People's Republic of China apply the principle of democratic centralism.' This organisational principle designates the relationship between central and local agencies, people's congresses and the government, courts and the procuratorate, as well as the organisation within government agencies (under the leadership responsibility system).[34]

Analysed from an institutional perspective, commentators on the meaning of democratic centralism in the Constitution follow the structure of article 3 to focus on the location of both democracy and centralism within the organisational structure of the state. Article 3.2 describes the National People's Congress and the local people's congresses at various levels as democratically constituted through democratic elections. They are responsible to the people and subject to their supervision. Articles 3.3 and 3.4 describe the centralist organisation under which all administrative, judicial and procuratorial organs of state are created by the people's congresses, to which they are responsible and by which they are supervised. It goes on to provide 'the divisions of functions and powers between the central

---

[32] Discussed most recently in Susan Whiting, 'Authoritarian "Rule of Law" and Regime Legitimacy' (2017) *Comparative Political Studies* 1.

[33] Ding, 'Law According to the Chinese Communist Party: Constitutionalism and Socialist Rule of Law', 331–334.

[34] Ling Ma (马岭), 'The Principle of Democratic Centralism in China's Current Constitution (Woguo Xianxing 'Xianfa" Zhong De Minzhu Jizhong Yuanze 我国现行《宪法》中的民主集中制原则)' (2013) 26(4) *Journal of Yunnan University, Law Edition [Yunnan Daxue Xuebao Faxue Ban 云南大学学报法学版]*. 2–14.

and local state organs is guided by the principle of giving full scope to the initiative and enthusiasm of the local authorities under the unified leadership of the central authorities'.[35] The constitutional principle of dual supervision organised both horizontally (under the people's congress at the same administrative level) and vertically (by the organ hierarchically superior) gives organisational form to the relationship between democracy and centralism.[36]

Even though the constitution suggests that horizontal supervision, exercised by people's congresses at each level, is the primary supervisory mechanism, constitutional scholar Jiang Shigong asserts that the core supervisory mechanism lies in the vertical relationship of subordination from local to central authority in the Party committees organised at each level. That is, centralised controls, represented by subordination to higher level agencies, are more important than democratic controls represented by accountability to the people's congresses. He draws on Mao Zedong's 1956 speech *On the Ten Major Relationships*, in which Mao prescribed consulting local authorities before policies are determined and relying on the initiative of local authorities, but ultimately subjecting localities to strict central control. Jiang argues that these prescriptions constitute a political interpretation of the constitution that is implemented in practice. This political principle forms part of what he describes as the 'unwritten constitution'.[37] Democratic centralism is thus not only articulated in the constitutional text, but also establishes extra-constitutional political practice that displaces the people's congresses (representing democratic principles) and reasserts the supremacy of the Party's vertical (and so centralist) control mechanisms.

A characteristic of Party organisation is the strength of vertical systems of accountability and control. Party discipline requires obedience to central instructions and policies, and institutes mechanisms of vertical control. For example, the Party personnel system is highly centralised. In allocating positions to Party members, it pays close attention to rank, which determines not only salary and benefits but also scope of

---

[35] Art. 3(4), Constitution of the PRC 1982.

[36] The constitutional provision of state organisation that combines vertical and horizontal modes of supervision, with horizontal control under the people's congress at the same level having priority, under the rubric: 条块结合以块为主. Party control systems on the other hand operate vertically.

[37] Shigong Jiang, 'Written and Unwritten Constitutions: A New Approach to the Study of Constitutional Government in China' (2010) 36 *Modern China* 12, 31–37.

decision-making power and position in the hierarchy of power.[38] Since the beginning of the Xi Jinping regime in 2012, recentralisation of power has seen the balance shift away from decentralisation and local autonomy to an increasingly centralised control of policy and administration.[39]

Many Chinese commenters assert that democratic centralism operates at the level of an organisational principle that is reflected in institutional arrangements of Party and state, and does not extend to influencing functional or operational principles of governance.[40] But the structural aspects of democratic centralism cannot help but have an impact on modes of governance; particularly on the ways both policy and law are drafted and enforced. As Flora Sapio has argued, constitutional basic principles 'produce their effects throughout the entire political and legal system'.[41] The question of what (if any) impact democratic centralism has on the mode of governance is explored in the following section.

8.3   Implications for Governance: Campaign-Style Enforcement as an Illustration

As the discussion so far has shown, since the establishment of the PRC and even before that, the ways in which the principles of democratic centralism have been given shape have been constantly in motion, both in China and other Leninist regimes. The acceptance of and shifts in the meaning of democratic centralism in the former Soviet Union, for example, is discussed in Chapter 3 of this volume. There has been movement over time between decentralisation and centralisation, between emphasising democracy and insisting on centralisation, as well as changes in the ways in which principles of democracy have been given form. The preceding discussion illustrates the important ideological and institutional effects of democratic centralism. From here, I ask how, if at all, the institutional and organisational principles of democratic centralism shape enforcement practice. At one extreme,

---

[38] Ling Li, '"Rule of Law" in a Party-State: A Conceptual Interpretive Framework of the Constitutional Reality of China' (2015) 2(1) *Asian Journal of Law and Society* 93, 100, 104–106.

[39] Sangkuk Lee, 'An Institutional Analysis of Xi Jinping's Centralization of Power' (2017) 26 (105) *Journal of Contemporary China* 325.

[40] Ma, 'The Principle of Democratic Centralism in China's Current Constitution', 2.

[41] Flora Sapio, 'Seeking Truth from Facts in Party Discipline Legislation', in *10th Annual Conference of the European China Law Studies Association* (Cologne, 25–27 September 2015), 11.

it could well be argued that democratic centralism permeates the whole edifice of rule of law and the functioning of the legal system as a whole. At the other, it might be argued that democratic centralism provides little assistance in understanding the ways in which rule of law is conceived and implemented in day-to-day governance, which might ultimately be explained in terms of command and control modes of administration. This next section seeks to make apparent the ways in which modes of law making and enforcement swing between favouring centralisation and decentralisation. But more than that, it explores the organisational and political aspects of campaigns that are explicable in terms of democratic centralism, and which go beyond ordinary forms of bureaucratic governance. The example of campaign-style enforcement illustrates the preference for centralised approaches to be taken during periods of perceived crisis, particularly where widespread failure of decentralised law enforcement has led to deep popular dissatisfaction, reflected in extensive public and socially disruptive protest.

8.3.1   The Problem: Wages Arrears

Many workers in China have difficulty getting paid – wages are paid late, with unauthorised or illegal deductions, and in some cases they don't get paid at all. In 2016, the Ministry of Human Resources and Social Security (MOHRSS) reported that this problem affected 2,369,000 migrant workers.[42] While wage insecurity is widespread, the impact falls mainly on workers in insecure and informal work environments, such as construction, infrastructure projects, labour intensive production and service sectors like hospitality and retail.[43] Migrant workers suffer disproportionately.[44] This problem has consistently attracted the attention and

---

[42]   Ministry of Human Resources and Social Security, 'Second Plenary Meeting of the Inter-Ministerial Joint Meeting on Efforts to Resolve the Problem of Wage Arrears [解决企业拖欠工资问题部际联席会议第二次全体会议召开]' (15 March 2017).

[43]   General Office of the State Council, *Opinion on Comprehensively Managing the Problem of Non-Payment of Migrant Workers' Wages [国务院办公厅关于全面治理拖欠农民工工资问题的意见]*, 2016, available at www.gov.cn/zhengce/content/2016-01/19/content_5034320.htm.

[44]   China Labour Bulletin, 'Wages and Employment' (2016) *China Labour Bulletin*; Sean Cooney, 'Making Chinese Labor Law Work: The Prospects for Regulatory Innovation in the People's Republic of China' (2007) 30(4) *Fordham International Law Journal* 1050; Gerard Greenfield and Tim Pringle, 'The Challenge of Wage Arrears in China' in Manuel Simón Velasco (ed.), *Paying Attention to Wages* (Geneva: International Labour Organisation, 2002).

concern of central authorities, at both Party and government levels.[45]
While this conduct is illegal and seriously harms the rights of large
numbers of workers, one of the main motivations for paying attention
to this problem has been that wage theft, including failure to pay wages
on time, in full or at all, causes a great deal of socially disruptive protest.
Wage-related disputes, in the form of strikes and protests, have risen
continuously since the introduction of labour market reforms.[46] Extra-
legal mobilisation, particularly where it disrupts social order, is bound to
attract the attention of local Party and state authorities. Their satisfactory
performance appraisal depends upon preventing or responding quickly
to dissipate disruptive conduct, and so they remain particularly sensitive
to signs of social instability.[47]

The increase in socially disruptive protests not only reflects the extent
of labour disputes, and disputes about wages in particular, but also
reflects the inability of established modes of dispute resolution to address
these systemic problems. A number of factors combine to cause this. The
first is that no good mechanisms exist for the negotiation of disputes
about economic interests (in contrast to legally defined rights), such as
wage increases and working conditions. Existing models of collective
negotiation are premised on strong trade union intervention to negotiate
on behalf of workers. However, beholden to both management at the
local level and required to implement Party policy at other levels, the
unions have been unequal to this task.[48] Unions are also required to
dissipate and resolve disputes, so they are unable to provide unequivocal

---

[45] See, e.g., 'The Challenge of Wage Arrears in China'. More recently [国务院办公厅]
General Office of the State Council, 'Opinion on Comprehensviely Managing the Problem of Non-Payment of Migrant Workers' Wages [关于全面治理拖欠农民工工资问题
的意见]', (17 January 2016); Biddulph, Cooney and Zhu, 'Rule of Law with Chinese
Characteristics'.

[46] China Labour Bulletin, 'Strike Map', available at http://maps.clb.org.hk/strikes/en; *China
Labour Bulletin*, 'Wages in China' (19 February 2008).

[47] Biddulph, *The Stability Imperative: Human Rights and Law in China*, p. 21.

[48] Feng Chen, 'Between the State and Labour: The Conflict of Chinese Trade Unions'
Double Identity in Market Reform' (2003) *The China Quarterly* 1006; Feng Chen,
'Individual Rights and Collective Rights: Labor's Predicament in China' (2007) 40(1)
Communist and Post Communist Studies 59; Feng Chen, 'Trade Unions and the Quadri-
partite Interactions in Strike Settlement in China' (2010) 102 *The China Quarterly* 104;
Eli Friedman and Ching Kwan Lee, 'Remaking the World of Chinese Labour: A 30 Year
Retrospective' (2010) 48(3) *British Journal of Industrial Relations* 507. Sarah Biddulph,
'Responding to Industrial Unrest in China: Prospects for Strengthening the Role of
Collective Bargaining' (2012) 34(1) *Sydney University Law Review* 35.

representation and support for workers in rights-based disputes either.[49] The second is that it remains difficult for an individual to obtain a quick and satisfactory resolution to a dispute about legally defined labour rights through the legally prescribed channels of mediation, labour arbitration and litigation, despite substantial changes to facilitate workers in the disputing process under the 2007 Labour Disputes Mediation and Arbitration Law.[50] The legal form of dispute resolution tends to individualise disputes and the capacity of workers to obtain legal assistance from union representatives, lawyers or worker activists is limited in a number of ways.[51] Third, labour laws also give primary responsibility for enforcement, including enforcement of pay entitlements, to MOHRSS.[52] However, the labour inspectorate is notoriously unwilling to enforce the law stringently or impose the maximum sanction permitted by law because it is understaffed, risk averse, subject to undue influence from local governments with competing priorities and, in some cases, corrupt.[53] Finally, where labour disputes become disruptive, local officials often circumvent the law in an effort to dissipate them.[54] This creates a

[49] Chen, 'Individual Rights and Collective Rights'; Anita Chan, 'Strikes in China's Export Industries in Comparative Perspective' (2011) 65 *The China Journal* 27.

[50] Sean Cooney, Sarah Biddulph and Ying Zhu, *Law and Fair Work in China* (London: Routledge, 2013). Mediation and Arbitration Management Division(调解仲裁管理司), 'The Responsible Person in the Ministry of Human Resources and Social Security Mediation and Arbitration Management Division Responds to a Journalist's Questions About the Opinion on Further Strengthening the Multidisciplinary Mechanism of Mediation and Arbitration of Labor and Personnel Disputes [人社部调解仲裁管理司负责人就《关于进一步加强劳动人事争议调解仲裁完善多元处理机制的意见》答记者问]', (1 April 2017).

[51] Aaron Halegua, 'Who Will Represent China's Workers? Lawyers, Legal Aid and the Enforcement of Labor Rights' (October 2016) *New York University School of Law U.S., Asia Law Institute*; Aaron Halegua, 'Getting Paid: Processing the Labor Disputes of China's Migrant Workers' (2008) 26(1) *Berkeley Journal of International Law* 254; Cooney, Biddulph and Zhu, *Law and Fair Work in China*, pp. 74–75.

[52] Halegua, 'Who Will Represent China's Workers?'; Cooney, Biddulph and Zhu, *Law and Fair Work in China*, pp. 64–69.

[53] Virginia Ho, 'From Contracts to Compliance? An Early Look at Implementation under China's New Labor Legislation' (2009) 23(1) *Columbia Journal of Asian Law* 35. Anita Chan, *China's Workers Under Assault* (Armonk, NY: M.E. Sharpe, 2001); Ching Kwan Lee, *Against the Law: Labor Protests in China's Rustbelt and Sunbelt* (Berkeley, CA: University of California Press, 2007). Cooney, Biddulph and Zhu, *Law and Fair Work in China*, pp. 73–74.

[54] Ching Kwan Lee and Yonghong Zhang, 'The Power of Instability: Unraveling the Microfoundations of Bargained Authoritarianism in China' (2013) 118(6) *American Journal of Sociology* 1475; Yang Su and Xin He, 'Street as Courtroom: State Accommodation of Labour Protest in South China' (2010) 44(1) *Law & Society Review* 157.

perverse incentive to behave even more disruptively in the hope that an extra-legal resolution will be forthcoming.[55]

In the construction industry, which predominately employs migrant workers, these problems are exacerbated by a widespread failure to enter into written labour contracts, as required by law. The construction industry is also characterised by many levels of subcontracting, from the head contractor down to the subcontractor who provides workers for the site. As a result, many workers are unable to identify their employer.[56] Even if they can, the subcontracting arrangement may be illegal or the subcontractor, if contracting as an individual, may not have legal status to enter into an employment relationship with the workers, thus rendering the protective provisions of labour law inapplicable and the worker the status of an independent contractor. Enforcing wage payment obligations in these circumstances faces almost insurmountable legal and practical hurdles.

Central authorities intervene where social order problems are acute and ongoing, and where local intervention has been ineffectual.[57] A repeating pattern has emerged in relation to wages arrears. During times when sensitivity about social order is high, when it is politically convenient and where the disruptive consequences of widespread problems of wage arrears reach the attention of central authorities, a centrally coordinated series of responses are undertaken, as they claim, to deal with the problem once and for all. In theory, there is a natural division between dispute resolution mechanisms and campaigns. The former is intended to resolve disputes after they arise, and the latter is directed towards addressing underlying systemic problems. In practice, the division is not as clear,

---

[55] Biddulph, *The Stability Imperative: Human Rights and Law in China*.

[56] Ngai Pun and Huilin Lu, 'A Culture of Violence: The Labor Subcontracting System and Collective Action by Construction Workers in Post-Socialist China' (2010) 64 *The China Journal* 143; Wei Deng, 'Resolving Unpaid Wages by Spring Festival: Mission Impossible?', *People's Daily Online*, 15 January 2004; Wanning Sun, 'Desperately Seeking My Wages: Justice, Media Logic, and the Politics of Voice in Urban China' (2012) 37(4) *Media, Culture and Society* 864, 867–868.

[57] The deleterious impact on social stability was a core motivating factor for the 2004–2007 Wages Campaign, discussed below and more recently in the General Office of the State Council, *Opinion on Comprehensively Managing the Problem of Non-payment of Migrant Workers' Wages* (国务院办公厅关于全面治理拖欠农民工工资问题的意见) issued on 20 January 2016; see also Benjamin van Rooij, 'Regulation by escalation: unrest, lawmaking and law enforcement in China' in Susan Trevaskes, Elisa Nessossi and Sarah Biddulph (eds.), *The Politics of Law and Stability in China* (London: Edward Elgar, 2014), p. 83.

as campaigns are also directed at resolving grievances that exist and have not yet been resolved, rectifying practical and bureaucratic impediments to enforcing labour law, and addressing the systematic problems that underlie wages disputes.

The next section in this Chapter reviews three illustrations of wage-related campaigns. The first is the 2004–2007 Wages Campaign. The second is the annual 'clean-up' to address problems of unpaid wages before Chinese Lunar New Year. The third is the concerted action launched by the State Council in January 2016.

8.3.2   What Is a Campaign? Past and Present

Campaigns were widely used as a mode of coordinated Party action in the pre-reform period (between 1949 and 1978), when they were frequently characterised by intensive mass mobilisation with revolutionary objectives of overcoming 'barriers to the progress of socialism'.[58] They are commonly viewed as Maoist. However, their form, as will become clear in the discussion below, draws on the organisational and institutional structure of democratic centralism and the mass line. They were a powerful ideological tool, intended to transform their target to assert the 'correct line', to change popular attitudes and social institutions, and to purge those officials seen to transgress.[59] Campaigns in the pre-reform period were not entirely antithetical to, nor disruptive of, the institutionalisation of power; however, they commonly operated with disregard for law or lawfulness.[60]

Early in the reform era, the campaign form was redeployed, most famously in the three-year Strike Hard (*Yanda*) *campaign against crime waged* between 1983 and 1986. In its initial phase, the Yanda campaign was lawless. However, Peng Zhen, a top Party leader in the law and order system at the time, quickly asserted that the campaign should be

---

[58] Gordon Bennett, *Yundong: Mass Campaigns in Chinese Communist Leadership* (Berkeley, CA: University of California Press, 1976), p. 18.

[59] Ibid. Also, Benjamin van Rooij, 'The Politics of Law in China: Enforcement Campaigns in the Post-Mao PRC' (2009) available at http://ssrn.com/abstract=136181; Julia Strauss, 'Morality, Coercion and State Building by Campaign in the early PRC; Regime Consolidation and After, 1949–1956' (2006) 188 *The China Quarterly* 891; Michael Dutton, 'Dreaming of Better Times: "Repetition with a Difference" and Community Policing in China' (1995) 3(2) *Positions: East Asia Cultures Critique* 418.

[60] Bennett, *Yundong*, p. 18. Strauss, 'Morality, Coercion and State Building by Campaign in the early PRC; Regime Consolidation and After, 1949–1956'.

conducted 'in accordance with law'.[61] Despite this demand, there remains a degree of tension between responding to the call to 'strike hard and fast' and the demands of the legal principles of substantive and procedural justice. In an era that purported to move away from Maoism and its revolutionary ideology and practice towards a more institutionalised and bureaucratised model of legalised justice, the question of whether the continued use of campaigns should be seen as a remnant 'of the politicised legal past'[62] remained. Michael Dutton has argued that it should not, characterising the campaign as now being a technocratic tool of punishment, rather than an ideological tool of transformation.[63] Despite transformation from ideological to technocratic tools, campaigns in the reform era continue to draw strongly on their pre-reform counterparts in terms of structure and method.

While campaigns differ in terms of degree of politicisation, geographical scope, extent and time, all campaigns in the reform era share the characteristics of 'coordinated operation' (tongyi xingdong), with intensified and focused enforcement activities by Party and state agencies at multiple levels, using the formula of 'striking hard and fast' against the targeted conduct or problems (congzhong congkuai daji). Coordination is achieved through the establishment of a central leadership group that determines and allocates tasks, and timing and performance targets, with corresponding leadership groups formed at local levels. Leadership groups organise and direct the campaign, and receive periodic reports on the performance of participating agencies against set targets. They combine propaganda, education and mobilisation of the public in support of campaign objectives. Nationwide campaigns are often divided into three one-year battles (zhanyi), each with their own targets and reporting requirements. Campaigns may be waged within the Party hierarchy or the state hierarchy. Or, more commonly for national level campaigns, they may involve coordinated Party, state and societal action.

While there is no straightforward typology of campaigns in the reform era, some examples illustrate their breadth of application. Probably the

---

[61] Zhen Peng, 'The Hard Strike against Crime Must Abide by the Law, Pay Attention to Policy and Strengthen Comprehensive Management', edited by the National Conference of Public Security Office and Division Heads (15–22 November 1983); Sarah Biddulph, *Legal Reform and Administrative Detention Powers in China* (Cambridge: Cambridge University Press, 2007). This rhetorical commitment has been reasserted periodically. See Xianguo Xiong, 'Yifa "Yanda" ("Strike Hard" According to the Law)', (Renmin Fayuan Bao [People's Court Daily], 2001).

[62] van Rooij, 'The Politics of Law in China', 5.

[63] Dutton, 'Dreaming of Better Times'.

best-known use of campaigns is against criminal behaviour.[64] Campaigns have also been waged against lesser forms of anti-social conduct. In addition to these nationwide campaigns, the justice organs of the state regularly conduct coordinated actions (*jizhong tongyi xingdong*), specialist struggles (*zhuanxiang douzheng*) and specialist rectifications (*zhuanxiang zhili*) dealing with more narrowly focused targets, often in a more constrained geographical area.[65]

Another well-known set of examples relate to problems of internal Party and state governance. The ongoing anti-corruption campaign is one example.[66] Campaign-style enforcement also draws on the campaign model in addressing serious problems in areas of economic and environmental regulation – regulatory failure campaigns.[67] These types of campaigns include those addressing problems such as environmental pollution, loss of rural land, food safety and pirating of famous brand name consumer products.[68] Wages campaigns fall within this category, as they are primarily responsive to social disruption arising out of regulatory failure.

8.3.3 The 2004–2007 Wages Campaign

From the late 1980s, the incidents of social protest and self-harm, and the instability related to labour abuses (such as widespread failure to pay wages) escalated. The construction industry was one of the areas of worst abuse.[69] In the early 2000s, a number of highly publicised episodes were reported sympathetically in the media, including the case of a migrant worker, Xiong Deming, seeking Premier Wen Jiabao's assistance in recovering unpaid wages, and another migrant worker threatening

---

[64] Susan Trevaskes, 'Severe and Swift Justice in China' (2007) 47(1) *British Journal of Criminology* 23; Susan Trevaskes, 'Yanda 2001: Form and Strategy in a Chinese Anti-Crime Campaign' (2003) 36(3) *Australian and New Zealand Journal of Criminology* 272; Murray Scot Tanner, 'State Coercion and the Balance of Awe: The 1983–1986 "Stern Blows" Anti Crime Campaign' (2000) 44 *The China Journal* 93; Biddulph, *Legal Reform and Administrative Detention Powers in China*.

[65] Biddulph, *Legal Reform and Administrative Detention Powers in China*.

[66] Xi Jinping launched this campaign in 2012 and it remains ongoing at the time of writing. See discussion in Willy Wo-Lap Lam, 'China's Anti-Graft Campaign in Review' (7 December 2015) 15 (23) *China Brief* 3.

[67] Biddulph, Cooney and Zhu, 'Rule of Law with Chinese Characteristics'.

[68] See, e.g., van Rooij, 'The Politics of Law in China'.

[69] Discussed in Biddulph, Cooney and Zhu, 'Rule of Law with Chinese Characteristics' 375, 379.

suicide over wage arrears.[70] The increasing activism and publicity surrounding efforts by migrant workers to get paid, coupled with spreading disruptive protest, was quickly identified as a threat to social order and attracted the attention of central Party and state leaders.[71] The 2004–2007 Wages Campaign shares characteristics with other campaigns in that it was initiated and led from the centre; it involved coordinated implementation with target setting and periodic reporting back; breaches were punished severely, quickly and publicly; and it was accompanied by extensive use of the media to educate the people and shame transgressors.

8.3.3.1   Central Leadership

The early 2000s were also a politically opportune time, as the new leadership of Hu Jintao and Wen Jiabao had signalled the importance of dealing with wage arrears as part of their policy to rebalance economic development with social development and equity, under the rubric of the Harmonious Society Policy.[72] The National People's Congress (NPC) Standing Committee had laid the groundwork through its investigation into the implementation of the Construction Law, carried out by its Internal and Judicial Affairs Committee in 2003. That report identified chronic and severe problems of failure to pay wages, which not only disrupted market order but also directly impacted on social stability. Li Tieying, the Standing Committee Vice-Chairman, demanded an urgent 'three year clean-up' (*sannian qingqian*) campaign to address compliance failures.[73]

---

[70] Sun, 'Desperately Seeking My Wages', 864–865.

[71] Jae Ho Chung, Hongyi Lai and Ming Xia, 'Mounting Challenges to Governance in China: Surveying Collective Protestors, Religions Sects and Criminal Organizations' (2006) 56 *The China Journal* 1; Wei Li, 'How to Prevent and Control the Masses Engaging in Collective Petitioning [Ruhe Yufang he Kongzhi Qunzong Jiti Shangfang]' (1999) 3 *The Secretary's Friend [Mishu zhi You]* 34.

[72] The Harmonious Society policy was formally adopted at the close of the Sixth Plenary session of the 16th CPC Central Committee meeting on 11 October 2006, in the *Resolution on Major Issues Regarding the Building of a Harmonious Socialist Society*, announced at www.china.org.cn/english/report/189591.htm. It was first raised by Hu Jintao in his inaugural report to the 16th CPC Congress in 2002; 'Strategic Intent to Build a Harmonious Society', *People's Daily*, 24 February 2005, available at http://politics .people.com.cn/GB/8198/70195/70203/4757848.html.

[73] NPC Standing Committee, 'NPC Standing Committee Law Enforcement Investigation Group 'Report on the Implementation of the PRC Construction Law' [Quanguo Renda Changweihui Zhifa Jiancha Zu Guanyu Jiancha '"Zhonghua Renmin Gongheguo Jianzhu Fa" Shishi Qingkuang de Baogao'] *China Construction Information Web*, 6 November 2003; *People's Daily Online*, 'The State Council Deploys to Rectify the Delayed Payment

8.3.3.2 Coordinated Implementation of Law Enforcement and Law Making

The campaign was directed by the Inter-Ministerial Liaison Committee on Resolving the Problem of Non-Payment of Construction Funds (the Inter-Ministerial Committee), under the leadership of Vice-Premier Zeng Peiyan. The Inter-Ministerial Committee issued documents that allocated targets for all participating agencies. It demanded that agencies 'crack down hard' (*yanli daji*) against all types of unlawful and criminal acts, and 'strengthen inspection and enforcement and assist migrant workers in recovering wages'; and that penalties be strengthened. The campaign was thus not merely about improving enforcement of legal regulations, but also achieving a substantive pro-worker objective. Documents setting out the timetable and a detailed division of responsibility between Party, state, judiciary and other social organisations responsible for implementing the campaign used military-style rhetoric of 'deploying the forces' (*bushu*). Corresponding committees at local levels were also established to oversee compliance with implementation and reporting requirements.[74]

A distinguishing feature of campaigns such as the 2004–2007 Wages Campaign is that they recentralise control, emphasising vertical control mechanisms (centralism) at the expense of local autonomy and as a way of overcoming inefficiencies in decentralised models of enforcement. It purposely breaks down institutional silos and blurs boundaries between state and judicial agencies and their spheres of authority; state and Party agencies and their spheres of operation; and state, Party and mass organisations, such as the All-China Federation of Trade Unions (ACFTU). For the duration of the campaign, priority must be given to the tasks of the campaign over other work. So, for example, the courts were required to give priority to cases involving wage claims, waive fees and find in favour of migrant workers where possible, as well as do their utmost to ensure enforcement of court judgements in this category of case. These instructions were subsequently set out in binding form in an urgent notice to all

---

of Construction Funds in the Construction Sector: Zeng Peiyan Emphasises that Before Spring Festival Each Region Must Pay Close Attention to Payment of Migrant Workers Unpaid Wages from the Previous Year', 3 January 2004; *Xinhua News Agency*, 'Resolving Delayed Payment of Wages in the Construction Sector: 5 Trump Cards in Blocking off the Deadbeats'Usual Escape Routes', 16 December 2003.

[74] See generally Biddulph, Cooney and Zhu, 'Rule of Law with Chinese Characteristics'.

courts issued by the Supreme People's Court.[75] In addition to coordinating and strengthening enforcement, agencies were instructed to draft new regulations to rectify regulatory gaps and inadequacies, so the campaign also had a direct impact on law reform.[76]

At the local level, provincial governments were responsible for evaluating performance of county governments and agencies against centrally set targets and the corresponding targets allocated in their own local plans. By setting enforcement targets, local agencies were given standards against which their performance was to be judged.[77] Where provinces failed to meet performance targets they were publicly named and shamed. These documents also made clear that leaders and other designated responsible people would be liable for punishment (both in terms of eligibility for performance bonuses and career promotion) if they failed to meet their performance targets or were not diligent in implementing the campaign. To ensure that local agencies did not merely report that the targets had been met without actually achieving them, both periodic and random inspections were carried out by the campaign leadership group, higher level agencies and other agencies such as the trade unions, people's congresses and the people's consultative committees.[78] Local governments thus ran the risk of being discovered if they completely fabricated their reports.

Despite the fact that local agencies are adept at giving the appearance of compliance while not actually changing their ordinary practices, the imposition of targets meant that the 2004–2007 Wages Campaign changed, albeit temporarily, the balance of autonomy and control between central and local authorities. As with other campaigns, the 2004–2007 Wages Campaign provided a systematic form of intervention by which central authorities could weaken foot dragging and obstruction inspired by local protectionism. A key aspect of such campaigns is that they are

---

[75] SPC *Urgent Notice on Concerted Action to Put in Order Cases on the Delayed Payment of Construction Funds and Wages of Migrant Workers*, December 2004.

[76] Biddulph, Cooney and Zhu, 'Rule of Law with Chinese Characteristics'.

[77] On performance controls generally, see Maria Edin, 'State Capacity and Local Agent Control in China: CCP Cadre Management from a Township Perspective' (2003) 173 *The China Quarterly* 35.

[78] See, e.g., http://www.scio.gov.cn/xwfbh/xwbfbh/wqfbh/2004/0826/Document/327084/327084.htm.

sporadic and so enable the centre to insist on its priorities for a defined period, while also allowing space for different and sometimes conflicting local objectives to be pursued outside of the period of the campaign.[79]

8.3.3.3   Propaganda and Education

As with all mass line activities, propaganda and education comprise key elements of the campaign. During the 2004–2007 Wages Campaign, the media was called upon to report egregious cases, publicise black lists of recalcitrant enterprises, educate people about the campaign and its objectives, and encourage active engagement with the campaign. Media and publicity also played a central role, beyond education about legal rights and responsibilities, and beyond the existence of the campaign and campaign objectives. This was an opportunity for the media to inculcate people with an appreciation for the care and concern the central authorities have for the welfare of working people.[80]

While the media initially reported sympathetically on worker action stemming from disputes about unpaid wages (including threatened suicide and murder), it later changed its focus to criticising their unlawful behaviour. To discourage this form of protest and to avoid exacerbating the already volatile situation, media reports criticised and mocked this behaviour as ignorant or merely attention seeking.[81] Media reporting was brought within the ambit of the campaign to fulfil its objectives of educating workers, shaming recalcitrant employers and promoting the achievements of the campaign and, more importantly, the Harmonious Society Policy of the then leadership of Hu Jintao and Wen Jiabao.[82] Of course, at the end of the campaign, the official declaration of its success in addressing problems of wages arrears was well publicised.[83]

---

[79] Xin He, 'Sporadic Campaigns as a Means of Social Control' (2003) 17(1) *Columbia Journal of Asian Law* 121.

[80] Sun, 'Desperately Seeking My Wages', 873; Biddulph, *The Stability Imperative*, p. 240.

[81] Sun, 'Desperately Seeking My Wages', 871–873.

[82] Biddulph, Cooney and Zhu, 'Rule of Law with Chinese Characteristics', 15–16; Sun, 'Desperately Seeking My Wages', 871–873.

[83] The then chairman of the NPC Standing Committee, Wu Bangguo, declared the campaign a success on 8 March 2008 at the second plenary meeting of the 11th NPC. China News Web, 'Most Provinces in China Have Already Fundamentally Resolved the Historical Problem of Delayed Payment of Wages', 8 March 2008.

8.3.4   Annual Wages Campaigns and the 2015 Harmonious Labour Relations Campaign

The common form of a regulatory failure campaign is explored in detail in the preceding discussion of the 2004–2007 Wages Campaign. Even though that campaign ended with a declaration that the problem of wage arrears had been resolved, it had not. In a sign that decentralised enforcement and individual dispute resolution mechanisms remain unequal to the task of addressing wages arrears, multi-agency centrally coordinated wages campaigns have been conducted annually since then during the period preceding the Lunar New Year holiday.[84] This is a sensitive time, as for many rural migrant workers it is their only opportunity to return home to visit the family members they have left behind. Failing to pay wages at this time of year is thus a much more serious transgression than at any other time.

A recent coordinated effort to address wages arrears dates from 21 March 2015, when the CCP Central Committee and the State Council jointly issued the 'Opinion on Building Harmonious Labour Relations'.[85] This document identifies failure to pay wages to migrant workers as a serious problem undermining social stability (among other problems). Again, we see articulated guiding principles and comprehensive programs to address wages arrears. Propaganda and education accompany these. In August 2015, both central and local levels of government launched a harmonious labour relations awareness month.[86] MOHRSS

---

[84] MOHRSS convened the annual multi-agency inter-ministerial meeting on 20 November 2015. Yujie 张玉洁 Zhang, 'MOHRSS convenes the 2016 annual work meeting on ensuring payment of migrant workers' wages prior to Spring Festival' [人社部召开 2016年春节前保障农民工工资支付工作视会], China Organisations and Personnel Daily [中国组织人事报], 23 November 2015.

[85] At http://china.lexiscn.com/law/law-english-1-2562627-T.html. Similar campaigns to strike hard against malicious refusal to pay wages have also been waged in 2012, 2013 and 2014. See www.mohrss.gov.cn/SYrlzyhshbzb/ldbk/laodongguanxi/laodongguan xixiediao/201202/t20120202_87337.htm, www.mohrss.gov.cn/SYrlzyhshbzb/zwgk/SYz hengcejiedu/201303/t20130309_87391.htm.

[86] See, e.g., in 内蒙古自治区自治区人力资源和社会保障厅 [Inner Mongolia Autonomous Region Office of Human Resources and Social Security], '自治区开展构建和谐 劳动关系宣传月活动' ['Autonomous Region Undertakes Construction of Harmonious Labour Relations Propaganda Month Activities'], Inner Mongolia Autonomous Region Human Resources and Social Security Web, 8 July 2015, available at http://m.jintang114 .org/view.php?aid=24241; www.mohrss.gov.cn/ldgxs/LDGXsanfangjizhi/LDGXhexielao donghuodong/201508/t20150824_218786.html.

issued a document setting out the recommended language and terms to be used during this month.[87]

On 20 November 2015, MOHRSS convened an inter-ministerial meeting on this issue. It was reported that each region and relevant agency was instructed to 'spring into action' (*xingdong qilai*), 'to quickly and comprehensively implement the concerted action' and 'to continually strengthen efforts' to deal with the problem of unpaid migrant worker wages.[88] As with concerted actions of this type, regions and agencies were required to strengthen investigation, enforcement and punishment, and to act in concert to achieve the designated objectives. All local labour bureaux were required to impose severe punishments on enterprises that failed to pay migrant worker wages, and to strengthen coordination with public security, procuratorial and adjudication agencies to ensure coordinated and rapid handling of criminal cases of refusal to pay wages. Labour mediation and arbitration agencies were required to establish a 'green channel' to simplify and expedite handling of wage disputes and to liaise with local unions and justice departments on provision of legal aid in wages cases. Repeat offenders and recalcitrant employers were to be entered on the 'black list', which was to be widely publicised in the media, alongside information about strengthened investigations and sanctions.[89]

In January 2016, the General Office of the State Council issued the 'Opinion on Comprehensively Managing the Problem of Non-payment of Migrant Workers' Wages', setting out a five-year agenda to address and redress the non-payment or delayed payment of the wages.[90] It directed the focus of this concerted action on the construction sector, labour intensive production and service sectors such as hospitality and retail where problems of wages arrears are concentrated, with work to be

---

[87] A link to this word document is at the bottom of this page www.mohrss.gov.cn/ldgxs/LDGXsanfangjizhi/LDGXhexielaodonghuodong/201508/t20150824_218786.html.

[88] Zhang, 'MOHRSS Convenes the 2016 Annual Work Meeting on Ensuring Payment of Migrant Workers' Wages Prior to Spring Festival [人社部召开2016年春节前保障农民工工资支付工作视会]'.There were reportedly 12 other agencies in attendance. Xingwei Sun (孙兴伟) 'Work to Ensure That the Wages Migrant Workers Should Receive Are Paid on Time and in Full [确保农民工按时足额拿到英得工资]' *China Labour Protection Daily (中国劳动保障报)* (21 November 2015).

[89] Zhang, 'MOHRSS Convenes the 2016 Annual Work Meeting on Ensuring Payment of Migrant Workers' Wages Prior to Spring Festival [人社部召开2016年春节前保障农民工工资支付工作视会]'.

[90] General Office of the State Council *Opinion on Comprehensively Managing the Problem of Non-payment of Migrant Workers' Wages* [国务院办公厅关于全面治理拖欠农民工工资问题的意见], 20 January 2016.

completed by 2020. Media reports from this time included praise for police who had helped migrant workers recover unpaid wages.[91]

On 15 March 2017, MOHRSS reported on the second inter-ministerial meeting of this campaign, receiving reports on work carried out in 2016. It resolved to persist in strengthening coordinated management and striking hard on the serious problem of non-payment of wages in the construction industry.[92] And so the pattern repeats.

8.4 Conclusion: The Significance of Campaigns and Campaign-Style Enforcement in the Chinese Legal System

Both democracy and centralism can be identified in the form and execution of these campaigns. The centralist aspects are illustrated by the centralised, vertical coordination between higher and lower level Party groups, and different agencies of state. The central leadership group allocates tasks and performance quotas across participating Party and state agencies and social organisations, and down the administrative hierarchy to local levels in a manner reminiscent of the central planning system. Significantly, the courts are also included and treated no differently to other administrative agencies, violating widely shared understandings of the separation of powers of liberal democratic societies.

In the orthodox model of democratic centralism, the Party gathers popular inputs as part of the democratic process, but ultimately makes decisions and policies in ways that do not necessarily respond directly to those inputs. In the case of the wages campaigns, the Party is responsive to the existence of public concerns and the failure to protect the lawful rights of migrant workers. It is also motivated by concerns about social stability and economic development. Once a decision has been made, full compliance is required. Propaganda and education, drawing on mass line techniques, are designed to raise public awareness of both the campaign and their legal rights, to shape and then mobilise public support for the campaign. The public message of these campaigns is that the central

---

[91] Jiaxin Zhao (赵家新), 'Xinghua: Create a Foundation for Stability Let the Masses, Stably Enjoy Peace [兴化：稳定根基 让群众"稳"享平安]', *People's Police Daily [人民公安报]*, 3 February 2016.

[92] Second Plenary Meeting of the Inter-ministerial Joint Meeting on Efforts to Resolve the Problem of Wage Arrears [解决企业拖欠工资问题部际联席会议第二次全体会议召开], available at www.mohrss.gov.cn/ldjcj/LDJCJgongzuodongtai/201703/t20170317_268101.html.

authorities are concerned about, and responsive to, the problems of the ordinary people – particularly vulnerable groups such as rural migrant workers. As campaigns all contain some moral message (in this case, sympathy and concern for the welfare of rural migrant workers), they are a vehicle to reiterate the Party's moral leadership, the link between Party and the people, and the link between the Party's moral leadership and law-based governance.[93]

Although there are a number of similarities with enforcement campaigns in Western countries, I would argue that Chinese campaigns are distinct from their Western counterparts. That is because they occur in a political context that permits periods of centralisation, which breaks down the institutional silos and obstacles to legal reform that may arise from a decentralised form of governance, including the separation of governmental functions and the division of function between central and local entities. Campaigns tend to conflate policy and law making, as well as party and state, judicial and administrative power.

What do campaigns tell us about Chinese rule of law with socialist characteristics? Are they an anomaly, or an artefact of transition that will fade as the Chinese legal system matures? Although they do not describe the whole of the legal system, the campaign as a response to periods of perceived crisis or regulatory failure appears to be both widespread and persistent. Campaigns can have a potentially constructive effect on the Chinese legal system. One outcome of the 2004–2007 Wages Campaign was the introduction of new rules by local governments to address non-payment of wages. It also provided the impetus for the drafting and passage of major national labour legislation that was more favourable to workers' interests than the Labour Law.[94] Campaigns also require a concentrated examination of the deficiencies in the existing legal and regulatory framework, and the formulation of responses to address those problems. However, this Chapter has also illustrated that the wages campaigns have been ineffective over decades to address the entrenched problem of wage arrears.

A more pressing problem might be that the continuing reliance on campaign-style enforcement perpetuates a political-administrative

---

[93] The link between governance by virtue and governance by law under the leadership of the Party is restated in the Fourth Plenum Decision.

[94] Biddulph, Cooney and Zhu, 'Rule of Law with Chinese Characteristics: The Role of Campaigns in Law-Making', 389–390.

approach to the development of China's legal system, which emphasises the central and coordinated role of the Party and state agencies. This has a number of consequences. The first is that even though state agencies lack the resources (and, in some cases, the will) to enforce the law at the local level, campaigns divert resources to focus on the problems and targets defined by central Party and state powers. This mode of governance is arguably detrimental to the development of more stable forms of regulation by mid and local level administrative agencies, which lose control over allocation of priorities and resources during campaign periods. Repeated campaigns are not popular. After suffering many years of law and order campaigns, the police renamed Yanda (严打, meaning 'Hard Strike') by using its homophone (厌打, meaning 'Can't Stand It Strike').[95]

The campaign is also at odds with the establishment of citizen-led, or bottom-up, modes of governance and the development of strong civil society actors to advocate for and assist migrant workers to protect their own rights. While the sporadic nature of campaigns allows local agencies to refocus on their own priorities after the campaign is finished, the campaign form creates instability and uncertainty for both regulatory agencies and those regulated. More generally, it subordinates a legal regulatory approach to the political.

Viewed in light of the principles of democratic centralism, we might see the form and ubiquity of the campaign as not just a question of political interference in the legal domain, but as more of a political and ideological *structuring* of that domain that has flow-on effects for the functioning of legal and regulatory systems. That said, it is important not to make too much of the example of wages campaigns or the more general example of campaigns. Certainly, they illustrate both the political-administrative orientation and the impact of democratic centralism on the legal system. They do not describe the whole of the legal system or the entirety of the ways in which the legal system functions; either in terms of

---

[95] Shengfu Sun, 'Guanyu Jianchi "Yanda" Fanzhen De Yixie Sikao [Some Reflections on Upholding the Guiding Principle of the 'Hard Strike']', in *Zhongguo Renmin Gong'an Daxue Xiaoqing Shi Zhou Nian Lunwen Xuanji [Selection of Essays for the Tenth Anniversary of the China People's Public Security University]* (Beijing: Zhongguo Renmin Gongan Daxue Chubanshe [China People's Public Security University Press], 1994). Sun uses the homophone of Yanda (严打) to express the degree to which police officers are fed up with carrying on campaigns (taoyan yanda [讨厌严厉打击] abbreviated to yanda [厌打]).

law making or law enforcement. Nevertheless, campaigns do focus our attention on the impact of democratic centralism on not only the institutional structure of the state and legal system, but also on modes of governance. In particular, campaigns seem to operate at times of perceived social crisis, which, due to the sensitivity of the party-state to social and political instability, is rather more often than we might anticipate.

Roots and Routes

Adapting the Soviet-Inspired Vietnamese Court and Procuracy System

PIP NICHOLSON AND PHAM LAN PHUONG

9.1 Introduction

Two critical 'socialist' influences impact the Vietnamese court and procuracy systems: socialist legality and democratic centralism. While borrowed from the Soviet Union, these principles have their own histories in Tsarist and Soviet Russia, and Vietnam. Since their introduction in the late 1950s, they have developed substantially in Vietnam. Through an analysis of socialist legality and democratic centralism in the Vietnamese courts and procuracies, we argue that democratic centralism remains palpable as a mechanism for party-state management of these legal institutions. Socialist legality, on the other hand, is transforming and, in turn, producing new 'legalities', including rising competition between the procuracy and court systems. This competition is a new development, with uncertain consequences for the courts and procuracies.

This Chapter focuses on two concerns. First, it explores the extent to which Soviet socialist structures and legalities were received in Vietnam in the late 1950s as a part of the Democratic Republic of Vietnam's socialist transformation. Second, it asks if and how Vietnamese courts and procuracies have adapted their socialist orientation in the contemporary period. In particular, we ask whether the 2013 court-procuracy reforms reflect new ideologies, or if they serve to re-package core tenets of Vietnamese socialism and socialist legality, and its management through democratic centralism.

We argue that, despite substantial reform of the courts and procuracies since their formal establishment in 1959, there remains a 'socialist' essence embedded within each institution. This is apparent in terms of ideologies and structures that have been deliberately retained across the period from 1959 to 2017. We suggest that democratic centralism remains a key party-state tenet in each institution. As we explain below, democratic centralism was initially introduced by the party-state as a bedrock ideology, subsequently morphing into a party-state (management) 'tool'. In contrast, we suggest that socialist legality has been changing across the same time period. This has produced new (and uncertain) notions of legality in contemporary Vietnam, resulting in competition between the courts and procuracies. The result of that competition is yet to be fully ascertained, but has, at least, challenged the Vietnamese received notion of Russian/Soviet supervisory legality set out in Chapter 3.

Some might argue that collective mastery was also a key party-state policy in Vietnam; however, it is not a focus of this Chapter, save to note its formative role in the adoption of socialism and its popularisation in the late 1950s:

> The practice of democracy has been developed to a high degree; the people are really the masters of the country. [...] All our people are aware that the present draft amended constitution is due to the Party – the organiser and leader of the past glorious victories and guarantor for future achievements – and to the unity of our entire people and the valiant struggle waged by them for national construction along the Party line.[1]

This Chapter focuses largely on ideology/policy and legal reform, and their impacts on the courts and procuracies to illustrate the ongoing relevance of democratic centralism and the changing nature of (socialist) legalities. We draw on issues arising primarily in the criminal jurisdiction to illustrate the tensions and developments these reforms produce within each institution, particularly as they impact socialist grassroots justice. There have also been very substantial changes to the ways in which legalities have changed and impacted courts and procuracies – in particular, the development of administrative review. We note this development briefly below, particularly as it impacts the supervisory work of the procuracy.

The observable resilience in each institution, however, also results from factors other than 'planning' and implementation of Communist Party of Vietnam (the Party or CPV) policy and state laws. Constraints on change, we argue, are also felt as a result of the conflict between the court and procuracy, and the outright rejection of a reduction in the

---

[1] Ho Chi Minh, 'Report on the Draft Amended Constitution' 18 December 1959, reprinted in *Ho Chi Minh Selected Writing* (Hanoi: The Gioi Publishers, 1994), pp. 229–230.

powers previously vested in the procuracy, particularly alongside the ongoing technical limitations of judges and procurators.

First, we explore the Vietnamese conception of the state and its regulation upon the adoption of socialism; focusing largely on the Soviet transplant of the courts and the procuracies to Vietnam in the mid-to-late 1950s.[2] Next, changes to each of the courts and procuracies (and their relationships) between 1991 and 2017 are explored, analysing how these reforms impact both democratic centralism and socialist legality. The Chapter offers an institutional account of law reform and the resilience of aspects of socialist doctrine and practice, concluding that there is targeted institutional reform, but that it does not challenge the critical role played by democratic centralism.

The influences on the Vietnamese legal system include Vietnamese and Chinese imperialism, French colonialism and socialism, together with contemporary reformism (shaped by diverse sources including, for example, international law, common law, Japanese law and European civil law).[3] The impacts have diverged across time, institutions, actors and practices. For example, within the courts and procuracies, we know different sites embraced or curtailed reform in different ways: adapting, rejecting, marginalising and re-interpreting.[4] Actors in all their variability (capacity, seniority, inclination) are a critical part of the legal institution reform 'mix'. And the factors that drive these responses and how they are interpreted by commentators also vary.[5] These arguments are well rehearsed, including in the literature on transplantation,[6] and will

---

[2] Pip Nicholson, *Borrowing Court Systems: The Experience of Socialist Vietnam* (Leiden: Brill Academic Publishers, 2007). Nicholson notes that there was dialogue with China and that it peaked during the land reform campaigns of 1953–1956. Subsequently the PRC was not a primary source of advice on the construction of legal institutions, at least during the period of socialist construction: at pp. 4–5.

[3] Mark Sidel, 'Vietnam', in Poh-Ling Tan (ed.), *Asian Legal Systems* (Sydney: Butterworths, 1997), pp. 356–389; Pip Nicholson, *Borrowing Court Systems*, pp. 201–222.

[4] Pip Nicholson and Sally Low, 'Local Accounts of Rule of Law Aid: Implications for Donors' (2013) 5 *Hague Journal on the Rule of Law* 143.

[5] Ibid.

[6] Otto Kahn-Freund argues political commitment to reform is critical to its take-up. Otto Kahn-Freund, 'On Uses and Misuses of Comparative Law' (1974) 37 *The Modern Law Review*, pp. 1–27. See also Alan Watson, 'Aspects of Reception of Law' (1996) 44 *The American Journal of Comparative Law* 335–351. Compare with Pierre Legrand, 'The Impossibility of Legal Transplants' (1994) 4 *Maastricht Journal of Comparative Law* 111–124. Gunther Teubner, building on systems theory, contends that legal systems develop their own modes of communication dynamically interacting with other modes of communication located in economics, for example. John Gillespie argues that discourse

not be taken up here, given our focus on socialist resilience and adaptation, whether intended or not.

This analysis of Soviet-inspired principle in the courts and procuracies does not assume that the retention of socialist-inspired principle and practices necessarily reflects a deep commitment to socialism. Authoritarian states also retain socialist features as 'control' mechanisms to avoid disruptive reform and retain the status quo. As noted in Chapter 1, there is generally a commitment to the retention of strongly state-led and managed legal institutions, to heighten the prospects of stable leadership. It is beyond the purview of this Chapter to explore the extent to which the institutional reforms discussed here are animated by a commitment to socialism and/or control. That is a project for another time.

9.2 Construction of the Vietnamese Socialist State: Policy and Law

9.2.1 Legal Borrowing: Democratic Centralism

Law must be built on the basis of the line and policy of the Party, employing the judicial experience of the past fifteen years and with reference to the social sciences of the friendly countries – mainly the Soviet Union.[7]

In the construction of Vietnamese socialism, made explicit after the defeat of the French at Dien Bien Phu and the partition of Vietnam in 1954, the Vietnamese borrowed heavily from the former Soviet Union, particularly Russia. This is evident in the establishment of the socialist state through the 1959 Constitution and the national court and procuracy systems in the former Democratic Republic of Vietnam (DRVN).[8]

---

analysis enables a mapping of the transplantation dynamic noting that legal discursive communication is not closed and reflects the attributes of discursive communities and the understandings generated between different epistemologies. See also Daniel Berkowitz, Katharina Pistor and Jean Francois Richard, 'Economic Development, Legality, and the Transplant Effect' (2003) 47(1) *European Economic Review* 165–195.

[7] Chief Judge of the SPC, BBC April 1961, pp. 9–10 (in Vietnamese).

[8] Pham Van Bach and Vu Dinh Hoe, 'The Three Successive Constitutions of Vietnam' (1984) 1 *International Review of Contemporary Law* 105–118; William J. Duiker, 'The Constitutional System of the Socialist Republic of Vietnam', in Lawrence W. Beer (ed.), *Constitutional Systems in Late Twentieth Century Asia* (Seattle, WA: University of Washington Press, 1992), pp. 331–362; Mark Sidel, *The Constitution of Vietnam: A Contextual Analysis* (Cambridge: Cambridge University Press, 2009), pp. 45–65. See also Pip Nicholson, 'Vietnamese Institutions in Comparative Perspective: Constitutions and Courts

The passage of the 1959 DRVN Constitution, the 1960 Law on the Organisation of People's Courts (LOOPC) and the 1960 Law on the Organisation of the People's Procuracies (LOOPP) reflected this legal 'borrowing'.[9] The 1960 statute of the Vietnam Workers' Party also reflected core ideological principles existing in the equivalent statutes of the Communist Party of the Soviet Union (CPSU) of 1952.[10]

Democratic centralism was recognised in the 1959 Constitution as a governing principle of the state: 'People's Councils at all levels and other State agencies shall adhere to the principle of democratic centralism.'[11] It was, however, not defined in the 1959 Constitution or subsequently. It was also unclear how the People's Councils and other state agencies should apply it. The principle, however, was clearly defined in the statute of the Vietnam Workers' Party. Like the equivalent CPSU statutes of 1952, the 1960 Statute of the Vietnam Workers' Party endorsed democratic centralism as the fundamental organising principle of the Party[12] and defined it as follows:

1. The leading bodies of the Party at various levels shall be established through elections. (These bodies shall only be nominated by the higher levels where, due to difficult situations, elections cannot be held.)
2. The highest leading body of the Party is the National Congress of Representatives.

   The leading body at local level is the local congress of representatives. The leading body of the grassroots organisation is the congress of representatives or congress of Party members of that grassroots organisation.

   Party committees are appointed at the congresses of representatives or congresses of Party members at all levels.

   Party committees shall be accountable for and report on their activities to the congresses at the corresponding levels.

Considered', in Kanishka Jayasuriya (ed.), *Law, Capitalism and Power in Asia* (London: Routledge, 1999), pp. 300–329.

[9] V. Kolesnikov, 'The Supreme People's Court – Highest Judicial Organ in the Democratic Republic of Vietnam'(1961) 3 *Byulletan Verkhognogo SSSR*, 36–40, Moscow, JPRS 4940.

[10] See William B. Simons, 'USSR', in William B. Simons and Stephen White (eds.), *The Party Statutes of the Communist World* (Leiden: Martinus Njihoff Publishers, 1984), p. 421 and Phuong-Khanh Nguyen, 'Vietnam', in William B. Simons and Stephen White (eds.), *The Party Statutes of the Communist World*, (Leiden: Martinus Njihoff Publishers), pp. 445–455.

[11] Art. 4, DRVN Constitution 1959; see also Art. 6, SRVN Constitution 1980.

[12] Preamble and Art. 10, Statute of the Vietnam Workers Party 1960. See Simons, 'USSR', p. 421 and Phuong-Khanh Nguyen, 'Vietnam', pp. 445–455.

3. Party organisations at all levels must strictly comply with the principle of combining collective leadership with division of tasks.
4. The work of the Party shall be conducted by competent Party bodies depending on the level of importance. Issues regarding guidelines, policies and important national political issues shall be decided by national leading bodies (National Congress and Central Committee). Local issues shall be decided by local leading bodies but not contrary to the resolutions of higher levels.
5. Resolutions of leading bodies of the Party shall be voted for by a simple majority of the members. Before the vote, every member shall be entitled to express his/her opinions.
6. Party resolutions must be implemented unconditionally. Individual Party members shall subject themselves to the Party organisation; the minority to the majority; the lower to the higher level; and the organisations in the whole Party to the National Congress of Representatives and the Central Committee.[13]

Democratic centralism was reaffirmed in subsequent Party statutes, with a minor change allowing Party members who hold 'opinions in the minority' (*ý kiến thuộc về thiểu số*) to outline their reservations and report these to higher level Party committees.[14] These reservations can proceed as high as the National Congress,[15] reflecting the 'democratic' aspect of democratic centralism. Members, however, are not allowed to maintain their disagreement after policy determination and are strictly prohibited from 'propagating' opinions contrary to Party resolutions.[16]

9.2.2   Legal Borrowing: Socialist Legality

Socialist legality was officially endorsed by the Party for the first time at its Third National Congress in 1960, becoming a constitutional principle in 1980.[17] Socialist legality requires the strict observance of the

---

[13] Art. 10, Statute of the Vietnam Workers Party 1960.
[14] Art. 9, Statute of the CPV 2011. See also Preamble. See also Preamble and Art. 10, Statute of the CPV 1976.
[15] Ibid.
[16] Ibid.
[17] Part IV (6), CPV National Congress Resolution 1960, available at http://dangcongsan.vn/tu-lieu-van-kien/van-kien-dang/van-kien-dai-hoi/khoa-iii/doc-492420152591056.html; Art. 12 SRVN Constitution 1980.

Constitution and the law by state agencies, government officials, social organisations and their staff, and citizens.[18] At this time, the law was characterised as an instrument to serve the proletariat, enable its dictatorship and prioritise the collective over the individual.[19] The Party, as the executive committee of the proletariat ('the ruling class') determined the content of law.[20] As a result, law was an instrument for the implementation of the Party line.[21] The DRVN and Russian constitutional provisions were almost identical regarding the leading role of the Party and the role and characterisation of the Party-led, popularly framed grassroots justice systems.[22]

While the 1960 and 1976 statutes of the Vietnam Workers' Party make no reference to law,[23] the 2011 CPV Statute makes one reference to law: '[a] Party organisation shall be entitled to decide on issues within its powers but not contrary to Party principles, guidelines and policies, state laws, and resolutions of higher levels.'[24] While ambiguous, it could be argued that law remained cast as inferior to Party principles, guidelines and policies, even in 2011. This contradicts the constitutional principles that the law binds the Party, its members and the state, an issue to which we return later.[25] In any event, socialist legality and democratic

---

[18] John Gillespie, 'Changing Concepts of Socialist Law in Vietnam', in John Gillespie and Pip Nicholson (eds.), *Asian Socialism & Legal Change: The Dynamics of Vietnamese and Chinese Reform* (Canberra: Australian National University E Press, Asia Pacific Press, 2005), p. 47.

[19] John Gillespie, 'Concepts of Law in Vietnam: Transforming Statist Socialism', in Randall Peerenboon (ed.), *Asian Discourses of Rule of Law*, (London: Routledge, 2004), pp. 150–151.

[20] Gillespie, 'Changing Concepts of Socialist Law in Vietnam', p. 47.

[21] The SRVN Constitution 1980, for example, states in its preamble: 'The Socialist Republic of Vietnam needs a constitution institutionalizing the current line of the Communist Party of Vietnam in the new stage. It is the constitution of the period of transition to socialism on a national scale'. See also Adam Fforde, 'The Unimplementability of Policy and the Notion of Law in Vietnamese Communist Thought' (1986) *Southeast Asian Journal of Social Science* 62. See also Le Duan, *Some Problems of Cadres and Organization in Socialist Revolution*, (speech in 1973), 1994, at p. 452.

[22] Preamble and Arts. 4 and 6, DRVN Constitution 1959. See also Arts. 2–4 and 6, SRVN Constitution 1980. For constitutional principles governing the organisation and functioning of state organs in socialist states see, e.g., Aleksandr Haritonovic Mahnenko and Boris Aleksandrovičl Strašun, *The State Law of the Socialist Countries*, Socialism Today (Moscow: Progress Publishers, 1976), pp. 247–267.

[23] Art. 10(4), Statute of the VCP 1960. See also Preamble. See also Preamble and Art. 10(4), Statute of the CPV 1976.

[24] Art. 9, Statute of the CPV 2011.

[25] Art. 4(3), SRVN Constitution 2013. See also Art. 4, SRVN Constitution 1992.

centralism required adherence to the Party line and policies, therefore ensuring that Party policies were given effect.[26]

9.2.3 Expanding Central Control

The newly introduced court system of 1959 replaced the system of War Administration Committees, Judicial Committees and the nascent Military Court (hearing crimes against the state alleged against civilians and the military).[27] It also succeeded the 'arbitrary and violent' abandoned land reform campaign, led by the mobile Special Courts.[28] The Special Courts were explicitly political, serving the war and contributing to the transformation of a democratic revolution into a socialist one.[29] These dispute resolution systems were highly fragmented, and a key ambition of the 1959 reforms was central control of and through these agencies.

The ambition to control was greatly assisted by the concurrent development of the Soviet-inspired procuracy. The institution of the procuracy has a long history in Russia, first developed in Tsarist times. It was, however, its Soviet incarnation that Vietnam borrowed.[30] Adopting Lenin's socialist ideology outlined in '"Dual" Subordination and Legality',[31] Ho Chi Minh established a procuracy 'to ensure that the law was

---

[26] Various leaders also note that the Party policies were given effect via the requirements for socialist ethics and morality. See Shaun Kingsley Malarney, 'Culture, Virtue and Political Transformation in Contemporary Northern Vietnam' (1997) 4 *The Journal of Asian Studies*, 899, 907 argues convincingly that part of the strength of socialist ethics lay in their continuity with Confucian ethics. The party-state only introduced two new elements, courage and incorruptibility, while maintaining much of the fabric of earlier ethical tenets, particularly benevolence, righteousness and knowledge. See Ho Chi Minh, *Selected Writings (1920–1969)* (Hanoi: The Gioi Publishers, 1994), pp. 195–208, pp. 352–354 (on revolutionary morality); Trường Chinh, *Selected Writings* (Hanoi: The Gioi Publishers, 1994), p. 552 at p. 604. Here Trường talks of the need to educate party cadres in '4 good principles' which include: implementing the party line and state policies along with maintaining the war for independence, caring for the people and integration with them and guiding production.

[27] Nicholson, *Borrowing Court Systems*, pp. 37–83.

[28] Ibid., pp. 67–70.

[29] Trường Chinh, *On the Vietnamese Revolution, Report of the Second National Congress of the Party, February in 1951, (Trường Chinh Selected Writings*, The Gioi Publisher, 1994), p. 294.

[30] Gordon Smith, *The Soviet Procuracy and the Supervision of Administration* (Alphen aan den Rijn, Netherlands: Sijthoff & Noordhoff, 1978), pp. 4–8. See also George Ginsburgs, 'The Soviet Procuracy and Forty Years of Socialist Legality' (1959) 18(1) *American Slavic and East European Review* 34–62.

[31] According to Lenin, the law must be uniform and a function of the procurators is 'to see that the law is really uniformly interpreted throughout the Republic, notwithstanding

observed strictly and uniformly, and people's democratic legality was maintained'.[32] The procuracy replaced the prosecution office, which was introduced during French colonisation and was modified after the signing of the Geneva Accord.[33] The procuracy served to implement socialist class-based justice. Like its *prokuratura* counterparts, the procuracies in Vietnam were guaranteed independence from other state agencies and exercised enormous supervisory power, essentially in two forms. The procuracy supervised the observance of the law by all state agencies and their staff, as well as citizens ('general supervision').[34] The Procuracy's supervision powers also extended to investigating crimes; supervising Public Security and other investigating agencies; supervising the courts' work through protests;[35] supervising detention centres' observance of law; and prosecuting important civil cases involving the state's or a citizen's interests (judicial supervision).[36]

As with the Constitution, the Vietnamese LOOPC and LOOPP mirrored the equivalent Soviet laws.[37] The three-tier court and procuracy structure reflected the levels of government (central, provincial and district), and were a part of the state apparatus, together with the military courts and procuracies. The court and procuracy systems were highly

differences in local conditions, and in spite of all local influences', V. I. Lenin, '"Dual" Subordination and Legality', available at www.marxists.org/archive/lenin/works/1922/may/20.htm.

[32] Art. 2, Law on the Organisation of the People's Procuracy (LOOPP) 1960. When Vietnam was unified in 1975, the procuracies were established in the south, creating a procuracy system in the entire country. See *The People's Procuracies of Vietnam 1960–2000* (National Political Publishing House, 2000), Part III – The People's Procuracies through different periods (1960–2000), available at www.vksndtc.gov.vn/kyyeu/kyyeu40ks.htm. Note William Partlett in this publication chronicles the split in Revolutionary Russia between the utopians and statists about the ongoing role of the Procuracy. Risking generalisation, we argue the Vietnamese Procuracy was envisioned along statist lines. Nicholson has argued elsewhere that Pashukanis' view of the ultimate 'withering' of law did not take hold in socialist Vietnam. Nicholson, *Borrowing Court Systems*, p. 199.

[33] The prosecution office that followed the French model was attached to the judicial body while the prosecution office established in 1959 belonged to the Government and enjoyed an equal position with other ministries. See *Phan hieu truong Dao tao boi duong Nghiep vu kiem sat tai thanh pho Ho Chi Minh* [Procuratorial Profession Training and Retraining School in Ho Chi Minh City], *Giao Trinh Nghiep Vu Kiem Sat [Procuratorial Profession Training Textbook]*, 2013, p. 5.

[34] Art. 105, DRVN Constitution 1959; Arts. 1, 3 and 18, Law on the Organisation of the People's Procuracy 1960.

[35] Art. 18, LOOPP 1960.

[36] Art. 3, LOOPP 1960.

[37] On courts see Nicholson, *Borrowing Court Systems*, pp. 173–175. On procuracy see George Ginsburgs, 'The Genesis of the People's Procuracy in the Democratic Republic of Vietnam' (1979) 5 *Review of Socialist Law* 187.

centralised. Local courts and procuracies were accountable to the superior courts and procuracies, and subject to the unified leadership of the Chief Judge or Chief Procurator, depending on the exigencies of war. The Procuratorial Councils established at the Supreme People's Procuracy (SPP) and local procuracies were claimed to reflect democracy in the system, but in fact served to enhance control and guidance of it.[38] A similar entrenchment of senior leadership of courts was managed through the Judicial Councils.[39] In effect, democratic centralism ensured subordination of lower to higher offices.

Both the courts and the procuracies explicitly existed to serve the Party and its now stated mission of 'socialist construction'.[40] Their decisions first rested on moral narratives, re-oriented to facilitate socialist/communist policies, or 'revolutionary consciousness'.[41] Later decisions reflected the Party line and common principles of socialist law.[42] Each of the Soviet and Vietnamese justice systems relied on the participation of people's assessors on court panels to illustrate their 'democratic' character, and the use of mobile hearings was bedrock to the 'popular justice' they sought to create.[43] The assessors were, at this time, appointed by local government as representatives of the 'masses'. We do not take up the role of the assessors across time in this Chapter.

[38] Ibid., 194.

[39] Nicholson, *Borrowing Court Systems*, pp. 110–112. Nicholson notes the Judges' Committee was to meet twice a month to review cases. See also Art. 2, Ordinance on the Organization of the People's Supreme Court and Local People's Courts, dated 23 March 1961.

[40] Ho Chi Minh, 'Opening the Third National Congress of the Vietnam Workers' Party' (speech held on 5 September 1960), in Bernard B. Fall (ed.), *Ho Chi Minh on Revolution: Selected Writings 1920–66* (London: Pall Mall Press, 1960), p. 348. See also *The People's Procuracies of Vietnam 1960-2000*, Part III. See also Bui Tin, *Following Ho Chi Minh: The memoirs of a North Vietnamese colonel* (Bathurst: Crawford House Publishing, 1995), p. 40. See also on Vietnamese courts, Nicholson, *Borrowing Court Systems*, pp. 120–124, 197. On procuracy, see George Ginsburgs, 'The Genesis of the People's Procuracy in the Democratic Republic of Vietnam' 193. On Soviet courts, see Stanislaw Pomorski, 'Communists and Their Criminal Law: Reflections on Igor Andrewjew's "Outline of the Criminal Law of Socialist States"' (1981) 7 *Review of Socialist Law* 10.

[41] On Vietnamese courts, see Nicholson, *Borrowing Court Systems*, pp. 120–124, 197. On procuracy, see Ginsburgs, 'The Genesis of the People's Procuracy in the Democratic Republic of Vietnam' 193. On Soviet courts, see Pomorski, 'Communists and Their Criminal Law: Reflections on Igor Andrewjew's "Outline of the Criminal Law of Socialist States"' 10.

[42] Ginsburgs, 'The Genesis of the People's Procuracy in the Democratic Republic of Vietnam' 196.

[43] Nicholson, *Borrowing Court Systems*, pp. 129–132, p. 197.

Relying on democratic centralism to give effect to the nascent conception of socialist justice (class-based justice), the institutions were staffed by those the Party approved – preferably members who had demonstrated loyalty to the party-state.[44] By 1962, it was claimed that the majority of judges and procurators were Party members.[45] Staff were selected in the hope of realising the 'correct' revolutionary morality. They were ideologically managed through highly active party cells that monitored the work of staff and reported on it to the higher equivalent bodies.[46]

Without legal training, procurators and judges had usually worked for the Party or other mass organisations, and included past soldiers and young people who had 'grown up and met the challenges of war'.[47] In 1960, only 0.3 per cent of the procuracy system's 800 staff held a bachelor degree (not necessarily in law).[48] In 1975, the number of procuratorial staff with a Bachelor of Law degree was 90 (out of 2,645), or 3.4 per cent.[49]

Legal training, with its focus on socialist justice, was first provided to senior officials of the procuracies and the courts via short courses led by experts from the Soviet Union in late 1960.[50] The trainees were later selected to train further generations of procurators and judges.[51]

9.2.4   Local Factors: Transforming Borrowings

The Vietnamese courts and procuracies were not carbon copies of the Soviet model.[52] Vietnam was a French colony prior to the Declaration of Independence in the North in 1945, with colonial power expressed differently in the north, middle and south of Vietnam.[53] Socialist Russia

---

[44] Ibid., p. 117, and Bui Tin, *Following Ho Chi Minh*, p. 40.

[45] Ginsburgs, 'The Genesis of the People's Procuracy in the Democratic Republic of Vietnam' 198.

[46] Bui Tin, *Following Ho Chi Minh*, p. 40.

[47] Procuracy University, Lịch sử hình thành phát triển của Trường Đại học Kiểm sát Hà Nội [The Establishment and Historical Development of the Procuracy University], available at http://tks.edu.vn/bai-viet/chi-tiet/34/lich-su-hinh-thanh-phat-trien-cua-truong-dai-hoc-kiem-sat-ha-noi. Nicholson, *Borrowing Court Systems*, p. 125.

[48] The People's Procuracies of Vietnam 1960–2000 (Hanoi: National Political Publishing House, 2000), Part IV.1.

[49] Ibid.

[50] Ibid.

[51] Ibid.

[52] Nicholson, Borrowing Court Systems, pp. 199–201.

[53] M. B. Hooker, *A Concise Legal History of South-East Asia* (Oxford: Clarendon Press, 1978); M. B. Hooker, *Legal Pluralism: An Introduction to Colonial and Neo-Colonial Laws* (Oxford: Clarendon Press, 1975); Milton Osborne, *The French Presence in Cochinchina and Cambodia* (Ithaca, NY: Cornell University Press, 1969).

expressly rejected the imperial legal system,[54] and yet retained the procuracy, which predated the revolution by some centuries.[55] These differences were present from the moment of legal borrowing and shaped how the borrowed institutions permuted. As the former CPV Secretary, Trường Chinh, noted, Vietnam adapted Marxism–Leninism in a 'creative manner to the concrete conditions prevailing in Vietnam'.[56] Vietnamese socialism might be described as opportunistic, with gradually increasing Marxist–Leninist characteristics reflecting Vietnam's geopolitical position as the war of independence became a war between Soviet-supported Vietnam and the Western allies: a cold war site.[57]

In addition, Vietnamese socialist construction took place during a protracted war. Divided into nine zones for military reasons, the construction of national institutions was challenged by fragmentation of the party-state and its preoccupation with military success. For example, during the first years after the procuracy was established in Vietnam, its general supervisory power was extensively exercised to serve the construction of socialism.[58] Vietnamese criminal justice focused on punishing counter-revolutionary acts such as destroying state property, obstructing the implementation of state policies and economic speculation.[59] With the escalation of war, however, the procuracy's focus shifted to the prosecution of treasonous behaviour and the fight against disobedience of wartime discipline.[60] These particular considerations were not replicated in Russia/the USSR.

[54] Mark Sidel, 'Vietnam', pp. 356–389.

[55] See Chapter 3 in this volume.

[56] Trường Chinh 'How Has Our Party Applied Marxism–Leninism in Viet Nam?' Speech at Cadres Conference to mark the 150th birthday of Karl Marx in 1968 (*Trường Chinh Selected Writings*, The Gioi Publishers, 1994), p. 554.

[57] Analyses of the DRVN Constitutions of 1945 and 1959 confirm the escalation of Vietnamese socialism over this period. Bui Ngoc Son, 'Restoration Constitutionalism and Socialist Asia' (2015) 37(1) *Loyola of Los Angeles International and Comparative Law Review* 21–27. Analysis of the Declaration of Independence in 1945 also suggests that the new Ho Chi Minh-led government was carefully inclusive of democratic as well as socialist principle. See David Marr 'Ho Chi Minh's Independence Declaration', in K. W. Taylor and John K. Whitmore (eds.), *Essays Into Vietnamese Pasts*, Studies on Southeast Asia, (Ithaca, NY: Cornell University, 1995), pp. 221–231. See also Pip Nicholson, 'Vietnamese Legal Institutions in Comparative Perspective: Contemporary Constitutions and Courts Considered', in Kanishka Jayasuriya (ed.), *Law, Capitalism and Power in Asia* (London: Routledge, 1999), pp. 300–329.

[58] *The People's Procuracies of Vietnam 1960–2000*, Part III.

[59] See Pham Diem, 'Growth of the Criminal Law through 1999', *Vietnam Law & Legal Forum*, 25 December 2007, available at http://vietnamlawmagazine.vn/growth-of-the-criminal-law-through-1999-4378.html.

[60] Ibid.

Socialist legality was operationalised by infusing 'legality' with socialist moral thinking. The development of 'ten golden words' (in Vietnamese) was attributed to Ho Chi Minh, and procurators were exhorted 'to memorise' them: *công minh, chính trực, khách quan, thận trọng, khiêm tốn'* (fair, upright, objective, cautious, modest). For the court, the 'eight golden words' (in Vietnamese) were *'phụng công, thủ pháp, chí công, vô tư'* (cherish justice, protect the law, public-spiritedness, impartiality). This particular training augmented general cadre training that applied to all Party members, including those servicing the courts and pro-curacies, requiring them to be 'good at helping the people in obeying the law and in the implementation of Party and state policies'.[61] Party cadre should also be good at fighting, good at caring for the masses and integration with them, and good at strengthening the work of the Party.[62] Reflecting its moral orientation, the courts privileged the state plan and policy over law in their cases: 'Generally speaking the law was only a subsidiary instrument while the policy and resolutions passed by the Party; administrative commands and planning documents were the main instruments in governing economic activities.'[63]

While these comments refer to the priority accorded economic poli-cies, the same approach held true in other types of cases: 'At present the people's courts only apply the new laws of the people's power. In the event of there being no legislative text they follow the principle of analogy or simply the general political line of the revolution.'[64]

9.2.5   Dynamics between Court and Procuracy: 1959–1991

The procuracy dominated, as it once did in the Soviet Union, in the early days of the DRVN and up until 1991. As the main enforcer of socialist legality, the procuracy closely supervised the observance of law by the courts to ensure consistent decision making in the interests of the party-state.[65]

---

[61] Trường Chinh, 'Forward along the Path Chartered By Karl Marx' in 1968, Speech at a Cadres Conference to mark the 150th birthday of Karl Marx, (*Truong Chinh Selected Writings*, The Gioi Poublishers, 1994), pp. 529–640 at p. 606.

[62] Ibid.

[63] Nguyen Nhu Phat, 'The Role of Law during the Formation of a Market-Driven Mechanism in Vietnam', in John Gillespie (ed.), *Commercial Legal Development in Vietnam: Vietnamese and Foreign Commentaries* (Sydney: Butterworths, 1997), pp. 397–412 at p. 398.

[64] Le Kim Que, 'The People's Courts', in *An Outline of the Institutions of the Democratic Republic of Vietnam* (Hanoi: Foreign Languages Publishing House, 1974), p. 99.

[65] Arts. 17–19, LOOPP 1960. Nicholson, *Borrowing Court Systems*, pp. 85–102.

Throughout this period, the courts were precluded from publicly determining the procuracy had acted improperly or beyond power.

Cooperation between the courts and the procuracies at this time resulted from the unclear division of responsibilities between the agencies, their embeddedness in the political structure and their shared joint mission to enable socialist legality. For example, after the passage of the first LOOPC and LOOPP in 1959, the courts did not know whether they could initiate criminal proceedings, or what their role was in the investigation of crimes.[66] The courts also queried when they should determine cases pre-trial or at the conclusion of the trial.[67]

A practice developed whereby cases were usually jointly reviewed by the procuracy and the court in advance of trials.[68] This practice continued after the promulgation of the 1988 Criminal Procedure Code. The Supreme People's Court (SPC) and the SPP agreed that, while not mandatory, pre-trial conferences assisted the agencies to cooperate and better perform their functions.[69] In the pre-trial conference, the responsible judge and the procurator met to discuss cases and, where necessary, leaders of the concerned court and procuracy could also meet.[70] In certain cases, investigators could also attend.[71] The pre-trial conference was often held when the court believed that further investigation was needed, or that a case should be suspended, ceased or transferred to another court. Pre-trial conferences were inevitable where the case was considered important *(vụ án điểm)* or complicated.[72]

Another instance of the close cooperation between courts and procuracies manifested in their close management of propaganda, which required the court to communicate the revolutionary morality fostered by their decisions.[73] While the courts had their own publications (the SPC, in particular, distributed internal guidance to judges in lower courts),[74] the

---

[66] Nicholson, *Borrowing Court Systems*, p. 97.

[67] Ibid.

[68] Nguyen Van Huong, 'Penal Procedure and Civil Procedure', in *An Outline of Institutions of the Democratic Republic of Viet Nam* (Hanoi: Foreign Languages Publishing House, 1974), pp. 217–218.

[69] Inter-circular No. 01-TANDTC-VKSNDTC/TTLT dated 8 December 1988 between the SPC and the SPP Guiding the implementation of some provisions of the Criminal Procedure Code, Part II.

[70] Ibid.

[71] Ibid.

[72] Ibid.

[73] Nicholson, *Borrowing Court Systems*, p. 97.

[74] Ibid., pp. 79–80, 123–132.

use of mobile courts (a strategy to take 'justice' to the people and educate them) and press reporting was negotiated with the procuracy.

Democratic centralism created an obligation to report to and seek guidance from higher procuratorial institutions and Party committees on high-profile cases.[75] High-profile cases may involve crimes against national security; issues of economic and social order; disruption to the implementation of party-state policy; or cases that have a politically negative effect on public opinion.[76] In these cases, the Chief Procurator must make sure that the case is assigned to a 'suitable' procurator who is experienced, capable and 'has a sense of responsibility'.[77] In a similar vein, lower courts sought and obtained advice from senior courts on how to handle cases.[78]

9.3   Adapting or Transforming? Courts and Procuracies 1991–2017

Since 1991, there have been three waves of legal reform in Vietnam. First, the meaning of socialist legality was changed, creating the possibility of a law-based state. Second, in 2001, there was a reduction in the ambit of the procuracy's supervisory power. At the same time, there was reform of both courts and procuracies in an attempt to create better managed and technically more competent institutions. Third, in the most recent reforms, commencing with a new Constitution in 2013, the authority of the procuracy was further reduced via the introduction of court-based supervisory powers and judicial power. Read together, these reforms do not lessen the party-state's hold on legal institutions through democratic

---

[75] Joint Circular 01/TTLN dated 15 October 1994 of Internal Affair Ministry, the Supreme People's Procuracy and the Supreme People's Court guiding the handling of high profile cases, Section III–IV. See also Joint Circular 06/TTLN dated 12 September 1990 of Internal Affair Ministry, the Supreme People's Procuracy and the Supreme People's Court guiding the handling of high profile cases.

[76] Joint Circular 01/TTLN dated 15 October 1994 of Internal Affair Ministry, the Supreme People's Procuracy and the Supreme People's Court guiding the handling of high profile cases, Section I.

[77] Joint Circular 01/TTLN dated 15 October 1994 of Internal Affair Ministry, the Supreme People's Procuracy and the Supreme People's Court guiding the handling of high profile cases, Section III.

[78] Pip Nicholson, 'Vietnamese Courts: Contemporary Interactions between Party-State and Law', in Stephanie Balme and Mark Sidel (eds.), *Vietnam's New Order: International Perspectives on the State and Reform in Vietnam* (New York, NY: Palgrave MacMillan, 2007), p. 190.

centralism, but they do erode, at least in part, the supervisory authority of the procuracy, and alter 'socialist legality' by elevating the courts' role in determining and publishing guidelines on the law. Let us now analyse these reforms more closely.

9.3.1   The Constitutions and Relevant Laws of 1992

Vietnamese constitutions are, in effect, aspirational documents with no mechanism for enforcement.[79] Yet they signal the movement of CPV policy to publicly proclaim law endorsed by the National Assembly. The new 1992 Constitution reflected the adoption at the CPV's 7th National Party Congress in 1991 of *nhà nước pháp quyền* (law-based state). For the first time, the 1992 Constitution provided that the Party was bound by law.[80] Although *nhà nước pháp quyền* has yet to be fully defined and is not a statement of the rule of law,[81] this change signalled that socialist legality had morphed into the 'socialist law-based state'.[82] Gillespie argues that 'law-based state' includes at least three elements: authoritative law; equality before the law; and the power of law to be used to manage the state.[83] As refashioned, socialist legality no longer solely reflected statist and class-based notions of law, and was increasingly relied upon to regulate social and economic relationships.[84] The adoption of the law-based state has, over time, required party-state-led reform of

---

[79] Bui Ngoc Son, 'The Discourse of Constitutional Review in Vietnam' (2015) 9(2) *Journal of Comparative Law* 191–221. See also Mark Sidel 'Analytical Models for Understanding Constitutions and Constitutional Dialogues in Socialist Transitional States: Re-Interpreting Constitutional Dialogues in Vietnam' (2002) 6(1) *Singapore Journal of International and Comparative Law* 42–89.

[80] Art. 4, SRVN Constitution 1992.

[81] See, e.g., John Gillespie, *Transplanting Commercial Law Reform: Developing A "Rule of Law" in Vietnam* (Aldershot: Ashgate Publishing Ltd., 2006), pp. 87–88; Tine Gammeltoft and Rof Herno, 'Human Rights in Vietnam: Exploring Tensions and Ambiguities', in Michael Jacobsen and Ole Bruun (eds.), *Human Rights and Asian Values: Contesting National Identities and Cultural Representations in Asia* (Richmond, Surrey: Curzon, 2000), p. 170; Karin Budmann, 'Building Blocks for the Rule of Law? Legal Reforms and Public Administration in Vietnam', in Stephanie Balme and Mark Sidel (eds.), *Vietnam's New Order: International Perspectives on the State and Reform in Vietnam* (New York, NY: Palgrave Macmillan, 1st edn., 2007).

[82] John Gillespie, 'Concept of Law in Vietnam', pp. 169–172.

[83] Ibid., pp. 151–152. Gillespie notes this mirrors changes in the 1980s Soviet Union.

[84] See Chapter 12 in this volume.

the legal system, including further clarification of the powers of each of the procuracies and courts, and the division of power between them, within the context of a unitary state.[85]

As noted at the outset, while this Chapter has discussed court and prosecutorial powers in relation to socialist legality and by reference to their criminal jurisdiction, there are, however, reforms that fundamentally impacted the power of courts and the procuracy in other jurisdictions. In particular, the establishment of the administrative courts in 1996 fundamentally changed the procuracy's supervision power and the role of the courts in handling grievances.[86] First, the new administrative courts challenged the procuracy's monopoly on supervision when the courts were given, at least in theory, an administrative review power to 'protect the legitimate rights of and interests of individuals, state agencies, and organisations and contribute to raising the effectiveness of state management'.[87]

Further, enabling (albeit limited) judicial review of administrative decision-making reflects a focus on citizens' 'rights', shifting the exclusive focus on compliance that had been under the procuracy's purview. The procuracy, however, continues to supervise the work of the Administrative Court.[88] That said, when introduced, administrative courts could only hear very limited types of cases, as a result of the narrow scope of administrative review and a lack of detailed procedural rules (including tight time limits limiting access).[89] Further limitations on administrative review included poor enforcement, together with a lack of qualified judges and ongoing court dependence on local government.[90]

---

[85] To Van Hoa, *Judicial Independence: A Legal Research on Its Theoretical Aspects, Practices from Germany, the United States of America, France, Vietnam, and Recommendations for Vietnam* (Lund: Jüristforlaget i Lund, 2006).

[86] See also Law on Amendments and Supplements to a Number of Articles of the LOOPC, 28 October 1995.

[87] Preamble, Ordinance on Procedures for the Settlement of Administrative Cases, 1 July 1996.

[88] Art. 3 and Arts. 20–22, LOOPP 2002, Arts. 4 and 27, LOOPP 2014. See also Ordinance on Procedures for the Settlement of Administrative Cases 1996 (amended in 1998 and 2006), Administrative Procedure Codes 2010 and 2015.

[89] Nguyen Van Quang, *A Comparative Study of the Systems of Review of Administrative Action by Courts and Tribunals in Australia and Vietnam*, Doctoral Thesis, Latrobe University (2007), pp. 265–280.

[90] Ibid.

9.3.2   The 2001 Constitutional Amendments: Diminishing the Power of the Procuracy and Professionalising the Judiciary

The 2001 amendment of the 1992 Constitution stripped the procuracy of its 'general supervision' power. In effect, the procuracy lost the power to supervise administrative agencies, agency staff and citizens. The procuracy was reduced to prosecuting and supervising 'judicial' activities, here a reference to the adjudication of cases by courts and the investigating activities.[91] The change was rationalised on several bases. First, it enabled the procuracy to focus on public prosecution and supervision of judicial activities; duties that cannot be entrusted to other agencies and are seen as pressing.[92] Second, the changes reduced the overlap between courts and the procuracy (arising in part because of the introduction of the administrative courts), and the procuracy with other supervisory institutions.[93] Third, it was alleged that the removal of this function would: '[R]educe the inconvenience suffered by agencies and organisations that are subject to the supervision, inspection and checks by the procuracy, so as to enable these agencies and organisations to be confident in their ability to operate, produce and carry on business in accordance with the law.'[94]

While providing the procuracy with the opportunity to focus on improving performance in the prosecution of crimes and supervision of judicial activities, the removal of its general supervision function also signified a change in ideology. The procuracy no longer monitored citizens and social organisations and their observance of the law. Legality in this period was being expanded also to regulate state power. Further, the introduction of the national inspectorate and auditing agency exemplified the rejection of a general supervisory agency, seeking to instil more

---

[91] Art. 1(23), Resolution No. 51/2001/QH10 dated 25 December 2001 of the National Assembly on Amending and Supplementing a number of articles of the 1992 Constitution of the Socialist Republic of Vietnam. Judicial activities are understood in a very broad sense, including investigative activities, the adjudication of cases by the court, the enforcement of sentences, and the operation of detention houses and prisons. The scope of the procuracy's supervision over judicial activities is not stipulated by the constitution but is set out in the Law on the Organization of the People's Procuracy.

[92] Report No. 310/UBTVQH on some amendments to the 1992 Constitution by the Standing Committee of the National Assembly to the National Assembly, dated 18 May 2011, Part V.2.

[93] Ibid. Other supervisory institutions include the State Auditing Authority and the Government Inspectorate.

[94] Ibid.

technically focused institutions with less central control held by one institution, although these institutions arguably remain party-managed.[95]

9.3.3   Policy and Law Reforms

Subsequent to the passage of the 2001 amendments to the Constitution, the CPV developed its legal reform agenda with Resolution 08 (2002) and Resolutions 48 and 49 (2005). These resolutions state that the Vietnamese party-state will 'combine the actual circumstances in Vietnam with carefully selected international experience'.[96] A strong role was retained for Party leadership over the courts and procuracies,[97] evidenced by the continuing accountability of courts and procuracies to the National Assembly. While there was a call for increasing technical skills (including that judges and procurators have a law degree),[98] this was to be accompanied by ongoing political and ethical commitments to the party-state.[99] Commitments were also given in these policies to reform of the system of courts and procuracies; procedure laws; and the publication and enforcement of judgements.

Consistent with the 2002 policy paper, the 2002 LOOPC did not seek to construct an independent court system, rather seeking to introduce a more self-managed and technically competent court system under Party leadership.[100] Judges were now required to have a Bachelor of Laws

---

[95] See Mark Sidel, *Law and Society in Vietnam*, p. 27.

[96] Section I.2.3, Resolution 48 and section I.2.4, Resolution 49. See also Pip Nicholson with Simon Pitt, 'Official Discourses and Court-Oriented Legal Reform in Vietnam', in John Gillespie and Pip Nicholson (eds.), *Law and Development and the Global Discourses of Legal Transfers* (Cambridge: Cambridge University Press, 2012), p. 222.

[97] Nicholson with Pitt, 'Official Discourses and Court-Oriented Legal Reform in Vietnam', pp. 202–236.

[98] Section II.B.3, Resolution 08; The 2002 LOOPP and the 2002 Ordinance on Procurators of the People's Procuracy.

[99] Pip Nicholson and Nguyen Hung Quang, 'The Vietnamese Judiciary: The Politics of Appointment and Promotion' (2005) 14(1) *Pacific Rim Law and Policy Journal* 1–34; Guideline 02/VKSTC-TCCB dated 2 January 2003 of the Chairman of the Supreme Procuracy on the procedure and dossier for the selection, appointment, removal and dismissal of procurator of the people's procuracy, military procuracy at all levels, chief and deputy chief procurator of local people's procuracy, deputy chief procurator of central military procuracy, chief and deputy chief procurator of zonal and regional military procuracy.

[100] Pip Nicholson, 'Renovating Courts: The Role of Courts in Contemporary Vietnam', in Jiunn-Rong Yeh and Wen-Chen Chang (eds.), *Asian Courts in Context*, (Cambridge: Cambridge University Press, 2015).

degree, coupled with legal experience and training in judging.[101] From 2002, the Chief Justice of the SPC, working with the Judicial Appointment Council, would appoint district and provincial judges, with the Chief Justice remaining a National Assembly appointment.[102] Judges were empowered to dismiss people's assessors, if the Fatherland Front agreed.[103] Court budgeting and staffing was transferred from the Ministry of Justice to the SPC, with the court applying for funds from the National Assembly.[104] The courts' adoption of technology was also encouraged.[105] While targeting competence and transparency in court work, these reforms leave Party leadership of courts and their supervision by the procuracy intact.

Similarly, the 2002 LOOPP sought to reform the competence of the procuracy. Procurators were required to have a Bachelor of Laws degree and legal experience.[106] As with the court, however, key determinants of the staff and shape of procuracy work remained unaltered, particularly democratic centralism.

Resolution 49 (2005) criticised the procuracy for wrongful investigation decisions, poor prosecuting and uneven capacity at trials.[107] This culminated in calls for reform, including the need to improve the quality of public prosecution. Resolution 49 went on to suggest that the procuracy might be transformed into a public prosecution office.[108] The policy also openly admitted the possibility of removing all supervisory functions.[109] The procuracy has, however, successfully resisted attempts to

---

[101] Art. 37, Law on the Organisation of People's Courts, 06/20002/L/CTN. Courts did not initially receive sufficient qualified applicants so judges were appointed on the basis that they would complete legal qualifications. See *Resolution 131/2002/NQ-UBTVQH11 On Judges, People's Assessors and Prosecutors*, 3 November 2002. See also Nicholson and Nguyen, 'The Vietnamese Judiciary', pp. 1–34.

[102] Arts. 25 and 40, Law on the Organisation of People's Courts 2002.

[103] Ibid.

[104] Ibid., Art. 42(1) and 44.

[105] Ibid., Art. 46.

[106] Art. 43, Law on the Organisation of People's Procuracy, 34/2002/QH10; Art. 2, Ordinance on Procurators of the People's Procuracy 2002.

[107] See Preamble, Resolution 49. See also UNDP's Report in 2004 reporting that the level of people's confidence in the procuracy is quite low – UNDP, *Access to Justice in Vietnam – Survey from a People's Perspective* (2004), p. 15, available at: www.vn.undp.org/content/ vietnam/en/home/library/democratic_governance/access-to-justice-in-viet-nam—survey-from-a-peoples-perspectiv0.html.

[108] s.II.2.2, Resolution 49.

[109] See, e.g., Bùi Ngọc Sơn, 'Viễn cảnh Viện kiểm sát ở Việt Nam' [the Future of the Procuracy of Vietnam] (2009) 20(157) *Tap chi Nghien cuu lap phap [Legislative Research*

reduce this function. In 2010, the Politburo concluded that the procuracy ought to retain the twin functions of prosecution and supervision of judicial activities.[110]

9.3.4 Contemporary Reforms

Under the Socialist Republic of Vietnam's new Constitution of 2013, the procuracy and the courts were no longer charged with the duty to protect socialist legality, as had previously been the case.[111] Instead, the courts (which remain in the same chapter as the procuracy, as has been the case since 1980[112]) are responsible for 'the protection of justice, human rights, citizen's rights, socialist regime, interests of the state, and legal rights and interests of organisations and individuals'.[113]

In similar terms, the procuracy is responsible for the 'protection of law, human rights, citizen's rights, socialist regime, interests of the state, and legal rights and interests of organisations and individuals, thus contributing to ensuring that laws are strictly and uniformly observed'.[114]

This fundamental reform, while not clearly defining human rights, requires both legal institutions to protect human rights and justice. In the case of the procuracy, this responsibility is broader than the past responsibility to protect 'the lives, property, freedom, honour and dignity of the citizen'.[115] To fulfil this responsibility, the procuracy was required to

---

Journal]; Trần Đại Thắng, 'Có nên chuyển đổi Viện kiểm sát thành Viện công tố?' [Should the Procuracy Be Transformed into the Prosecution Office?] (2006) (6/11/2006) *Tap chi Nghien cuu lap phap dien tu [Legislative Research Journal]*, available at www .nclp.org.vn/nha_nuoc_va_phap_luat/co-nen-chuyen-111oi-vien-kiem-sat-thanh-vien-cong-to/?searchterm.

[110] Conclusion 79-KL/TW dated 28 July 2010 of the Politburo on reforming the organisation and operation of the People's Court, the People's Procuracy and the Investigating Body.

[111] Compare with Art. 126, SRVN Constitution 1992. See also Art. 127, SRVN Constitution 1980 where the procuracy and courts had to protect the 'socialist legal system, the socialist system'.

[112] The courts and procuracy are both under the same chapter heading in the 1959 Constitution also, although their tasks are more clearly separated in subsequent constitutions. Chapter VIII, DRVN Constitution 1959.

[113] Art. 102(3), SRVN Constitution 2013. See also Art. 2(1), LOOPC 2014.

[114] Art. 107(3), SRVN Constitution 2013 and Art. 2(2), LOOPP 2014. Note, however, that the LOOPP inexplicably retains the procuracy's responsibility to protect socialist legality. Art. 75, LOOPP 2014 which provides that 'being determined to protect socialist legality' is a criterion for procurator.

[115] Art. 126, SRVN Constitution 1992. See also Art. 2, LOOPP 2002.

ensure that all criminal acts be handled on time, that cases targeted the real offender and that 'justice' was served for the innocent.[116] The procuracy now, at least in theory, must ensure not only the 'correct' result arising from a prosecution, but also an obligation to respect individual rights through due process. In addition, the procuracy is charged with protecting human rights when exercising its supervisory power.

The introduction of the need to protect the 'socialist regime' suggests each institution must continue to protect the state's interests – particularly its economic interests, along with the party-state's social and political orientation and commitments. This is illustrated by the procuracy's supervisory role which has it appear in first instance civil cases in which public assets or interests are involved. The procuracy seeks to ensure cases are 'quickly and lawfully' handled.[117] In these cases, the procuracy can comment on the settlement of cases by the court; request the court to collect evidence (in certain circumstances); and collect evidence to protest against courts judgements or decisions according to appellate, cassation or re-opening procedures.[118]

Prosecutorial structural conflicts (a duty to prosecute to safeguard the state accompanying a duty to protect the rights of those it prosecutes), along with ideological and technical barriers to the implementation of a meaningful set of human rights protections may limit the protection of human rights in practice. Similarly, it is anticipated that the courts will struggle with the protection of human rights given the ways in which lawyers are marginalised generally, including at trials,[119] as well as technical and ideological limitations about the meaning of human rights and justice. Nevertheless, the party-state is signalling that the concept of a socialist law-based state fosters individual due process in theory, even where that might fall short in practice.

The 2013 Constitution also introduced 'judicial power', while leaving that term undefined.[120] The 2014 LOOPC further defined judicial power to include the courts' power to supervise the procuracy.[121] More

---

[116] Art. 126, SRVN Constitution 1992; Art. 23, Criminal Procedure Code (CPC) 2003.

[117] Art. 21, Civil Procedure Code.

[118] Art. 21, Art. 57, Art. 58, Art. 97, Art. 106, 2015 Civil Procedure Code.

[119] Tim Lindsey and Pip Nicholson, *Drugs Law and Legal Practice in Southeast Asia* (Oxford: Hart Publishers, 2016), pp. 252–257.

[120] Art. 102(1) and Chapter VIII, SRVN Constitution year.

[121] Art. 2, Law No. 62/2014/QH13 passed by the National Assembly on 24 November 2014 on the Organisation of the People's Court (LOOPC, 2014).

specifically, it explains that judicial power includes the courts' power to supervise the work of the procuracies in criminal cases.[122] The courts' power has also been expanded to include reviewing the work of investigators and procurators during the investigation, prosecution and trial; reviewing the legal basis of evidence; returning case dossiers to the procuracies for further investigation; requesting procuracies to review or provide supplementary evidence; and the presentation of matters related to cases at hearings.[123] These powers are echoed in the 2015 Criminal Procedure Code (CPC) that will come into effect on 1 January 2018.[124]

The 2013 Constitution confirmed that the procuracy retained the power, along with its prosecution function, to supervise the work of the courts and investigative agencies.[125] This supervisory power of the procuracy is defined in the 2014 LOOPP.

> [S]upervising judicial activities is an activity of the procuracy to supervise the legality of the actions and decisions of state agencies, organisations and individuals in judicial activities. It starts with the receiving and dealing with denunciation and information about the crime, requesting the initiation of the case and continues during the criminal process; in the settlement of administrative, civil, marriage and family, business, commercial and labour cases; in the execution of judgements and settlement of complaints and denunciations about judicial activities; and in other judicial activities in accordance with the law.[126]

---

[122] Art. 2(3), LOOPC 2014. The constitutional debates included a wider court supervision function of the procuracy, but that was not ultimately adopted. Pham Lan Phuong, 'The Procuracy as a Subject of Constitutional Debate' (2016) *Asian Journal of Comparative Law*, pp. 319–320.

[123] Art. 2(3), LOOPC 2014.

[124] See, e.g., Art. 284, CPC 2015 on the power to request the procuracy to supplement documents and evidences; Art. 296 on the power to summon investigators and persons implementing procedure; Art. 298 on the power to substitute more serious crimes than those alleged by the procuracies, which may be exercised when the courts return case dossiers to the procuracies, but procuracies determine not to alter the prosecution; Art. 313 on the power to listen to or watch the audio or video records to test the legal basis of evidence. Note the 2015 CPC was scheduled to come into effect on 1 July 2017 but was suspended awaiting the passage of the revisions to the 2015 Criminal Code, which was suspended for having too many errors. When the National Assembly passed the revisions to the 2015 Criminal Code on 20 June 2017, it was decided that the 2015 CPC would come into effect on 1 January 2018.

[125] Art. 107, SRVN Constitution 2013. For an analysis of the constitutional debates see Pham Lan Phuong, 'The Procuracy as a subject of Constitutional Debate: Controversial and Unresolved Issues', (2016) 2 *Asian Journal of Comparative Law*, 319–320, where it is reported that over 97 per cent of comments made to the Procuracy about its powers suggested that general supervision powers should be reinstated.

[126] Art. 4, LOOPP 2014.

To protect these powers, the procuracy placed more emphasis on supervising judicial activities (as understood in a broad sense).[127] Concurrently, the procuracy was also given more power to supervise the investigation of criminal cases.[128]

As we have seen, the introduction of 'judicial power' changes the court hierarchy and gives the courts power to supervise the work of the procuracy – producing mutual supervisory power between the procuracy and the court.[129] Judicial power is also defined to include the power to make recommendations about law reform to law-making agencies (such as the National Assembly),[130] and to ensure the uniform application of law, through the publication of cases.[131] In short, the power of the courts has been escalated at the expense of the procuracy, while a tight hold remains on personnel (see Section 9.3.6). We suggest the basis for these new powers is ultimately the transformation of socialist legality into the evolving notion of a socialist law-based state.

9.3.5 Court Procuracy Dynamics

As a matter of practice, the courts and the procuracy have also become generally more independent of each other, except in 'important cases'. It is claimed that judges and procurators no longer meet before trials to determine the outcome of cases or to discuss the possibility of returning the case dossiers for further investigation.[132] Instead, the courts and the

---

[127] See, e.g., Lê Hữu Thể, 'Mot So Van De Sua Doi, Bo Sung Cac Quy Dinh Ve Vien Kiem Sat Trong Hien Phap Nam 1992' ['Some Issues on Amending the Provisions About the Procuracy in the 1992 Constitution'] (2012) 1 *Tap chi Kiem sat [Procuratorial Journal]*; Lê Thành Dương, 'Mot So Van De Ve Chuc Nang, Nhiem Vu Cua Vien Kiem Sat Nhan Dan Trong Bo May Nha Nuoc Cong Hoa Xa Hoi Chu Nghia Viet Nam Trong Tien Trinh Sua Doi Hien Phap Nam 1992' ['Some Issues About the Functions, Duties of the People's Procuracy in the State Machinery of the Socialist Republic of Vietnam in the Process of Revising the Constitution 1992'] (2012) 13 *Tap chi Kiem sat [Procuratorial Journal]* 34 at 35–36.

[128] See, e.g., Part II 2.2, Resolution 49, and more recently Art. 2(3) Resolution 96/2015/QH13 of the National Assembly dated 25 June 2015 on Enhancing the measures to prevent and tackle criminal injustice and misjudgment and ensure compensation for persons suffering damage in criminal proceedings.

[129] See section 2.1, Conclusion 92 on Continuing to implement Resolution No. 49-NQ/TW, dated 2 June 2005, of the Politburo term IX on the Judicial Reform Strategy to 2020, dated 14 February 2014.

[130] Art. 2(7), LOOPC 2014.

[131] Art. 104(3), SRVN 2013 Constitution and Art. 2(8), LOOPC 2014.

[132] Nguyễn Ngọc Kiện, 'Mối quan hệ giữa Toà án và Viện kiểm sát trong tố tụng hình sự' ['The Relationship between the Courts and the Procuracies in Criminal Proceedings'],

procuracies and other relevant bodies meet only to discuss difficult issues (such as those caused by vagueness in the law) and to organise mobile hearings.[133] One of the catalysts for this change was the public condemnation of pre-determined cases (án bỏ túi). Further, the courts identified that relying on the procuracy was risky; potentially leaving the court liable for compensation for injustice and poor judgements.[134] The courts have also been increasingly reluctant to determine guilt based on the view of the procuracy alone.[135] The return of case dossiers for further investigation by the courts in recent drug cases, despite objection by the procuracies, is an example of the court exercising these new powers.[136]

There have also been structural adjustments giving the courts more power to manage the evolving nature of law and the socialist law-based state; for example, the 2014 LOOPC introduced a new level of court – the High Court.[137] This new court hierarchy enables the development of a newly imagined ultimate court – the Supreme People's Court (SPC), which can, in turn, develop the law. The newly introduced High Courts (sitting under the SPC), established in Hanoi, Da Nang and Ho Chi Minh City, have jurisdiction to hear appeals and protests from judgements

---

available at MOJ website, www.moj.gov.vn/tcdcpl/tintuc/Lists/ThiHanhPhapLuat/View_detail.aspx?ItemID=368.

[133] Ibid.

[134] Resolution 388 No. 388/2003/NQ-UBTVQH11 dated 17 March 2003 of the Standing Committee of the National Assembly on Compensation for Damage Caused to Unjustly Condemned People by Competent People in Criminal Proceedings and Law No. 35/2009/QH12 passed by the National Assembly on 18 June 2009 on state compensation liability.

[135] According to the statistics of the SPP and SPC, in 2014, twenty-one defendants charged by the procuracies were held not guilty by the first-instance courts. The corresponding numbers in 2015 and 2016 were twenty-seven and ten, respectively. Report No. 03/BC-TA dated 15 January 2013 of the SPC on the work in 2014 and focal duties of court work in 2015, Section A.I.1.1; Report No.152 dated 27 December 2016 of the SPP on procuracy work in 2016, Section II.4. For discussion of a particular case see: See Gia Khánh, 'Viện đề nghi chung thân, tòa tuyên vô tội' ['The Proccuracy Proposed Life Imprisonment, the Court Declared Not Guilty'], Thanh Nien Newspaper, Issue 237 (7185), 25 August 2015, p. 3.

[136] See Vũ Thanh Tùng, 'Vấn đề giám định hàm lượng ma túy và những bất cập cần giải quyết' ['The Evaluation of Drug Concentration and Problems That Need to Be Solved'], Viện Kiểm sát Bắc Giang (Việt Nam) [(Vietnamese) Bac Giang Procuracy], availalble at vksbacgiang.gov.vn/chuyendephapluat/61/3545.

[137] This is set out in Conclusion 79-KL/TW, dated 28 July 2010 of the Politburo and in Conclusion 92 on Continuing to implement Resolution No. 49-NQ/TW, dated 2 June 2005, of the Politburo term IX on the Judicial Reform Strategy to 2020, dated 14 February 2014.

of the provincial courts within their territorial jurisdiction.[138] Effectively, they assume the work of the former appellate courts of the SPC, leaving the SPC to hear only cassational reviews[139] and to reopen cases. The procuracy system has also been adjusted accordingly, with the introduction of the High Procuracies and changes to the scope of the SPP's work.[140]

There has not been sufficient time since the 2013 Constitution, the 2014 LOOPC, the 2014 LOOPP and the 2015 CPC to appraise how these developments are generally impacting practice. However, the changes to date herald structural adjustments to the original roots of the courts and procuracy. Ideologically, we have seen that judicial power has been introduced while continuing the commitment to democratic centralism,[141] a socialist state and Party leadership. Socialist justice has been supplanted by the requirement that these institutions protect 'justice', human rights and the socialist regime.

9.3.6 Maintaining Party Control

The clearest manifestation of Party control, however, lies in the status and management of judges and procurators as Party functionaries. As Nicholson and Nguyen note, democratic centralism – the mechanism by which functionaries account to institutions senior to them in the hierarchy and by which the Party institutes its management of personnel – thrives to this day.[142] Judges and procurators are considered civil servants,[143] although with particular selection criteria, such as having a law degree.[144] Loyalty to the party-state is a core qualification assessed by peers in the current workplace, in addition to demonstration

---

[138] Art. 344, CPC 2015.

[139] Broadly speaking, a cassational review is afforded where an inquiry is one-sided, or the court's decision fails to fit the facts or there is a violation of a procedural law or a breach of law or a combination of these.

[140] Art. 41, LOOPC 2014.

[141] Pip Nicholson and Nguyen Hung Quang, 'Independence, Impartiality, and Integrity in Vietnam', in H. P. Lee (ed.), *Asia-Pacific Judiciaries* (forthcoming) [Copy on file with author].

[142] Ibid.

[143] Arts. 7–8, Decree 06/2010/ND-CP dated 25 January 2010 of the Government Defining Civil Servants (Decree 06/2010).

[144] Art. 67(1), LOOPC 2014; Art. 75(2), LOOPP 2014.

of political knowledge, and political and ethical qualities.[145] As a civil servant, a judge or a procurator can be disciplined for infringing 'obligations, ethics and the communication culture applicable to civil servants'.[146] Punishments include demotion, warning, suspension or dismissal.[147] The Law on Complaints and the Law on Denunciations also applies to judges and procurators.[148] The Party statute exists over and above state laws, and breaching it attracts Party disciplinary proceedings.[149]

Democratic centralism continues to impose obligations on individual procurators to report to and comply with the leadership of the Chief Procurator in individual cases.[150] The procuracies also bear a duty to report to and seek guidance from the procuracy senior to them in specific cases.[151] The types of reports include preliminary reports *(báo cáo ban đầu)*, urgent or unplanned reports *(báo cáo đột xuất)*[152] and reports to

---

[145] Art. 13, Resolution No. 929//2015/UBTVQH13 of the Standing Committee of National Assembly providing Working Regulation of the National Council for Judicial Selection and Supervision. See also Art. 75, LOOPP 2014.

[146] Art. 3, Decree No. 34/2011 dated 17 May 2011 of the Government on Stipulating the Discipline of Civil Servants ('Decree 34/2011'). On acts that can see a Chief Justice or Deputy Chief Justices demoted see Art. 13.

[147] Ibid., Art. 8.

[148] Law No. 02/2011/QH13 of the Standing Committee of National Assembly dated 11 November 2011 on Complaints; Law No. 03/2011/QH13 dated 11 November 2011 of the Standing Committee of National Assembly on Denunciations.

[149] Direction No. 09-HD/UBKTTW of the Politburo's Central Commission of Inspection dated 6 June 2013 on Implementation of Some Articles of Regulation No. 181/QD-TW dated 30 March 2013 on Discipline Applying to Party Members. See also Statute of the Vietnam Communist Party, 2011.

[150] Art. 83(1), LOOPC 2014. See also duties and powers of the Chief Procurator and procurator in the CPC 2015 (Arts. 41 and 42).

[151] Art. 7, Decision 379/QĐ-VKSTC dated 13 July 2012 of the Chief Procurator of the SPP promulgating the Regulations on mechanisms for the information, report and management of work in the procuracy sector.

[152] In general, the procuracies bear a duty to report regularly on weekly, monthly, quarterly, or yearly basis to senior procuracies. However, there are certain circumstances where they must report immediately to the senior procuracy. These circumstances include extremely serious cases which happens in the locality; cases where investigating agencies and the procuracies acquit suspected persons; cases which are suspended by investigating agencies or the procuracies on the ground that the suspected persons did not commit the crimes; cases where the courts find the defendants not guilty; and other cases upon requests of the senior procuracy. Arts. 11, Decision 379/QĐ-VKSTC dated 13 July 2012 of the Chief Procurator of the SPP promulgating the Regulations on mechanisms for the information, report and management of work in the procuracy sector.

seek guidance *(báo cáo thỉnh thị)*.[153] The need to report cases depends on the nature of the crime and/or the profile of the defendant involved, but in general the control of procuratorial reporting has escalated, reflecting the increasing control over procuratorial work.[154]

There is also a system of reward for judges who demonstrate 'emulation' excellence.[155] Put briefly, this requires judges to voluntarily make an 'effort' in the 'construction and protection of the Fatherland'.[156] The courts are divided into groups for the purpose of determining emulation targets and certifying who will receive rewards.[157] Institutional targets are set for resolving cases and doing so without findings of corruption.[158] There are also individual targets, such as having no more than 1.16 per cent of cases of any one judge set aside and no more than 4.2 per cent of a single judge's cases amended.[159] Failure to participate in these activities may mean a judge is not reappointed.[160] Similarly, the procuracy set its institutional and individual emulation targets.[161] These targets are based

---

[153] Arts. 10–12, Decision 379/QĐ-VKSTC dated 13 July 2012 of the Chief Procurator of the SPP promulgating the Regulations on mechanisms for the information, report and management of work in the procuracy sector.

[154] Compare Arts. 10–12, Decision 379/QĐ-VKSTC dated 13 July 2012 of the Chief Procurator of the SPP promulgating the Regulations on mechanisms for the information, report and management of work in the procuracy sector, List A and List C with Section I, Joint Circular 01/TTLN dated 15 October 1994 of Internal Affair Ministry, the Supreme People's Procuracy and the Supreme People's Court guiding the handling of high profile cases, Section I. See also Joint Circular 06/TTLN dated 12 September 1990 of Internal Affair Ministry, the Supreme People's Procuracy and the Supreme People's Court guiding the handling of high profile cases.

[155] Nicholson and Nguyen, 'Independence, Impartiality, and Integrity in Vietnam'.

[156] Art. 3, Law No. 15–2003-QH11 dated 26 November 2003 on Emulation and Commendation ('Law on Emulation and Commendation 2003').

[157] Official Letter No. 62/TANDTC-TDKT guiding some contents of emulation and commendation in the people's court sector, 25/04/2012; Decision No. 220/QD-TA-TDKTon assigning the managers and deputy managers of emulation groups of the people's court sector in 2014, 25/12/2013. The courts are divided into seven emulation groups – roughly provinces per group and a seventh group comprising the central courts.

[158] Nicholson and Nguyen, 'Independence, Impartiality, and Integrity in Vietnam'.

[159] Official Letter No. 62/TANDTC-TDKT dated 25 April 2012 Guiding Some Contents of Emulation and Commendation in the People's Court Sector ('Official Letter 62/2012'); Decision No. 220/QD-TA-TDKT dated 25 December 2013 on Assigning the Managers and Deputy Managers of Emulation Groups of the People's Court Sector in 2014.

[160] Ibid.

[161] Decision 307/QĐ-VKSTC dated 3 July 2008 of the Chief Procurator of the SPP promulgating the emulation and commendation Regulations in the People's Procuracy Sector.

on a work assessment system that is set out in detail[162] – for example, there is an institutional target for having no defendant found 'not guilty' by the courts.[163] There is also a target for having no case set aside to reinvestigate or retry due to the procuracy's error.[164]

9.4 Socialist Legal Institutions: Continuity and Tension

We argue that the Democratic Republic of Vietnam received the mid-1950s Soviet institutions: the courts and procuracies. As noted, it is not suggested that these Vietnamese institutions are a replica of the Soviet order, but their introduction reflected Soviet legal borrowing. Since that time, there has certainly been momentum for institutional reform within and between the courts and procuracies. This has resulted in some structural changes and is also increasingly producing more educated and technically informed staff, whether at the courts or the procuracies. Democratic centralism remains a key principle operating within the procuracies and courts. It has not been abandoned either in Party policies, the new Constitution, the LOOPC or the LOOPP.

Both the courts and procuracies reflect their early construction. Throughout this period, judges and procurators remain almost 90 per cent Party members with very real political obligations to the Party, set out in the CPV Statute 2011. The preamble provides:

> [. . .] The Party is a close-knit organisation united in willpower and action, takes democratic centralism as the fundamental organisational principle, practises collective leadership and individual accountability, self-criticism and criticism, treasures comradeship, implements proper discipline, preserves unity on the basis of the Political Program and the Party Statutes, maintains close relationship with the people, operates in the framework of the Constitution and the laws. The Communist Party of Vietnam is a party in power.[. . .] The Party exercises leadership over the political system while being an integral part of it.[165]

---

[162] Decision 379/QĐ-VKSTC dated 10 October 2017 of the Chief Procurator of the SPP promulgating the system of basic criteria to assess the professional work in the procuracy system (Decision 379).

[163] System of basic criteria to assess the professional work in the procuracy system attached to Decision 379, Criterion 25.

[164] System of basic criteria to assess the professional work in the procuracy system attached to Decision 379, Criterion 24.

[165] Preamble, Statute CPV 2011.

We suggest that the transition is from the post-Leninist, pre-Gorbachev Soviet socialist model imported to Vietnam to a socialist-based Vietnamese model. There have been policy statements, as explained, articulating reforms to the courts and procuracy, but in each case the institutions are not overhauled. Reforms, including the introduction of judicial power, do not challenge the party-state's leadership, nor do they diminish democratic centralism. Rather, they operationalise clearer processes, more institutional accountability to the public (most noticeably the legal profession) and to the National Assembly, and more transparency.

They concurrently reshape the socialist legality of the 1950s. The increase in the status of the SPC to determine the law and proclaim it, and also to supervise the work of the procuracy, shifts the socialist conception of justice from implementing the Party line – with the Party above the law – to a law-based model of socialist state. This is most clearly articulated through invoking the duty to protect 'justice', albeit undefined, and the socialist regime, rather than 'socialist justice'. This change also shifts the balance of power between court and procuracy. As the debates about reform of the procuracy reveal, the procuracy has resisted these reforms, just as some court leadership has arguably encouraged them.[166] The introduction of the administrative courts and their (limited) power to review the legality of some state acts, further corrodes procuratorial authority, just as the introduction of other agencies, such as the State Audit Authority and Government Inspectorate, reduces its remit.

That said, there are currently limits on the ways in which the party-state has transformed 'socialist legality'. A reduction of the procuracies' supervision power over courts would signal real change, although even this might be cast as supporting the socialist law-based state.[167] As noted, this was not introduced in the 2013 Constitution, but it has been debated since as early as 1992. Instead, the courts were given power to supervise the procuracy; perhaps a small step to curtail the lack of transparency and process within the investigation and prosecution of crimes, but not a fundamental reform. And party cadres and elites staff these agencies. These cadres retain obligations to the Party, set out in the 2011 Party Statute.

As noted at the outset, there are also practical constraints limiting intended reforms. Both the procuracy and the courts are conservative organisations with low levels of training and technically limited staff,

---

[166] Pham, 'The Procuracy as a subject of Constitutional Debate', p. 320. This change was most strongly supported by the Ministry of Justice.
[167] Gillespie, 'Concept of Law in Vietnam', p. 152.

despite recent investment.[168] This is especially evident when trying to develop and implement strategies to enable the mooted adversarialism or to render court decisions more transparent. The court system has a limited budget, low salaries and a high level of central 'guidance'.[169] The procuracy system also suffers from low salaries and procurators' dependence on the Chief Procurators of their office.[170] The procuracies do not have sufficient resources, and procurators have a very heavy workload due to the increasing number and complexity of cases.[171] There is not space here to chronicle practical constraints at any length, but they are real.

The focus on Vietnamese socialist policies, laws, mores and practices, combined with the realities of incremental reform, given technical and resource constraints, culminates in the resilience of the Vietnamese socialist roots of courts and procuracies. While reforms target particular aspects of these institutions, they do not confront the bedrock role played by democratic centralism. The changes to conceptions of socialist legality, particularly the move to protect justice, signals a disaggregation of politics and law as one – to a politics potentially bounded by law. But this change is, and will remain, led and managed by the party-state through the principles of democratic centralism. These principles enable the party-state to lead, manage, expel and appoint officers in each institution. The remaining question is: Who monopolises the protection of justice – the procuracy or the courts? As we have seen, there is ongoing and robust debate between the courts and the procuracy over who has the more prominent role, with the Ministry of Justice acting as the greatest champion for change that favours an increase in the courts' powers. Its ambitions have not yet been realised.

---

[168] Lê Hữu Thể, Công tác nghiên cứu khoa học và công tác đào tạo, bồi dưỡng cán bộ Ngành kiểm sát trong giai đoạn mới [Scientific Research and the Training and Fostering of the Procuracy's Cadres in the New Period], Procuratorial University website: http://tks.edu.vn/thong-tin-nghiep-vu/chi-tiet/82/49.

[169] Nicholson and Nguyen, 'Independence, Impartiality, and Integrity in Vietnam'.

[170] Viện kiểm sát nhân dân tối cao [The Supreme People's Procuracy], Báo cáo tổng kết thực tiễn thi hành Luật tổ chức Viện kiểm sát nhân dân năm 2002, Pháp lệnh kiểm sát viên năm 2002 (sửa đổi năm 2011), Pháp lệnh Tổ chức Viện kiểm sát quân sự năm 2002 [Report on the Implementation of the 2002 Law on the Organization of the People's Procuracy, the 2002 Ordinance on the People's Procurator (Amended in 2011), the 2002 Ordinance on the Organization of the Millitary Procuracy] (9 January 20144 2014). (2014). Part II. 2.

[171] Ibid.

PART V

Labour

PART V

Labour

What Is Socialist about Labour Law in China?

CYNTHIA ESTLUND AND AARON HALEGUA

10.1 Introduction

What, if anything, is 'socialist' about contemporary labour law in the People's Republic of China? The question is one crucial facet of a larger question: What is 'socialist' about the 'socialist market economy' that China claims to be constructing since opening its doors to foreign capital and private enterprise under Deng Xiaoping? Rephrasing the question along those lines reminds us that 'socialism' is sometimes defined in contrast to a market economy, particularly in regard to the treatment of labour. There is little doubt that China's is largely a market economy. The past four decades have seen China's abandonment of central planning, the rise of commodified labour exchanged through labour markets, the dramatic growth of private profit-seeking corporations and their share of the labour force, and the gradual development of regulatory constraints on labour standards and practices. In the modern era of semi-regulated labour markets in a mostly non-state economy, what differentiates China's labour regime from those of other regulated market economies? And, whatever that is, is it 'socialist'?

As this last question suggests, we intend to proceed from China's particularities to the more abstract definitional question of what makes a labour law regime 'socialist', rather than attempting to define 'socialism' at the outset and looking for signs of its presence. We will begin by briefly reviewing some basic changes in China's labour policies since the end of the Maoist era, changes that raise the question of whether China is best seen as 'post-socialist' in its labour policies and practices. Then we will turn to two distinctive institutional features of China's labour law regime, both legacies of the Maoist era and both reflecting constitutional commitments: first, the strong commitment to Party control of the collective representation of workers through a single monopolistic trade union organisation, the All-China Federation of Trade Unions (ACFTU); and, second, 'democratic management' of enterprises, mainly through Staff and Worker Representative Congresses (SWRCs). The latter, which might genuinely qualify as 'socialist', is very weakly institutionalised. The former, which may or may not be considered 'socialist', pervades and shapes nearly every aspect of China's contemporary labour regime. That is evident in China's multifaceted response to labour disputes, which include the mediation and adjudication of rights disputes, a formal system of collective consultation and the ad hoc response to wildcat strikes and protests. Each of these systems is shaped by the government's commitment to monopolising collective representation and maintaining stability. We will conclude by reflecting on the definitional question posed by our title.

10.2   What Is *Not* Socialist about China's Labour Regime: The Rise of Labour Markets, Private Capital and Regulation

In a market economy, labour is a commodity bought and sold in labour markets. Labour in China's planned economy under Mao was the antithesis of this. Workers in the state-owned and state-planned economy were not labour market actors, but near-permanent members of a work unit, or *danwei*, which supplied workers and their families with food, housing, education, health care and other basic requisites of daily life. But that socialist economy has been thoroughly dismantled, even in the large remaining state-owned sector. The 'corporatisation' of state-owned enterprises (SOEs), with or without privatisation, famously shattered the *danwei* system and the 'iron rice bowl' that its members enjoyed in favour of commodified labour and labour markets.[1] That long, painful 'reform' process triggered widespread feelings of betrayal and massive labour unrest in China's industrial heartland, culminating in the early 2000s.[2] The state still owns many of China's most important enterprises, with an effective monopoly in certain strategic industries; but even workers in the state sector are undoubtedly labour market actors who sell their labour through contracts.

---

[1] Mary E. Gallagher, *Contagious Capitalism: Globalization and the Politics of Labour in China* (Princeton, NJ: Princeton University Press, 2007); William Hurst, *The Chinese Worker after Socialism* (Cambridge: Cambridge University Press, 2009); Tim Pringle, *Trade Unions in China: The Challenge of Labour Unrest* (Abingdon: Routledge, 2011), pp. 56–86.

[2] Hurst, *The Chinese Worker after Socialism*; Ching Kwan Lee, *Against the Law: Labour Protests in China's Rustbelt and Sunbelt* (Berkeley, CA: University of California Press, 2007).

In the meantime, as China 'corporatised' its state sector, it fostered the growth of an even larger non-state sector.[3] China's 1982 Constitution declares that 'socialist public ownership of the means of production' is to remain the 'dominant' form of ownership, and that China remains on a path towards eliminating 'the system of exploitation of man by man' and effectuating 'the principle of "from each according to his ability, to each according to his work"'.[4] But these rhetorical invocations of socialism were increasingly defied by the facts on the ground.

Beginning with 'special economic zones' in the Pearl River Delta and elsewhere along the coast, China opened its borders to foreign capital, often as part of joint ventures. Collectively owned 'township and village enterprises' began to operate much like private firms, and domestic entrepreneurs were allowed to go into business, often as suppliers to large foreign corporations.[5] Those foreign corporations flocked to China in pursuit of cheap labour supplied by a steady flow of poor rural migrants, whose wages and working conditions were largely unregulated for the first decade or two of capitalist-led growth. The jarring spectacle of those Dickensian sweatshops seemed to make a cruel hoax of China's claim to the banner of 'socialism'. China's workers have responded as workers eventually do to exploitation, staging some spectacular and increasingly well-organised strikes that seem more reminiscent of labour's response to twentieth century development under Western capitalism than redolent of 'socialism'.

Because the reform of the state sector lagged behind the opening of the private sector, China's 'socialist market economy' initially looked like two separate economies: a socialist economy still planned and administered by the state; and a market economy ruled by managers on behalf of profit-driven capitalist owners. Since the early 1990s, however, the two sectors have largely converged towards one based on regulated markets,

---

[3] Whereas 25 per cent of China's total labour force was employed by SOE in 1996, this number dropped to 7 per cent by 2003. Mimi Zou, 'Evolution of Collective Labour Law in China', in Roger Blanpain, Ulla Liukkunen and Chen Yifeng (eds.), *China and ILO Fundamental Principles and Rights at Work* (Kluwer Law International, 2014), p. 61. As for China's industrial labour force, only 12 per cent still worked in state-controlled firms by 2013. Barry Naughton, 'Is China Socialist?' (2017) 31(1) *Journal of Economic Perspectives*, 3, 7.

[4] Article 6, 宪法 [Constitution] 1982 (P.R.C.) (http://www.npc.gov.cn/englishnpc/Constitution/node_2825.htm). The current Constitution was adopted in 1982, and was amended in 1988, 1993, 1999, 2004, 2007 and 2018.

[5] Yasheng Huang, *Capitalism with Chinese Characteristics: Entrepreneurship and the State* (Cambridge: Cambridge University Press, 2008), pp. 73–77.

including rather familiar formal labour standards that apply across all enterprises. The advent of regulation has been a drawn-out affair and is still incomplete. In the planned economy, in which all productive enterprises were owned and administered by the party-state and its appointed managers, there was no need for regulatory institutions as we know them.[6] So China has had just a few decades to construct regulatory institutions virtually from scratch.[7]

In some respects, China's labour policies since 'reform and opening' mirror the 'double movement' that is characteristic of modern capitalism: the social construction of markets and the countermovement for social protection from markets.[8] The regulatory dimension of the 'double movement' has been compressed in China and is ongoing. In the meantime, as we will discuss later, China is strongly resisting another crucial dimension of the 'double movement'; that is, the legitimation and accommodation of workers' own organisations.[9]

Before 1994, 'labour law' in China consisted of 'a myriad of confusing and often contradictory laws, regulations, notices, directives and so on'.[10] The national Labour Law of 1994 was a breakthrough in its imposition of a single basic labour regime – one founded on regulated labour contracts and labour markets – across the state and non-state sectors.[11]

---

[6] Benjamin van Rooij, 'Regulation by Escalation: Unrest, Lawmaking and Law Enforcement in China', in Susan Trevaskes, Elisa Nesossi, Flora Sapio and Sarah Biddulph (eds.), *The Politics of Law and Stability in China* (London: Edward Elgar, 2014), p. 86.

[7] Sean Cooney, Sarah Biddulph and Ying Zhu (eds.), *Law and Fair Work in China* (Abingdon: Routledge, 2013).

[8] Karl Polanyi, *The Great Transformation: The Political and Economic Origins of Our Time* (Boston, MA: Beacon Press, 1957). Regarding the 'double movement' in China, see Eli Friedman, *Insurgency Trap: Labour Politics in Postsocialist China* (Ithaca, NY: ILR Press, 2014); and Shaoguang Wang, 'Double Movement in China' (2009) 43 *Economic and Political Weekly* 51–59.

[9] Eli Friedman argues in his book, *Insurgency Trap*, that China's regime is trapped at the 'insurgency' phase of the countermovement, unable or unwilling to continue to the 'institutional' phase.

[10] Susan Leung, 'China's Labour Contract System from Planned to Market Economy' (2012) 3 *Journal of Law, Ethics & Intellectual Property*, 1, 2.

[11] There are still differences between these sectors at the level of enforcement or implementation, but not all of them cut in the expected direction. For example, although SOEs are generally thought to maintain higher labour standards than most private enterprises, they are also among the largest users of temporary agency workers, as they seek to reduce the portion of their workforce eligible for various costly entitlements. *See* Wenjuan Jia, 'The Making of Dualistic Labour Regime: Changing Labour Process and Power Relations in a Chinese State-Owned-Enterprise under Globalization', in Mingwei Liu and Chris Smith (eds.), *China at Work: A Labour Process Perspective on the Transformation of Work and Employment in China* (Basingstoke: Palgrave, 2016), pp. 76–97 (describing firms in Guangzhou).

It supplanted both direct administration of labour in the planned economy, and the near–*laissez faire* that prevailed in the non-state sector in the early period of liberalisation, with sharply divergent consequences for workers in the two economies. In the state sector, the Labour Law's embrace of labour contracts formalised the demise of the *danwei* system and the demotion of workers from 'masters' of the enterprise to mere employees – a drastic decline in status and security. But for migrant factory workers in the growing non-state sector, the Labour Law was a major step toward better labour standards. China's embrace of regulated labour markets represented a convergence, not only between China's own two economies, but also between China and the world's advanced market economies.[12] Thereafter China proceeded along a fairly well-trodden path towards higher minimum labour standards, and better procedures for enforcing standards and adjudicating employment disputes. The 2007 enactment of the Labour Contract Law was another big step along that path, though its higher formal labour standards might have exacerbated the severe 'enforcement gap' that continues to fuel unrest.[13]

Let us return to the opening question with this background under our belts: What, if anything, is 'socialist' about China's now mostly unified labour law regime and the treatment of labour in the 'socialist market economy'? It is not the use of centralised planning in place of market ordering; the former has decreased drastically since the pre-reform era.[14] Nor is it (for most workers) state ownership of the employing enterprise. Could it be a generally pro-worker labour regime? Certainly not in the early years of liberalisation, which fostered egregious exploitation of workers in the new export-oriented factories. One might argue that the legislative enactments in 1994 and especially 2007 represented a 'socialist' turn towards more protective labour laws and higher labour standards. But that shift brought China closer to, not further away from, the labour

---

[12] Mary E. Gallagher and Baohua Dong, 'Legislating Harmony: Labour Law Reform in Contemporary China', in Sarosh Kuruvilla, Ching Kwan Lee and Mary E. Gallagher (eds.), *From Iron Rice Bowl to Informalization: Markets, Workers, and the State in a Changing China* (Ithaca, NY: ILR Press, 2011).

[13] Mary E. Gallagher, *Authoritarian Legality: Law, Workers, and the State in Contemporary China* (Cambridge: Cambridge University Press, 2017).

[14] However, as Barry Naughton notes, state involvement in the economy today is not insignificant: 'The government in China has much more influence over the economy than in virtually any other middle-income or developed economy. State firms and state banks remain prominent. Government five-year plans command attention, both domestically and internationally.' Barry Naughton, 'Is China Socialist?', 4.

law regimes of the developed market economies of the West, which all regulate work hours, minimum wages, health and safety, discrimination and so on. In that respect, China's 'socialist market economy' looks more and more like modern regulatory capitalism.[15]

In the meantime, China's economy has grown from one of the world's poorest to one of its most powerful, and from one of its most egalitarian to one of its most unequal.[16] A recent study found that the richest 1 per cent of households own one-third of the country's wealth, while the poorest 25 per cent of households own just 1 per cent of total wealth.[17] It is worth asking whether modern China is best understood as 'post-socialist' in its labour policies (as many informed commentators now describe it).[18] First, however, we must examine two dimensions of continuity between China's socialist past and its market-infused present.

10.3   Two Leninist Legacies: The ACFTU and the SWRCs

Not everything about China's socialist past has been thrown over in the rush to embrace markets and pursue economic growth. The first 'general principle' of its Constitution provides that China is 'a socialist state under the people's democratic dictatorship led by the working class and based on the alliance of workers and peasants'. Official rhetoric, including the Constitution, continues to invoke the leadership of the Communist Party of China (CCP) and the guidance of Marxism–Leninism and Mao Zedong Thought (as well as 'Deng Xiaoping Theory and the important thought of Three Represents').[19] But, when it comes to institutions that affect the working lives of its citizens, there are two important manifestations of continuity with the Maoist era: first and foremost, the ACFTU,

---

[15] Chinese leaders maintain that China is not capitalist but is in the primary stage of socialism. Alan R. Kluver, *Legitimating the Chinese Economic Reforms: A Rhetoric of Myth and Orthodoxy* (Albany, NY: State University of New York Press, 1996), pp. 71–72.

[16] Approximately 260 million rural residents were living in poverty at the start of the 1990s, compared to only 56 million by 2015. Barry Naughton, 'Is China Socialist?', 16.

[17] Gabriel Wildau and Tom Mitchell, 'China Income Inequality among World's Worst', *Financial Times*, 14 January 2016, available at www.ft.com/content/3c521faa-baa6-11e5-a7cc-280dfe875e28 (noting China's Gini coefficient for income by 2012 was 0.49, which the World Bank considers an indicator of severe income inequality).

[18] See, e.g., Friedman, *Insurgency Trap*; Hurst, *The Chinese Worker after Socialism*; Pun Ngai, *Migrant Labour in China: Post-Socialist Transformations* (Malden, MA: Polity, 2016).

[19] 'Preamble', 宪法 [Constitution].

which embodies the Party's official leadership of the working classes; and, to a far lesser degree, SWRCs, which embody the constitutional commitment to 'democratic management'.[20] Let us turn now to them.

10.3.1   The ACFTU and Its Official Monopoly on Collective Representation of Workers

The ACFTU, through its many branches and chapters, is not only the official representative of China's workers in collective labour relations, it is China's only lawful trade union – if it is a trade union at all. For the ACFTU is above all a branch of the Party. Its hierarchy mirrors the organisation of the Party, and its officials are appointed by, and answerable to, the corresponding party branch. Party control of the ACFTU operates horizontally, from the national CCP to the national ACFTU, from provincial party organisations to provincial ACFTU chapters, and so on down to the local level; that horizontal control dominates vertical control from higher to lower levels of the ACFTU.[21] In that very concrete sense, the ACFTU is an arm of the Party, not a representative of the workers.

The enterprise trade union chapters, or 'grassroots unions', have a rather different character. Reflecting in part their origins in the planned economy, in which managers were Party officials, the enterprise trade unions have been almost uniformly dominated by management.[22] That is so despite a long-standing formal mandate that trade union officers within the enterprise, unlike those outside the enterprise, are supposed to

---

[20] This commitment first appeared in the post-Mao 1982 Constitution. But Deng Xiaoping, in his 1980 speech calling for the institutionalisation of the SWRCs noted, that this had been 'decided long ago'. Deng Xiaoping, Speech on 18 August 1980, from 'Selected Works of Deng Xiaoping: Modern Day Contributions to Marxist–Leninist Theory', available at https://dengxiaopingworks.wordpress.com/2013/02/25/on-the-reform-of-the-system-of-party-and-state-leadership/.

[21] Lee, *Against the Law*, pp. 57–59. Strictly speaking, the provincial and local branches of the ACFTU are not 'All-China' but are instead regionally identified; for example, the Guangdong Federation of Trade Unions. But for the sake of readability, we refer to them as ACFTU or ACFTU branches.

[22] Yujuan Zhai, 'Thoughts on the Labour Side of China's Collective Consultation', paper presented at Labour Relations Conference, Renmin University (2011); Stanley Lubman, 'China Real Time Report: The New Challenge of the Strikes Won't Go Away', Wall Street Journal, 14 July 2010.

be elected by worker-members. In practice, management has typically appointed one of its own, usually a high-level manager, to lead the enterprise union.[23]

Between management domination at the enterprise level and Party domination at higher levels, it is not surprising that workers typically describe the official trade unions as 'useless' in their own struggles for better wages and working conditions. Party domination remains unquestionable, but management domination of the enterprise unions has come under more pressure as labour unrest has grown. In particular, there have been numerous calls for, and some moves towards, more democratic elections of enterprise trade union officers by workers. But those moves have been limited, halting and fragile. As things stand, trade union representatives are rarely electorally accountable to workers at the lowest level, and never above that level.[24]

Although it may be 'useless' to workers in their labour disputes, the ACFTU and its official monopoly on collective worker representation casts a very heavy shadow over any other organisations that would seek to represent workers, including non-governmental organisations (NGOs) that advocate for individual workers and their rights. By their very existence, such organisations seem to challenge the dogma that the Party itself, through its labour arm the ACFTU, is the true voice of the workers. Their treatment is in some ways illustrative of the tenuous standing of 'civil society' in China.

The ACFTU is one of the stronger surviving components of what once was a comprehensive system of Party control of collective social activity, through which whole segments of the population – women, youth, workers – were each represented through a single hierarchically organised official channel under the control of the CCP.[25] Each of these national 'mass organisations' stood atop a pyramid of provincial and local branches, and was charged with the dual mission of conveying the

---

[23] Simon Clarke, Chang-Hee Lee and Qi Li, 'Collective Consultation and Industrial Relations in China' (2004) 42 *British Journal of Industrial Relations* 235.

[24] Cynthia Estlund, *A New Deal for China's Workers?* (Cambridge, MA: Harvard University Press, 2017), pp. 149–173; Cynthia Estlund and Seth Gurgel, 'Will Labour Unrest Lead to More Democratic Trade Unions in China?', in Blanpain, Liukkunen and Chen (eds.), *China and ILO Fundamental Principles and Rights at Work*.

[25] Anita Chan, 'China's Trade Unions in Corporatist Transition', in Jonathan Unger (ed.), *Associations and the Chinese State: Contested Spaces* (Armonk, NY: M.E. Sharpe, 2008), pp. 69–85.

interests of the masses up to party leaders and conveying the 'party line' down to the masses. While that Leninist 'transmission belt' system has been loosened considerably in many domains of civil society since the Maoist era, it continues to constrain the legal and political space for independent social organisations.[26]

Labour groups occupy a distinct zone of China's civil society land-scape, owing to both ideology and history: Official Communist ideology exalts workers and their interests, but it still condemns their collective representation outside of official channels. In view of the history of independent labour movements across the world, the regime regards organisations of workers as politically threatening, even if they avoid any overt challenge to party rule or the ACFTU's monopoly. Groups and individuals that are found to be organising across enterprise boundaries, or in multiple enterprises, still court prosecution or detention.[27] Even organisations that steer clear of organising across workplaces, and con-fine themselves to representation of workers in their individual rights claims, are closely watched. Under the dual registration system in place for most NGOs, labour groups must secure a party-state sponsor (such as a local branch of the ACFTU or justice bureau) in order to register as a civic organisation. But few can do so. Many labour NGOs register as business entities – that requires no official sponsor, but it also affords no protection against official harassment, and may be seen as an evasion of the social management system.[28] The level of enforcement of the regis-tration requirement for labour NGOs varies over time and across regions, but enforcement, as well as harassment of non-registered labour NGOs, has intensified in recent years.[29] And since 2014, several NGO-based

---

[26] See generally, Karla W. Simon, *Civil Society in China: The Legal Framework from Ancient Times to the 'New Reform Era'* (Oxford: Oxford University Press, 2013).

[27] See, e.g., 'A letter to the People's Daily on China Labour Bulletin's work with labour activists in China', *China Labour Bulletin*, 12 January 2016, available at www.clb.org .hk/en/content/letter-people's-daily-china-labour-bulletin's-work-labour-activists-china (describing the organising activities of Zeng Feiyang, who along with several former colleagues was detained in December 2015 and later criminally prosecuted).

[28] Simon, *Civil Society in China*. It also means that any revenues are taxable, which can lead to both financial and legal difficulties.

[29] Labour NGOs in Beijing were 'reminded' in 2009 of their obligation to register. In 2010 and 2011, those in Guangzhou were invited to meet with local ACFTU officials, who touted the advantages of formal affiliation but did not demand it. In Shanghai, sources indicate that no independent labour NGOs have managed to operate for any significant period of time.

labour activists – especially those involved with labour protests or strikes – have suffered arrest, detention or other forms of official pressure and harassment.[30]

The ACFTU's official monopoly on collective worker representation, and the Party's control of the ACFTU (subject to management domination within the enterprise), begin to capture a dimension of China's labour law system that sharply differentiates it from those of 'regulatory capitalism' – the continuing insistence on monopolistic Party control of organised labour. That insistence stands in defiance of international labour law's commitment to the freedom of association,[31] and in ironic contrast to China's more liberal treatment of 'organised capital'.

In China's planned economy, the Party administered both capital and labour through managers and union officers, all party cadres. (By contrast, in the West, both unions and corporations are relatively autonomous, though regulated to varying degrees.) 'Reform and opening' entailed a loosening of control over 'organised capital', which is now *regulated* but not directly administered by the state. Capital and capitalists are comparatively free to associate. Individuals may aggregate their capital by incorporating. China also has over 70,000 trade associations, or groups of businesses, and has called for them to sever their government connections.[32] Under reforms announced in 2013, trade associations will be subject to a streamlined registration process, with no need for an official sponsor.[33] Yet organised labour is still subject to direct party-state control through the ACFTU.

China has managed to reconcile its self-proclaimed socialist commitments with private ownership of much of the means of production,

---

[30] *See* Eli Friedman, Aaron Halegua and Jerome A. Cohen, 'Cruel Irony: China's Communists Are Stamping Out Labour Activism', *Washington Post*, 3 January 2016.

[31] International Labour Organisation, Committee on Freedom of Association, Case No. 2031 (China), Report No. 321 ¶ 165 (June 2000) (noting that provisions of China's Trade Union Act 'resulted in the imposition of a trade union monopoly and that the requirement that grass-roots organisations be controlled by higher-level trade unions and that their constitutions should be established by the National Congress of Trade Union Members constituted major constraints on the right of unions to establish their own constitutions, organise their activities and formulate programmes' and therefore 'were contrary to the fundamental principles of freedom of association'.)

[32] Nectar Gan, 'Beijing to cut its ties to trade associations', *South China Morning Post*, 9 July 2015, available at www.scmp.com/news/china/article/1835512/beijing-cut-its-ties-trade-associations.

[33] Article 48, Decision of the Central Committee of the Communist Party of China on Some Major Issues Concerning Comprehensively Deepening the Reform, adopted 12 November 2013, English translation online at www.china.org.cn/china/third_plenary_session/2014-01/16/content_31212602.htm.

substantial entrepreneurial autonomy for capital and Party membership for capitalist owners. China has cultivated the loyalty of the domestic capital-owning class, and party-state officials have acquired large private stakes in China's business enterprises.[34] The intertwined membership and interests of business and Party elites have enriched both, and have helped to defuse challenges to Party rule from the 'bourgeoisie'. But workers have not been sharing in the feast. The powers that be in China fear that, if workers were permitted to organise themselves, they would threaten the stability of the political-economic status quo. That fear virtually rules out loosening of Party control of the official trade unions and casts a heavy shadow over any form of collective labour activity outside that structure.

The official party-state monopoly on representation of 'organised labour', and the commitment to both suppressing and pre-empting independent labour organising outside that monopoly, is a genuinely distinctive feature of China's labour law regime – one that holds true across state and non-state sectors alike, and that distinguishes it from 'regulatory capitalism' in the democratic market economies. We do not mean to say that this feature is unique to China; other authoritarian regimes have sought to maintain an official monopoly on worker organising.[35] Nor is it clear that this feature of China's labour law regime makes it 'socialist', a point to which we will return in the conclusion. But it is clear that China's distinctive posture towards organised labour and worker mobilisation shapes several dimensions of China's labour law regime, and especially its approach to resolving labour disputes. Before returning to this point, let us briefly take note of another distinctive feature of China's labour law regime: the commitment, at least in principle, to 'democratic management' of enterprises through direct worker participation.

10.3.2   The SWRCs and Democratic Management

The notion that workers should have a meaningful role in the governance of the enterprises in which they work has good socialist credentials.[36] But it has been embraced in various forms across much of the world, not just

---

[34] Bruce J. Dickson, *Red Capitalists in China: The Party, Private Entrepreneurs, and Prospects for Political Change* (Cambridge: Cambridge University Press, 2003).

[35] See, e.g., Angie Tran, 'The Third Sleeve: Emerging Labour Newspapers and the Response of the Labour Unions and the State to Workers' Resistance in Vietnam' (2007) 32 *Labour Studies Journal* 257.

[36] Karl Marx and Friedrich Engels, *The Communist Manifesto* (Chicago, IL: Charles H. Kerr, 1888); John E. Elliott, 'Karl Marx: Founding Father of Workers' Self-Governance?' (1987) 8 *Economic and Industrial Democracy* 293.

in countries that identify as 'socialist'. At one end of the spectrum, US labour law fosters collective bargaining through independent unions, but only if a union gains majority support over (lawful) employer opposition. Even then, employers are required to bargain only over a limited range of issues, and workers' ability to exact concessions depends on their collective market power within the 'free play of economic forces'. In Germany, by contrast, in addition to sectoral collective bargaining through independent unions over economic issues, workers are entitled, upon a modest showing of interest, to participate in enterprise governance through elected works councils. Works councils have legally prescribed rights of 'co-determination', or consultation, on a wide range of issues, though their actual power varies greatly across enterprises.

One might judge a system of worker participation to be more 'socialist' the more it is a matter of right (versus voluntarist struggle), and the wider the range of governance issues within its competence. By that yardstick, China's system of 'democratic management' is modestly socialist on paper, though very weak in its actual operation.

To begin with, China's current Constitution prescribes 'democratic management' in state and 'collective' enterprises (though not clearly in foreign or private enterprises).[37] The primary institutional embodiment of that principle is the SWRCs,[38] which (more than the trade union chapters) were meant to allow workers to exercise their authority as 'masters of the enterprise'. Ironically, these 'socialist' institutions were institutionalised within the SOEs only in the waning years of the planned economy under Deng.[39]

As of 1986, regulations called for the SWRCs to be directly elected, with leading cadres or managers making up no more than 20 per cent, and with a 'suitable' proportion of women and younger workers.[40] Nominally, these bodies had the power to supervise and even replace top

---

[37] Articles 16–17, 'General Principles', 宪法 [Constitution], available at www.npc.gov.cn/englishnpc/Constitution/2007-11/15/content_1372963.htm.

[38] The Chinese term (职工代表大会) has several translations. 'Staff and Workers' Representative Congress,' though unwieldy, captures the inclusion of all employees of an enterprise, including workers, technicians, management and party cadres.

[39] Cynthia Estlund, 'Will Workers Have a Voice in China's 'Socialist Market Economy'? The Curious Revival of the Workers Congress System' (2015) 36 *Comparative Labour Law and Policy Journal* 69; Estlund, *A New Deal for China's Workers?*, pp. 176–177.

[40] Articles 10 and 12, 全民所有制工业企业职工代表大会条例 [Regulation on State-Owned Enterprise SWRCs], 15 September 1986, effective 1 October 1986, available at www.34law.com/lawfg/law/6/1189/law_250917172417.shtml.

managers, though this power was rarely exercised. In both their composition and their selection procedures, the SWRCs were far more representative of the workforce than the trade union. But they were effectively subordinate to the trade union, which convened the SWRCs' infrequent meetings and exercised their powers in between those meetings. In the 1980s and 1990s, some SWRCs were active and influential, and their meetings 'protracted and elaborate'; but most served as little more than a 'rubber stamp' for management.[41]

As the SOEs were 'corporatised' and profit-driven managers took the helm, whatever power the SWRCs had quickly faded.[42] Institutions of democratic management came to be seen, on one account, as 'anachronistic relics of a bygone era, not suited for a modern corporate environment'.[43] Two 1994 laws, both covering state and non-state enterprises alike, set out the new arrangements: the Company Law reassigned most of the SWRCs' formal powers to a corporate board of directors and supervisory committee, and reduced the notion of 'democratic management' to a vague recommendation of consultation.[44] The Labour Law clarified what little was left: new workplace rules and some other employment-related matters had to be 'submitted to the [SWRCs] *or all the employees* for discussion and adoption'.[45] But the highlighted

---

[41] Malcolm Warner, *Changing Workplace Relations in the Chinese Economy* (London: Macmillan, 2000), pp. 27–28. *See also* Jackie Sheehan, *Chinese Workers: A New History* (New York, NY: Routledge, 1999), p. 201.

[42] Joel Andreas, 'Losing Membership Rights: The Impact of Eliminating Permanent Job Tenure on Power Relations in Chinese Factories', paper presented at the American Sociological Association Annual Meeting, New York, NY, 11 August 2013, p. 8; Cooney, Biddulph and Zhu, *Law and Fair Work in China*, pp. 68–69.

[43] Andreas, 'Losing Membership Rights', p. 19.

[44] Article 38, 中国人民共和国公司法 [Company Law of the People's Republic of China] (promulgated by the National People's Congress, 29 December 1993, effective 1 July 1994) [hereinafter Company Law], available at www.lawinfochina.com (reassigning to shareholders the function of supervising managers and their appointment and dismissal); article 55 (providing that workers' opinions *should* be solicited on matters tied to their interests, and members of the trade union or SWRC should be invited to attend relevant meetings as *non-voting delegates*) (emphasis added); article 63 (SOE's board of directors 'should have' a democratically elected SWRC member) (emphasis added). See also, Ronald C. Brown, *Understanding Labour and Employment Law in China* (Cambridge: Cambridge University Press, 2009), p. 46 (citing article 16 of the Company Law).

[45] Article 33, 中国人民共和国劳动法 [Labour Law of People's Republic of China] (promulgated by the Standing Committee of the National People's Congress, 5 July 1994, effective 1 January 1994), available at www.lawinfochina.com.

phrase, which is repeated in the Labour Contract Law of 2008,[46] left it ambiguous whether SWRCs had to be established at all in the non-state sector; and in most private and foreign-invested enterprises, SWRCs existed on paper only, if at all.[47]

In recent years, there have been tentative signs of a modest revival of the SWRCs.[48] Policy makers, including the national ACFTU, have begun to press for the establishment of SWRCs in all enterprises, and a few courts have given some teeth to the Labour Contract Law's requirement that workplace rules be reviewed by the SWRC (by invalidating dismissals based on rules that have not been submitted).[49] It remains to be seen whether these modest moves will do anything to invigorate the SWRCs as vehicles of worker participation in workplace governance. If that were to happen, the SWRCs could become a mechanism for the prevention or early resolution of workplace disputes before they escalate into open conflict. Robust SWRCs would also become key indicators of the 'socialist' character of China's labour laws. But for now, the feeble and ineffectual SWRCs suggest instead that China's leaders pay lip service to a tenet of socialism while empowering capital and its appointed managers to govern enterprises as they choose, within external regulatory constraints but without meaningful internal participatory mechanisms.

But let us return to the crucial question of how labour disputes are resolved in China today. For while the SWRCs make barely a cameo appearance, and the ACFTU and its enterprise chapters are marginal participants, the regime's commitment to avoiding any rival form of worker representation plays a decisive role in these dramas.

10.4   The Resolution of Labour Disputes, Formal and Informal

The term 'labour dispute' can be confusing, for it may refer to either formal legal complaints or strikes and street protests. It may also refer to

---

[46] Articles 4 and 51, 中国人民共和国劳动合同法 [Labour Contract Law of the People's Republic of China] (promulgated by the Standing Committee of the National People's Congress, 29 June 2007, effective 1 January 2008), available at www.lawinfochina.com.

[47] Furthermore, some lawyers advised firms that, in the absence of an SWRC, the duty to consult with 'all the employees' could be fulfilled by posting new rules in the workplace or in an employee manual; and, an individual's continued employment at the firm could be taken as consent to those rules. See Estlund, A New Deal for China's Workers?, pp. 174–194.

[48] Estlund, 'Will Workers Have a Voice in China's "Socialist Market Economy"?'; Estlund, A New Deal for China's Workers?, pp. 174–194.

[49] Estlund, 'Will Workers Have a Voice in China's "Socialist Market Economy"?'.

either 'rights disputes' (based on claims that employers have broken the law or contractual promises) or 'interest disputes' (based on workers' demands for more than they are currently entitled to by law or contract). The distinction is important because, although both types of disputes might lead to disorderly protests, their *orderly* resolution calls for rather different institutions. China has done little to institutionalise the resolution of interest disputes, as we will see later in the Chapter; however, it has invested heavily in the resolution of rights disputes through formal legal channels. All the while, official concerns over stability and fears about the collective mobilisation of workers both shape and constrain the mechanisms for handling both rights and interest disputes.

10.4.1   Averting Unrest by Resolving Rights Disputes

The regime is well aware that unresolved rights disputes can trigger strikes and mass protest incidents. In fact, most strikes appear to stem from disputes over unpaid wages, a quintessential rights dispute. That has been a major motivation behind China's efforts to improve channels for resolving legal disputes. On the surface, China's official system for handling workers' rights disputes largely resembles those of other market economies. This consists of various bodies that seek to resolve disputes through mediation and, when the parties cannot agree upon a resolution, labour dispute arbitration committees (LDACs) and courts. Obviously, the government far prefers workers to pursue their claims in the courtroom versus the street.[50] There is nothing surprising or nefarious in that – all law-based societies (and almost all of their citizens) prefer orderly dispute resolution procedures to boisterous agitation. What distinguishes China from other regulated market economies is the overriding preoccupation with squelching any form of collective worker activity outside of official party-state channels, a preoccupation that shapes and limits the efficacy of official dispute resolution procedures.

One manifestation of this preoccupation is China's enormous emphasis on mediating labour disputes. China has a long tradition of relying on mediation to resolve conflicts.[51] In the early reform era, virtually all civil disputes were handled through mediation of some form. With China continually emphasising the need to develop its legal system and rule

---

[50] Yang Su and Xin He, 'Street as Courtroom: State Accommodation of Labour Protest in South China' (2010) 44 *Law & Society Review* 157.

[51] Jerome A. Cohen, 'Chinese Mediation on the Eve of Modernization' (1966) 54 *California Law Review* 1201.

the country by law, and disputants more willing to use the courts, fewer cases were mediated year upon year in the 1990s.[52] However, for at least the last decade, China has sought to re-establish mediation as the predominant means of dispute resolution through what it calls 'grand mediation'.[53] Mediation services are now offered by a wide variety of institutions, including mediation committees within enterprises, community organisations, local justice bureaus, legal aid offices and trade union offices. LDACs and courts have their own mediation windows, too.

Why this huge investment in mediation? In part, it aims simply to relieve the burden on the LDACs and courts. More importantly, however, mediation is viewed as better promoting order and stability.[54] It allows disputes to be nipped in the bud – resolved early and quickly, before they escalate. Moreover, parties are more likely to accept and implement a mediated solution to which they voluntarily consented. By contrast, a worker who is unsatisfied by an arbitration or court decision, or is unable to enforce it, may complain, petition or protest to the local government. In fact, recognising that mediation can promote stability in this way, in 2010, the central government made 'preventing social instability through proper mediation' a metric that could be used to veto the promotion of a local official.[55]

Although mediation is formally voluntary under the law, it has sometimes veered towards compulsion. Chinese mediators are encouraged to proactively identify and intervene in conflicts before the parties seek out their services, or even before any complaint is filed. Some jurisdictions in China make participating in mediation a prerequisite to commencing litigation. Even after a case is filed, the arbitrator or judge will (again) attempt mediation. The city of Qingdao has provided that arbitration cases are to be mediated four times: prior to filing, prior to the hearing, during the hearing and before the award is issued.[56]

---

[52] Aaron Halegua, 'Reforming the People's Mediation System in Urban China' (2005) 35(3) *Hong Kong Law Journal* 715.

[53] Wenjia Zhuang and Feng Chen, "Mediate First": The Revival of Mediation in Labour Dispute Resolution in China' (June 2015) 222 *China Quarterly* 380–402.

[54] Carl Minzner, 'China's Turn Against Law' (2011) 59 *American Journal of Comparative Law*, 935, 957–959.

[55] Zhuang and Chen, "Mediate First", 388.

[56] 法院首次联合仲裁发布劳动人事争议处理白皮书 [Arbitration and Court Jointly Issue White Paper on Handling Labour Disputes for the First Time], 27 January 2016, available at www.qdxin.cn/qingdao/2016/62071.html.

The emphasis on mediation underscores that the fundamental object-ive of the formal dispute resolution system is just that – dispute reso-lution. The goal is to settle the conflict so that stability is maintained. Concerns over fairness, justice or legality are often secondary. In fact, mediation gives the mediator, arbitrator or judge leeway to achieve a resolution distinct from what the law requires. Even efficiency is a secondary consideration. Authorities may choose to mediate a dispute multiple times, instead of simply issuing an arbitration award that runs the risk of leaving a party dissatisfied or upset.

When mediation cannot resolve the dispute, or appears to be futile, the government seeks to steer parties into the LDACs and courts – and off the streets. To this end, China has gone to great lengths to make these forums more accessible. For instance, in 2007, new legislation lengthened the statute of limitations for labour disputes and eliminated or greatly reduced filing fees. In one case, in response to 300 workers agitating for back wages, the local government actually brought the courtroom to the workers – dispatching judges to the street to accept the case.[57] In a more recent dispute, when workers were camping outside the labour bureau to protest unpaid wages, the local court replied to the workers' social media post with its own message asking them to put trust in the legal system.[58] Another aspect of the effort to draw workers from agitation into litiga-tion is offering them a free lawyer through an ever-expanding legal aid program, discussed later in this Chapter.

However, alongside these 'carrots', or efforts to make litigation more accessible and attractive, China has also used 'sticks' against protesters who disrupt social order. In a 2016 case, local authorities criminally prosecuted eight workers who allegedly blocked traffic and attacked police while protesting their unpaid wages, and then conducted a public sentencing rally to deter such actions by other aggrieved workers.[59] And numerous individuals who were deemed to have instigated workers to

---

[57] Yang Su and Xin He, 'Street as Courtroom', 164.

[58] 'Anhui Workers Left Out in Cold Seeking Government Help', *China Labour Bulletin*, 7 October 2016, available at www.clb.org.hk/content/construction-workers-become-des perate-run-golden-week-holiday.

[59] Chun Han Wong, 'Chinese City Publicly Shames Migrant Workers Who Protested Unpaid Wages', *Wall Street Journal*, 18 March 2016, available at http://blogs.wsj .com/chinarealtime/2016/03/18/chinese-city-publicly-shames-migrant-workers-who-pro tested-unpaid-wages/.

protest – even if the workers had legitimate legal claims – have been criminally prosecuted in recent years.[60]

In the meantime, the LDACs and courts have made considerable progress in formalising procedures and raising the competency of arbitrators and judges over the past decade. Nonetheless, these bodies are still beholden to the Party and its goals. In the view of the authorities, litigation – like mediation – serves the instrumental purpose of preserving stability. This is vividly borne out in how these institutions treat collective disputes. The authorities are not satisfied simply with channelling group claims into litigation instead of agitation. They still worry that litigation itself can be a mobilising experience and are disturbed by the prospect of a group of aggrieved individuals united under the leadership of a lawyer or other advocate. Therefore, courts will often break down large collective cases into multiple, smaller cases or even individual ones.[61]

Moreover, it is crucial to recall that cases are not decided by independent, neutral arbiters. Arbitrators and judges are essentially civil servants, beholden to the local government and supervised by the local Party politics and law committee (the Party institution that oversees domestic security operations), which may dictate the outcome in a given case. Sometimes this means protecting SOEs or businesses with close connections to the government; but political interference may also sometimes benefit workers. For example, in a case involving 500 workers alleging wage arrears, two days after the arbitration hearing, the municipal-level politics and law committee held a meeting to discuss how to 'properly handle' the case and 'reached a consensus'. Four days later, the arbitrators issued an award for plaintiffs in the amount of 5.8 million RMB (over US $850,000).[62]

---

[60] One worker, Wu Guijun, was detained for 100 days after leading workers in demanding severance from a relocating factory. Charges were later dropped, and he was paid compensation for his wrongful detention. 'Worker Wu Guijun won his appeal and received compensation for wrongful detention', Hong Kong Confederation of Trade Unions, available at http://en.hkctu.org.hk/mainland-china/position-and-analysis/after-more-than-one-year-of-wrongful-detention-worker-wu-guijun-won-his-app.

[61] Fu Hualing, 'Human Rights Lawyering in Chinese Courtrooms' (2014) 2 *Chinese Journal of Comparative Law* 270, 281 ('There is no class action in practice, and workers' collective grievances are broken down into individual cases when they are accepted by courts.'); Feng Chen and Xin Xu, '"Active Judiciary": Judicial Dismantling of Workers' Collective Action in China' (January 2012) 67 *China Journal* 87 (same).

[62] Yang Shuxin and Lin Xida, '20年一遇特大群体性劳资纠纷广州法援15天快速应急成功化解' ['Encountering a collective labour dispute after 20 years, Guangzhou legal aid speedily resolves the matter in 15 days'], Guangzhou Legal Aid Bureau, 4 February 2016, available at www.gzsfj.gov.cn/webInfoPublicity/newsDetail/8272.html.

In its effort to ensure that litigation remains a means for neutralising conflicts, not escalating them, China has also tightened controls over who may represent workers and how they may do so. One element of this strategy was the virtual elimination of 'citizen agents' or 'barefoot lawyers'.[63] In China, as elsewhere, workers are often unable to afford the fees charged by licensed attorneys. One study found that 40 per cent of workers who make it to court have no legal representation.[64] Some turned to 'barefoot lawyers' – individuals without any formal legal training or licence, but with a modicum of experience and expertise, who charge lower fees than lawyers to provide representation. In some sense, they helped to bring law to the masses, expanding access to litigation for workers. But these barefoot lawyers sometimes encouraged workers to use extra-legal methods in conjunction with their lawsuit to push their demands, such as petitioning the government or protesting outside its offices – clearly inconsistent with the authorities' stability maintenance program. Not beholden to any bar association or government licensing authority, barefoot lawyers also felt more free to resist mediation efforts by officials, arbitrators and judges, and to pursue collective cases and administrative lawsuits against the government. Perhaps most troubling to the authorities was that staff members of independent labour NGOs, particularly in Guangdong, were acting as barefoot lawyers to represent workers in litigation. The government was already anxious about these groups' potential for mobilising workers outside the official representation system; eliminating their ability to provide legal aid was another way to weaken them.[65]

The government has sought to fill the gap in legal representation for workers through its own legal aid program. When a case is approved for legal aid, justice bureau officials either represent the party themselves or assign the case to a private lawyer, who receives a small stipend for the

---

[63] The term 'citizen agent' (公民代理人) is derived from the term actually used in the Civil Procedure Law and Administrative Procedure Law. For a discussion of how these acts were amended to limit the role of citizen agents in the legal system, see Aaron Halegua, 'China's Restrictions on Barefoot Lawyers could Backfire, Leading to More Unrest', *South China Morning Post,* 30 March 2015, A13.

[64] Aaron Halegua, 'Who Will Represent China's Workers? Lawyers, Legal Aid, and the Enforcement of Labour Rights', U.S.–Asia Law Institute, NYU School of Law, October 2016, available at https://usali.org/chinaworkers/.

[65] Investigative Report of Guangdong Province on the Question of 'Professional Citizen Legal Agents' (issued by the Guangdong Provincial Committee on Politics and Law of the Chinese Communist Party, January 2009), translated version available through China Labour News Translations (explaining the nexus between legal representation by citizen agents and the growth of labour NGOs as perceived by the Guangdong authorities).

work. Previously, many localities refused legal aid to individuals from other provinces and required all legal aid applicants to produce documentation of financial need. But with frustrated migrant workers increasingly taking their rights disputes to the street – petitioning or protesting the government, and even threatening suicide and self-immolation – the central government instructed local governments in 2006 that any migrant worker with a wage arrears or work injury claim should be deemed eligible for a free lawyer, and that legal aid budgets should be increased accordingly. This was part of an effort to steer these disputants into the formal legal system and occurred around the same time that arbitration and court filing fees for labour cases were being eliminated. Results were dramatic: in 2005, under 76,000 migrant workers received legal aid, but the number nearly doubled in 2006 and climbed to over 476,000 by 2014.[66] The ACFTU also has its own program for providing workers with free lawyers, and has reportedly done so in 250,000 cases from 2011 to 2015.[67] This constitutes a not insignificant portion of the nearly 1.1 million labour disputes filed in arbitration and courts in 2014, a number that continues to climb.[68]

While expanding legal aid for poor workers is obviously a good thing, and most countries have a legal aid program, China's motivations for this expansion are somewhat distinct. The government grew the legal aid program in part because it sees licensed attorneys as safer and less likely to make a ruckus than barefoot lawyers or NGOs. Private lawyers and law firms are subject to rules issued by local bar associations (branches of the party-state) and rely upon the local justice bureau for their licences. For instance, they must notify the authorities when taking on a 'mass case' of ten or more people. The rules in some localities explicitly prohibit lawyers handling labour cases from provoking workers to protest, petition (*xinfang*) or otherwise disrupt social order, and require them to report the possibility of these acts occurring.[69] In effect, lawyers are viewed as part of the stability maintenance apparatus – obliged to inform the government

---

[66] Halegua, Who Will Represent China's Workers?, 23.

[67] Ibid., 30.

[68] Ibid., 14–15 (noting 374,000 court cases and 715,000 arbitration disputes in that year). The growth in labour dispute cases has been quite steady throughout the 2000's, except for a sharp spike immediately after the passage of the Labour Contract Law that subsequently levelled off.

[69] Articles 5 and 105, 广东省律师办理劳动争议案件操作指引 [Guangdong Province Operational Guidelines for Lawyers Handling Labour Disputes] (promulgated by Guangdong Lawyers' Association, 2014).

of potential unrest and to encourage their clients to accept the mediated resolution of the authorities. This is even clearer when the government is the one selecting and paying the lawyer, as it is in legal aid cases.

In sum, the government prefers to handle rights disputes through formal legal channels of mediation and litigation, and has taken measures – some helpful to workers, others less so – to encourage workers to select this path, instead of more socially disruptive means of addressing their grievances. The primary focus of these institutions is simply to get conflicts resolved; fairness or justice is far less important than avoiding collective mobilisation or disgruntled, protesting litigants. Moreover, litigation is attractive to the authorities because they can control nearly every aspect of the process – the parties, the advocates and the outcomes.

Yet things do not always go according to plan. Both individual workers and groups of workers sometimes choose to press their demands through a strike, slow-down or protest, instead of in the courtroom. Other workers may try litigation but then, frustrated with the process or dissatisfied with· the results, resort to extralegal means. We will turn shortly to the question of how the government addresses these rights disputes once they erupt into strikes or other public protest. But at that point, the distinction between rights disputes and interest disputes fades into the background as the authorities seek to quell unrest and maintain stability by whatever means possible. So, before turning to how the government reacts to strikes or protest incidents that have erupted, let us first look briefly at the other side of China's efforts to address labour unrest: preventing interest disputes through 'collective consultation' and collective contracts.

10.4.2   Collective Bargaining with Chinese Characteristics

China's leaders might have preferred to avoid the whole subject of interest disputes, collective bargaining and strikes, or at least to postpone it for a few more cycles of economic growth. They might have preferred instead to address workers' rising demands wholly by enacting higher minimum labour standards and expanding official channels for adjudicating 'rights claims'. But then came the Honda strikes. In May 2010, over 1,800 workers at the Nanhai Honda transmission factory in Foshan, China, went on strike. They demanded both higher wages and (later) the right to elect the leaders of the plant's official trade union. The strike stalled work in three downstream Honda assembly plants for nearly two weeks, and cost Honda up to 2.4 billion RMB (about US $350 million) a day. It was followed by strikes at another Honda component factory and several other foreign and domestic automakers.[70] In all, some twenty-five factories and many thousands of workers were affected by the strike wave.[71]

In the wake of those strikes, China's labour law establishment was gripped by the question of how to modernise China's collective labour relations system and, in particular, how to peacefully resolve 'interest disputes' between employers and workers who want more – more than they are getting and more than the law guarantees them. A conventional time-tested solution to this problem in industrial societies is collective bargaining between employers and workers' organisations, with the possibility of industrial conflict, and its risks and costs for both sides, driving the parties towards agreement. But in China, workers have no organisations of their own, and are not allowed to form such organisations; and industrial conflict occurs under a cloud of illegitimacy. Strikes obviously occur, and scholars debate whether they are technically legal or illegal. But clearly there is no 'right to strike' as Western labour cognoscenti know it.[72] In practice, the state may detain and prosecute strike leaders. And when employers prohibit strikes, and discipline or discharge workers who violate those rules, the courts generally back them up.[73] Moreover, far from leading or threatening strikes as leverage for getting a better deal for workers, the official unions are charged with avoiding or ending any work stoppage that disrupts production. When strikes do occur, they are invariably self-organised by workers outside of, and to some degree in conflict with, the trade union that supposedly represents them.

Even basic terminology underscores the Chinese authorities' aversion to industrial conflict. The official term for what is supposed to take place between workers and managers in determining wages and other matters is not 'collective bargaining' (jiti tanpan), but 'collective consultation' (jiti xieshang), which connotes a less combative and more consensus-based process, in keeping with the official aspiration to 'harmonious labour-management relations'.[74]

[70] Friedman, Insurgency Trap, pp. 140–156.
[71] Kevin Gray and Youngseok Jang, 'Labour Unrest in the Global Political Economy: The Case of China's 2010 Strike Wave' (2015) 20 New Political Economy 594.
[72] Kai Chang and Fang Lee Cooke, 'Legislating the Right to Strike in China: Historical Development and Prospects' (2015) 57 Journal of Industrial Relations 440 (discussing the legality of strikes under Chinese law over time).
[73] Tianyu Wang and Fang Lee Cooke, 'Striking the Balance in Industrial Relations in China? An Analysis of 308 Strike Cases (2008–2014)' (2016) 59 Journal of Industrial Relations 22.
[74] Estlund, A New Deal for China's Workers?, pp. 124, 147.

Given the bureaucratic nature of the trade unions and the aversion to industrial conflict, it may be unsurprising that 'collective consultation' in China entails a routinised and bureaucratic process of concluding collective agreements. Without engagement of workers or collective leverage on the labour side, the agreements were typically boilerplate, consisting largely of a restatement of those entitlements already guaranteed by the labour laws, along with a few minor additions, such as extra breaks for female workers or holiday celebrations.

In the wake of the 2010 Honda strikes, the ACFTU vowed to reform and rejuvenate the process for securing collective agreements; but the operational result was that local trade union organisations were enjoined to fill their quotas of signed agreements, still with little or no give-and-take and no input from the workers. The post-Honda arc of reform efforts was most dramatic in Guangdong itself. In 2010, provincial officials proposed a more realistic legal framework for collective bargaining that recognised a right to strike. But after much debate and several revisions, the final regulation issued in 2015 largely preserved the formalistic status quo.[75]

In the meantime, increases in legal minimum wages (which are set in China at the local level) have surely done more to address workers' economic demands than the denatured form of 'collective consultation'. The ongoing wave of minimum wage increases, together with the bureaucratic process of securing boilerplate collective agreements (which incorporated those wage increases), might be meant as a prophylactic response to labour unrest — an effort to pre-empt worker discontent over wage levels and perhaps head off some strikes. However, unlike collective bargaining as it is known and practised in the West, the wage increases and resulting collective agreements do not reflect the economic power that workers in any particular enterprise or industry can muster by threatening a strike.

Yet strikes have been critical in securing gains for workers in China. Anxiety about rising strike levels is helping to drive both minimum wage increases and the ACFTU's effort to expand the reach of collective contracts. And, as shown in the next section, when workers do strike, they are often able to achieve significant gains.[76] But there is still no effective

---

[75] Aaron Halegua, 'Strike a Balance', South China Morning Post, 26 February 2015, A15.

[76] Manfred Elfstrom and Sarosh Kuruvilla, 'The Changing Nature of Labour Unrest in China' (2014) 67 Industrial & Labour Relations Review 453, available at http://digital commons.ilr.cornell.edu/cgi/viewcontent.cgi?article=2014&context=articles.

mechanism, much less an officially sanctioned one, by which workers can deploy the *threat* of a strike as leverage to gain concessions (and perhaps avoid an actual strike). That requires labour organisations that represent workers and are willing and able to speak for workers and fight for them. Those do not exist in China.

10.4.3   Firefighting: Ending Strikes and Quelling Protest[77]

When formal mechanisms fail to prevent or resolve disputes, both rights and interest disputes often end up spilling into the streets. Many strikes arise out of a mix of complaints about unenforced minimum standards and demands above and beyond those standards. For strikes of any significant magnitude or duration, the authorities bring roughly the same toolbox and the same anxieties to the scene of worker protest incidents, whether they originate in demands for compliance with law, or for more than the law requires, or both.

The government's response to strikes has been ad hoc, highly interventionist and aimed above all at pacifying workers. The typical chronology is as follows: first, there is a strike, self-organised by workers outside any union structure; then, local officials swoop in to figure out what the workers want, and to try to extract enough concessions from management – sometimes including wage increases – to induce the workers to go back to work. So, far from sitting back while the parties exercise their economic muscle in an effort to reach an agreement, as may happen in some market economies, the government actively approaches disputants and seeks to mediate the dispute. This approach has been well described as a 'firefighting' strategy – the strike sets off an alarm bell and officials rush to the scene to try to put out the conflagration.[78] This work is often carried out by the 'stability maintenance' (*weiwen*) committees established by local governments, comprised of officials from multiple departments that step in to resolve disputes over land confiscation, property demolitions or any other collective

---

[77] This section draws heavily on Estlund, *A New Deal for China's Workers?*, pp. 123–148.

[78] Tim Pringle, 'Trade Union Renewal in China and Vietnam?', Working Paper, 26th International Labour Process Conference, 2006, available at http://web.warwick.ac.uk/fac/soc/complabstuds/russia/ngpa/Trade%20Union%20Renewal%20in%20China%20and%20Vietnam.doc.

unrest or 'mass incident'.[79] But the response to labour unrest – strikes in particular – has some distinct features.

The union often plays a key role in the 'firefighting', but less as the representative of the workers than as a mediator or go-between. Indeed, the neutral connotations of the term 'mediator' arguably overstate the weight of workers' interests in the union's equation, for traditionally the union has performed this function on behalf of managers. The Trade Union Law instructs the trade union, in the event of a slowdown or strike, to help the enterprise 'restore the normal order of production and other work as soon as possible'.[80] In the Honda strikes of 2010, far from seeking to empower or represent the workers, union officials were dispatched to persuade the workers to return to work, which resulted in violent confrontations with the workers.[81]

The local government and trade union use not only their mediating skills, but also a 'mix of cash, coercion and pledges of redress' to defuse worker unrest.[82] They often pressure employers to pay outstanding wages.[83] In the 2014 Yue Yuen strike – the largest in China's modern history, involving seven factories and as many as 40,000 workers – the employer was compelled to pay over 190 million RMB (US $31 million)

---

[79] Jonathan Benney, 'Weiwen at the Grassroots: China's Stability Maintenance Apparatus as a Means of Conflict Resolution' (2016) 25 *Journal of Contemporary China*, 389, 401 (the *weiwen* committee may include representatives from the labour department and trade union).

[80] Article 27, 中国人民共和国工会法 [Trade Union Law] (Amended 2001) provides as follows:

> [I]n case of work-stoppage or slow-down strike in an enterprise or institution, the trade union shall, on behalf of the workers and staff members, hold consultation with the enterprise or institution or the parties concerned, present the opinions and demands of the workers and staff members, and put forth proposals for solutions. With respect to the reasonable demands made by the workers and staff members, the enterprise or institution shall try to satisfy them. The trade union shall assist the enterprise or institution in properly dealing with the matter so as to help restore the normal order of production and other work as soon as possible.

[81] Chris King-Chi Chan and Elaine Sio-leng Hui, 'The Development of Collective Bargaining in China: From "Collective Bargaining by Riot" to "Party State-led Wage Bargaining"' (March 2014) 217 *China Quarterly*, 221, 228.

[82] Chun Han Wong and Mark Magnier, 'China Mixes Cash, Coercion to Ease Labour Unrest', Wall Street Journal, 15 March 2016.

[83] Benney, 'Weiwen at the Grassroots', 398.

in unpaid social insurance contributions.[84] In other cases, even without any rights violations in sight, the authorities might push management to grant wage increases, as they did at Honda. In smaller cases, if an employer is unable to come up with the money to resolve a matter, local authorities might 'buy stability', using their own funds to satisfy workers' demands.[85] The willingness to deploy state resources in this way demonstrates the importance that authorities attach to quelling labour unrest and any expressions of collective discontent.[86] Like China's litigation system, there is little evidence that the government necessarily strives to achieve the most just, fair or legally consistent outcome in defusing these collective disputes.[87] Similarly, such government actions are not driven by an ideological allegiance to the plight of the working class. Getting workers off the streets appears to be the paramount objective.[88]

Of course, China also uses a range of coercive tools, poorly constrained by the 'rule of law', in its 'firefighting' efforts. Even ordinary strikers may face arrest (though rarely). In 2014, for example, over seventy Walmart workers protesting inadequate severance payments were detained for a week, and eleven Guangdong security guards were convicted of 'disturbing public order' after a dispute with their employers.[89] But criminal sanctions are mainly deployed against strike leadership. The sheer availability of those coercive sanctions surely inhibits some potential leaders from stepping forward. And authorities have become more willing to resort to those sanctions since 2015, especially for activists who show up

---

[84] Liyan Qi, 'Yue Yuen Strike Is Estimated to Cost $60 Million', *Wall Street Journal,* 28 April 2014.

[85] Wong and Magnier, 'China Mixes Cash, Coercion to Ease Labour Unrest'; Yang Su and Xin He, 'Street as Courtroom', 168.

[86] Benney, 'Weiwen at the Grassroots', 398 (describing several cases that 'demonstrate the extent to which local governments are prepared to draw from "stability maintenance funds"' in order to prevent conflicts reaching courts or petitioning, and to prevent larger-scale mass incidents or long drawn-out public displays of dissent').

[87] In fact, Zhuang and Chen note that local officials often prefer mediation because it allows them to broker the result they want, which may be inconsistent with what the law dictates. Zhuang and Chen, 'Mediate First', 382 ('to serve the goal of stability maintenance as well as the preferences of local authorities, the state-directed mandatory mediation aims more at defusing conflicts than at having justice done.')

[88] Benney, 'Weiwen at the Grassroots', 392. See Shahla Ali, 'The Jurisprudence of Responsive Mediation: An Empirical Examination of Chinese People's Mediation in Action' (2013) 45 *Journal of Legal Pluralism & Unofficial Law* 227.

[89] Tom Mitchell and Demetri Sevastopulo, 'China Labour Activism: Crossing the Line', *Financial Times,* 7 May 2014; Tom Mitchell, 'China Crackdown on Labour Activism Bolstered by Court Ruling', *Financial Times,* 15 April 2014.

in multiple strikes across different enterprises. Even short of arrest and detention, other sanctions – cancelled leases and eviction, 'visits' from the police and the like – may keep activists off balance and on guard; and they may do so without provoking a heated backlash, either from workers or from the international community. All of these activities are merely one dimension of China's sprawling 'stability maintenance' effort, spending on which surpassed the defence budget as of 2011.[90]

The regime faces a real dilemma here: genuine grassroots leaders and organisations can be useful to the government and to employers in bringing an end to an industrial dispute; but they also increase the risk that strikes will spread from one factory to another, and that industrial activism will coalesce into something more politically consequential and dangerous. China's efforts to keep potential leaders off balance, on guard and scarce helps to keep strikes from spreading. But it also ensures that strikes are usually chaotic and disorganised, and impedes the emergence of a more lasting solution to industrial conflict. That is a trade-off that China's leaders appear willing to make for now, and perhaps for some time.

On the whole, this ad hoc mix of appeasement and targeted repression may do more to encourage than to prevent strikes. Workers have learnt that the best route to securing a wage hike is a strike that grabs the government's attention. Indeed, in a system lacking any orderly means for collective bargaining or resolving grievances, striking is often the only way to air disagreements, whether over interests or rights. That does not make for a viable industrial relations strategy. As a stability maintenance strategy, however, the 'firefighting' approach has its virtues. It allows authorities to keep most strikes quite short and confined to a single factory, and thus keep unrest from spreading or intensifying to a dangerous degree, without having to open the door to independent unions. After all, it is the escalation and spread of labour unrest that the government fears most.

10.5 Conclusion

This brief and partial overview of China's labour laws, policies and practices makes it clear that the goal of preventing independent mobilisation

---

[90] Edward Wong, 'Beijing Goes Quiet on Rise of Local Security Budgets', The New York Times, 6 March 2014, available at https://sinosphere.blogs.nytimes.com/2014/03/06/beijing-goes-quiet-on-rise-of-local-security-budgets/?_r=0.

of workers outside the official ACFTU structure casts a heavy shadow, even over issues that would seem to have little to do with collective labour relations. That goal is a facet of the regime's broader commitment to 'stability maintenance'. Anything that carries the slightest whiff of independent collective action among workers is subject to close scrutiny, restrictive regulation and often repression.

To be sure, the commitment to avoiding the rise of independent labour activism has also been a major impetus for party-state actions advancing workers' interests, including both ad hoc concessions to workers who raise a ruckus and more systemic reforms that aim to forestall unrest. We have mainly focused here on efforts to raise labour standards, improve official avenues of redress and expand government-sponsored legal aid for workers, as well as efforts, largely symbolic so far, to promote the SWRC system in the non-state sector. But the shadow cast by the aversion to independent labour activism is visible across all of those areas of reform, as well as in the immediate response to unrest, for that aversion constrains and sometimes hobbles reform as well as motivating it (as one of us argues at length elsewhere).[91] One poignant illustration of this dynamic can be seen in the severe restrictions on collective litigation and independent advocacy, especially by 'barefoot lawyers' and NGOs. Despite the expansion of official legal aid, these restrictions leave many frustrated workers unable to enforce their legal rights through formal channels and push them onto the streets to air their grievances.

China's efforts to mollify workers, address their grievances, strengthen their legal protections, and enhance their access to certain legal services and legal remedies do provide some benefit to workers. But when pursuit of those aims poses even the glimmer of a threat to the ultimate aims of stability maintenance and regime preservation, the latter hold sway. The regime's assiduous and well-resourced commitment to preventing independent organising by workers contrasts with its half-hearted and formalistic implementation of the constitutional commitment to 'democratic management'. The idea that workers should have a significant role in the governance of the enterprise for which they work has good socialist credentials. But the main institutional embodiments of that principle in China – the SWRCs – are widely seen as 'rubber stamps' for management in all but the rarest cases.

---

[91] Estlund, *A New Deal for China's Workers?*

We return finally to the question with which we began: What, if anything, is 'socialist' about China's labour laws and policies? There is little doubt that China's commitment to monopolistic control of organised labour through a party-controlled 'trade union' reflects a Leninist legacy from the era of the planned economy. That legacy has survived the transition to a mixed economy in which private capital has a great deal of autonomy and profits flow overwhelmingly, and sometimes through corrupt channels, to a politically wired elite. But does that Leninist legacy make China's labour law regime 'socialist'?

To address that question, we must take sides in a longstanding debate about whether socialism is embodied in the 'actually existing socialism' of the old Soviet Union and other Leninist regimes in its mould or is rather a normative ideal against which any purportedly socialist society should be judged. In Chapter 2 of this volume, Michael Dowdle puts himself squarely in the latter camp, arguing that 'socialism' stands for a normative ideal that pursues substantive equality and opposes subordination of workers in the sphere of production (in part by affording them a collective voice in enterprise governance). Dowdle warns against debasing the concept of socialism by conflating it with nationalism, Leninism, state capitalism or other features of societies that claim the mantel of socialism without pursuing the values it stands for. A similar view animates the numerous scholars of Chinese labour relations who assert that China entered a 'post-socialist' phase with the opening to private capital.[92] The premise is that a society that allows private capital to profit richly from the exploitation of commodified labour, as China has done since the 'reform and opening', does not deserve to be called 'socialist'.

China's leaders might object by pointing to the unprecedented reduction in poverty since the close of the Maoist era. If advancing the interests of the labouring masses is what identifies a society as 'socialist', then surely the higher living standards of China's labouring masses should count in its favour, even if political and economic elites have captured the lion's share of GDP gains. But that comes perilously close to echoing 'trickle-down' arguments for capitalism and market ordering as engines of growth that will benefit all, albeit to highly unequal degrees. 'Socialism' as an ideal concerns itself with the gap between rich and poor, as well as with poverty, and with the status, security, dignity and power of workers, as well as with their incomes.

[92] Ibid.

Since the mid-2000s, China might also point to rising labour standards and legal protections for individual workers, which are strong by international standards, as evidence of their 'socialist' credentials.[93] China's laws strictly limit overtime, grant generous paid maternity leave and give most workers substantial job security (including a right to a 'non-fixed term contract', terminable only for good cause, once workers have concluded two consecutive fixed-term contracts). The central government's enactment of such measures may well reflect pro-worker sentiment among some top officials (as well as concerns about unrest and stability). But there are two difficulties with calling China's labour law regime 'socialist' on those grounds: first, China's formal labour standards largely mimic those of regulated market economies across the world; second, the persistence of pervasive noncompliance on the ground undercuts whatever 'socialist' credentials might otherwise follow from having strong formal labour standards on paper.

We are sympathetic to the effort to insulate the normative ideal of 'socialism' from the baggage accumulated in the history of 'actually existing socialism' in China and elsewhere. We are thus inclined to view the central distinguishing features of modern Chinese labour law and policy – in particular, strict Party control of the official trade union, with an enforced monopoly on collective representation of workers – as Leninist but not necessarily socialist. The Leninist features of China's labour law system entrench one-party rule, and they do so in part by suppressing the efforts of workers to help themselves – as workers have sought to do throughout the history of industrialisation – by joining together, forming associations and taking action together. It would be ironic to pin China's 'socialist' credentials to those features.

But it might go too far to say that those Leninist features of China's labour regime necessarily refute its claim to being socialist. At least in theory, a one-party state could use its entrenched power to pursue a 'socialist' agenda, even within a mostly capitalist economy – to empower workers within enterprises, to lift up the conditions and opportunities of ordinary working people, and to restrain the efforts of elites to further enrich themselves. China's official rhetoric, including provisions in its Constitution, continues to embrace that 'socialist' agenda. There might even be something to be said for a one-party state that consistently

---

[93] See, e.g., OECD Indicators of Employment Protection, available at www.oecd.org/els/emp/oecdindicatorsofemploymentprotection.htm (China ranks higher than many OECD countries in terms of its legislative protection of workers against dismissal).

pursued those socialist ideals as a matter of constitutional commitment, as compared to a multiparty electoral democracy that leaves those ideals up for grabs as it veers between liberal social democracy and populist nationalism.

In the end, however, we should follow Deng Xiaoping's call to 'seek truth from facts',[94] and judge China's socialist bona fides by observing the real operation of its labour law regime, as well as the real maldistribution of wealth and power in the country. The latter has little to do with China's labour law regime, but it risks rendering farcical China's claim to the banner of socialism. Perhaps China will change course, and commit its daunting governmental power to reigning in wealthy elites, redistributing more of the nation's wealth to the poor and the working classes, and empowering labour relative to capital both within enterprises and beyond. But that seems unlikely to happen without the active political engagement of strong labour organisations that are actually accountable to workers.

---

[94] While this phrase had been used by Mao Zedong and its roots date back even earlier, it was popularised by Deng Xiaoping, who adopted it as his mantra in reforming and opening China and spoke of a 'seek-truth-from-facts school' (实事求是派). Kwok-sing Li, *A Glossary of Political Terms of the People's Republic of China*, trans. Mary Lok (Hong Kong: The Chinese University Press, 1995), pp. 413–414.

11

Strike Settlement in Transitional Vietnam and the Persistence of Socialist and Marxist–Leninist Influences

DO HAI HA

11.1 Introduction

The transition from a centrally planned economy to a socialist-oriented market economy (*kinh tế thị trường định hướng xã hội chủ nghĩa*) in 1986 – usually known as *Đổi mới* – has considerably reshaped Vietnamese labour law. With the dismantling of the centralised system of workforce management, the extensive system of administrative regulations that predetermined all terms and conditions of employment was largely abolished.[1] Instead, new laws were introduced to set out minimum standards for individual contracts of employment; mechanisms for interaction between employers, employees and unions; and processes and institutions to manage labour disputes.[2] Consequently, Vietnamese labour law today is substantially comparable to its counterparts in capitalist market economies.

However, as the term 'socialist-oriented market economy' suggests, the Vietnamese party-state has never meant to break with the legacy of the high socialist era. The question that then arises is to what extent this legacy has shaped post-*Đổi mới* labour law and its implementation. This Chapter seeks to address this question by assessing how local authorities settled strikes, a common form of labour conflict in market economies, from 1995 to 2013. It argues that strike management in the socialist-oriented

The author would like to thank Professors Pip Nicholson, John Gillespie and Fu Hualing for their thoughtful feedback on the early versions of this Chapter. Sincere gratitude is also dedicated to Professors Pip Nicholson and Sean Cooney for their constructive guidance throughout my doctoral study, which has resulted in this work.

[1] For an account of this transition, see Ying Zhu and Stephanie Fahey, 'The Impact of Economic Reform on Industrial Labour Relations in China and Vietnam' (1999) 11(2) *Post-Communist Economies* 173.

[2] See generally Labour Code 1994; Trade Union Law 1990.

market economy essentially reflected political, economic and legal ideas of the high socialist era, including fundamental socialist thinking and, in particular, the Marxist–Leninist view of socialism. This Chapter also demonstrates that socialist and Marxist–Leninist influences were eroded over time, coinciding with the emergence of more practical, pro-capitalist and liberal thinking.

This Chapter elicits data from qualitative interviews conducted during my doctoral study. From March 2012 to October 2013, I interviewed and re-interviewed 58 people who were involved in the making of strike laws and/or the actual management of strikes in Bình Dương, Đồng Nai and Hồ Chí Minh City (HCMC). These localities were chosen because they accounted for the most strikes nationwide[3] and, as a result, they have played an important role in the regulatory innovation of industrial relations.[4]

The Chapter contains seven sections. The second offers a snapshot of Vietnamese labour law in the high socialist era, showing that it essentially reflected socialist and Marxist–Leninist influences. The third recaps labour law changes after Đổi mới, with some focus on strike regulation. The fourth highlights the prevalence of unlawful wildcat strikes and the marginalisation of legal institutions in industrial conflict management. The fifth explores the actual approach of local regulators to strike resolution from 1995 to 2006 and the epistemic logics behind this approach. It reveals that strike settlement during this period largely replicated regulatory ideas of the high socialist era. The sixth section investigates the continuities and changes in strike resolution from 2006 to 2013, and demonstrates that, while remaining strong and significant, Marxist–Leninist and socialist influences gradually declined. The final section concludes.

11.2   Vietnamese Labour Law in the High Socialist Era: Some Historical Background

As a result of the rising influence of the People's Republic of China and the Soviet Union on the Democratic Republic of Vietnam (DRV), the installation of Soviet-style labour law and practice in Vietnam began in

---

[3] Ministry of Labour, War Invalids and Social Affairs (MOLISA), *Số liệu Đình công 1995–2013* [Strike Statistics 1995–2013] (2014), showing that more than 70 per cent of strikes in this period took place in these provinces and city. File provided by an official from the MOLISA's Legal Department.

[4] Do Quynh Chi, *Understanding Industrial Relations Transformation in Vietnam: A Multi-Dimensional Analysis*, PhD Thesis, University of Sydney (2011), pp. 308–313.

the early 1950s.[5] This was accelerated after the DRV asserted control
of territory north of the 17th Parallel in 1954 and committed its intention to construct socialism.[6] The adoption of a Soviet-style labour law
system was fundamentally completed by the mid-1960s.[7] Following
national reunification in 1975, this system was imposed on the whole
country – the Socialist Republic of Vietnam (SRV) – and remained in
place until the initiation of Đổi mới.[8]

Like its Chinese and Soviet parents, Vietnamese labour law in the high
socialist period was constructed on two ideological conceptions. The first
proposed that social control of the means of production is a must for
material equality, social cooperation and community solidarity.[9] Behind
this central tenet of socialism is the fundamental criticism of capitalism
that private ownership of production and free market competition generates exploitative and unfair distribution of wealth and power, leading to
material inequality and social alienation.[10]

Reflecting this socialist thinking, pre-Đổi mới labour law endorsed
a centralised labour system, in which the government assigned jobs,
determined wages and working conditions, and provided free cultural
and social welfare to workers.[11] There was limited space for contractual
labour relations, whether in law or practice.[12] Further to this, it was
declared that workers were the master of their enterprises, exercising

[5] Tuong Vu, 'Workers and the Socialist State: North Vietnam's State–Labour Relations,
1945–1970' (2005) 38 *Communist and Post-Communist Studies* 329, particularly
332–336. See also Arturo Bronstein, *International and Comparative Labour Law: Current
Challenges* (Basingstoke: Palgrave Macmillan, 2009), pp. 212–215 for an account of
Soviet-style labour law and labour relations.

[6] See Phạm Công Trứ, 'Luật Lao động – Một Ngành Luật Độc lập trong Hệ thống Pháp
luật Việt Nam' ['Labour Law – An Independent Branch of the Vietnamese Legal System']
in Phạm Công Trứ (ed.), *Giáo Trình Luật Lao Động Việt Nam* [*Vietnamese Labour Law
Textbook*] (Hanoi: Nhà Xuất bản Đại học Quốc gia Hà Nội [Hanoi National University
Publisher], 1999), p. 52.

[7] Ibid.

[8] Ibid., p. 53.

[9] See John Murphy (ed.), *Socialism and Communism* (New York, NY: Britannica Educa-
tional Publlishing, 2015), pp. 17–18. For the influence of this idea in Vietnam, see Lê
Duẩn, 'Làm chủ Tập thể Là Bản chất và Bản lĩnh của Giai cấp Công nhân' ['Collective
Mastery Is in the Nature and Ability of the Working Class], speech delivered at the Fifth
Congress of the Vietnamese Trade Union, May 1978.

[10] Murphy, *Socialism and Communism*, p. 26.

[11] Hoàng Thế Liên, Đặng Đức San and Nguyễn Văn Phần, *Về Bộ luật Lao động của Việt
Nam năm 1994* [*On Vietnam's 1994 Labour Code*] (Viện Nghiên cứu Khoa học Pháp lý
[Institute for Legal Research], 1995), pp. 3–7. See also Art. 58, Constitution 1980.

[12] Hoàng Thế Liên, Đặng Đức San and Nguyễn Văn Phần, ibid., pp. 3–5.

their managerial right – at least on paper – via trade unions and other mechanisms like workers' assemblies, enterprise committees and, above all, the socialist state.[13]

The other ideological conception that shaped Vietnamese labour law before Đổi mới derived from the Marxist–Leninist perception of socialism. That is, socialist construction requires a centralised state under the exclusive control of a 'vanguard' party – the communist party.[14] This differentiated Vietnamese trade unions from those in capitalist market economies. Vietnamese workers were not allowed to establish unions outside the structure of the Vietnam General Confederation of Labour (VGCL), which was closely connected to the communist party.[15] Nor were these unions viewed primarily as the representatives of workers. More often, they were considered the 'political backup' (cơ sở chính trị) of the party-state, as encapsulated in the Soviet-inspired slogan: 'Trade unions are a school of communism'.[16]

Hence, the prioritised function of Vietnamese unions was not protecting labour, but educating and mobilising workers to fulfil state production plans.[17] Nor was their protective function discharged in the same way as in capitalist market economies. While portraying itself as the protector of workers' interests, the VGCL had no intention to challenge either management or the party-state.[18] Rather, its major means to protect labour was participating in policy and decision making at workplace and governmental levels, and administrating cultural and social welfare for workers.[19]

Marxist–Leninist thinking also underpinned the prohibitive approach of the party-state to strike action. As in the USSR, strikes were seen to

---

[13] Lê Duẩn, 'Làm chủ Tập thể Là Bản chất và Bản lĩnh của Giai cấp Công nhân' ['Collective Mastery Is in the Nature and Ability of the Working Class']. See also Decree 205-HDBT of the Ministerial Council dated 12 July 1985 Promulgating Regulations on the Organisation and Operation of Enterprise Committees; Trade Union Law 1957.

[14] Murphy, Socialism and Communism, p. 19.

[15] Art. 3, Trade Union Law 1957.

[16] Ibid. For the Soviet-inspired slogan, see Sarah Ashwin and Simon Clarke, Russian Trade Unions and Industrial Relations in Transition (Basingstoke: Palgrave Macmillan, 2003), p. 11.

[17] Irene Nørlund, 'Trade Unions in Vietnam in Historical Perspective: The Transformation of Concepts' in Rebecca Elmhirst and Ratna Saptari (eds.), Labour in Southeast Asia: Local Processes in a Globalised World (Abingdon: RoutledgeCurzon and International Institute of Social History, 2004), pp. 107, 113–117.

[18] Tim Pringle and Simon Clarke, The Challenge of Transition: Trade Unions in Russia, China and Vietnam (Basingstoke: Palgrave Macmillan, 2011), pp. 9–10.

[19] Arts. 5–8, 18, Trade Union Law 1957.

impede the fulfilment of state economic plans.[20] Further, strikes were regarded as a form of political defiance, which might entail counter-revolutionary conspiracy.[21] The negative attitude towards strikes was also inspired by socialist ideology, as indicated in the argument that strikes were unnecessary in a socialist economy because the interests of labour, management and the socialist state were congruent.[22]

In short, until the late 1980s, Vietnamese labour law was built predominantly on socialist and Marxist–Leninist notions. Socialist influence was particularly evident in the existence of a centralised labour system and mechanisms for employee participation in management. Meanwhile, the subordination of union organisations to party leadership, their co-optation into the party-state system and the prohibition of strike action closely reflected the impact of Marxism–Leninism.

11.3 Post-*Đổi Mới* Labour Law Developments and the Legalisation of Strikes

Vietnamese labour law underwent important developments after the transition to a socialist-oriented market economy. The centralised labour system was essentially dismantled. Workers were no longer allocated jobs on state-determined terms and conditions, but were free to choose their own jobs, with terms and conditions subject mainly to negotiation with their employers.[23] They were no longer entitled to free social and cultural welfare as they had been in the past.[24] They now had to buy social insurance and pay for their living expenses.[25] Similarly, labour law no longer declared workers the masters of their enterprises, but expressly required that employees be subordinate to their employers.[26] These

---

[20] 'Tổng hợp Ý kiến Xây dựng Dự án Bộ luật Lao động' ['Compiled Comments on the Labour Code Bill'], Sài Gòn Giải phóng [*Liberated Saigon*], 20 May 1994, p. 2. See also Jozef Wilczynski, *Comparative Industrial Relations: Ideologies, Institutions, Practices and Problems under Different Social Systems with Special Reference to Socialist Planned Economies* (London: Macmillan, 1983), p. 177, for the Soviet perception of strikes.

[21] Mê Linh, 'Quan hệ Lao động trong Cơ chế Thị trường và Vấn đề Đình công' ['Labour Relationship in a Market Economy and the Strike Issue'] (1993) (8) *Tạp chí Lao động và Xã hội* [*Journal of Labour and Social Affairs*] 19, 20.

[22] Interview with retired leader of the Vietnam General Confederation of Labour (VGCL) (Hanoi, 22 March 2012); Interview with veteran labour law expert from the Ministry of Justice (Hanoi, 22 August 2012).

[23] See generally Labour Code 1994.

[24] Ibid.

[25] Ibid.

[26] Art. 7(3), ibid.

developments represent a remarkable departure from fundamental socialist ideals and policies.

Trade union law was also reformed, demonstrating greater emphasis on the representative function of unions, growing union autonomy vis-à-vis the party-state and creating scope for union involvement in law and policy making.[27] There were also attempts to legalise and promote collective bargaining and dialogue between labour, management and the government.[28] Nevertheless, the VGCL remains the solely lawful federation, tightly controlled by the Communist Party and operating as a transmission belt between the Party and workers.[29] Unlike core socialist ideas, Marxist–Leninist political principles continue to have strong impact on labour legislation after Đổi mới.

Another prominent change of post–Đổi mới labour law is the reintroduction of the right to strike into labour statutes. However, these statutes have concurrently severely restricted the exercise of this right. Politically related and secondary strikes are not permitted, as strikes must arise from collective labour disputes, fall within the scope of labour relations and take place within one enterprise.[30] Similarly, unofficial strikes are precluded because strikes have to be organised by trade unions.[31] Procedural restrictions also exist, including strike ballots, prior notice and the compulsory use of statutory conciliation and arbitration.[32] Further, strikes are prohibited in three circumstances, namely: where employees are public servants;[33] where employees work for enterprises serving the public or enterprises important to the national economy or national security and defence; or where the Prime Minister decides to stay or suspend a strike due to concerns about detriment to the national economy or public safety.[34]

To sum up, the post–Đổi mới period witnessed remarkable developments in Vietnamese labour law. These developments demonstrate that, while socialist influences on labour law have declined drastically, Marxist–Leninist

---

[27] Anita Chan and Irene Nørlund, 'Vietnamese and Chinese Labour Regimes: On the Road to Divergence' (1998) (40) *The China Journal* 173, 185–187. See also Arts. 2, 4–6, 8, Trade Union Law 1990.

[28] Pringle and Clarke, *The Challenge of Transition*, pp. 76, 96–102.

[29] Arts. 1–2, Trade Union Law 1990.

[30] Arts. 173–176, Labour Code 1994; Arts. 215, 220–221, Labour Code 2012.

[31] Art. 173, Labour Code 1994; Art. 210, Labour Code 2012.

[32] Art. 176, Labour Code 1994; Arts. 211–213, 215, Labour Code 2012.

[33] Arts. 2, 4, Labour Code 1994; Arts. 2–3, Labour Code 2012 excluding public servants from the governing scope of labour law and, therefore, legal protection of the right to strike.

[34] Arts. 175–176, Labour Code 1994; Arts. 220–221, Labour Code 2012.

Table 11.1 *National Strike
Numbers 1995–2013*[35]

Year	Strike numbers
1995	60
1996	59
1997	59
1998	62
1999	67
2000	71
2001	89
2002	100
2003	139
2004	125
2005	147
2006	387
2007	541
2008	762
2009	310
2010	424
2011	981
2012	539
2013	327

influences remain strong and significant. Yet, the legalisation of strike action
and a certain degree of union reform suggest that the party-state has, to
some extent, loosened its adherence to Marxist–Leninist political principles.

11.4   The Prevalence of Unlawful, Wildcat Strikes
and the Marginalisation of Legal Mechanisms

Industrial conflicts grew remarkably in the transitional era. As shown
in Table 11.1, strike rates increased by 5.45 times between 1995 and
2013. More specifically, the number of strikes began to rise in 2001
and increased rapidly from 2006. Strike numbers hit a peak in 2011 but
decreased markedly in the subsequent years.

Industrial conflicts did not only grow in quantity – their nature also
transformed over time. Empirical studies reveal that there was a gradual

---

[35] MOLISA, *Số liệu Đình công 1995–2013* [*Strike Statistics 1995–2013*].

shift in the character of strikes from rights to interest based during the 2000s,[36] which continued until at least 2013. According to the statistics of the Ministry of Labour, War Invalids and Social Affairs (MOLISA), only 10.2 per cent of strikes between 2007 and 2011 were purely rights-based.[37] Meanwhile, 70.35 per cent of strikes involved interest-based demands and the rest (19.45 per cent) involved both rights and interest-based strikes.[38] My fieldwork in Bình Dương, Đồng Nai and HCMC between 2012 and 2013 re-confirms this tendency, indicating that strikers usually demanded wage increases, bonuses and better shift meals.[39]

Despite the increase in strikes, legal mechanisms for managing industrial conflict, which were set out in the 1994 Labour Code and its successors, have had limited actual impact. Notwithstanding the lack of comprehensive statistics, it is consistently noted that collective disputes were seldom resolved by labour conciliation, labour arbitration, labour courts or, from the 2006 Labour Code reform, the Chairmen of People's Committees.[40] Most, if not all, strikes that took place were wildcat and unlawful.[41] This is not only because workers rarely had recourse to compulsory legal processes before going to strike.[42] Workers also frequently failed to observe the requirements of secret ballots and prior

---

[36] Lee Chang-Hee, 'Industrial Relations and Dispute Settlement in Vietnam', Discussion Paper (Geneva: ILO, June 2006), pp. 3–4.

[37] MOLISA, *Số liệu Đình công 1995–2013* [Strike Statistics 1995–2013].

[38] Ibid.

[39] Interviews with fourteen labour officials (L1–L14) and twelve union officials (U1–U12) in Bình Dương, Đồng Nai and HCMC. See also Đồng Nai Department of Labour, War Invalids and Social Affairs (DOLISA), *Báo cáo Số 65/BC-LĐTBXH Đánh giá Tình hình Thực hiện các Quy định Pháp luật về Giải quyết Tranh chấp Lao động, Đình công* [Report No. 65/BC-LDTBXH on Assessment of the Implementation of Legal Regulations on Dispute Resolution and Strikes] (14 April 2011), p. 3. Note that L1–L6 and U1–U7 were from HCMC, L7–L10 and U8–U10 were from Bình Dương, L11–L14 and U11–U12 were from Đồng Nai. These interviews were conducted from 6 April 2012 to 28 October 2013.

[40] Interviews with L1–L14, U1–U12. See also Bình Dương DOLISA, *Báo cáo Số 51/BC-SLĐTBXH về Tình hình Thực hiện các Quy định Pháp luật về Giải quyết Tranh chấp Lao động, Đình công* [Report No. 51/BC-SLDTBXH on the Implementation of Legal Regulations on Dispute Resolution and Strikes] (9 April 2011), p. 7; Đồng Nai DOLISA, *Báo cáo Số 65/BC-LĐTBXH Đánh giá Tình hình Thực hiện các Quy định Pháp luật về Giải quyết Tranh chấp Lao động, Đình công* [Report No. 65/BC-LDTBXH on Assessment of the Implementation of Legal Regulations on Dispute Resolution and Strikes], pp. 9–11; MOLISA, *Báo cáo Tổng kết Số 68/BC-BLĐTBXH Đánh giá 15 Năm Thi hành Bộ luật Lao động* [Summative Report No. 68/BC-BLDTBXH on Assessment of the Fifteen Years of Implementation of the Labour Code] (6 September 2011), pp. 27–28.

[41] Interviews with L1–L14, U1–U12; MOLISA, ibid., 27–28.

[42] Ibid.

notification.[43] Further, strikes were hardly ever organised by trade unions or representatives elected by workers, as required by law.[44] Nor did employers request the courts to stop illegal strikes and order compensation.[45]

11.5 The Emergence of Multi-Sector Task Forces as the Principal Mechanism for Strike Resolution from 1995 to 2007 and Their Reflection of Socialist and Marxist–Leninist Influences

While legal mechanisms were marginalised, local authorities in Bình Dương, Đồng Nai and HCMC gradually developed their own mechanism to handle unlawful wildcat strikes. This mechanism is often referred to as multi-sector task forces for strike settlement (đoàn/tổ công tác liên ngành giải quyết đình công).[46] As we shall see, the constitution and operation of these task forces essentially replicated Marxist–Leninist and socialist political, economic and legal conceptions.

Functioning as a 'firefighting' mechanism, strike task forces were set up when local authorities became aware of strikes and then dissolved upon their resolution.[47] Key members of a strike task force were usually labour officials from the provincial labour administration (that is, the Department of Labour, War Invalids and Social Affairs – DOLISA) and when the strike took place in an industrial zone, from the Provincial Industrial Zones Authority,[48] together with union officials from

---

[43] Ibid.

[44] Ibid.

[45] Interviews with L1–L2, L5, L7–L14, U1–U2, U4–U6, U8–U9, U11.

[46] Interviews with L1–L14, U1–U12. See also Bình Dương People's Committee, Temporary Regulation on Cooperation in Resolution of Labour Disputes in Bình Dương (Regulation 190/2003), issued in conjuntion with Decision No. 190/2003/QD-UBND dated 24 July 2003; Đồng Nai People's Committees, Regulation on Coordination between the People's Committees of Bien Hoa City or Other Districts and Provincial Departments and Organisations in Initial Resolution of Collective Labour Disputes in Enterprises in Đồng Nai Province (Regulation 1596/2003), issued in Conjunction with Decision No. 1596/2003/QD.UBT dated 3 June 2003; HCMC People's Committee, Regulation on Initial Resolution of Strikes Not in Compliance with Labour Law in HCMC (Regulation 35/2006), issued in Conjunction with Decision No. 35/2006/QD-UBND dated 2 March 2006.

[47] Interviews with L1–L2, L7–L9, L11–L12, U2, U8, U11.

[48] The Provincial Industrial Zones Authority is a special administrative agency created to promote (foreign) investment in export-processing, industrial and high-tech zones. To save time for investors, this organ has been authorised to discharge functions of various provincial administrative agencies, including the labour administration. The Industrial Zones Authorities of Bình Dương, Đồng Nai and HCMC all contain a division responsible for labour matters.

the Provincial Federation of Labour.[49] Strike task forces also typically included representatives from organisations at lower levels, including the People's Committee (the local government committee) of the relevant district, the union organisation of the relevant district, industry or industrial zone, and the relevant representative office of the Provincial Industrial Zones Authority.[50] The major tasks of lower-level officials were maintaining order, mobilising strikers and exploring strikers' demands.[51]

Multi-sector task forces for strike settlement operated without a legal basis for several years. Nevertheless, the provincial authorities of Bình Dương, Đồng Nai and HCMC enacted their own regulations to formalise this mechanism between 2003 and 2006 – in part, because foreign investors repeatedly questioned its legality.[52] The mechanism was partially recognised by the central government in the 2006 Revised Labour Code, which came into effect in mid-2007.[53]

11.5.1 Strike Resolution by Multi-Sector Task Forces

Typically, the settlement of a strike by a multi-sector task force followed three basic steps. At first, the task force would talk with workers to calm them down and engage with their requests.[54] Then, they would meet with management to negotiate for a settlement.[55] Strikers were seldom allowed to participate in this meeting.[56] Finally, the settlement would be announced to striking workers.[57] The task force, sometimes together with the employer, then explained the settlement to workers and mobilised them to return to work.[58] If workers remained unsatisfied, the task force would keep working with both parties until the issue was resolved.[59]

---

[49] Interviews with L1, L7–L9, L11–L12, U2, U8, U11; Lee, 'Industrial Relations and Dispute Settlement in Vietnam', p. 6.

[50] Interviews with L1, L7–L9, L11–L12, U2, U8, U11; Lee, 'Industrial Relations and Dispute Settlement in Vietnam', p. 6.

[51] Interviews with L1–L2, L7, L11, U2, U8, U11.

[52] See Regulation 190/2003; Regulation 1596/2003.

[53] See Art. 159(3), Labour Code (Revised) 2006 encouraging local authorities to proactively intervene in work stoppage arising from rights disputes.

[54] Interviews with L1, L5, L7–L10, L12, L14, U2, U11.

[55] Interviews with L1, L5, L7–L8, L14, U11; Lee, 'Industrial Relations and Dispute Settlement in Vietnam', p. 6.

[56] Interviews with L5, L7–L8, L10, L12, L14, U2, U11; Lee, 'Industrial Relations and Dispute Settlement in Vietnam', p. 6.

[57] Interviews with L1, L5, L7–L8, L11–L12, L14, U11.

[58] Interviews with L8, L11–L12, U11.

[59] Interviews with L5, L8, L11–L12, U2, U11.

Strike resolution by multi-sector task forces was characterised by five features. First, the priority was not resolution of the underlying disputes, but ending the strike quickly. For example, these task forces regularly intervened in strikes immediately, rather than waiting for a request for help in settling the dispute from employers or labour collectives.[60] Further, they tended to concentrate on 'key [rather than all] demands of workers, the settlement of which would stop the strikes'.[61] In addition, strike task forces frequently supported workers' requests and pressed management to accept them to bring about a prompt end to the unrest.[62]

Second, multi-sector task forces usually adopted a rights-based approach to resolve disputes. Quite often, they considered requests without legal grounds (that is, interest-based requests) as 'illegitimate' or 'unreasonable', and excluded such requests from the resolution.[63] The strike waves in 2005 and 2006 offer a prominent example of this practice. When strikes for higher wages exploded in foreign-invested enterprises, the HCMC People's Committee recommended that these enterprises delay wage increases until the government announced a rise in the minimum wage rates for the foreign sector.[64] When this increase incited another wave of strikes in domestic private enterprises, provincial officials explained to workers that their demands for wage increases had no legal basis, as the new minimum wages applied only to foreign-invested companies.[65]

This approach is also demonstrated in cases where strike task forces (that is, multi-sector task forces) recast workers' interest-based demands as rights-based ones. For instance, disputes over production rates were reframed as complaints about breaches of overtime and wage regulations, since local officials reasoned that setting heavy production rates was a

---

[60] Interviews with L1–L2, L7–L9, L11–L12, U2, U8, U10–U11; Lee, 'Industrial Relations and Dispute Settlement in Vietnam', p. 5.

[61] Interviews with L3, L8, L11, L14, U11.

[62] Interviews with L8, L11–L12, U6; Interview with E1 (HCMC, 14 May 2012); Interview with M1 (Bình Dương, 29 May 2012); Lee, 'Industrial Relations and Dispute Settlement in Vietnam', p. 6. E1 was a senior official of the Vietnam Chamber of Commerce and Industry (VCCI). M1 was the HR manager of a foreign-invested company.

[63] Interviews with L12, L14, U2, U8; Lee, 'Industrial Relations and Dispute Settlement in Vietnam', p. 6.

[64] KH B and H N, 'Kiên quyết Xử lý những Hành vi Quá khích' ['Severe Punishment for Extreme Action'], Sài Gòn Giải phóng [Liberated Saigon], 5 January 2006, available at www.sggp.org.vn/xahoi/nam2006/thang1/88264/.

[65] Nam Dương, 'Giải quyết Đình công Vẫn còn "Thủng Đầu Vá Đó"' ['Strike Settlement Remains Reactive'], Người Lao động [The Labourer], 26 June 2006, available at https://nld.com.vn/quyen-va-nghia-vu/giai-quyet-dinh-cong-van-con-thung-dau-va-do-155620.htm.

tactic to force workers into unpaid overtime.[66] Likewise, requests for a seniority-based pay system were considered as requests for the adoption of wage scales as prescribed by law.[67] In a similar vein, complaints about the reduction or termination of wage allowances unilaterally set out by employers were reinterpreted as demands to enforce oral agreements.[68]

Third, strike task forces maintained an interventionist approach, which largely disregarded collective bargaining, party autonomy, right to participation and other due process requirements. As previously shown, these task forces regularly filtered the requests of workers, and rarely permitted them or their representatives to directly negotiate a resolution with employers. Moreover, as the priority was prompt settlement, employers had little opportunity to defend their position. Nor were there processes to appeal the resolutions reached by strike task forces, including those on compliance issues.[69]

Fourthly, multi-sector task forces generally tolerated strike action and favoured striking workers. Despite the unlawful nature of strikes and the authorities' concern over these incidents, police rarely took action against strikers and their leaders.[70] And, as previously noted, strike task forces frequently pushed employers to satisfy workers' key requests. Further to this, they often criticised employers vigorously for exploiting workers and/or violating labour standards, rather than taking a neutral position between labour and capital.[71]

However, this does not mean that the authorities entirely accepted strike action. On occasion, those alleged to 'coerce' or 'instigate' workers to strike or 'incite strikers to violence' were summoned, detained,

---

[66] See, e.g., Interview with U11; Phạm Hổ, 'Đưa Định mức Cao Để Không phải Trả Tiền Phụ trội' ['Setting High Production Rates to Avoid Overtime Payment'], Người Lao động [The Labourer], 9 August 2001, http://suckhoedinhduong.nld.com.vn/71002p1010c1012/dua-dinh-muc-cao-de-khong-phai-tra-tien-phu-troi.htm.

[67] See, e.g., Interview with L3; Nguyễn Hữu Cát, 'Đình công: Nguyên nhân & Giải pháp' ['Strikes: Causes and Solutions'] (2006) 288 Tạp chí Lao động và Xã hội [Journal of Labour and Social Affairs] 48. Under Art. 58 of the 1994 Labour Code, private enterprises had to enact wage scales and register them with the authorities. Art. 4(1) of Decree 114/2002/ND-CP further provided that such scales were set out in view of workers' jobs, skills and experience. This provision was interpreted as workers' entitlement to annual wage increase.

[68] Interview with L1.

[69] See Regulation 35/2006; Regulation 190/2003; Regulation 1596/2003.

[70] Interviews with L1–L3, L10–L11, L14, U2; Lee, above 'Industrial Relations and Dispute Settlement in Vietnam', p. 6.

[71] Interviews with E1, M1.

threatened or beaten by the police.[72] This was usually done in an informal and secret manner.[73]

Finally, multi-sector task forces preferred to use compromise and flexibility when settling strikes. This is demonstrated by task forces often making concessions to both labour *and* capital. On the one hand, they supported workers' requests and tolerated breaches of strike laws.[74] On the other hand, they rarely sanctioned employers for violating labour standards, but permitted them to fix violations within a certain period.[75] Further, strike task forces tended to flexibly apply – rather than strictly adhere to – legal principles. While tolerating workers and employers' breaches of labour laws, they relied on labour laws to press employers to accept strikers' demands, with a view to ending the incidents promptly.

11.5.2   Regulatory Ideas behind Multi-Sector Task Forces for Strike Settlement and the Domination of Socialist and Marxist–Leninist Thinking

The composition of multi-sector task forces and their approach to strike settlement significantly and substantially reflected political, economic and legal ideas of the high socialist era, especially Marxist–Leninist views about socialist construction. The inclusion of trade union delegates in strike task forces exemplifies this. By participating in these task forces, trade unions took on the role of the regulator of labour relations, rather than the representative of workers. In fact, most local officials with whom I spoke in Bình Dương, Đồng Nai and HCMC automatically referred to trade unions as 'responsible authorities' (*cơ quan chức năng*) for labour-related matters, including strike management.[76] This thinking closely resembled the Leninist conception of trade unions, in which union organisations were viewed more as a part of the party-state than the representative of their members.

Originating from Marxist–Leninist thinking, the fear that strikes would damage economic development and political stability also had important impact on the operation of multi-sector task forces. It nurtured a widespread perception among regulators that prompt and proactive

---

[72] Interviews with L1–L2, L10, L14, U2.
[73] Interviews with L2, L14, U2.
[74] Interviews with L1, L7–L8, L11–L12, U6, U8–U9; Lee, 'Industrial Relations and Dispute Settlement in Vietnam', pp. 29–30.
[75] Interviews with L7, L10, L12, U2, U8.
[76] Interviews with L1–L3, L5, L7–L12, L14, U1–U2, U4–U6, U8–U11.

intervention was necessary to reduce the detrimental effect of strikes to business activities and the likelihood of political disorder.[77] This perception in turn encouraged local regulators to intervene immediately once strike action had commenced. Further, it encouraged strike task forces to focus on selected – rather than all – requests of workers, and to frequently apply pressure on employers to accept such requests.[78]

The emphasis on prompt settlement also relates to the frequent ignorance of collective bargaining, party autonomy, the right to participation and other due process requirements in strike settlement. According to several officials, they did not organise direct negotiation between labour and management because this would prolong the settlement process.[79] One official further explained that if strikers participated in resolution meetings, they would know exactly how their entitlements were breached and, therefore, would become angrier, making it harder to settle strikes.[80]

Another Marxist–Leninist idea shaping the practice of strike resolution is the notion of a socialist state extensively intervening in economic and social affairs.[81] Conversations with local officials reveal that their preference for proactive intervention into strikes was based partly in the conception that local governments had an *ex officio* power and responsibility to intervene in social conflicts.[82] This is particularly evident when some officials stressed that 'the state [had] an obligation to intervene when two individuals [were] fighting'.[83]

---

[77] See Interviews with L1–L3, L5, L11–L12, L14, U1–U2, U11; Government Office, *Notice No. 134/TB-VPCP on Conclusion of Prime Minister Nguyễn Tấn Dũng at the Discussion Meeting regarding Measures for Strike Management in the Forthcoming Period* (29 August 2006); HCMC DOLISA, Báo cáo số 910/BC-SLĐTBXH-LĐ về Tình hình Đình công, Lãn công 3 năm (2003–2005) và từ Tháng 12/2005 đến 23/02/2006 Của Các Doanh nghiệp Ngoài Khu Chế xuất – Khu Công nghiệp Trên Địa bàn Thành phố Hồ Chí Minh [*Report No. 910/BC-SLDTBXH-LD on the Situation of Strikes [and] Slowdowns in 2003–2005 and from December 2005 to 23 February 2006 in Enterprises outside Industrial Zones in HCMC*] (23 February 2006), pp. 9–10; HCMC Union, *Report on Collective Labour Disputes and Strikes in HCMC between 1995–1998* (15 April 1999), p. 4; VGCL, *Resolution No. 5A/NQ-BCH on Promotion of Trade Unions' Legal Works in the New Situation* (7 July 2005), p. 5.

[78] Interviews with L3, L8, L11, L14, U11.

[79] Interviews with L5, L7, U8, U11.

[80] Interview with L2.

[81] See Janos Kornai, *The Socialist System: The Political Economy of Communism* (Oxford: Oxford University Press, 1992), pp. 56–57 explaining the paternalistic nature of the socialist state.

[82] Interviews with L11, U1–U2, U11.

[83] Interviews with U1–U2.

The emphasis on state intervention into economic relations, usually known as 'state economic management' (quản lý nhà nước về kinh tế),[84] was also linked with the rights-based approach of strike task forces. As some industrial relations experts observed, this approach stemmed from the unfamiliarity of local regulators with market concepts like collective bargaining and interest disputes,[85] which had roots in the pre-existing socialist planned economy. While these concepts imply that workers may collectively negotiate with management for better terms and conditions, it was the state that would unilaterally decide all terms and conditions of employment in the centrally planned economy. Despite market reforms from the late 1980s, this practice remained influential until at least the mid-2000s. As demonstrated previously, although the HCMC authorities supported workers' demands for wage increases in the 2005 and 2006 strikes, they recommended employers delay such increases until the central government announced new minimum wage rates.

Meanwhile, underlying the local regulators' tolerance of strikers and their demands was pro-worker sentiment. These regulators often explained their pro-worker approach using five narratives. First, although workers violated strike laws, exploitative and law-breaking employers were the main culprits of strikes.[86] Second, workers merely violated procedural requirements; their requests were substantively legitimate.[87] Third, workers' breaches of strike laws derived in part from complex and impractical legal procedures.[88] Fourth, the state was partially responsible for the miseries that prompted workers to strike.[89] Last, the socialist state was obliged to advocate workers, who constituted the foundation of the socialist society.[90] These narratives strongly echoed the socialist criticism of capitalism and the Leninist ideology that the state represented the working class.

Pro-worker sentiment not only promoted a tolerant approach to strike resolution, it also contributed to the emphasis on settling strikes quickly, as local officials believed that the tardy resolution of strikes would

---

[84] See John Gillespie, 'Changing Concepts of Socialist Law in Vietnam', in John Gillespie and Pip Nicholson (eds.), Asian Socialism & Legal Change: The Dynamics of Vietnamese and Chinese Reform (Canberra: ANU Press, 2005), pp. 56–60.
[85] Interview with VGCL official (Hanoi, 31 March 2012); Interview with former VGCL official (Hanoi, 26 March 2012); Interview with Vietnamese industrial relations researcher (Hanoi, 9 October 2013).
[86] Interviews with L1, L12, L14, U1.
[87] Interviews with L1, L11–L12, U1.
[88] Interviews with U4–U5.
[89] Interviews with L5, U2.
[90] Interviews with L3, L7.

seriously impact the lives of workers and their families.[91] It should be stressed, however, that the most frequently cited reasons for prompt action were based on economic and political concerns about industrial action.

Strike resolution was also inspired by the instrumentalist conception of law inherent in Marxist–Leninist legal theory. In this conception, law is a mere tool of the party-state[92] and can therefore be disregarded if it does not serve its objectives. The impact of this view on strike resolution can be found in the broad use of multi-sector task forces, despite the extra-legal nature of this mechanism. Although local regulators were aware of the lack of a legal basis for these task forces, they did not see this as a major problem.[93] Rather, there was a strong belief that strike task forces were necessary because legal processes were unworkable and the parties, especially workers and enterprise unions, had little experience in negotiation.[94]

Legal instrumentalism also contributed to the disregard for party autonomy, neutrality and due process requirements in strike settlement. Interviews with local officials indicate that these legal principles were ignored because they did not serve (or might impede) the prioritised objective of local regulators: a quick end to strikes.[95] Viewed in this light, it is unsurprising that, while utilising labour laws to press employers to satisfy workers' demands, multi-sector task forces usually avoided fining strikers and employers for breaching labour laws. The logic was that this flexibility would facilitate the speedy resolution of strikes.[96]

Moreover, strike resolution by multi-sector task forces closely resembled the Maoist method of mass mobilisation (vận động quần chúng). In explaining this method, Hồ Chí Minh said:

> Mass mobilisation . . . is, first and foremost, using all means to explain to people that the task [that they should do or are assigned to] is for their interest and [is] their duty [so that] they will try the best to complete it.[97]

Hồ Chí Minh implies that some compromise of interests among people and between people and the party-state is necessary to achieve the party-

---

[91] Interviews with L14, U1, U5.

[92] Gillespie, 'Changing Concepts of Socialist Law in Vietnam', p. 47.

[93] Interviews with L8–L9, L12, U2, U11; HCMC DOLISA, Báo cáo số 4925/SLĐTBXH-LĐ về Tình hình Đình công Từ 01/01/2006 Đến Nay [Report No. 4925/SLDTBXH-LD on the Situation of Strikes from 1 January 2006] (16 August 2006), pp. 6–7.

[94] Ibid.

[95] Interviews with L2, L5, L7, L14, U8, U11.

[96] Interviews with L2, L10–L11, L14, U6, U11.

[97] Hồ Chí Minh, Toàn tập – Tập 5 [Complete Works – Vol 5] (Hanoi: Nhà Xuất bản Chính trị – Quốc gia [National Political Publishing House], 1995), p. 698.

state's objectives. But in so doing, he prioritises the objectives of the party-state over the interests of other actors. Hồ Chí Minh also suggests that, while explanation is generally preferred to coercion, party-state officials may employ any means that suit their objectives. Mass mobilisation, therefore, promotes compromise, flexibility and an outcome-oriented approach, rather than a principled-based approach to legal problems.

The idea of mass mobilisation strongly influenced strike task forces. Local regulators repeatedly stressed that 'mobilisation' (vận động) and 'persuasion' (thuyết phục) were the main ways to settle strikes.[98] Significantly, their resolution of strikes replicated Hồ Chí Minh's approach to mass mobilisation in many important ways. In my conversations with local officials, it was often noted that strike resolution had to compromise the interests of three parties: labour, capital and the party-state.[99] As a corollary, strike task forces often made concessions to both labour and capital. Yet, these conversations also indicate that such concessions were to serve the party-state's priority of promptly ending strikes.[100] Further, as shown earlier in this Chapter, local regulators generally preferred settling strikes via persuasion, rather than hard-line measures like administrative fines or police suppression. But they still applied such measures from time to time, when they thought it necessary. In short, the idea of mass mobilisation played an important role in the compromising and flexible approach of strike task forces.

The compromising and flexible approach of strike task forces was also - justified by local regulators, based on the interrelation of interests between labour, capital and the state. Specifically, it was reasoned that fining law-breaking employers would displease investors, harming economic growth

[98] Interviews with L11–L12, L14, U1; Bình Dương People's Committee, Decision No. 1052/ QD-UBND on Establishment of the Direction Board for Resolution of Collective Labour Disputes and Strikes Not Following Procedures Prescribed by Law in Bình Dương (17 March 2006), p. 2; Regulation 1596/2003 art 5.4; HCMC DOLISA, Báo cáo số 910/ BC-SLĐTBXH-LĐ về Tình hình Đình công, Lãn công 3 năm (2003–2005) và từ Tháng 12/2005 đến 23/02/2006 Của Các Doanh nghiệp Ngoài Khu Chế xuất – Khu Công nghiệp Trên Địa bàn Thành phố Hồ Chí Minh [Report No. 910/BC-SLDTBXH-LD on the Situation of Strikes [and] Slowdowns in 2003–2005 and from December 2005 to 23 February 2006 in Enterprises outside Industrial Zones in HCMC], p. 9.

[99] Interviews with L5, U1, U6; HCMC DOLISA, Báo cáo số 910/BC-SLĐTBXH-LĐ về Tình hình Đình công, Lãn công 3 năm (2003–2005) và từ Tháng 12/2005 đến 23/02/ 2006 Của Các Doanh nghiệp Ngoài Khu Chế xuất – Khu Công nghiệp Trên Địa bàn Thành phố Hồ Chí Minh [Report No. 910/BC-SLDTBXH-LD on the Situation of Strikes [and] Slowdowns in 2003–2005 and from December 2005 to 23 February 2006 in Enterprises outside Industrial Zones in HCMC], pp. 4–5.

[100] Interviews with L2, L10–L11, L14, U6, U11.

and, thus, workers' job security.[101] Meanwhile, strict measures against strikers would damage the morale of workers, pose threats of riot and social unrest and, therefore, hamper the business activities of employers, economic development and political stability.[102] To some extent, these arguments reflected the socialist ideal about social cooperation.

It should be noted that the approach of strike task forces was not only inspired by Marxist–Leninist and socialist thinking, it was also shaped by other political, economic and regulatory perspectives. One of them is Asian-style developmental thinking, which includes an emphasis on the importance of economic growth and foreign investment.[103] Gaining influence in Vietnam from the early 1990s,[104] this thinking contributed to the fear of strikes that underpinned the prompt and interventionist approach to strike resolution. This is demonstrated in the prevalent belief among local regulators that strikes affected the investment environment and economic development negatively.[105] In addition, Asian-style developmental thinking discouraged the regulators from penalising breaches of labour laws by foreign investors.[106]

---

[101] Interviews with L10, U6, U11; HCMC DOLISA, Báo cáo số 910/BC-SLĐTBXH-LĐ về Tình hình Đình công, Lãn công 3 năm (2003–2005) và từ Tháng 12/2005 đến 23/02/2006 Của Các Doanh nghiệp Ngoài Khu Chế xuất – Khu Công nghiệp Trên Địa bàn Thành phố Hồ Chí Minh [*Report No. 910/BC-SLDTBXH-LD on the Situation of Strikes [and] Slowdowns in 2003–2005 and from December 2005 to 23 February 2006 in Enterprises outside Industrial Zones in HCMC*], pp. 4–5.

[102] Interviews with L5, L11, U6, U11; HCMC DOLISA, Báo cáo số 910/BC-SLĐTBXH-LĐ về Tình hình Đình công, Lãn công 3 năm (2003–2005) và từ Tháng 12/2005 đến 23/02/2006 Của Các Doanh nghiệp Ngoài Khu Chế xuất – Khu Công nghiệp Trên Địa bàn Thành phố Hồ Chí Minh [*Report No. 910/BC-SLDTBXH-LD on the Situation of Strikes [and] Slowdowns in 2003–2005 and from December 2005 to 23 February 2006 in Enterprises outside Industrial Zones in HCMC*], p. 4.

[103] See Gong Ting and Chen Feng, 'The Rise of Developmentalism across the Taiwan Strait', in Yu Bin and Chung Tsungting (eds.), *Dynamics and Dilemma: Mainland, Taiwan and Hong Kong in a Changing World* (New York, NY: Nova Science Publishers, 1996), pp. 19, 20–23 for an account of Asian developmentalism.

[104] Le Thanh Vinh, *Competition Law Transfers in Vietnam: From a Interpretive Perspective*, PhD Thesis, Monash University (2012), p. 131.

[105] See, e.g., Interviews with L1, L7–L8, U11; HCMC DOLISA, Báo cáo số 910/BC-SLĐTBXH-LĐ về Tình hình Đình công, Lãn công 3 năm (2003–2005) và từ Tháng 12/2005 đến 23/02/2006 Của Các Doanh nghiệp Ngoài Khu Chế xuất – Khu Công nghiệp Trên Địa bàn Thành phố Hồ Chí Minh [*Report No. 910/BC-SLDTBXH-LD on the Situation of Strikes [and] Slowdowns in 2003–2005 and from December 2005 to 23 February 2006 in Enterprises outside Industrial Zones in HCMC*], p. 7; Vĩnh Tùng, 'Đình công Tự phát: Doanh nghiệp và Người Lao động Đều Thiệt' ['Wildcat Strikes: Both Enterprises and Workers Are Affected'], *Người Lao động* [*The Labourer*], 13 June 1998, p. 2.

[106] Interviews with L10, U6, U11.

Multi-sector task forces were also inspired by virtue-rule thinking, which has existed in Vietnam for centuries and has been selectively adapted by the communist party to support its leadership and state governance.[107] As already seen, the tolerant and pro-worker approach to strike resolution was based primarily on regulators' perceptions regarding the extent to which employers, workers and the state were morally responsible for strike incidents. Notwithstanding this, it is safe to conclude that the main and most influential ideas behind multi-sector task forces derived from socialist-inspired perspectives, especially Marxist–Leninist views about socialism.

11.6 Limited Transformation in Strike Resolution from 2007 to 2013 and the Erosion of Socialist and Marxist–Leninist Influences

Multi-sector task forces remained the principal mechanism to handle unlawful wildcat strikes in Bình Dương, Đồng Nai and HCMC between 2007 and 2013.[108] Yet compared to the earlier period, this mechanism operated on a sounder legal foundation (a consequence of the 2006 and 2012 Labour Code reforms).[109]

There were only two changes in the composition of strike task forces.[110] The first was an increase in the participation of officials from party-state organisations in charge of mass mobilisation, such as the Department of Mass Mobilisation, the Fatherland Front, the Youth Union and the Women's Union (though key members were still labour and union officials).[111] This indicates that mass mobilisation was still seen as a major means for strike management.

The second change in the composition of strike task forces was the declining involvement of provincial authorities. The escalation of strikes from the mid-2000s caused these authorities to become overloaded,

---

[107] Gillespie, 'Changing Concepts of Socialist Law in Vietnam', pp. 60–61; Penelope (Pip) Nicholson, *Borrowing Court Systems: The Experience of Socialist Vietnam* (Leiden: Martinus Nijhoff, 2007), pp. 224–227.

[108] Interviews with L1–L14, U1, U4–U6, U8–U12.

[109] See Art. 158, Labour Code (Revised) 2006; Art. 222, Labour Code 2012.

[110] Interviews with L1–L14, U1, U4–U6, U8–U12; Bình Dương DOLISA, *Báo cáo Số 51/BC-SLĐTBXH về Tình hình Thực hiện các Quy định Pháp luật về Giải quyết Tranh chấp Lao động, Đình công* [Report No. 51/BC-SLDTBXH on the Implementation of Legal Regulations on Dispute Resolution and Strikes], p. 8; Đồng Nai DOLISA, *Báo cáo Số 65/BC-LĐTBXH Đánh giá Tình hình Thực hiện các Quy định Pháp luật về Giải quyết Tranh chấp Lao động, Đình công* [Report No. 65/BC-LDTBXH on Assessment of the Implementation of Legal Regulations on Dispute Resolution and Strikes], pp. 8–9.

[111] Interviews with L4–L6, L13, U4, U6.

urging them to shift the task of strike resolution to lower organisations.[112] Nonetheless, provincial involvement remained considerable due to insufficient personnel at district and equivalent levels, and the provincial authorities' frequent concern about strikes.[113]

11.6.1 Changes and Continuities in the Operation of Multi-Sector Task Forces

As in the period from 1995 to 2007, the resolution of unlawful wildcat strikes by multi-sector task forces in Bình Dương, Đồng Nai and HCMC followed three basic steps: exploring workers' requests and stabilising the situation; working with management for a settlement; and announcing the settlement to workers and getting them back to work.[114] Despite this, several changes emerged.

First, there was an increasing acceptance of interest-based disputes. Unlike preceding years, multi-sector task forces did not automatically exclude such requests, but usually communicated them to management.[115] Additionally, they often attempted to push employers to accept the whole or a part of these requests.[116] This was usually done by way of persuasion, in which local officials invoked both economic and moral reasons, such as inflation, market rates and practices, benefits of a quick settlement, workers' misery and the 'good' of profit sharing between labour and capital.[117]

Second, local regulators adopted a more decisive approach to rights-based disputes. Unlike in the past, they often revisited strike-affected enterprises to ensure that the employers had ceased their breaches of labour laws.[118] In Bình Dương, the Provincial People's Committee also directed multi-sector task forces to maintain a more resolute attitude towards employers violating labour standards.[119]

Third, strike task forces became less favourable to workers and more favourable to employers. They now refrained from strongly criticising

---

[112] Interviews with L1–L14, U1, U4–U6, U8–U12.
[113] Ibid.
[114] Interviews with L1–L14, U1, U4–L12.
[115] Ibid.
[116] Interviews with L2–L3, L5–L6, L9, L11–L14, U5–U6, U10–U12.
[117] Ibid.; Interview with M2 (HCMC, 18 April 2012). M2 was the general manager of a domestic private enterprise and a senior member of the American Chamber of Commerce in HCMC.
[118] Interviews with L2, L7–L14, U5–U6, U8, U10.
[119] Interviews with L7–L10. Interviewees reported the time of issuance of this direction differently (late 2011 or early 2012). It was not possible to obtain this document from local officials.

employers and blaming strikes solely on them.[120] And they often intentionally chose not to advocate all the interest-based demands of workers.[121]
Where strikes were prolonged, many task forces did not push management
to make further concessions until workers were satisfied, as they had in the
past.[122] Instead, they recommended that management ask workers to return
to work within five working days to avoid likely dismissal.[123]

Bình Dương offers the most remarkable example of declining task
force support for workers. In late 2011 or early 2012, the Bình Dương
People's Committee expressly directed multi-sector task forces to be
tougher on strikers.[124] From then on, local officials increasingly merely
communicated interest-based demands to management, leaving them to
determine their own responses to workers.[125] Additionally, they often
encouraged employers to stage a stronger response to workers, believing
that this would prevent strikes in the long run.[126] In particular, task forces
usually encouraged employers to resist changing their initial response to
workers' interest-based demands and to dock their pay for the striking
days.[127] Some even urged employers to reject interest-based requests.[128]

Finally, multi-sector task forces utilised a more patient and less interventionist approach to strike settlement, which permitted a greater – though still
limited – space for collective bargaining, the autonomy of disputing parties
and workers' right to participation. This is demonstrated in workers having
more opportunities to participate in settlement meetings. According to
several local officials, they allowed representatives that had been nominated
by workers to attend such meetings, though these representatives were not
always permitted to negotiate with management.[129] Sometimes, strike task
forces also arranged for the employer to negotiate directly with the whole
labour collective.[130] Further, as mentioned earlier, strike task forces ceased to

---

[120] Interviews with E1, L5, M1, U8.
[121] Interviews with E1, L1–L3, L5, L7, L11–L12, L14, U6, U8–U9.
[122] Interviews with L4–L5, L7–L8, L13, M1–M2, U6, U9, U12.
[123] Interviews with L4–L5, L7–L8, L13, M1–M2, U6, U9, U12. This recommendation stemmed
from Art. 85(1) of the 2006 Revised Labour Code, which permitted an employer to dismiss an
employee who took five days off in one month without acceptable reasons. However, some
officials did not advocate this approach: Interviews with L14, M1.
[124] Interviews with L7–L10, U7–U9.
[125] Interviews with L7–L8, L10, M1.
[126] Interviews with L7–L10, M1, U8–U9.
[127] Interviews with L7–L10, M1, U8–U9.
[128] Interviews with U9.
[129] Interviews with L1–L2, L5–L7, L9, L11, U4–U6, U8; Interview with worker (Đồng Nai,
22 April 2012).
[130] Interviews with L12, U5–U6, U10–U11.

broadly disregard interest-based requests. During my field visits, some – but not all – local officials stressed that they communicated all requests of strikers to management, whether they supported those requests or not.[131] As noted, the principal way to resolve interest-based requests was to persuade, rather than compel, employers.

Moreover, local officials did not always visit a strike-affected factory immediately as they had previously, but might give workers and management one or two days to settle the incident themselves.[132] One district official in HCMC noted that she encouraged employers and in-house unions to work together before seeking state help, and this was successful in some cases.[133] In Bình Dương, from late 2011 or early 2012, if a task force's first attempts to resolve a strike were unsuccessful, they would leave the parties alone for a few days (while retaining police presence to maintain order), rather than work with them continuously, as they had in the past.[134] This also occurred in Đồng Nai and HCMC, but did not reflect the extent of the changes in Bình Dương.[135]

Notwithstanding the foregoing developments, the approach of local regulators to strike settlement remained essentially unchanged. Multi-sector task forces were still under pressure to extinguish strikes.[136] Thus, they continued to intervene in strikes proactively, kept concentrating on 'key demands' of workers and regularly pushed employers to satisfy such demands.[137]

Furthermore, strike task forces did not completely abandon their rights-based approach to interest-based disputes. They frequently explained to strikers that interest-based demands had no legal basis and, therefore, depended on employers' discretion.[138] Additionally, task forces often discouraged interest-based demands that they deemed 'excessive',[139] such as workers requesting wage increases beyond employers' capacity or considerably higher than market rates, or interfering with managerial issues like the appointment of managers and the selection of shift meal providers.[140] In several cases, 'excessive requests' were

---

[131] Interviews with L8, L13, U6.
[132] Interviews with L2, L5, L11, L14, U4, U11.
[133] Interview with U4.
[134] Interviews with L7–L10, U8. These interviewees reported the time of change differently. Some said late 2011 while the others mentioned early 2012.
[135] Interviews with L5, L14, U11.
[136] Interviews with L1–L14, U1, U4–U6, U8–U12.
[137] Interviews with L1–L14, U1, U4–U6, U8–U12.
[138] Interviews with L2–L3, L5, L7–L14, U5–U6, U8, U10.
[139] Interviews with L3, L8, L11–L13, U2, U6, U8, U10.
[140] Interviews with L3, L8, L11–L13, U2, U6, U8, U10.

excluded from resolution meetings.[141] In other cases, task forces tried to persuade workers to withdraw such requests, but still conveyed them to management if workers refused to do so.[142] On occasion, they communicated the requests but encouraged employers to reject them.[143]

Likewise, local regulators kept recasting interest-based demands as rights-based.[144] Two HCMC officials, for example, told me that wage increase demands indicated rights disputes because wages had to 'be paid in consideration of the rate of production, and the quality and result of the work performed'.[145] The well-known strike that occurred in Pou Chen Corporation (Đồng Nai) in 2010 offers another illustration. Instead of negotiating with management to resolve the case, the relevant district union publicly criticised the company for enacting illegal wage scales to push for wage increases.[146]

Moreover, strike task forces still maintained an interventionist approach that permitted little space for collective bargaining, party autonomy, right to participation and other due process requirements. Though to a lesser degree, these task forces still filtered out workers' requests and preferred to work with labour and capital separately.[147] In addition, they made extensive use of administrative/coercive measures to resolve interest-based disputes. Several task forces deployed the existence of employers' breaches to pressure them into accepting interest-based demands.[148] Others threatened management that their companies would be inspected on compliance issues or left alone with the incidents, including the possibility of workers resorting to sabotage and violence.[149] As in the period from 1995 to 2007, there remained limited – though greater – chance for workers and management to negotiate with each other. Further, strike task forces continued to largely disregard due process principles such as neutrality, the right of self-defence and the right to appeal.[150]

---

[141] Interviews with L3, L8, L11–L13, U2, U6, U8, U10.

[142] Interviews with L8, L13, U6.

[143] Interview with U9.

[144] Interviews with L1–L3, U1.

[145] Interviews with L1–L2, citing Art. 55, Labour Code (Revised) 2006.

[146] See Nam Dương, 'Công nhân Pou Chen VN Vẫn còn Ngừng việc' ['Workers of Pou Chen Vietnam Are Still Stopping Working'], Người Lao động [The Labourer], 7 April 2010, available at http://nld.com.vn/2010040611514302p1011c1010/cong-nhan-pou chen-vn-van-con-ngung-viec.htm.

[147] Interviews with L1, L3–L5, L7–L14, U1, U5–U6, U8–U12.

[148] Interviews with E1, L2–L3, L6, L13.

[149] Interviews with L2, L5, U2.

[150] Interviews with L1–L14, U1, U4–U6, U8–U12. See also Regulation 35/2006; Bình Dương People's Committee, Temporary Regulation on Organisation and Operation of the

Similarly, local regulators still tolerated unlawful wildcat strikes (while police attempts were still made from time to time to threaten, punish and separate strike activists from workers).[151] Further, they continued to fail to take a neutral position. All officials I met in HCMC appeared to enthusiastically support strikers.[152] Most Đồng Nai officials exhibited a similar attitude, though to a lesser extent.[153] Meanwhile, as noted, Bình Dương officials gradually came to favour management starting in late 2011 or early 2012. And strike task forces continued to prefer methods of compromise and flexibility, tolerating both workers' and employers' breaches with a view to obtaining a quick resolution.[154]

11.6.2   The Persistent but Eroding Impact of Socialist and Marxist–Leninist Thinking on Multi-Sector Task Forces and the Emergence of New Modes of Thought

Interviews with local officials reveal that, from 2007 to 2013, Marxist–Leninist and socialist ideas continued to dominate the view of local regulators about strike management, which is similar to their views between 1995 and 2007.[155] That is why the composition of multi-sector task forces and their approach to strike resolution remained fundamentally unchanged. Field research, however, reveals certain erosion in the impact of some Marxist–Leninist and socialist ideas, which coincided with the growing influence of new modes of thinking. As shown below, changes in the operation of strike task forces between 2007 and 2013 were closely linked with this epistemic transformation.

The reduction in the support for workers is a case in point. In justifying this, local officials – especially those from administrative agencies – often reasoned that the state had to take a 'middle position' (cửa giữa)

Provincial Direction Board for Resolution of Collective Labour Disputes and Strikes Not Following Procedures Prescribed by Law, and on the Responsibility for Cooperation between the Provincial Direction Board and Relevant Bodies and Organisations in Prevention and Resolution of Labour Disputes and Strikes in Bình Dương, issued in Conjunction with Decision No. 149/2006/QD-UBND dated 13 June 2006; Đồng Nai People's Committee, Regulation on Resolution of Collective Labour Disputes Not Following Procedures Prescribed by Labour Law in Enterprises in Đồng Nai Province, issued in Conjunction with Decision No. 22/2009/QD-UBND dated 2 April 2009.

[151] Interviews with L1–L14, U1, U4–U6, U8–U12.
[152] Interviews with L1–L6, U1–U6.
[153] Interviews with L11–L13, U11–U12.
[154] Interviews with L1–L14, U1, U4–U6, U8–U12.
[155] Ibid.

when settling disputes.[156] Additionally, they believed that satisfying all of the workers' requests would encourage them to strike again in the future.[157] These arguments indicate that local officials became less influenced by the notion of the workers' state and more in line with the liberal concept of the state as a neutral umpire and the lessons drawn from their practical experience.

Meanwhile, underpinning the growing support for employers was the erosion of the socialist criticism of capitalism and the emergence of pro-capitalist thought. During my interviews, several party-state officials explicitly challenged the notion of exploitative employers, or explained strikes without referring to employers' failures or with greater emphasis on other causes.[158] Further to this, many strongly condemned workers as abusing strike action and causing undue difficulties for employers.[159]

The erosion of the notion of the workers' state and the concept of exploitative capitalists is particularly evident in the case of Bình Dương. Unlike in Đồng Nai and HCMC, most officials that I met in this province expressed a negative attitude towards strikers and a sympathetic attitude towards employers.[160] This explains why Bình Dương regulators endorsed not only a reduction in labour protection, but also tough measures against strikers. Arguably, the transformation in Bình Dương reflected its longstanding policy of promoting private business and foreign investment.[161] Yet the economic slowdown in 2008 was a catalyst, pressing Bình Dương authorities to implement bolder measures to support investors.[162]

Nevertheless, the changing attitude towards labour and capital also replicated old-style thinking. In explaining this transformation, many officials reasoned that workers did not always strike because of their

---

[156] Interviews with L4, L5, L8, L11–L12, U4, U6, U8.

[157] Interviews with L2, L4, L7, L9, L11, U6.

[158] Interviews with L1–L2, L7–L10, U6, U9–U10; Interview with C1 (Hanoi, 20 March 2012); Interview with C2 (Hanoi, 29 March 2012). C1 and C2 were senior officials of the MOLISA.

[159] Interviews with L7–L10.

[160] Interviews with L7–L10, U9–U10.

[161] See Edmund L. Malesky, 'Push, Pull, and Reinforcing: The Channels of FDI Influence on Provincial Governance in Vietnam', in Benedict J. Tria Kerkvliet and David G. Marr (eds.), Beyond Hanoi: Local Government in Vietnam (Copenhagen: NIAS Press; Singapore: Institute of Southeast Asian Studies, 2004), p. 308; Nguyen Van Thang and Nick J. Freeman, 'State-Owned Enterprises in Vietnam: Are They "Crowding out" the Private Sector?' (2009) 21(2) Post-Communist Economies 227, 238, for Bình Dương's longstanding support for private business and foreign investment, including comparative reference to Đồng Nai and HCMC.

[162] Interviews with L7, U9.

needs, but due to coercion and encouragement from 'bad elements' (that is, strike instigators).[163] This suggests that regulators retained a negative attitude towards independent worker activism, which had roots in the Leninist conception of trade unionism.

Further, the change in attitude towards labour and capital reflected the continual inspiration by ethical (right/wrong) perspectives. This is demonstrated by local officials, who justified reducing their support for strikers by pointing out that strikes decreasingly involved breaches by employers'.[164] Some further stressed that, whereas employers had improved compliance with labour standards, workers kept violating strike laws.[165]

Moral perspectives also underpinned the more decisive approach to employers' breaches in strike settlement. This is exhibited in the explanation of local officials that (foreign) employers could no longer cite lack of legal knowledge to avoid legal liability because they had several years of doing business in Vietnam and had been provided with the relevant legal information.[166] However, the adoption of stricter measures against employer violation was also inspired by local officials' reflection of practical experience, as some officials noted that the tolerance of employer violation contributed to the recurrence of strikes.[167]

The emergence of a more patient and less interventionist approach to strike resolution offers another illustration of weakening Marxist–Leninist and socialist influences. The 2007–2013 period saw a rising recognition, especially among labour and union officials, that strikes were a normal industrial relations phenomenon that rarely posed a political threat to the party-state.[168] Concurrently, there emerged a perception that strikes could have positive side effects, such as informing the authorities of labour and social problems, redistributing profits between labour and capital, or preventing labour disputes from escalating into political unrest.[169] The slight reduction in anxiety about strikes enabled a more patient and less interventionist approach to strike resolution.[170]

The decreasing emphasis on quick and proactive intervention in strike settlement also demonstrates the erosion of 'state economic

---

[163] Interviews with L7–L10.
[164] Interviews with L11–L12, U6, U10.
[165] Interviews with L8, L11.
[166] Interviews with L2, L10, U6.
[167] Interviews with L7–L9.
[168] Interviews with L2, L4–L5, L14, U4, U8.
[169] Interviews with L2, L5, L7, L11, U8.
[170] Interviews with L2, L4–L5, L14, U4, U8.

management', and the greater impact of 'practical lessons' and more liberal thinking. Increasingly, local regulators realised that task force intervention had weakened the role of in-house unions, and they encouraged workers to utilise industrial action and state intervention, rather than collective bargaining, to settle industrial disputes.[171] In addition, it was decided that labour and capital could and should be allowed to settle disputes by themselves, mostly through collective negotiation.[172]

The push to diminish state intervention appeared to intensify in relation to interest-based disputes. Local officials consistently noted that compelling employers to accept workers' interest-based requests 'did not accord with the law of a market economy' and might cause further disputes in future.[173] Many officials (mostly from Bình Dương) went even further, arguing that employers should be left alone to determine interest-based requests because these were economic issues.[174] This explains why several Bình Dương task forces simply communicated workers' interest-based requests to management, rather than enter into negotiations for them.

Given that the disregard for interest-based disputes had roots in planned economic practice, it is likely that the erosion of state economic management contributed to the increasing acceptance of these disputes. Nonetheless, the rather swift acceptance of interest-based disputes in the period from 2007 to 2013 suggests that the incorporation of this concept into the 2006 Revised Labour Code had significant influence on the mindset of regulators.[175]

In summary, the limited transformation in strike resolution from 2007 to 2013 substantially reflected two interconnected epistemic changes. One is the erosion of some Marxist–Leninist and socialist ideas, including the concept of state economic management, the notion of the state representing the working class and the socialist criticism of capitalism. The other is

---

[171] Interviews with L2, L7, L11, L13; Đồng Nai DOLISA, Báo cáo số 65/BC-LĐTBXH Đánh giá Tình hình Thực hiện Các Quy định Pháp luật về Giải quyết Tranh chấp Lao động, Đình công [Report No. 65/BC-LDTBXH on Assessment of the Implementation of Legal Regulations on Dispute Resolution and Strikes], p. 11.

[172] Interviews with L1–L2, L7, L14, U4, U6, U9.

[173] Interviews with L7–L8, U4, U6.

[174] Interviews with L7–L8, L10, L14.

[175] Interviews with L1–L9, L11–L14, U1, U4–U6, U8–U12 showing that local officials understood rather well why and how rights and interest disputes should be handled differently.

the emergence of new modes of thought, which exhibited more practical, pro-capitalist and liberal ideas about strikes and strike management.

11.7 Conclusion

The transition to a socialist-oriented market economy in Vietnam resulted in extensive reforms in labour law, which demonstrated a drastic decline in socialist influences and a certain relaxation of Marxist–Leninist principles. However, scrutiny of strike resolution in Vietnam between 1995 and 2013 reveals that the regulatory ideas of the high socialist era continued to dominate the actual management of labour conflicts in the socialist-oriented market economy. As previously argued, the methods for resolving unlawful wildcat strikes remained inspired by socialist conviction of capitalism, and socialist ideals about labour protection and social cooperation. In addition, they substantially, and perhaps more frequently, reflected Marxist–Leninist political, economic and legal ideas, including the Leninist perception of socialist unions, the discouragement of industrial action and worker activism, the notion of the workers' state and its paternalistic role, the instrumentalist view of law and the idea of mass mobilisation.

Nonetheless, the foregoing analysis also shows that some of these ideas – such as the criticism of capitalism, the ideology of the state representing the working class and the concept of state economic management – gradually declined in influence. Meanwhile, regulators were increasingly inspired by more practical, pro-capitalist or liberal perspectives, which lead to limited changes in strike settlement between 2007 and 2013.

PART VI

Regulatory Approaches

Is Vietnam Transitioning Out of Socialism or Transforming Socialism?

Searching for Answers in Commercial Regulation

JOHN GILLESPIE

12.1 Introduction

This Chapter explores a central question: is Vietnam transitioning out of socialism and/or transforming socialism? For decades, commentators have confidently predicted that Vietnam is transitioning out of socialism towards 'market-Leninism'.[1] While acknowledging that the party-state steadfastly clings to Leninist ideology and institutions, they argue that economic reforms following Đổi mới (renewal) in the mid-1980s excited wide-ranging institutional and regulatory change. For evidence, they point to the end of socialist command planning and agricultural cooperatives, as well as governance through market institutions and market-based strategies of accumulation. In their estimation, economic liberalisations are synonymous with institutional and regulatory liberalisations.

This Chapter argues that political, legal and economic changes have not entirely transformed the institutional structures and epistemic settings that supported socialism. Reforms changed some structures while leaving others relatively intact. Case studies considered in this Chapter demonstrate striking continuities in the objectives and methods used by the party-state to govern the pre- and post–Đổi mới economies. They suggest that, rather than experiencing a linear transition out of socialism, Vietnam is undergoing a highly variegated and complex transformation of socialism.

The inquiry into whether Vietnam is transitioning out of socialism and transforming socialism is complicated by five factors. First, it is

---

[1] See generally Jonathan London, 'Vietnam: The Making of Market Leninism' (2009) 22 (3) *Pacific Review* 375–395; Brian Van Arkadie and Raymond Mallon, *Viet Nam: A Transition Tiger?* (Canberra: Asia Pacific Press, 2003).

surprisingly difficult to differentiate socialism from capitalism – Cold War propaganda exaggerated difference and ignored shared historical origins.[2] Soviet command planning, for example, drew from Taylorist management techniques developed in the United States,[3] and functioned with a thick veneer of socialist rhetoric overlaying a thriving underground market economy. Thus, socialism and capitalism often drew on similar regulatory practices.

Second, it is difficult to unravel socialism from Marxism–Leninism. Although French radicals imported a broad range of socialist ideas into Vietnam during the early twentieth century, on gaining power, the Vietnamese Communist Party (VCP, or Party) methodically suppressed independent progressive thinking.[4] As a consequence, contemporary Party narratives conflate Leninist organisational practices, such as democratic centralism and the leading role of the Party, with socialism.

Third, in a related concern, it is important to bear in mind that socialist economic regulation in Vietnam did not begin when the Democratic Republic of Vietnam imported command planning technologies from the Soviet Union during the 1960s.[5] It has a much older genealogy that reflects longstanding patterns of interaction between state, bureaucracy and markets.[6] What we understand as socialist regulation did not so much control behaviour directly, as coordinate and interact with preexisting pre-colonial and colonial regulatory orders.

Fourth, another methodological difficulty is distinguishing continuity from change. This requires a framework for measuring change. There are several possibilities: one is change relative to pre-Đổi mới economic regulation, while another possibility is change reflecting imported neoliberal or East Asian regulatory ideas.

Fifth, this inquiry focuses on regulatory rather than legal change. To more accurately understand how the Party and state governs the economy, this Chapter abandons the image of the state as a constitutionally

---

[2] Elisabeth Dunn and Katherine Verdery, 'Dead Ends in the Critique of (Post)socialist Anthropology: Reply to Thelen' (2011) 31 (3) *Critique of Anthropology*, 251, 253.

[3] See Kendall Bailes, 'Alexei Gastev and the Soviet Controversy over Taylorism 1918–1924' (1977) 24(3) *Soviet Studies* 373–394.

[4] See Keith Weller Taylor, *A History of the Vietnamese* (Cambridge: Cambridge University Press, 2013), pp. 500–511.

[5] See John Gillespie, *Transplanting Commercial Law Reform* (Aldershot: Ashgate, 2006), pp. 62–64.

[6] See Gerard Sasges and Scott Cheshier, 'Competing Legacies: Rupture and Continuity in Vietnamese Political Economy' (2012) 20 *South East Asia Research* 5–33.

defined set of institutions and instead searches for regulation wherever rules are present, authority is perceived and behaviour is modified.[7]

To explore whether Vietnam is transitioning out of socialism or transforming socialism, this Chapter poses the following questions: has the shift from a centrally planned economy to a mixed market affected how economic regulation is understood, calculated and acted upon? Does the privatisation of state-owned enterprises (SOEs) signify the retreat of the party-state and more autonomy for the Vietnamese people to regulate market activities? Has there been a shrinking of the regulatory space in which the state projects power? Or, rather than a decline in state power, has there been a redeployment and diversification of state regulation over the economy? Finally, have macro-level regulatory liberalisations been offset by reregulation in specific industries at the micro-regulatory level?

12.2 Sequencing Regulatory Change in Vietnam

After the partition of Vietnam in 1954, the North and South followed radically different regulatory paths. In 1958, the Democratic Republic of Vietnam announced a three-year economic plan to transform the economy along socialist lines – with the people as owners, the Party as leader and the government as managers.[8] Over the following decades, North Vietnamese leaders imported a facsimile of the Soviet command economy, with few concessions to local conditions.[9] Following Lenin's injunction that 'the only possible economic foundation of socialism is large-scale machine industry',[10] Party leaders industrialised the rural economy and diverted scarce resources to new industries such as steel production.[11] Thousands of Vietnamese were sent to Eastern Bloc countries to

---

[7] Julia Black, 'Regulatory Conversations' (2002) 29(1) *Journal of Law and Society* 163–196.

[8] See Ho Chi Minh, 1959 'Report on the Draft Amended Constitution', December 18, 1959, reproduced in *Ho Chi Minh Selected Writings* (1920–1969), 214, 221.

[9] See Hoang Hao, 'Phap Luat va Kinh Te' [Law and Economy], Tạp chí Cộng sản [Communist Review], 24–28 December 1987; Tran Duc, 'Ve Cac Luat Kinh Te Trong thoi Ly Qua Do Len Chu Nhia Xa Hoi' ['Economic Laws in the Transition Period to Socialism'], Tạp chí Cộng sản, May 1987, pp. 69–73.

[10] Vladimir Lenin, *Collected Works* (Moscow: Progress Publishers 1965), vol. 32, p. 492 cited in Le Duan, *Selected Writings (1960–1975)* (Hanoi: The Gioi Publishers, 1994) p. 247.

[11] See Le Huu Tang and Liu Han Yue (eds.), *Economic Reform in Viet Nam and in China: A Comparative Study* (Hanoi: The Gioi Publishers, 2006), pp. 14–23.

learn how to manage a command economy. After unification in 1975, the victorious North imposed command economic regulation on the South.[12]

Unlike the Soviet Bloc, the VCP did not proclaim the end of socialism with the fall of the Soviet Union. Đổi mới reforms in 1986 officially recognised a mixed market, and although some aspects of the centrally planned economy were abandoned, other parts were reformed and retained. For example, the National Assembly still prepares detailed five-year socio-economic plans guiding national development. Far from withering away under a policy of privatisation, a reduced number of state-owned companies have maintained their share of the national economy.[13] In fact, the party-state continues to insist that Vietnam is a socialist state.[14]

In another difference from the Soviet Bloc, market reforms in Vietnam did not bring about political collapse.[15] The VCP penetrates the state apparatus and still attempts to dominate, govern and regulate most aspects of social life. Following Lenin's organisational model,[16] the Party organises cells in every branch of government and in every institutional arena and, beyond the formal remit of state administration, into neighbourhood units, economic units, universities, schools and hospitals.

As discussed in Chapter 1 in this volume, Truong Chinh's address to the 1986 National Congress of the Communist Party outlined the reasons for the legal turn in Vietnam. Legal scholars argued for a comprehensive legislative framework to govern the mixed-market economics.[17] Laws were needed, they reasoned, to unleash entrepreneurial creativity and push innovation to new heights. In 1991, the Party adopted the law-governed state (Nhà nước pháp quyền) policy, which prescribed stable,

---

[12] Le Huu Tang and Liu Han Yue, p. 16.

[13] The General Statistics Office reported a total of 3,135 SOEs in 2013, down from nearly 5,800 in 2000. Vietnam Briefing, 3 January 2014, available at www.vietnam-briefing.com/news/decline-state-owned-enterprises-vietnam.html. Also see Edmund Malesky and Jonathan London, 'The Political Economy of Development in China and Vietnam' (2014) 17 Annual Review of Political Science 395, 411–412.

[14] Article 2 of the recently amended Constitution 2013 proclaims 'the Socialist Republic of Vietnam is a socialist state'.

[15] Dang Phong and Melanie Beresford, Authority Relations and Economic Decision-Making in Vietnam: An Historical Perspective (Copenhagen: NIAS Publications, 1998).

[16] Janos Kornai, The Socialist System: The Political Economy of Communism (Oxford: Oxford University Press, 1992).

[17] See Lê Minh Thông, 'Mấy vấn đề lý luận chung về pháp luật trong thời kỳ quá độ ở Việt Nam' ['Some Issues with the General Theory of Law in the Transitional Period in Vietnam'], Nha Nuoc Phap Luat, No. 3, 1988, pp. 41–45.

authoritative and compulsory law; equality before the law; and the use of law to constrain and supervise the enforcement and administration of law.[18] Rather than breaking from the past, this reform carried forward decades-old socialist concepts, such as socialist legality (*nhà nước pháp quyền xã hội*) and democratic centralism (*tập trung dân chủ*).

Over the intervening decades, Marxist–Leninist tenets associated with the class struggle, such as dictatorship of the proletariat and collective mastery, have withered away, leaving firmly in place Leninist organisational structures that ensured the leading role for the Communist Party.[19] Without institutions such as a constitutional court to review Party power, law emanated from and served the Party and state. It evolved into an instrument through which the party-state could strengthen its grip on society and avoid the fragmentation that occurred in post-socialist Europe.

In reforming the economy, the party-state did not simply remove legal controls over private enterprises and get out of the way, as neo-liberal commentators urged. Instead, Party leaders consciously designed new markets, frequently with complex rules and regulations, to promote specific state socio-economic policies, such as economic efficiency and state control over particular economic sectors. In strategic sectors – areas important to national security and technical advancement – the party-state has centralised regulatory controls. In less strategic sectors, the party-state has relinquished some central control, decentralised policymaking to local authorities and encouraged private investment. A central claim in this Chapter is that state regulation functions differently in three distinct economic sectors: the 'commanding heights of the economy',[20] the foreign investment sector, and the small-scale trading and service sector.

12.3   Conceptualising Socialist Regulation

An epistemological dilemma haunts every attempt to determine what is socialist about economic regulation: Is socialism fundamentally different

---

[18] See Do Muoi, *Sua Doi Hien Phap Xay Dung Nha Nuoc Phap Quyen Viet Nam, Day Manh Su Nghiep Doi Moi* [*Amending the Constitution, Establishing a Law-Based-State and Promoting Doi moi Achievements*] (Hanoi: Nha Xuat Ban Su That, 1992), pp. 30–38.

[19] See John Gillespie, *Transplanting Commercial Law Reform: Developing a "Rule of Law" in Vietnam* (Aldershot: Ashgate, 2006), pp. 76–105.

[20] Lenin used the term 'commanding heights of the economy' to refer to core economic sectors, such as steel production, transport and communication, that are considered vital to economic development.

from capitalism, or are the differences a matter of degree? Rather than assuming there is a single determinative socialist criterion, this Chapter focuses on a range of ideals, processes and practices that have enabled culturally and historically varied forms of socialism.[21] Applying this multi-component analysis, socialist economic regulation falls along a continuum. Soviet command planning occupies one end of the continuum, while other types of governance that emphasise state economic guidance, such as the East Asian developmental state and Scandinavian social democracies, occupy other positions on the continuum.[22]

To explore continuities and changes in economic regulation, this Chapter divides regulation into two basic modalities:

1. regulatory signalling – the ideological and normative messages sent by state regulation; and
2. regulatory technologies – the methods and logics of regulation.

Regulatory technologies are further subdivided into five categories: statutory rights protection, relational regulation, the criminalisation of commerce, data collection and monitoring, and mass movements. To ascertain what (if anything) is socialist about the modalities, the discussion first explores how the modalities functioned under the command economy and then searches for continuities and changes in the post–Đổi mới economy.

12.4   Regulatory Signalling

Regulation signals the kind of economic behaviour regulators desire.[23] It makes broad statements about the objectives of governance and the future direction of policies, as well as economic, political and legal ideology. Regulatory signalling is most effective in shaping behaviour where the signals appear credible, consistent and legitimate.

---

[21] See generally Michael Burawoy and Katherine Verdery (eds.), *Uncertain Transition: Ethnographies of Change in the Postsocialist World* (Lanham, MD: Rowman and Littlefield, 1999).

[22] Peter Hall and David Soskice, *Varieties of Capitalism: The Institutional Foundations of Comparative Advantage* (Oxford: Oxford University Press, 2001); Bob Jessop and Ngai-Ling Sum, *Beyond the Regulation Approach: Putting Capitalist Economies in Their Place* (Cheltenham: Edward Elgar, 2006), pp. 152–156.

[23] Cass Sunstein, 'On the Expressive Function of Law' (1996) 144 *University of Pennsylvania Law Review* 2021–2053.

12.4.1   Equality

A core characteristic of socialism is its commitment to an egalitarian society.[24] Ho Chi Minh emphasised this ideal when he opined that '[p]lainly and briefly speaking, socialism is first and foremost helping laboring people escape poverty, providing everyone with jobs, making everyone wealthy and securing everyone a happy life'.[25] Command regulation in Vietnam did not countenance absolute economic equality, as income differentials were retained to encourage performance. Nevertheless, the state tightly managed the accumulation of wealth by strictly controlling the size of houses people could own and by prohibiting leasing and other renter activities.[26]

Orthodox Marxist–Leninism prescribed state ownership as the primary method for achieving social equality. *The Communist Manifesto* claimed that a communist revolution 'cannot be effected without means of despotic inroads on the rights of [private] property' and proposed the '[a]bolition of property in land and application of rents of land to public purposes'.[27] Party leaders in Vietnam put this injunction into practice by placing land under people's ownership (*sở hữu toàn dân*), nationalising large corporations, establishing cooperative farms and SOEs (see Chapter 15 in this volume), and criminalising private commerce.[28]

Contemporary Party theorists struggle to reconcile mixed-market reforms with socialist objectives of equality.[29] They argue, for example, that the mixed-market economy is a necessary stage in the transition to socialism. Market mechanisms develop and modernise the economy

---

[24] Michael Newman, *Socialism: A Very Short Introduction* (New York, NY: Oxford University Press, 2005).

[25] Ho Chi Minh, *Ho Chi Minh Toan Tap* [*Ho Chi Minh Collected Works*] (Hanoi: Chinh Tri Quoc Gia [National Political Publishing House], 2000), vol. 10, p. 17.

[26] Circular No. 713 TTg on Land Management Authorizing State Management Policies 1963. Also see Phung Minh, *40 Nam Quan Ly Nha Cua O Ha Noi* [*40 Years of Housing Management in Hanoi*] (Hanoi: unpublished paper, 14–18 October 1998).

[27] Karl Marx, *Karl Marx Selected Writings* (Indianapolis, IN: Hackett Publishing, 1994), p. 175.

[28] Ho Chi Minh, 'Report on the Draft Amended Constitution', 18 December 1959, reproduced in *Ho Chi Minh Ho Chi Minh's Collected Works* (Hanoi: National Politics Publishing House, 1959), pp. 214–221.

[29] See Vũ Văn Phúc, 'Developing the Socialist-Oriented Market Economy in Viet Nam: Theoretical Awareness, Practices and Recommendations', Tạp chí Cộng sản, No. 858, April 2014, available at http://english.tapchicongsan.org.vn/Home/Socialist-oriented-Market-Economy/2014/425/Developing-the-socialistoriented-market-economy-in-Viet-Nam-Theoretical-awareness-practices-and.aspx.

without compromising equality because the state can harness capitalism's positive features and discard the negative ones.[30] In this view, private ownership over commodities and the means of production is permitted only insofar as it supports Party socio-economic policies.[31] Theorists argue that private land ownership goes too far, as it will permit rapid wealth accumulation and compromise the socialist project.[32]

12.4.2   Community and the Individual

Socialism favours the community – its aims and values – over those of the individual.[33] Marx stressed universal social and moral perspectives rather than individual perspectives.[34] Although socialist texts do not deny that humans are self-interested, they nonetheless maintain that, with appropriate party leadership, people can develop altruistic motivations that subordinate personal interests to community.

Party leaders in Vietnam followed the Soviet lead and sought to promote communitarian and altruistic values by engineering socialist men. As Ho Chi Minh observed: 'If you want to build socialism then you must first of all have some socialists.'[35] Party leaders sought to harness neo-Confucian aphorisms, such as 'people are a totality of their social relationships', to support socialist communitarianism.[36] Socialist

---

[30] Lê Huu Nghia, 'The Tenth National Party Congress and Awareness of the Path towards Socialism in Vietnam', Nhân Dân (People), 3 July 2006, available at www.nhandan .com.vn/english/news/030706/domestic_tenth.htm.

[31] Vu Ngoc Nhung, 'Role of the State in Market Economy with Socialist Orientation' (1999) 6 Vietnam Social Sciences 19–23; Phạm Ngọc Quang, 'Vai trò của Nhà nước trong nền kinh tế thị trường định hướng xã hội chủ nghĩa ở Việt Nam hiện nay' ['The Role of State in the Socialist-oriented Market Economy of Vietnam Today'], Tạp chí Cộng sản, No. 798(8), 2009.

[32] See Vũ Văn Phúc, 'Sở hữu toàn dân về đất đai: Tất yếu lịch sử trong điều kiện nước ta hiện nay' ['Public ownership of land: A historical necessity under the current conditions of our country'], Tạp chí Cộng sản, 20 March 2013 available at www.tapchicongsan.org .vn/Home/Tieu-diem/2013/20653/So-huu-toan-dan-ve-dat-dai-Tat-yeu-lich-su-trong.aspx.

[33] See Nguyen Chi My, 'Chu Nghia Ca Nhan va Cuoc Dau Tranh De Khac Phuc No' ['Individualism and the Struggle to Overcome It'], Tạp chí Cộng sản, No. (6), 1989, pp. 36–40.

[34] Karl Marx, 'Alienated Labor', in Lawrence H. Simon (ed.), Karl Marx: Selected Writing (Indianapolis, IN: Hackett, 1994), pp. 58–68.

[35] Ho Chi Minh cited in Le Duan, Selected Writings (1960–1975), p. 240.

[36] See Hoang Quoc Viet, Can Dam Bao Cho Phap Luat Duoc Ton Trong Trong Cong Tac Quan Ly Linh Te Cua Nha Nuoc [We Must Ensure the Enforcement of Law in State Economic Management] (Hanoi: Truth Publishing, 1964), pp. 35–36.

men were expected to transcend 'feudal' culture, respect public property, oppose capitalist individualism and promote the collective spirit.[37]

Contemporary Party leaders remain optimistic about the perfectibility of human nature and the capacity of the state to engineer epistemic transformations.[38] This belief in social engineering contrasts with neo-liberalism, which reifies self-interest as an immutable human condition that resists state-directed social change. Neo-liberalism treats state regulation as an inferior form of social coordination, with the potential to impair the workings of private modes of economic regulation.

Although recent economic policies in Vietnam emphasise 'wealth-making individuals' (người làm giàu), they have stopped well short of embracing Hayek's neo-liberal proposition that society has no material existence.[39] Party pronouncements still caution against the evils of individualism and actively promote communitarian values in the market economy.[40] Reflecting on the tension between communitarianism and individualism in Vietnam, Christina Schwenkel and Ann Marie Leshkoich concluded: '[t]he imbrication of the individual in a collectivity in turn involves multiple ideologies that work to produce subjects who are neither fully state determined nor liberally autonomous, neither public nor private.'[41]

12.4.3   Cooperation and Competition

The preference in socialism for cooperation and solidarity over competition is predicated on an optimistic view about the capacity of humans to collaborate with one another.[42] It valorises self-sacrifice and presupposes a society based on communal reciprocity. This preference for cooperation is

---

[37] Le Duan, *Selected Writings (1960–1975)*, p. 246.

[38] Christina Schwenkel and Ann Marie Leshkowich, 'How is Neo-Liberalism Good to Think Vietnam? How is Vietnam Good to Think Neoliberalism?' (2012) 20 (2) *Positions: East Asia Cultures Critique* 379–401.

[39] Friedrich Hayek, 'The Atavism of Social Justice', in Friedrich Hayek (ed.), *New Studies in Philosophy, Politics, Economics and the History of Ideas* (Chicago, IL: University of Chicago, 1978), pp. 57–68.

[40] Pham Huy Ky, 'Chu Nghja Ca Nhan: Dac Diem Bieu Hien va Bien Phap Khac Phuc' ['The Ways of Avoiding Individualism in Society'] (1999) 2 *Nghiem Cuu Ly Luan* [*Journal of Theoretical Studies*] 46–48. John Gillespie, 'Human Rights as a Larger Loyalty: The Evolution of Religious Freedom in Vietnam' (2014) 27 (1) *Harvard Journal of Human Rights* 107–149.

[41] Schwenkel and Leshkowich, 'How is Neo-Liberalism Good to Think Vietnam?', 395.

[42] G. A. Cohen, *Why not Socialism?* (Princeton, NJ: Princeton University Press, 2009), pp. 35–40, 67–70.

antithetical to neo-liberalism. In socialism, it is the guiding hand of the
party and state, rather than the market, that is supposed to secure the
common good.[43] Economic activity is planned to satisfy basic social needs
and aims to minimise the self-interest and inequality generated by market
competition. Socialism does not prohibit competition; rather, competition
is conceived of as a process by which everyone rises and falls together.

Following *Đổi mới*, some Party writers argued that markets were the
site of knowledge production and that law needed to facilitate competition so as to generate the exchange of ideas.[44] This notion is similar to
Hayek's claim that 'competition is essentially a process of the formation
of opinion'.[45] Faith in the capacity of economic competition to galvanise
innovation did not displace the Party's reliance on state ownership over
key economic sectors. This duality is reflected in the 2013 Constitution,
which proclaims a 'market economy following a socialist orientation'
(*nền kinh tế thị trường theo định hướng xã hội chủ nghĩa*).[46] The 2013
Constitution then juxtaposes the socialist notion that the 'state economy plays the leading role' with the liberal notion that '[e]veryone
has the right to freedom of enterprise in the sectors and trades that are
not prohibited by law'.[47] As we will see, the state still actively manages
competition in key markets and sends mixed messages about private
competition in other markets.

12.4.4   Continuity and Change in Regulatory Signalling

A comparison between pre– and post–*Đổi mới* regulatory signalling points
to continuities, recurrences and cross-fertilisations, which suggests that
socialism is responding and adapting to the mixed-market economy.
Encouraging continuity, the party-state insists that the market should
not fundamentally disrupt social equality. It emphasises communitarian

---

[43] Katherine Verdery, 'What is Socialism, and why did it Fall?', in Katherine Verdery, *What Was Socialism, and What Comes Next?* (Princeton, NJ: Princeton University Press, 1996), pp. 26–30.

[44] Phạm Ngọc Quang, 'Để bảo đảm quyền con người – cần đổi mới nhận thức về nhân tố con người trong chủ nghĩa xã hội' ['Change our Conception of Human Agency in Socialism to Ensure Human Rights'] (1989) 10 *Nhà Nước Pháp Luật* 20–28.

[45] Friedrich Hayek, *Individualism and Economic Order* (Chicago, IL: University of Chicago Press, 1948), p. 106.

[46] Article 51, Constitution of Vietnam 2013. Also see Nguyen Phu Trong, 'Strong Determination and Great Effort to be Made!', Closing Speech of the 5th Meeting of Central Party Committee, 16 May 2012.

[47] Article 33, Constitution of Vietnam 2013.

values in the market place and vigorously rejects the neo-liberal preference for market individualism. In key economic sectors, state agencies pro-actively manage competition and encourage market collaborations. As the following discussion reveals, socialist signals have enduring power, not only because they are promoted by state rhetoric, but also because many people within and outside the state find socialism familiar and credible.

Increasing levels of social inequality have undoubtedly eroded the credibility of socialist signals such as equality.[48] But it is unclear whether neo-liberal regulatory signals are taking their place. As we shall see, the credibility of neo-liberal ideas imported in commercial laws is under-mined by the regulatory technologies used by the state.

12.5   Regulatory Technologies

Officials need technology to implement regulatory signals. As Michel Foucault observed, the technology of governance 'is to structure the possible field of action of others'.[49] It involves the transformation of complex, illegible and diverse local practises into simplified, legible and standardised processes.[50] Regulatory technologies determine people's rights and obligations, and specify what courses of action are available.[51] They differ from regulatory signals, because their epistemological logics are often elusive, subtle and mistaken for mindless process and habit.[52]

It is possible to identify five distinct regulatory technologies that evolved during the command economy and continue to order economic behaviour. They are statutory rights protection, relational regulation,

---

[48] The GINI coefficient increased from an egalitarian 20 in 1980 to a more unequal 39 in 2013; see World Bank World Bank GINI Index, available at http://data.worldbank.org/indicator/SI.POV.GINI?page=4. For a comparison of social equality in China and Viet-nam, see Qin Gao, Martin Evans and Irwin Garfunkel, 'Social Benefits and Income Inequality in Post-Socialist China and Vietnam', in Douglas J. Besharov and Karen Baehler (eds.), *Chinese Social Policy in a Time of Transition* (Oxford: Oxford University Press, 2013), pp. 48–67.

[49] Michel Foucault, 'The Subject and Power', in Hubert Dreyfus and Paul Rabinow (eds.), *Michel Foucault: Beyond Structuralism and Hermeneutics* (Chicago, IL: University of Chicago Press, 1982), p. 221.

[50] See James Scott, *Seeing Like a State: How Certain Schemes to Improve the Human Condition Have Failed* (New Haven, CT: Yale University Press, 1998), pp. 11–22.

[51] See Martha Lampland and Susan Leigh Starr (eds.), *How Quantifying, Classifying and Formalizing Practices Shape Everyday Life* (Ithaca, NY: Cornell University Press, 2008).

[52] Annalise Riles, 'The Anti-Network: Private Global Governance, Legal Knowledge, and the Legitimacy of the State' (2008) 56 (3) *American Journal of Comparative Law* 605–630.

the criminalisation of commerce, data collection and monitoring, and mass-mobilisation campaigns.

12.5.1   Statutory Rights Protection

One of the main distinctions between socialist and neo-liberal regulation is the way in which law is used to regulate the economy. In neo-liberal theory, the 'rule of law' disciplines the economy by forcing entrepreneurs to calculate the potential costs and benefits of complying with the law.[53] Property rights are also thought to play a key role in protecting investments against abuse by holders of political power and other market actors, and in promoting saving, investment and creative endeavour.[54] As the varieties of capitalism literature shows, the role reserved for property rights varies according to the value different societies place on social, as opposed to individual, goals.[55] Vietnam, it is argued, has only selectively absorbed the neo-liberal preference for individual wealth maximisation and property rights.

Commercial law and property rights played a peripheral role in regulating the command economy in Vietnam. In a radical break from the past, Truong Chinh argued during the Sixth Party Congress in 1986 that '[t]he management of the country should be performed through laws rather than moral concepts'.[56] Responding to his call, the National Assembly embarked on a massive legislative program. Having begun economic reforms earlier than the Soviet Union, Vietnam turned elsewhere for legislative inspiration. In retrospect, Chinese laws appear the obvious choice but, at the time, borrowing from China was politically sensitive and the Chinese economic model had not yet demonstrated a capacity for sustained growth.[57] Instead, lawmakers initially copied French law, and then looked more widely for inspiration from Japan, Southeast Asia and the international donor community. Compliance

---

[53] Nikolas Rose, *Powers of Freedom: Reframing Political Thought* (New York, NY: Cambridge University Press, 1999), p. 155.

[54] Lee Hoskins and Ana Eiras, 'Property Rights: Key to Economic Growth', in Gerald O'Driscoll, Kim Holmes and Mary O' Grady (eds.), *Index of Economic Freedom* (Washington, DC: Heritage Foundation, 2002), pp. 37–48.

[55] Hall and Soskice, *Varieties of Capitalism*.

[56] Truong Chinh, 'Introduction to the Political Report', Part 4, *Vietnam News Agency*, 15 December 1986.

[57] Jorn Dosch and Alexander Vuving, 'The Impact of China on Governance Structures in Vietnam', Discussion Paper, Bonn, 2008, p. 24.

with international treaties (such as the ASEAN Free Trade Area and the World Trade Organization)[58] has also been a powerful driver of legislative reforms.

Vietnam has now enacted a legislative framework that covers most aspects of a capitalist economy. Although there is formal convergence with international legal models, there is less functional convergence in the way the law is interpreted and implemented.[59] Entrepreneurs consequently struggle to calculate the costs and benefits of legal compliance, and imported commercial law does not perform the neo-liberal function of disciplining the economy.[60]

12.5.2   The Regulatory Technology of Legislation

The party-state uses commercial legislation to determine which markets are open to private commerce and which markets remain under tight government management. Three distinct regulatory arenas are discernable.

12.5.2.1   Commanding Heights of the Economy

Legislation reserves the commanding heights of the economy for state-owned and controlled enterprises.[61] It protects key economic sectors such as telecommunications and electricity generation from private competition. In conjunction with relational regulation (discussed in the next section), legislation also loosely coordinates interaction between state agencies and SOEs.

12.5.2.2   Foreign Investment Sectors

Many commercial laws were enacted to comply with international treaty obligations and selectively open economic sectors to foreign competition and investment.[62] Although foreign investors primarily use transnational regulatory systems to shape their transactional environment, they also

---

[58] Joint Donor Report, *Business: Vietnam Development Report*, Vietnam Consultative Group, Hanoi, 2006, pp. 109–111.

[59] John Gillespie, *Transplanting Commercial Law Reform*, 2006.

[60] See John McMillan and Christopher Woodruff, 'Interfirm Relationships and Informal Credit in Vietnam' (1999) 114(4) *Quarterly Journal of Economics* 1285–1320.

[61] UNCTD, *Investment Policy Review: Vietnam* (New York, NY: United Nations, 2008), pp. 31–42.

[62] John Gillespie, 'Exploring the Role of Legitimacy in Framing Responses to Global Legal Reforms in a Transforming Socialist Asia' (2011) 28 (2) *Wisconsin Journal of International Law* 534–579.

rely on domestic laws for rights protection. Commercial litigation reveals stark differences in the way statutory rights function in the different economic sectors.[63] Judges reflexively advance the state interest (*lời ích của nhà nước*) by protecting SOEs from private, especially foreign, competition.[64] At the same time, most commercial litigation is initiated by foreign investors seeking to protect property from local partners.[65]

12.5.2.3 Small-Scale Trading and Service Sectors

The party-state is reluctant to permit law to function as a framework to facilitate private transactions among small- and medium-sized enterprises (SMEs). A recent study showed that 70 per cent of SMEs surveyed avoided official registration and other forms of legislative regulation.[66] Without formal registration, firms cannot litigate or legally enforce statutory rights. As discussed later in this Chapter in more depth, many entrepreneurs believe that relational connections with officials deliver more favourable regulatory outcomes than the legislative framework. Not only are statutes complex and contradictory, they often restrict profitability by limiting how businesses can access and exploit markets.

12.5.2.4 Rights Protection or Rights Management

The discussion so far suggests that statutory rights are selectively enforced in the three key economic sectors in Vietnam. But, does rights protection for foreign investors foreshadow a neo-liberal 'regulatory state'? As Kanishka Jayasuriya has shown, regulatory states not only protect commercial rights, they also shield markets from the 'corrosive influence' of politics with arms-length politically neutral institutions, such as courts, central banks and competition agencies.[67] Movement in this direction is constrained in Vietnam by the Leninist aversion to politically neutral regulatory agencies. Not only does the party-state keep the courts under tight control, it does not permit agentification and politically independent regulatory agencies. For example, the party-state has

---

[63] Commercial cases increased from 1,978 cases in 2006 to 14,767 cases in 2013. See Vietnamese Supreme People's Court, available at http://toaan.gov.vn/portal/page/portal/tandtc/5901712.

[64] Interviews with judges and lawyers.

[65] Interviews with judges and lawyers.

[66] Jean-Pierre Cling, *The Informal Sector in Vietnam: A Focus on Hanoi and Ho Chi Minh City* (Hanoi: The Gioi Editions, 2010), pp. 173–175, 196–169.

[67] Kanishka Jayasuriya, 'Governance, Post-Washington Consensus and the new Antipolitics', Southeast Asian Research Centre, Working Paper Series No. 2, April 2001, City University Hong Kong, p. 1.

intervened to prevent the Competition Agency from prosecuting market monopolies operated by state-owned or -controlled firms, such as interest rate collusion among state-owned banks, a steel industry cartel and collusion among life insurance companies.[68]

As Marxist–Leninist orthodoxies have faded, the party-state has attempted to derive legitimacy by adopting the facade and ritual of legality. Legislation in Vietnam performs three main regulatory functions. As we have seen, it signals regulatory intentions. It also coordinates market activities by determining the rules governing market entry and exit. The third regulatory function – rights protection – remains highly selective and does not promote legal transparency, equality before the law and the enforcement of statutory rights against the state. If legislation is an unreliable signpost of party-state policy and the 'rule of law' does not discipline the economy, how does the state regulate commerce?

12.5.3   Relationally Embedded Regulation

During the command economy, Party leaders encouraged officials to personalise administrative rule by getting 'in touch with the people' (đường lối quần chúng).[69] Echoing Confucian morality rule, officials were obliged to instruct and guide those with lower-class awareness.[70]

State planning and morality rule were conflated into a regulatory practice called 'state economic management' (quận lý nhà nước kinh tế). Originally devised in the Soviet Union to link planning and economic production, Vietnam's state economic management gave Party cadres 'prerogative' powers to regulate economic production.[71] Party leaders rejected calls by reformers in the 1970s to codify state economic management, arguing that officials needed personal relationships to 'organically

---

[68] Le Thanh Vinh, *Competition Law Transfers: From an Interpretive Perspective*, PhD Thesis Monash University, 2012, pp. 255–288.

[69] Thanh Duy, 'Co So Khoa Hoc va Van Hoa Trong Tu Tuong Ho Chi Minh Ve Nha Nuoc va Phap Luat' ['Scientific and Cultural Basis of Ho Chi Minh's Ideas of State and Law'], Tạp chí Cộng sản, January 1997, pp. 26, 27–28.

[70] See Ho Chi Minh, *Complete Works* (Hanoi: The National Political Publishing House, 1995), vol. 5, p. 338.

[71] Hoang Quoc Viet, 'Can Dam Bao Cho Phap Luat Duoc Ton Trong Trong Cong Tac Quan Ly Linh Te Cua Nha Nuoc' ['We Must Ensure the Enforcement of Law in State Economic Management'] in *Nghien cuu Nha Nuoc va phap quyen* [*Studies about State and Law*] (Hanoi: Truth Publishing, 1964), pp. 8–12; Le Thanh Nghi, *Mot So Van De Co Ban Trong Quan Ly Kinh Te Xa Hoi Chu Nghia* [*Several Basic Maters on Socialist Economic Management*] (Hanoi: Nhan Xuat Su That [Truth Publishing House], 1975).

link' production with state plans.[72] Although command planning is long
gone, relational regulation remains a key regulatory technology in the
three main economic sectors.

12.5.3.1   Regulating the Commanding Heights
of the Economy

Following Đổi mới reforms, the Party decided to rationalise SOEs. The
'grasp the large and release the small' policy concentrated efforts on large
SOEs – general corporations (GCs) that dominated the 'commanding
heights of the economy'.[73] Smaller SOEs in less strategic industries were
scheduled for privatisation.

As previously noted, legislation only loosely coordinates the activities
of SOEs. Instead, the state relies on personal relationships to fine tune
SOEs. Modelled on Soviet institutions, the Central Party Organising
Committee (Ban Tổ Chúc Trung Uống) operates a nomenklatura system
(công tác tổ chúc cán bộ) that controls the recruitment and promotion
of senior government and SOE officials.[74] Although the Law on State-
Owned Enterprises 2003 gives the board of management of SOEs broad
powers to formulate corporate policies, in practice key decisions are
determined through nomenklatura networks.[75] Studies attribute the
party-state's regulatory power to a combination of personal influence
projected through the nomenklatura system and training that stresses
loyalty to Party superiors. As Scott Cheshier and Jonathan Pincus
observed: '[h]abits acquired during the period of central planning still
condition the behavior of General Corporations (GCs) more than two
decades after the advent of reform.'[76] Although powerful SOEs such as

---

[72] Nguyen Nien, 'Several Legal Problems in the Leadership and Management of Industry Under
the Conditions of the Present Improvement of Economic Management in Our Country'
(1976) 33(14) Luat Hoc [Juridical Science], translated by J.P.R.S., 30 September 1976, 34–36.

[73] Martin Painter, 'The Politics of Economic Restructuring in Vietnam: The Case of State-
owned Enterprise "Reform"' (2003) 25(1) Contemporary Southeast Asia 20–43.

[74] See Martin Gainsborough, Vietnam: Rethinking the State (London: Zed Books, 2010),
pp. 102–113; Scott Cheshier, Jago Penrose and Nguyen Thi Thanh Nga, The State as
Investor: Equitisation, Privatisation and the Transformation of SOEs in Viet Nam (Hanoi:
UNDP, 2006) Policy Paper.

[75] Cheshier, Penrose and Nguyen, 19–22.

[76] Scott Cheshier and Jonathan Pincus, 'Minsky au Vietnam: State Corporations, Financial
Instability and Industrialisation', in Daniela Tavasci and Jan Toporowski (eds.), Minsky
Crisis and Development (Basingstoke: Palgrave Macmillan, 2010) pp. 188–206. Also see
John Gillespie 'Managing Competition in Socialist Transforming Asia', in Michael
Dowdle, John Gillespie and Imelda Maher (eds.), Competition, Regulation and Capitalism
Lessons from Asia. (Cambridge: University of Cambridge Press, 2013) pp. 164–195.

PetroVietnam can leverage Party connections to resist state directions,[77] most SOEs are tightly controlled by state-dominated relational regulation. This raises the question: If relational regulation relies on Party networks for control, can it order privatised enterprises?

12.5.3.2   Managing Privatised State-Owned Companies: Politically Embedded Regulation

Although privatisation in Vietnam is often portrayed as a retreat by the state, empirical studies suggest that it is better viewed as a continuation and redeployment of state economic management.[78] Studies show that state authorities continue to use relational connections to guide privatised firms. Beresford and Dang Phong observed that 'as the markets became open and established ... personal relations [forged under planning] developed into more or less organized and institutionalized networks, albeit still often based on connections between family members, neighbors and colleagues'.[79]

Privatisation did not sever personal relationships with the party-state. One study found that senior officials in privatised firms spent ten to twenty years (that is, their formative years) working in the government.[80] Directors still referred to the state as the 'controlling institution' and reported to supervising state authorities.[81] Privatised firms wanted to retain the trust and support of state regulators, not only to secure state resources and support, but also as insurance against future problems.

Other studies have found that the capacity of Party and state officials to determine outcomes varies according to the size and financial capacity of the privatised firms.[82] Firms in the textile industry, for example, are highly dependent on government support for credit and export quotes,

---

[77] See Jonathan Pincus and Vu Thanh Tu Anh, 'Vietnam Feels the Heat', *Far Eastern Economic Review*, May 2008, available at https://theeconomics.wordpress.com/2008/05/18/vietnam-feels-the-heat-far-eastern-economic-review/.

[78] Martin Gainsborough, 'Privatisation as State Advance: Private Indirect Government in Vietnam' (2009) 14 *New Political Economy*, 257, 265–267.

[79] Melanie Beresford and Dang Phong, *Economic Transition in Vietnam: Trade and Aid in the Demise of a Centrally Planned Economy* (Cheltenham: Edward Elgar, 2000), pp. 152–153.

[80] Gainsborough, 'Privatisation as State Advance', 265–267.

[81] Gainsborough, *Vietnam*, p. 101.

[82] Scott Cheshier and Jonathan Pincus, 'Minsky au Vietnam: State Corporations, Financial Instability and Industrialisation', Cheshier and Pincus 197–201.

and have little bargaining power.[83] Similarly, firms in the construction industry require close relational connections with the Party and state to gain insider knowledge about state tenders.[84] In contrast, privatised firms in the computer and software industry exhibit much higher levels of autonomy from the state. Yet, as the following discussion suggests, as reliance on the state diminishes, Party and state officials find other means of extending relational controls over firms.

12.5.3.3   Managing Private Firms: Socially Embedded Regulation

Officials responded to the mixed-market economy by using business licences to project relational controls over private enterprises. In a far-reaching reform, the Enterprise Law 1999 abolished business licences and unleashed the entrepreneurial skills and energies of individuals.[85] However, this law did not fundamentally curtail longstanding relational practices.[86] Rather than relinquishing prerogative powers over private entrepreneurs, studies show that officials shifted relational controls from market entry to sub-licences covering health and safety, environmental standards, and fire and building controls.[87]

Over the last two decades, the party-state has extended legislative recognition to a vast array of commercial activities. Commercial life is now bound in a dense network of laws, regulations, directives, rules and pronouncements. But the thickets of statutory regulation often confuse as much as they protect commercial rights.

Officials use the regulatory uncertainty generated by ambiguous regulations to create 'asking–giving' (*xin–cho*) relationships.[88] To minimise regulatory risk, entrepreneurs cultivate 'relationship friendships' (*quan hệ*) with officials.[89] Entrepreneurs invite officials to karaoke parlours, and

---

[83] See Scott Cheshier and Jago Penrose, *Top 200: Industrial Strategies of Viet Nam's Large Firms* (Hanoi: UNDP, 2007), Policy Paper, pp. 14–15.

[84] John Gillespie, 'Exploring the Role of Legitimacy in Framing Responses to Global Legal Reforms in a Transforming Socialist Asia' (2011) 28 (2) *Wisconsin Journal of International Law* 559–563.

[85] Gillespie, *Transplanting Commercial Law Reform*, pp. 155–160.

[86] Le Huu Tang and Liu Han Yue, *Economic Reform in Viet Nam and in China*, pp. 72–75.

[87] CIEM, *Comparative Provincial Performance in Private Business Development*, VIE01/025, November (Hanoi: CIEM, 2003), p. 23.

[88] John Rand and Finn Tarp, *Firm-Level Corruption in Vietnam*, United Nations University, World Institute for Development, Working Paper, 2010. Cling, *The Informal Sector in Vietnam*, p. 173.

[89] See Gillespie, 'Exploring the Role of Legitimacy in Framing Responses to Global Legal Reforms in a Transforming Socialist Asia' 534–579.

offer goodwill payments (*khoản tiền chi*) and gifts on special occasions such as weddings, birthdays and *Tet* (Lunar New Year).[90] According to recent surveys, over the last decade, entrepreneurs have expanded 'relationship payments' to officials,[91] leading to a significant increase in the perception of commercial corruption.[92]

Entrepreneurs use the term *làm luật* (literally, 'make law') to describe relational regulation. *Làm luật* has the positive connotation of finding flexible solutions to rigid centrally imposed laws, and the negative implication of inventing rules to extract rents.[93] In return for 'goodwill payments', officials are expected to reconcile local business interests with state laws and policies. For example, entrepreneurs expect advance warning about inspections, and officials turn a blind eye to minor regulatory violations.

12.5.4 Regulating Consumer and Environmental Standards

During the command economy, state planners used relational regulation to control consumer and environmental standards. As central controls were relaxed and private commerce flourished, the state searched for new regulatory mechanisms. Over the last twenty years, the state has incrementally introduced a broad range of consumer, food safety and environmental protection standards. These laws have now consolidated standards, recognised a range of consumer rights and established regulatory agencies at the provincial/city level.[94]

Studies suggest that central standards have been relatively unsuccessful in shaping business behaviour. One problem concerns the overlapping

---

[90] World Bank, *Corruption from the Perspective of Citizens, Firms and Public Officials* (Hanoi: National Political Publishing House, 2012), pp. 42–47; Cling, *The Informal Sector in Vietnam*, p. 173, 202–204.

[91] An Dien, 'Business as Usual: Bribery Remains a Way of Life in Vietnam', *Thanh Nien News*, 16 April 2015, available at www.thanhniennews.com/politics/business-as-usual-bribery-remains-a-way-of-life-in-vietnam-42245.html.

[92] UNDP, *PAPI 2014: The Vietnam Provincial Governance and Public Administration Performance Index* (Hanoi: UNDP, 2014), pp. 11–13, available at www.vn.undp.org/content/dam/vietnam/docs/Publications/PAPI2014_FinalReport_SmallSize_ENG.pdf.

[93] See Kirsten Endres, 'Making Law: Small-Scale Trade and Corrupt Exceptions at the Vietnam–China Border' (2014) 116 (3) *American Anthropologist* 611–625.

[94] Law on Consumer Protection No. 59/2010/QH12; Law on Food Safety No. 55/2010/QH12 and Law on Quality of Products and Goods No. 5/2007/QH12. See John King and Tu Ngoc Trinh, 'Vietnam', in Luke Nottage and Sakda Thanitcul (eds.), *ASEAN Product Liability and Consumer Product Safety Law* (Bangkok: Winyuchon Publication House, 2016), pp. 305–333.

responsibilities between coordinating ministries. For example, five different ministries share responsibility for certifying and regulating food
safety, and have issued conflicting and confusing sub-laws.[95] Another
problem concerns the use of relational regulation to control consumer
and environmental standards. Local government agencies have turned
to sub-licences and permits to control consumer standards.[96] As a
sunglasses trader explained:[97]

> Everyone knows that the sunglasses are fake or smuggled and econo-
> mic police and market control authorities pretend to look for certificates
> of origin. I *vui vẻ* [literally 'pacify', but implying bribery] the inspectors
> in my area. But for this to happen I must remember them before they
> remember me. The main reason for the visits is to remind me who they
> are. This is a mandarin mentality that tells me that the law is something
> that is very far away from people.

Although officials claim that relational regulation is necessary to fill
the regulatory vacuum left by confusing statutory standards, studies
suggest that local officials have reverted to the regulatory technology
with which they are most familiar. As Sasges and Cheshier remind us,[98]
in Vietnam, strong relational connections between state and businesses
pre-date socialism.

In summary, the relational regulation that evolved during the command economy continues to order many facets of the mixed-market
economy. Officials use personal interactions to blur distinctions between
the public and private sectors and embed regulation in complex networks of political and social relationships. Both norm-setting and
regulatory enforcement operate through case-by-case processes of
private negotiation between the regulator and the regulated. The relationship between the regulator and the regulated is interdependent
rather than hierarchical; relational and collegial rather than impersonal; intimate rather than arms-length. In an environment dominated

---

[95] For a description of the monitoring and regulatory process, see Russin and Vecchi
Lawyers, 'Food Law in Vietnam: Part 2', 14 March 2015, available at www.mondaq
.com/article.asp?articleid=125098.
[96] Nguyen Sa, 'Licenses Torment Businessmen', Vietnamnet, 15 October 2007, available at
http://vietnamnet.vn/service/printversion.vnn?article_id=719758.
[97] This statement was presented to the Private Sector Forum in April 2010 by a sunglasses
trader and recorded by lawyers working for Leadoc, a Hanoi based law firm.
[98] Sasges and Cheshier, 'Competing Legacies'.

by relational regulation, rights-based regulation grounded on principled sets of norms are superfluous.[99]

12.5.5   Criminalising Commerce

During the command economy, private commerce constituted a criminal offence. Party officials vilified private traders as conspirators (*móc ngoặc*) and smugglers (*buôn gian bán lận*).[100] State force was used to confiscate trading assets and imprison offenders.[101] Although private trading was decriminalised in 1988, the state continues to use criminalisation (*hình sự hóa*) as a regulatory technology.[102]

Criminalisation works by extending by analogy the reach of criminal law to commercial activities that are not directly proscribed by the law.[103] The line between economic crimes prohibited by the law, such as theft and embezzlement, and criminalisation is blurred. Take, for example, the campaign orchestrated by the government to pressure Qantas Airways to divest shareholding in Jetstar Pacific. In 2010, police arrested the managing director of Jetstar Pacific for 'irresponsibly causing serious losses to socialist property'.[104] This criminal charge related to losses incurred in hedging fuel transactions, a standard commercial practice in the aviation industry. Police extended by analogy the crime of 'causing losses

---

[99]   See Melanie Beresford, 'The Development of Commercial Regulation in Vietnam's Market Economy', in John Gillespie and Albert Chen (eds.), *Legal Reforms in China and Vietnam: A Comparison of Asian Communist Regimes* (London: Routledge, 2010), pp. 264–266.

[100] Vũ Quốc Tuấn, 'Phát triển doanh nghiệp- Suy nghĩ về một quá trình' ['Enterprise Development – Thinking over a Process'], in Đào Xuân Sâm and Vũ Quốc Tuấn (eds.), *Đổi mới ở Việt Nam- Nhớ lại và suy ngẫm* [*Đổi Mới in Vietnam-Rethinking and Reflection*] (Hanoi: Nhà Xuất bản Tri thức [Knowlegde Publishing House], 2008), p. 131.

[101] Đặng Phong, *Tư duy kinh tế Việt Nam: Chặng đường gian nan và ngoạn mục 1975–1989* [*Vietnam's Economic Thingking: A Hard and Incredible Road 1975–1989*] (Hanoi: Nhà Xuất bản Tri thức [Knowlege Publishing House], 2008), pp. 216–228.

[102] World Bank, *Corruption from the Perspective of Citizens, Firms and Public Officials* (Hanoi: National Political Publishing House, 2012), pp. 40–41. Also see John Gillespie, 'Testing the Limits to the "Rule of Law": Commercial Regulation in Vietnam' (2009) 12(2) *Journal of Comparative Asian Development* 245–272.

[103] See John Gillespie, 'Self-Interest and Ideology: Different Explanations for Bureaucratic Corruption in Socialist Transforming East Asia' (2001) 3(1) *Australian Journal of Asian Law* 1–36.

[104] Leithen Francis, 'Jetstar Pacific Execs held in Vietnam Following Fuel Hedging Losses', *Flightglobal* 8 January 2010, available at www.flightglobal.com/news/articles/jetstar-pacific-execs-held-in-vietnam-following-fuel-hedging-336897.

to socialist property' to criminalise an otherwise lawful commercial practice.[105] The criminalisation formed part of a state-orchestrated campaign to persuade Qantas to divest shareholding in Jetstar Pacific to Vietnam Airlines, the state-owned carrier.

Criminalisation is a potent regulatory technology, because the mere threat of criminal prosecution transforms calculable commercial risk into incalculable criminal risk and encourages entrepreneurs to cultivate relational connections with state officials. Despite widespread calls inside and outside the state to abandon this practice,[106] officials routinely use criminalisation to manage powerful enterprises that are proving intractable to other forms of regulation.

12.5.6 Data Collection and Monitoring

In transitioning into socialism, central agencies developed five-year plans that sought to balance production with social needs.[107] Although statistical information is important in every economic system, in centralised command economies the production of timely and accurate data is vital. Vietnamese planners were profoundly influenced by Lenin's faith in modern scientific technologies to realise the socialist project.[108] Central agencies developed statistical and accounting techniques to standardise processes, collect information and monitor production.[109] Officials compared numerical data collected from samples and audit inspections against predetermined production criteria.

---

[105] Tuoi Tre, 'Charges Dropped Against Former Jetstar Pacific Director', *VietnamNet*, 6 November 2010, available at http://english.vietnamnet.vn/fms/society/1369/charges-dropped-against-former-jetstar-pacific-director.html.

[106] Bàn thêm về thuật ngữ Hình sự hóa [More on the Terminology of Criminalisation], *Canh Sat Nhan Dan*, 26 May 2015, https://www.flightglobal.com/news/articles/jetstar-pacific-execs-held-in-vietnam-following-fuel-hedging-336897/.

[107] Cong Tac Ke Hoach, 'Carrying Out Good National Economic Planning and Summarizing National Economic Planning Well,' JPRS 67923, 9–11 April 1976, pp. 16–22.

[108] Vladimir Lenin, 'The Capitalist System of Modern Agriculture', in *Collected Works*, 4th edn., (Moscow: Progress Publishers, 1967 [1910]), vol. 4, p. 432. Also see Alice Her-Soon Tay and Eugene Kamenka, 'Marxism, Socialism and the Theory of Law' (1985) 23 *Columbia Journal of Transnational Law* 217.

[109] See Kendall Bailes, 'Alexei Gastev and the Soviet Controversy over Taylorism 1918–1924' (July 1977) 24(3) *Soviet Studies* 373–394. Morris Bian, *The Making of the State Enterprise System in Modern China: The Dynamics of Institutional Change* (Cambridge, MA: Harvard University Press, 2005), pp. 1–17.

Despite increasing technical sophistication, data collection consistently distorted statistics.[110] Efforts by central planners to gain accurate information from SOEs often resulted in fabricated data.[111] Losses from the state budget were treated as criminal offences, promoting strategic reactions and tactical manoeuvring by firms to place assets beyond central scrutiny. Mistrust regarding the veracity of information supplied by SOEs encouraged central planners to redouble their efforts to strengthen central control through tighter administrative oversight.[112] Inspection teams (đội công tác kiểm soát) were dispatched to conduct impromptu performance audits, which often lead to further tactical manoeuvring by firms. In response, the state devised additional layers of documentation, monitoring and accountability rituals that only deepened the culture of mistrust.

As Gerschenkron[113] noted about the Soviet Union and Naughton[114] noted about China, deviations from central planning were endemic to socialist states. Even during the height of command planning in the 1970s, state officials in Vietnam engaged in 'fence breaking' (phá rào) to experimentally combine state and private markets.[115] Central planners negotiated off-plan with managers, and by 1986 less than 40 per cent of manufactured consumer goods passed through state-controlled trading networks.[116] Party leaders condemned plan evasion in official pronouncements, while unofficially condoning these practices. Spontaneous markets

---

[110] Đặng Phong, Tư duy kinh tế Việt Nam: Chặng đường gian nan và ngoạn mục 1975–1989 [Vietnam's Economic Thinking: A Hard and Incredible Road 1975–1989] (Hanoi: Nhà Xuất bản Tri thức [Knowledge Publishing House], 2008), p. 86.

[111] Ken MacLean, The Government of Mistrust: Illegibility and Bureaucratic Power in Socialist Vietnam (Madison, WI: University of Wisconsin, 2013), pp. 89–110.

[112] See Suzy Paine, 'The Limits of Planning and the Case for Economic Reform', in David Marr and Christine White (eds.), Postwar Vietnam: Dilemmas in Socialist Development (Ithaca, NY: SAP Cornell University, 1988), pp. 133–146.

[113] According to Gerschenkron, 'the normalcy of Soviet mercantilism, was concealed beneath a general veneer of socialist phraseology'. Alexander Gerschenkron, 'Industrial Enterprise in Soviet Russia' in Alexander Gerschenkron, Economic Backwardness in Historical Perspective: A Book of Essays (Cambridge, MA: The Belknap Press of Harvard University, 1962), p. 295.

[114] Barry Naughton, Growing Out of the Plan: Chinese Economic Reform 1978–93 (Cambridge: Cambridge University Press, 1996), pp. 23–24.

[115] See Le Huu Tang and Liu Han Yue, Economic Reform in Viet Nam and in China, pp. 44–45.

[116] See Vo Van Kiet, 'Report to the National Assembly in the 1985 Socio-Economic Development Plan', Hanoi Domestic Service, 26 December 1986 (trans. FBIS Asia and Pacific Daily Report, 30 December), p. 9.

were needed to fulfil plans,[117] and coexisted with and underpinned the official state economy. By the close of the command economy, data collection and monitoring institutionalised disinformation and mistrust.

In the post–*Đổi mới* economy, the state has sought to augment macro-economic levers over SOEs, with data collection and monitoring technologies.[118] Auditing in the command economy stressed upward accountability, in which SOEs were encouraged to focus on centralised plans and directives to enhance performance. More recently, the state has turned to neo-liberal auditing practices that stress downward accountability.[119] The aim is to increase personal accountability in areas where central agencies have insufficient information to efficiently monitor SOEs.

Neo-liberal auditing has not made directors more personally accountable.[120] The core problem is that the state has been unable to take directors out of a bureaucratic context in which they are managed by superiors and place them into market-like contexts, in which their behaviour is disciplined by private sector incentives. In a recent example, the directors of Vinashin, a large-scale state-owned enterprise, used Party connections to conceal income from state auditors and inspectors.[121] Funds totalling hundreds of millions of dollars were then side-streamed to private companies associated with senior Party officials. Party structures created a command and control architecture, which undermined the autonomous choices encouraged by neo-liberal auditing.

---

[117] See MacLean, *The Government of Mistrust*, pp. 81–88.

[118] Dwight Perkins and Vu Thanh Tu Anh, *Vietnam's Industrial Policy: Designing Policies for Sustainable Development*, UNDP Policy Dialogue Paper No. 3, 2009, pp. 22–23.

[119] See Nikolas Rose, *Inventing Our Selves: Psychology, Power and Personhood* (New York, NY: Cambridge University Press, 1996).

[120] Gregory Smith, Binh Le Duy, Jim Colvin and Rab Habib, *Transparency of State Owned Enterprises in Vietnam: Current Status and Ideas for Reform* (Washington, DC: World Bank Group 2014). http://documents.worldbank.org/curated/en/2014/01/19902783/transparency-state-owned-enterprises-vietnam-current-status-ideas-reform 31–32.

[121] VOV, 'Xử vụ án tại Vinashin: Thiệt hại kinh tế gần 950 tỷ đồng' ['Hearing the case at Vinashin: economic losses nearly 950 billion'], *Voice of Vietnam*, 2012, available at http://vov.vn/Phap-luat/Xu-vu-an-tai-Vinashin-Thiet-hai-kinh-te-gan-950-ty-dong/204387.vov; PV, 'Bộ Chính trị: Không để sụp đổ Vinashin' ['The Politburo did not let Vinashin Collapse'], *VietnamNet*, 8 August 2010, available at http://vietnamnet.vn/chinhtri/201008/Bo-Chinh-tri-ra-ket-luat-ve-Vinashin-927611; 'The Unlearnt Lesson', *The Saigon Times Daily*, 26 May 2012, available at http://english.thesaigontimes.vn/23653/The-unlearned-lesson.html.

12.5.6.1   Regulation through Metrics

The government has enthusiastically embraced the use of key performance indicators to rank and standardise provincial governance. The Provincial Competitiveness Index, for example, ranks commercial governance in Vietnamese provinces.[122] In a departure from the command system, which relied on rules and punishments, regulation through metrics uses neo-liberal notions of soft law that shapes behaviour by ranking performance standards.[123] Provinces that fail to meet the performance targets or that rank below others in the key indicators are 'shamed' into improving their records.

Although sometimes providing grounds to oppose neo-liberal regulation, regulatory technologies developed during the command economy can also normalise metrics regulation. In particular, the scientism encouraged by Lenin and command planners made metrics and performance indicators appear familiar and appropriate to contemporary regulators. In another continuity, the added layers of neo-liberal regulation encourage directors[124] to collude and fabricate responses to data collection and monitoring in ways that resemble the manufacture of data to meet production targets during the planned economy. Data collection and monitoring thus entrench the politically and socially embedded regulatory practices that they were designed to displace.

12.5.7   Mass-Mobilisation Campaigns

Mass-mobilisation campaigns copied from China have been used in Vietnam since the early 1950s to rectify social wrongs and communicate with the 'masses'.[125] Mass organisations controlled by the Party, such as the Vietnam Fatherland Front, were enlisted as one-way communication channels to persuade (*thuyết phục*) and educate (*giao dức*) the masses. The Party sought to inculcate the virtues of the new regime, critique shortcomings in the old regime and transform social epistemologies. For example, moral rectification campaigns demanded 'selfless'

---

[122] Trang Mae Nguyen, 'Grading Regulators: The Impact of Global and Local Indicators on Vietnam's Business Governance' (2013) 88 *New York University Law Review* 2254–2285.

[123] See Grainne De Burca, 'New Governance and Experimentalism: An Introduction' (2010) 2010(2) *Wisconsin Law Review* 227–238.

[124] See, e.g., PV, 'The Politburo did not let Vinashin Collapse'.

[125] Chris Dixon, 'State, Party and Political Change in Viet Nam', in Duncan McCargo (ed.), *Rethinking Viet Nam* (London: RoutledgeCurzon, 2004), pp. 15–26.

commitment to resist foreign reoccupation, purged French cultural influences (1946–1952), reformed land ownership (1953–1956) and attacked 'feudalistic property ethics and Confucian morals'.[126] Party leaders modelled slogans on pre-revolutionary Confucian proverbs that assembled related ideas into groups of three. Using this technique, Confucian truisms, such as the three 'relations' and the three 'obediences', morphed into the three revolutions (*ba cuộc cách mạng*) and the three responsibilities (*Ba đảm đang*).[127] Mass-mobilisation campaigns during the command economy relied on exemplary individuals to act as role models (*người gương mẫu*) for the masses to emulate (*thi đua*). The emergence of the mixed-market economy did not signal a retreat from mass mobilisation, but rather a reconfiguration of how the Party sought to persuade and educate the masses.[128]

12.5.7.1 Mass Mobilisation through the Vietnam Chamber of Commerce and Industry

The Party established the Vietnam Chamber of Commerce and Industry (VCCI) in 1963 to assist Vietnamese SOEs to trade with socialist bloc countries. Following *Đổi mới* reforms, it was reconfigured as 'an independent, non-government organisation' to represent state and private enterprises.[129] As a member of the Vietnam Fatherland Front, it retains strong formal and informal linkages with the Party and state. Vu Oanh, the Politburo member responsible for mass mobilisation, confirmed this close relationship when he described VCCI as the 'highest representative of the business community and the appropriate instrument for the party

---

[126] Oskar Weggel, 'The Vietnamese Communist Party and Its Status under Law', in Dietrich Loeber (ed.), *Ruling Communist Parties and their Status Under Law* (The Hague: Martinus Nijhoff, 1986), p. 415.

[127] See Shaun Kingsley Malarney, *Culture, Ritual and Revolution* (Honolulu, HI: University of Hawaii Press, 2002), pp. 74–76; Phan Đại Doãn and Nguyễn Quang Ngọc (eds.), *Kinh nghiệm tổ chức quản lý nông thôn Việt Nam trong lịch sử* [*Experience on Organizing and Governing the Rural Areas in Vietnam in History*] (Hanoi: Nhà Xuất bản Chính trị Quốc gia [National Political Publishing House], 2002), pp. 44–45.

[128] See Le Phuong, 'Civil Society: From Annulment to Restoration', unpublished paper, 'Vietnam Update Conference: Doi Moi, The State and Civil Society', 10–11 November 1994, p. 5.

[129] VCCI, 'Strengthening the Organisation and Activities of the Chamber of Commerce' (unpublished paper No. 11, Hanoi, 1993), p. 3.

and state to gather and guide the business community for all economic sectors of the country in the cause of building the economy'.[130]

VCCI is positioned at the apex of a hierarchical structure that controls industry-specific employer associations. It explains government policies and laws to members associations, which are then expected to convey this information to individual firms. It also transmits information in the other direction and assists members to access state subsidies, such as concessional taxation and land finance.

Although VCCI advocates business interests to state agencies and critiques commercial law drafts, it does not act like a member-directed organisation. There is ample evidence that VCCI filters complaints from members to ensure that private commercial interests do not disrupt state policy.[131] For example, VCCI enlisted support from family-based corporations to abolish business licences in the Enterprise Law but ignored their request for two-tiered corporation laws with minimal reporting requirements for family-based corporations. VCCI was influenced by the neo-liberal idea that family corporations are less efficient and modern than public corporations run by knowledge professionals. While VCCI has changed in response to the mixed-market economy, it continues to function like a Leninist mass organisation in giving the Party leverage over business activities that lie beyond the reach of other regulatory technologies.

12.5.8 Emulation Campaigns

Party leaders have reinvented emulation campaigns to regulate the post–Đổi mới market economy. Although the Party exalts the masses as the cultural base of society, they also believe the masses lack the knowledge required to participate in the modern economy. This is a longstanding concern. Even during the high socialist period (1954–1986) Party officials considered the masses 'ignorant' (*ngu dốt*), 'backward' (*lạc hậu*) and

---

[130] Vu Oanh, 'Phong Thuong Mai da Tro Thanh Mot To Chuc Tin Cay de Tap Hop, Van Dong, Giup Do Ho Tro va Bao Ve Loi Ich cac Doanh Nghiep Trong Su Nghiep Kinh Doanh' ['The Chamber of Commerce has Become a Reliable Organisiation for Gathering, Mobilizing, Assisting and Protecting the Interests of Enterprises in Business Affairs'], Dien Dan Doanh Nghiep, 22 September 1995, p. 12.

[131] John Gillespie, 'Localizing Global Rules' (2008) 33(3) *Law and Social Inquiry* 673–707.

'uncivilised' (vô văn hóa).[132] To develop a modern economy, the Party encourages the masses to raise their cultural level to centrally proscribed standards. Party leaders use emulation campaigns to 'civilise' (văn minh), modernise and counter the damaging moral influences unleashed by global integration and the market economy.[133]

Consider the use of emulation campaigns to promote 'urban civilisation' (văn minh dô thi).[134] In an illustrative example, Erik Harms described the transformation of Turtle Lake in central Ho Chi Minh City. During the 1990s, a large and diverse group of informal traders and cafés jostled for space around the lake.[135] The area attracted people from a wide range of socio-economic backgrounds. An urban civilisation campaign designed to modernise the city for the 2003 Southeast Asian Games encouraged formal cafés and restaurants to replace the street traders.

Interviews with the former customers of the informal traders revealed considerable support for the campaign.[136] Informants adopted the language used in the campaign to portray the informal cafés as 'insufficiently civilised' (thieu văn minh), and described the formal cafés as 'safe', more 'civilised' and more 'hygienic'. Harms concluded that public support for government campaigns to clarify public and private property boundaries increased with rising property values. He found that '[t]he new cafés are run by, and increasingly patronised by, people who have proprietary relations to space'.[137] Informal trading blurred public–private boundaries and threatened the ability of people to accumulate and consolidate private capital. The campaign succeeded because it linked notions of civility and modernity with market-based notions of private ownership.

[132] Le Thanh Nghi, Mot So Van De Co Ban Trong Quan Ly Kinh Te Xa Hoi Chu Nhgia [Several Basic Matters on Socialist Economic Management] (Hanoi: Nhan Xuat Su That [Truth Publishing House], 1975); MacLean, The Government of Mistrust, p. 20.

[133] See Vu Ngoc Hoang, 'On building Vietnamese Culture and Man', Tạp chí Cộng sản, 26 January 2015, available at http://english.tapchicongsan.org.vn/Home/Culture-Society/2015/762/On-building-Vietnamese-culture-and-man.aspx. Also see Stephen Mc Nally, 'Bia Om and Karaoke: HIV and Everyday Life in Urban Vietnam', in Lisa Drummond and Many Thomas (eds.), Consuming Urban Culture in Vietnam (London: Routledge, 2003), pp. 110–122.

[134] Erik Harms, Saigon's Edge: On the Margins of Ho Chi Minh (Minneapolis, MN: University of Minnesota, 2011), pp. 20–21, 201–204; Ann Marie Leshkowich, 'Standardized Forms of Vietnamese Selfhood: An Ethnographic Genealogy of Documentation' (2014) 41(1) American Ethnologist 143–162.

[135] Erick Harms, 'Vietnam's Civilizing Process and the Retreat from the Street: A Turtle's Eye View From Ho Chi Minh City' (2009) 21(2) City & Society 182–206, 182.

[136] Ibid., 192–193.

[137] Ibid., 200.

Echoes of socialist paternalism are apparent in contemporary mass-mobilisation campaigns. The party-state still claims the right to shape the national character. As Katherine Verdery noted, in the past, cradle-to-grave social welfare provided the ideological justification for socialist paternalism.[138] Following Đổi mới reforms, the Party no longer provides universal welfare for its citizens,[139] but it continues to engineer social thought.

12.6   Conclusions

After three decades of market reforms, commercial regulation in Vietnam might seem an unlikely home for socialism. What this Chapter shows is that socialist-era norms and regulatory technologies remain deeply, if unevenly, embedded in commercial regulation. In some economic sectors, new regulatory practices have partially, although not entirely, displaced or reconfigured socialist-era regulation. In other sectors, socialist-era regulation has continued almost unchanged. One consequence of this variegated regulatory landscape is that Vietnam is simultaneously transitioning out of socialism *and* transforming socialism.

Regulatory signalling reflects this variegation. Among the glaring contradictions are enough continuities, cross-fertilisations and adaptions to suggest that the core socialist tropes of equality, community and cooperation are transforming rather than withering away. This ideological flexibility has opened political space for a wide range of market reforms. For example, although the party-state retains controls over the commanding heights of the economy, transnational investment and trade has penetrated and now dominates certain markets. The party-state responds to the increasingly self-conscious demands of an emerging propertied class by allowing them more autonomy to regulate market activities. It also selectively responds to media campaigns protesting egregious violations of consumer[140] and environmental

---

[138] Verdery, *What was Socialism, and What Comes Next?*, pp. 24–25; Kornai, *The Socialist System*, p. 56.

[139] Workers took strike action in 2014 to protest the weak Law on Social Insurance 2014 that restricted rights to benefits. See Angie Ngoc Tran, 'Small Victory, Systemic Problems', *New Mandela*, 30 April 2015, available at www.newmandala.org/small-victory-systemic-problems/.

[140] Virginie Pedregal and Nguyen Ngoc Luan, 'Is Fresh Milk Powdered Milk? The Controversy over Packaged Milk in Vietnam', in Adam Lindgreen, Martin Hingley and Joelle Vanhomme (eds.), *The Crisis of Food Brands* (London: Routledge, 2016), pp. 65–86.

standards.[141] However, the Party is careful to prevent the nascent consumer and environmental movements from developing a public voice that might interfere with the state's ambitious industrialisation and modernisation plans.[142]

Reflecting deep internal divisions, after three decades of market reforms, the party-state has yet to develop a coherent ideological discourse to justify the subordination of private commercial rights to party policies and directives. In contrast, there is a broad consensus that Marxist–Leninist class conflict should quietly recede into the background. Dictatorship of the proletariat and collective mastery are incompatible with a party-state led by cadres who, more than anyone else, have appropriated the benefits of market reforms.[143]

If regulatory signals are ambiguous, the regulatory technologies used to manage the economy more clearly reveal their socialist origins. Regulation through data collection and monitoring arose from Lenin's preoccupation with techno-scientific governance. More recently, this regulatory technology has assimilated neo-liberal notions of efficiency and quality. This assimilation is not an entirely top-down process, as new regulatory ideas are also absorbed through complex interactions in transnational supply chains.[144]

Neo-liberal ideas have not fundamentally changed the underlying regulatory logic. Some neo-liberal ideas, such as governing from a distance, calculability and the promotion of self-activating subjects, reinforce existing regulatory technologies.[145] But party-state leaders have been reluctant to implement neo-liberal reforms that might dis-embed SOEs from the political-bureaucratic matrix and allow private sector incentives to instill personal accountably.

One of the ironies of market reforms designed to remove bureaucratic oversight is that relational regulation adapted, evolved and extended

---

[141] See Linh Tong, 'Vietnam Fish Deaths Cast Suspicion on Formosa Steel Plant', *The Diplomat*, 30 April 2016, available at http://thediplomat.com/2016/04/vietnam-fish-deaths-cast-suspicion-on-formosa-steel-plant.

[142] See Pedregal and Nguyen Ngoc Luan, 'Is Fresh Milk Powdered Milk?'

[143] Benedict Kerkvliet, 'Government Repression and Toleration of Dissidents in Contemporary Vietnam', in Jonathan London (ed.), *Politics in Contemporary Vietnam* (London: Palgrave Macmillan, 2016), pp. 100–134.

[144] See John Gillespie, 'New Transnational Governance and the Changing Composition of Regulatory Pluralism in Southeast Asia' (2014) 9 *Asian Journal of Comparative Law* 65–95.

[145] Andrew Kipnis, 'Audit Cultures: Neoliberal Governmentality, Socialist Legacy, or Technologies of Governing?' (2008) 35(2) *American Ethnologist* 275–289.

bureaucratic power into every facet of the new economy. It is strongest in the commanding heights of the economy and the small trading and service sector, where it almost entirely displaces other regulatory technologies. In the foreign direct investment sector, where political pressure constrains bureaucratic power, relational regulation co-exists in an uneasy alliance with statutory rights and transnational regulation. Capitalism in Vietnam has not decoupled the economy from the polity.

Differing from the East Asian and the neo-liberal regulatory models, the bureaucracy in Vietnam functions like an extension of the political elite. Rather than arms-length regulation, relational governance creates spheres of mutual constitution, juxtaposition and coexistence between state and non-state actors. This interaction blurs distinctions between public and private, and between socialism and capitalism. Entrepreneurs bargain outcomes with state regulators, creating space for firms to engage in seemingly autonomous behaviour under the watchful gaze of the state.

Where relational regulation fails to influence businesses, the party-state uses criminalisation as a regulatory cudgel. Criminalisation enables officials to project state force into arenas that are not directly regulated by legislation. Despite its legalistic veneer, criminalisation is a regulatory technology that pre-dates and undermines the post–*Đổi mới* experiment with the law-based state.

In another regulatory continuity, the party-state uses mass organisations and emulation campaigns to shape what people think. With the introduction of the mixed-market economy, the message has shifted from emulating model socialist workers to preparing the masses for the global economy. A key difference between social steering in Vietnam and elsewhere in East Asia (with the exception of China) is the party-state's moral conviction in its mission to guide society.

What this Chapter has revealed are clear continuities in the regulatory technologies used to order the economy. The technologies do not exclusively aim for avowedly socialist objectives, nor do they necessarily produce the socialist objectives of equality, community and collaboration. However, many epistemic assumptions about what constitutes the proper way to regulate the economy, which evolved during the high socialist period, continue today.

One way of understanding how these epistemic assumptions and habits are changing is to explore how regulation evolves.[146] Regulatory

---

[146] Sally Engel Merry and Susan Coutin, 'Technologies of Truth in the Anthropology of Conflict' (2014) 41(1) *American Ethnologist* 1–16.

technologies come into existence through a large number of material arrangements and technical adjustments. Crafting regulation for the post–*Đổi mới* economy involved selecting elements from pre-existing regulatory technologies and redeploying them to govern new commercial ideas and practices. This repurposing borrowed texts and technologies that had already acquired legitimacy and authority and applied them to emerging market practices. Each new regulatory iteration was thus a composite of prior norms, measurements, rankings and negotiations. Past regulatory templates guided developments in the future, and eventually the regulatory layers fused into something new.

Attention to the layering furnishes insights into the trajectory of regulatory reform. Past regulatory technologies are brought into the present and given new meanings. In addition, external ideas are borrowed to resolve current commercial problems. Over time, the new regulatory layers come to be seen as appropriate and natural ways of ordering commerce. This shift in regulatory knowledge renders some business practices and problems that were invisible and illicit in the command economy visible and licit in the mixed market. But the pre-existing layers do not disappear, and they continue to influence the accumulation of the regulatory knowledge through which governance occurs. Market forces have not displaced socialist norms and regulatory technologies. Instead, the pre-existing regulatory layers have influenced the redeployment and diversification of state regulation over the mixed-market economy. Vietnam is reinventing socialist-era regulation to suit an increasingly globalised mixed-market economy.

The Influence of Socialist Principles on the Legal Regulation of Markets in China

The Anti-Monopoly Law

WENDY NG

13.1 Introduction

When China embarked on economic reform and opening up in 1978, it did not completely dismantle its socialist command-style system. Instead, it decided to build a market economy out of its existing socialist system.[1] A market grew out of the planned economy, and the state's involvement in and control over the economy decreased significantly.[2] After nearly forty years of reform, although China's economy is increasingly reliant on markets to allocate resources and coordinate economic outcomes and is integrated into the global economic system, it is an economy that operates within a socialist system and under the state's influence, though diminished.[3] To regulate and support the market economy, China has needed to formulate relevant laws and legal institutions, as its legal system was effectively abolished during the Cultural Revolution.[4] A question that therefore arises is whether and how China's commitment to socialism has influenced the way in which the law is developed, understood and applied to regulate markets in China.

This Chapter considers this question by exploring whether and how fundamental socialist principles have influenced the use of competition law to regulate markets in China. It should be noted at the very outset

---

[1] See, e.g., Victor Nee, 'The Role of the State in Making a Market Economy' (2000) 156 *Journal of Institutional and Theoretical Economics* 64.

[2] Barry Naughton, *Growing Out of the Plan* (Cambridge: Cambridge University Press, 1995); Barry Naughton, 'Is China Socialist?' (2017) 31(1) *Journal of Economic Perspectives* 3.

[3] Nee, 'The Role of the State in Making a Market Economy', 65.

[4] See generally Stanley Lubman, 'Bird in a Cage: Chinese Law Reform after Twenty Years' (2000) 20 *Northwestern Journal of International Law & Business* 383; Donald C. Clarke, 'Legislating for a Market Economy in China' [2007] (191) *The China Quarterly* 567.

that, in examining this question, this Chapter does not engage with the literature and debates relating to normative conceptions of socialism and whether China remains consistent with or has transformed socialism due to its adoption of, inter alia, market principles. China resolutely regards itself as a socialist state, with economic and legal systems that are socialist in nature.[5] This Chapter therefore takes China's own understanding of socialism and explores its implications for the legal regulation of markets in China, using competition law as its case study.

The Anti-Monopoly Law (AML) is China's first comprehensive competition law, and it is a principal law governing the operation of markets and the market economy in China. Competition law is a legal instrument typically used in market economies to maintain and protect competition and ensure the proper functioning of markets. Its operation in a socialist market economy where the state has been, and continues to be, instrumental to the introduction and development of the market economy[6] can provide important insights into understanding how socialist principles influence the nature, role and enforcement of competition law, and legal regulation of markets more generally, in China.

After this introduction, Section 13.2 examines the understanding of socialism in China. It finds that two principles – the leadership of the party and the dominance of public ownership – are fundamental to the concept of socialism in China and that adherence to these principles at the same time as introducing market mechanisms into the economy means that the state both directly participates in and regulates the market. It also considers how these socialist concepts interact with the state apparatus that carries out market regulation. Section 13.3 provides an overview of the AML. The dual roles of the state and their influence on the way that the AML is understood and implemented are examined in Sections 13.4 and 13.5. Section 13.4 examines how the AML has been enforced against state-owned enterprises (SOEs), which are the state's vehicles for direct participation in the market. Section 13.5 considers how the state is using the AML to carry out its role as market regulator, both of market activities and of exercises of regulatory power that impact the market.

This Chapter argues that the dual and leading roles of the state in the economy both constrains and promotes the enforcement of the AML and, as a corollary, the legal regulation of markets in China. The

---

[5] See, e.g., 中华人民共和国宪法 [Constitution of the People's Republic of China], preamble, arts. 1, 5–6.
[6] See generally Nee, 'The Role of the State in Making a Market Economy'.

embedded positions of SOEs within governmental and political structures, their relationships with other government actors, and the dynamics that shape such interactions constrain the ability of competition authorities to enforce the AML against SOEs. Conversely, the enforcement of the AML is promoted and enhanced by the state's macroeconomic control because the AML is regarded as a legal mechanism for supervising market actors and activities, as well as administrative regulatory power. Further, the AML has been used to help clarify the boundaries of the respective roles of the government and the market in the economy and, more broadly, to balance and modulate the relationship between the market and the state.

13.2 The Understanding of Socialism in China and Implications for the State and Markets

An examination of key policy documents of the Communist Party of China (CPC) shows that there are two key principles that are fundamental to socialism in China. The CPC regards the leadership of the party as the most essential feature of 'socialism with Chinese characteristics'.[7] This means that although the CPC, which is the dominant party in China, and the state apparatus are organisationally distinct, in reality the CPC controls, has authority over and supervises state affairs, including all aspects of legal governance.[8]

There are several mechanisms that enable the CPC to exercise control and supervision of state institutions. Through the *nomenklatura* system,[9] the CPC controls the appointment of senior positions at a wide range

---

[7] 中共中央关于全面推进依法治国若干重大问题的决定 [Decision of the Central Committee of the Communist Party of China on Some Major Issues Concerning Promoting the Governance of the Country According to Law] (People's Republic of China) Fourth Plenary Session of the 18th Central Committee of the Communist Party of China, 23 October 2014.

[8] Ibid.; Jianfu Chen, *Chinese Law: Context and Transformation*, revised and expanded edn. (Leiden: Brill Nijhoff, 2015), pp. 121–122, 180–181; Randall Peerenboom, *China's Long March Toward Rule of Law* (Cambridge: Cambridge University Press, 2002), p. 214; Manuél E. Delmestro, 'The Communist Party and the Law: An Outline of Formal and Less Formal Linkages Between the Ruling Party and Other Legal Institutions in the People's Republic of China' (2010) 43 *Suffolk University Law Review* 681 at 682–690.

[9] The *nomenklatura* system consists of 'lists of leading positions over which party committees exercise the power of appointment, lists of reserve cadre for the available positions, and the institutions and processes for making the appropriate personnel changes': John P. Burns, 'China's Nomenklatura System' (1987) 36(5) *Problems of Communism* 36. See also Hon S. Chan, 'Cadre Personnel Management in China: The Nomenklatura System, 1990–1998' (2004) 179 *The China Quarterly* 703.

of state institutions such as the National People's Congress, the State Council, the ministries and commissions under the State Council, the courts, the procuratorate, provincial governments and SOEs.[10] This means that the CPC can appoint its own members to senior positions within state institutions; indeed, many top government officials are also CPC leaders.[11] In addition, the CPC supervises government work from within state institutions through party committees and party groups.[12] This creates a de facto parallel system of party governance within state institutions, and ensures that CPC policies are communicated and implemented, important decisions are deliberated and made, the conduct of CPC members is supervised, and party discipline is upheld and enforced within state institutions.[13] Further, party control and supervision mechanisms are reinforced by 'leading small groups', which are established under the Central Committee of the CPC and link the CPC's leadership with party and state institutions within key functional areas.[14] It is believed that leading small groups are responsible for policy formulation, coordination and implementation in key policy areas.[15] As such, these

[10] Chan, 'Cadre Personnel Management in China', 719–734.

[11] For example, the Premier and the Chairman of the National People's Congress are both members of the Standing Committee of the Political Bureau of the Central Committee. See also Chen, *Chinese Law: Context and Transformation*, p. 178.

[12] Li-Wen Lin and Curtis J. Milhaupt, 'We Are the (National) Champions: Understanding the Mechanisms of State Capitalism in China' (2013) 65 *Stanford Law Review* 697 at 737; Benjamin van Rooij, 'China's System of Public Administration', in Jianfu Chen, Yuwen Li and Jan Michael Otto (eds.), *Implementation of Law in the People's Republic of China* (The Hague: Kluwer Law International, 2002), pp. 332–333; Susan L. Shirk, *The Political Logic of Economic Reform in China* (Berkeley, CA: University of California Press, 1993), pp. 59–60.

[13] 中国共产党章程 [Constitution of the Communist Party of China] (People's Republic of China) National Congress of the Communist Party of China, 21 October 2007, arts. 29–32; Carol Lee Hamrin, 'The Party Leadership System', in Kenneth G. Lieberthal and David M. Lampton (eds.), *Bureaucracy, Politics, and Decision Making in Post-Mao China* (Berkeley, CA: University of California Press, 1992), p. 97; Hon S. Chan, 'Politics Over Markets: Integrating State-owned Enterprises into Chinese Socialist Market' (2009) 29 *Public Administration and Development* 43 at 50; Shirk, *The Political Logic of Economic Reform in China*, p. 58; Delmestro, 'The Communist Party and the Law', 694.

[14] Constitution of the Communist Party of China, art. 22; Alice Miller, 'The CPC Central Committee's Leading Small Groups' [2008] (26) *China Leadership Monitor* 1 at 1, 3; 周望 [Zhou Wang], 中国'小组'政治模式解析 [China's "Small Group" Political Model Analysed] [2010] (3) 云南社会科学 [Social Sciences in Yunnan] 14 at 16–17; Kenneth Lieberthal, *Governing China: From Revolution Through Reform*, 2nd edn. (New York, NY: W. W. Norton, 2004), pp. 215–217.

[15] Miller, 'The CPC Central Committee's Leading Small Groups', 1, 3; Lieberthal, 'Governing China', p. 217; Zhou, 'China's "Small Group" Political Model Analysed', 16–17.

control and supervision mechanisms enable the CPC to connect to, control and lead the state apparatus.

Another principal tenet of socialism in China is the dominance of public ownership. The Chinese Constitution provides that public ownership is the foundation of China's socialist economic system, and the CPC regards public ownership as an important pillar of 'socialism with Chinese characteristics'.[16] Public ownership is manifest in SOEs, which are important material and political foundations of 'socialism with Chinese characteristics'.[17] While SOEs operate in a wide variety of industries (strategically important, regulated and/or competitive) and their share of the economy has decreased, they are dominant in industries that are considered key to the national economy (so-called 'lifeline industries' or the 'commanding heights' of the economy) and national security.[18] The CPC has made it clear that SOEs have leading roles in the economy and that their vitality, controlling force and influence will be continually improved and developed.[19]

The introduction of market principles into the Chinese economy while remaining committed to key socialist principles means that the state has dual – and at times conflicting – leading roles vis-à-vis the market: it is both a direct participant and the regulator. In relation to SOEs, their leading role is recognised, protected and enhanced by policy measures. At the same time, the state has, and continues to, reform SOEs and industries dominated by SOEs, as such reform is considered essential to the development of China's socialist market economy. SOE reforms have largely focused on commercialising and consolidating SOEs, and

---

[16] Constitution of the People's Republic of China, arts. 6–7; 'Decision of the Central Committee of the Communist Party of China on Some Major Issues Concerning Promoting the Governance of the Country According to Law', ch. 2.

[17] 习近平在全国国有企业党的建设工作会议上强调:坚持党对国企的领导不动摇 ['Xi Jinping Emphasises Persistence and Unwavering Party Leadership in SOEs at Nationwide SOE Party Building Conference'], 新华社 [*Xinhua News Agency*], 11 October 2016, available at http://news.xinhuanet.com/2016-10/11/c_1119697415.htm.

[18] Kellee S. Tsai and Barry Naughton, 'Introduction' in Barry Naughton and Kellee S. Tsai (eds.), *State Capitalism, Institutional Adaptation, and the Chinese Miracle* (Cambridge: Cambridge University Press, 2015), pp. 3–4; Naughton, 'Is China Socialist?', 7–10.

[19] 中共中央关于全面深化改革若干重大问题的决定 [Decision of the Central Committee of the Communist Party of China on Some Major Issues Concerning Comprehensively Deepening Reform] (People's Republic of China) Third Plenary Session of the 18th Central Committee of the Communist Party of China, 12 November 2013, ch. 2.

improving their corporate and enterprise management, efficiency and competitiveness.[20] Therefore, the participation of SOEs in the market can lead to tension between protecting and recognising their dominant and leading role while also subjecting them to market forces and competition.

Similarly, although China is transitioning from a command economy to a market-based economy, the economy nonetheless remains subject to the state's macroeconomic regulation and control.[21] The transition process has been gradual, incremental and experimental. Initially, market mechanisms were introduced and implemented within and alongside various sectors of the planned economy. Eventually, planned production and distribution ended in favour of markets.[22] While the state's direct control over and intervention in the economy has decreased significantly, it still has strong influence over the economy and the capacity to intervene to shape economic outcomes.[23] For example, the CPC and the state uses five-year plans to guide China's economic, social and technological development, an economic management practice that has persisted since 1953. Each five-year plan is a national blueprint for the economy over a five-year cycle and it contains guidelines, policy frameworks and targets for officials at all levels of government.[24] Therefore, while market forces are allocating and distributing resources, determining outcomes and imposing market discipline, the state is also intervening to achieve particular outcomes and ensure the proper functioning of the market. The delineation, balance and potential tension between the roles of the market and the state in the economy are recognised by the CPC as key reform issues. At the Third Plenum of the 18th Central Committee of the

---

[20] Yingyi Qian, 'The Process of China's Market Transition (1978–1998): The Evolutionary, Historical, and Comparative Perspectives' (2000) 156 *Journal of Institutional and Theoretical Economics* 151 at 163–164; Donald C. Clarke, 'Corporate Governance in China: An Overview' (2003) 14 *China Economic Review* 494 at 496; Chenxia Shi, 'Recent Ownership Reform and Control of Central State-owned Enterprises in China: Taking One Step at a Time' (2007) 30 *UNSW Law Journal* 855 at 857–858; Xiaofei Mao, 'An Overview of the Anti-Monopoly Practice in the People's Republic of China', in Hassan Qaqaya and George Lipimile (eds.), *The Effects of Anti-Competitive Business Practices on Developing Countries and Their Development Prospects* (New York, NY: United Nations Conference on Trade and Development, 2008), p. 523.

[21] Constitution of the People's Republic of China, art 15; Decision of the Central Committee of the Communist Party of China on Some Major Issues Concerning Comprehensively Deepening Reform', art. 14.

[22] See generally Naughton, *Growing Out of the Plan*.

[23] Naughton, 'Is China Socialist?', 10.

[24] Ibid., 11–13.

CPC held in November 2013, the CPC stated that the market plays a decisive role in allocating resources, whereas the government's role is to, inter alia, strengthen market oversight, maintain market order and remedy market failures.[25] Thus the CPC's approach is for the decisive role of the market in resource allocation to sit alongside the state's oversight and supervision (and in limited circumstances, intervention) role.

To explore and illustrate the ways in which market regulation is shaped by the dynamics of the relationship, interaction and tension between socialist and market principles within the economy, this Chapter examines the implementation of China's competition law. In particular, it considers how the AML reflects, responds to and is challenged by the dual roles of the state in the economy.

13.3   An Overview of the Anti-Monopoly Law

The AML has the attributes of a legal transplant that is based upon competition law models of advanced Western capitalist states.[26] Similar to those competition laws, the AML prohibits horizontal and vertical anti-competitive agreements, abuses of dominance and anti-competitive mergers.[27] As Haley observes, these competition law models focus on the conduct of private actors and generally do not address state power or the need for the state to create conditions that enable effective competition.[28] However, the AML is being implemented in an economy where, in addition to market forces, the party and the state have leading roles. In part, as a reflection of this, the AML also prohibits anti-competitive

---

[25] 'Decision of the Central Committee of the Communist Party of China on Some Major Issues Concerning Comprehensively Deepening Reform'; 习近平 [Xi Jinping], 关于《中共中央关于全面深化改革若干重大问题的决定》的说明 [An Explanation of 'Decision of the Central Committee of the Communist Party of China on Some Major Issues Concerning Comprehensively Deepening Reform'], Third Plenary Session of the 18th Central Committee of the Communist Party of China, 15 November 2013.

[26] Wentong Zheng, 'Transplanting Antitrust in China: Economic Transition, Market Structure, and State Control' (2010) 32 *University of Pennsylvania Journal of International Law* 643 at 648.

[27] 中华人民共和国反垄断法 [Anti-Monopoly Law of the People's Republic of China] (People's Republic of China) Standing Committee of the National People's Congress, 30 August 2007, chs. 2–4.

[28] John O. Haley, 'Competition Policy for East Asia' (2004) 3 *Washington University Global Studies Law Review* 277 at 277.

abuses of administrative power (also known as administrative monopolies),[29] which are not typically included within the scope of other jurisdictions' competition laws.[30]

The AML was adopted in response to growing demand for a competition law to regulate the socialist market economy. Competition law – popularly referred to as an 'economic constitution' – is considered by the Chinese government to be an essential part of a legal system that is required to support the functioning of a market economy because it protects market competition, maintains market order and enables the market to fulfil its role to allocate resources.[31] It also regards competition law as an important tool of economic policy to regulate the market economy.[32] Throughout the drafting process, the lawmakers emphasised that the AML should not only be consistent with international competition law norms and practices, it must also reflect and suit China's national conditions.[33] As a result, the AML is generally consistent in form and substance with prevailing international competition law norms, with many of its provisions being similar to or reflecting approaches taken in the competition/antitrust laws of the United States, European Union and Germany.[34] At the same time, there are some provisions in the AML that are tailored to China's specific needs and circumstances. Examples include the prohibition on administrative monopoly noted earlier in the Chapter, the divided administrative enforcement structure

---

[29] Anti-Monopoly Law, ch. 5.
[30] Examples of countries whose competition laws also cover public restraints on competition are Ukraine, Russia and Hungary.
[31] 关于《中华人民共和国反垄断法 (草案)》的说明 [An Explanation of China's Anti-Monopoly Law (Draft)], 22nd Session of the Tenth Standing Committee of the National People's Congress, 24 June 2006; 发言摘登: 反垄断法草案 [Speech Excerpts: Draft of the Anti-Monopoly Law], 22nd Session of the Standing Committee of the Tenth National People's Congress, 27 June 2006; Ming Shang, 'Antitrust in China – A Constantly Evolving Subject' (2009) 3 Competition Law International 4 at 4.
[32] An Explanation of China's Anti-Monopoly Law (Draft), 24 June 2006.
[33] Ibid., 反垄断法二审稿更加符合我国国情 – 分组审议反垄断法草案发言摘登 (一) [Anti-Monopoly Law Second Deliberation Draft More Compatible with Our National Conditions – Speech Excerpts of the Group Deliberations of the Draft Anti-Monopoly Law (1)], 28th Session of the Standing Committee of the Tenth National People's Congress, 25 June 2007; Zhenguo Wu, 'Perspectives on the Chinese Anti-Monopoly Law' (2008) 75 Antitrust Law Journal 73 at 77; Xiaoye Wang, 'Highlights of China's New Anti-Monopoly Law' (2008) 75 Antitrust Law Journal 133 at 134–135.
[34] See generally Wendy Ng, The Political Economy of Competition Law in China (Cambridge: Cambridge University Press, 2018), ch. 2.

that reflects the pre-AML competition-related experiences and responsibilities of the competition authorities, and the several provisions that provide for the consideration of public interest, industrial policy, economic development and social factors.[35] The leading role of the state in the economy, as participant and regulator, is also recognised and protected in the AML.[36]

Before examining and exploring how the two dimensions of the state's leading role in the economy influences the AML and its enforcement, it is imperative to understand several key aspects of its implementation.

First, the administrative enforcement of the AML is divided among three ministries.[37] The competition authorities are the Ministry of Commerce (MOFCOM), the National Development and Reform Commission (NDRC), and the State Administration for Industry and Commerce (SAIC). The MOFCOM is responsible for merger review and enforcement, whereas the NDRC and the SAIC share enforcement responsibility for anti-competitive agreements and abuses of dominance along price-related and non-price-related lines, respectively. Within each ministry, a central-level department is allocated the responsibility for AML enforcement. The Anti-Monopoly Bureau (MOFCOM Bureau) is the responsible department at the MOFCOM, the Bureau of Price Supervision and Anti-Monopoly (NDRC Bureau) is the responsible department at the NDRC, and the SAIC has allocated its enforcement responsibility to the Anti-Monopoly and Anti-Unfair Competition Enforcement Bureau (SAIC Bureau). Whereas the MOFCOM has centralised its AML enforcement work, both the NDRC and the SAIC have delegated AML enforcement authority to its provincial-level authorities.[38] In contrast, responsibility

---

[35] An Explanation of China's Anti-Monopoly Law (Draft), 24 June 2006; Speech Excerpts: Draft of the Anti-Monopoly Law, 27 June 2006.

[36] 全国人大法律委员会关于《中华人民共和国反垄断法(草案)》修改情况的汇报 [Report of the Law Committee of the National People's Congress on the Revision of the Anti-Monopoly Law of the People's Republic of China (Draft)], 28th Session of the Standing Committee of the Tenth National People's Congress, 24 June 2007.

[37] An intergovernmental body has also been established (the Anti-Monopoly Commission) to organise, coordinate, and guide AML-related work, but it is not involved in the day-to-day enforcement of the AML: Anti-Monopoly Law, art. 9.

[38] The NDRC has delegated its AML enforcement authority to provincial-level price authorities outright, whereas the SAIC delegates AML enforcement authority to provincial-level AICs on a case-by-case basis, with the exception of administrative monopolies, where provincial-level AICs automatically have authority to handle such cases. See 反价格垄断行政执法程序规定 [Regulation on Anti-Price Monopoly Administrative Enforcement Procedures] (People's Republic of China) National Reform and Development Commission, Order No. 8, 29 December 2010, art. 3; 工商行政管理机关

for enforcing the administrative monopoly prohibition lies with the superior authority of the administrative organ whose conduct is in question, and the competition authorities can only make non-binding recommendations to the superior authority on how to handle the case under the AML.[39]

Second, while mergers that reach a particular threshold must be notified to the MOFCOM for anti-monopoly review,[40] it is up to the NDRC and the SAIC to initiate investigations into non-merger conduct.[41] The outcomes of merger review and investigations into non-merger conduct also differ. The MOFCOM can prohibit a proposed merger if it results or may result in the elimination or restriction of competition, or it can attach conditions to its approval to eliminate or reduce the anti-competitive effects or approve a merger unconditionally.[42] For anti-competitive agreements and abuses of dominance, the NDRC and the SAIC can order investigated parties to stop their illegal conduct, confiscate illegal gains and impose fines, or they may accept commitments from investigated parties and suspend an investigation without making a finding or imposing a penalty.[43] As noted prior, the competition authority's role in enforcing the prohibition against anti-competitive abuses of administrative power is limited to making non-binding recommendations.[44]

查处垄断协议，滥用市场支配地位案件程序规定 [Regulation of the Administration for Industry and Commerce on the Procedures Relating to the Investigation of Monopoly Agreement and Abuse of Dominance Cases] (People's Republic of China) State Administration for Industry and Commerce, Order No. 42, 26 May 2009, art. 2; 工商行政管理机关制止滥用行政权力排除，限制竞争行为程序规定 [Regulation of the Administration for Industry and Commerce on Procedures Relating to the Prevention of the Abuse of Administrative Power to Eliminate or Restrict Competition] (People's Republic of China) State Administration for Industry and Commerce, 5 June 2009, art. 2.

[39] Anti-Monopoly Law, art. 51.

[40] 国务院关于经营者集中申报标准的规定 [Regulation of the State Council on the Notification Thresholds for Concentrations of Business Operators] (People's Republic of China) State Council, Order No. 529, 3 August 2008, art. 3.

[41] Since the AML came into effect on 1 August 2008, the Chinese competition authorities have made over 100 publicly known investigations or decisions relating to non-merger conduct.

[42] Anti-Monopoly Law, arts. 28–29; 经营者集中审查办法 [Measure on the Review of Concentrations of Business Operators] (People's Republic of China) Ministry of Commerce, Order No. 12, 15 July 2009, art. 12.

Of the 1,657 mergers that were reviewed and concluded as at 31 December 2016, 1,627 (98.19 per cent) were unconditionally approved, 28 (1.69 per cent) were approved subject to conditions and 2 mergers (0.12 per cent) were prohibited.

[43] Anti-Monopoly Law, arts. 45–47.

[44] Ibid., art. 51.

13.4   The Anti-Monopoly Law and State-Owned Enterprises

The tension between the state's direct participation in the market and regulation to ensure its compliance with the law is demonstrated in both the text of the AML and in the way that it has been enforced against SOEs. This tension is intensified by the position and status of SOEs within the political economy. As SOEs are part of the political structure, they derive power not only from their own positions within the hierarchy but also from their relationships with other government authorities. The application of the AML to SOEs illustrates how these dynamics influence the legal regulation of markets in China.

13.4.1   Express Recognition and Protection of the State in Certain Industries

The AML expressly recognises and protects the state's controlling position in certain industries. Article 7 provides that the state protects the lawful business activities of businesses operating in industries that relate to the national economic lifeline and national security and which are controlled by the state-owned economy, or which are subject to state-granted monopolies.[45] Such industries, which are regarded by the state as strategic or important, are dominated by SOEs. This article, which was added to the AML during the final stages of drafting, reflects a compromise to balance two competing needs – protecting the dominance of SOEs in important and strategic industries, and prohibiting their anti-competitive conduct.

There were concerns that Article 7 would result in the exemption or favourable treatment of SOEs under the AML[46]; however, this has not

---

[45] Article 7 of the AML is as follows: 'The state will, in industries that relate to the national economic lifeline and national security that are controlled by the state-owned economy or which are subject to exclusive operations and sales according to the law, protect the lawful business activities of such operators, supervise and regulate the conduct and price of goods and services of those operators according to the law, protect consumer interest, and promote technological progress. Operators in these industries must operate their business according to law, act in good faith, engage in strict self-discipline, accept public supervision, and not use their controlling position or monopoly status to harm consumer interest.'

[46] See, e.g., Deborah Healey, 'An Anti-Monopoly Law for China: Weapon or Mirage?' (2008) 16 *Competition & Consumer Law Journal* 220 at 228–229; Nathan Bush, 'Constraints on Convergence in Chinese Antitrust' (2009) 54 *Antitrust Bulletin* 87 at 113–114; Eleanor M. Fox, 'An Anti-Monopoly Law for China – Scaling the Walls of Government Restraints' (2008) 75 *Antitrust Law Journal* 173 at 192–193; H. Stephen Harris Jr. et al.,

occurred in enforcement. The Chinese competition authorities have investigated a variety of SOEs for potential breaches of the AML; both centrally-owned and locally-owned SOEs, operating in industries where SOEs are dominant and those that are competitive where SOEs compete with privately-owned businesses. Further, the SAIC's local authority in Liaoning province, relying on Article 7, confirmed that state-granted monopolies are not exempt from the AML[47] and the NDRC's local authority in Hubei province interpreted Article 7 as imposing a positive obligation on SOEs operating in those industries to act in good faith and be self-disciplined.[48] Thus, although the AML recognises the leading and dominant position of SOEs in certain industries, this does not mean that their conduct is not subject to scrutiny under the AML.

13.4.2   Institutional and Political Constraints

However, competition authorities face institutional and political constraints when seeking to enforce the AML against SOEs. Such constraints arise from the positions, stature and relationships of SOEs within the political structure that extend beyond the state's ownership interest in SOEs.[49]

First, the SOEs that are more likely to attract scrutiny under the AML are those that are larger and more economically powerful, and operate in strategic or natural monopoly industries. These SOEs are therefore themselves powerful economic and political actors within the state that are capable of challenging or resisting AML enforcement efforts.

Second, SOEs may have the support of industry regulators.[50] The industries and sectors overseen by industry regulators tend to be those

---

Anti-Monopoly Law and Practice in China (New York, NY: Oxford University Press, 2011), pp. 195–197.

[47] 辽宁省烟草公司抚顺市公司滥用市场支配地位案 [Liaoning Tobacco Company Fushun Subsidiary Abuse of Dominance Case] (People's Republic of China) Liaoning Province Administration for Industry and Commerce, Order No. 2, 1 June 2015.

[48] National Development and Reform Commission, 湖北省物价局依法查处武昌盐业分公司强制搭售案件 [Hubei Price Bureau Investigates the Wuhan Salt Industry Group Branch Forced Tying Case According to Law] (News Release, 15 November 2010).

[49] Curtis J. Milhaupt and Wentong Zheng, 'Reforming China's State-owned Enterprises: Institutions, Not Ownership', in Benjamin L. Liebman and Curtis J. Milhaupt (eds.), Regulating the Visible Hand?: The Institutional Implications of Chinese State Capitalism (New York, NY: Oxford University Press, 2016).

[50] SOEs will also find support from the government authorities under which they are owned, such as the State-owned Assets Supervision and Administration Commission.

where SOEs are the major or only players. A close relationship between them exists, and industry regulators often protect regulated businesses from competition and seek economic advantages for them.[51] Further, the interests of SOEs and industry regulators are aligned when it comes to AML matters. Some sector-specific laws that are administered by industry regulators contain competition-related provisions; hence, they have incentives to protect their regulatory turf from encroachment by the AML. Similarly, SOEs prefer to be subject to sector-specific laws, regulations and supervision, as those arrangements are generally regarded as being favourable to their interests.[52] Therefore, the support of industry regulators, who are key players within their areas of regulatory power, can add to the political weight opposing or resisting AML enforcement.

Third, the relationships and interactions between the competition authorities and SOEs are shaped by their positions within the hierarchy of power. This is reflected in the ranking system, in which each government and CPC institution – including the competition authorities and SOEs – has a bureaucratic rank, each government and CPC official holds an individual rank, and the political power wielded by a government or CPC institution is determined by its own rank and the rank of its leaders.[53] Higher-ranked entities can issue binding orders to, and compel cooperation from, lower-ranked entities. In contrast, lower-ranked entities cannot bind higher-ranked entities, and they may find it difficult to seek cooperation from higher-ranked entities; the same applies for entities of an equal rank.[54] The position of a government authority

---

[51] *OECD Reviews of Regulatory Reform: China: Defining the Boundary between the Market and the State* (Organisation for Economic Co-Operation and Development, 2009), p. 99; Margaret Pearson, 'The Business of Governing Business in China: Institutions and Norms of the Emerging Regulatory State' (2005) 57 *World Politics* 296 at 308–309; 江涌 [Jiang Yong], 警惕部门利益膨胀 ['Be Wary of the Expansion of Industry and Sector Interests'] [2006] (41) 瞭望新闻周刊 [Outlook] 33 at 35; Shen Jia, 'The Invisible Obstacle', *News China Magazine* (January 2011).

[52] 李莫言 [Li Moyan], 让反垄断法少些遗憾 [Let Anti-Monopoly Law Have Fewer Defects] [2006] (7) 大经贸 [Foreign Business] 24 at 24; Philip Wen, 'China's Xi Jinping Compared to Deng Xiaoping as His Power Base Grows', *The Age*, 18 November 2013, available at www.theage.com.au/world/chinas-xi-jinping-compared-to-deng-xiaoping-as-his-power-base-grows-20131117-2xp3y.html.

[53] Kenneth Lieberthal and Michel Oksenberg, *Policy Making in China: Leaders, Structure, and Processes* (Princeton, NJ: Princeton University Press, 1988), pp. 142–145; Chen, *Chinese Law: Context and Transformation*, pp. 178–181.

[54] Susan V. Lawrence and Michael F. Martin, 'Understanding China's Political System' (Congressional Research Service, 31 January 2013), p. 15.

within the administrative hierarchy is therefore very important. While the competition authorities are ministry-level entities, the responsibility for enforcing the AML has been allocated to – and therefore, the actual work of enforcement is carried out by – bureaus within the central ministry and their local offices, which are ranked lower than the ministry level. Moreover, interactions between state institutions are shaped by the CPC's strong vertical systems of accountability and control and the manner in which democratic centralism is reflected in the institutional arrangements of the CPC and the state and governance, which result in periods of centralisation and decentralisation; this is discussed in Chapter 8 in this volume. Hence, a competition authority's ability to enforce the AML against a SOE, and its effectiveness in doing so, is affected by its position vis-à-vis that SOE.

The effect of these constraints and dynamics on AML enforcement can be seen in merger and non-merger cases. In the non-merger context, the competition authorities have taken enforcement action more frequently against local SOEs than central SOEs. At the end of 2016, none of the SAIC's published decisions have concerned the activities of central SOEs, whereas more than twenty of its forty-eight published administrative penalty decisions have involved the conduct of local SOEs. Most of the NDRC's publicly known investigations involving SOEs have pertained to local SOEs, however it has taken two cases against central SOEs. While these enforcement statistics may, in part, reflect the fact that there are fewer central SOEs than local SOEs, another explanation is that it is politically easier for competition authorities to take action against local SOEs than central SOEs.

Even though local SOEs can be important players in their locality or region and have the support of local government, in most cases, the visibility and power of local SOEs is generally less than central SOEs and local regulators are less likely to interfere in the decision-making of competition authorities. Further, while most investigations of local SOEs are undertaken by the competition authorities' local offices, in practice, they are quite closely supervised and supported by the central authority.[55] This helps to overcome issues relating to rank and political pressures that arise in relation to investigating SOEs, as the NDRC Bureau and the SAIC Bureau are likely to be as, if not more, politically powerful than the local SOEs their local offices are investigating, and

---

[55] Interviews with Chinese competition law experts and stakeholders.

the central authorities are less likely to be implicated in local political structures and issues. The effectiveness of central authority support in overcoming local-level opposition was illustrated in, for example, *Moutai RPM*, *Wuliangye RPM* and the *Shanghai Gold and Platinum Jewellery Cartel* cases. In the *Moutai RPM* and *Wuliangye RPM* cases, which involved powerful local SOEs, the AML investigations were initiated by the NDRC Bureau, which later delegated enforcement authority to its local offices. These cases resulted in the SOEs being fined.[56] In the *Shanghai Gold and Platinum Jewellery Cartel*, the NDRC's Shanghai bureau was aware of the price fixing conduct of several local SOEs in the gold industry for over a decade, but had been unable to take action against them because their conduct was supported by the local government. However, in 2013 the NDRC's Shanghai bureau successfully investigated and sanctioned the price-fixing arrangement when it had the support of the NDRC's central-level bureau, which had directed it to initiate the AML investigation.[57]

In contrast, central SOEs are generally larger and more powerful SOEs that operate in important and strategic sectors of the economy, where the interests of relevant industry regulators are likely to be implicated. Depending on the central SOE being investigated, it may be more highly ranked than the competition authority. These dynamics can make it more difficult for competition authorities to act against central SOEs, and this was seen in the *China Telecom/China Unicom* and *TravelSky* cases, the two publicly known AML investigations involving central SOEs to date. In *China Telecom/China Unicom*, the NDRC Bureau investigated two of the largest telecommunications companies in China and powerful central SOEs, China Telecom and China Unicom, for potentially abusing

---

[56] Sichuan Development and Reform Commission, 五粮液公司实施价格垄断被处罚2.02 亿元 [Wuliangye Fined RMB 202 Million for Implementing Price Monopoly] (News Release, 22 February 2013); 公告 (2013年第1号) [Announcement (No. 1 of 2013)] (People's Republic of China) Guizhou Price Bureau, Order No. 1, 22 February 2013; Angela Huyue Zhang, 'Bureaucratic Politics and China's Anti-Monopoly Law' (2014) 47 *Cornell International Law Journal* 671 at 700.

[57] Angela Huyue Zhang, 'Taming the Chinese Leviathan: Is Antitrust Regulation a False Hope?' (2015) 51 *Stanford Journal of International Law* 195 at 223–225. See 上海黄金饰 品行业协会及部分金店实施价格垄断被依法查处 [Price Monopoly Agreement Implemented by the Shanghai Gold Jewellery Industry Association and Some Jewellery Stores Investigated According to Law] (13 August 2013) National Development and Reform Commission, available at www.sdpc.gov.cn/fzgggz/jgjdyfld/jjszhdt/201308/t20130813_553443.html.

their dominance.[58] The two SOEs had the public support of one of the most important industry regulators, the Ministry for Industry and Information Technology (MIIT).[59] Similarly, the Civil Aviation Administration of China (CAAC) supported the investigated parties in the *TravelSky* case,[60] which involved TravelSky – the CAAC's ticketing website that also issues the tickets for major Chinese airlines – and several Chinese SOE airlines. In addition to the opposition by industry regulators, the SOEs investigated in both cases had a higher rank than the NDRC Bureau. China Telecom, China Unicom and some of the investigated SOE airlines are classified as important backbone SOEs, which means they have at least vice-ministerial rank;[61] while the NDRC Bureau is ranked at the next level down (at least). The position and status of the investigated SOEs and their supporting industry regulators combined would have made it difficult for the NDRC Bureau to compel cooperation from the investigated SOEs and to resist political pressure, unless more highly ranked and politically powerful officials within the NDRC weighed in.

Moreover, investigations involving SOEs might be more likely to be resolved in favour of suspension or termination, rather than financial sanctions, as compared to investigations of private domestic companies and foreign companies. In cases involving SOEs, accepting commitments (such as to adopt measures that undo or mitigate the adverse effects of the conduct) and effectively settling the case might be regarded as a more realistic outcome for the competition authority. This resolution allows the competition authority to both address the adverse effects of the anti-competitive conduct and deliver benefits to consumers (in the form of reduced prices or improved services, for example), and resolve

---

[58] 国家发改委就价格监管与反垄断工作情况举行新闻发布会 [NDRC Holds News Conference on Price Supervision and Anti-Monopoly Work] (19 February 2014) available at www.china.com.cn/zhibo/2014-02/19/content_31502397.htm.

[59] 赵谨, 李蕾 [Zhao Jin and Li Lei], 工信部下属两家媒体驳电信联通涉嫌垄断报道 [Two Media Outlets Under the MIIT Refute Reports of Alleged Monopolisation by China Telecom/China Unicom], 新京报 [*The Beijing News*], 12 November 2011, available at www.chinanews.com/it/2011/11-12/3455659.shtml.

[60] 林红梅 [Lin Hongmei], 中国民航局澄清: 中国民航运价政策没有发生变化 [Civil Aviation Administration of China Clarifies: China's Civil Aviation Pricing Policy Has Not Changed], 新华社 [*Xinhua News Agency*], 21 April 2009, available at www.gov.cn/fwxx/ly/2009-04/21/content_1291265.htm.

[61] "国有重要骨干企业" 有哪些? [Which are the "Important Backbone SOEs"?], 新华网 [*Xinhuanet*], 30 January 2015, available at http://news.xinhuanet.com/video/sjxw/2015-01/30/c_127440169.htm.

the pressures it faces from SOEs and other government departments. For example, this appears to have been influential in how the NDRC Bureau decided to resolve its *China Telecom/China Unicom* investigation. The NDRC had reportedly made its preliminary findings and decided to fine the two SOEs. However, this position apparently changed after the NDRC Bureau consulted with the State Council Legislative Affairs Office, the Supreme People's Court, the MIIT, and the State-owned Asset Supervision and Administration Commission (SASAC).[62] The NDRC Bureau ultimately accepted China Telecom's and China Unicom's commitments to adopt corrective measures and expand their bandwidth, reduce prices and improve interoperability.[63] The Director-General of the NDRC Bureau later acknowledged that it had faced pressure from all sides during the investigation, which hints that the consultation process is likely to have led the NDRC Bureau to decide to accept commitments rather than impose fines.[64] More broadly, a number of investigations of SOEs, especially at the central level, have resulted in their suspension or termination. The majority of the investigations that have been suspended or terminated following the offering and/or implementation of commitments have involved local and central SOEs, with most resulting in no fines, and some without a formal decision or public announcement

[62] 新华社调查电信联通涉嫌垄断案, 称系"神仙战" ['Xinhua Investigates China Telecom/China Unicom Suspected Monopoly Case, Calls it the "Battle of the Gods"'], 中国日报 [*China Daily*], 12 November 2011, available at www.chinadaily.com.cn/hqpl/zggc/2011-11-12/content_4349426.html; 发改委否认宽带垄断案和解, 称已获得核心证据 ['NDRC Denies Settling Broadband Monopoly Case, Says it has Already Gathered Core Evidence'], 新京报 [*The Beijing News*], 22 November 2011, available at http://finance.sina.com.cn/g/20111122/075410857808.shtml; 'Editorial: Anti-Monopoly Investigations Should be Conducted Openly and Independently', *News China Magazine*, (January 2012).

[63] China Telecom Corporation Limited, 'Announcement' (Hong Kong Stock Exchange Announcement, 2 December 2011); China Unicom (Hong Kong) Limited, 'Announcement' (Hong Kong Stock Exchange Announcement, 2 December 2011); 国家发改委就价格监管与反垄断工作情况举行新闻发布会 ['NDRC Holds News Conference on Price Supervision and Anti-Monopoly Work'] (19 February 2014), available at www.china.com.cn/zhibo/2014-02/19/content_31502397.htm.

[64] 发改委反垄断局: 继续督促电信联通反垄断整改 限期3–5年 ['NDRC Anti-Monopoly Bureau: Continues to Urge China Telecom and China Unicom to Undertake Anti-Monopoly Rectification, Time Limit of 3–5 Years'], 证券时报 [Securities Times], 25 September 2013, available at www.cs.com.cn/xwzx/hg/201309/t20130925_4153920.html. See also Xiaoye Wang, 'The China Telecom and China Unicom Case and the Future of Chinese Antitrust', in Adrian Emch and David Stallibrass (eds.), *China's Anti-Monopoly Law: The First Five Years* (Alphen aan den Rijn, The Netherlands: Kluwer Law International, 2013), p. 485.

relating to their outcome.[65] In contrast, most of the cases where the investigated parties had made commitments and were also sanctioned by the competition authority involved the conduct of private companies.[66]

Similarly, the MOFCOM faces challenges in merger enforcement involving SOEs, as merger enforcement activity involving SOEs appears to be disproportionately low. According to Sobel, during the period 1 August 2008 to 31 December 2015, just over 6 per cent of the total number of mergers approved during that period were domestic mergers involving SOEs.[67] However, SOEs have been active in mergers since the AML came into effect in August 2008. For example, the SASAC has been restructuring and consolidating the central SOEs under its administration, reducing that number from 149 to 102 in the period from 1 August 2008 to 31 December 2016 through mergers, acquisitions and other restructuring activities.[68] As the merger notification thresholds are relatively low in China, many of those mergers would have likely required notification to the MOFCOM for anti-monopoly review.[69] However, only nine of these mergers involving central SOEs were so notified.[70] Therefore, there is an apparent discrepancy between the merger enforcement statistics and the

---

[65] Publicly known cases involving local SOEs that were suspended or terminated are *Wuchang Salt Tying, Inner Mongolia Mobile Unreasonable Conditions, Inner Mongolia Unicom Tying, Ningxia Broadband Internet Tying,* and *Hai'an Electric Power Unreasonable Conditions.* The two cases involving central SOE (*TravelSky* and *China Telecom/ China Unicom*) were also apparently settled. Publicly known cases involving private companies that were suspended or terminated are *Qinghai Tianlu Dairy RPM, Inter-Digital, Cixi Energy Saving Testing Cartel, Beijing Shankai Sports Tying.*

[66] Such publicly known cases involving private companies are the *Japanese Auto Parts Cartel, Japanese Ball Bearings Cartel, Ningxia Courier Cartel, Infant formula RPM, Lens Manufacturers RPM.* The local SOEs in the *Shanghai Gold and Platinum Jewellery Cartel* were also sanctioned and had made commitments.

[67] Yuni Yan Sobel, 'Domestic-to-Domestic Transactions – A Gap in China's Merger Control Regime?' [2014] (February) *The Antitrust Source* 1 at 4; Yuni Yan Sobel, 'Domestic-to-Domestic Transactions (2014–2015) – A Narrowing Gap in China's Merger Control Regime' [2016] (February) *The Antitrust Source* 1 at 4.

[68] 中央变更 [Central SOE Changes], State-owned Assets Supervision and Administration Commission, available at www.sasac.gov.cn/n2588035/n2641579/n2641660/index.html; 央企名录 [Central SOE Directory], State-owned Assets Supervision and Administration Commission of the State Council, available at www.sasac.gov.cn/n2588035/n2641579/n2641645/index.html.

[69] Sobel, 'Domestic-to-Domestic Transactions – A Gap in China's Merger Control Regime?', 5–6.

[70] *General Electric/Shenhua, Anshan Iron and Steel/Panzhihua Iron and Steel, China Power Investment/State Nuclear Power Technology, China North Locomotive & Rolling Stock/ China South Locomotive & Rolling Stock, China Minmetals/China Metallurgical, Baosteel/ Wuhan Iron and Steel, China National Travel Service/CITS, China National Building Materials/Sinoma, COFCO/Chinatex.*

actual level of SOE-related merger activity. This suggests that SOEs simply do not notify their mergers to the MOFCOM for anti-monopoly review, even where it is strictly required to do so under the AML.[71]

Even though the MOFCOM has the power to investigate, fine or make other orders in relation to non-compliance with the AML notification requirements,[72] the political and institutional constraints facing the MOFCOM Bureau seem to provide SOEs with some cover from investigation or sanction. Much like the situation facing the NDRC Bureau and the SAIC Bureau, the MOFCOM Bureau might be ranked lower than the SOEs that it is seeking to investigate and take enforcement action against. The MOFCOM Bureau might also face opposition from other government departments if it sought to investigate or sanction a SOE for implementing a merger that was approved by other government departments such as industry regulators, the SASAC (for central SOEs) or maybe even the State Council. It would also be more difficult for the MOFCOM Bureau to investigate or sanction a merger that was taken as part of industry-wide reforms or plans adopted by the government. For example, the merger between China Netcom and China Unicom, which were two leading telecommunications central SOEs, in October 2008 was completed pursuant to a restructuring of the telecommunications industry undertaken by the MIIT, the NDRC and the Ministry of Finance. The merger was also approved by the State Council and other government departments, including the securities regulator.[73] Therefore, even though the merging SOEs had not obtained the MOFCOM's anti-monopoly

---

[71] Interviews with Chinese competition law experts and stakeholders. See also D. Daniel Sokol, 'Merger Control under China's Anti-Monopoly Law' (2013) 10 *New York University Journal of Law & Business* 1 at 21–22; 王毕强 [Wang Biqiang], 国资委人士称央企重组不需商务部反垄断审查 ['SASAC Official Says MOFCOM Anti-Monopoly Review Not Required in Central SOE Restructuring'], 经济观察网 [*Economic Observer Online*], 2 August 2008, available at http://finance.sina.com.cn/roll/20080802/09455160451.shtml.

[72] 未依法申报经营者集中调查处理暂行办法 [Interim Measure for Investigating and Handling Concentrations of Business Operators Not Notified in Accordance with the Law] (People's Republic of China) Ministry of Commerce, Order No. 6, 30 December 2011.

[73] 中国联通与中国网通重组 国资委监管企业调整为141户 [China Unicom and China Netcom Reorganises, SASAC Supervised Businesses Adjusts to 141 Units] (7 January 2009) State-owned Assets Supervision and Administration Commission, available at www.sasac.gov.cn/n2588035/n2641579/n2641660/c3753973/content.html; China Unicom, 'The Red Chip Companies of China Unicom and China Netcom are Successfully Merged and China Unicom Telecommunications Corporation Limited is Established in Beijing' (News Release, 15 October 2008); 灵戈 [Ling Ge], 联通网通合并案涉嫌违法? 追究责任要全面彻底 ['China Unicom/China Netcom Merger Suspected Illegal? Quest for Accountability Must Be Complete and Thoroug'h], 人民网 [*People's Daily Online*], 4 May 2009, available at http://it.people.com.cn/GB/42891/42895/9232735.html.

approval despite reaching the notification thresholds,[74] it was unlikely that the MOFCOM could have taken action against them if it had wanted to. Nevertheless, the MOFCOM has been able to take some action against SOEs for non-compliance. Five of its nine published administrative penalty decisions concern mergers involving SOEs, which cover both local SOEs and subsidiaries of central SOEs.[75]

13.5   The Anti-Monopoly Law and the State as Regulator

The regulatory role of the state, together with its adjustment and rebalancing vis-à-vis the market, shapes the way in which the AML is viewed, understood and implemented. The macroeconomic control of the state is not only reflected in Article 4 of the AML, it expressly contemplates that the AML will further that macroeconomic control.[76] At the same time, the drafters of the AML recognised that the government could impede competition in carrying out its regulatory role and included a prohibition against the abuse of administrative power to restrict or eliminate competition in the AML.[77] Therefore, the AML is regarded as a mechanism to supervise market activities as well as the exercise of administrative power.

13.5.1   Supervision of Market Activities

The competition authorities have enforced the AML in a manner that helps to further the macroeconomic control of the state. Consistent with the Chinese government's view that its role in the market is predominantly one of supervision, the AML has been used to help competition authorities monitor and supervise prices and the conduct of merging parties in the post-merger period.

---

[74] 姜伯静 [Jiang Bojing], 商务部警示联通网通合并涉嫌违法凸显中国法制进步 ['MOF-COM Warns China Unicom/China Netcom Merger Might be Illegal, Highlights Progress in China's Legal System'], 人民网 [People's Daily Online], 4 May 2009, available at http://it.people.com.cn/GB/42891/42895/9229575.html.

[75] Tsinghua Unigroup/RDA Microelectronics, BesTV/Microsoft, Fujian Electronics/Shenzhen Zhongnuo, CSR Nanjing Puzhen/Bombardier Transportation, Beijing CNR/Hitachi.

[76] Article 4 of the AML provides that the state 'establishes and implements competition rules that are compatible with the socialist market economy, strengthens and perfects macroeconomic supervision and control, and develops a unified, open, competitive and orderly market system'.

[77] Anti-Monopoly Law, arts. 8, 32–37.

Price supervision and regulation are important aspects of market regulation.[78] The NDRC, in addition to enforcing the AML, regulates prices (which includes controlling and stabilising general price levels) and administers the *Price Law*.[79] The NDRC views its AML enforcement activities as helping to carry out its role as price regulator, as the AML is a component of the legal system on price regulation and price-related monopoly conduct investigations are undertaken to strengthen price regulation, maintain overall price stability and curb inflation, as well as maintain fair competition.[80] The positioning of the AML within the price regulation legal framework is also reflected in the fact that the NDRC bureau responsible for enforcing the AML is the same bureau that is responsible for price supervision.

This conception of the AML as an instrument of price supervision is evident in many of the NDRC's AML investigations. The NDRC has expressly employed the AML to help it monitor and supervise drug prices in the wake of pricing reforms that took effect on 1 June 2015.[81] To address concerns that drug prices would increase with the lifting of price controls,[82] the NDRC ordered its local authorities to undertake two

---

[78] 关于建立完善价格监管机制的意见 [Opinion on Establishing and Perfecting the Price Supervision Mechanism] (People's Republic of China) National Development and Reform Commission, Order No. 2099, 22 October 2013.

[79] 中华人民共和国价格法 [Price Law of the People's Republic of China] (People's Republic of China) Standing Committee of the National People's Congress, 29 December 1997, art. 26.

[80] 李镭 [Li Lei], 总结经验，继往开来，开创制止价格垄断工作新局面 [Lessons Learned, Continue Opening Up, Create a New Situation to Stop Price Monopoly] (22 July 2008) National Development and Reform Commission, available at www.sdpc .gov.cn/fzgggz/jggl/zhdt/200808/t20080829_248411.html; 坚持稳中求进，锐意改革创新，促进经济持续健康发展和社会和谐稳定 – 全国发展和改革工作会议在京召开 [Insist on Progress Whilst Maintaining Stability, Commit to Reform and Innovation, Promote Sustained and Healthy Economic Development and a Harmonious and Stable Society – National Development and Reform Commission Work Conference Held in Beijing], 15 December 2013, available at www.sdpc.gov.cn/xwzx/xwfb/201312/ t20131215_570441.html; Fei Deng, H. Stephen Harris, Jr and Yizhe Zhang, 'Interview with Xu Kunlin, Director General of the Department of Price Supervision under the National Development and Reform Commission of People's Republic of China' [2011] (February) *The Antitrust Source* 1 at 3–4.

[81] 推进药品价格改革意见 [Opinion on Promoting Drug Price Reform] (People's Republic of China) National Development and Reform Commission, National Health and Family Planning Commission, Ministry of Human Resources and Social Security, Ministry of Industry and Information Technology, Ministry of Finance, Ministry of Commerce, and China Food and Drug Administration, Order No. 904, 4 May 2015.

[82] Yin Pumin, 'Medicine Price Reforms', Beijing Review, 23 June 2015, available at www.bjreview.com.cn/nation/txt/2015-06/23/content_693280.htm.

consecutive six-month inspection campaigns targeting collusion, price fixing, unfairly high prices and anti-competitive agreements, all of which are price-related activities prohibited under the AML.[83] As a result of the inspection campaigns, the NDRC investigated and sanctioned cartels relating to allopurinol tablets and estazolam active pharmaceutical ingredients and tablets and abuse of administrative power in drug procurement by hospitals and other public health institutions pursuant to the AML.[84] The NDRC has also relied on both the AML and the *Price Law* in a number of published decisions involving price-related monopoly conduct.[85] There have also been at least two cases where the NDRC took action under the *Price Law* and indicated that, had the facts of the cases been slightly different, it might have taken action under the AML instead.[86] For example, although the NDRC Bureau took action against Unilever under the *Price Law* for fabricating and disseminating information about price increases, it noted that Unilever's actions could have also amounted to concerted pricing conduct, and therefore is potentially caught under the AML.[87] While these cases illustrate the overlap and complementarity between these two laws within the price regulation legal framework, they also suggest that the NDRC views them as relatively

[83] 关于加强药品市场价格行为监管的通知 [Notice on Strengthening Supervision of Market Prices of Drugs] (People's Republic of China) National Development and Reform Commission, Order No. 930, 4 May 2015; 关于在全国开展药品价格专项检查的通知 [Notice on Carrying Out National Drug Price Inspections] (People's Republic of China) National Development and Reform Commission, Order No. 1101, 22 May 2016.

[84] *Allopurinol Tablet Cartel, Estazolam Tablet Cartel, Bengbu Health and Planning Commission Drug Procurement Administrative Monopoly, Sichuan and Zhejiang Health and Planning Commissions Drug Procurement Administrative Monopoly.*

[85] *Guangxi Rice Noodle Cartel, Zhejiang Paperboard Cartel, Hainan and Yunnan Tourism Cases, Xiamen Courier Cartel, Wuhan BMW Pre-Delivery Inspection Fee Cartel.*

[86] National Development and Reform Commission, 六家境外企业实施液晶面板价格垄断被依法查处 [Six Overseas Businesses Investigated and Punished for Implementing LCD Panel Price Monopoly] (News Release, 4 January 2013); National Development and Reform Commission, 联合利华散布涨价信息扰乱市场秩序受到严厉处罚 [Unilever Severely Punished for Disseminating Price Increase Information and Disrupting Market Order] (News Release, 6 May 2011); 我委有关负责人就查处联合利华(中国)有限公司散布涨价信息扰乱市场秩序的有关问题答记者问 [NDRC Responsible Person Answers Reporters' Questions on the Investigation into Unilever for Spreading Price Increase Information and Disrupting Market Order] (6 May 2011) National Development and Reform Commission, available at www.ndrc.gov.cn/fzgggz/jggl/zhdt/201105/t20110506_410564.html.

[87] [NDRC Responsible Person Answers Reporters' Questions on the Investigation into Unilever for Spreading Price Increase Information and Disrupting Market Order].

interchangeable for targeting price-related monopoly conduct and carrying out its price supervision function.

The NDRC's use of the AML as an instrument of price supervision fits in with the Chinese government's clarification of its role in the economy and declaration that it will reduce and limit its intervention. The NDRC, with its history as the state's economic planner, has tended to adopt an interventionist approach to address economic concerns.[88] However, the NDRC is adapting its approach to market regulation to one that is based more on supervision, with Naughton observing that it wants to demonstrate and ensure that it has an important and continuing role to play in deepening market reform.[89] The NDRC's handling of pricing concerns in the infant formula and auto industries is in keeping with this adjustment from intervention to supervision. In response to rising prices of imported infant formula,[90] the NDRC initially adopted interventionist measures such as restricting profit margins and prices and meeting with foreign infant formula producers to have an 'informal talk' about prices and costs.[91] However, these measures did not stop price increases, and the NDRC changed its approach and later initiated an AML investigation into the pricing conduct of nine domestic and foreign infant formula producers. In contrast to the ineffectiveness of the interventionist measures to address rising prices, the infant formula producers voluntarily committed to decreasing prices in response to the NDRC's AML investigation, even before the NDRC handed down its final decision.[92] The

---

[88] Barry Naughton, 'Since the National People's Congress: Personnel and Programs of Economic Reform Begin to Emerge' [2013] (41) *China Leadership Monitor* 1 at 2; Angela Huyue Zhang, 'Bureaucratic Politics and China's Anti-Monopoly Law', 695.

[89] Naughton, 'Since the National People's Congress', 2.

[90] See, e.g., Dai Lian, 'Food Safety Regulators Reshuffled', Caixin, 18 November 2011, available at www.caixinglobal.com/2011-11-18/101016303.html; Edward Wong, 'Contaminated Milk Is Destroyed in China', *The New York Times*, 26 December 2011, available at www.nytimes.com/2011/12/27/world/asia/contaminated-milk-is-destroyed-in-china.html; 'Infant Formula Found Contaminated', *China Daily*, 22 July 2012, available at http://usa.chinadaily.com.cn/china/2012-07/22/content_15606682.htm.

[91] 国家发展改革委发出紧急通知 要求切实加强婴幼儿奶粉价格监管 [NDRC Issues Emergency Notice, Requests Strengthening of Infant Formula Price Supervision] (News Release, 19 September 2008) available at www.ndrc.gov.cn/xwtt/200809/t20080919_236575.html; 发改委约谈六家 "洋奶粉" 企业表示属例行工作 ['NDRC Talks with Six Foreign Infant Formula Businesses, States that it is Routine'], 广州日报 [*Guangzhou Daily*], 9 May 2011, available at www.chinanews.com/cj/2011/05-09/3024728.shtml.

[92] National Reform and Development Commission, 合生元等乳粉生产企业违反《反垄断法》限制竞争行为共被处罚6.6873亿元 [Biostime and Other Infant Formula Producers Restricted Competition and Violated the Anti-Monopoly Law, Fined a Total of RMB

NDRC, which found that the infant formula producers had breached the AML by engaging in resale price maintenance, claims that this investigation resulted in consumer savings of more than RMB 2.4 billion.[93] Similarly, China's auto industry has also traditionally been subject to a high degree of government intervention.[94] However, instead of intervening directly to address concerns about the high prices of imported cars, the NDRC monitored anti-competitive conduct in the auto industry over a number of years[95] and instituted a series of high-profile AML investigations into car manufacturers, local dealers and auto parts manufacturers.[96] Just as with the infant formula investigation, a number of car manufacturers voluntarily reduced their prices in response to the investigations.[97] Therefore, the use of the AML in these situations not only

668.73m] (News Release, 7 August 2013); 惠氏奶粉最高降价二成 洋奶粉反垄断调查效应初现 ['Wyeth's Maximum Price Decrease of 20 per cent, Foreign Infant Formula Anti-Monopoly Investigation Sees Initial Effects'], 南方日报 [*Southern Daily News*], 4 July 2013, available at http://finance.chinanews.com/cj/2013/07-04/5001321.shtml; 叶碧华 [Ye Bihua], 发改委释疑惠氏免遭重罚: 首先降价率队认错 ['NDRC Explains Why Wyeth Was Exempt from Penalty: First to Reduce Price and Make Admissions'], 21世纪经济报道 [*21st Century Business Herald*], 8 August 2013, available at http://finance.sina.com.cn/chanjing/gsnews/20130808/022816379184.shtml.

[93] National Development and Reform Commission, 顺利实现价格预期调控目标,价格改革和监管工作取得积极成效 ['Price Control Targets Successfully Reached, Price Reform and Supervision Work Achieved Positive Results'] (News Release, 24 January 2014) available at www.sdpc.gov.cn/xwzx/xwfb/201401/t20140124_576928.html.

[94] See, e.g., Hua Wang, 'Fluctuation of the Chinese Automobile Market During and After the Financial Crisis', in Bruno Jetin (ed.), *Global Automobile Demand: Major Trends in Emerging Economies*; vol. 2 (Basingstoke: Palgrave Macmillan, 2015).

[95] 卢延纯: 反垄断法要促进行业经济发展 ['Lu Yanchun: Anti-Monopoly Law Needs to Promote Industry Economic Development'], *Auto.sina.com.cn*, 29 November 2012, available at http://auto.sina.com.cn/news/2012-11-29/12241071631.shtml; 发改委彻查进口豪车 "低价设限" 车价全球最高被疑垄断 ['NDRC Thoroughly Investigates Imported Luxury Cars "Minimum Price Restrictions", Car Prices are Highest Globally, Suspected Monopoly'], 人民网 [*People.cn*], 19 August 2013, available at http://news.ifeng.com/gundong/detail_2013_08/19/28768765_0.shtml; 发改委就发展生产性服务业促进产业结构升级召开新闻发布会 ['NDRC Holds Press Conference on Developing and Promoting the Structural Upgrade of Producer Service Industries'] (6 August 2014) available at www.china.com.cn/zhibo/2014-08/06/content_33139708.htm.

[96] *Shanghai Chrysler Cartel and RPM, Japanese Auto Parts Cartel, Japanese Ball Bearings Cartel, FAW-Volkswagen and Audi Cartel and RPM, Mercedes-Benz Cartel and RPM, Dongfeng Nissan Cartel and RPM, Hanook Tire RPM, SAIC General Motors RPM.*

[97] Li Fangfang and Li Fusheng, 'Automakers Lower Prices Following Monopoly Concerns', China Daily, 29 July 2014, available at http://usa.chinadaily.com.cn/epaper/2014-07/29/content_18206559.htm; Samuel Shen and Pete Sweeney, 'Japanese Car Makers Cut Parts Prices in China after Anti-Monopoly Probe', *Reuters*, 9 August 2014, available at www.reuters.com/article/us-china-autos-antitrust-idUSKBN0G90H520140809.

enabled the NDRC to achieve its desired outcome to reduce prices, it also demonstrated that it could adopt a regulatory approach that is equally – if not more – effective as intervention.

Similarly, many of the conditions attached by the MOFCOM to its merger approvals allow it to monitor and supervise the conduct of merging parties after the merger has been completed. Typically, the types of merger conditions that the MOFCOM imposes fall into two broad categories: structural conditions, which are one-off and seek to restore or preserve the competitive structure of the market that existed before the merger; and behavioural conditions, which are ongoing and designed to modify or constrain behaviour.[98] Behavioural conditions require the MOFCOM to monitor and supervise compliance with the conditions over a long-term period, whereas structural conditions generally do not. Competition agencies in other countries tend to strongly prefer structural over behavioural conditions because they are reluctant to monitor and supervise the merged firm on an ongoing basis.[99] In contrast, the MOF-COM expresses no such preference, which is consistent with administrative culture and practice in China where administrative agencies are accustomed to supervising and guiding the conduct of private actors.[100] As such, in practice it has more often used behavioural conditions over structural conditions in merger enforcement.

The MOFCOM has imposed a range of conditions that modify or constrain the behaviour of merging parties. Some conditions aim to control market outcomes. The MOFCOM has required that merged firms supply or provide access to certain products or assets.[101] It has

---

[98] 关于经营者集中附加限制性条件的规定（试行）[Regulation on the Imposition of Restrictive Conditions on Concentrations of Business Operators (Trial)] (People's Republic of China) Ministry of Commerce, Order No. 6, 4 December 2014, art. 3; International Competition Network Merger Working Group: Analytical Framework Subgroup, 'Merger Remedies Review Project' (Report for the Fourth ICN Annual Conference, Bonn, June 2005), p. 7.

[99] International Competition Network Merger Working Group: Analytical Framework Subgroup, 'Merger Remedies Review Project', 7.

[100] Fei Deng and Yizhe Zhang, 'Interview with Shang Ming, Director General of the Anti-Monopoly Bureau Under the Ministry of Commerce of the People's Republic of China' [2014] (April) *The Antitrust Source* 1 at 3; 商务部反垄断局负责人关于《关于经营者集中附加限制性条件的规定（试行）》的解读 [Head of the Ministry of Commerce Anti-Monopoly Bureau's Interpretation of the 'Regulation on the Imposition of Restrictive Conditions on Concentrations of Business Operators (Trial)'] (People's Republic of China) Ministry of Commerce Anti-Monopoly Bureau, 17 December 2014, available at http://fldj.mofcom.gov.cn/article/j/201412/20141200835988.shtml.

[101] See, e.g., *General Motors/Delphi, Uralkali/Silvinit, Glencore/Xstrata, Google/Motorola Mobility, ARM joint venture, Microsoft/Nokia*.

also often stipulated, or restricted the merging parties' freedom to determine, the terms (such as price or volume) of this access or supply.[102] Other conditions limit the merging parties' ability to engage in particular types of conduct, such as exercise shareholders' rights,[103] enforce intellectual property rights,[104] expand their business in China[105] or even fully integrate their businesses post-merger.[106] Moreover, some conditions effectively pre-empt future breaches of the AML. For example, in some cases, merging parties are required to not engage in exclusive dealing or certain tying and bundling conduct[107] (which might be considered abuse of dominance) or to terminate an agreement with a competitor[108] (which could potentially aid coordination and collusion).

These merger conditions facilitate market supervision in at least several ways. In addition to resolving concerns about the potential anticompetitive effects arising from a merger, these merger conditions are regulatory in nature and allow the MOFCOM to monitor and supervise the conduct of merging parties over a long-term period and intervene to ensure compliance with the conditions. The merging parties are generally required to periodically report to the MOFCOM on their implementation and compliance with merger conditions. While the type of information that the merging parties would need to provide to demonstrate compliance would vary depending on the type of condition, it will likely involve disclosure of information relating to price, volume, costs and customers. The periodic provision of such information helps the MOFCOM to monitor market activity and conditions. The merging parties must also obtain the MOFCOM's prior approval if they wish to vary or revoke the conditions,[109] which provides the MOFCOM with an additional avenue for monitoring the merging parties' activities, regardless of its power under the AML or other laws and regulations.

---

[102] See, e.g., *Henkel/Tiande, Uralkali/Silvinit, Glencore/Xstrata, Google/Motorola Mobility, Microsoft/Nokia, NiMH battery joint venture, Thermo Fisher/Life*.

[103] *Panasonic/Sanyo, MediaTek/MStar*.

[104] *Microsoft/Nokia, Nokia/Alcatel-Lucent*.

[105] *InBev/Anheuser-Busch, Mitsubishi Rayon/Lucite, Novartis/Alcon, Wal-Mart/Newheight, MediaTek/MStar*.

[106] *Seagate/Samsung, Western Digital/Hitachi, Marubeni/Gavilon, MediaTek/MStar*.

[107] *General Motors/Delphi, Seagate/Samsung, Western Digital/Hitachi, General Electric/ Shenhua, Merck/AZ Electronics, Microsoft/Nokia*.

[108] *Novartis/Alcon, Baxter/Gambro*.

[109] Regulation on the Imposition of Restrictive Conditions on Concentrations of Business Operators (Trial), arts. 25–26.

As such, these merger conditions help the MOFCOM to carry out the government's role of market supervision.

13.5.2   Supervision of Exercises of Administrative Power

The Chinese government realises that, in fulfilling its regulatory functions, its actions can hamper the effective functioning of the market. For example, a government department or industry regulator could adopt regulations that favour local businesses over businesses from other regions, prevent the free flow of goods and services between regions, restrict entry into particular sectors or favour incumbent businesses over new entrants. These acts of local protectionism and industry monopoly are examples of abuses of administrative power. The abuse of administrative power is widely regarded as the main barrier to furthering China's economic reforms and creating a unified and open national market, the latter of which is necessary to enable the market to play a decisive role in allocating resources.[110] As such, there is broad consensus within government and the general public that the abuse of administrative power needs to be combatted and eliminated.[111]

Government restrictions, however, are not typically addressed by competition laws. This was one of the main reasons why the inclusion of abuse of administrative power within the ambit of the AML was a controversial and intensely debated topic during the drafting process. Those opposing its inclusion argued that the AML should be consistent with international practice and suit a market economy. They also believed that administrative monopoly required economic, political and administrative

---

[110] An Explanation of China's Anti-Monopoly Law (Draft), 24 June 2006; Speech Excerpts: Draft of the Anti-Monopoly Law, 27 June 2006; Dai Yan, 'Making of Anti-Trust Law is Speeded Up', China Daily, 28 October 2004, available at www.chinadaily.com.cn/ english/doc/2004-10/28/content_386300.htm; Vanessa Yanhua Zhang, 'Interview with Mr Handong Zhang, Director General of the National Development and Reform Commission (NDRC) of PR China' [2017] (3) *CPI Antitrust Chronicle* 1 at 1.

[111] 谢晓冬 [Xie Xiaodong], 《反垄断法》草案减负 "反行政垄断" 被整体删除 [Draft Anti-Monopoly Law Reduces its Burden, 'Administrative Monopoly Prohibition' is Entirely Deleted], 新京报 [Beijing News], 11 January 2006, available at http://finance1 .people.com.cn/GB/1037/4017283.html; 赵杰 [Zhao Jie], 反垄断法草案删除关于行政性垄断章节 [Anti-Monopoly Law Draft Deletes Administrative Monopoly Chapter], 第一财经日报 [*First Financial Daily*], 8 June 2006, available at http://finance.people .com.cn/GB/1037/4448654.html.

system reform, which was beyond the abilities of competition law to address.[112] In contrast, others believed that the reality of China's national conditions was that government restrictions are pervasive and do impede and distort competition, making it inappropriate for the AML not to address a form of conduct that is in fact very harmful to the Chinese economy.[113] Ultimately, the imperative to acknowledge, and signal opposition to, the economic harms that might be caused by the government's exercise of regulatory power prevailed,[114] and the AML prohibits various types of conduct constituting abuses of administrative power.

In doing so, the AML helps the state to supervise exercises of administrative power. By prohibiting abuses of administrative power that are anti-competitive, the AML determines the bounds of appropriate government regulation of, and intervention in, market activities. Further, this helps to clarify the government's role in the economy, which is an important aspect of the supervisory function of the AML that has led to a clear and significant increase in AML enforcement involving abuses of administrative power. Enforcement of this prohibition was limited in the first few years after the AML came into effect. Prior to September 2014, there was only one published administrative enforcement case involving abuse of administrative power, which was released by the SAIC in July 2013.[115] However, there has been a noticeable increase in AML

---

[112] An Explanation of China's Anti-Monopoly Law (Draft), 24 June 2006; Wu, 'Perspectives on the Chinese Anti-Monopoly Law', 93–94; Xiaoye Wang, 'Issues Surrounding the Drafting of China's Anti-Monopoly Law' (2004) 3 *Washington University Global Studies Law Review* 285 at 293; 刘娜 [Liu Na], 反垄断法如期初审,行政性垄断内容再写入草案 [Initial Review of the Anti-Monopoly Law as Planned, Administrative Monopoly Content Restored in Draft], 经济观察报 [Economic Observer Online], 24 June 2006, available at http://finance.sina.com.cn/g/20060624/22332678790.shtml; Xie, 'Draft Anti-Monopoly Law Reduces its Burden'.

[113] An Explanation of China's Anti-Monopoly Law (Draft), 24 June 2006; Harris *et al.*, *Anti-Monopoly Law and Practice in China*, p. 44; Wu, 'Perspectives on the Chinese Anti-Monopoly Law', 94; Xie, 'Draft Anti-Monopoly Law Reduces its Burden'; Liu, 'Initial Review of the Anti-Monopoly Law as Planned'.

[114] An Explanation of China's Anti-Monopoly Law (Draft), 24 June 2006.

[115] 会议纪要指定经营者,工商机关首次行使建议权 《反垄断法》剑指地方政府排除限制竞争 – 广东省工商局调查滥用行政权力排除、限制竞争案纪实 ['Minutes of Meeting Designate Operators, SAIC Authorities Target Their Recommendation Powers under Anti-Monopoly Law at Local Governments that Eliminate or Restrict Competition for the First Time – Case Report of Guangdong AIC's Investigation of Abuse of Administrative Power to Eliminate or Restrict Competition'],中国工商报 [*China Business News*], 27 July 2011, available at www.saic.gov.cn/zt/jg/fldybzdjz/201209/t20120918_219847.html.

enforcement activity against abuse of administrative power since the latter half of 2014. As at 31 December 2016, the NDRC and its local offices have published a total of twelve recommendations and outcomes relating to its investigations into abuse of administrative power.

This has coincided with the Chinese government's increased focus on and commitment to rebalancing and clarifying the respective roles of the government and the market in the economy and establishing a unified, fair, open and competitive market.[116] In particular, the AML prohibition of anti-competitive abuses of administrative power has been expressly linked to the fair competition review system, which was first discussed in June 2014 and adopted in June 2016.[117] The fair competition review system is another mechanism for the oversight of government regulatory activities, and it was adopted to improve the handling of the relationship between the government and the market and to better define their respective roles, thereby creating and maintaining an environment conducive to fair competition.[118] It also helps to break down acts of local protectionism and industry monopoly in favour of a national, unified and open market. Whereas the AML provides for ex-post examination of government actions for their impact on competition, the fair competition review system largely provides for ex-ante self-assessment and review. It requires policymaking bodies at the central and local levels and the State Council to evaluate proposed regulations and policies against specific criteria before adoption, to ensure that they do not eliminate or restrict competition or impede the creation of a unified national market.[119] As such, the fair competition review system operates

---

[116] The State Council released an opinion in June 2014 on improving the market regulation system and promoting fair competition, in which it called for, inter alia, the breaking up of local protectionism and industry monopoly: 关于促进市场公平竞争维护市场正常秩序的若干意见 [Some Opinions on Promoting Fair Market Competition and Maintaining Normal Market Order] (People's Republic of China) State Council, Order No. 20, 4 June 2014.

[117] 关于在市场体系建设中建立公平竞争审查制度的意见 [Opinion on Establishing a Fair Competition Review System in the Construction of a Market System] (People's Republic of China) State Council, Order No. 34, 1 June 2016. See also Vanessa Yanhua Zhang, 'Interview with Mr Handong Zhang, Director General of the National Development and Reform Commission (NDRC) of PR China', 2–3.

[118] Vanessa Yanhua Zhang, 'Interview with Mr Handong Zhang, Director General of the National Development and Reform Commission (NDRC) of PR China', 1.

[119] Opinion on Establishing a Fair Competition Review System in the Construction of a Market System.

alongside, complements and enhances the AML in regulating anti-competitive government behaviour.

13.6 Conclusion

China regards itself as a socialist state, with a socialist market economy and a socialist legal system. The CPC identifies two features that are essential to socialism in China: the leadership of the CPC and the dominance of public ownership. At the same time, China has adopted market principles in its economy. Adherence to both socialist and market principles results in the state having participatory and regulatory roles in the economy. This places the state in dual and potentially conflicting roles and impacts the way in which the law applies to regulate the market. This Chapter has examined this issue through the lens of China's competition law, which is one of the key laws governing the operation of markets and market actors in China. It has shown that the nature, understanding and enforcement of the AML have been significantly influenced by both dimensions of the state's role. In particular, the state has hindered, as well as supported and fostered, AML enforcement.

Although it is clear that the AML applies to SOEs to prohibit them from engaging in anti-competitive conduct, the ability of the competition authorities to enforce that prohibition is constrained. Such constraints arise not from the mere fact that SOEs are owned by the state, but rather from the position, status and relationships with other state actors that SOEs enjoy, in large part because they are an entrenched part of the political structure. Therefore, while the AML aims to ensure that the state itself does not engage in anti-competitive conduct in its business activities and that SOEs compete in the market on equal footing with privately-owned businesses, in practice, the achievement of those objectives is hampered. In contrast, the state's regulatory role promotes and furthers the enforcement of the AML. The AML is regarded not only as a means to maintain and encourage competition, but also as a mechanism to supervise markets and administrative regulatory power. As such, it has been enforced to further the supervision of prices, the conduct of merging parties after their merger is completed and the exercise of administrative power. In doing so, the government is using the AML to create and maintain market conditions that are conducive to competition, as well as to limit the state's regulatory interventions to those that ensure the proper functioning of the market and which do not have an anti-competitive impact, which in turn allows market forces to play a greater role in allocating resources and coordinating outcomes. Thus, the AML is being applied in a manner that helps to clarify and better define the respective roles of the market and the government in the economy, thereby balancing and improving the government's handling of the relationship between the market and the state.

PART VII

Land

PART VII

Land

14

The Evolution of the Property System in China

Between the Socialist Heritage and Liberal Market

LEI CHEN

14.1 Introduction

While much has been written on the importance of property rights to economic development, relatively little seems to be understood about the processes of change in complex property systems. Law and economics rhetoric applies a cost–benefit analysis to predict the evolution of property systems towards efficiency and net social welfare amid competitive conditions.[1] However, this optimistic picture does not appear to be matched by reality in many developing/transitional countries.[2] Rather, it seems to provide only a general conceptual framework, and the extent to which it operates to a particular country depends on the government-driven policies, economic development level, customs and other relevant factors. This view of property change describes private property as a story of evolutionary success. That said, property systems do become more efficient under the influence of competitive conditions.[3]

In contrast, the pessimistic view of property change sees that property transitions take place through political processes.[4] This is a public choice

The chapter was supported by a grant from the Research Grants Council of the Hong Kong Special Administrative Region, China [Project No. CityU 11400814].
[1] Harold Demsetz, 'Toward a Theory of Property Rights' (1967) 57 *American Economic Review* 347.
[2] Daniel Fitzpatrick, 'Evolution and Chaos in Property Rights Systems: The Third World Tragedy of Contested Access' (2006) 115 *Yale Law Journal* 996.
[3] *See* Thomas W. Merrill, 'Introduction: The Demsetz Thesis and the Evolution of Property Rights' (2002) 31(2) *Journal of Legal Studies*, 331, 331 ('The Demsetz thesis can be seen as an anticipation of the idea that the common law evolves towards efficient rules').
[4] Richard A. Epstein, 'The Allocation of the Commons: Parking on Public Roads' (2002) 31 *Journal of Legal Studies*, 515, 516 ('The public choice dynamic, so dominant in human affairs, plays a far more powerful role in the definition and transformation of property rights systems than Demsetz attributed to it.').

conception of property as a product of competition among interest groups. Powerful interest groups induce property change in order to capture a disproportionate share of its benefits.[5] They may favour a constituency or interest group without necessarily incurring the costs of compensating those who lose under the new property regime. The result is a less optimistic view than evolutionary perspectives, as it encompasses change that favours well-connected interest groups that are more likely to influence property policy.

However appealing these theories are in helping to understand the various factors that affect a property system, the role of law in property change is worth examining. Many anthropological and sociological studies have challenged the efficacy of the formalisation of property rights as disregarding cultural and social variations of place.[6] Law itself seems to be less effective for resolving property-related conflicts than the cultural–ethical legitimacy in which law is embedded.[7] Black-letter or bright-line approaches to property rights distinguish between formal law (state law) and informal law (local norms and practices). This binary approach does not adequately capture the dynamics of the interrelationship between various factors – cutural or historical, social or moral – in public and private spheres.[8] Consequently, expecting a miracle cure or searching for one-size-fits-all solutions that are modelled on rules in developed countries is, at best, idealistic.

Nevertheless, recognising cultural variations and informal factors does not deter legal formalisation. Kennedy cautiously suggested that the revived law and development theory should focus on economic assumptions and political choices embedded in policy-making.[9] From the government's perspective, respecting property rights, holding policy accountability and maintaining state intervention for good governance

---

[5] Stuart Banner, 'Transitions Between Property Regimes' (2002) 31 *Journal of Legal Studies*, 359, 361.

[6] Chris Hann, *Property Relations: Renewing the Anthropological Tradition* (Cambridge: Cambridge University Press, 1998); Fitzpatrick, 'Evolution and Chaos in Property Rights Systems'.

[7] Daniel Abramson, 'Transitional Property Rights and Local Development History in China' (2011) 48(3) *Urban Studies*, 553, 555.

[8] John Gillespie, 'Commentary: Theorising Dialogical Property Rights in Socialist East Asia' (2011) 48(3) *Urban Studies*, 595, 596.

[9] David Kennedy, 'Laws and Development', in John Hatchard and Amanda Perry-Kessaris (eds.), *Law and Development: Facing Complexity in the 21st Century: Essays in Honour of Peter Slinn* (London: Cavendish Publishing, 2003), pp. 17–19.

are indispensable for sustainable development.[10] Legislation is a precise and reliable tool for distributing power to individuals and thus an efficient solution to the problem of lack of legal institutions, which cannot be left to good conscience, informal rules or traditional civil customs.[11] More fundamentally, the solution to incomplete property systems is to incorporate the property systems that already exist in the informal sectors to create a 'unified property system'.[12] The real question then is not whether the law needs to reflect and respond to the inter-action and compromise among legal and sub-legal/extra-legal factors, and state and non-state actors, in underlying property regimes. Rather, it is about how the state, users and rights-holders use the legislation to ensure a smooth transition from mismatched social norms to a law-oriented and well-coordinated property system.

The purpose of this Chapter is twofold. First, it traces the historical development of land laws and policies in China, and explores the debates around the evolution of the land title system. Second, drawing on land-taking and rural land-transfer issues, it explores the extent to which the state continues to maintain public control over land use and land markets. It maintains that despite economic growth, the institutional structures of the land system have not been transformed. As a conse-quence, epistemic assumptions supporting socialist approaches to land remain. Rather than a linear transition to private ownership, the insti-tutional reform of rural land markets in China is more complex than what economic theory or law and development theory suggests.

So, how do property rights evolve in a transitional socialist jurisdiction like China? For Ajani, law was seen as an instrument of social engineer-ing; a precondition of a free market when he evaluated the transitional processes in Russia and Eastern Europe in the mid-1990s.[13] Upon closer

---

[10] Ann Seidman and Robert Seidman, *State Law in the Development Process* (London: McMillan Press, 1994), pp. 5–22.

[11] Ronald Keith, *China's Struggle for the Rule of Law* (New York, NY: St. Martin's Press, 1994), pp. 137–141; Elinor Ostrom, *Governing the Commons: The Evolution of Insti-tutions for Collective Actions* (Cambridge: Cambridge University Press, 1990), pp. 15–20; Donald Clarke, 'Economic Development and the Rights Hypothesis: The China Problem' (2003) 51 *American Journal of Comparative Law*, 89, 111.

[12] Hernando De Soto, *The Mystery of Capital: Why Capitalism Triumps in the West and Fails Everywhere Else* (New York, NY: Basic Books, 2000), pp. 52–54.

[13] Gianmaria Ajani, 'By Chance and Prestige: Legal Transplant in Russia and Eastern Europe' (1995) 43(1) *American Journal of Comparative Law* 93.

scrutiny, private law design – in particular, land reform – in post-socialist Russia and Eastern Europe is more complex than many legal comparatists suggested.[14] Without a clear understanding of how domestic institutional arrangements cope with transplanted foreign laws, it would be difficult to provide a meaningful answer on how a legal system evolves. Therefore, a detailed depiction of the existing institutional context in a transitional society by way of socio-economic analysis is indispensable.[15] This reminds us of Hayek's argument that in order for a market economy to be effective, it must operate within a framework of liberal institutions of governance that provide security of title and stability of the legal framework.[16]

More than two decades after the collapse of the Berlin Wall, how relevant are these theories to China and the Chinese land system? China is a particularly important, yet understudied, jurisdiction. Important changes in the last few decades in both the People's Republic of China (PRC) land law and the dynamics of land transactions/expropriations in China further highlight the importance of the China case study. A gap exists between the PRC land law's underlying assumptions and the modern reality of how property rights are often created and enforced. This Chapter aims to explain the choices made between socialist heritage and liberal markets in China. The research findings are useful in assessing current Chinese law and may inspire possible statutory reforms.

This Chapter draws on three institutions of China's property system in order to illustrate the non-linear transition from a socialist regime to a liberal market: rural land transfers, land expropriations and urban home purchase restrictions. This Chapter aims to explore to what extent the state continues to maintain public control over land use, housing and land markets. Secondly, it attempts to portray how the state law interacts with the pre-existing norms and customs. It helps explain why the institutional structures of the land system have not been liberalised despite economic growth. As a consequence, epistemic assumptions supporting socialist approaches to land remain.

---

[14] Michele Graziadei, 'Legal Transplants and Frontiers of Legal Knowledge' (2009) 10(2) *Theoretical Inquiries in Law* 723.

[15] Gunther Teuber, 'Legal Irritants' (1998) *Modern Law Review*.

[16] Friedrich A. Hayek, *Individualism and Economic Order* (Chicago, IL: University of Chicago Press, 1948); Peter Boettke, 'Hayek and Market Socialism: Science, Ideology, and Public Policy' (2005) 25(4) *Economic Affairs* 54–60.

14.2   Historical Background

14.2.1   A Bifurcation of Urban Public Land Ownership and Rural Collective Land Ownership (1954–1984)

Prior to the formation of the People's Republic of China (PRC) in 1949, most of the rural land belonged to feudal landlords and rich farmers; peasants were only tenant farmers and did not own any land.[17] At this time, the Chinese Communist Party (CCP) was greatly influenced by the Soviet Union in engineering its land tenure system.[18] This was evident from the first PRC Constitution enforced in 1954, which shared a high degree of similarity with the 1936 USSR Constitution regarding the content and treatment of the land tenure system. Liu Shaoqi, the then PRC President, told the National People's Congress (NPC) at their first plenary session, during which the 1954 Constitution was passed:

> When the Constitution Drafting Committee worked on the draft, it used as reference materials the earlier and later constitutions of the Soviet Union and the constitutions of other people's democracies. Obviously, the experience of the advanced socialist countries headed by the Soviet Union has been of great assistance to us. Our draft constitution combines Chinese experience and international experience. Our draft constitution is not only the product of the people's revolutionary movement in our nation, but it is also a product of the international socialist movement.[19]

Unlike the Eastern European countries that retained most of their original legal frameworks after their communist revolutions,[20] all the legislation enacted by the Guomindang regime was obliterated once the PRC was founded. Consequently, the regime that allowed affluent bourgeois landlords to consolidate land and resources was abolished. For the purpose of opening up the production forces hampered by the oppressive Guomindang era, plots of land and housing were issued to peasants and

---

[17] See Wang Wenjia, *Zhongguo Tudi Zhidu Shi* [*The History of Chinese Land Systems*] (Cheng Chung Book, 1988).

[18] Lei Chen, 'Legal and Institutional Analysis of Land Expropriation in China', in H. Fu and J. Gillespie (eds.), *Resolving Land Disputes in East Asia: Exploring the Limits of Law* (Cambridge: Cambridge University Press, 2010), p. 61.

[19] Albert Chen, 'Socialist Law, Civil Law, Common Law, and the Classification of Contemporary Chinese Law', in Jan Otto, Maurice Polak, Jianfu Chen and Yuwen Li (eds.), *Law-Making in the People's Republic of China* (The Hague: Kluwer Law International 2000), p. 57.

[20] John Quigley, 'Socialist Law and the Civil Law Tradition' (1989) 37 *American Journal of Comparative Law* 781, 802.

the proletariat masses.[21] They were also guaranteed a wide range of property rights, such as the right to farm and reside on the land and to buy, sell or transfer the land to another party.[22] In a similar vein to what occurred in the Russian Revolution,[23] the Chinese Agrarian [Land] Reform Law (Land Reform Law)[24] was one of the first pieces of legislation promulgated by the new regime.[25] Article 1 of the Land Reform Law provides that 'the land ownership system of exploitation by the landlord class shall be abolished and the system of peasant land ownership shall be introduced in order to set free the rural productive forces, develop agricultural production and thus pave the way for New China's industrialisation.'[26] In particular, article 30 recognises the notion that land in the hands of peasants and farmers is considered their private property: 'After the agrarian reform is completed, the People's Government shall issue title deeds and shall recognise the rights of all land owners to manage, buy, sell or rent out land freely.'[27]

Subsequently, the 1954 Constitution abandoned the socialisation of land, which was the crux of Bolshevik land policy and codified the peasants' right to own land.[28] However, as private ownership of land was incompatible with the basic Marxist creed of public ownership, the Communists decided to establish collective farms.[29] So, apart from some extremely small private plots around the peasants' houses, private ownership was converted into collective ownership.[30]

During the 1950s, there was a period referred as the 'Golden Age' of the construction of the PRC legal system, where the PRC endeavoured to acquire various ideologies, institutions and practices from the Soviet Union in the arenas of political, economic and social life.[31] The Soviet

---

[21] Ding Chengri, 'Land Policy Reform in China: Assessment and Prospects' (2003) 20 *Land Use Policy* 109–120.

[22] Zhang Jialin, 'China's Slow Motion Land Reform' (2010) 159 *Policy Review* 59, 60.

[23] William E. Butler (ed.), *The Legal System of the Chinese Soviet Republic 1931–1934* (Dobbs Ferry, NY: Transnational Publishers, 1983), p. 77.

[24] Albert Blaustein, *Fundamental Legal Documents of Communist China* (South Hackensack, NJ: F.B. Rothman, 1962), p. 276.

[25] Butler, *The Legal System of the Chinese Soviet Republic 1931–1934*, p. 90.

[26] Blaustein, *Fundamental Legal Documents of Communist China*.

[27] Ibid., p. 279.

[28] Article 8, PRC Constitution 1954.

[29] James Tsao, *China's Development Strategies and Foreign Trade* (Lexington, MA: Lexington Books 1987), p. 14.

[30] Ibid.

[31] Jerome Cohen, *The Criminal Process in the People's Republic of China 1949–1963* (Cambridge, MA: Harvard University Press, 1968), p. 11.

model was also adopted in legal matters – for example, some Soviet legal scholars were invited to teach in law schools in China and Soviet legal literature was translated into Chinese for use as teaching materials.[32] In addition, Soviet legislative texts were usually referred to when drafting laws.[33]

One of the key features of Soviet influence during this era was the doctrine of socialist ownership, which comprised both ownership by cooperatives and mass enterprises and state ownership.[34] Following 'socialist legality', all land and natural resources in the PRC became the subject of socialist public ownership. This came in two forms: rural land that was held in collective ownership by labouring masses; and urban land that was held in state ownership.[35] Such transformation in land ownership was attained either by the confiscation of the land remaining during the period of the Nationalist rule[36] or through the policy of socialist transformation that began in 1953.[37] In the latter strategy, private enterprises that owned much of the remaining land in urban areas were forced to join state-private enterprises. By the end of 1956, the Central Government finished nationalising those joint enterprises.[38] The two procedures simultaneously complemented the state's consolidation of land in urban areas.

The process of collectivising land carried on during the era of Mao Zedong's Great Leap Forward. As part of the overall scheme to strengthen communism, the agricultural cooperatives were integrated and amalgamated into the larger People's Communes, the grassroots collective units in rural China since 1958.[39] While private ownership of land and houses was abolished, the communes took over the management of domestic animals and 'tools for private economic activities'.[40] Unlike the Soviet Union, where the state had an exclusive title to all land and assigned its perpetual use to different land users,[41] the Chinese state

---

[32] Joan Liu, *Finding Chinese Law on the Internet* (New York, NY: GlobaLex, 2005), ch. 1.
[33] Chen, 'Socialist Law, Civil Law, Common Law, and the Classification of Contemporary Chinese Law', p. 57.
[34] William E. Butler, *Soviet Law* (London: Butterworths, 1988), pp. 180–181.
[35] Articles 8 and 10, PRC Constitution (amended in 2004).
[36] Victor Lippit, The Economic Development of China (M.E. Sharpe 1987) 109.
[37] Ibid., 110.
[38] Ibid.
[39] Marsh Marshall, *Organizations and Growth in Rural China* (London: Palgrave Macmillan, 1986), pp. 46–47.
[40] Ibid., 47.
[41] Chen, 'Socialist Law, Civil Law, Common Law, and the Classification of Contemporary Chinese Law', p. 80.

only retained the title to urban and industrial land, and left the rural land to the collectives. It is contended that the Chinese system resembled the Romanian land framework in which a bifurcation of the land title system existed: the state merely claimed the title to urban and industrial land, and conferred ownership of rural areas to the tillers.[42]

The current PRC Constitution has clearly embraced the notion of public ownership of land in China: 'Land in the cities is owned by the state. Land in the rural and suburban areas is owned by the collectives ... No organisation or individual may appropriate, buy, sell or otherwise engage in the transfer of land by unlawful means.'[43]

14.2.2 The Introduction of the Household Responsibility System in Rural Farmland

Due to the failure of the People's Commune system, the decentralisation of collective ownership to the production team (*sheng chan dui* 生产队) was carried out in the early 1960s.[44] As a result, the production team became the de facto manager of the land in most villages up until the mid-1980s.[45] When the Cultural Revolution ended, China steered a new course with dramatic economic and social changes. An integral part of Deng Xiaoping's reforms was the Household Responsibility System (HRS), a family-oriented farming system in villages, which replaced the People's Commune system.[46] Under the HRS, land is contracted to individual households for fifteen to thirty years. The decentralisation of land use from the collective to the household level provided incentive for peasants to improve farming productivity. As a consequence, agricultural production boomed and rural incomes increased rapidly.[47] The HRS was

---

[42] John Hazard, *Communists and Their Law: A Search for the Common Core of the Legal System of the Marxian Socialist States* (Chicago, IL: University of Chicago Press, 1969), p. 157.

[43] Article 10, PRC Constitution 2004.

[44] Dali L. Yang, *Calamity and Reform in China: State, Rural Society, and Institutional Change since the Great Leap Famine* (Stanford, CA: Stanford University Press, 1996).

[45] See Chris Bramall, 'Chinese Land Reform in Long-Run Perspective and in the Wider East Asian Context' (2004) 4 (1) (2) *Journal of Agrarian Change* 107–141.

[46] See James K. S. Kung, 'Choice of Land Tenure in China: The Case of a County with Quasi-Private Property Rights' (2002) 50 (4) *Economic Development and Cultural Change* 793–817.

[47] This was so despite the fact that its success was short lived for various reasons. Some attributed this to the tenure insecurity. See Roy Prosterman, Tim Hanstad and Ping Li, 'Can China Feed Itself?' (1996) 5 *Scientific American* 90–96. Others thought the reason

initially conducted as an experiment in several designated areas but, due to its success, it was quickly introduced nationwide.

14.2.3   Transforming Rural Land Use

From the mid-1980s to the end of the 1990s, the Chinese Central Government encouraged village collectives to utilise agricultural land for building Township and Village Enterprises (TVEs).[48] Rural peasants were encouraged to leave the land but not the countryside in order to work in the newly initiated TVEs. This essentially allowed agricultural land to be used for non-agricultural (mainly manufacturing) purposes. The Rural Land Contracting Law (RLCL), implemented in 2002, aimed to secure households' rights of use and possession by enforcing thirty-year land-use contracts, which prevents large-scale arbitrary reallocations of land and allows transfers of land between households.[49] Generally, under the current land system, farmers have two rights of use over rural land.

14.2.4   Reforms for Social Stability and a Market Economy

With the development of the market economy and the emergence of private property interests, the CCP perceived a need to tone down public power and distribute more private interests, wealth and status to people.[50] From the government's perspective, respecting property rights, showing policy accountability and maintaining state intervention for good governance are indispensable for sustainable development.[51]

---

was due to the low farm-gate price instead of property rights. See James Kung, 'Equal Entitlement versus Tenure Security under a Regime of Collective Property Rights: Peasants' Preference for Institutions in Post-reform Chinese Agriculture' (1995) 21 *Journal of Comparative Economics* 82–111. Whatever the reason, this necessitated further rural land reform, which is discussed in the subsequent parts of this article.

[48] This policy eventually became a piece of legislation to the same effect. See articles 12 and 28 of the TVE Law of 1996.

[49] Li Ping, 'Rural Land Tenure Reforms in China: Issues, Regulations and Prospects for Additional Reform' (2003) 3 *Land Reform (special edition)*, available at www.fao.org/ docrep/006/y5026e/y5026e06.htm. See also Li Ping and Roy L. Prosterman, 'From Collective to Household Tenure: China and Elsewhere' in Roy L. Prosterman, Robert Mitchell, and Timothy Hanstad (eds.), *One Billion Rising: Law, Land and the Alleviation of Global Poverty* (Amsterdam: Leiden University Press, 2009).

[50] Kennedy, 'Laws and Developments', pp. 17–19.

[51] Seidman and Seidman, *State Law in the Development Process*, pp. 5–22.

The promulgation of the 2007 Property Law reflected state commitments and responded to middle class appeals to clarify and demarcate private property rights.[52] It was essential in setting up a legal and institutional framework that recognises existing property rights, enforces them at low cost and facilitates the exercise of those rights to enable broader social benefits.[53]

In 2008, the Hu Jintao administration proposed a policy to allow farmers to lease or transfer land use rights.[54] In the same year, the third full meeting of the 17th Central Committee proposed to 'gradually unify the construction of land use markets in urban areas and rural areas'; and asserted that 'legally acquired, collectively-owned rural construction land should have rights equal to those of state-owned land'.[55] Five years later, in the third plenary session of the 18th Central Committee, the government stated (again) that, in the future, farmers will be allowed to enjoy more property rights, namely to mortgage their land or transfer use rights. It also stated that there should be a unified market for construction land.[56]

In 2014, the No. 1 Central Document of the CCP Central Committee stressed the intention to intensify rural land reform and accelerate the modernisation of agriculture in China.[57] Specifically, while emphasising

---

[52] Lei Chen, 'Private Property with Chinese Characteristics: A Critical Analysis of the Chinese Law on Property of 2007' (2010) 18(5) *European Review of Private Law* 983–1004; Yun-chien Chang, 'Property Law with Chinese Characteristics: An Economic and Comparative Analysis' (2012) *Brigham-Kanner Property Rights Conference Journal* 345–372.

[53] Thomas Merrill and Henry Smith argue that property rights are good against the whole world, thus requiring rules that reduces the costs of information for a broad-ranging yet unspecified group of potential violators. Thomas Merrill and Henry Smith, 'Making Coasean Property More Coasean' 54(S4) *Journal of Law and Economics* S77–104.

[54] Jim Yardley, 'China Enacts Major Land-Use Reform', *The New York Times*, 2008, available at www.nytimes.com/2008/10/20/world/asia/20china.html.

[55] Xiao Zhao, 'Why China Should Proceed Cautiously On Land Reform', *Chinadialogue.net*, 2013, available at www.chinadialogue.net/article/show/single/en/6469-Why-China-should-proceed-cautiously-on-land-reform; see also '中共中央关于推进农村改革发展若干重大问题的决定 [CCP Central Committee's Decision On Several Crucial Questions About Promoting Rural Reform]', *China.com.cn*, 2008, available at www.china.com.cn/policy/txt/2008-10/20/content_16635093_3.htm.

[56] 'Decision of the Central Committee of the Communist Party of China on Some Major Issues Concerning Comprehensively Deepening the Reform', *China.org.cn*, 2014, available at www.china.org.cn/china/third_plenary_session/2014-01/16/content_31212602.htm.

[57] Qing Shen, 'No.1 Central Document Targets Rural Reform', *Xinhua News*, 2014, available at http://news.xinhuanet.com/english/china/2014-01/19/c_133057121.htm.

that the rural land contracting system must be stable, the document called for the granting of rights to use, occupy and generate income to farmers, and allow the land to be subject to mortgages or liens.

In November 2016, the government issued a guideline to promote and standardise 'the transfer of the right to use from rural residents to commercial entities'[58] in return for yearly payments. The guideline also recommended the separation of the land ownership rights, contracted rights and operation rights,[59] which the Agricultural Minister Han Changfu opined would 'help[ ] guide the orderly transfer of land operating rights and lay[ ] a system foundation for appropriate-scale agricultural operations in development and modern agriculture'.[60] However, the Chinese government was still unwilling to change the rural collective ownership system: '[n]o matter how the government changes the land system, it cannot break down the rural collective ownership system.'[61]

In early 2017, the No. 1 Central Document was devoted to agriculture and rural areas for the fourteenth consecutive year. It reinforced 'the implementation of a rural land reform which separates farmland ownership rights, contract rights and operating rights, allowing farmers to earn more by transferring their land rights to individuals or conglomerates'.[62] It called for the establishment of the construction land market, a system of land registration and stressed the importance of the collective ownership as the basis of reforms.

[58] 'China Promotes Transfer of Farmland Use Right', *English.gov.cn*, 2016, available at http://english.gov.cn/policies/latest_releases/2016/10/31/content_281475479420893.htm.

[59] Elias Glenn and Kevin Yao, 'China Loosens Land Transfer Rules To Spur Larger, More Efficient Farms', *Reuters*, 2016, available at www.reuters.com/article/us-china-economy-landrights-idUSKBN12Y09F; see also '30 Years On, China Embarks On New Rural Land Reforms', *China.org.cn*, 2016, www.china.org.cn/china/2016-11/01/content_39612474.htm.

[60] 'China Eases Land Transfer Rules To Spur Larger, More Efficient Farms', *South China Morning Post*, 2016, available at www.scmp.com/news/china/policies-politics/article/2042636/china-eases-land-transfer-rules-spur-larger-more.

[61] 'China Land Reform Opens Door to Corporate Farming', *Financial Times*, 2016, available at www.ft.com/content/9d18ee2a-a1a7-11e6-86d5-4e36b35c3550.

[62] 'China Focus: China To Deepen Reform In Agricultural Sector', Ministry of Agriculture of the People's Republic of China, 2017, available at http://english.agri.gov.cn/news/dqnf/201702/t20170206_247179.htm; see also '中共中央国务院关于深入推进农业供给侧结构性改革加快培育农业农村发展新动能的若干意见 [Guidelines Of The CCP Central Committee And State Council On Deepening Supply-Side Structural Reform Of Agriculture And Accelerating The Cultivation Of New Growth Drivers For Agriculture And Rural Areas]', *Xinhua News*, 2017, available at http://news.xinhuanet.com/politics/2017-02/05/c_1120413568.htm.

This timeline reveals that the Chinese government has recognised the inadequacies and drawbacks of the land system and started implementing various land reforms in recent years.

14.3   Institutional Analysis of Non-Linear Transition

14.3.1   Rural Land Transfer

As we have seen, China employs a bifurcated system of land-use rights, differentiating between urban land and rural land. China's land tenure system has allowed the commercial transfer of urban land since the 1988 constitutional amendments, while the transfer of rural land has been frozen. Under the HRS, rural households are allocated land use rights, but not the right to dispose of the land – that is, rural land cannot be transferred or used as collateral to obtain a loan. Moreover, under the HRS, land parcels are subject to periodic reallocation at the discretion of village leaders, in view of changes in population and the formation of new households.[63] Further, tenure insecurity has worsened due to land expropriation for urban expansion and infrastructure development.[64] These limited property rights have dampened farmers' investments in the sense that there are no guarantees that 'those who invested to improve the land would be the long-term beneficiaries of such investments'.[65]

Rural land has remained under collective ownership overseen by local governments via village committees. Farmers are not allowed to (privately) buy, sell or mortgage the land on which they live. Property rights in rural China are weak and vulnerable to the dictates of local government policies.[66] Even urban residents, who have 'stronger' property rights (in the sense of market transfer), are sometimes restricted under the housing policy. In economic terms, an effective way to reduce title insecurity or uncertainty, and thereby enhance market efficiency, is to provide landholders with titles backed by a legal system that enforces

---

[63] See Katrina Mullan, Pauline Grosjean and Andreas Kontoleon, 'Land Tenure Arrangements and Rural-Urban Migration in China' (2011) 39 (1) *World Development* 123–133; Loren Brandt, Jikun Huang, Guo Li and Scott Rozelle, 'Land Rights in Rural China: Facts, Fictions and Issues' (2002) 47 *The China Journal*, 67–97, 74.

[64] Tao Ran and Xu Zhigang, 'Urbanization, Rural Land System and Social Security for Migrants in China' (2007) 43 (7) *The Journal of Development Studies* 1301–1320.

[65] See Jean C. Oi, 'Two Decades of Rural Reform in China: An Overview and Assessment' (1999) 159 *The China Quarterly* 616–619.

[66] Ethan Michelson, 'Climbing the Dispute Pagoda: Grievances and Appeals to the Official Justice System in Rural China' (2007) 72 *American Sociological Review* 459–485.

property rights. However, under the current legal model, the demand for rural land in China is satisfied through state expropriation and converting the legal status of land, rather than through direct commercial dealings based on private land-use rights. Mass expropriations of land (which is a major income source for local governments, as they sell the land to developers at a far higher price) have increased tensions between farmers and government officials, thus affecting social stability. Such tensions are projected to increase as the Chinese government pushes for urbanisation.[67] Rural land reform is crucial in order to address social unrest and drive rural-to-urban migration.[68]

The lack of clear property rights leaves farmers and rural residents prone to seizures of farmlands from 'state-linked and economically powerful actors who coerce or underpay existing rights-holders'.[69] It has been argued that the complete privatisation of land is a more appropriate means to encourage more efficient use of land and urbanisation,[70] as legal rights 'are an essential weapon of the weak, albeit a heretofore disappointing one'.[71] Some pilot experiments have been conducted in designated areas in order to transfer rural land. In 2007, for example, the State Council (PRC Central Government) allowed Chengdu to conduct pilot projects in relation to the registration and transfer of agricultural land.[72] This was recognised as a gradual establishment of a 'unified urban and rural market'.[73] Since then, Chengdu municipality has

---

[67] See Dinny McMahon, 'Beijing Moves to Break Down the Rural-Urban Divide', *Wall Street Journal*, 2013, available at https://blogs.wsj.com/chinarealtime/2013/11/15/beijing-moves-to-break-down-the-rural-urban-divide/.

[68] See 'China's Land Reform Will Be Neither Quick Nor Clean', *Stratfor*, 2015, available at www.stratfor.com/analysis/chinas-land-reform-will-be-neither-quick-nor-clean.

[69] Jacques deLisle, 'Law in the China Model 2.0: Legality, Developmentalism and Leninism under Xi Jinping' (2016) 26 *Journal of Contemporary China* 68–84.

[70] Zhou Qiren, 周其仁：The Current Land Title System Causes Social Unrest: Reform or Collapse, 土地制度引发社会冲突 再不改革会面临崩溃, 经济观察报, 2011年 07月22日.

[71] DeLisle, 'Law in the China Model 2.0'.

[72] National Development and Reform Commission (NDRC), The Circular approving Chongqing and Chengdu as the Special Experimental Zones for Coordinated Rural and Urban Development areas (Fā gǎi jīng tǐ [2007] No. 1248). This Notice was dated 7 June 2007. The Chinese version of this notice is available at www.sdpc.gov.cn/zcfb/zcfbtz/2007tongzhi/t20100511_346231.htm.

[73] 'Notice of Establishing Urban-Rural Integration Areas in Chengdu and Chongqing', *Fa Gai Jing Ti* No [2007] 1248, issued by the National Development and Reform Commission of the PRC on June 7, 2007.

been implementing and fine-tuning many concrete policies to set up a legal and institutional framework that recognises rural property rights.[74]

There are some reasons to explain the piecemeal 'provincial laboratory' approach impacting rural land transfer. First, the hindrance of privatisation might be ideological. The insistence on collective ownership is a legacy of the Soviet Union, as previously mentioned. Critics of the proposed land reform have warned that 'weakening the existing system of collective village ownership could deprive peasants of the security of having a piece of land and possibly lead to millions of landless farmers'.[75] It has been argued that privatising land would see conglomerates and companies acquiring vast areas of land, leading to unemployment for farmers.[76] It is clear that current land reform continues to be limited by the conception of collective ownership.

The issue of equality for farmers may be one of the factors contributing to the reluctance to privatise land. One of China's important policies on agriculture is grain security and self-sufficiency. In order to implement this policy and prevent the loss of valuable agricultural land, state involvement in land transactions is considered necessary to encourage local governments to maintain agricultural land for grain production. Despite 'the many possible loopholes for abuse and malpractice',[77] the local government's involvement 'is still deemed necessary as its presence may continue to serve as leverage for state regulation',[78] thus providing another disincentive to privatise farmlands.

The discussion now considers whether the current land reform is path dependent and, if so, to what extent. While the government's reform is based on collective ownership, it has deviated from collective ownership in some areas in order to create more flexibility in the current system – for example, separation of ownership, contractual management and operating rights, granting more property rights to landowners, establishment of a construction land market and allowing the transfer of use rights to

---

[74] See Guo Xiaoming, *Coordinating Urban and Rural Development and Rural Land Transfer Reform: An Empirical Study on Chengdu Model* (Beijing: China Science Press, 2012).

[75] Yardley, 'China Enacts Major Land-Use Reform'.

[76] '分析：中國土地改革的夢想與現實 [Analysis: The Dreams And Realities Of China's Land Reform]', BBC Chinese, 2015, available at www.bbc.com/zhongwen/trad/china/2015/02/150206_china_land_reform.

[77] Ray Yep, 'Containing Land Grabs: A Misguided Response to Rural Conflicts Over Land' (2013) 22(80) *Journal of Contemporary China* 273.

[78] Guiding Opinions of the General Office of the People's Government of Sichuan Province on the Construction of Market System for Rural Property Right Transfer Transactions (June 15, 2015).

conglomerates. However, such suggestions have been raised for a number of years; they were stated in various government documents repeatedly but not implemented, or that they were implemented at a rather slow rate. It is contended that the current land reform involves incremental changes rather than an overhaul to address changed economic conditions. The state is willing to change its role to act as a market facilitator, but only at times where 'the exchange or transfer of farmland contracts among peasants has no impact on the aggregate land available for agricultural production'.[79] It is thus concluded that there is a high degree of path dependence in China's current land reform. The reason for this path dependence is twofold. First, it is socialist ideological inertia. While experiments on rural land transfer have been gaining momentum in many provinces, the notion of collective ownership of rural land is enshrined in the Constitution, and the government's documents repeatedly highlight the collective ownership of rural land as a baseline for any further reforms. As a consequence, there is a threefold rights structure in Chinese rural land – namely, collective land ownership, contractual management rights by individual households and operation rights held by outside investors. The purpose of this legal design is to not only stabilise the land contract management rights of farmers, but also to commercialise the right to operate the land by allowing farmers to use this operation right to finance mortgages from financial institutions.[80] While the contractual management rights have been defined as a limited genuine right, the nature and scope of the operating rights held by outside investors remain uncertain. Second, the government is extremely cautious to maintain social stability. Many government officials fear that once the rural farmland becomes transferrable in the market, it could generate land concentration problems, and many farmers could lose their land and future livelihood, thereby jeopardising China's social stability.

14.3.2   Land Takings

For years, urban regeneration in China has been synonymous with home evictions, provoking residents' grievances and complaints.[81] Individual homeowners are perceived to be weak and vulnerable to infringement of

---

[79] Yep, 'Containing Land Grabs'.

[80] Qianxi Wang and Xiaoling Zhang, 'Three Rights Separation: China's Proposed Rural Land Rights Reform and Four Types of Local Trials' (2017) 63 *Land Use Policy* 111–121.

[81] Eva Pils, 'Land Disputes, Rights Assertion, and Social Unrest in China: A Case from Sichuan' (2005) 19(1) *Columbia Journal of Asian Law* 235.

their property rights by the local government and property developers. Land expropriation (and the subsequent sale of land to property developers) has become a major source of revenue and financing for local governments, as peasants are drastically undercompensated for their expropriated land.[82] Thus, conflict over expropriation of land continues to fuel the simmering hotpot of social unrest in China.[83] Currently, demand for land in rural China is satisfied by state-based models of expropriation and converting the legal status of rural land, rather than through impersonal exchanges of property rights. The current model is a cause of widespread land conflicts in China, as state officials appropriate the benefits of transitions to higher value uses of land. It can be vividly described as 'going private for government gains'.[84]

In 2011, the Regulations for Expropriation and Compensation for Houses on State-Owned Land (2011 Expropriation Regulations) were introduced[85] to replace the 2001 Demolition Regulations, which had in many respects contravened China's 2007 Property Law.[86] The 2011 Expropriation Regulations were heralded as taking a big leap forward in China's legal framework for state-oriented expropriations.[87] First, the different types of public interest that justify and legitimise mandatory expropriation were set out. Moreover, before an expropriation decision is made, the regulations ensured that a coordinated review was conducted by a number of departmental agencies of the local government to verify whether the proposed expropriation fulfils the public interest requirement. The legislative intent behind the 2011 Expropriation Regulations is to regulate the procedure governing expropriation and compensation, while upholding public interest and protecting the legal interests of property owners. This is dramatically different from the 2001 Demolition Regulations, which leaned in favour of the smooth operation of urban development.[88]

---

[82] See generally Wang Cailiang's blog, 'Annual Report of Expropriations in China 2012', available at http://blog.caijing.com.cn/expert_article-151549-46704.shtml.

[83] See Yu Jianrong, 'Land Issue Became the Focal Point of Peasant's Rights Maintainance' (2005) 8 The World of Research and Study (Diao Yan Shi Jie) 22–23.

[84] Chen, 'Legal and Institutional Analysis of Land Expropriation in China'.

[85] Kennedy, 'Laws and Development'.

[86] See Cui Jianyuan, 'Comparing Housing Demolition with Real Estate Expropriation', in Fang Shaokun and Wang Hongping (eds.), Real Property Expropriation (Beijing: China Legal Publishing House, 2009), pp. 309–311.

[87] Chen, 'Legal and Institutional Analysis of Land Expropriation in China'.

[88] Article. 1 of the 2001 Regulation. See details in Table 1.

Second, in relation to compensation (the most contentious part for any expropriation), payment levels would now have to take into account the location of the property and market value based on an independent third-party assessment. Third, the 2011 Expropriation Regulations introduced some detailed procedural safeguards, including public hearings, ensuring participation of the affected property owners, the selection of a property appraiser and dispute settlement provisions during an expropriation process. Any homeowner objecting to an expropriation procedure can file an administrative lawsuit.

Finally, under the 2011 Expropriation Regulations, it is the housing expropriation department, as a government agency, that signs off on expropriation and compensation agreements with individuals. The implication is that the government is the party who enjoys exclusive authority to expropriate, rather than the property developers or any other intermediaries, as was provided for in article 17 of the 2001 Demolition Regulations.

While the 2011 Expropriation Regulations provide protection from abuses of land seizures by the government in respect of urban land, the same protection for rural land remains lacking. The 2011 Expropriation Regulations are not applicable to rural land expropriations, and many forced evictions and land disputes are still taking place in rural areas. The root cause is the artificial differentiation of transferable urban land and non-transferable rural land. It is therefore not uncommon to have collusive alliances among the village collective, local government and commercial developers. Performance assessments of local governmental officials place a heavy emphasis on factors such as GDP growth, fiscal revenues and urban infrastructure building. There is a lack of incentive to offer equal protection of rural land rights given that it may serve as a hindrance should the local government choose to reclaim rural land for redevelopment. As a result, peasants are prone to forced evictions with inadequate compensation and insufficient provision of social security.

One question persists: Why is rural land excluded from the 2011 Expropriation Regulations? Ho argued that China's land tenure system is a 'deliberate institutional ambiguity', which allows local governments to adapt and respond quickly to a variety of pressures and the rapid changing of conditions.[89] Hence, there has never been a land policy

---

[89] See Peter Ho, *Developmental Dilemmas: Land Reform and Institutional Change in China* (London: Routledge, 2005).

which has been 'uniform and consistent' throughout China.[90] That said, the national land law and policy is intentionally broad so that different localities may implement their own land rules to cater for local demographic and economic conditions.

There are two policy choices faced by Chinese lawmakers: one is to undertake a systematic overhaul and the other is a piecemeal approach. A systematic overhaul is required to truly transform the land market, based on the principle of equal rights for both rural and urban land. It should enable collective rural land to be openly bought and sold in the market. However, this approach has not gained ground, mainly due to the fear of losing farmland and the threat of grain security. Under the current state-dominant land-supply model, almost all of the land used for urban purposes must be acquired by the local government from collective farmland and then converted into urban land. The decrease in farmland as a result of urbanisation has begun to threaten China's grain security.[91] Although the Central Government has promulgated regulations to protect agricultural land, these regulations have failed due to various manipulations of the rules by local governments.[92]

14.3.3   Urban Home Purchase Restrictions

Urban home prices have surged in major Chinese cities, causing property bubbles and lack of affordability. The policy of home purchase restrictions (HPR) has been one of China's harshest housing market interventions to tackle speculative demand and dampen soaring home prices.[93] Property prices in economically advanced cities like Beijing and Shenzhen have often been higher than those in major Western markets due to

---

[90] See George C. S. Lin and Samuel P. S. Ho, 'The State, Land System, and Land Development Processes in Contemporary China' (2005) 95 (2) *Annals of the Association of American Geographers* 411–436.

[91] Yingling Liu, 'Shrinking Arable Lands Jeopardizing China's Food Security', *World Watch Institute* (April 2006) April, available at www.worldwatch.org/node/3912.

[92] George C. Lin, Samuel P. Ho, 'The State, Land system, and Land Development Processes in Contemporary China' (2005) 95(2) *Annals of the Association of American Geographers* 411–436.

[93] Yang Ge and Pan Che, 'China's Legislators take on Zombie Companies, Real Estate', *China File*, 3 March 2017, available at www.chinafile.com/caixin-media/chinas-legislators-take-zombie-companies-real-estate.

rampant speculation.[94] China took steps to cool the market after rapid price increases in recent years, mostly by placing limits on potential buyers (the demand side). These new tightening measures include higher down-payment requirements on second homes and restrictions on the purchase of second or third homes. More recently, however, local governments tightened controls over the sales policy of real estate developers, limiting the supply side.

At the Central Leading Group on Finance and Economic Affairs meeting in February 2017, Xi Jinping stated: 'Houses are built to be lived in, not for speculation.'[95] In the past year, various cities in China have announced HPR policy due to the increased heat in their property markets. Such restrictions were implemented in mid-September 2016 for Hangzhou,[96] and in late September to early October 2016 for Zhengzhou, Guangzhou, Beijing, Shanghai and Shenzhen.[97] These cities were chosen for analysis as their governments introduced HPR at around the same time. Cities from both the first and second tier were chosen[98] in order to reflect a broad view of changes in the demand and supply of the housing market.

China's housing price growth was expected to slow significantly in 2017 due to the continued implementation of government limits and tighter credit conditions, which reduced land sales and property investment growth.[99] Changes in sales price indices for newly constructed residential buildings, newly constructed commercialised buildings and second-hand residential buildings were selected as indicators of the effects of home purchase restrictions, as prices reflect the meeting point between demand and supply, and those restrictions mainly targeted the

---

[94] Gwynn Guilford, 'China Has the Most Unaffordable Housing in the World', *The Atlantic*, available at www.theatlantic.com/business/archive/2013/07/china-has-the-most-unafford able-housing-in-the-world/277428/.

[95] http://news.xinhuanet.com/english/2017-02/28/c_136092232.htm.

[96] '杭州重启限购外地人限购1套房 9月19日起实施', *Sina Finance*, 2016, available at http://finance.sina.com.cn/chanjing/2016-09-18/doc-ifxvyqwa3403202.shtml.

[97] '4天9城密集出台楼市新政 多地重启限购限贷', *中国新闻网* [*China News*], 2016, available at www.chinanews.com/gn/2016/10-04/8022103.shtml.

[98] The following website is referred to when determining the tiers of each city: Marco Hernández, 'Urban Legend: China's Tiered City System Explained', *South China Morning Post*, available at http://multimedia.scmp.com/2016/cities/.

[99] 'China Property Sales Surge Despite Efforts to Cool the Market', *VOA*, 14 March 2017, available at www.voanews.com/a/china-property-sales/3764872.html.

purchase of residential homes.[100] The change in sales of commercialised buildings was also selected as one of the indicators because it reflects the change in demand of home buyers.

14.4 Conclusion

Although recent reforms to property rights may have been influenced by liberal ideas and market-driven concepts, they were grafted onto the pre-existing institutional framework and economic structures. This Chapter posits that political, legal and economic developments in China have not entirely transformed the institutional structures and epistemic settings that supported socialist law and institutions. At the risk of oversimplification, it is a phenomenon of 'going private but staying public'. Reforms that were intended to drastically change behavioural routines did in fact effect change, but not always in an expected manner.

Rural land transactions offer a potential alternative to state-based mechanisms of property rights exchange. However, allowing the contractual transfer of rural land use rights is a sensitive socio-political topic in China, not only because of unrests arising from smallholder farmers losing their land, but also because it raises issues of citizens' engagement with the state.

While significant statutory improvements have been made to address the land-taking issues, the scope of application for the new rules remains confined to urban land. The Chinese government and legislature are resistant to a legislative overhaul – this perhaps reinforces my main argument that, due to the contested institutional interactions between laws, norms, customs and government policies in China, rural property rights have been intentionally fuzzy.

The Chinese government's visible hand in the market is ubiquitous – the housing purchase restriction policy is an example of this. In order to achieve a policy agenda (political or economic), local governments often intervene in the housing market, without paying much heed to the national legislation. Interestingly, Chinese courts, through their judicial decisions or other binding documents, uphold local rules when they are in conflict with the national legislation.

---

[100] Note that the term 'newly constructed commercialized buildings' translates to '新建商品 住宅' in Chinese. It can be reasonably comprehended that such buildings also have a residential purpose.

Due to the legal and institutional limitations on the transfer of property rights, the rural land market in China has been undeveloped. Given the evolution of the Chinese rural land tenure system, it seems that the two radical options of abandoning the land collective in favour of either full privatisation or nationalisation are not viable. Rather, the Chinese Central Government has taken a piecemeal approach to enhance farmers' ownership of their land, such as the three rights separation scheme. However, there is still no clearly defined answer to the legal nature of operation rights granted by farmers to outside investors. Should the operation rights be a right *in rem*, which makes farmers' contract management rights akin to private ownership in effect? Whether this will turn out to be the solution China is seeking and, if so, how this will eventually reconcile with the socialist ideal of the collective productive use of land resources, remains to be seen.

The ambiguity of the operation rights may be justified from sociological and political perspectives. For rural land reform in China, the bright-line law itself seems to be less effective for resolution of property-related conflicts than the cultural-ethical legitimacy in which the law is embedded. Black-letter approaches to property rights distinguish between formal law (state law) and informal law (local norms and practices), but do not adequately capture the dynamics of the interrelationship among various factors (such as cultural or historical, social or moral, market liberalism and social stability–oriented socialism in public and private spheres). Consequently, expecting a miraculous cure and searching for one-size-fits-all solutions modelled on the most recent rules in China is, at best, idealistic. This Chapter has explored the paradoxes and fuzziness of land ownership in China through institutional studies and what they reveal about the persistence of socialist land policies in a Chinese-style market economy. However, more nuanced studies are warranted to demonstrate how the complex relations between different stakeholders (such as local government, village collectives, individual farmers, outside investors/renters and institutional lenders) can be reformulated to benefit farmers.

15

From Revolution to Evolution

The Changing Meanings of Socialist Land in Vietnam

JOHN GILLESPIE AND TOAN LE

15.1 Introduction

Given Vietnam's history of land revolution,[1] it is unsurprising that the socialist trope of people's ownership of land has laid down deep roots. According to the communist party's foundational mythology, the revolution was fought to secure 'land for farmers' (*ruộng cho dân cầy*).[2] From the 1980s onward, internal and external forces have compelled reluctant party leaders to selectively recognise private rights to land. This Chapter explores how these forces have shaped communist party thinking and concludes by speculating about the future of land ownership.

We argue that three interrelated factors are changing how party leaders conceptualise land. First, during the late 1970s, failures in the collective agricultural system convinced some party leaders that farmers needed private land use rights to stimulate productivity.[3] Experimentation with the agricultural contract system led to the collapse of socialist collective farming and the eventual allocation of fifty-year land use rights to farmers.[4]

---

[1] See, e.g., Edwin Moise, *Land Reform in China and North Vietnam: Consolidating the Revolution at the Village Level* (Chapel Hill, NC: University of North Carolina Press, 1983).

[2] Ngoc Luu Nguyen, *Peasants, Party and Revolution: The Politics of Agrarian Transformation in Northern Vietnam 1930–1975*, Thesis (Amsterdam: University of Amsterdam, 1987).

[3] See, e.g., Le Huu Tang and Liu Han Yue (ed.), *Economic Reform in Viet Nam and in China: A Comparative Study* (Hanoi: The Gioi Publishers, 2006), pp. 14–23.

[4] Dang Phong, *Pha Rao Trong Kinh Te Vao Truoc Dem Doi Moi [Fence-Breaking in Economic Arena Prior to Economic Renovation]* (Hanoi: Tri Thuc Publisher, 2011), pp. 164–196.

Second, following *Đổi mới* (renewal) economic reforms during the 1980s, the state encouraged citizens to satisfy their own housing needs.[5] This policy proved spectacularly successful in producing a vibrant residential land market and an ascendant middle class, who are now clamouring for property rights. Although steadfastly refusing to recognise private land ownership, party leaders have incrementally granted tenure rights to urban residential land, which now closely resemble private ownership.

Third, over the last decade, the area of land taken from farmers for urban and industrial developments has exceeded one million hectares, significantly greater than the 810,000 hectares redistributed during the socialist land reforms of the 1950s.[6] The widespread and sometimes violent protests from dispossessed farmers[7] have compelled party leaders to debate whether state economic development policies are undermining the original goal of the revolution – to secure 'land for farmers'.

In this Chapter, we first trace the history of land ownership. After reaching a zenith under French colonialism, the communist revolution rapidly swept away private land ownership in northern Vietnam. In the euphoria of the communist victory in 1975, the socialist land tenure regime seemed unassailable, but within a few decades it too came under pressure. By 2001, the chairman of the Hanoi People's Committee publicly lamented that most land problems in the capital were caused by the socialist land management system.[8] Next, we discuss how simmering concerns about people's ownership of land resurfaced in constitutional debates during 2012 and 2013. Despite strong public support, the party leadership ruled out any shift to private land ownership. In the final section of this Chapter, we argue that socialist land tenure is not merely an elite ideology, as it remains deeply embedded in the thinking of judges and land officials. We conclude that, although the forces for change are gathering momentum, socialist land tenure policies are so

---

[5] See, e.g., Trinh Duy Luon and Nguyen Quoc Vinh, 'Tac Dong Kinh Te Xa Hoi Cua Doi Moi Trong Linh Vuc Nha O Do Thi Vietnam' ['Social and Economic Impact of Reforms on City Residential Areas in Vietnam'] (1996) 15(2) *Xa Hoi Hoc* 17–19.

[6] Vu Tuan Anh, 'Land Issues in the Process of Implementing the 1992 Constitution' (2012) 8 *Vietnam Economic Review* 16–27.

[7] Benedict Kerkvliet, 'Protests over Land: Rightful Resistance and More' (2014) 9(3) *Journal of Vietnamese Studies* 14–34.

[8] Huy Duc, 'Thi Truong Soi Dong Nghi Truong Than Trong' ['The Market Is Vibrant, Why Is the Political Debate Cautious?'], *Thoi Bao Kinh Te Sai Gon*, 31 May 2001, pp. 17–18.

deeply entrenched that they are likely to influence party and state leaders for decades to come.

15.2 Land Ownership Narratives

15.2.1 A Quick Overview of Land Ownership (1092–2013)

15.2.1.1 Customary Land

Private land ownership has a long history in Vietnam. Land and tax records established formal state recognition of private ownership from 1092.[9] By the nineteenth century, privately owned land (*ruộng tư*) had surpassed public land holdings (*ruộng công*).[10] During imperial rule, the emperor was the legal owner of all land. However, in practice, there was a settled understanding that the people possessed proprietary rights to land. In short, land ownership was established by community recognition of land occupation and was protected by imperial decree.[11]

15.2.1.2 Colonial Land Titles

State protection of private land ownership reached a zenith under French colonialism (1862–1954). The colonial government introduced a Torrens title by registration system,[12] which based land transfers and ownership on cadastral planning and written records. Under this system, land became a tradable commodity that could be purchased and sold in the colonial market economy. Land titling also increased the number of landless peasants, as the French and indigenous Vietnamese elite accumulated land from the rural poor.[13] Eventually, 53 per cent of peasants became landless, and land ownership became a sensitive political issue.[14] During the 1920s, the Indochinese Communist Party tapped into this disenchantment to build a political platform to overthrow French

---

[9] Phan Dai Doan, *Lang Xa Vietnam: Mot So Van De Kinh Te Van Hoa Xa Hoi* [*Village Vietnam: Some Issues Relating to Economic, Culture and Society*] (Hanoi: Political Publisher, 2010), p. 44.

[10] Ibid., 45.

[11] Dao Minh Quang, 'History of Land Tenure in Pre-1954 Vietnam' (1993) 23(1) *Journal of Contemporary Asia* 84.

[12] Jean Louis Bassford, *Land Development Policy in Cochin China under the French (1865–1925)*, PhD Thesis, University of Hawaii, 1984.

[13] Quang, 'History of Land Tenure in Pre-1954 Vietnam', 89–90.

[14] Nguyen Van Linh 'Panorama des Mouvements Paysans Vietnamiens', in Pierre Brocheux (ed.), *Histoire de l 'Asie du Sud-Est: Révoltes, Réformes, Révolutions* (Lille: Presses Universitaires de Lille,1981), pp. 83–110, cited in Quang, 'History of Land Tenure in Pre-1954 Vietnam', 90.

colonialism. A core promise made to attract support from the peasants was to secure 'land for farmers'.[15]

15.2.1.3 Introducing Socialist Land Tenure

Although independence from France's rule was not achieved in North Vietnam until 1954, the government in exile passed the (Agrarian) Land Reform Law in 1953.[16] This law aimed to destroy the ownership rights of French colonialists and trials were convened to 'eliminate the private ownership of the landlord class'.[17] At this time, hundreds of Chinese advisers were invited to explain how the Chinese communist party managed the transition to collective land management.[18] In his memoir, Bui Tin described being made to watch films and plays that depicted landlords as greedy and cruel – the evil hands of imperialism.[19] 'Everything was black and white', Bui Tin recalled.[20] For a brief period of three years, peasants were provided with private land ownership. However, by 1956, the Party took land ownership from the peasants. Land collectivisation was influenced by Marxist–Leninist theory, which proposed that land is a special commodity that only the state should own and control.[21]

From 1956 to 1975, agricultural collectivisation was imposed in North Vietnam.[22] During this period, peasants were 'encouraged' to transfer ownership of their land to farming collectives. The state used a points system to reward labour and inculcate the principles of collective labour, collective land ownership and equity in land distribution.[23] Following reunification in 1975, the victorious Northern regime transferred land collectivisation into South Vietnam, despite the acknowledged shortcoming of this system.[24]

---

[15] Phuong Tran, 'The Land Reform' (1965) 7 *Vietnamese Studies*, 153, 155; Bui Tin, *Following Ho Chi Minh: memoirs of a North Vietnamese colonel* (London: C. Hurst, 1995), p. 23.

[16] Democratic Republic of Vietnam, Luat Cai Cach Ruong Dat [Agriculture Land Reform Act], 4 December 1953. Available at http://moj.gov.vn/vbpq/lists/vn%20bn%20php%20 lut/view_detail.aspx?itemid=1106, accessed 7 November 2016.

[17] Article 1, Agriculture Land Reform Act 1953.

[18] Tin, *Following Ho Chi Minh*, pp. 23–24.

[19] Ibid., p. 24.

[20] Ibid.

[21] Xuan Son Bui, 'On the Present Situation of Land Administration and Exploitation', *Tap Chi Cong San*, 4 February 1999, pp. 5–8.

[22] Phong, *Pha Rao Trong Kinh Te Vao Truoc Dem Doi Moi*, pp. 164–196.

[23] Ibid.,166.

[24] The Republic of South Vietnam was an independent country from 1955 to 1975 and it adopted the French's capitalist laws on land. For a detailed discussion on the shortcomings of land trials, see for example, Edwin Moise, *Land Reform in China and North Vietnam*.

15.2.1.4   Collectivisation and Peasant Resistance

Vietnamese peasants resisted the collectivisation of agricultural land by withdrawing their labour. This contributed to a food shortage and led to several decades of incremental reforms. In 1979, Vietnamese leaders acted to 'abandon immediately policies that were irrational and that caused obstacles for production'.[25] The leaders restored 'producers' rights in agricultural production. A new system of 'product contracts' was implemented that returned decision making in relation to agricultural production to the tiller.

Contradicting liberalisations in farm management, the passage of the new Constitution in 1980 replaced private land ownership with people's land ownership. Some commentators argue this Constitution reflected Soviet influence in Vietnam and resembled the 1936 Constitution of the USSR.[26] The Vietnamese Constitution followed article 6 of the 1936 Soviet Constitution which states 'land, its natural deposits, waters ... are state property, that belong to the whole people';[27] article 19 of the 1980 Constitution of Vietnam provides 'land, forest, river ... all belong to the people'. In contrast to the Maoist-inspired land policies that more narrowly focused on agrarian land collectivisation as a strategy to build and consolidate political power, the Vietnamese land laws developed after 1980 recognised the importance of achieving broader economic industrialisation objectives.

Although the preceding discussion reveals Maoist and Soviet influences, Vietnamese land ownership laws assumed a distinctive form that reflected local experimentations in granting peasants limited land use rights.[28] Most significantly, unlike the Chinese law that prohibited trade in collective land, Vietnamese law returned collective land to rural

---

[25] Phong, *Pha Rao Trong Kinh Te Vao Truoc Dem Doi Moi*, p. 207.

[26] Petition 72, 2013, Kien Nghi Ve Sua Doi Hien Phap 1992 [Proposal to Change the 1992 Constitution], available at http://boxitvn.blogspot.com.au/2013/01/kien-nghi-ve-sua-oi-hien-phap-1992.html, accessed 7 November 2016; Ha Quang, *Đất đai không chỉ là tài sản vật chất thuần tuý* [*Land is Not Merely a Financial Asset*] (Hanoi: Bao Dau Tu, 2013) available at http://diaoconline.vn/tin-tuc/thi-truong-dia-oc-c18/dat-dai-khong-chi-la-tai-san-vat-chat-thuan-tuy-i35843, accessed 7 November 2016.

[27] 1936 Constitution of the USSR, available at www.departments.bucknell.edu/russian/const/1936toc.html, accessed 7 November 2016.

[28] For the Chinese land ownership reform, see for example, Jia Lin Zhang, 'China's Slow-Motion Land Reform' (March/February 2010) *Policy Review* 59–70.

households.[29] Reforms also set more reasonable production targets and enabled peasants to receive fair prices for agriculture harvest.[30]

In another significant reform, the Ordinance on Residential Housing 1990 recognised private ownership of residential dwellings. It also set in motion ongoing legal uncertainty about the status of home ownership.[31] Local state officials and citizens recognised that land transactions 'occurred as a natural course of life' and that householders circumvented the prohibition on transferring land by selling or bequeathing houses together with the underlying land.[32] Although the separation of land and house ownership was compatible with a command economy in which the state planned and supplied housing, it was increasingly unsuited to Vietnam's mixed-market economy where the people were responsible for satisfying their own housing needs.[33] It also created complex legal and administrative problems. For example, land and houses were separately valued, surveyed and measured for land registration, and different dispute resolution bodies resolved land and housing complaints.

Despite the legal recognition of home ownership, party leaders maintained the socialist trope of people's ownership of land to retain control over rural land. To support this position, they referred to Marx's maxim that land is a 'natural resource, a resource for all of humanity in which no individuals have the right to make it their own'.[34] In addition, they argued that people's ownership of land is embedded in Vietnamese history and culture. For example, it has been stated that 'recognising people land ownership is necessary as land is connected to the battles that our forebears had fought in order to construct and defend the country. Our land is the result of the blood and bones of many generations'.[35]

---

[29] Phong, *Pha Rao Trong Kinh Te Vao Truoc Dem Doi Moi*, pp. 224–226.

[30] Ibid., pp. 351–352.

[31] Personal interview with high ranking former Ministry of Natural Resource and Environment (MONRE) official, 8 February 2013. File with author.

[32] Personal interview with high-ranking MONRE official, 5 February 2013. File with author.

[33] Pham Cao Nguyen, 'Thị Truong Bat Dong San' [Real Estate Markets], unpublished paper, CIME Conference on Fixed-Asset Markets Hanoi, paper delivered by the Director of Housing and Land Department, Ministry of Construction, 10 January 2001.

[34] Tran Cong Thanh, 'Doi Moi Nhan Thuc ve Dat Dai' ['Reforming our Viewpoint on Land'], 6 September 2011, available at http://vietnamnet.vn/vn/thoi-su/38227/doi-moi-nhan-thuc-ve-dat-dai.html, accessed 7 November 2016.

[35] Ho Nguyen Quan, Dat Dai Thuoc So Huu Toan Dan [Land is Owned by the Entire People] http://moj.gov.vn/qt/tintuc/Pages/nghien-cuu-trao-doi.aspx?ItemID=1610 See also http://plo.vn/thoi-su/chinh-tri/co-nen-cho-so-huu-tu-nhan-ve-dat-dai-bai-1-so-huu-toan-dan-qua-mu-mo-142892.html [Should Private Land Ownership be Recognised?]

In summary, private land ownership existed prior to socialist rule. From the 1950s, socialist leaders attempted to eliminate private land ownership and promote the socialist trope of people's land ownership. Party leaders responded to popular resistance to cooperative agriculture by returning rural land to private control and recognising private home ownership. However, they have steadfastly refused to contemplate private land ownership.

The next section examines the state's incremental recognition of private land rights from 1992 to 2013, and continuing party support for people's ownership of land.

15.2.2 The Incremental Recognition of Private Land Use Rights (1992–2012)

From the late 1980s, party leaders accepted the need to change the land tenure system. This incremental recognition of private land rights gained momentum following Đổi mới mix-market reforms, which gained official approval at the Sixth National Party Congress in 1986.[36]

Notwithstanding the growing social pressure to recognise private land ownership, party leaders remained committed to socialist ideology. In the lead-up to Vietnam's 1992 Constitution, party leaders resolved that the system of people's ownership of the 'means of production' and people's ownership of land should remain, even though the state now recognised private ownership over the 'means of production' in other social spheres.[37] This meant that the state continued to view land use rights as public assets allotted by the state to households. Authorities allocated land on a case-by-case basis according to a planning hierarchy, the nature of the land use and the status of the grantee (households/individuals and organisations).[38] As a consequence, land use rights functioned

---

[36] Vu Dinh Bach, *Kinh Te Thi Truong Dinh Huong Xa Hoi Chu Nghia o Viet Nam* [*Market Economy with Socialist Orientation in Vietnam*] (Hanoi: Political Publisher, 2008), p. 153.

[37] CPV, *Cương lĩnh xây dựng đất nước trong thời kỳ quá độ lên chủ nghĩa xã hội* [*Political Manifesto to Accelerate the Country in the Socialist Transition Period*], 6 October 2015. Available at http://dangcongsan.vn/tu-lieu-van-kien/tu-lieu-ve-dang/sach-ve-cong-tac-dang/books-110620153463956/index-5106201534538563.html, accessed 7 November 2016.

[38] Articles 15 and 16, Land Law 1993, *Socialist Republic of Vietnam*, available at http://thuvienphapluat.vn/van-ban/Bat-dong-san/Luat-Dat-dai-1993-24-L-CTN-38481.aspx, accessed 7 November 2016.

more like licences – contractual privileges to do something that would be otherwise illegal, rather than propriety interests enforceable against the world.

The 1993 Land Law represented a turning point because it recognised that landholders possessed disposal rights in land, including the right to transfer, mortgage, lease, exchange, bequest and inherit land use rights.[39] The creation of these rights allowed land to be used as collateral to finance private commerce. As the Minister of Agriculture, Nguyen Cong Tan, acknowledged: 'the practice has confirmed that land has a price, our people say "a centimetre of land is a centimetre of gold".'[40] Amendments to the Land Law in 1998 and again in 2001 further extended and clarified five land use rights. In particular, business organisations were permitted to hold land use rights – a major break from Marxist–Leninist policies, which criminalised private commerce in respect of land.[41]

Without losing faith in core socialist ideals, party leaders became skilled at flexibly adjusting socialism to promote a mixed-market economy. For example, the 1993 Land Law was remarkable for maintaining socialist egalitarian principles, with article 2.3 asserting that the state guarantees landholders engaging in agriculture access to land. This article also reflects the socialist principle of allocating land according to need. By contrast, article 10.3 of the 2003 Land Law more loosely defined this principle, merely suggesting that 'the state has a policy to create opportunities for agriculture producers to access land'.

While party leaders have quietly downgraded the socialist ideal of allocating land according to need in some areas, they have entrenched the ideal in other areas. For example, urban residential land use rights are still limited to a maximum area of 200 square metres. The law also reflects the socialist trope of collective ownership. For example, the concept of household ownership appears in both the Land Law and the Civil Code.[42] It establishes joint household administration over property contributed by family members and reflects the socialist principle that

---

[39] Ibid.
[40] Legal Committee, 'Bao Cao Tham Ra Cua Quy Ban Phap Luat Ve Du An Dat Dai' [Report of the Legal Committee on the Draft Land Law Project], 16 June 1993. File with author.
[41] Allotted land is the highest form of land use rights.
[42] Articles 15 and 16, Land Law 2003, *Socialist Republic of Vietnam*, available at http://moj.gov.vn/vbpq/lists/vn%20bn%20php%20lut/view_detail.aspx?itemid=19439, accessed 7 November 2016; arts. 108–109 *Bộ luật dân sự* [*Civil Code*] (Vietnam).

family property constitutes a 'means of production' that should be managed collectively.[43] Like other attempts to adapt socialism to a mixed-market environment, it has generated conceptual confusion. Surveys show that over 70 per cent of judges, lawyers and litigants struggle to differentiate household property from individual property.[44]

Despite decades of market reforms, people's ownership of land remains deeply entrenched in elite party thinking. Nowhere is this clearer than in the powers claimed by the state for the compulsory acquisition of land. States around the world reserve 'eminent domain' powers to compulsorily acquire land for public purposes, such as transport infrastructure and hospitals. In these cases, the state pays 'just' compensation. In Vietnam, the state treats the compulsory acquisition of land as an administrative withdrawal of rights (*trung dung*). Because householders do not own the land, but rather hold an administrative licence, the state can withdraw land use rights without paying market compensation.

State-sanctioned land grabs and land corruption has angered peasants.[45] In 2012, images of more than fifty police and military servicemen attempting to evict a farmer by the name of Doan Van Vuon produced an unprecedented response of public outrage from Vietnamese social media.[46]

---

[43] Mai Thị Thanh Xuân and Đặng Thị Thu Hiền, 'Phát triển kinh tế hộ gia đình ở Việt Nam' ['Promoting Household Economics in Vietnam'] (2013) 29(3) *Tạp chí khoa học* [*Sciences Journal*] 1.

[44] Bộ tư pháp [Ministry of Justice], *Thực tiễn thi hành một số chế định của Bộ luật Dân sự năm 2005 phục vụ công tác xây dựng và hoàn thiện pháp luật dân sự* [*Survey on the Implementation of 2005 Civil Code for the Development of Civil Legislation*], 2013, pp. 55 and 94.

[45] Toan Le, 'Perspectives of Land Grabbing Vietnam', in Andrew Harding and Connie Carter (eds.), *Land Grabs in Asia: What Role for the Law?* (London: Routledge, 2015), pp. 158–164. For cases on systematic land corruption, misappropriation and economic exploitation in relation to land administration, see 'Hoang Khue, Tham Nhung Dat Dai Do Son Thiet Hai Hon 23 Ty Dong' [Land Corruption in So Son of Over 23 Trillion Dong], 2 April 2007, available at http://vnexpress.net/tin-tuc/phap-luat/tham-nhung-dat-dai-do-son-thiet-hai-hon-23-ty-dong-2088584.html, accessed on 7 November 2016; Viet Anh, "Hơn 1.300 cán bộ bị khởi tố vì tham nhũng đất đai [Over 1300 Cadres Persecuted for Land Corruption] 7 November 2005, available at http://vietbao.vn/Xa-hoi/Hon-1.300-can-bo-bi-khoi-to-vi-tham-nhung-dat-dai/10932504/157/; D Thanh 'Giam Doc So TNMT Mat Trom 1.6 Million Dong' [Director of Ministry of Natural Resource and Environment Loses 1.6 Million Dong], 11 August 2014, http://tuoitre.vn/tin/phap-luat/20140811/giam-doc-so-tn-mt-tphcm%C2%A0mat-trom%C2%A016-ty-dong/632884.html, accessed on 7 November 2016.

[46] Analysis of the Doan Van Vuon case and other key developments can be found in Toan Le, 'Interpreting the Constitutional Debate Over Land Ownership in the Socialist Republic of Vietnam (2011–2013)' (forthcoming) *Asian Journal of Comparative Law*.

This case illustrated the injustice arising from the people's land ownership regime. The Doan Van Vuon dispute showed that, notwithstanding
decades of promoting people's ownership of land, some people were
unwilling to accept a land tenure regime where the state could withdraw
land use rights at will. A series of other high-profile land protests in
Hung Yen,[47] Xuan Thanh,[48] Duong Noi,[49] Long An, Ho Chi Minh City[50]
and Hanoi[51] suggest a bifurcation between state and public understandings about land ownership.[52]

15.2.3   The Push for Land Ownership

Responding to public discontent, senior leaders were forced to revisit
land ownership at the Eleventh National Party Congress in January
2011. The Minister of Planning and Investment, Vo Van Phuc, led
the push for reform. He noted that Marx and Lenin taught students to
assess theory based on practice and not according to a dogmatic adherence to ideology:[53]

---

[47] Thanh Phuong, 'Nông dân Hưng Yên và Đắk Nông biểu tình ở Hà Nội phản đối các vụ
trưng thu đất' [Hung Yen and Dak Nong Peasants' Protests Over Land Eviction in
Hanoi], 21 February 2012, available at http://vi.rfi.fr/viet-nam/20120221-nong-dan-
hung-yen-va-dak-nong-bieu-tinh-o-ha-noi-phan-doi-cac-vu-trung-thu-dat, accessed 7
November 2016.

[48] Anonymous, 'Cưỡng chế đất cho dự án sân golf tại xã Xuân Thành,huyện Nghi Xuân (Hà
Tĩnh)' [Land Eviction for Golf Course in Xuan Thanh District], 12 December 2013,
available at www.youtube.com/watch?v=xl_4iJM5vwc, accessed 7 November 2016.

[49] Anonymous, 'Dan Oan Noi Duong Bieu Tinh Doi Dat Dai Cuong Che' [Innocent
Citizens of Noi Duong Protest Seeking the Return of Evicted Land], 22 January,
2013 available at http://vietinfo.eu/tin-viet-nam/dan-oan-duong-noi-bieu-tinh-doi-d%
E1%BA%A5t-dai-cuong-che.html, accessed on 7 November 2016.

[50] Tra Mi, 'Bieu Tinh Tai Saigon Trong Ngay Dau Nam' [Protests in Saigon in the first days
of New Year], available at www.voatiengviet.com/content/bieu-tinh-tai-saigon-trong-
ngay-dau-nam-moi/1822003.html, accessed on 7 November 2016.

[51] Anonymous, 'Hàng trăm nông dân biểu tình khiếu nại đất đai tại Hà Nội' [Hundreds of
Peasants Protests Over Land in Hanoi], available at www.rfa.org/vietnamese/in_depth/
land-prot-i-hanoi-05222013094633.html, accessed 7 November 2016.

[52] John Gillespie, 'Transforming Land-Taking Disputes in Socialist Asia: Engaging an
Authoritarian State' (2017) 39 Law and Policy 280–303.

[53] Nghia Nhan, 'Thao luan dan chu, cong khai Dai Hoi X!: Dai Bieu Vo Van Phuc Noi Loi
Tam Huyet' [Democratic discussion at the Eleventh National Party Congress: Delegate
Vo Hong Phuc Said His Heartfelt Words], Phap Luat Phanh pho Ho Chi Minh, available
at http://phapluattp.vn/thoi-su/theo-dong/dai-bieu-vo-hong-phuc-noi-loi-tam-huyet-
385498.html, accessed 7 November 2016.

> There is the viewpoint that the foundation of socialism is ownership. But I believe that the foundation of socialism must be social justice, income re-distribution. To view ownership as the foundation, we will make the mistake of following the same path as the Soviet Union and Eastern Europeans.[54]

Vo Van Phuc argued for a radical departure from Marxist–Leninism in which state ownership of the 'means of production' constituted the core mechanism for achieving social equity. Senior party leaders publicly rebuked Vo Van Phuc. For example, Nguyen Phu Trong, the incoming Party Secretary, forcefully argued for the retention of the Marxist theory of people's ownership. He cautioned that 'delegates should vote for change only when there is absolute unity for change and the conditions for change had not ripened'.[55]

The final vote revealed a shift in thinking: 65 per cent favoured removing from the Political Manifesto the requirement that only the people can own the means of production.[56] A new Political Manifesto was drafted that adopted similar wording to the Political Report of the Tenth National Congress in 2006. Despite the clear majority favouring change, the new wording used meaningless language that presented a face-saving strategy. It says that socialist society in Vietnam consisted of 'a highly developed economy based on modern production forces and improved [*tiến bộ*] production relations that suits the development level of the production forces'.

In summary, party thinking about land ownership has slowly evolved in response to *Đổi mới* mixed-market reforms. The discussion has shown that, although the party-state has incrementally introduced private land use rights, the socialist ideal of people's ownership of the materials of production and household ownership remain deeply embedded. Party thinking about the allocation of land according to need has undergone more change. On the one hand, the party-state has progressively moved towards socialisation policies that make the people, rather than the state,

---

[54] Ibid.

[55] Anonymous, 'Bieu Quyet ve Cong Huu Tu Lieu San Xuat' [Vote on the Public Ownership of the Means of Production], 18 January, 2011, available at http://phapluattp.vn/thoi-su/theo-dong/bieu-quyet-ve-cong-huu-tu-lieu-san-xuat-385339.html, accessed 7 November 2016.

[56] Luu Nghia Son, 'Thông qua Nghị quyết Đại hội lần thứ XI của Đảng và Điều lệ Đảng sửa đổi, bổ sung' [Passing the 11th National Party Congress Resolution], Saigon Giai Phong, available at www.sggp.org.vn/chinhtri/tientoidhd/2011/1/248984/, accessed 7 November 2016.

responsible for housing and other social needs. On the other hand, the state has retained controls over agricultural land that, in theory, if not always in practice, protects farmers from the wholesale dispossession that fuelled the socialist revolution last century.

The next section will examine the constitutional and Land Law debates in 2012 and 2013, which saw a concerted push for private land ownership.

15.2.4 The 2012–2013 Constitutional Debates

The government initiated discussion about land reforms by announcing a period of public consultation in the lead-up to constitutional reforms in 2013.[57] In the outline presented to the National Assembly, the senior leadership expressly limited the scope of land reform, reaffirming people's ownership.[58] In addition, senior leaders stressed that 'the state will not return land that has been redistributed to organisations, households and individuals in the process of carrying out land policies'.[59] According to one prominent participant, although the consultation process was open, public opinions were filtered by politics.[60] He further claimed that, 'although the public position was that there were no restrictions on the terms of consultation about land ownership reforms, in fact restrictions were imposed'. Supporting the view that the party had no intention of fundamentally changing land policies, land officials interviewed during the consultation period insisted that there would be no change to recognise private land ownership.[61] Two land officials

---

[57] Uy BanThuong Vu Quoc Hoi, *Nghi Quyet ve Viec To Chuc Lay Y Kien Nhan Dan Doi voi Du Thao Luat Dat Dai (sua doi)* [*Resolution on Public Consultation on Land Law Reform*], document No. 563/NQ-UBTVQH13, 21 January 2013; Nguyen Hung, 'Lay Y Kien Nguoi Dan Ve Luat Dat Dai' [Public Consultation on Land Law], 30 January 2013, VN Express, available at http://vnexpress.net/tin-tuc/thoi-su/lay-y-kien-nguoi-dan-ve-luat-dat-dai-2420971.html, accessed 7 November 2016.

[58] Government of Vietnam, *To Trinh Ve Du An Luat Dat Dai (sua doi)* [*Presentation on the Project to Change the Land Law*], document No. 222/TTr-CP, 6 September 2012.

[59] Ibid.

[60] Personal interview, former senior land official, 10 February 2016.

[61] Interviews with Officials from MONRE, Hanoi, 1 February 2013. The officials recognise problems caused by the current regulations but attribute them to procedural irregularities and corrupt land officials. One deputy vice minister believes that peasants are interested in secure land rights, not private land ownership. Another deputy vice minister recognises the merits and disadvantages of the Chinese and American approach to land ownership regulation and suggests Vietnam should adopt a middle course. A more junior official confirmed that there will be no change to private land ownership as this would upset the spirit of the revolution and cause instability.

intimated that one of the reasons for protecting the status quo was the fear of 'instability'.[62] In addition, there appears to have been concern that the party would lose its political legitimacy to rule if it abandoned the socialist land revolution.

Undaunted by attempts to control the discussion, a broad range of actors took part in public deliberations, including intellectuals, retired officials, national assembly delegates, citizens, business bodies and international agencies. The content of the submissions varied enormously; however, most adopted a pro-farmer position.[63] For example, the United Nations Development Programme (UNDP) argued that farmers needed secure land tenure to protect them from compulsory land acquisitions.[64] It also called for 'major reform' to provide more transparency and curb land corruption.[65] In addition to the UNDP, Vietnamese actors pushed strongly for radical land reforms. A group of seventy-two eminent scholars submitted a landmark petition known as Petition 72.[66] They argued that the new Constitution must give people rights to determine access to land and should recognise private land ownership. In addition, they thought that state ownership of land should be abandoned in the interest of the people, especially farmers.

> If private, collective and community ownership are not recognised alongside state ownership, the people will be robbed of a fundament right to own property. To equate state ownership with people's ownership of land is to create the conditions for public administrators at the various levels to engage in corruption, abuse public powers and enter into alliances with private developers to cause financial harm to the people, especially the farmers.[67]

In short, Petition 72 called for radical changes to land ownership and linked this issue to broader reforms affecting the standing of the party in society.

---

[62] Ibid.

[63] Dang Hung Vo, Thong Qua Luat Dat Dai: Y Kien cua Dan va nhung Dieu Can Suy Ngam [Passage of the Land Law: The Opinion of the People and Things to Ponder], 21 June 2013, available at https://hienphap.wordpress.com/2013/06/23/thong-qua-luat-dat-dai-y-kien-cua-dan-va-nhung-dieu-can-suy-ngam-dang-hung-vo/, accessed 7 November 2016.

[64] UNDP, 'Land Should Not Be Revoked for Private Investor Projects', available at www.vn.undp.org/content/vietnam/vi/home/presscenter/undp-in-the-news/land-should-not-be-revoked-for-private-investor-projects–undp-e0.html, accessed 7 November 2016.

[65] Ibid.

[66] Petition 72, 'Proposal to Amend the Constitution', 14 April 2013, available at http://boxitvn.blogspot.com/2013/01/kien-nghi-ve-sua-oi-hien-phap-1992.html, accessed 7 November 2016.

[67] Ibid.

Petition 72 provoked a strong rebuke from the Party General Secretary, Nguyen Phu Trong. He denounced people who proposed ideas that undermined the stability of the state as engaging in 'acts of political, ideological and moral deterioration'.[68] Senior party leaders showed no signs of abandoning the socialist ideology of 'people's' ownership of the means of production.

In contrast to the cautious leadership, many rank-and-file National Assembly delegates argued for controls that might prevent government officials from taking land under the guise of economic development. They wanted a secret ballot so that delegates were free to express their views.[69] Although party leaders initially allowed these debates, the final debate was abruptly cancelled. On 28 November 2013, when the delegates voted by pushing a button on their computer screen, 97 per cent voted in favour of the draft constitution, which preserved both state land ownership and one-party rule. Only two delegates abstained from the vote.[70] The Land Law was passed on 29 November 2013, with a similar majority of almost 90 per cent.[71] The new law retained the key socialist ideas of people's ownership, and continued to treat land as a special commodity, giving the state powers to recover land for economic development purposes.

In summary, private land tenure rights have incrementally increased since *Đổi mới* reforms. Despite widespread public support for private land ownership, the political elite clings steadfastly to people's ownership of land to prevent 'instability' and further damage to the legitimacy of the party.

Socialist ideas concerning land have shifted from the traditional Marxist–Leninist socialist trope that land is a 'special commodity' without a market value. While maintaining people's ownership, land policies have effectively recognised land as a tradable commodity. The remaining

---

[68] Anonymous, 'TBT Trọng nói về sửa đổi Hiến pháp' ['TBT Trong talks about Amending the Constitution'] *BBC*, 26 February 2013, available at www.bbc.com/vietnamese/viet nam/2013/02/130226_nguyenphutrong_constitution.shtml, accessed 7 November 2016.

[69] Nguyen Le, 'Đề xuất bỏ phiếu kín vẫn để còn khác nhau về Hiến pháp' ['Proposed secret ballot on various issues still in debate about the Constitution'], *VnEconomy*, 4 November 2013, available at http://vneconomy.vn/thoi-su/de-xuat-bo-phieu-kin-van-de-con-khac-nhau-ve-hien-phap-20131103100819208.htm, accessed 7 November 2016.

[70] Tien Dung-Nam Phuong, 'Quoc Hoi Thong Qua Hien Phap Sua Doi', *VN Express*, 28 November 2013, available at http://vnexpress.net/tin-tuc/thoi-su/quoc-hoi-thong-qua-hien-phap-sua-doi-2916328.html, accessed 7 November 2016.

[71] Ibid.

question is whether this faith in socialist land ideals is limited to the political elite, or does it extend down into the party-state cadres who manage the land tenure system?

15.3   Implementing Socialist Land Law

So far, the discussion has examined elite-level discourse. In the second part of the Chapter, we turn to the implementation of socialist land law. Ho Chi Minh opined that without ideology the party and state are 'like a person without wisdom or a ship without a compass'.[72] We will argue that following *Đổi mới* reforms, political expediency has steered state ideology well away from its socialist moorings. While political elites have clung to the socialist ideal of 'people's ownership of land', for decades state officials and judges have creatively imbued socialist land law with pre-colonial and capitalist regulatory ideas.

15.3.1   Inheritance Cases

Inheritance cases illustrate the flexible application of socialist ideology. A decade after the 1980 Constitution nationalised land, two ordinances reopened the door for private property ownership. The Ordinance on Residential Housing 1990 permitted private ownership of residential accommodation, while the Ordinance on Inheritance 1990 recognised the right to bequeath houses. The Ordinances reflected the individual-isation and commodification of land and housing unleashed by *Đổi mới* market liberalisations.[73] Court judgements that deal with inheritance disputes provide glimpses into how the party-state reconciles the socialist ideal of 'people's ownership' with market liberalisations.

15.3.2   The Changing Nature of Inheritance Regulation

Contemporary Vietnamese inheritance laws were modelled on European civil law ideas about private property rights and self-determination.[74]

---

[72] Do Muoi, 'Building and Perfecting the State' (1995) 1(6) *Vietnam Law and Legal Forum*, 3, 5.

[73] Hue-Tam Ho Tai and Mark Sidel (eds.), *State, Society and the Market in Contemporary Vietnam: Property, Power and Values* (London: Routledge, 2013).

[74] Nguyễn Mạnh Bách, *Tìm hiểu pháp luật: Chế độ hôn sản và thừa kế trong luật Việt Nam [Study Vietnamese Laws: Regulations on Marriages and Inheritance]* (Ho Chi Minh City:

Unlike the pre-socialist inheritance law, which reflected the Confucian preoccupation with maintaining family lineages, contemporary legislation aims for the orderly and equitable distribution of assets. The Civil Code 2015, for example, promotes testamentary freedoms and establishes clear rules for the distribution of intestacies.[75] Underlying these civil law objectives is the socialist notion that inheritance should promote the productive use of household assets, while preventing a concentration of private wealth that might rival party and state power.

The number of cases involving inheritance disputes rapidly increased during the 1990s.[76] Commentators attribute this upsurge to several main factors.[77] The value of land and housing increased many times during the 1990s, generating tensions within families. At the same time, the Ordinance on Inheritance 1990 disrupted long-standing customary practices grounded on Confucian patrilineal succession. Many of the inheritance cases involved women asserting newly granted inheritance rights for themselves and their children. What is striking about the court cases is how judges blend law, socialism and customary precepts to find socially acceptable outcomes.

15.3.3 The Enduring Legacy of Socialist Thinking in Inheritance Disputes

A wide-ranging review of inheritance cases found that judgements dating from the mid-1990s reflected the socialist principle that land belonged to the state.[78] Consistent with the socialist trope that land is a special commodity, judges ruled that buildings, but not the underlying land, formed part of testamentary estates. As the land market gained momentum in the new millennium, judges were compelled to rethink the

---

Nhà xuất bản Thành Phố Hồ Chí Minh [Ho Chi Minh City Publishing House], 1993), pp. 124, 184.

[75] Article 4, Bộ luật dân sự 91/2015/QH13 2015 [Civil Code of Vietnam].

[76] Over a period where the population has almost doubled, civil law disputes have increased from 5,470 in 1976 to 94,932 in 2013; see Penelope (Pip) Nicholson, *Borrowing Court Systems: The Experience of Socialist Vietnam* (Leiden: Martinus Nijhoff Publishers, 2007), p. 133: Tối cao Toà án nhân dân [Supreme People's Court website] available at http://toaan.gov.vn/portal/page/portal/tandtc/lienhe, accessed 7 November 2016.

[77] For a wide-ranging discussion see Bui Bich Thi Lien, *Regulatory Interaction in Court-Based Resolution of Inheritance Disputes in Vietnam*, PhD Thesis, Monash University (2016).

[78] Lien, *Regulatory Interaction in Court-Based Resolution of Inheritance Disputes in Vietnam*, pp. 183–216.

socialist fiction that houses are privately owned while the underlying land remains a public asset.[79]

Despite the gradual strengthening of private rights to land, socialist thinking periodically resurfaces in inheritance cases. Take, for instance, the Supreme People's Court (SPC) decision in *Ms Bản* v. *Mr Hải*.[80] In this case, the SPC overturned a decision by the Hà Nội City Court that gave Ms Bản financial compensation but allocated family land to her stepbrother, Mr Hải. The SPC ruled that the family's land was sufficiently large to accommodate two households and, by excluding Ms Bản from the land, the inferior court had not properly considered her 'benefits'. Also evincing the socialist egalitarian principle of distribution according to personal need, the People's Supreme Procuracy argued that Ms Bản did not need more land because she had already inherited a house from another relative. What is instructive about this case is that the court officials disregarded the inheritance law, which clearly stipulated that property should be distributed equally, regardless of personal need. Court officials followed socialist egalitarian principles calling for the equitable redistribution of housing and land – principles that are no longer enshrined in the civil law.

Inheritance cases involving ancestral worship land (*Hương hỏa*) further illustrate how judges balance competing socialist, market and Confucian/traditional customary influences. During the fifteenth century, the Lê Code introduced detailed provisions regulating the inherence of ancestral worship land.[81] It stipulated that this type of land should pass to the eldest male heir, who in return was expected to conduct rituals to venerate clan ancestors.[82] Ancestral worship property could not be sold or transferred to outsiders. Following this tradition, it became commonplace for clan members to refer to lineage trees (*gia phả*) to legitimise claims to clan land.[83] Overturning centuries of established practice,

---

[79] Although some judges still claim that land use rights cannot form part of intestacies because they constitute a public asset. See Trần Thế Hợi, 'Quan điểm khác nhau về vụ kiện thừa kế quyền sử dụng đất [Different Views on Inheritance Disputes Regarding Land Use Rights]' (2005) 11 *Dân chủ và pháp luật* [*Democracy and Law*] 10.

[80] Decision No. 14/2009/DS-GDT, 16 July 2009 (Supreme People's Court).

[81] Articles 388–400, Lê Code.

[82] Mai Văn Hai, 'Gia đình, dòng họ và thôn làng với tư cách là các gía trị cơ bản của văn hoá làng Việt' ['Family, Clan, Village as Core Values of Vietnamese Village Culture'] (2009) 1 *Xã hội học* [*Sociology*] 36.

[83] '*Sổ đỏ là cái gì? chúng tôi có cả gia phả dòng họ từ nhiều đời nay để lại có thể chứng minh rõ nguồn gốc đất*'. See Bình Minh, 'Tranh chấp nhà thờ họ ở Ngọc Mỹ, Quốc Oai: Cuộc chiến giữa "lý" và "tình"!' ['Dispute Involes Temple Clan in Ngoc My, Quoc Oai: a Battle between "Reason" and "Sentiment"'], *Tầm nhìn: tri thức và phát triển* [*Vision: Knowledge and*

article 670 of the Civil Code 1995 created a dilemma for the courts. Judges were caught between community expectations of patrilineal inheritance and a law that treated ancestral worship property no differently from other classes of property.

A district court case demonstrates how judges often reconcile competing claims to ancestral worship property.[84] The presiding judge ordered a clan to subdivide ancestral worship property by giving one-third of the land to the occupants. He argued that the clan's claim that the land should pass to the eldest male heir contravened a 'constitutional right to housing'. The judge ruled in favour of a poor clan member who had resided on the property for many years. The legal basis for the judgement is unclear. Article 62 of the 1980 Constitution required the state to provide housing for citizens, but this socialist principle was quietly dropped from the 1992 Constitution. Le Kim Que, the clan's lawyer, later speculated that the judge invoked the constitutional principle to legitimise the socialist principle that land should be distributed according to need.[85] This decision was later reversed on appeal when the SPC upheld patrilineal secession rights for ancestral worship property.

Judges often refer to the nebulous concept of 'inner beliefs' (niềm tin nội tâm) to justify decisions that are not clearly grounded in law. The term covers subjective interpretations that range from intuitive 'gut feelings' through to more concrete socialist and community norms. In a regulatory environment where land laws are vague and lack guiding legal principles,[86] judges search for meaning from myriad sources that include socialist, customary and market precepts.

15.3.4 Land-Taking Cases

Like judges in inheritance cases, officials involved in land-taking disputes search well beyond the law for regulatory solutions. Over the last decade,

Development], 2 June 2014, available at http://www.nguoitieudung.com.vn/tranh-chap-nha-tho-ho-o-ngoc-my-quoc-oai————————————————————————————————cuoc-chien-giua-ly-va-tinh-d20632.html, accessed 7 November 2016.

[84] An So 52/ DSST, 2 October 1995, People's District Court Tu Liem; An So 20 PTDS, 31 January 1996, People's Court, January 1, 1996.

[85] Personal interview with Le Kim Que, President of the Hanoi Bar Association, Hanoi, July 1998. File with author.

[86] John Gillespie, 'Exploring the Limits of the Judicialization of Urban Land Disputes in Vietnam' (2011) 45 (2) *Law and Society Review* 241–275; Lien, *Regulatory Interaction in Court-Based Resolution of Inheritance Disputes in Vietnam*.

the state has compulsorily acquired land from over nine million farmers, constituting over 10 per cent of the population.[87] As mentioned previously, the Land Law 2013 grants officials extensive powers to 'withdraw' (*trứng dung*) private land use rights without paying market compensation. Many farmers have not left quietly, and land-taking disputes that pit citizens against the state have erupted throughout the country. What is remarkable about these contests is that, despite the central state's opposition to regulatory pluralism, and its insistence on top-down legal powers, customary land traditions have proved surprisingly resilient and adaptable. Rather than socialist precepts displacing custom, land-taking disputes reveal an accommodation between socialist, market and customary claims to land.

A series of case studies demonstrates how intermediaries have leveraged their party connections to negotiate settlements to land-taking disputes. In one representative case, a dispute erupted when the state sought to relocate more than 100,000 Thái Đen ethnic minority villagers from highland river valleys.[88] Land officials in this Sơn La case study established Resettlement Persuasion Taskforces (*Ban Vận động Di dân*), comprised of Thái Đen people seconded from local party cells and mass organisations. The taskforces were expected to convince the villagers to abandon their customary claims to land and peacefully relocate to resettlement zones. Rather than strictly enforcing the law, which afforded the state extensive powers to take the land, the taskforces acted like double agents. They explained state powers to the villagers but also communicated the villagers' concerns about relocating away from ancestral land up the chain of command to provincial land officials. The intermediation transformed how the officials and villagers conceptualised the dispute, giving the villagers more say in planning the resettlements. The case is instructive in showing how intermediaries convinced land officials to look beyond the socialist trope that land is a public asset and consider customary claims to land.

In an analogous case,[89] retired state officials acted like intermediaries in brokering a resettlement deal for disposed farmers. Provincial officials compulsorily acquired land in Đông Dương village, near Hanoi, for a factory development. Following procedures established in the Land Law

---

[87] Kerkvliet, 'Protests over Land', 19–54.

[88] John Gillespie, 'Social Consensus and the Meta-Regulation of Land-Taking Disputes in Vietnam' (2014) 9(3) *Journal of Vietnamese Studies* 91–124.

[89] Gillespie 'Transforming Land-Taking Disputes in Socialist Asia'.

2003, the officials offered compensation based on state-mandated land valuations, which were well below prevailing market prices. According to socialist theory, since land is a 'special commodity', it does not have a market value. Farmers were incensed that state officials and developers refused to share the windfall profits generated from the conversion of their farmland.

To settle the dispute, retired state officials drew on party connections to claim more compensation for the farmers. Rather than relying on the Land Law 2003, which favoured the interests of state officials and developers, the intermediaries engaged the officials in *thỏa đáng* – a traditional form of dispute resolution that encourages *biết điều* (reasonableness), normative flexibility and compromise. State institutions assimilated *thỏa đáng* decision-making techniques during the high socialist period (1945–1986), and it remains influential within official circles today.[90]

The intermediaries persuaded the officials to consider the underlying morality of land taking and treat the Land Law 2003 as just one of many sources of authority. For example, they invoked socialist rhetoric to remind the officials that 'the revolution aimed to provide life-time security for farmers', and that it was their duty as party members to assist farmers. In addition, they sought to delegitimise the land development by portraying the investors as 'capitalists who would seize any opportunity to exploit others for their own benefits'.[91] To support this moral argument, they tapped into rich party narratives that attribute rising social inequality in Vietnam to the commodification of land in the market economy.[92] Eventually, the officials recognised the farmers' moral claims to the land and increased the land compensation.

What these case studies demonstrate is that socialist land policies give way to customs in the ambiguous regulatory space where state and village land tenure systems overlap. In this contested space, state authority is attenuated, its roles and boundaries blurred or nebulous, and multiple modes of land regulation co-exist. This ambiguity affords intermediaries opportunities to experiment with new regulatory forms. For example, intermediaries in the Sơn La case convinced the officials that Thái Đen

---

[90] Gillespie, 'Exploring the Limits of the Judicialization of Urban Land Disputes in Vietnam', 262–266.

[91] Interviews with retired male officials, Đông Dương Commune, Thái Bình Province, Vietnam, 2–3 March, 2012, 3–4 October 2012, April and September 2013.

[92] Nguyen Van Suu, 'Industrialization and Urbanization in Vietnam: How Appropriation of Agricultural Land Use Rights Transformed Farmers' Livelihoods in a Peri-Urban Hanoi Village', EADN Working Paper No. 38, 2009.

culture stood outside the state land tenure system. The officials temporarily stepped outside of the state land tenure framework, suspended socialist top-down planning and allowed villagers to relocate some customary land practices to the resettlement zones. Similarly, intermediaries in the Đông Dương case invoked socialist revolutionary ideology to persuade local officials to flexibly apply the state land tenure system. They invited local officials to treat property rights as 'fuzzy'[93] and contingent entitlements, rather than rigid and fixed legal categories. Officials responded by temporarily suspending state law and accepting a land tenure regime that accommodated community perceptions about just access to land.

The case studies demonstrate that the state land tenure system is unable to displace non-state land tenure systems and provide a common epistemic framework to resolve land-taking disputes. This results in regulatory ambiguity that gives intermediaries opportunities to suspend the socialist trope that land is a public asset with no market value, and bring customary and market norms into regulatory settlements.

The case studies reveal a duality in the land law. While party leaders repeat socialist tropes in high-level political discourse, judges and land officials have for decades quietly recalibrated socialism to suit customary and market precepts. Equally, market forces have not banished socialist ideas from land regulation, as they have in some other regulatory arenas. Rather, socialism has adjusted to a wide range of customary and market regulatory precepts. In some circumstances, socialist ideas seem to prevail. For instance, judges routinely allocate inheritance property to those most in need, and land officials 'withdraw' land use rights without paying market-based compensation. In other circumstances, both socialism and imported rights-based notions of property have given way to customary and religious claims to land. Judges, for example, routinely suspend the inheritance law to ensure patrilineal succession for ancestor worship property. What is missing from these cases is evidence that socialism is in conversation with other regulatory ideals. Rather than forming regulatory hybrids that combine socialism and other regulatory precepts to create new regulatory norms and procedures, syncretic combinations are more common. Judges and land officials selectively draw on socialist

---

[93] John Gillespie, 'Narrating Land Disputes in Three Vietnamese Communities' in Hualing Fu and John Gillespie (eds.), *Resolving Land Disputes in East Asia: Exploring the Limits of Law*, (Cambridge: Cambridge University Press, 2014), pp. 291–314.

ideas where they produce contextually appropriate outcomes, while turning to customary or market precepts in other contexts.

15.4 Conclusion

It is interesting to reflect on whether socialist ideas are more deeply ingrained in land regulation than in other regulatory arenas. We have seen in previous Chapters that socialist tropes, such as state ownership of the means of production and the allocation of resources according to need, have all but vanished outside the 'commanding heights' of the economy. Market-based laws, strongly intermediated by relational regulation, now regulate vast swathes of the economy.

In contrast, socialism still maintains a strong presence over land regulation. Despite increasingly strident calls from reformers for private land ownership, party leaders remain committed to 'people's ownership' of land. We have argued that three forces – agricultural reforms, vibrant land markets and land protests – are driving change. Yet, as the constitutional debates during 2012 and 2013 illustrate, party leaders are prepared to stare down public protest to preserve people's ownership of land.

It is notoriously difficult to predict the trajectory of regulatory policies. However, there are reasons for believing that party leaders are unlikely to embrace private land ownership in the near future. We have identified several factors inhibiting change. First, senior party leaders remain haunted by the possibility that private land ownership will lead to landless peasants and the social instability that fuelled the socialist revolution seventy years ago. Second, for decades, the party invoked the socialist land revolution to secure legitimacy and support from farmers. For many farmers, the adoption of private land ownership would constitute a betrayal of the revolution and raise the question: what did people fight for?

Third, people's ownership of land is not just a chimera in the minds of the party leadership, as judges and land officials throughout the country regularly use socialist ideas to formulate responses to land disputes. What is remarkable is that some socialist ideas, such as allocation according to need, remain in the official repertoire long after they were dropped from the law. Any movement away from socialist land tenure by the ruling elite risks alienating party cadres in key state agencies and the judiciary. It also threatens to disrupt land dispute settlements that have woven together ideas from the past and present, socialism and capitalism, and state and community.

Nowhere have socialist ideas more deeply worked their way into the fabric of regulatory life than in land regulation. Even if the party-state was to recognise private land ownership, echoes of the socialist project, such as distribution according to need, are likely to remain part of the regulatory landscape.

At the same time, the political elite must accommodate growing public support for private land ownership. It is likely that future reforms will incrementally adopt procedures that improve transparency in land takings. The gradual enlargement of private land tenure rights is possible, with perhaps the recognition of long-term land leasehold rights, similar to those issued in Hong Kong and Singapore. Nevertheless, the social trope of people's ownership of land is likely to cast a shadow for decades to come.

INDEX

429